D0883201

CURRICULUM PLANNING

Integrating Multiculturalism, Constructivism, and Education Reform

Fourth Edition

Kenneth T. Henson

The Citadel

Long Grove, Illinois

To Isabelle

For information about this book, contact:
Waveland Press, Inc.
4180 IL Route 83, Suite 101
Long Grove, IL 60047-9580
(847) 634-0081
info@waveland.com
www.waveland.com

Cover: James R. Henson, *Blue Figure*, 2007.

10-digit ISBN 1-57766-609-7
13-digit ISBN 978-1-57766-609-7

Printed in the United States of America

7 6 5 4 3

CONTENTS

PREFACE

Approach

As a graduate student, I found my curriculum texts to be among the most difficult of all my texts, not because the subject matter was inherently complex, but because these books were written in a jargon-laden, convoluted style that most of us found awkward, unclear, and sometimes even pompous. I wasn't impressed, and I always thought that I could do better. This fourth edition of *Curriculum Planning* is part of my continuing attempt to do so.

Perhaps, like me, at some time in your life you have heard someone comment, "He (or she) must be really smart, because I listened to the whole presentation and didn't understand a single word." I believe that this type of thinking is wrong. The best authors and teachers don't make things sound complicated; on the contrary, they do just the opposite, making complex subjects clear and easy to understand. Only then can the study of various disciplines become enjoyable. To that end, this book is not filled with jargon and complex sentence structure designed to impress. My goal for this text has been to remove the mystery from curriculum development and make it a clear and exhilarating experience. Effective thinkers make their thinking visible (Ritchhart & Perkins, 2008). Good writers do, too. To make my thinking clear, I use a graphic organizer to introduce each chapter.

Many of the curriculum books I used as a student had a second common weakness; they lacked currency. The twenty-first-century curriculum developer must have a firm grasp of the latest knowledge bases in curriculum study and its foundations. Major concepts, principles, and theories must be examined and explained, not to be memorized but to be used by today's educators to critically examine the many reform practices that are occurring in their local school districts. This book is well documented with the latest insights in the literature.

A Balanced View

My tone is intentionally encouraging, because lasting improvements in the nation's schools require the support of those of you enrolled in this course: designated curriculum directors, administrators, instructional supervisors, and teachers—especially teachers, because successful reform requires an unprecedented level of teacher involvement and leadership. But my encouraging language should not—must not—be interpreted as blind support for all education reform or as failure to recognize the many flaws and weaknesses that characterize many reform reports. On the contrary, I have long been concerned about the many unsound practices recommended by the nation's many reform reports, as clearly expressed in my *USA Today* article, "America's public schools: A look at the recent reports" (1986) and in the subsequent article, "Why curriculum development needs reforming" (*Educational Horizons*, Summer 1996).

Simple, quick-fix solutions usually occur only in an environment of ignorance, and the effects of such changes usually disappear with equal speed. Sound curriculum development requires an awareness and understanding of theories based on a solid knowledge of educational foundations. Consequently, good curriculum development is seldom quick or easy. But it can and should be very satisfying. The overriding aim of this book is sound curriculum development for lasting improvement.

Themes of the Text

Education Reform

This book is written to help supervisors, administrators, teachers, and other educators meet the paramount challenge of twenty-first-century education, which is to help all students succeed, both academically and socially. The No Child Left Behind legislation is only the latest of many reform reports with which educators and curriculum planners must familiarize themselves in order to meet this challenge. This goal will require a special type of education reform. Because many reform practices are far from good, this book provides the foundations needed to make judicious decisions regarding the implementation of reform practices. Most reform practices have both strengths and limitations. The readers of this text are provided opportunities to review the merits and criticisms of many popular reform practices and are then pressed to weigh these carefully to make their own value judgments about the worth of each to their local school district. Good education reform is designed to help maximize the academic and social development of all students.

Multicultural Education

Throughout the country, teachers encounter students of widely varied backgrounds. By the year 2020, half of the nations' public school students will be minorities, but only about 5 percent of the teachers will be minorities (Meyer & Rhodes, 2006). Students from all cultural backgrounds leave their marks on the schools' honor rolls and lists of valedictorians and salutatorians; at the same time, because of language barriers and negative home environments, many youths from all cultures hold low expectations for themselves. Successful curriculum development in the twenty-first century must prepare teachers to help *all* students succeed. For example, English language learners (ELLs) require additional classes to prepare them to communicate better, but that alone won't meet their needs; these students must have quality instruction (Christie, 2008). This book provides opportunities to apply curriculum foundations and practices to some of the many problem situations faced by today's students, situations that challenge all contemporary teachers. In a democracy, all students must be educated to their highest potentials, and all citizens have a right to feel proud of their heritage. As used in this text, multicultural education refers to establishing and maintaining a classroom climate or culture in which students appreciate diversity and allow themselves to be enriched by the opportunity to work with students from many cultural backgrounds, including differences in ethnicity, political affiliation, socioeconomic status, ability level, and religion.

Constructivism

The research has shown that the best teachers have a depth of understanding about a variety of curriculum theories and models, and they are prepared to choose and use the combination that works best with the particular educator at a particular school at a particular time (Reed, 2010). Therefore, this book takes an eclectic approach, introducing a variety of curriculum and learning theories. Research has also shown that we learn best that which we are able to connect to our prior knowledge and use to create or "construct" new understanding.

Constructivists believe that true understanding happens only when we tie new information to previously acquired understanding and that the teacher's role is to help this happen. Each time we learn, we shape our existing understanding, making the current state of our knowledge temporary. Learning is the result of our discovering relationships between new and old information while confronting new information. Constructivists believe that this event (learning) happens best when learners help each other, motivated by an internal desire to learn. Russian psychologist Lev Vygotsky called the process of learning together "socially negotiating meaning." Grouping has the best results when each group has learners representing the racial, cultural, and gender makeup of the entire class (Armstrong et al., 2009).

Integration of the Themes

The themes of **education reform, multiculturalism,** and **constructivism** are woven throughout the content of each chapter. All three themes are addressed in the Focus Questions, Additional Learning Opportunities, Suggested Activities, and concluding sections of each chapter. The following tables illustrate the integration of the themes. The numbers shown in each table represent the sequence in which the objective, question, or suggested activity refers to particular content found in the body of the respective chapter.

Education Reform

Focus	Questions	Additional Learning Opportunities	Suggested Activities
Chapter 1	3	6	4
Chapter 2	2	3	1
Chapter 3	2	3	3
Chapter 4	4	1	2
Chapter 5	1	2	1
Chapter 6	2	1	1
Chapter 7	1	1	2
Chapter 8	5	3	3
Chapter 9	2	2	1
Chapter 10	1	2	1
Chapter 11	1	1	2

Multiculturalism

Focus	Questions	Additional Learning Opportunities	Suggested Activities
Chapter 1	1	2	1
Chapter 2	2	2	4
Chapter 3	1	1	1
Chapter 4	3	1	1
Chapter 5	2	1	1
Chapter 6	1	1	1
Chapter 7	3	1	2
Chapter 8	2	1	2
Chapter 9	2	1	1
Chapter 10	4	2	3
Chapter 11	1	1	1

Constructivism

Focus	Questions	Additional Learning Opportunities	Suggested Activities
Chapter 1	1	2	2
Chapter 2	1	1	1
Chapter 3	2	1	0
Chapter 4	2	2	1
Chapter 5	2	1	0
Chapter 6	3	1	1
Chapter 7	3	1	1
Chapter 8	1	1	1
Chapter 9	2	3	1
Chapter 10	4	2	3
Chapter 11	1	1	1

Case Studies

A special feature of this text is the inclusion of *case studies*. In his article, "The Essential Cognitive Backpack," Mel Levine (2007) says that case studies should be used to model balanced critical thinking. As noted by L. Darling-Hammond and J. Baratz-Snowden (2007), cases can help teachers develop reasoning skills. Each chapter begins with a short vignette entitled "The Case of . . . ," and later in the chapter a second case study appears. Unlike the introductory vignettes, which are based on actual events but perhaps are unintentionally embellished over time, *the case studies detail contemporary curriculum planning experiences occurring throughout the country.* Each is written by educators who are directly involved with the experiences described.

Each case study contains a description of the school and the surrounding environment, which enables the reader to see how much the appropriateness of reform practices depends on the existing conditions at a particular school, in a particular community, or at a particular time. The case is then followed by a section entitled "Issues for Further Reflection and Application" that helps the reader examine the case information, focus on relevant issues, and practice making decisions about educational reform practices. The inclusion of the case studies is intended to give the reader an appreciation of the demands educators face, always requiring decisions and often without all the information needed to make wise choices.

Tips

New to this edition are tips, included in each chapter from educators across the country. After teaching in self-contained public school classrooms, I was surprised to discover that other teachers had some highly effective activities and strategies I was never aware of. I have since discovered that this is also true of curriculum workers, who have some unique ways to achieve their goals. As a result, I invited curriculum workers from all across the United States to share their favorite activities to help teachers improve their curricula. I am amazed at the creativity educators are able to unleash when given the opportunity.

To the Reader

Newspapers, magazines, books, and reports regularly describe problems in our schools. In some places, legislators and educators are suing their states for failing to provide the type of education needed to prepare students for life and work in the twenty-first century. Schools and teachers are being measured, not by their own performance but rather by the performance of their students on national exams. The people are calling for a national curriculum, and NCLB is ensuring that national standards are met. To say the least, these are exciting and challenging times.

As a twenty-first-century educator, you are no longer restricted to teaching the textbook content to the students in your class. The teacher's role has moved from the classroom to the total school (restructuring), to the community, and to the world (reform). Your job is to prepare your students to ask new types of questions, think new kinds of thoughts, dream new dreams, and reach new goals. In effect, you must play a major role in shaping the future.

To be sure, this new role requires mastering content, and knowledge of the principles of curriculum development is an indispensable part of this content. But, if indeed you are to use this course and this book to prepare the students at your school for the world, you will need content mastery *and more*. You must have the courage and stamina to ask yourself and seek the answers to many questions:

- What is it about education reform that perplexes me (after all, nobody fully understands all the reform elements)? Which reform practices in my district do I support?
- What insights about learners do I have that I can use to contribute to designing a new type of educational system? What is wrong with our current system? What is right with it?
- What is wrong with our world? How can I help change it? How can I use the answers to these questions to increase the impact I can have on shaping our schools?
- What have been my greatest learning experiences? What made them so?
- Who is the best teacher I have ever had? Why? Exactly how did that teacher reach me? How can I help others use this teacher's strengths and methods?
- What is the difference between knowledge and wisdom? Why is this important to curriculum planners?
- What are my fondest memories from elementary school? Secondary school? What were my most traumatic educational experiences? How can I influence the shape of curricula to accentuate the former and eliminate the latter? How can I best use all of these memories and experiences to help others?
- How is each discipline different? Does each discipline have a best route to mastery? How can this route be discovered? For what disciplines is each teaching method best suited?
- What other kinds of questions should I be asking myself so that I can ride the crest of the reform wave and experience success instead of wallowing in dissatisfaction? How can I remain passionate about reform and yet avoid falling prey to the politicians' empty rhetoric and to the flawed recommendations that characterize so many of the reform reports?
- How can I keep my concern for the welfare of every student of every nationality and every social level as the reason and guide for all my decisions? How can I help all students realize their strengths, their self-worth, and their importance and obligations to the community?
- What is it about me that makes me different from any other human being who has ever lived, and how can I understand and harness this uniqueness

to direct my energies and those of my colleagues to make a positive difference in our schools and in our world?

This book might raise more questions than it answers. The poet Antonio Machado once wrote, "Life is a path you beat while you walk it." Curriculum improvement is the same. There is no step-by-step manual, no algorithm or recipe. Instead, with each answer comes the arrival of new questions, if we keep our minds open. Does curriculum planning require a knowledge base and a depth of understanding? You bet. The challenge remains hidden, waiting to be discovered, and therein also lie the excitement and fun. Never lose the excitement that comes from discovering a new insight. For, indeed, those who enjoy shaping the curriculum in their schools will tell you that the joy in the journey of curriculum improvement is to be found not only at the destination but also in the ongoing trip. Because I fully believe that neither you nor I will ever know all the answers, my advice is that you ask a lot of questions and, while you are seeking the answers, try to relax and enjoy the trip.

chapter one

An Introduction to Curriculum Development

the integrated themes

- constructivism
- multiculturalism
- education reform

the importance of curriculum

defining and interpreting curriculum

- a document
- planned experiences
- social implications
- as an end
- short and long definitions
- live or dead
- interpreting curriculum
- the hidden curriculum

the negative impact of reform reports

- overemphasis on test scores
- misleading test-score interpretations
- narrow view of reform reports
- flawed overall purposes
- educationally unsound recommendations
- the legacy of *A Nation at Risk:* No Child Left Behind

positive outcomes of education reform

- teacher involvement
- parental involvement
- administrator involvement
- advances in teacher education
- identification of true weaknesses
- an emphasis on constructivism

Focus Questions

1. What elements in your school's hidden curriculum work against minority students, and how can this be remedied?
2. How is the No Child Left Behind (NCLB) Act improving school leadership?
3. What is the strongest evidence of the power of the hidden curriculum that you have witnessed?
4. What must principals, teachers, and others know about the curriculum development process to enhance their school's reform efforts?
5. What qualities make some curriculum definitions more useful than others, and how do you define curriculum development?
6. What is constructivism, and how is it important to curriculum development?
7. What major curriculum practices differentiate U.S. schools from their counterparts in those nations whose schools lead in science and mathematics?

The Case of Eastwood Middle School

Eastwood Middle School is in many ways a typical American middle school. Its 26 teachers and 425 students in grades 5 to 8 make it average in size. Its culturally diverse student body and predominantly white administration and faculty contribute to its typical qualities. Eastwood Middle serves a primarily working-class population. Unfortunately, like other communities, Eastwood has its share of broken homes, single-parent families, and latchkey children. The students do not always receive the level of encouragement needed to convince them to achieve their maximum potential. Those who do receive encouragement at home are often told to "get an education so you can get a good job."

Eastwood is in the town of Madisonville, which has its right and wrong sides of the tracks. Madison has several pockets of ethnic groups, and its residents are stereotyped according to their sub-communities, each with its own ethnic culture.

As is true of schools throughout the country, Eastwood Middle School is the hub of the community, not in the sense of its being the meeting place for citizens to gather, but because it is the one place where the community's youth from all backgrounds come together.

Eastwood Middle School is located in a state where education reform is occurring at record speed, with each week bringing new dimensions of reform. In two years of rapid reform, the schools in this state have been introduced to such innovations as authentic assessment, curriculum alignment, nongraded primary curriculum, site-based decision making, alternative testing, performance evaluation, research-based teaching, educational technology, and valued outcomes. A new statewide tax increase has financed these and other changes.

To say that teaching at Eastwood Middle School during the last two years has been an exciting experience would be the understatement of the year. Highlighting the motivation for Eastwood teachers has been a series of articles in the local newspaper on a continuing "school reform" theme. Eastwood's senior faculty members remember times when the only news items on local schools were stories about the decline of local standardized test scores, the failure of the schools to enforce discipline codes, or an occasional drug bust.

Drug problems initially shocked this small Midwestern community, but as alcohol and drugs slowly invaded the town, their presence later became accepted as an unfortunate sign of the times.

In spite of these problems, good things have been happening at Eastwood, and recently even the television news programs have featured special stories on some of the curriculum reforms at Eastwood Middle. The senior faculty members agree that it is time for some positive stories about their school, and these reform stories are welcomed and appreciated by many.

As with all schools, education reform at Eastwood Middle School has its detractors. Eastwood Middle has its share of naysayers, faculty members who announce daily in the teachers' lounge that this new reform won't work. Some of the reasons they give for predicting the education reform movement's early demise include:

- Sure, all of the reform elements sound great in theory, but once they are removed from the master drawing board and put in the real world, they'll never work."
- "The recently generated monies fueling this education reform movement will soon run out, and when this happens the reform will stop."
- "This school reform movement is just another bandwagon fad. The legislators are using it to build their own support base. Once they stop getting publicity, they'll withdraw their support."
- "The principal is using the reform movement to get another feather in her hat. She'll press for its implementation just long enough to get all the media coverage she can get, and then she'll find another way to get publicity."
- "We teachers are being falsely enticed to go along with all the reform issues. We are receiving more and more work assignments with no more pay, and all of us are already overworked. Soon we'll come to our senses and say, 'Enough is enough.'"
- "This reform is holding us teachers accountable for the performance of *all* our students and, let's face it, some students will never succeed. The movement was doomed to fail before it started."

Although in numbers these naysayers are in the minority, they are a loud and determined group. The principal often muses over how much this group of teachers could contribute to reforming the school if only they would channel all of their energy positively.

Like most schools, Eastwood Middle also has its group of innovators who are standing ready to take on new challenges. These faculty members seem tireless. Instead of being exhausted from overwork, these teachers seem to get even more energy from working hard. Eastwood's principal wishes this group had more members.

Most of Eastwood's teachers are somewhere between these two extremes. They hear the rumblings, and they read and hear about the success stories. They are suspended between the two points of view, waiting to see whether they should invest their energy and time in the reform movement. They know that successful reform will require a big commitment of everybody's time and energy, and they want to improve their school, but since their schedules are already taxing, before making personal investments in reform they want to be sure the reform movement will not run out of steam or money before it succeeds.

Susan Carnes has just completed her undergraduate program and has accepted her first full-time teaching assignment at Eastwood Middle. After serving on this faculty for only two months, Susan can see the political forces at work. In addition to recognizing the distinct social groups, she has noticed that different individuals have their own reasons for wanting the education reform movement at Eastwood Middle to succeed or fail.

Carlos Garcia is a soft-spoken, polite science teacher who seems immune to the daily gossip. He is a good listener who seems to empathize with all the complainers, but he, himself, never complains. It seems clear that when the chips are down, Carlos will support the administration and the reform practices. At the other extreme is Frances Watson, whose tongue seems to be loose at both ends. Frances is a large, boisterous teacher who demands everyone's attention wherever she goes, regardless of the purpose of the meeting. In faculty meetings when all 26 are present, Frances speaks every time anyone else speaks, as though she considers her ability to contribute to the conversation at least equal to that of the other 25 teachers combined. Susan is amazed that the rest of the faculty members permit one individual to dominate them. Apparently, they are willing to acquiesce to her overwhelming personality just to avoid the unpleasant complaining that would surely follow if she did not get her say.

This bothers Susan. After all, these are supposed to be professional people, and professional teachers are supposed to put the welfare of their students ahead of concerns for themselves and their colleagues. Susan doesn't see concern for the students as a force behind any of this faculty's decisions. In fact, she doesn't see any efforts being made to address the needs of the minority students. Two months is a short time to be on a faculty, and Susan is sure that she has much more to learn, both about this school and about her new colleagues, and she can tell that success here will require her to learn more about both. Susan feels that as a professional, she must be committed to helping the local reform efforts succeed if, indeed, those efforts might improve the plight of the students at Eastwood. In any case, since implementing reform was the state's decision and she is a state employee, she has concluded that perhaps it is up to her to find ways to make the reform serve the students.

Susan wonders whether she should express her position on this local school reform issue and perhaps search out others who are also committed to its success. Also, Susan desperately wants to talk to someone about the school's multicultural needs. At this time, just having a peer to talk to and the ability to share her feelings would bring some much-needed relief, yet she wonders if this would lead to friction with those who oppose reform.

• • •

As reflected in this description of Eastwood Middle School, curriculum reform does not occur easily. Most faculties are divided over change of any kind, and reluctance is common, especially where heavy commitments of time and energy are required. Reform is energy-hungry, as reflected in John Goodlad's (1997, p. 102) comments, "Even with reform efforts close to and involving teachers from local schools, a major part of the net result appears to be added work and stress for teachers seeking to cope with matters that do not support their teaching." Intelligent schoolwide involvement in education reform will require a good grasp of the meaning of curriculum and will require familiarity with the development of the current wave of school reforms.

The Integrated Themes

The three themes of this book, constructivism, multiculturalism, and education reform, are closely related. *Constructivism* is the belief that learning occurs only when the learner ties newly acquired information to previously gained understanding. *Multiculturalism* refers to establishing and maintaining a classroom climate where students with many differences in background, potential, and challenges learn to work with all of their classmates and learn to appreciate their uniqueness. *Education reform* refers to systematic approaches at the national, state, or local level to make significant improvements in education. Good education reform, as viewed by the author, uses practices or activities that help all students meet the goals of constructivists and multiculturalists.

One quality that aligns constructivism with multiculturalism is the common belief that *all students can and will learn*. The No Child Left Behind Act of 2001 reflects this belief. Many teachers, even highly experienced teachers, find this concept difficult to accept, yet it is absolutely essential for maximum effectiveness in today's classrooms. Sooner or later, our basic beliefs translate into action. Such ideas are more than political rhetoric. If teachers reject the postulate that all students can learn, these teachers will eventually, perhaps unwittingly, lower the expectations they hold for students perceived as less capable and, as a result, they may provide them less assistance. Teachers who believe that all students can succeed will never give up on their students or surrender their willingness to help any students succeed to their maximum capacities. Principals who accept this postulate will continue searching for ways to improve their school's curriculum to meet this goal.

We know that good education reform uses many practices considered essential by constructivists and multiculturalists. One of these common practices is the use of *small-group assignments*, in which each member helps all other group members. Constructivists say that small-group activities enhance learning. Multiculturalists say that small-group activities enhance the development of social skills and even increase students' self-confidence because the value of each group member is recognized by all other members of the group.

Both constructivists and multiculturalists recognize that increased learning and socialization result only when all group members cooperate to help the other members of their group. Thus, another quality that ties constructivism to multiculturalism is *cooperation*, as opposed to the traditional belief that learning occurs best in a competitive environment. Multiculturalists believe that cooperation strengthens students' self-images.

One activity that helps us understand the positive impact that cooperative, small-group work has on learning is *student discourse* (i.e., students talking and sharing teaching strategies). Discourse in the classroom pulls together concepts, ideas, and conclusions. Eminent Russian psychologist Lev Vygotsky (1896–1934) referred to small-group discussions as *negotiating meaning*. For example, a common technique used by constructivists to promote discourse in diverse settings is storytelling. One way of employing this strategy is by engaging students in discussions about cultures that may be excluded from curriculum materials.

Gerald Campano (2007) says, "In short, the deepest intellectual resources in classrooms are the students themselves. And one of the most powerful ways students can share their knowledge, partake in their own education, and intervene on their own behalf is by telling their stories" (p. 50). Egan and Judson (2008) remind us that as a cognitive tool, story structuring enables us to shape our stories, creating images so that our audience can feel our meanings. These images can be highly motivating.

In contrast to traditional education, which depended on teacher-directed instruction with passive students, many contemporary education reform programs use *student-centered approaches*. For example, the most commonly used learning activity in constructivist classrooms is problem solving. Even the approaches used to solve problems have changed significantly. Instead of traditional step-by-step, formula-driven problem solving, many contemporary education reform programs favor a more flexible, nonlinear approach that takes students from the simple-recall learning level to higher-order thinking.

Another activity that ties the themes of this book together is the type of *assessments* used in many reform programs. During the early twentieth century, schools almost exclusively gave objective tests to hold students accountable for remembering "taught" information. To be candid, many contemporary education reformers have continued to use assessment to hold students, teachers, administrators, and even schools, districts, and state education systems accountable; but there is good news: Many contemporary education reformers have endorsed the use of *authentic assessments*. The big difference is that authentic assessments require students to use the information they have learned to solve lifelike problems (Tomlinson, 2007/2008). *Self-assessment* has also become an accepted practice, using portfolios, exhibits, and other activities that require students to track their own progress. Furthermore, the assessment instruments are being used *in a continuous, daily manner*, unlike the traditional practice of testing at the end of instruction, when it is too late to adjust methodologies to enhance learning.

Perhaps the most significant aspect of the change to continuous assessment is the purpose for which assessment is being used. In addition to the increased use of authentic assessment, progress reporting, and self-assessment, contemporary educators are also using feedback from these continuous assessments to improve the curriculum, teaching, and learning.

Multiculturalists are quick to endorse practices that are used for the purpose of assisting students. Assistive instruction is often misinterpreted as making efforts to help by lowering the standards for challenged and nonmainstream students. In fact, multiculturalists encourage teachers to hold the same standards for all students and find ways to help students with special barriers to overcome, whether they are language barriers (for example, students who live in homes where English is not spoken); barriers resulting from homes or community cultures that may be dissonant with the school's culture; or barriers caused by physical, mental, and/or emotional challenges.

Although the No Child Left Behind Act of 2001 (NCLB) has a goal of total equity and the performance levels of minority and mainstream students have been narrowed somewhat (Good & Brophy, 2008), according to the National Center for Education Statistics (NCES) (2007), white students continue to outperform black, Hispanic, and Native American students (see box 2.2 in chapter 2). The national high school dropout rate of Latino students (30%) is twice the rate of that for African Americans and three times the rate of that for European Americans (Lindholm-Leary, 2005). The sooner minority students are introduced to the reform curriculum the better. There has been progress; more minority group members are taking advanced science and mathematics courses than ever before.

Another activity that ties the themes in this book together, and a reason for much hope, is the expansion of the learning arena. Formerly classroom-bound education has now expanded to become schoolwide, communitywide, and even worldwide education. *Partnerships* are being formed that include teachers, administrators, parents, universities, and other community members. There is good news: Ironically, paralleling the expansion of national goals and standards, there is evidence of decentralization, especially at the state and local levels. NCLB provides funding to increase community involvement in education, particularly in impoverished communities.

As the education arena has expanded, so has the power of each player, including students. Constructivists believe that students should be active participants in shaping their education. Teachers are being empowered by the late twentieth-century invention of site-based school councils that are often given power to make all types of important decisions, including major decisions about curriculum matters. Students, too, are being empowered. Although they have an inquisitive nature, students don't always act on their inquisitiveness. Learning to do so is empowering. A major source of student empowerment is the constructivist belief that the only way to really understand is through solving problems, thereby creating new understanding. Thus, the realization that teachers cannot "give" understanding to passive students has also been a strong factor in efforts to purposefully empower students.

These are only a few of the ways that this book's themes of *constructivism*, *multiculturalism*, and *education reform* are interrelated. As you read this book, learning about others' decisions and making decisions yourself, consider the effects that each decision will have on the goals of multiculturalism and constructivism.

The Importance of Curriculum

The important role of the curriculum in meeting the school's mission cannot be overemphasized. Since curriculum is the primary vehicle for achieving the goals and objectives of a school, a focus on curriculum planning and development is naturally a top priority of education reform. And since teachers' roles in curriculum planning are expanding beyond their own classrooms, they cannot choose to ignore education reform. Therefore, it's important for all teachers to understand as much as possible about the overall national reform movement and about the specific reform elements (practices) that are occurring in their particular state. Historically, major curriculum changes have been made largely because of pressure, by hunches, or in terms of expediency instead of being based on research. This old-fashioned basis for curriculum planning has changed. Because of its complex nature and the constantly changing environment in which it takes place, curriculum development is one of the most challenging facets of education reform.

The Challenges of Curriculum Reform

Curriculum development has been described as a messy process. One reason that curriculum development is so complicated is that it is aimed at facilitating teaching, and teaching itself is an enormously complex and fluid process. These complexities serve as barriers to curriculum change and have contributed to a curriculum that many describe as archaic. With ready access to the Internet, today's students know how archaic their school curriculum really is. Many have come to the conclusion that it's not what they learn *in* school but what they learn *after* school that prepares them for the future (Prensky, 2008).

Another variable that complicates curriculum development is the environment in which it occurs, which is highly complex and constantly changing. To remain effective, the curriculum must be designed and modified to reflect the changes in society at large, changes in the local community, changes in the local school, and changes in the students. Failure to consider and adjust for these changes would be tantamount to learning how to operate a car without ever putting it in traffic.

In addition to curricular change being a highly complex process (Bintz & Dillard, 2007), the perception and definition of curriculum can be interpreted in a multitude of ways.

Box 1.1 Early Attempts at Reform

Curriculum developers in the twenty-first century need an awareness of some of the history of the education reform movement of the 1980s and 1990s. This wave of education reform was started in a sporadic fashion, with a few states introducing reform legislation. It has its origin in a climate of dissatisfaction and lack of confidence in local school boards and local educators. This is not all bad; without a recognized need for change, there would be little improvement.

Some people find it comforting to believe that this recent wave of reform had its origin in research, but nothing could be further from the truth. The 1980s and 1990s reform wave was born in a climate of politics. There is good news, however. Research shows that (1) to be effective, education programs must empower (and many contemporary programs *are* empowering) teachers; and (2) all teachers can share this power and, in fact, must do so if education reform efforts are to be effective. Bernauer (1999, p. 69) says, "Unless they [teachers] are empowered to deliver high quality, there is little chance that meaningful educational improvement will occur." Teachers need to be given control of their profession, and teachers should be prepared to be researchers into the practice that they control (Clement & Vandenberghe, 2000). So, even though research was not at the root of the current call to reform, it is seen as an important part of the reform process.

Former governor William Winter of Mississippi is credited with having introduced the first bold, statewide education reform movement. Governor Winter's major concern was with improving the state's economy, which he believed possible only through improving education. His Accountability in Instructional Management (AIM) program required all teachers to get together with fellow faculty members in their discipline and design a grade 1–12 curriculum. In every school and in all disciplines, each curriculum was to include objectives, content, teacher activities, student activities, materials, and test items *for every day's lesson.* Mississippi teachers were given five years to develop this new curriculum.

Defining and Interpreting Curriculum

Curriculum definitions are important because they convey educators' perceptions and, in turn, these perceptions affect how a curriculum is used and, indeed, even whether it is used at all. McNeil (2003) defines unused curricula as *dead curricula* and used curricula as *live curricula:* ". . . the live curriculum is when teachers and students engage in classroom activities that they find meaningful" (p. 13).

The term *curriculum* is a Latin word that originally meant "racecourse." When used in education, curriculum has many meanings. Traditionally, the term meant a list of courses, but through the years it has expanded, taking on several new meanings. Curriculum developers who have a clear mental grasp of several of these meanings can perform a wider range of curriculum development activities and can do so more effectively than those who have only a vague idea of what is meant when the word curriculum is mentioned.

Curriculum: A Program of Studies

Curriculum has never had a uniform and monolithic definition (Bintz & Dillard, 2007). Most earlier definitions of curriculum were quite general. In its early application to American education, curriculum meant a program of studies. When asked to describe a curriculum, a layperson is likely to list a sequence of courses. This view of curriculum is seen in most college catalogs, which often list a definite sequence of courses to describe a particular program of studies.

Curriculum: A Document

Some educators perceive the purpose of curriculum as being the improvement of instruction, and they define it accordingly. For example, James Macdonald defined curriculum as "planned actions for instruction" (Foshay, 1969). Such a definition implies that curriculum is a document. When an accrediting team makes a site visit, the chair or another team member may ask to see the science curriculum. Usually, this person would expect the school officials to produce a document describing the school's science program.

Curriculum: Planned Experiences

To other educators, the term curriculum means a school's planned experiences. Caswell and Campbell (1935) defined curriculum as all the experiences children have under the guidance of teachers. Thompson and Gregg (1997, p. 28) have said that "Curriculum embraces every planned aspect of a school's educational program." Saylor and Alexander (1966, p. 5) distinguished between the school's actual activities and its planned activities: "Curriculum encompasses all learning opportunities provided by the school" versus "A curriculum plan is the advance arrangement of learning opportunities for a particular population of learners." Saylor and Alexander said that a *curriculum guide* is a written curriculum plan.

Others have defined the curriculum as experiences:

> A sequence of potential experiences is set up by the school for the purpose of disciplining children and youth in group ways of thinking and acting. This set of experiences is referred to as the curriculum. (Smith, Stanley, & Shores, 1957)

> The curriculum is now generally considered to be all of the experiences that learners have under the auspices of the school. (Doll, 1996, p. 15)

This change from an emphasis on content to an emphasis on experiences reflects a general change in thinking that occurred during the Progressive Education Era (the 1920s to the 1940s), when the curriculum emphasis shifted from being subject-centered to being student-centered.

Some contemporary educators recognize curriculum as both a plan and the experiences spelled out in that plan. Curriculum is often defined as the planned or formal specification of content and skills to be taught (Armstrong et al., 2009, p.140). Marsh and Willis (2003) defined curriculum as ". . . an interrelated set of plans and experiences that a student undertakes under the guidance of the school" (p. 13). Parkay, Hass, and Anctil (2010) define curriculum as "all of the educative experiences learners have in an educational program, the purpose of which is to achieve broad goals and related specific objectives that have been developed within a framework of theory and research, past and present professional practice, and the changing needs of society" (p. 3).

Curriculum: Social Implications

By the 1980s, the concept of curriculum expanded even more, to include changes in social emphasis, for example:

> [Curriculum is the] learning experiences and intended outcomes formulated through systematic reconstruction of knowledge and experience, under the auspices of the school, for the learners' continuous willful growth in personal-social competence. (Tanner & Tanner, 1994, p. 189)

> If we are to achieve equality, we must broaden our conceptions of curriculum to include the entire culture of the school—not just subject matter content. (Gay, 1990, pp. 61–62)

Curriculum: As an End

The preceding definitions portray curricula as content to be learned or experiences to be had as a means toward an end. In contrast, other definitions (e.g., Popham & Baker, 1970, p. 48) present curriculum as an end unto itself: "Curriculum is all the planned learning outcomes for which the school is responsible."

Curriculum: Short and Long Definitions

Some definitions of curriculum are much more general than are others. This is even true for definitions written by the same author. For example, Armstrong et al. (2009) define curriculum as "An overall plan for learning" (p. 172). However, as noted earlier, these same authors also describe curriculum as the "specification of skills and content to be taught" (p. 140). Taba (1962), in contrast, had this to say about curriculum:

> A curriculum usually contains a statement of aims and of specific objectives; it indicates some selection and organization of content; it either implies or manifests certain patterns of learning and teaching, whether because the objectives demand them or because the content organization requires them. Finally, it includes a program of evaluation of the outcomes. (p. 11)

Curriculum: Live or Dead?

Curriculum definitions are important because they convey educators' perceptions and, in turn, these perceptions affect how a curriculum is used—indeed, even whether it is used at all. Recall McNeil's (2003) definition of "dead" curricula as unused, and "live" curricula as engaging students in meaningful classroom activities. Kieran Egan and Gillian Judson (2008, p. 25) explain live curriculum by saying, "Everything in the curriculum is human knowledge—a product of human hopes, fears, and passions. If we want to make that knowledge engaging to students, we have to share it in the context of the hopes, fears, and passions from which it has grown and in which it finds a living meaning."

Interpreting Curriculum

At this point, the logical mind strives to impose some order on the evolution of the meaning of the word *curriculum*. Unfortunately, this is not possible, because the development of curriculum theory has not followed a straight, logical path. Although we might desire a single, accepted definition, a variety of definitions exist because many educators work with curricula in diversified ways, and each definition brings a unique perspective to the field. Instead of a clean definition of curriculum, we now offer a series of *interpretations* of curriculum given by Oliva (2009, p. 3) to conclude this discussion:

- Curriculum is that which is taught in school.
- Curriculum is a set of subjects.
- Curriculum is content.
- Curriculum is a program of studies.
- Curriculum is a set of materials.
- Curriculum is a sequence of courses.
- Curriculum is a set of performance objectives.
- Curriculum is a course of study.
- Curriculum is everything that goes on within the school, including extra-class activities, guidance, and interpersonal relationships.
- Curriculum is that which is taught both inside and outside the school and directed by the school.
- Curriculum is everything that is planned by school personnel.
- Curriculum is a series of experiences undergone by learners in the school.
- Curriculum is that which an individual learner experiences as a result of schooling.

Figure 1.1 shows various definitions of curriculum categorized into thematic groups, showing some of the extremely diverse ways in which curriculum is viewed.

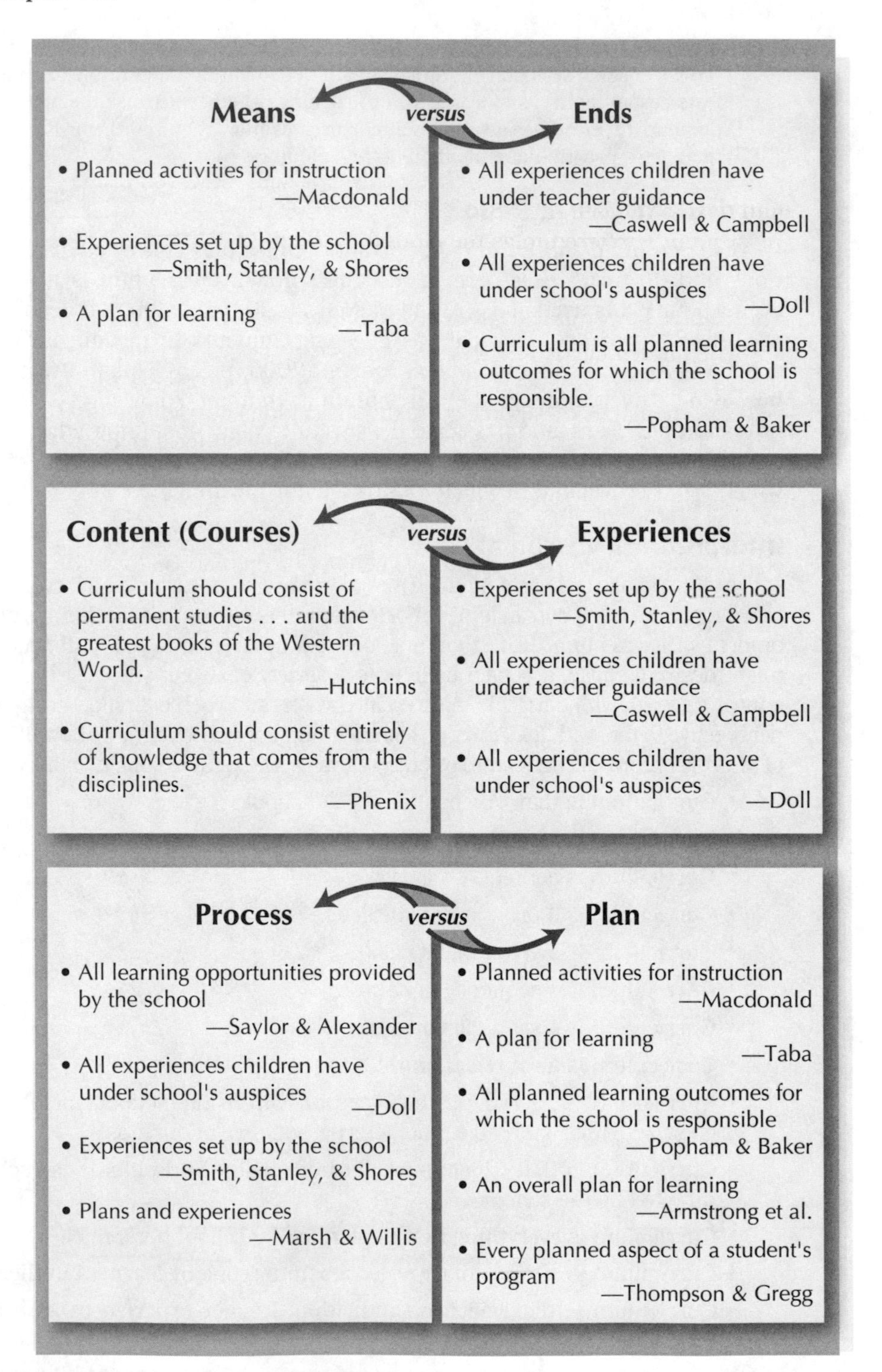

Figure 1.1 Categorizing Definitions of Curriculum

The Hidden Curriculum

The curriculum that we have been attempting to define and interpret, though varied in many respects, has at least one implied commonality: It is visible, whether it is a document or an ongoing set of activities. But, like the moon, curriculum also has a face that is never openly exposed—or, if you prefer, every curriculum has a hidden dimension. That more obscure, less visible part of the curriculum is referred to as the *hidden curriculum*—that which is taught implicitly, rather than explicitly, by the school experience.

The Subtle Power of the Hidden Curriculum

The hidden curriculum carries subtle messages that go on continuously, and the task of grasping a clear concept of the hidden curriculum is difficult. Not so difficult, though, is the ability to see that the hidden curriculum is a powerful force in any school, and it may reinforce school, state, and local reform efforts and the school's stated mission. Or it may militate vigorously against the two, or it may even support some parts of local reform practices and the school's mission while simultaneously working against other parts of the reform and mission. Armstrong et al. (2009) caution of its power, "The content we choose to teach, the rules we implement, the way we organize the classroom, and the methods we use to teach the content all send messages to students" (p. 141).

The socialization process that comes from the school itself, as a community, is a significant part of the hidden curriculum. At some schools, this process teaches that competition is the road to success in the United States; at other schools, students learn that cooperation is preferred. At some schools students learn to appreciate diversity; at others, students learn to avoid students with back-

FYI Environmental Scanning

Victoria Robinson • University of Northern Iowa

Teachers need to be acutely aware of the hidden curriculum that exists in their classroom and in their building. A teacher's actions often speak louder than words and, as Theodore Sizer reminded us, "The students are watching."

In order to provide practice for my students in identifying both helpful and harmful hidden curriculum in their own classroom and building, I ask my graduate students to conduct an environmental scan focused on my Curriculum, Assessment and Instruction class. Working in teams of three, the students list specific routines, procedures, social interactions, feedback, assignments, assessments, teacher behavior, class activities, and unspoken expectations. After twenty minutes, each team of three joins another team. This team of six then analyzes the two lists to determine what is silently communicated to them in this class. Teams report their analysis to the large group at the end of the class session. Students report that this activity caused them to be much more aware of the hidden messages being sent to students in a class. (Note: I also receive valuable feedback through this activity as students uncover for me the hidden curriculum in my class!)

grounds different than their own. These are just two of the hundreds of lessons taught at every school through the hidden curriculum.

Although hidden curriculum is often called *unplanned curriculum*, sometimes it is planned, and with positive results. Without purposeful planning, however, the hidden curriculum can be (and often is) damaging. According to Ornstein, Behar, and Pajak (2003), "The hidden curriculum fosters conformity and passivity, while seldom encouraging critical thinking, ethical behavior, and civic courage" (p. 385). Martin Haberman expressed concern for what he considers severe hidden curriculum damage on a national level (see Haberman & Bracey, 1997; Haberman, 1999). He argued that the 120 largest school districts in the United States offer curricula that unintentionally and perhaps unknowingly prepare students to fail in the workplace. For example, he says that in our efforts to be compassionate we often lead students to conclude that it is acceptable to be absent or tardy if they have a good excuse. Later, when these same students try this at the workplace, they are puzzled when they receive pink slips.

Haberman (1999, p. 73) asks the following questions:

1. Are we rewarding students on the quality of their excuses? Or do we reward students for making up work they have missed?
2. Are we rewarding students who do not like each other by separating them? Or do we reward students who show they can work with people they might not necessarily like?
3. Are we rewarding students for only working when a teacher is present? Or do we reward students for being productive without having direct supervision?

Haberman's concerns give credibility to the claim that the effect of the hidden curriculum is powerful, perhaps even more so than that of the visible curriculum. The hidden curriculum includes what a school does *not* do. The investigators of one school reported that their school does little to encourage contact among students of different backgrounds (McCarthy & Kuh, 2006). Ask yourself: What experiences do I remember most from my school days? Were these planned activities/planned content or were they unplanned, such as important relationships between you and your teachers and classmates, the unwritten behavior code among students, or maybe just the overall culture of your school?

Positive Effects of the Hidden Curriculum

Although, as we have seen, the hidden curriculum can be a powerful negative force, with careful planning the hidden curriculum can work favorably for all students. Schools with successful reform programs have cultures with a prevailing attitude of experimentation, the attitude of having nothing to lose by trying a new approach. Even the smallest of changes can have a marked impact. For example, teachers who always return tests promptly and follow up on all homework assignments silently communicate to their students that these activities are important. Teachers who bring in daily news clippings and articles from current journals are letting their students know that their teachers are readers and lifelong learners. Teachers who hound their students until they turn in their assignments communicate multiple messages, including, "I have faith in your ability and you are too important for me to let you miss the opportunities that my class promotes."

If we are able to recognize the hidden curriculum and acknowledge its power, we can then harness it to plan effectively in our schools.

Impact on Multicultural Education

In the absence of an appreciation for differences, the hidden curriculum unfortunately can also have a negative or prejudicial influence on students. Oliva (2009, pp. 505–506) addresses this concern:

> Multiracial committees and entire faculties find that in order to eliminate negative attitudes and conflicts, they must analyze all aspects of the school, including the "hidden curriculum"—the school climate, social relationships among individuals and groups, values and attitudes held by both students and faculty, rules on student conduct, unspoken expectations, and unwritten codes of conduct.

The mostly covert nature of the hidden curriculum may or may not be intentional. One part of the hidden curriculum is the dialogue that occurs among members of minority ethnic groups. Members of the mainstream may be critical of some minorities' tendency to gather in small groups. They may perceive such groups as prejudiced against the mainstream, never realizing that the minority group members may feel like victims of prejudice themselves and are trying to satisfy some cultural and psychological needs. Thoughtful and careful curriculum planning can help meet some of these needs.

The hidden curriculum offers opportunities to communicate important positive multicultural messages. Domestic diversity and an unprecedented influx of immigrants have created a vibrant mixture of cultural, ethnic, linguistic, and experiential plurality (Gay, 2006). By providing a positive role model, teachers can show their appreciation for the opportunities a multicultural class offers to enrich life experiences. All teachers who choose to do so can have multicultural classrooms, even teachers whose students are all white, all black, all Hispanic, or indeed any other ethnic background, or whose students are all male or all female, so long as the teacher leads students to tolerate, appreciate, and celebrate diversity.

The Negative Impact of Reform Reports

Soon after the education reform process was underway in a few states, a reform explosion occurred. Dissatisfied with the performance of American students on standardized achievement tests, then-secretary of education Terrel Bell initiated the National Commission on Excellence in Education. In 1983, this committee released its report, *A Nation at Risk*, to the president and to the public at large. Within a year after the report was published, reform initiatives were underway in every state (Kretovics, Farber, & Armaline, 2004).

During the early and mid-1950s, Russian and U.S. scientists were competing to see who could put the first satellite into space. In October of 1957 the Russians launched *Sputnik* and were perceived as winning the "space race." This caused a feeling of malaise that bordered on panic among the American people, who blamed the schools (Bracey, 2007), concluding that U.S. high schools must be far inferior to those in Russia and perhaps in other developed nations. The result of these American fears was the legislation known as the Elementary and Secondary Education Act (ESEA) of 1965, which poured high amounts of funding into public education. This support led to aggressive behavior as congress stepped up its involvement with public schools. According to Phillip Schlechty (2008, p. 1), the No Child Left Behind legislation "is nothing more or less than the latest reauthorization of the 1965 legislation."

The space race continued and the level of competition increased, contributing to the general cold-war paranoia and prompting a series of reports calling for major reform of U.S. schools. The tone of *A Nation at Risk* set the stage: "If an unfriendly foreign power had attempted to impose on America the mediocre educational performance that exists today, we might well have viewed it as an act of war" (p. 5). This report also stated that American schools were "drowning in a rising tide of mediocrity."

Almost two decades later, the *A Nation at Risk/Goals 2000* agenda was, right or wrong, still at heart a movement founded on the establishment and broad implementation at the state and local levels of some form of nationally approved, uniform, world-class academic standards at all grade levels (Clinchy, 1998, p. 276; Borko & Elliott, 1999). Orlich (2000, p. 469–470) has summarized the report:

> *A Nation at Risk* recommended (1) a tougher set of academic basics for high school graduation, (2) higher standards for universities, (3) a longer school year and/or school day, (4) merit pay for top teachers, and (5) more citizen participation.

Orlich (2000) pointed out that this report was issued by a group dominated by people who did not work in the public schools. He listed eight negative qualities of most reform reports:

1. The reforms are politically inspired and coerced by state governments.
2. The stress on higher student achievement is based on standards-based reports that were prepared by professional associations, not by local school boards.
3. Content standards tend to be collections of outcomes or student behaviors, assembled in a nonsystematic manner and without content hierarchies clearly shown.
4. Cost-benefit analyses are lacking from the reports on state school reforms.
5. Control of education has shifted to the national and state levels and away from localities.
6. The reform agendas, though fragmentary, are broad in scale and encompass most of the 50 states.
7. Politically inspired as the education reform movement has been, it must still be classified as being atheoretical—that is, its basic premises are grounded not in empirically sound studies but rather in political enthusiasms and intentions.
8. Implied within these reforms is the conclusion that, as a consequence of standards and high-stakes state testing and assessment programs, there should be a dramatic increase in student achievement. (pp. 469–472)

These shortcomings are discussed below.

Overemphasis on Test Scores

The overemphasis on standardized test scores can take its toll on teachers. The No Child Left Behind legislation has intensified this concern, continuing to rely on test scores as evidence of school success. At least one incident has been documented where teachers were encouraged by administrators to assist students in cheating on tests for the purposes of achieving higher scores. Had they not been found out, those teachers and administrators would have received financial rewards if their schools improved their test scores. (The district superintendent, for example, would have received a $20,000 bonus!)

Twenty-first century educators must avoid concluding that the American schools or American teachers have been inferior to schools or teachers in other nations based on standardized test scores when, in fact, the American students who have taken these tests have competed against the top few percent of selected students in other countries who have gone on to pursue formal secondary education programs. On the contrary, the proficiency demonstrated by American students is an accomplishment of great magnitude, and we should celebrate the work of twentieth-century teachers. Throughout the twentieth century, American schools attempted to educate *all* of the country's youth. Granted, no country has reached perfection in this goal, but more important, until recently no other country had even aspired to this goal. Furthermore, our schools have been successful in retaining an increasing number of students. Of the 1,015 colleges responding to a recent survey (Habley & McClanahan, 2004), 479 colleges (47.2%) reported that they had established a goal for improvement in the first- to second-year retention rate, and 336 colleges (33.1%) reported that they had established a goal for improvement in the five-year degree completion rate.

Misleading Test-Score Interpretations

After a decade of negative reports, a couple of incidents occurred that exposed the intentional misuse of testing to portray the schools negatively. Consequently, Gough (1993, p. 108) predicted an upturn in the public's perception of American education:

> The public's perception of our profession took a turn for the better in 1991. That's when the first "Bracey Report" on the condition of education ("Why Can't They Be Like We Were?") appeared in the pages of the *Kappan*. That's also when the third draft of a report on the condition of American education, written by researchers at the Sandia National Laboratories, began to circulate informally throughout the education community—and then beyond it, to a broader audience.
>
> The Sandia researchers, employees of the Department of Energy, had no vested interest in defending education. . . . [They] found, in the process, essentially the same thing that Gerald Bracey had found: the schools were not in the state of collapse that some critics had claimed. . . . Thus, the Sandia study helped shift conventional wisdom. The "oh-ain't-the-schools-awful" refrain quickly began to give way to today's more realistic assertion that the schools are doing just about as well as they ever did. . . .

For years, the National Assessment of Educational Progress (NAEP) has been called "the nation's report card." Isolated results on this test have been used as evidence of the deterioration of American schools. Yet, when viewed over a twenty-year span, they are very stable (Bracey, 1991). While the performance of white students has remained constant, the performances of African Americans and Hispanics have actually improved.

The U.S. Department of Education Institute of Education Science's 2008 National Center for Education Statistics Report, "The Condition of Education" (2009a), shows that the mathematics scores for 9- and 13-year-olds are higher than in all previous assessment years. At age 9, the average score in mathematics in 2008 was 4 points higher than in 2004 and 24 points higher than in 1973 (NCES, 2009a). The 2008 NAEP report informs us that U.S. schools' enrollment is rising to an all-time high, and the student body is becoming more diverse. More individuals of all races are enrolling in college and are earning more bachelor's degrees than in the past. Compared to 1986, the percentage of 13-year-olds taking algebra increased from 16 to 30% (NCES, 2009a).

In addition, the public seldom sees how the population who takes the SAT is determined. Since the test is taken voluntarily, and since it is used for college admission, the annual audience is whoever shows up Saturday morning to take it. Considering the increase in the number and range of students who take this test, it is remarkable that the scores have held steady. For example, when the test was initiated in 1941, the subjects were 10,654 mostly white, male students headed for Ivy League and other prestigious private universities. During the 1988–1990 school years, one and a quarter million students (1,025,523), of which 27% were minorities, took the test. Furthermore, 52% were females, who historically have not scored as well as males on the SAT. In 2006, of 1.5 million students who took the SAT, 39% were minorities (Pytel, 2007). According to an article in *The Washington Post* (Glod & Chandler, 2008), SAT performance held steady for 2008 high school graduates even as participation rose among minority students and those who are part of the first generation in their families to go to college.

Narrow Views of Reform Reports

Since the National Commission on Excellence (1983) released *A Nation at Risk*, over four hundred national- and state-level reform reports have followed. Most share the flaws that characterized their grandparent report, and most have additional flaws. Naturally, such reports represent the interests of their authors. Most reform reports have been written by committees whose interests or agenda have ranged from economics to defense. Because reports are written by special-interest groups and because most of these groups are politically based, many of the reports are narrow in their perspective. Whatever the purposes of our schools—and there is no implication that there is, could ever be, or should be universal agreement on their purposes—American schools do not exist with the sole purpose of producing competitive workers, or superior soldiers, or world-competitive economists. Because many of the reports view the purpose of the schools in light of the mission of their interest group, the reports are too narrow in perspective.

Flawed Overall Purposes

Another flaw in many of the education reform reports concerns the overall intended purpose of the reports, that is, the reasons for their existence and their intended effects. The language used is significant. Some of the reform efforts use inflammatory language, which does not suggest an honest effort to inform or enlighten the public. This type of rhetoric may be an attempt to excite and alarm. Recall, for example, the grandparent report, *A Nation at Risk*—which set the tone for later reports—referring to an "unfriendly foreign power" and portraying American schools as "drowning in a sea of mediocrity." Another major report, *Action for Excellence* (Education Commission of the States, 1983), which appeared at about the same time, speaks of "a need for survival" and uses such terms as "emergency" and "urgency." Well intentioned or not, the use of exaggeration and inflammatory language misleads the public. The concern about the use of reform reports continues. The act of planning reform at the state and national levels and then imposing it on local schools causes teachers and principals to further question the purpose of the reforms.

Educationally Unsound Recommendations

Another common flaw in many twentieth-century education reform reports was in their recommendations. Because most of the reports were written by laypeople, most of whom are not educators, many of their recommendations are not educationally sound. For example, *A Nation at Risk* recommended both a longer school day and a longer school year. In other words, the critics were basically saying the performance of the schools is mediocre (meaning "very poor"), so give us more of it, which is illogical. Most of the reports call for more math and science at the expense of the arts and humanities. Most appear to address only the secondary curriculum, on the assumption that whatever is good for secondary students and teachers is good for their elementary counterparts.

Few of the earlier reports addressed the fact that a large number of students abuse drugs. Few addressed the fact that teachers are overworked. Few mentioned the need to discover ways of motivating students. Until recently, few of the reports mentioned societal problems that must be addressed and overcome before the schools can reach their academic goals. However, we now have some startling statistics to ponder.

- As of 2007, 39% of U.S. children were living in poverty. Sixty percent of black children, 61% of Latino children, and 57% of American Indian children were living in poverty-stricken circumstances. Fifty-four percent of these children were living in single-parent households; 5% of them in households with no parent present (National Center for Children in Poverty, 2008).
- In the United States, 1.35 million children are homeless in America (Institute for Children and Poverty, 2008). According to the National Coalition for the Homeless (2000), 14% of homeless children are diagnosed with learning disabilities—double the rate of other children. Twenty-one percent repeat a grade because of frequent absence from school and/or frequent school transfers.

If we take into consideration the substantive economic challenges that have recently occurred in the United States, it is quite likely that these numbers have increased.

Neuroscientists have found that many children growing up in very poor families with low social status experience unhealthy levels of stress hormones, which impair their neural development, affecting language development and memory (Krugman, 2008). Obviously, such impairments are likely to result in children with learning problems. Further, Paul Krugman (2008) states that "In modern America parental status trumps ability: Students who did very well on a standardized test but came from low-status families were slightly less likely to get through college than students who tested poorly but had well-off parents." Henry Levin (2007) affirms that "poverty and educational failure have been inextricably linked in American education. Students from low-income backgrounds experience relatively low levels of academic achievement and fewer years of educational attainment relative to students from higher-income categories."

High-Stakes Testing

Referring to the standardized tests used to hold teachers and schools accountable for student learning, Marion Brady (2008, p. 67) has said, "Of all the obstacles to improving student thinking, these [high-stakes tests] are surely the most damaging" (p. 66). By the early 1980s the national focus on improving the schools moved forward at irreversible speed by the National Commission on Excellence in Education. Educators Joseph Kretovics, Kathleen Farber, and William Armaline (2004, p. 213) have summarized the effects of the test-driven movement introduced by *A Nation at Risk:*

> Over the past twenty years, both the generals and the casualties of this war on public education have been many. . . . Test-driven accountability has raised academic standards for poor and minority children but has done little to change a system that virtually guaranteed their failure. The failure of school-reform movements, thus far, is largely a failure to identify the root cause of educational problems; to understand the complexities of public education; to understand the social, cultural, political, and economic forces that help structure education at the local level; and to identify and overcome barriers to improved academic and social performance.

We should weigh dubious advantages derived from improving test scores against the real examples that high-stakes testing can be detrimental to our youth. Too much emphasis on test-driven accountability can make teachers powerless and shift the focus of education away from students (Armstrong et al., 2009); yet twenty-first-century educators know that they must keep the total welfare of students at the center of their thoughts and goals. We must avoid this harmful practice of putting concern for output above concern for input (or what happens to learners in the school). For example, Eric Jensen (2008) remarks that ironically, while "The current high-stakes testing environment means that some educators are eliminating recess, play, or physical education from daily agendas. . . . The weight of evidence is that exercise is strongly correlated with increased brain mass, better cognition, mood regulation, and new cell production" (p. 412). Other school curricula are cutting back on the fine arts, although evidence has shown that these types of courses are most effective in enhancing higher-level thinking and creativity in students—two of the most valued aspects of learning. Audry Amrein-Beardsley (2007, p. 64) says that there is virtually no evidence to support the conclusion that high-stakes tests increase student achievement.

One major mistake that NCLB is making in its attempt to hold schools accountable is the use of end-of-year tests, because these tests do not tell us what the students know at the beginning of the year or how much knowledge was acquired outside the school (Barton, 2007/2008). C. Thomas Holmes (2006) made a good point by saying that instead of being used to hold students accountable, standardized test results should be used for identifying areas in curriculum that need improvement.

Inadequate Support

Perhaps the most serious and damaging shortcoming of the reform reports has been their failure to acknowledge the unwillingness of our lawmakers to provide adequate financial support for our schools. Unlike American lawmakers and policy makers, their counterparts in the world's leading schools have taken responsibility for providing adequate financial support. The importance of this difference is addressed in the Council of Chief State School Officers' 2008 Report and Recommendations for Educational Policymakers: "Clearly, a major factor in the success of Singaporean students is the monetary investment in their education by their leaders and policymakers" (CCSSO, 2008, p. 6).

The Legacy of *A Nation At Risk:* No Child Left Behind

In the twenty-first century, it's an unfortunate fact that legislators have convinced the public that the answer to improving our schools lies in increased testing and in punishing those schools that do not measure up to continually growing expectations. A case has been made that the latest legacy of *A Nation at Risk* is the *No Child Left Behind Act* of 2001 (Schlechty, 2008; Wood, 2002), the end product of a half-century of increased criticism of U.S. schools. This bill, signed into law in 2002, continues to rely heavily on high-stakes testing that determines promotion to the next grade level and graduation from high school (Oliva, 2009); it also punishes schools to force them to improve. Many of these tests on which NCLB relies use basically numerical scores. James Popham (2007/2008) cautions us that "The perception that our education tests are precise because they yield numerical scores is fundamentally mistaken" (p. 88) and has remarked that when all one has to work with are numbers representing learners' scores, one lacks the information needed to change conditions to bring about improvement.

High-stakes tests have seriously damaged the learning process. For many educators, the appeal of having data on student growth to guide instruction is overshadowed by fear that the numbers will be used to penalize schools and teachers whose students are standing still. Many consider NCLB among the reform programs that were never intended to improve schools. Consider the following complaints. "District-mandated pacing guides and timeliness of data results impede

Box 1.2 No Child Left Behind

The No Child Left Behind database, which the Education Commission of the States (ECS) maintains, records actual policy enactments and calculates trends by quarter. At a glance, visitors to the Web site can see how the nation as a whole is progressing on the seven NCLB categories, how individual states are faring, and how states compare to one another. According to the ECS:

> This groundbreaking report contains information you won't find anywhere else about how implementation of NCLB is playing out in states. It includes results from ECS's comprehensive database, which tracks and reports state implementation activity on 40 NCLB indicators; trends within and across states; issues and challenges facing states; and recommendations.

To learn more about this report and to access the NCLB database online, visit the ECS Web site (http://www.ecs.org/NCLB).

support for teachers to analyze student work and use data for instruction (Hanson & Moir, 2008, pp. 457–458). According to Bracey (2003), "NCLB is a weapon of mass destruction used to launch a campaign of shock and awe against the schools and against the children" (p. 163).

In an article titled "Vonnegut warned us," Clare Fugate (2007) draws a parallel between a Kurt Vonnegut story, *Harrison Bergerson*, and NCLB. Vonnegut's story features a Handicapper-General who, in attempting to level the playing field [the way NCLB does], requires all beautiful women to wear masks, the graceful to drag around bags of bird shot tied to their legs, and those with beautiful voices to squeak and cackle so that eventually everyone will be "equal." Like the Handicapper-General, NCLB requires schools to hold (*not lead*) all students to the same proficiency level.

Excessive Demands on Schools

In addition to the increased use of high-stakes testing, an equally disturbing factor is the number and variety of expectations placed on schools. NCLB legislation ill-defines terms such as *highly qualified teacher*, actually leaving it up to each state to define them, and then makes teachers accountable for taking student performance to impossible levels. NCLB sets expectations for students that schools and school districts find impossible to reach, some because the expectations are vague, others because they are impossibly high. Using the term *adequate yearly progress* (AYP), NCLB requires schools and districts to disaggregate test scores for groups such as ethnic minorities, special-education students, and economically disadvantaged students. To make AYP, each group must exceed its previous year's performance on standardized tests. Schools that do not meet these goals within two years will be declared in need of improvement. If after three years they don't improve, the curriculum and/or the staff can be replaced (Woolfolk Hoy & Hoy, 2009). It only stands to reason that schools can exceed their previous year's performance only so many times before it becomes impossible to do better.

A recent national poll found that over two-thirds (69%) of the public believe that current emphasis on standards will cause teachers to teach to the tests. About four-fifths of the public believe that this is a bad thing (Rose & Gallup, 2007). Critics say that grouping students, giving them impossible expectations, and then labeling them as failures hurts these students, their teachers, and their parents, and it militates against current efforts to create a nurturing, personalized curriculum.

According to David Marshak (2004),

> The public school system that we have today was constructed during the first two decades of the 20th century. . . . These "industrial schools" were structured to maximize competition between students and to minimize the depth of relationships between students and their teachers. . . . The bulk of our culture is already in or racing toward postindustrial forms. For schools, this will mean personalization, small schools, strong relationships developed over several years, common goals for all students, individual goals for every student, and many and varied uses of communication technologies in ways that are intensely student-centered. . . . The tragic irony of the 1990s and of the present moment is that we have the knowledge in our culture to create schools that will educate every child with respect and to good ends. Indeed, we have exemplary schools all over the nation that are doing so right now. . . . These good schools all have high standards, and they have accountability. But they also respect and value the inevitable diversity of the human population. And everything that happens in them starts with personal long-term relationships between adults and children. (pp. 229–231)

Reform is rapidly changing the roles and lives of teachers, administrators, parents, counselors, designated curriculum leaders, instructional supervisors, and students. Representatives from all of these groups are responding to the demands of education reform in many ways, ranging from desperate panic in efforts to meet the reform challenges to absolute refusal to comply with reform demands, to unprecedented levels of enthusiasm, energy, and ownership over cutting-edge innovations. The outcome of these increased demands and role changes brought about by reform remains to be seen.

Positive Outcomes of Education Reform

Not all of the outcomes of education reform efforts have been negative. On the contrary, there is much good news to report, and it is growing daily.

Teacher Involvement

A shift in the scope of teacher involvement has occurred, from the isolated classroom to the broader school curriculum-planning arena. An inversion is currently sweeping the country, moving reform initiatives from state and federal bureaucracies to local districts and schools. NCLB has mandated that twenty-first century educators at all levels must base their practices on research, which the U.S. Department of Education explains "means there is reliable evidence that the program or practice works." As a result, more teachers are becoming involved with research, which in the past has been noticeably neglected by many educators. Dixon-Kraus (2003, quoted in Franco, 2007) believes that action research can be considered as the "scientifically based research" required by NCLB. Teachers who conduct action research studies learn from their own experiences and can share their knowledge with their peers. Initiatives supported by research offer the most promising ways to develop school improvement programs. (Chapter 8 discusses the changing scope of teacher involvement and the increasingly important role of teachers as researchers.)

The education reform reports provide the education profession a great service when they reaffirm the importance of education in the public's mind. Consequently, in several states the level of financial support has been raised. The reform reports also focus teachers' attention on the broader curricula across the school. Historically, most teachers have not been involved with curriculum development beyond the limits of their own classroom. Until recently, most teachers have not been prepared or permitted to get involved with schoolwide planning. Involvement in their school's total curriculum should enable teachers to avoid or at least minimize disruptions and duplications between their classes and those of other teachers, particularly those classes that students take during the years just prior to and just following the teacher's classes.

Parental Involvement

Equally important, the increased public awareness of the importance of education has raised the overall level of parental support. In his February 28, 2009, address before Joint Session of Congress, President Barack Obama underscored the importance of parental involvement when he said:

> In the end, there is no program or policy that can substitute for a parent—for a mother or father who will attend those parent/teacher conferences, or help with homework, or turn off the TV, put away the video games, read to their child. I speak to you not just as a president, but as a father, when I say that responsibility for our children's education must begin at home. That is not a Democratic issue or a Republican issue. That's an American issue.

Increased parental participation is a necessity for maximum academic gains. Many parents want to help their children succeed but feel unqualified (Wherry, 2007). The No Child Left Behind legislation provides increased opportunities for parents to become involved in a variety of ways. For example, administrators and teachers must use language that parents understand, and parents are now discovering that they have a stake in determining the learning strategies selected to increase their children's achievement level, as well as the content being taught. More and more ways are being discovered to use technology to involve parents in their children's education.

Administrator Involvement

There is more good news: Administrators, too, have become more involved with curriculum planning. Recognizing the need for administrators to be directly involved in instructional and curriculum planning, former secretary of education Terrel Bell (1993) said, "It is futile to even try to improve a school if the leadership

FYI Fortune Cookie

Janice M. Walker • Drake University

A good way for students to summarize the supervision process or clarify the supervisor's role in the evaluation cycle is to participate in the following activity. Divide your students into pairs, and give each student a fortune cookie. Each student reads his or her fortune aloud, and then together the pair designs a statement that combines both fortunes and highlights key ideas of supervision. We write the statements on large chart paper and discuss what the key ideas were or the most important ideas to remember.

is lackluster" (p. 597). During the 1980s and 1990s the level of involvement of school administrators in curriculum and instruction reached heights unprecedented since the days of the one-room school. Research on effective schools has made educators aware of the need for administrators—particularly building principals—to be at the center of instructional and curriculum planning. The No Child Left Behind legislation provides Title II grant money for the recruitment, training, and development of high-quality principals.

To serve students from a wide range of diverse backgrounds, administrators must make their schools inviting to everyone, taking a proactive stance and not just waiting for parents and other community members to become involved. Administrators also must encourage teachers and students to take risks (Keefe & Amenta, 2005). A positive school culture that encourages risk taking does not fault mistakes, but rather treats them as part of the learning experience.

Advances in Teacher Education

In the 1980s and 1990s the focus of education reform programs was mainly on elementary and secondary schools; however, in the twenty-first century this focus has broadened to include the higher education institutions. Teacher education colleges and departments have three major responsibilities in the education reform movement. First, they must prepare students to be knowledgeable about the major reform practices in their state and must be skilled in implementing these elements. Effective implementation of school reform requires that teachers, designated curriculum directors, instructional supervisors, administrators, parents, and counselors (1) be comfortable and confident in their ability to carry out reform, and (2) acquire and maintain a positive attitude toward the reform movement. Teacher education colleges and departments must provide students with opportunities to develop these necessary understandings, skills, and attitudes.

State and local reform initiatives have raised the bar for student learning, which places greater demands on teachers. Preparing new cohorts of teachers for these heightened expectations will require reforms in teacher education programs. Colleges and universities should strengthen the academic course requirements for prospective teachers and should provide them with high-quality education and practice in effective teaching methods. School districts should provide support for new teachers, such as mentoring (Center on Education Policy and the American Youth Policy Forum, 2000).

The second goal of education colleges and departments is to help teachers assess the value of each reform practice for their school and their students. Frankly, some reform practices should never have been implemented. Unfortunately, some of the earlier reform reports attempted to convince the public that the underlying cause of the perceived failure of American schools is weak teachers. The good news is that later reports have not reinforced that belief. A decade after *A Nation at Risk* was published, its initiator, Terrel Bell (1993), wrote:

> We have foolishly concluded that any problems with the levels of academic achievement have been caused by faulty schools staffed by inept teachers and by fixing the schools we can attain the levels of success we so desperately need in this decade. (p. 595)

Bell continued by saying, "We also know that teacher leadership of and involvement in school improvement must become a more integral part of our plans" (p. 597). Indeed, it is important to recognize that teachers and other school personnel hold unique power to exert leadership and shape student lives. For more on the evolving and expanding role of teachers, see chapter 8.

A third major goal of teacher education in the education-reform process is to help *in-service teachers* (who have graduated and are teaching full time), administrators, curriculum developers, instructional supervisors, and counselors to gear up to perform the reform requirements in their state. Teachers, particularly, hold the key to success or failure in reforming the schools. No one can reform our schools for us. If there is to be authentic reform in American education, it must be a *grassroots movement*. This is precisely the viewpoint of this book. We hope to familiarize readers with the nature of the curriculum development process and the nature of education reform, and to prepare them to apply sound foundations and principles of curriculum development to meet their responsibilities in implementing major education reform. Keep in mind at all times the two major purposes of U.S. schools: learning and socialization.

Identification of True Weaknesses

Current education reform efforts have resulted from perceived weaknesses in American schools. Although, as already stressed, some of these perceptions are dead wrong, some of the reform reports actually identify major weaknesses that permeate the schools. Separately and collectively, these weaknesses prevent American students from reaching their maximum potential. Correcting these conditions will require some major curriculum adjustments within and beyond the classroom which, in turn, will require changing the ways teachers and other educators use the curriculum development process in their classrooms and in the school at large.

As you prepare to launch your own program to contribute to education reform, a logical way to begin your reform efforts is by examining the weaknesses in the current education system. The following paragraphs discuss some of the areas that many educators say need to be improved.

One area in which many educators see a need for improvement is the failure to use research—a practice that is called for in The No Child Left Behind Act of 2001. Ironically, this same law pressures teachers to cover an extensive list of required topics, and many are frustrated by their lack of time for anything else—including research. Yet there are teachers who actively conduct research. Some teacher education colleges and some departments, such as those found at Michigan State University and the University of Maryland, have histories of school–university partnerships, collaborating with local schools in conducting meaningful action research studies. (Action research is small, expedient research aimed at improving current practices. For a more in-depth discussion, see chapter 8). If reform is successful, this practice will become commonplace in twenty-first-century schools. Teacher education colleges and departments must assume major responsibility for graduating students who are prepared as both conductors and consumers of research—two skills that are prerequisite to developing an appreciation for research.

The relationship between the role of the schools and the way educators view research is ironic. From the perspective of the reconstructionist, a major role of the schools is to lead or shape society, yet other areas in society seem to be more involved than the schools in the use of research. It is unthinkable that the advancements made in industry, architecture, business, agriculture, engineering, medicine, or any other profession could have occurred without the major role that research plays in these professions. How could anyone think of education as an exception?

Graduate curricula for educators reflect a recognition of the importance of research to education in that almost all graduate degree programs require one or more courses in research, and most advanced graduate programs require all candidates to conduct their own research studies, usually in the form of a major thesis or dissertation. Teacher educators must involve their students in authentic problem solving to ensure that they view their research courses and assignments not as obstacles in their programs to be overcome, but as powerful tools to be developed and used on a daily basis in the schools where they will teach. It is perhaps even more critical that undergraduate teacher education programs engage all students in research, both as a subject to be studied and as a project to be carried out.

The No Child Left Behind Act calls for *scientifically-based* curriculum and instruction. Later in this book you will also see that, ironically and unfortunately, the area of education where research lags most is the area in which research could most improve education. Can you identify that area? You can test your hypothesis when we return to the topic in a later chapter.

To end this discussion of research on a negative note would be shortsighted, for the picture is rapidly changing; many schools are making remarkable progress with action research and are using it to restructure their entire curriculum. After pointing out the inability of research to prescribe infallible teaching practices, James Popham (2007/2008, p. 79) concludes by saying, "It's clearly better to use teaching practices that probably will succeed than to use those that probably won't." The following case study by David Stine is a good model that other school faculties can follow.

case study

Action Research as an Instrument of Change

David Stine
California State University–San Bernardino

Background Information

Many of the U.S. border states are confronted with a dramatic change in the demographics of students in the public schools. Increasing numbers of new students enroll with limited ability to read or speak the English language. Some arrive in the upper grades or even high school without ever having been in a formal school setting. The newly enrolled students often represent a variety of the cultures from Asia, South and Central America, and Mexico. Teachers are faced with classes of students with a wide range of differences in their understanding of English and of American culture, and teachers in turn often have a limited understanding of the students' cultures.

In many schools there is no longer a predominant majority of any race of students, and there is a multiplicity of cultures and ethnic backgrounds to consider. Many schools are using the same textbooks, the same teaching methods, and the same assessment instruments in their classrooms that were introduced before these demographic changes occurred.

The Educational Community

With compulsory attendance policies in place and political pressure for minimal dropout rates ever present, schools are committed to providing appropriate education for all students, but class sizes are increasing and new funding is nonexistent. The faculty, administration, and staff are not sure how to cope with this changing student environment, and the community is concerned about dropping test scores.

At the state level there are debates in the legislature regarding the usefulness of bilingual education and of teaching English as a second language (ESL), how to teach reading, and even how to build student self-esteem. The state school board association also studies these problems, and the professors at the local universities can offer a variety of solutions to these concerns verified by their own research, but they seldom agree on any issue. The real challenge for the career educator is to determine what needs to be done to provide the most powerful teaching and learning environment for the students and then to take action.

The School

San Antonio High School is a large suburban comprehensive school of 3,000 students in grades 9 to 12. It is the original school in a union high school district that has spawned six other schools in neighboring communities and cities as the population has fled the urban center. Affordable housing, an increased service market, and major transportation links have made this area attractive for newcomers. A new principal who has been hired to replace a retiring one has been given the challenge to energize the faculty, assess the student needs, improve test scores, and build community relations.

The Principal

The new principal was the first administrator to be hired from outside the district in the last 12 years. The central administration and the board of education wanted to hire an experienced, proven leader who had a track record of positive relations with faculty and a person who believed in a decentralized organization where teachers would be included in the decision-making process. The principal they chose had a demonstrated record of shared decision making and teacher empowerment in his previous schools. In addition, his references had praised his high energy and his work with parents and community. He was noted for his organizational ability and problem-solving skills.

The Case

Upon arriving on the job in the summer, when the faculty and students were enjoying vacation time, the new principal wanted to use this time to meet parents, get acquainted with local business owners, and invite faculty in for individual conferences. His intent was to discover the perceptions of the various stakeholders about the school. Two key questions he asked were, "What are you proudest of at SAHS?" and "What needs our attention?"

In an effort to introduce himself to parents, the principal visited the local newspaper, and an article was published that profiled him and included his offer to meet with parents in their homes "any time—morning, noon, or night—during the first three weeks of August." Key parents who had held leadership positions or whose students were in leadership roles in school were also contacted individually. These key parents included booster club supporters, parents of scholarship winners, parents of student council members, and parents of incoming freshmen who had been active in the middle schools. The principal also held 17 coffee klatches, and their locations were recorded on a map of the school district that the principal later used for strategizing. The goal was to reach as many parents as possible and to learn about the demographics and living conditions of the students. This strategy also revealed the languages spoken in the homes. A guest book was available at each of the 17 homes where gatherings were held, and participants listed their names and the names and grade levels of their children in school. The mapping provided a geographic profile of the school district and clarified where centers of parent interest were and where additional outreach might be needed in the future. Four additional parent meetings were held after a second list of invitations was extended to parents of special education students, Chapter 1 students, and bilingual students. The same two questions were asked at each meeting, and this completed the data gathering from the parents' needs assessment.

The principal also visited local businesses, service clubs, and special interest groups, including the Kiwanis, Rotary, Lions, Soroptomists, Toastmasters, American Association of University Women, Business and Professional Women, Veterans of Foreign Wars, American Legion, Chamber of Commerce, Hispanic Chamber, Salvation Army, and the local YMCA. In addition, the principal contacted city and county governmental agencies, including the regional offices of elected state and county government officeholders. At each visit the principal's message was similar: "I'm here and listening. What is good about our school, what needs attention, and how can we work together?"

About one-third of the faculty and staff accepted the invitation to come in and meet the new principal in an informal setting. After inquiring about their professional backgrounds, the principal asked about their current teaching assignments, about any extracurricular positions they might hold, and especially about any special interests or abilities they might have. The purpose was to determine the potential of the staff and faculty to become involved in future changes at the school. After the preliminary conversation, the principal asked the same broad questions he had posed to parents and business owners, and then he did a lot of listening. This technique set the stage for collaboration and demonstrated a collegial approach to problem solving. An underlying message from the principal was his belief in the philosophy that "Power with is stronger than power over." Conversations with faculty included inquiry about what they felt needed "fixing" at the school and what contributions each might make. Much of the feedback from faculty could be summarized as, "Things are not the way they used to be. Changes are going to have to happen. And we are all part of the solution."

The stage was now set, with the initial information gathered and the climate for positive change in place, so that real collaborative research could be conducted with the administration and faculty working together. The ultimate goal was the improvement of teaching and increased learning for all students at the school. The faculty was ready to be included in the action research model of problem solving.

As the weeks of summer slipped away, more and more faculty and staff returned to work. As soon as the three co-administrators and the six counselors arrived, a half-day retreat was held. Again, the initial focus was to inquire about everyone's perceptions of the school and of what needed attention. After a period of brainstorming and summarizing, the new information was combined with the data gathered from parents, faculty, and other community members. During the last hour of the session, the members present explored what people, agencies, institutions, or other sources were available that could assist in interpreting all of the information that had been gathered. Responses included key personnel at other schools, district office staff, county educational office staff, and university professors. Members of the counseling staff and an assistant principal volunteered to work with faculty to assess previous test scores to diagnose areas of weakness in student achievement. A second assistant principal took the leadership role in working with department chairs, and especially with foreign language teachers and bilingual staff, to identify what curricular changes might be useful to assist students with special needs.

A powerful statement was issued that included the endorsement of the group and stated that there was substantial talent and competency within the faculty, and that they had been waiting to be asked for their input and participation and to explore creative means to meet the new challenges with which they were being confronted. It was now time to open school and to begin the informal process of planning and continuing the action research already begun. Planning teams of volunteer faculty and department chairs began to review summaries of all the data that had been gathered. The principal introduced the teams to a seven-step model that included: (1) defining the problem, (2) proposing a method, (3) data collection, (4) data analysis, (5) reporting results, (6) action planning, and (7) evaluation. As faculty members discovered, action research is merely an organized, step-by-step approach to solving a problem.

The initial step was to determine what was the most significant problem facing the school. After considerable deliberation, it was concluded that students with limited fluency in English needed extra help and a specialized program. With this focus it was then determined that an internal search for ideas and talent would be made to find the appropriate methods to solve this problem. Test scores were reviewed, specialists were consulted, and alternatives were considered. The data that had been collected were reviewed and analyzed to determine whether the school needed to be reorganized. The suggestions and results were then reported to the entire faculty and to the appropriate district staff to solicit their reactions and their suggestions.

The final recommendation was to develop a "newcomers' school" on campus, where students with limited English speaking proficiency would be placed for three periods per day. These students would attend regular classes for the remaining three periods. The core courses would include reading, writing, and spoken English and would incorporate social science and mathematics. Students would be immersed with regular students in physical education and two elective classes. The basic classes would be limited to 20 students, and funds from various categorical programs would be utilized to finance the program. It was a clear consensus that the classes should be held on the regular campus and that the students should be a part of the regular student body. Evaluation would be a key component, and records of tests given before and after participation in the program would be maintained. Routine assessment of student progress would be done on a weekly basis. Samples of student work would also be kept to verify progress, and a report to the board of education would be made at the end of the year.

With the program in place by the second semester, administrators, counselors, and faculty made special efforts to ensure accurate and thorough communication concerning student progress and overall program effectiveness. The faculty members felt good about their participation in planning the program and recognized that they were an integral part of the solution. As a follow-up measure, plans were made to communicate to the community about the program and to invite its parents to the school to observe the classes. Press releases would be written at regular intervals, and the entire faculty would be kept apprised of the status and progress of the program.

Issues for Further Reflection and Application

1. How would you involve faculty members in the general data-gathering stages?
2. What are some ways to involve students in the problem-solving process that may have been overlooked?
3. Do you think the action research model may have been short-circuited in any way? If so, explain your answer.
4. Were the parents and community connected to the school by this process?
5. What is your assessment of the principal's utilization of time during the summer?
6. Would you object if your son or daughter were placed in this "newcomers' school"?
7. What might be the adverse consequences of a "school within a school"?
8. Could you use the action research model to solve a problem at your school? If so, describe the problem and how it might be solved.
9. What are some alternative problem-solving strategies that might have been used in this case?

Suggested Readings

Brady, M. (2008). Cover the material—or teach students to think? *Educational Leadership, 65*(5), 64–676.

Rose, L. C., & Gallup, A. M. (2007). The 39th annual Phi Delta Kappa/Gallup poll of the public's attitudes toward the public schools. *Phi Delta Kappan, 89*(1), 33–48.

The principal discussed in the case study took several initiatives to reach out to members from various segments of the community. Do you think any of his strategies will be more effective than others? Which strategies would work best in your community? Greg Gibbs (2010) recommends building your own case studies. Self-made cases are authentic, they target real problems, and they help teachers become more familiar with the community.

Effective schools research has found that parent involvement is directly linked with academic success. Although constructivists believe that each student must link newly acquired information to previously acquired understanding, the principal and teachers in the case study did not have to prescribe a method for involving parents in the creation of new knowledge. Instead, this principal chose to use action research, letting the parents and other community members design their own strategies for helping students learn. What advantage do you see in this more open approach?

Fear is a major deterrent to teachers using research. Many teachers feel insecure, perhaps believing they lack the skills required to conduct complex research studies like the ones they studied in graduate school. As seen in this case study, however, teachers needn't conduct such complex studies, nor must they do their research alone. On the contrary, some of the best research that teachers do is in collaboration with their former professors and other teachers; *collaborative research* is empowering. Also, some of the best studies are not highly complex. Rather, they are simple, practical studies about practical problems teachers have encountered. Did you notice that the teachers in this case study began simply by identifying a problem? What effect do you think this had on reducing their fear?

An Emphasis on Constructivism

Another positive reform quality is the emphasis on constructivism. Elementary and secondary curricula in the twenty-first century are dynamically changing as a result of the following three key educational forces: omnipresent use of evolving technologies, acute focus on the value of diversity, and professional emphasis on constructivist principles. Constructivists describe learning in terms of building connections between prior knowledge and new ideas and claim that *effective teaching* helps students construct an organized set of concepts that relates new and old ideas. Making connections between ideas, facts, and procedures suggests a conceptual emphasis (TIMSS Video Mathematics Research Group [TIMSS], 2003). Based on the TIMSS test scores and what they saw when they visited the world's leading schools in Singapore, the Council of Chief State School Officers

Box 1.3 Constructivism

According to Elizabeth Murphy:

> numerous researchers, educators and authors are actively engaged in using constructivist principles to design and implement new learning environments. Technology is increasingly being touted as an optimal medium for the application of constructivist principles to learning. Numerous online environments and technology-based projects are showing that theory can effectively guide educational practice.

Murphy's Web site, *Constructivism: From Philosophy to Practice* (http://www.ucs.mun.ca/~emurphy/stemnet/cle.html), highlights attempts at integrating constructivist characteristics into the practice of teaching and learning. Here Murphy offers discussion on constructivist epistemology and learning theory; characteristics of constructivist learning and teaching; and a list of projects, activities, and environments that possess these characteristics.

The Maryland Collaborative for Teacher Preparation has compiled a comprehensive online list of links to essays on constructivism and education (http://www.towson.edu/csme/mctp/Essays.html).

FYI No Buts

Janice M. Walker • Drake University

Words such as "but" and "and" can enhance or impede communication. To demonstrate this concept, I have the students divide into pairs. They must decide who will be Partner A and who will be Partner B. The pairs are told that they are going on an all-expenses-paid vacation to a destination of their choice, and at a time that is good for both partners. Partner A begins the vacation discussion by starting out, "I think we should go to_________ because__________ . . . ." Partner B must interrupt Partner A, beginning by using the word, *but,* and talk about where he/she wants to go instead, until Partner A interrupts with the word *but.* The students continue the conversation, interrupting each other each time by beginning with the word *but.* After one minute, I stop the conversation. Then the pairs have the same conversation, but they now must interrupt each other using the word *and.* Students are amazed at how difficult it is to have a conversation without the word *but* and at how frequently *but* can be a conversation blocker and create tension. After this activity we discuss the quality of our conversations with others.

(CCSSO, 2008) said that "Memorization of constantly changing factual knowledge, instead of analyzing and application, has frequently led to disconnects between what is taught in the classroom and what students need in the real world" (p. 10).

Teaching students to connect new information with existing understanding requires purposeful planning. Planning sufficient time for learning each concept allows students to engage in different kinds of learning experiences. Teachers must give assignments that require students to describe the process they use to explore new content as it relates to what they already know. Armstrong et al. (2009, p. 372) define constructivism as "a perspective on teaching that holds that learners are not passive responders to the environment but rather individuals who engage it purposefully as they seek to extract personal meaning."

Although schools have many varied purposes (discussed in detail in chapter 3), a universally recognized purpose is to educate. One perception of *education* is the process through which individuals learn to alter their environments and their own behavior to better cope with life situations. These goals require both academic and social growth. This process involves the constructivist practice of acquiring new information and changing it into meaningful knowledge. Indeed, as perceived by constructivists, this is the purpose of curriculum content. *Content* may even be defined as information that is selected to be changed into useful knowledge at a later time. Similarly, activities are selected to become meaningful experiences to students. These processes will be discussed further in chapter 7.

* * *

One final suggestion that will serve twenty-first-century teachers well is for educators to keep a balance in emphasis on all subjects. There is a tendency to emphasize one or two sources of the curriculum and neglect the others. Ninety-six percent of all Americans support the current heavy emphasis on science and mathematics, and half of those citizens believe the emphasis should be increased (Rose & Gallup, 2007). However, it is not the sciences but the arts that contribute most to the development of positive personal traits: social behavior, self-discipline, self-motivation, self-esteem, and social interaction (Henson, 2010).

An additional suggestion for future educators is to realize that lasting, meaningful reform must begin within the schools. Successful reform is something that teachers initiate. Good leaders encourage and support changes that teachers perceive as necessary (Oliva & Pawlas, 2007).

Examine the current reform practices in your local schools. Have they grown out of real teacher or student needs? Are these practices supported by research? Could/should the local teachers test them to see if they are working?

Overall, although many concerns still need to be addressed, we really do have a lot to feel good about, as the NAEP 2008 "Nation's Report Card" has shown.

Conclusion

Some of the advances made and concerns raised about the topics discussed in this chapter are summarized below.

Advances

- More minority group members than ever before are taking advanced science and mathematics courses.
- NCLB provides funds to increase community involvement.
- Today's educators know that constructivist teaching strategies such as problem solving can enhance learning.
- Domestic diversity and an unprecedented influx of immigrants have created a vibrant mixture of cultural, ethnic, and linguistic plurality.
- Students are naturally inquisitive and, given the opportunity, they will enjoy investigating the unknown.
- Used properly, the hidden curriculum can become a powerful tool to reach a variety of goals.

Concerns

- NCLB withholds money from districts whose students fail to excel in science and mathematics.
- NCLB withholds funds from districts that fail to show progress in any category.
- Increased use of standardized tests robs teachers and students of time needed to use constructivist methods.
- If ignored, the increased opportunity for cultural enrichment can instead create problems of unprecedented magnitude.
- Current curricula do not enable students to put a voice to their inquisitiveness.
- When ignored, the hidden curriculum fosters conformity and passivity.
- The funding for American schools continues to be woefully inadequate.

As applied to education, the term curriculum traditionally meant a "list of courses." However, through the years it has come to mean many things to different people. To some, the curriculum is a written document that purports to guide students' learning; to others it is the activities themselves. Still others view the curriculum as a statement of objectives or expected outcomes.

Whatever the definition, educators agree that if it is to be worthwhile, the curriculum must be more than a document that is prepared, filed, and ignored. An awareness of the different definitions enhances the curriculum planner's ability to plan, execute, evaluate, and improve curricula, and purposeful planning is both difficult and essential. Other educators agree: If what is most worthwhile is to be reached in ways other than chance, curriculum planning is necessary. Furthermore, a sound, comprehensive understanding of curriculum is needed today to guard against the narrow view of some reformers who may aspire to use the curriculum to achieve their narrow goals.

The presence of a hidden curriculum—that is, the impressions and attitudes that are taught implicitly—amplifies each teacher's need to have a firm grasp of the concept of curriculum. A sound understanding of curriculum will prepare teachers to better support positive reform changes while suppressing undesirable trends. Teachers in diverse settings have a special need to eliminate the negative effects of the hidden curriculum and to instead use the hidden curriculum to provide positive experiences for all students. To strengthen our youth and our nation all teachers, including those with homogeneous classrooms, must prepare all students to live and work positively in diverse settings. Special effort should be made to involve parents from all segments of the community, thus developing a sense of ownership among all.

Many of the 1980s and 1990s reform reports followed the pattern set by *A Nation at Risk* in defining single-minded, self-centered goals for America's schools. Nevertheless, reform efforts overall have made citizens aware that teachers are the essential key to making major improvements in our schools and, as such, must be the leaders in reforming the curriculum. The No Child Left Behind legislation has intensified twenty-first-century educators' need for good research skills and a sound understanding of curriculum if they are to be prepared to support the positive goals of school reform and avoid its pitfalls.

In the 1990s, schools experienced a strong swing toward constructivism to meet higher standards set at national, state, and local levels. In the twenty-first century, parental involvement is considered essential for maximum academic and social achievement; essentially, learning must be the cooperative endeavor of teachers, students, and parents forming a learning community by solving problems cooperatively.

Additional Learning Opportunities

1. What must teachers and others know about school reform in their state to promote sound school reform through curriculum development?
2. Considering your experience in schools, the definitions in this chapter, and your role in education, how would you define curriculum?
3. What would you find helpful to your efforts to conduct research at your school?

4. What must teachers and others know about human behavior, politics, and the nature of schools to garner the support of their colleagues in education reform?
5. What political factors in your school might inhibit or promote reform?
6. Among the reform practices or policies in your state, what features can you identify that will serve all student needs?
7. Can you identify features in local reform efforts that can be used to meet the special needs of minority students? If so, what are these features, and how can they be used more effectively toward this end?
8. How can your faculty increase its political influence on education reform in your state and district?
9. What evidence of constructivism have you seen in school curricula?

Suggested Activities

1. Select a topic in your teaching field and identify and list the major concepts in a week's lessons.
2. Research the literature on effective schools and make a list of the qualities common to these schools.
3. Select an important concept in your teaching field and grade level, preferably one that students find difficult to comprehend, and devise a step-by-step method to help students relate this concept to prior knowledge.
4. Examine the list of definitions of curriculum in figure 1.1. Create your own definition, using the definitions provided in the figure and text to support it.
5. Make a list of the major education reform practices in your state.
6. Assess your own reasons for taking this course, and identify at least two important professional aims or goals that will give you direction and motivation throughout the course.
7. Examine the list of reasons the Eastwood Middle School naysayers gave as to why teachers resist education reform, and restate each reason so that it supports education reform.
8. Interview a local school superintendent, principal, or counselor and get a list of the major education reform laws in your state. Select one or more of these practices that you would like to support. Between now and the end of this course, build a strong case of support for this reform practice.
9. Develop a strategy to increase your faculty's political influence in your community and state.
10. Design an activity to educate your students about contributions that each of several local cultures has made to the larger community or to the entire country.

chapter two

Social and Technological Foundations of Curriculum

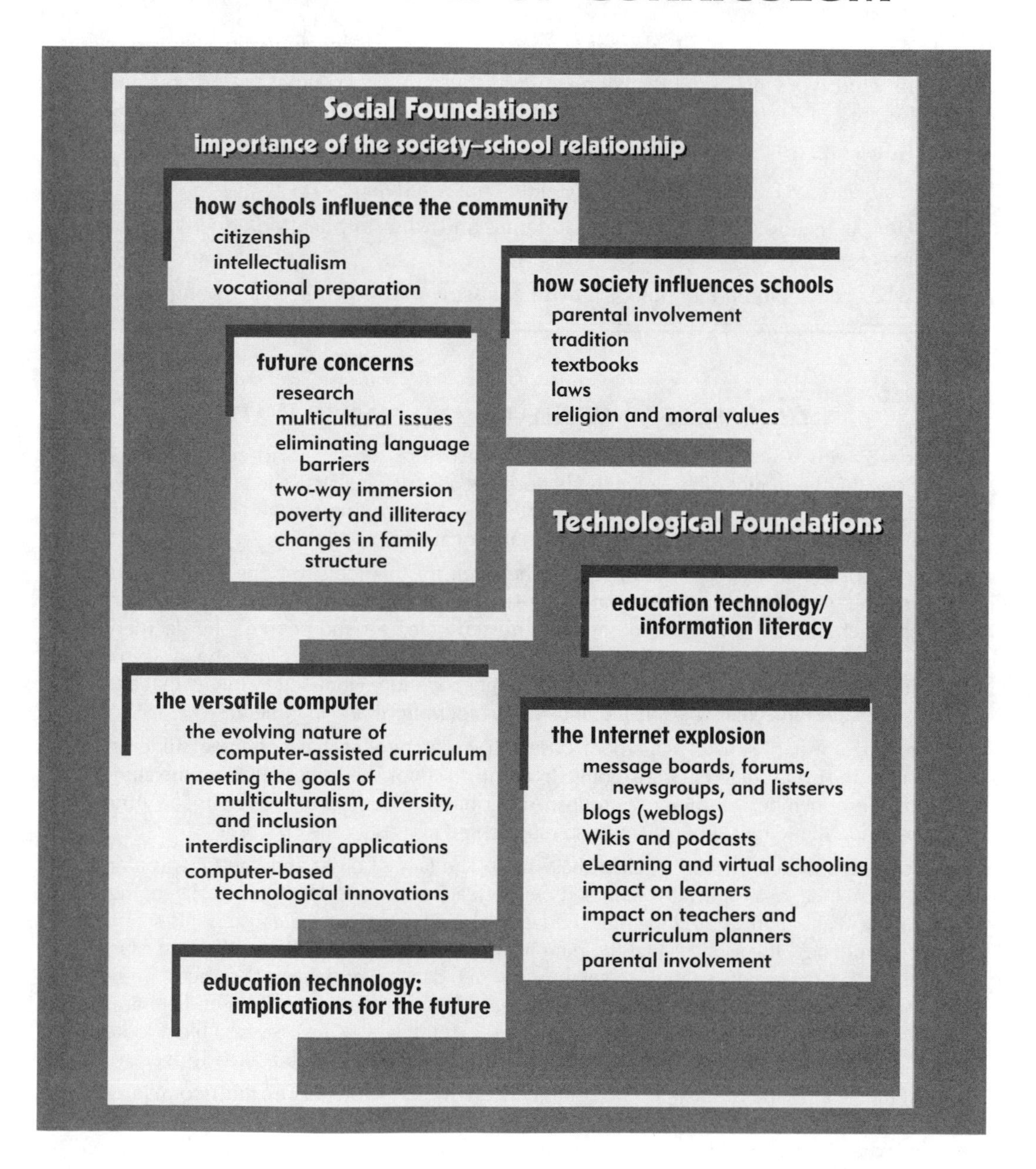

Focus Questions

1. How would you define cultural discontinuity? How does it affect students?
2. How can you use technology to address multicultural concerns?
3. In your opinion, what is the most important thing a school can do to develop good citizens?
4. What evidence do you have that your school's culture affects its curriculum?
5. In what types of school decisions should the public participate? Can you name an area of decisions in which the public should be excluded?
6. How can curriculum development be used to empower teachers? Students?
7. How can we use technology to promote constructivism?
8. How is technology empowering students, and what implications does this have for teachers?
9. What roles should technology play in ensuring that no child is left behind?

The Case of Linda Blevins and Marvin Watts

Linda Blevins was in her senior year of college before she began to consider the job options that her major offered. She had chosen economics because she enjoyed studying the subject. Upon graduating, Linda accepted the first position for which she had been interviewed, in the home mortgage division of a local bank.

Linda found that her major had prepared her well for this job; from the beginning, she found the work easy. But by the end of her second year, she was extremely bored. Linda spent each day doing paperwork, and she missed being around people. She decided to return to school to pursue a master of arts in teaching (MAT) degree. Since she lived in the inner city and depended on the city buses for transportation, Linda felt fortunate that a university extension center was located only a few blocks from her apartment.

The program had a major classroom observation component that permitted students to observe in several different classrooms. In the first school she visited, 90% of the student body were members of minority groups. About half of the students were African Americans, and other ethnic groups were also represented in most of the classes.

Linda was shocked by the first class she visited. The lack of order and control was alarming, and Linda was especially surprised by the teacher. Marvin Watts was a large, cigar-smoking white man who, Linda quickly deduced, had been hired because of his size and self-confidence. It was clear that the man feared nothing. In their first conference Marvin told her that his goal was simply to get through each day and each year. "You see," he said, "it would be different if these kids wanted to learn, but they don't. Hey, half of them are on dope or booze. The other half will drop out. Look at it this way, teachers are hired to keep these kids off the streets and out of thc prisons which, as you know, are already overfull.

"Let me give you a little advice," he continued. "Nowadays you hear all this reform jargon. Let me tell you something: most of those reports were written by politicians who have no idea what the real world is like. Give me a break. Half of these kids are on crack, and even they aren't as spacey as the politicians responsible for NCLB. And talk about turning over the school to the parents and site-based councils. Hey, most of these kids don't have parents. Those that do don't speak enough English to order a meal at McDonald's. Could you imagine asking them if they think the curriculum should be integrated? They would probably think they had been insulted. And they're supposed to help the kids with their education. That's a joke. The kids who *do* have parents go home and help *them*!"

Linda noticed two Asian students who sat at the same table each day. Neither paid any attention to Mr. Watts as he lectured in a monotone. She could understand their choosing to ignore Watts, for that was her own method of tolerating his dull lectures, but she didn't understand why he was willing to ignore them, until she had an opportunity to ask.

"It's simple," Watts replied. "They don't understand a word of English. The sup will probably ship them to another school if he ever gets around to it. Right now, they're just as well off here as they would be anywhere else."

Linda was appalled at this attitude. At least Watts was honest, but how could he be so irresponsible? Linda was angry. Later, her shock and anger turned into concern. All she could think about were the waste of time and energy and the unfairness to these students. If they didn't prepare for the future while here at school, how would they ever improve their lot in life? Linda knew the answer to that question.

Linda also noticed that she could count the different ethnic groups in any room because the members of each group seemed to be drawn to each other like drops of oil on water. Mr. Watts showed no concern about this student-selected grouping.

Once she overcame her shock at the lack of respect these students showed to the teacher and to each other, Linda began to notice that none of the strategies she had learned about in her recent college courses were evidenced in any of the classrooms in this school. It was as though topics such as curriculum alignment, valued outcomes, research-based teaching, metacognition, research-based education, authentic assessment, performance evaluation, and, yes, cultural pluralism had never penetrated the walls of this school or the heads of any of its teachers.

Back at the university, Linda related each topic she studied to what she had observed in the classrooms. She could see that, once she graduated, if she decided to remain in this community (and that was a big if), the culture of the schools would work against any efforts she would make to implement the curriculum and instructional strategies she was learning. Although she wanted to help bring about change, she wondered whether she could fight the powerful forces of tradition that permeated this school and community.

Knowing that first-year teachers are often viewed with a jaundiced eye, Linda wanted to avoid being perceived as an overzealous novice who expects to save the world. She believed she needed a strategy that would provide gradual, long-lasting improvement for all students at this school without alienating her fellow teachers, but she didn't know how to begin developing such a plan.

• • •

Maximum effectiveness of all school personnel, including teachers and other curriculum developers, requires an understanding of the context in which a school resides. First, ***context*** *refers to the school's physical surroundings. A school located in a small, rural community has potential advantages and disadvantages compared to an urban ghetto school. Maximum effectiveness in either setting requires planning to (1) capitalize on the resources of the community and (2) overcome the community's weaknesses.*

PART I: SOCIAL FOUNDATIONS

> Life at school and life outside school are simply too far apart. We need to go back, then, and build up anew from the foundations of democratic values, social realities, and our knowledge of human growth and development.
>
> —J. H. Lounsbury

We are taught that a school is, theoretically, a microcosm of the local community and of society at large, but many teachers in urban schools find little comfort in this statement. Our schools are microcosms of good communities only when we strive to make them so. Each school is complex (Woolfolk Hoy & Hoy, 2008) and each curriculum is unique. Although we may think of the uniqueness of each school as the differences in subjects taught and activities pursued, uniqueness comes from a much broader arena known as culture, and each school has its own unique culture. *Culture* has been defined broadly as "a people's entire way of life" (Ornstein & Hunkins, 2004, p. 373). It is more than just a fancy word—it means that a school's culture can make the school an enjoyable place to be or it can make some students' world a continuous nightmare. It can welcome ethnic diversity, or it can harbor and nurture prejudices. It can stimulate minds, or it can anesthetize entire beings. As our society continues to become more diverse, the curricula must change to reflect the new differences. Experienced teachers realize that the school's culture and curriculum are tied to the culture of the community and society. We must measure schools by what they can contribute to their students and their communities, and we must measure communities and societies by what they contribute to their students and their schools. Educators should consider the effects that community changes have on the culture of a school and on the culture of the classrooms.

Importance of the Society–School Relationship

Both society and the schools are in a continuous state of change. The relative power of social forces on the schools shifts, and the relative power that the schools have to shape society also waxes and wanes, requiring teachers, principals, and other curriculum directors to be constantly aware of the school's relationships within society. The society–school relationship is important in at least two general ways. First, many Americans believe that the school has some responsibility for shaping society, although they disagree on how much. Social reconstructionists believe that schools must completely reform society, while others question whether the school's role as an agent of change should be so extreme. At the opposite extreme are those who believe the school's primary role is to conserve society. These people would have society return to the "good old days." Whether one believes that schools should change society or preserve it, perhaps most people would agree that the schools should protect some qualities and change others.

The second major relationship between the school and society is the cumulative effects that society has on the schools. Any attempt to develop curriculum or improve the climate in classrooms without considering the impact of society on the schools is bound to fail.

A clear understanding of the relationship between the schools and society begins with the realization that the school is an institution that was created by and for society, and that the school is an institution that is supported by society. Schools mirror society; they do not drive it. Trouble is inevitable for anyone who fails to recognize that the community owns and supports the schools. In his book, *The Water Is Wide*, Pat Conroy (1972) describes his own failure to understand this relationship. While a first-year teacher, Conroy refused to heed the advice of his supervisor, who told him, "Son, I can replace you just as easily as replacing a light bulb." And he did. Conroy, an excellent teacher who loved his students and his job, was fired. Working in an institution that belongs to society, teachers and other school officials must work for and with the community.

It would be simple if the educator's responsibility were only to his or her employer (i.e., society). This is not the case, however, because the school was also created for another purpose: to serve the students. Public and private school educators have two masters to serve: the society and the students, and the demands of the two are not always compatible. On the contrary, serving society may be, and frequently is, in direct conflict with the teacher's responsibility to serve the students. For example, some schools are encouraged to change the curriculum to produce world-class workers, and others to prepare students to do well on tests—which, as critics sometimes point out, is not in the best interest of students. This conflict can be seen further by examining the school's purposes.

How Schools Influence the Community

Some of the traditional ways that schools influence the community include citizenship, intellectualism, and vocational preparation (see figure 2.1).

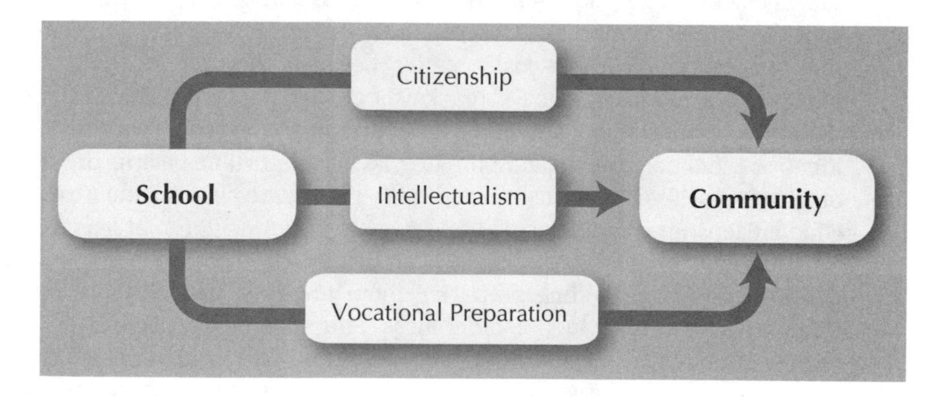

Figure 2.1 Some Ways Schools Influence Society

Citizenship

More than two thousand years ago Aristotle stressed the need to guide the development of citizenship in youth. The need for teaching citizenship in contemporary society has not diminished. As John Goodlad (2003/2004) has said,

> It would be the height of folly for our schools not to have as their central mission educating the young in the democratic ideals of humankind, the freedom and responsibilities of a democratic society, and the civil and civic understandings and dispositions necessary to democratic citizenship. (p. 20)

The Cardinal Principles of Secondary Education, which also apply to elementary schools, include citizenship as an important aim for the nation's schools. Although few people would question the value of this aim for American schools, many disagree about what the aim encompasses. Some of the more generally accepted responsibilities of schools in developing citizenship are:

- teaching social studies,
- developing national allegiance,
- acquiring skills,
- developing a desire to protect society,
- developing a desire to improve society,
- developing social responsibility, and
- developing moral values.

Some of these responsibilities might be met indirectly through the hidden curriculum (discussed in chapter 1). These seven aims encompass nearly every aspect of human existence.

Daphna Oyserman (2008) believes that in order to succeed, students must incorporate future goals into their self-concepts (e.g., the "clever" self who passed the algebra test, the "fat" self who failed to lose weight, the "fast" self who fell in with the "wrong" crowd; see Oyserman, Bybee, & Terry, 2006). Oyserman believes that "future self-relevant goals matter because they shape the strategies one chooses to achieve one's goals" (Parkay et al., 2010, p. 534). This kind of self-regulation is not possible if students' self-concepts are not congruent with their social identities. School culture and climate play an important part in the development of positive self-concepts associated with the healthy social identity that makes good citizenship possible.

Curricula that prepare citizens for living in a democracy must involve students in decision making, preparing them to think critically and discuss their opinions openly, allowing for differences, and showing respect for all. They must engage students in service, with the school and the local community serving as microcosms of the larger society, and they must acquaint students with various community institutions. Civic education must also prepare students to respect, embrace, and defend democracy and liberty.

Service-learning programs are a good example of curricula that help students connect to their communities. Gary Hopkins (2004) provides meaningful definitions of service learning from two different educators. Laurel Singleton says that "service learning is a teaching method that combines academic content with direct service experiences in which students provide genuine service to their school or community while extending or deepening their understanding of curricular content." Arden Moon comments,

> Service learning is learning experientially through structured integration of service and subject matter that is part of a planned curriculum. . . . If service learning is structured correctly, it is academically demanding and provides opportunities to learn about social development and citizenship It also prepares students for the work world by teaching them teamwork, problem solving, about diversity, and interpersonal skills. The service-learning experience becomes a source of knowledge.

The case study in chapter 4 features an example of community-based learning and also a list of Web sites where you can learn more about community service.

Intellectualism

To Thomas Jefferson, an educated citizen was nothing less than indispensable to a democratic society: "If a nation expects to be ignorant and free in a state of civilization, it expects what never was and what never will be." Jefferson used the word *ignorant* to mean the opposite of *knowledgeable* or *intellectual*. The pursuit of wisdom is as old as philosophy itself, and, as we'll see in chapter 3, wisdom and philosophy are inseparable. During the golden age of intellectualism in Greece, the belief in the value of knowledge for knowledge's sake was common. Throughout most of the civilized world, intellectualism is still prized.

In the United States, unfortunately, intellectualism is often viewed skeptically unless it leads directly to practical ends. Nevertheless, through the years Americans have been dedicated to serving individual students. Even in the face of lofty, unrealistic expectations set by the states, many teachers have continued to meet the personal and social needs of their students. Mary Antin, the daughter of European immigrants, understood the unique, education-for-all goal of American schools. Antin was unable to speak English, but that did not prevent her from attending the Boston public schools. Later, reflecting on her experience, she wrote (1912, p. 186):

> Education was free . . . it was the only thing my father was able to promise us when he sent for us; surer, safer than bread or shelter. . . . No application made, no questions asked, no examinations, rulings, exclusions, no machinations, no fees. The doors stood open for every one of us.

This belief in the importance of education for all of the nation's youth is the distinguishing factor of education in the United States. A poll of educational leaders (Elam, 1996) contained the question, "What do you consider to be the most important achievements of public education in America?" Most respondents cited the goal of maintaining and extending democracy as a way of life by providing free education without regard to race, class, religion, gender, or ideology. S. M. Elam, one of the poll's authors, summarized, "We are one of a very few countries that attempt to teach all the children of all the people; against great odds, we have achieved almost universal education" (p. 611). When we hear critics downgrade our schools, or when we are tempted to replace our school system with that of another country, we would do well to remember the words of Keefe and Amenta (2005, p. 537):

> Make no mistake about where we stand: the American public school system has been one of the world's spectacular success stories. The notion that every girl and boy, of whatever socioeconomic background, is entitled to equal educational opportunity is so startling that most of us who live in this society fail to appreciate its implications. No other country in the world, except for our neighbor and traditional partner, Canada, offers anything comparable to the American secondary system. And much of the rest of the world, seeing its validity and value, is following in our footsteps. The American model is a deliberate attempt to educate the masses. At its best, it is an exemplar for the world. But it is not indestructible. It can and must continue to evolve to meet the needs of each succeeding generation. This kind of evolution can only be accomplished by dedication, by commitment to the future, and by hard work.

When coupled with the belief that intellectual superiority is essential to maintaining national security and a strong economy, this historically unprecedented commitment to all students has resulted in a revived appreciation for the importance of intellectualism in the schools. The language used in the reform reports of the 1980s and 1990s reflected this feeling; two of the most frequent words used in the more than 400 reports were *rigor* and *excellence*. To that end, initiatives such as the Twenty-first Century Learning Community Centers Program offer a wide variety of grant opportunities to fund after-school programs for civic and intellectual enrichment. Such programs range from drug and violence prevention to the fine arts (Alliance for Excellent Education, n.d.).

Vocational Preparation

The first American school was established to prepare young men for entrance into Harvard College, where they would study for the clergy. The vocational role of the school was reaffirmed in 1918 by the Cardinal Principles of Secondary Education. In the United States, the vocational force is so strong that students at all levels often give as a reason for taking a particular class the fact that it is required for graduation, and their reason for wanting to graduate is to increase their ability to get a job and earn more money.

During the 1980s and 1990s, the impact of business and industry on the curriculum increased substantially. Apple (1990, p. 526) addresses this influence:

> The public debate on education and on all social issues has shifted profoundly to the right . . . (and) the effects can be seen . . . in the consistent pressure to make the needs of business and industry the primary concerns of the education system.

But the role of the worker has changed drastically in the last decades, shifting from *Taylorism* (breaking each job down into small parts and closely supervising the worker to ensure that each function is performed precisely according to instructions) to group problem solving. Arthur Wirth (1993, p. 1) described a major contrast in the roles of educators during the 1990s and the world-connected, group-oriented, problem-solving skills that work would require of employees in the future. He says:

> Under Secretary Bennett's banner of "back to basics" and test score accountability, the 1980s produced the hyper-rationalization that Arthur Wise warned us about . . . the style of the 1980s was based, more than anything else, on control: "to control reading, to control language, to control learners, to control teachers. . . ." At the end of the 1980s Lauro Cavazos (Cooper, 1989), Bennett's successor, acknowledged, "We tried to improve education by imposing regulations from the top down, while leaving the basic structure of the school untouched. Obviously, that hasn't worked."

In contrast, modern businesses are turning away from the race to outperform the international competition and are using computer-facilitated processes, digital communication, and aerospace technology to solve problems. Robert Reich's book, *The Work of Nations: Preparing Ourselves for 21st Century Capitalism* (1991, pp. 224–225), lists four skills that are required of today's workers:

- *abstraction*—the capacity to order and make meaning of the massive flow of information, to shape raw data into workable patterns;
- *system thinking*—the capacity to see the parts in relation to the whole, to see why problems arise;
- *experimental inquiry*—the capacity to set up procedures to test and evaluate alternative ideas; and
- *collaboration*—the capacity to engage in active communication and dialogue to get a variety of perspectives and to create consensus when that is necessary.

Modern Career and Technical Education

Over a century ago John Dewey advocated practices that served students' personal, social, and intellectual needs, advocating that authentic or lifelike problem solving should be the main vehicle for delivering the curriculum. Unlike the general curriculum, career and technical education (CTE) programs have continued to rely on problem solving as a fundamental learning tool. Perhaps this explains their endurance and their high success rate.

Bill and Melinda Gates Foundation researchers (The Value of CTE, 2008) report that approximately 81% of dropouts interviewed said they might have stayed in school had they experienced more "real-world learning." This is a key focus of modern CTE curricula, with on-the-job training through school-to-work and other programs for career preparation. The focus of CTE curriculum seems to have good results: The dropout rate for career and technical education programs is about 16% below the overall dropout rate (Howlett, 2008).

How Society Influences Schools

Although the relationship between the schools and society is symbiotic, the schools have the responsibility for monitoring the social forces that affect them and for seizing opportunities to impact the community. Stated differently, at all times teachers, administrators, and other curriculum developers should be proactive, having the ability to foresee obstacles and opportunities and changing the curriculum accordingly.

Too frequently, we educators (K–university level) have remained passive and reactive, going about our daily business without concern for what is happening in the world around us. The result, of course, is that instead of presenting a steady, positive image of our profession, we always seem to be reacting and defending ourselves and the schools. Such reactionary educational policy results in a curriculum that has no relevance in the world populated by today's students. Later on in the chapter, we will see how technology is a way to break through the barriers that separate learning from the real world.

Societal changes constantly impact student lives and must be addressed by the school's curricula. Unfortunately, many factors that put children at risk are beyond educators' control. Many children live in emotionally barren homes and unsafe neighborhoods. Many arrive at school only to find themselves in an even more threatening world, for the public continues to recognize discipline as one of the greatest problems in today's schools (Bushaw & Gallup, 2008). Some important problems that curriculum developers should be concerned about center around poverty, breakdown in family structure, drug abuse, and multicultural issues. They should seek opportunities to understand and combat these problems by using action research in the classroom and promoting modern relevance in the curriculum through the use of technology.

Society's impact on the schools is substantial, constantly reshaping the mission of education. Education reform is making some long overdue improvements. Educators have an important responsibility to ensure that the changes intended in their schools are educationally sound—that is, validated by research. Consequently, several significant improvements are being made.

Parental Involvement

The 2001 No Child Left Behind Act requires schools to keep parents informed of their children's performance, with federally sponsored programs to provide increased opportunities for parents to be involved in the shaping of their children's learning activities. Just as schools can have a major impact on family and community connections to help students achieve, when parents take responsibility for their children's learning and are allowed input into what and how their children learn, schools can respond accordingly with the result that learning becomes a more meaningful, real-world, community-based initiative.

The combined roles of teachers and parents in curriculum planning are expanding. The benefit of involving teachers and parents is substantiated by research. Research has constantly indicated that parent and family involvement significantly contributes to learning, and it is critical to the academic success of many children (Medirata, Fruchter, & Lewis, 2002; Wilson & Corbett, 2000). A good example of a nationwide program improvement supported by research involves the creation of child-care centers and teen centers. Even the practice of validation through research is part of many reform programs, including NCLB. Some state reform programs require teachers to select and use methods that have been validated by research. One of the most frequent suggestions for improving the schools is for parents to take more responsibility for their children's schooling. However, this should not be interpreted to mean the more involvement—regardless of the circumstances—the better. Parents must consider the level of difficulty of the assignment, the ability level of the student, and the student's age.

Generally, the older the student is, the less help is needed. The principal in the case study in chapter 1 provided an excellent model to guide the involvement of parents in planning to improve the learning in their children's school, giving consideration to each parent's expertise and limitations. In this chapter, the opening vignette in Part II reflects the role of technology in involving parents.

Educators bear the responsibility for communicating clearly with parents, which often is exceedingly difficult, especially when non-English-speaking parents are involved. The problem of communications between teachers and non-English-speaking parents is often underestimated. Teachers and administrators must ensure that parents are not asked to perform tasks such as reading to their children, if the parents themselves are nonreaders or very poor readers.

At any given moment, many forces are working to keep the school curriculum the way it is; simultaneously, many counterforces are aimed at changing the curriculum, including tradition, textbooks, laws, religious beliefs, multicultural concerns, poverty, the expansion of knowledge, and growth in technology (see figure 2.2).

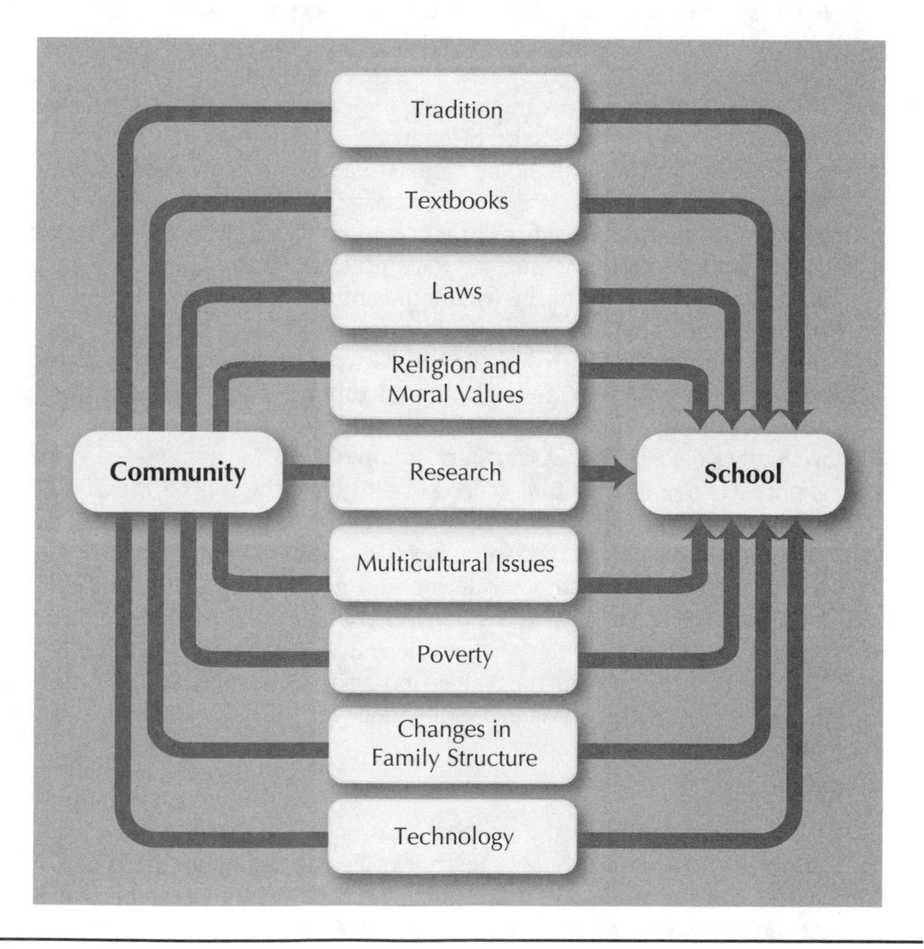

Figure 2.2 Some Ways Society Influences Schools

Tradition

One of the oldest and strongest forces in any society is tradition. For example, the musical *Fiddler on the Roof* showed the powerful role that tradition played in nineteenth-century Russia. Tradition is a strong force in all societies, including our own. When teachers try to introduce change at their schools, the first resistance they often hear is the voice of tradition:

"But we've never done that at this school."
"It will never work."
"They won't like it." (*They* are seldom identified.)
"The administration will never buy it."

Tradition can be a stumbling block to progress when new ideas are not given a chance because of fear of failure or a fear of the unknown. One of the greatest obstacles to efforts to improve schools is parental nostalgia for schools as they used to be. Tradition is an equally strong force *within* the schools. Much of the curriculum of most schools is there simply because it has always been there. Because teachers, principals, students, and even the school itself are part of the community at large, it is not surprising that the powers of tradition are at work inside the school as well as in the outside community.

Tradition also serves the schools in positive ways. It acts as a stabilizer, preventing "change for the sake of change"; in doing so, it protects the tried and proven. For example, consider the massive reform movements that are reshaping the curricula in all states. Some necessary questions in undertaking such reforms are: Is this particular reform practice good? What evidence is available to show that it works? What evidence suggests otherwise? Do we really need this reform? Why? Toward the end of the twentieth century, one commonly heard answer was, "Because the Japanese are doing it." After all, perhaps no other country had experienced such rapid improvement and earned the respect of the business world as completely as the Japanese. But could this be a sound reason for change? For educators in the United States to respond to Asian competition by imitating what we perceive to be the Asian curriculum would be a mistake. Japan and Singapore—two countries that scored at and near the top on the 2009 TIMSS tests (Gonzales, 2008)—have reduced their emphasis on subject-matter testing in favor of curriculum reforms that will meet their nations' needs for individuals who can work cooperatively, demonstrate high-order thinking skills, and show creativity. Ironically, while our intent has been to emulate the practices in these highly successful countries, as they work to become more personalizing our teachers are being pressured to turn their attention away from meeting the personal needs of students. For further caveats about change for the sake of change, see the opening vignette in chapter 5.

Textbooks

For four centuries the textbook has been the number-one curriculum determiner in American schools. Textbooks heavily influence both the selection and sequencing of content. First, textbooks are highly accessible, making reading assignments very easy. A second advantage that textbooks offer is organization, with the content in each chapter building on the content in previous chapters.

FYI Using Old Textbooks

Barbara Morgan-Fleming • Texas Tech University

When teaching curriculum history, I start by bringing in old/antique textbooks. (I generally find them at garage sales and thrift stores, rarely spending over $1.00). I have each student select a book, browse through it and report on the underlying premises of the book (e.g., What is knowledge? What is the purpose of learning in the subject presented? Who is the audience for the book?)

After all have reported, I have them select a current textbook and go through the same process, this time asking how someone from the future would complete the above exercise on this book, and what their answers to the questions would be.

Finally, I have the students form curriculum committees (by curriculum subject) looking at both sets of books. They decide the strengths and weaknesses of each book, and whether they would adopt any of the textbooks. The committees then put together their own textbook, choosing sections/topics from all the books, and adding sections that will be needed for present and future students.

This makes course organization easy. Even when a syllabus is required, the textbook often provides the pattern for the sequencing of the syllabus.

Textbooks allow teachers to demonstrate their knowledge of a subject. By mastering the stable content in the textbook and then lecturing, the teacher can demonstrate expertise in content and organization, and making students aware of the teacher's expertise gives the teacher expert power. Students expect and want their teachers to have mastery over the content they teach.

The textbook facilitates the alignment of instruction and assessment. By using the text to construct tests, a teacher can ensure coverage of the content studied. Even when the teacher fails to address some of the topics in class, content validity is enhanced by aligning the content on the test with the content in the text. But this does not mean that textbooks do not have inherent weaknesses. Textbooks are highly standardized, making them a limited tool for stimulating creativity (Abell, 2007).

Laws

The power of legislation affecting schools is not constant. During one era, federal laws may be the dominating social force on schools. In another era, state laws, local developments, or other influences may dominate. For example, during the mid-1950s the *Brown v. Board of Education* decision, which required integration in the public schools, was perhaps the strongest force affecting the curriculum. In 1975 Public Law 94-142, the Education for all Handicapped Children law, dominated. During another era, increased funding or the absence of financial support may be the overriding force shaping the schools. For example, the Elementary and Secondary Education Act of 1965 was the most influential of any law on education in the 1960s. In the twenty-first century, NCLB is having a powerful effect.

Religion and Moral Values

A wide variety of social forces may dominate the shaping of schools from year to year. For example, during the 1980s lack of funding forced a shorter school year in parts of West Virginia and Florida. However, values have been and continue to be the most consistent and prominent social influence on our schools. The 1990s were characterized by politicians stressing "family values," a political position that is still prominent in the twenty-first century—to the point of becoming a crucial issue in national elections. Although these values are not clearly defined, such rhetoric, although empty, affects education. The 1990s gave far too little attention to the ideas and ideals of democracy and education.

Because the first American school was established to prepare students for admission to a divinity college, values have always been a force shaping the curriculum. At times, the question of how much influence religious institutions should have on the selection of values to be taught has caused controversy in communities. On some occasions, the controversy has been so extreme as to draw the attention of the entire nation. The most notable example was the Scopes trial (the so-called "monkey trial") in Tennessee in 1925 regarding the teaching of evolution in the classroom. (For a detailed treatment on the Scopes trial and other related issues, see Linder, 2002.)

A widely perceived deterioration of the moral fiber in the United States has made the moral responsibilities of schools a special concern to some educators. For example, John Lounsbury (1991, p. 5) gives some examples of values that are prized by civilizations throughout the world, values that in his opinion should be everyday features in our schools; yet he warns against the schools dictating particular values.

> We need classrooms in which beauty is savored, truth honored, compassion practiced, and fellowship honored; classrooms where creativity is encouraged. . . . The school must not attempt to dictate a particular set of values, but must assist young adolescents in exploring their values, attitudes, and standards.

These comments exemplify the paradox involved in the curriculum planner's role in teaching values education. Morality is indispensable, and merely providing definitions of *value* is not enough. Theodore Roosevelt said, "To educate a man in mind and not in morals is to educate a menace to society." Character education remains critical at a time when its critics want to talk about evil or injustice in the greater world without considering our own character (Glanzer, 2008).

G. A. Davis (1993, p. 32) gives credence to Lounsbury's words of caution:

> Schools always have taught values and always will. Values relating to patriotism, hygiene, and health, appreciation for the sciences, the arts, one's culture, and education itself are common substance for affective education in the classroom. Other values are equally non-controversial and warrant teaching: honesty, responsibility, trustworthiness, a sense of fairness, and respect for the rights and property of others.

Most teachers would probably agree that the schools share some of the responsibility for influencing these values, for values are continuously being taught in our schools, whether or not we mean to do so.

At the beginning of the twentieth century, socialization was deemed by many to be a more important function of the schools than intellectual development. Many thought that the 'real' purpose of schools was to serve as an engine of social reform. Certainly, some of the practices in many of today's schools would be shocking to those who hold the schools accountable for the welfare of society.

Future Concerns

In the twenty-first century, influence of society on schools continues to evolve, and different concerns are becoming more prominent. Following is a discussion about these issues and their potential to effect curriculum reform.

Research

This book stresses the need for research-based decisions in education, but therein lies a natural trap. The design of most educational studies is correlational, not causal. Consequently, research findings do not always lend themselves to linear application. A second trap can be the tendency of consumers to focus on research studies that support a favored practice. Special effort is needed to report and use those studies that question or contradict the favored positions.

Of equal concern is the contemporary practice of focusing most on those studies that examine effects on test scores. Interestingly, when W. J. Burke (1967) interviewed national teacher-of-the-year finalists over a seven-year period, he learned that all 54 finalists attributed their success to their relationships with students and, in particular, to their ability to transmit a sense of efficacy to each student. Burke (1967, p. 206) wrote, "My microscopic examination of fifty-four separate school systems encouraged me to believe that nothing in American life can match the vigor and importance of the classroom confrontation of minds. Therein lies our future."

The qualities that Burke described do not appear on test scores. Such widespread testimony of the need to consider non-test-related measures of achievement is too convincing to be ignored. Referring to NCLB, Tom Allen (2004) echoes McNeil's earlier concern for the loss of creativity in American schools due to the use of high-stakes tests: "A heavy reliance on these high-stakes tests forces schools to 'teach to the test' at the expense of more creative kinds of learning" (p. 397).

E. W. Eisner (1985, p. 27) perceived the dependence on quantitative test scores to be so extreme that he referred to it as *scientism*, the belief that unless something can be quantified it cannot be truly understood or known. Faith in scientism as applied to education is considered one of the major forces affecting the curriculum.

Unfortunately, a broad focus will result only if curriculum workers insist on gathering and using qualitative data in their decision making. Every nation, every state, and every institution needs a stabilizer to keep it on course. A good example of an effective stabilizer would be the practice of researching each reform practice before permanently adopting it. Without such a stabilizer, we would discard the good along with the bad as we take up first one practice and then another.

Multicultural Issues

In a democratic society, a major purpose of the schools—perhaps the most important purpose of all—is to promote and protect democracy. A truly democratic society values diversity and requires dissent to maintain its vitality. One way to view the multicultural concerns of teachers is by recognizing that students from minority backgrounds live in two very different worlds. The lack of harmony between these worlds, or cultures, can cause continuous problems for minority students. Each culture has certain expectations and makes certain demands of the student. These expectations and demands can be mutually exclusive, and they can be imposed directly or indirectly. Perhaps the worse of the two types is indirect expectations, because they include conflicting forces that make conflicting demands on students. If ignored, the opposing expectations cause a type of alienation known as *cultural discontinuity*.

Teachers who understand that these conflicts exist can learn more about the difficulties these students face by helping them become involved with the curriculum and helping them to accept the curriculum by modifying it to make it resemble the "practical" learning that happens outside the school. Unless teachers understand that students' backgrounds, needs, and perspectives toward education are different, the needs of *at-risk students* will go unmet.

The movement toward multicultural education has grown rapidly and would have grown even faster were there not widespread confusion over the meaning of the term *multicultural*. But whatever definitions are used, whenever students of any background perform below their potential, society suffers. Maximum human productivity requires tolerance, a quality that is still lacking in our society. Without the quality of tolerance, our society simply will not survive. The overlap among the social and nonsocial factors that pressure the curriculum is clearly and abundantly evident. By presenting simple stereotypes of minorities, textbooks retard curriculum changes needed to address ethnic and gender issues positively.

If tolerance is to be developed, our curricula must be adjusted to promote it. But the multicultural role of schools must go beyond the development of tolerance; future curricula must promote an appreciation for diversity. Each ethnic group should learn to value the uniqueness of other ethnic groups, and all groups must see the strength that diversity offers our nation. Good social and emotional programs are grounded in theory and research, teach students to apply emotional skills and ethical values in daily life, build connections between students and their schools, address the affective and social dimensions of learning, and involve families and communities as partners.

Human rights must remain a major concern of all teachers, for all teachers share the responsibility for promoting among students an appreciation for others' rights. Students cannot be taught to appreciate and protect the rights of others through didactic methods, however. *Social contracts* such as the one shown in box 2.1 can be used like a blueprint to guide the management of classroom behavior.

Multicultural education is more than just curriculum reform that involves changing or restructuring the curriculum to include content about ethnic groups, women, and other cultural groups. According to James Banks (2006), we must understand the various dimensions of multicultural education more thoroughly if we are to implement it successfully. Banks (2006) defines the following five dimensions of multicultural education.

Box 2.1 Social Contract

The classroom operates as a community of scholars who are engaged in learning. The individual's right to learn is protected and respected by all scholars. Scholars should initiate learning and teachers should initiate instruction, balancing the rights of individuals with the rights of other individuals in the community.

Right To Exist, or safe occupancy of space. The classroom is a physically safe learning environment. The teacher:

- does not allow students to physically harm each other or engage in other risky behavior that endangers any student.

Right To Liberty, or freedom of conscience and expression. The teacher:

- allows students to assert their opinions.
- fosters respectful student dissent as a means for rational understanding of issues and divergent opinions.
- fosters students' self-examination of their ethnic or cultural heritages. Teachers should help students become "ethnically literate" about their own individual cultural backgrounds and those of others.

Right To Happiness (or self-esteem): The classroom is an emotionally safe learning environment, fostering high self-esteem among students. The teacher:

- does not allow name-calling, elitist, racist, or sexist slurs, or stereotypical expressions in the classroom.
- disciplines students equitably, ensuring that minority and majority group students are punished similarly for the same infractions.
- shows cultural respect by using linguistically and culturally relevant curriculum materials and instructional strategies, and by telling the students that their languages and cultures are welcome in the classroom community.
- encourages students to understand their differences and similarities.

From *Kappa Delta Pi Record, 30*(21), 70. © *Kappa Delta Pi.*

1. *Content integration.* Banks lists many ways in which multiculturalism can be promoted across the disciplines—not just in social studies and language arts. Creative teachers can discover ways to integrate the math and science curriculum with ethnic and cultural concepts, for example.
2. *The knowledge construction process.* Banks says that teachers can help students to understand how knowledge is created and how it is influenced by the racial, ethnic, and social-class positions of individuals and groups.
3. *Prejudice reduction.* Students' racial attitudes can be modified by encouraging the development of more democratic attitudes and values. Banks mentions several interesting studies resulting in interventions to develop more positive attitudes and values.
4. *An equity pedagogy.* "An equity pedagogy exists when teachers modify their teaching in ways that will facilitate the academic achievement of stu-

dents from diverse racial, cultural, ethnic, language, and gender groups" (Banks & Banks, 1995, p. 342).

5. *An empowering school culture and social structure.* School culture (see chapter 8) and the hidden curriculum (chapter 1) have a huge impact on the social structure within schools. Each of the four dimensions discussed directly above deals with a certain aspect of a cultural or social system.

Eliminating Language Barriers

An examination of the demographic shift in cultures in the United States shows that there will be a new ethnic majority in the new millennium. Every major metropolitan area now has a "minority majority," but the white ethnic majority that has dominated the teacher ranks throughout the nation's existence continues to do so.

A special handicap faced by many minority students is the language barrier. The United States trails most of the civilized world in the teaching of foreign languages. Some educators recommend requiring all students to be proficient in two or more languages, and most citizens (85%) share this opinion (Rose & Gallup, 2007). Too often, foreign students are ignored because they speak little or no English. Perhaps the most urgent need of these students is a change in the attitudes of their teachers.

Jeff Zwiers (2005) alerts educators that English-as-a-second-language students are handicapped by a third language, academic English. Academic language is the language that gives meaning to academic tasks, texts, and tests. Teachers must help these students by teaching them to scope out the context in which these words are used, recognize words that describe thinking skills, read challenging but understandable materials, converse with native speakers about academic topics, and take risks with their evolving language.

Several myths must be dispelled. For example, the common belief that learning an additional language interferes with one's native language must be disproved. Another common myth is that success in learning a language is proportional to the time spent studying the language. Time-on-task is only one of many factors that affect learning a language.

In addition to fostering appropriate attitudes, schools should alter policies to promote language development and the academic success of students who are handicapped by a language barrier. For example, the No Child Left Behind Act requires that members of all ethnic groups be held to the same academic expectations. The law makes it clear that students who struggle with English will be expected to achieve to the same standards as native English-speaking students. Nichols and Berliner (2007) address this weakness: "We note in passing that only people who have no contacts with children could write legislation demanding that every child reach a high level of performance, thereby denying that individuals exist. Only those same people would also believe that all children would reach high levels of proficiency at precisely the same rate of speed" (p. 36). Academic success requires a special kind of language development—that of an academic vocabulary, which requires about five to seven years to master. Policy should ensure that these students are given the necessary support during this developmental period.

Multicultural expectations can be met in a variety of ways. Scott (1993, p. 2) says that students need an opportunity to develop their own theories based on experiences in multicultural classrooms:

> What is needed for teacher evaluation is a conceptualization of teacher education pedagogy in which theory and practice are interactive. "Practices draws theory" as much as "theory draws practices." Such a pedagogy would require that prospective teachers have sufficient practice to build principles of action, an understanding by theory to guide decision-making, and the recognition that teaching situations are multi-faceted ones in which there is seldom a perfect match between theory and practice. By defining teaching as dilemma-driven, teacher educators can better prepare teachers to cope with situations where there is often no one right way, or even best way, to act.

Two-Way Immersion

Students in bilingual programs learn as much or more than students in English-only classes (Genesee, Lindholm-Leary, Saunders, & Christian, 2006). Furthermore, students in two-way bilingual classes excel academically and have improved attitudes.

Two-way bilingual immersion (TWI), also known as *dual language programs*, are programs that take place in two languages, with non-English being used for at least 50 percent of instruction; involve both English and non-English work assignments; and place English language learners and native English speakers together for most content instruction (Lindholm-Leary, 2005). A study of seventh graders in California showed that students in these programs scored higher than their traditionally taught counterparts in all subjects on the Stanford Achievement Test.

As shown in figure 2.3 (on the following page), the number of TWI programs increased dramatically over the past few decades, from 30 programs documented in the mid-1980s to 335 documented programs in 2007 (Center for Applied Linguistics, 2009). With the increasingly diverse population in the United States, such programs are an educational alternative that has the potential to expand even further, given our current demographics and societal needs.

Poverty and Illiteracy

Throughout their existence American schools have been challenged by poverty. The Franklin Academy, with its practical and relevant curriculum, lost its position as the most popular school in the country because it charged tuition, and the vast majority of families could not afford to send their children to the academy. For decades, many schools have been too poor to afford their students even such basic necessities as textbooks, pencils, paper, and chalk.

In the environments surrounding the schools, poverty has taken its toll on millions of children. The child poverty rate in the United States is among the highest in the developed nations (Thomas & Bainbridge, 2002). This is most painfully apparent in low-income and minority groups. In 2007, the percentage of Hispanic families living below the poverty level was 21.5; the percentage of black families was 24.5; Asians, 10.2, and non-Hispanic whites, 8.2% (U.S. Census Bureau, 2008). Present demographic trends indicate that this situation will continue for many years. With the downturn in the economy, these percentages will almost certainly worsen. Extreme poverty often manifests itself in malnourishment, high rates of mortality, and even suicide. The number of behavioral problems directly correlates with the degree of poverty.

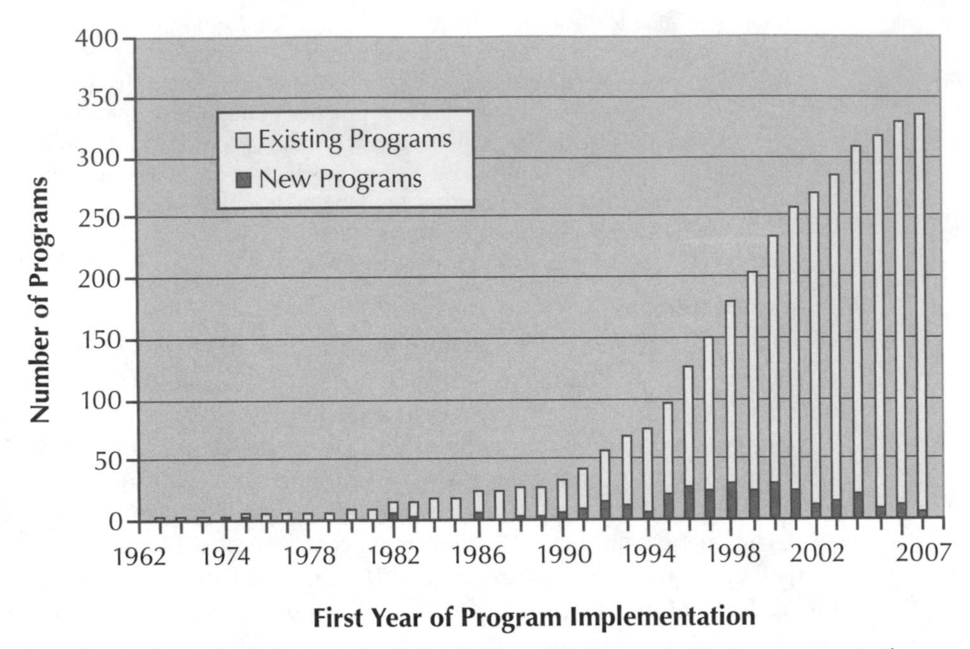

From the Center for Applied Linguistics (2009), *Directory of two-way immersion programs in the United States* (http://www.cal.org/twi/directory).

Figure 2.3 Growth of Two-Way Immersion Programs in the U.S., 1962–2007

The No Child Left Behind legislation focuses on schools located in poor communities, and many of the grant opportunities are limited to such schools. The success of the programs that are funded will be measured on the performance of these students compared to student performance in other schools. According to Doorey and Harter (2002/2003), the goal of bringing all schools to the same level of performance will be a monumental challenge: "Throughout the United States, the challenge of ensuring equity in our schools will increase as the income gap widens and pressure for high achievement increases" (p. 25). Recent Texas reform illustrates the need for this concern. There, the 1990s test-driven approach has produced a much increased dropout rate among minority students (Neill, 2003). Teacher turnover is also about 50% higher in high-poverty schools, "consigning students to a continual parade of ineffective teachers" (Darling-Hammond, 2003, p. 9).

Box 2.2 Closing the Achievement Gap

According to Gay (2004), disparities in educational opportunities and outcomes among ethnic groups have caused the achievement gap to reach crisis proportions, due in part to socioeconomic factors. Closing the gap between white and Asian students and their black and Hispanic counterparts is a major twenty-first-century challenge. According to the National Center for Education Statistics (NCES) (2009b),

In reading, the achievement gap between White-Black 4th-graders was smaller in 2007 than in any previous assessment. However, the gap between White-Hispanic 4th-graders was not measurably different in 2007 compared with 1992. In 2007, at the 4th-grade level, Blacks scored, on average, 27 points lower than Whites (on a 0–500 scale), and Hispanics scored, on average, 26 points lower than Whites. At 8th grade, there was no measurable difference in the White-Black or White-Hispanic reading achievement gaps in 2007 compared with 1992 or 2005. In 2007, at the 8th-grade level, Blacks scored, on average, 27 points lower on the reading assessment than Whites, and Hispanics scored, on average, 25 points lower than Whites.

In mathematics, the achievement gap between White-Black 4th-graders was lower in 2007 than in 1990 (26 vs. 32 points), but there was no measurable change over the last two years. The gap between White-Hispanic 4th-graders increased in the 1990s before decreasing in the first half of the 2000s, but the gap in 2007 (21 points) was not measurably different from that in 1990. Among 8th-graders, a similar trend existed in both the White-Black and White-Hispanic score gaps: increases occurred in the 1990s before decreasing to the current levels, which are not measurably different from those in 1990. The White-Black 8th-grade mathematics gap was lower in 2007 than in 2005, but there was no measurable change in the White-Hispanic gap. In 2007, among 8th-graders, the White-Black mathematics gap was 32 points, and the White-Hispanic gap was 26 points.

A major factor contributing to this problem is the fact that teachers in schools with high minority enrollments or high poverty levels are somewhat less likely to have a master's degree or a college major or minor in their main field of assignment than teachers in schools with few minority children or low poverty levels (Peske & Haycock, 2006). Fortunately, as of July 2006, "For the first time, leaders in every state must deliver to the Secretary of Education their plans for ensuring that low-income and minority students in their states are not taught disproportionately by inexperienced, out-of-field, or uncertified teachers" (Peske & Haycock, 2006, p. 1). The Education Trust makes the following recommendations to states and school districts on how to solve this problem of teacher inequality (Peske & Haycock, 2006):

1. Overhaul hiring practices for teachers, giving priority to recruiting and hiring teachers for high-poverty and high-minority schools who have academic backgrounds and full certification in the fields they are teaching;
2. Pay effective teachers more in high-needs schools, give them reduced student loads so they have more time for individual instruction, collaboration with colleagues, and coaching and induction.
3. Rethink the current policies (a) on paid sabbaticals, recognizing that teachers in high-need schools must be allowed to recharge their intellectual and emotional batteries; and (b) on tenure, reserving it for those teachers who demonstrate effectiveness at producing student learning.
4. Place the best principals in the schools that need them most. Supportive, collaborative principals are hugely important to attracting and holding strong teachers in high-poverty schools.
5. Ban unfair budgeting practices. More advantaged schools should not be allowed to "buy" more than their share of the most highly paid teachers. Set staff budgets at the school level, proportionate with student needs.

One profound impact of poverty on youth is the incapacitating effect it has on the ability to read. By the end of fourth grade, poor students of all races are two years behind their peers in both reading and math (Rebell, 2008). In poor communities, many parents themselves either are illiterate themselves or are too busy working to take the time to model reading for their children. Too many of our students, particularly those in high-poverty schools, struggle to become fluent readers. This inability to read, in turn, restricts students' growth in all academic areas. The expectations that teachers hold for their students tend to be lower in rural schools and in schools with high minority student enrollments (Weiss & Pasley, 2004). Carefully planned workshops can enhance participants' awareness of how poverty is impacting their schools.

Such circumstances pressure educators to try to design the curricula to help children overcome the harm they suffer daily as a result of poverty. Knapp and Shields (1990) identify some ways that curricula in impoverished areas can be strengthened: (1) maximize time-on-task, (2) set high expectations, (3) strengthen the involvement of parents in the support of instruction, (4) plan content in small, discrete parts structured in sequence, (5) provide whole-group or small-group formats, and (6) integrate the curriculum, giving students in all subjects opportunities to write, read, and discuss.

Box 2.3 Motivation and Learning

Without motivation learning is impossible. Although maximum learning depends on motivation (Woolfolk Hoy & Hoy, 2008), most contemporary youths do not receive strong motivation and encouragement outside the classroom. The home environment of many students does not contribute to a desire for learning. Confronting students' lack of motivation has become an increasing challenge. Many unmotivated students are retained in a grade, and a substantial number of these students will subsequently drop out. According to Jane David (2008), retention can increase the likelihood that a student will drop out of school: Students who drop out are five times more likely to have been retained than those who graduate.

> In 2007, about 10% of students in kindergarten through grade 8 had ever been retained in a grade during their school career. A greater percentage of black students than either white or Hispanic students had ever been retained in this year. . . . The percentage of K–8 students who had ever been retained was greater among students from poor families. The percentage of students from poor families who had ever been retained was higher in 2007 (23%) than in 1996 (17%), while the percentage of students from nonpoor families who had ever been retained was lower in 2007 (5%) than in 1996 (7%) (NCES, 2009b).

Although many of these children's circumstances outside the classroom are beyond the control of the educator, research has shown that teachers can influence student motivation. Teachers' attitudes toward their students can improve the students' self-concepts, which has been associated with improved motivation in the classroom (Brewster & Fager, 2000). Students should feel welcome and supported in their schools. The school climate should "recognize individual differences, encourage creativity, and give both teachers and students a sense of autonomy" (Brewster & Fager, 2000). Mastery learning can also help bolster student self-confidence. Constructive feedback and praise for work well done are equally important in fostering good student self-concepts.

Noncompetitive evaluation criteria are also important. When correctly designed, tests can be used to motivate students' interest in content. The power of tests and other evaluation procedures to shape students' perceptions of their teachers' expectations cannot be overestimated. As teachers fulfill their new education reform roles—using valued outcomes, alternative assessment, performance evaluation, and portfolios—many new ways of motivating students will be available to those who are cognizant of the need to use evaluation and other means to motivate.

FYI Creating Personal Learning Webs: The Power of Reflection in Mentoring

Ellen Reames • Auburn University

When mentoring new faculty members, a useful strategy is to have the "mentee" and mentor each create a *personal learning web*, which is a pictorial representation of how past experiences have influenced one's present knowledge and place. Mentors and mentees who are able to clearly reflect on past experiences are more likely to learn, improve their practice, and become productive members of a learning community. The only rule for this activity is that the drawing must focus on how the individuals see the development of their personal and professional learning experiences and how these developments have influenced where they are presently. To create the learning web, participants can use any shapes they wish (e.g., circles, ovals, squares, triangles, stars) and any types of lines (e.g., dotted, solid, and arrow lines) to show how these experiences have influenced and impacted their present knowledge. A simple example is shown below.

My personal web: What influences my present knowledge about teaching and learning?

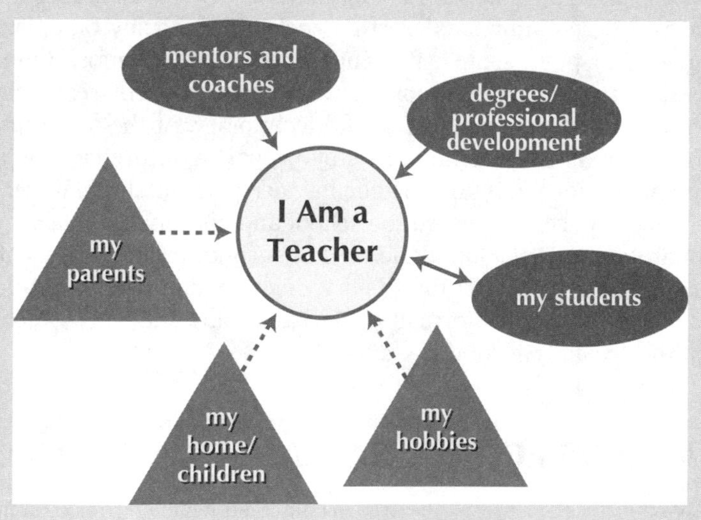

Changes in Family Structure

Through the years, the family unit has been a profound strength in the American culture. In the past, the responsibility for transforming kids into competent adults was mainly the job of the family. The typical concept of family has changed radically in the past few decades, however. As far back as 1989, a survey by the Massachusetts Mutual Life Insurance Company (Seligmann, 1989) asked 1,200 randomly selected adults what the word family meant to them. Only 22% picked the traditional definition of "a group of people related by blood, marriage, or adoption." About 75% selected "a group of people who love and care for each other." Most of today's youths—not just those in impoverished circumstances—have no concept of the traditional family that existed throughout the first half of the twentieth century—that is, the natural mother and father (no divorce, no stepparents), the father being the breadwinner for his family, and the mother being a homemaker who did not have a job outside the home.

Contemporary curricula must reflect these changes. Homework assignments must be compatible with the realization that most of today's youths do not have the support fostered in the traditional family and setting—for example, a quiet, lighted study area; ample time to give to homework assignments; and parents who are available, willing, and able to help students understand their assignments. Perhaps more realistically, many of today's youth have no adult role models at home who read books for information and pleasure, and many have no parents to encourage them and remind them of the importance of education.

A Final Thought on Social Foundations

Our schools may never close the achievement gap without changing our society. "Raising the achievement of lower-class children requires the amelioration of the social and economic conditions of their lives, not just school reform" (Rothstein, 2004, p. 110). A balance is maintained between the forces that schools and their respective communities exert on each other. At any time, every community has forces that push against its schools. Some of the more influential of these forces include tradition, textbooks, laws, religious beliefs, research, multicultural concerns, poverty, family changes, and technology. At the same time, the schools exert pressure on their communities by preparing future citizens and promoting intellectualism. Ideally, a homeostatic balance is maintained. When this balance is lost, problems develop between the school and community.

In addition to social foundations, there is another influence which, although it appeared relatively late in the history of curriculum planning, looms large on today's curriculum transformation horizon. This influence—technology—is the topic of the second part of this chapter.

PART II: TECHNOLOGICAL FOUNDATIONS

> We educators must resist the urge to talk about technology, or even think about it, without concern for how it can be used to enhance learning.
>
> —K. Henson

THE CASE OF O'DONNELL SCHOOL: TECHNOLOGY GOES HOME @ SCHOOL BUILDS PARENTAL INVOLVEMENT

Background

In the Technology Goes Home @ School Program, administered through the Boston Public Schools, families attend an initial informational meeting at their child's school, and program training is in a group setting with peers. The child's teacher conducts the training, creating an opportunity for parents and teachers to communicate regularly and get to know each other.

The goals of the TGH @ School program are:

- to help children improve their academic performance,
- to encourage parents and children to work together toward a common goal,
- to enhance the relationship between parents and teachers, and
- to help adults prepare for better employment opportunities.

The O'Donnell Elementary School in East Boston is using technology training to create a culture of parental involvement. The results are both impressive and surprising—for parents, teachers, and the school as a whole.

"Working with the Boston Digital Bridge Foundation's Technology Goes Home@School program (TGH@S)," explains O'Donnell's Principal, Dr. Robert Martin, "we offer 12 weeks of computer training for students and their parents. Three years ago, we started with the idea that demystifying computers would be a good thing. What we've discovered is that this powerful learning experience also demystifies the school. As parents meet teachers and other parents, they become engaged in other school activities and more willing to take on leadership roles. In fact, virtually all of the school's site council parents and a majority of the parent council members are TGH@S alums."

"TGH@S has clearly become a gateway to greater parental involvement," says Ellen Cooper, O'Donnell's computer teacher, a TGH@S instructor, and a 2005 Boston Public School Teacher of the Year. "For many of our parents, English is a second language. At first, they were shy about interacting. But as they found that the teachers were actually there to help, shyness gave way to confidence."

"You can just see the comfort level of the parents go up," says fourth-grade teacher Ellen Howe, who is a TGH@S instructor. "And as it does, you see their involvement go up. The lesson plans for TGH@S are based on the school curriculum, and this gives parents insights into what their children are studying, as well as opportunities to discuss school curriculum with teachers. A mutual respect grows as kids and parents learn together."

Tech Boston bilingual high school students served as TGH@S assistants and were instrumental in bridging the language gap. The younger students looked up to these interns, who became positive role models. Students also helped overcome language barriers, often serving as interpreters for the parents.

"Parent involvement is crucial," Principal Martin says. "TGH opens a door so parents feel involved and empowered. They appreciate the teachers, value the educational experience for

Tech Boston Assistant Christina Osorio works with student Sonia Penna on her PowerPoint presentation, "What is a tsunami?"

their kids, and want to be more involved. They take on leadership roles and it makes all the difference in the world. When parents are involved, we see kids become better learners and teachers become better teachers. The technology training is great. The increased parental involvement is even better. It's a huge bonus."

Martha Velez, mother of a fourth grader, says, "TGH@S is helping me learn English. I've also signed up for the school's ESL class." In addition, Martha has become an active member of the School Site Council. Parent Gloribell Mota adds, "I loved the computer classes and the collaborative learning with my son, Edward. It made me feel connected to the school, the teachers, and other parents. That's why I joined the School/Parent Council and the School Site Council."

Martha Velez and her daughter Michelle Perez. Martha is a member of the School Site Council and Parent Council, and she has become an advocate for other Spanish-speaking families. Michelle has been accepted to Advanced Work Class for next year.

Dong Young Kim is happy that he and his fourth-grade son are improving their English and writing skills through TGH, and he is also finding that it's fun to help out with school field trips and meet other parents. Shawnda Pugliese says that TGH has brought her closer to her daughter and made it easier for her to attend parent/teacher conferences and other school meetings.

In its fifth year, in May of 2003 the TGH@S program graduated a class of 263 families (comprised of 526 individuals).

For more information:
http://www.bostondigitalbridgefoundation.org
Jackie Collins, Program Director
(617) 201-6316
jcollins@boston.k12.ma.us

Ellen Howe works with Dong Young Kim, his daughter, Jung In, and his son, Joo Yoeb, during their afternoon-school class.

Shawnda and Amber Pugliese put final touches on their PowerPoint project titled "Hurricanes." They will make their presentation to their class on the final-night celebration of their 12-week TGH@S program.

• • •

Sometimes educators who spend their lives working in schools don't realize how uncomfortable some parents and other community members (especially English-as-a-second-language parents) feel when they enter the school building. Some parents do not have computers and don't know how to use them, and this lack of technology and skills can further diminish their confidence. Projects like Boston's Technology Goes Home program provide a good entrée to the school world for these parents, and a good entrée to their children's worlds.

This highly successful project was designed to serve the mission of its school. For this same reason, technology has helped Singapore turn its very young schools into world leaders. Using the theme, "Teach Less and Learn More," Singapore uses its technology to promote lifelong learning, energize students, promote higher-level thinking, and promote independent learning (CCSSO, 2008). As you read the rest of this chapter, keep your school's mission in mind. As each type of technology and each program are discussed, consider the effects that they would have on promoting your school's mission.

The explosion of technology on the education scene in the past few decades has been astronomical. Toward the end of the twentieth century, one of the most frequent suggestions educational leaders made for improving schools was the integration of technology into the teaching and learning process. Although substantial progress has been made, this integration is still far from complete, even at the college level.

Today, the power of technology to change the curriculum is almost beyond comprehension, and the movement for technologically induced changes in the curricula of American elementary and secondary schools is expanding at lightning speed. As reported by Bernauer (1999, p. 70), "Findings confirm that motivation and achievement improved after technology was integrated into the curriculum." Research studies on *information technology* reported the following gains in students' advanced skills:

- explored and represented information dynamically and in many forms
- became socially aware and more confident
- communicated effectively about complex processes
- became independent learners and self-starters
- worked well collaboratively
- knew their areas of expertise and shared expertise spontaneously
- used technology routinely and appropriately
- increased their writing skills
- increased their understanding of, and gained a broader view of, math
- evidenced the ability to teach others
- evidenced greater problem-solving and critical thinking skills (see Stockard, 2001, pp. 212–213).

Education Technology/Information Literacy

> The allure of engrossing digital tools, entertaining experiences and social networking communities outside of school is making it increasingly difficult for educators to motivate and engage a large majority of students in academic learning with traditional pedagogy. Schools must create learning environments that are as engaging and relevant as the ones that students gravitate to outside of school. Research also shows that students are more engaged and more successful when they can connect what they are learning to situations they care about in their community and in the world. Technology provides access to real-world data, tools, and resources, and can help students link learning to life.
>
> —Partnership for 21st Century Skills

History is full of "new" technologies that promised to revolutionize education (Baines, 2007). Although some of the earlier attempts may have been less than effective, in this century new doors are opening into a technological world with virtually boundless potential in the field of education. The No Child Left Behind legislation provided $15 million for a five-year research study to identify the conditions necessary for technology to improve student achievement using scientifically based research methods. The USDE Office of Educational Technology (www.ed.gov/technology) produced Helping Practitioners Meet the Goals of No Child Left Behind, a guide for educators who are considering the use of technologies to meet various requirements of the law.

In 2004, the U.S. Department of Education undertook a strategic review and revision of the National Educational Technology Plan (NETP) of 1999, based on the thoughtful input from thousands of students, educators, administrators, technology experts, and officials of numerous educational organizations. The outcome was *Toward a New Golden Age in American Education—How the Internet, the Law and Today's Students Are Revolutionizing Expectations,* If you have not been excited about technology's role in education so far, this report will change the way you feel. The official Web site of NETP features a downloadable version of the entire report as well as a browse-friendly online version, student perspectives, action steps and accompanying recommendations, state and district success stories, and several blogs (visit http://www.ed.gov/about/offices/list/os/technology/plan/2004/site/edlite-default.html).

To take full advantage of the benefits that education technology offers, educators must become information literate, enabling the construction of new knowledge in an increasingly diverse, multicultural student population. *Information literacy* is the ability to identify what information is needed, understand how the information is organized, identify the best sources of information for a given need, locate those sources, evaluate the sources critically, and share that information. According to the National Forum on Information Literacy (2009),

> Information literacy . . . is a critical competency necessary for America to compete successfully in an increasingly interdependent global economy which is bound together by an interconnected information and communication technology infrastructure that seamlessly networks a variety of peoples, institutions,

> and organizations in all sectors, regardless of creed, color, age, gender or socio-economic status. . . . It fosters the successful transformation of traditional teaching-centered modes to modern learning-centered strategies within our rapidly and radically changing information and communication technology universe.

The remainder of this chapter addresses some of the most promising and exciting innovations in education today, all centering around computer-based technology.

The Versatile Computer

The most obvious facet of educational technology is the computer—particularly in its service-providing role as gateway to the Internet and World Wide Web, which enables everyone to access information from distant sources. Educational computer use has expanded astronomically over the past decade or two. According to the National Center for Education Statistics (2007), nearly 100% of schools and 92% of classrooms in this country are now connected to the Internet—an astounding increase when compared with only 35% in 1994. In 2003, 10% of public schools provided a handheld computer to students or teachers (U.S. Department of Education, 2004). This increased computer use has heavily impacted curricula in secondary and elementary schools, characterizing the education reform movement in most states.

The Evolving Nature of Computer-Assisted Curriculum

At first, curriculum planners introduced computer-based technology gradually over the years. Word processing was the simplest and most versatile of computer tools and, for that reason, was initially the most used in classroom situations. Studies indicated that word-processing software encouraged writing and led to increased motivation and improvement in their writing skills (Van Scoter, Ellis, & Railsback, 2001).

At that time, teachers were challenged to write computer-based assignments that required the use of problem-solving skills and creativity. Today, in contrast, there is an almost overwhelming amount of lesson plans available online. In addition, most educational software vendors are aligning their curricula to teacher needs and to state standards (Mercurius, 2003). For several downloadable examples of standards-based, curriculum-based projects (K–8), visit the Web site of Technology Solutions for Schools (http://www.k8technologyprojects.com/_Home.html). For Edutopia's teacher-rated list of the best online plans, read their online list (http://www.edutopia.org/best-site-download-free-lessons-2007).

In chapter 6, we discuss the various levels of the educational taxonomies and examine examples of objectives at each level in each domain. By focusing computer activities at the upper levels of the taxonomies, teachers can effectively use the computer to meet one of the schools' most critical needs, that of raising the level of student thinking. As just a few examples, stories in which students share their values (through listservs, blogs, message boards, and forums—discussed later in the chapter) can become topics of multicultural discussions. Languagearts students have used the computer to create open-ended scenarios that help them develop particular skills, including advanced-level thinking, and enable them to tie current information to prior knowledge.

Hewett (2004) reports that when students share their accomplishments via digital portfolios, their motivational levels increase. In addition, According to Merkley, Schmidt, Dirksen, and Fulher (2006), "parent-teacher communication might be enhanced using a Web-based system that manages student reading artifacts along with teacher insight and explanation" (p. 12).

Why integrate technology into the curriculum? According to the George Lucas Educational Foundation (Edutopia.org), the reasons are many:

> Integrating technology into classroom instruction means more than teaching basic computer skills and software programs. . . . Effective tech integration must happen across the curriculum in ways that research shows deepen and enhance the learning process. . . . It must support four key components of learning: active engagement, participation in groups, frequent interaction and feedback, and connection to real-world experts. Effective technology integration is achieved when the use of technology is routine and transparent and when technology supports curricular goals. . . .
>
> Technology also changes the way teachers teach, offering educators effective ways to reach different types of learners and assess student understanding through multiple means. It also enhances the relationship between teacher and student. When technology is effectively integrated into subject areas, teachers grow into roles of adviser, content expert, and coach. Technology helps make teaching and learning more meaningful and fun.

Visit Edutopia's technology integration Web page (http://www.edutopia.org/tech-integration) for a mind-boggling amount of timely and useful information, including videos of real-life success stories, a keyword-searchable database, and a constantly updated "Big List" of nearly 100 technology integration articles.

Today's curricula must help teachers to assess software to ensure that it is educationally sound. Good software prompts students to produce charts, written responses, and other products and processes that require higher-level thinking. Two decades ago, Siegel and Davis (1986) feared that commercial developers would probably not improve the quality of software as quickly as they should. Such fears have proved to be unfounded, and choices of educational software abound. For an extensive list of educational software, including links to reviews and manufacturers, visit *Educational Software Reviews: Your Guide to Educational Software Reviews on the Web* (http://www.educational-software-directory.net/reviews.html). Edutopia's results from their 2007 survey on best education software can be found at http://www.edutopia.org/best-education-software-2007.

Perhaps more important than the programs teachers choose to use is how the computer programs/applications are introduced to students. The computer should be a learning tool that enables students to explore without fear of criticism.

Meeting the Goals of Multiculturalism, Diversity, and Inclusion

In addition to its invaluable role as an instructional tool, the computer can play multiple roles in developing and maintaining a classroom climate that encourages all students to accept, appreciate, and celebrate all types of differences. Many businesses have programs designed to enhance multicultural relationships among employees. In the classroom, guest speakers who represent ethnic and gender diversity and who use computers to facilitate their presentations to the class can expand students' own application of computers while also providing positive role models.

There is also value in interacting with the community by sending teacher-education students into schools with diverse populations. For at least four decades, teacher-education colleges have been increasing the number of hours students spend in the schools. These experiences can be enriched by reflective assignments that prompt teacher-education students to notice how computers are being used by a diverse body of students. Too often, we assume that our role is to know what students should be doing with computers and to guide them in that direction. But this is only partly true; we can and should also watch students to learn what they find interesting and stimulating about computers. Student self-concepts can be strengthened by involving them in the selection of computer activities. Given the opportunity to choose their own computer projects, what they choose may give us insight on the most effective ways in which students can use computers to learn.

There is inherent value in using interactive strategies to enhance multicultural education (Nagel, 1998). Some programs partner students with counterparts in other countries for ongoing e-mail exchanges (a technological twist on the familiar "pen pal" idea that has long benefited foreign-language students). One organization that promotes such exchanges is ePals. Founded in 1996 and recently having

FYI Tower Building

Jacques Singleton and Gwendolyn Neal • Arkansas State University

Inclusion can be frustrating for both the student and teacher. To help teachers gain a better understanding of the frustration, we often employ an activity that is fun and interactive. We have used the following activity as a part of our introduction to special education courses as a way of detailing some of the possible mistakes teachers make when including all students in the regular education classroom.

The activity is called the Build a Tower Game. The class is divided into groups of four, whose task is to build a tower with straws and tape as high as possible on a table. The four group members are each assigned one of the following roles: a "normal"-functioning person, a person who cannot use the dominate hand, a blindfolded person, and a person unable to speak. Once the activity is complete, the members discuss in small group first and then with the whole group the following questions: How did they feel? Did they participate in the group? Were they treated differently? What did they learn? Through this discussion, teachers experience some of the frustration that students with disabilities feel when trying to work with their nondisabled peers in the regular education classroom. The major objective is for teachers to take these experiences back to their classrooms and consider them when planning activities for the entire classroom.

undergone a twenty-first-century makeover, ePals offers its updated communications platform to schools free. The ePals Global Learning Community includes some thirteen million students and teachers in 200 countries, making it the largest online community in K–12 education (Boss, 2008). With such programs, Students from different cultural backgrounds can be paired together, and assignments stemming from such relationships enable students to counteract stereotypes and promote reflection about each other's cultures. Autobiographic essays to stimulate student reflections about their own cultures can be shared by blogging (discussed later in the chapter) or e-mail and also with classmates and teachers within the same room. Depending on the level of teacher expertise and the sophistication of available equipment, students can prepare multimedia presentations, not only in the classroom but also for school assemblies or after-school functions where parents and other family members can attend.

A large variety of technology products exists to improve language skills of ESL students. Computer programs/applications to teach phonics, phonemic awareness, articulation, and pronunciation are available. Some programs can record audio of the students reading, make corrections, document errors, evaluate comprehension, and provide extensive data for monitoring student progress. According to one teacher interviewed by Maya Payne Smart (2008c, p. 3),

> With a password, [teachers] can access audio files of any district student reading aloud to monitor his or her progress over time. Teachers can even e-mail the sound clips to parents. Some students progress from reading twenty words per minute to seventy words per minute.

Students also testify that technology has improved their language skills and makes school fun: "We go to the computer lab and make PowerPoint presentations and write a lot of letters and essays. I like writing on the computer better than writing with a pencil" (Smart, 2008c, p. 2).

Computerized assistive technology can be a great equalizer for individuals with disabilities that might otherwise prevent full participation in school.

> Text and graphics enhancement software can enlarge sections of a monitor enough to be seen by persons with vision impairments. Text can be read electronically by a digitized voice synthesizer for a person who is blind. For persons with hearing impairments, amplification devices can filter extraneous noise from the background or pick up an FM signal from a microphone on a teacher's lapel. (Behrmann, 1998, p. 2)

Word processing, with its accompanying editing, spelling, and grammatical tools, facilitates the inclusion of students with learning disabilities. With Internet access, students can interact in real time via on-screen messaging, video, and audio transmissions. In most of these learning situations, a disability makes no difference at all.

Interdisciplinary Applications

Teachers who believe in integrating the disciplines know that computers can be used in and across various disciplines and cultures. For example, English writing assignments can easily focus on science, social studies, and other disciplines. Social studies teachers, for another example, could begin a story about problems urban dwellers have because of their cultural differences. Computers could be used to help students analyze the problems from the viewpoints of different cultures. Once the stories are complete, role playing, simulations, and discussions placing students of varied backgrounds into cooperative working relationships can follow. A follow-up assignment might involve students using the computer to develop a profile of their value systems, listing their own beliefs that came to light during the previous exercises. By sharing these value profiles with others (often via the Internet), students can generate multicultural discussions.

One of the biggest benefits of integrated studies is that it allows students to solve problems and construct knowledge in ways that mimic real life. According to the Edutopia staff (2008),

> In today's dynamic global economy, centered on the development and exchange of knowledge and information, individuals prosper who are fluent in several disciplines and comfortable moving among them. Creativity, adaptability, critical reasoning, and collaboration are highly valued skills. When it comes to fostering those skills in the classroom, integrated study is an extremely effective approach, helping students develop multifaceted expertise and grasp the important role interrelationships can play in the real world.

Other Technological Developments

The computer revolution is part of a much broader development that includes a number of other digital inventions, several of which are contributing much to curriculum development. Paradoxically, although some schools cannot afford the expenses required to make their students technologically current, a significant advantage offered by that very technology is its ability to save money over time.

Because they use computerized technology to create and "develop" pictures, digital cameras are more convenient and user friendly than traditional cameras. The once-prohibitive cost of digital cameras is decreasing from year to year, and many teacher-education colleges now find that they can afford digital cameras and color printers. Digital cameras have unlimited uses. Prospective teachers can record what they observe during visits to school campuses for use in reports and in their portfolios. Teachers can visit businesses and agencies in the community and visually record diverse community leaders using technology, thus making the connection between technology in the schools and in the outside community. Classroom photos now regularly grace copies of e-newsletters to parents.

Consider another application of the digital camera: Accrediting agencies such as the *National Council for Accreditation of Teacher Education* (NCATE) require teacher education programs to promote diversity and multicultural education. With that goal in mind, teachers can use digital cameras to make a permanent visual record of activities that promote these values. The results can be made available on displays or in portfolios kept in the accreditation site team workroom. For example, if a college has minority student-recruitment summer workshops, or perhaps an exchange program with a college with many students from different cultures, or if an institution holds multicultural or international events, any of these events can be easily recorded using a digital camera. They are also a handy tool for creating student portfolios.

Since it was first introduced it in 2001, Apple has expanded the capabilities of the iPod far beyond that of a portable format for mp3 music files. According to Maya Payne Smart (2008a),

> Many programs are available free from iTunes U, a new section of Apple's iTunes Store, which offers downloads for MP3 players. The online repository, launched in July [of 2008], contains everything from course curricula and professional-development tips to student-journalism podcasts and school announcements. The State Educational Technology Directors Association, a national organization that promotes leadership in technology to support lifelong learning, and several state education agencies have provided Apple with the K–12 content. So far, contributors in Arizona, California, Florida, Maine, Michigan, New Jersey, Pennsylvania, and Utah have uploaded materials to the site. . . . iTunes U helps teachers quickly identify materials they can use as references in their courses. For example, a chemistry teacher seeking resources on hydrogen can perform a search for the element using the iTunes Store's Power Search tool, and she can limit it to return only iTunes U results. She can then add the appropriate links to her course page and encourage students to download the audio to study. This feature will become increasingly useful as the content library grows.

The Internet Explosion

The most important contribution of the computer to education is through the Internet and the World Wide Web. Just a few of the many educational tools and services available through this medium are message boards, listservs and forums, school portals, blogs, eLearning/virtual schooling, cyberlibraries, virtual field trips, and WebQuests.

Message Boards, Forums, Newsgroups, and Listservs

In 1978, a system was perfected for programming computers to transfer files from one machine to another via modems and telephone lines, and software and hardware was developed for doing so. The resulting software–hardware combination was named the Computerized Bulletin Board System (CBBS). It operated like a virtual "thumb-tack" bulletin board: participants could post messages to a public "board," and others could read and respond to those messages, creating an ongoing virtual discussion (*What Does a Network Do?* n.d.) Soon, virtual *bulletin boards* popped up all over the country and were given the generic name BBS (for bulletin board system). By the early 1990s most BBSs had become connected to the Internet, vastly expanding the possibilities of users. Such systems (sometimes referred to as the USENET) are called *message boards, forums,* or *newsgroups*.

The *listserv*, a popular automatic mailing list server, is another communication-enhancing tool that benefits educators. People sharing an interest may "subscribe" to a given discussion, and other subscribers' contributions to the thread are distributed to the entire subscriber base via e-mail. The result is similar to a newsgroup or forum, except that the messages are transmitted as e-mail and are therefore available only to individuals on the list. Up-to-date listserv information for the entire Internet is available from CataList (http://www.lsoft.com/lists/listref.html), which calls itself "the official catalog of Listserv lists." It features a database of over 53,000 public listservs searchable by specific topic. Those with interests such as computers and the Internet, curricula, distance education, education and technology, and multiculturalism are certain to find a listserv to suit their purposes.

Through these technologies, students have been able to share and discuss their projects worldwide. Message boards, forums, newsgroups, and listservs also are effective vehicles through which curriculum planners and teachers from different schools can collaborate on curricula, lesson plans, and a multitude of other subjects. The technology has proved useful in strengthening communication among culturally different schools and universities.

> Many schools have easy access to such services through their own specially created portals, which can be used by teachers, students, and/or parents. A portal is a gateway or entrance to the Web. This Web site or service commonly offers a broad array of resources and services, such as e-mail, message boards, forums, and search engines. In some communities, parents are encouraged to use these sites to stay informed of student assignments and school news. . . . Portal sites for individual grade levels, subjects, or courses are frequently part of a school's larger portal site. . . . Portals especially for teachers can include links to associations representing their specific academic interests, offer professional development opportunities, and feature links to ERIC clearinghouses and other resources. (Stockard, 2001, p. 210)

However, more and more teachers and students are exploring the possibilities of an even later development—the blog.

Blogs (Weblogs)

By now, just about everyone is familiar with the concept of blogging—including teachers. John Franklin (2005) has recommended blogging as a mentoring tool to support new teachers and a tool for collaboration with colleagues. (To read the entire article see Henson, 2006, pp. 58–70.) Armstrong, Berry, and Lamshed (2003) and DeLuca (2005) explored the range of potential applications of blogging technology in education and training for student and teacher communication, delivery of learning materials, the provision of mentoring to students, collaboration and professional development for teachers, and knowledge management. Helena Echlin (2007) describes the many uses of blogs in education, including classroom management, assessment, class discussion, and many other applications. David Carraher (2003), who blogs on teacher education, curriculum development, and research about teaching and learning at Harvard, comments on the rapidly expanding role that blogging has in education:

> The implications of blogging in curriculum development are exciting and virtually limitless. "Curriculum developers could access examples of students', teachers' and researchers' thinking. . . . Teacher educators could discuss examples from actual classrooms. Teacher educator weblogs would document the evolution of their thinking over time."

Several online sites show teachers how to set up blogs to help meet learning goals. Two of the most highly recommended free blog services are WordPress.com and Blogger.com, both of which were selected by Google Scholar eLearning as one of the Top 10 (out of 100) tools for 2008. Edublogs.org (another highly ranked in the Top 100) is geared toward education, helps teachers learn how to use blogs with their students, and offers lively forums where educators at all levels of technological acuity swap tips. Fifty useful blogging tools for teachers can be found at TeachingTips.com (2008).

Wikis and Podcasts

Wikis are collaborative Web sites that enable people to edit or add to their content. Some teachers use password-protected Wikis to create their own textbooks and resource sites (Richardson & Mancabelli, 2007).

Podcasts are digital broadcasts that teachers or students can produce using a computer, a microphone, and editing software. Students can add music, and can even paste their podcasts to blogs to share with their peers and families. Ann Marie Dlott (2007) has tried all of these activities and reports that the results are well worth the effort.

case study

Listening to Themselves: Podcasting Takes Lessons Beyond the Classroom

Maya Payne Smart

Brent Coley's fifth-grade students' eyes light up when they learn that their schoolwork can be heard in Apple iTunes, the program that allows them to compile their favorite artists' music.

Although the Tovashal Elementary School students, in Murrieta, California, won't be jamming on guitars or drums in Coley's class, their studies of poetry, the solar system, and the early English settlements in North America become exciting when they're posted on a class Web site and saved in iTunes as ColeyCasts, room 34's take on podcasting.

Web distribution of their work motivates students to put their best foot forward. "My Web site has been viewed in all fifty states and eighty-seven foreign countries," Coley says. "I use that to my advantage. When I show the kids statistics and recent visitor numbers, it tells them that I'm not the only person who is going to hear what they're doing. People in Australia and England are going to hear it."

With minimal technology, Coley gives his students a global audience. And he's not alone. Teachers across the nation are helping their students produce an impressive array of downloadable educational material. Directories such as the Education Podcast Network and *iTunes U K–12* try to organize that material. (See the *Edutopia* article "In One Ear: iTunes U Puts iPods to Good Use" at http://www.edutopia.org/itunes-u-professional-development) And award programs, such as the KidCast Podcasting in the Classroom Awards, honor the best of it.

Access to digital educational content at school, at home, and on the go is growing. The Pew Internet & American Life Project reported in September 2008 that 74% of kids ages 12–17 own an iPod or another MP3 player, up from 51% two years ago. The portability of digital content available for MP3 players such as the iPod and Microsoft's Zune player boosts instructional time by making course content available anywhere. Fort Sumner Municipal Schools students who took part in a Zune media player pilot study used the technology to study during long bus and car rides and to access study materials including video, audio, and Microsoft PowerPoint slides in their rural part of New Mexico. This learning on the go pushed Spanish I grades "through the roof," according to Superintendent Patricia Miller.

Podcasting Defined

At the end of a social studies or science unit, Coley breaks the class into groups of two or three students so they can develop podcast scripts by discussing and summarizing what they've learned. Coley reviews the scripts for accuracy and helps students record audio on the classroom computer or on his iPod using a Griffin iTalk Pro voice recorder. Coley adds an introduction and music between each segment before playing the finished product for the class and posting it on iTunes and mrcoley.com.

"I've received emails from teachers all over the country who have found the site in a link and listened to it," Coley says. "I pass the messages on to the kids, and it keeps them motivated to do their best work."

Podcasts are simply audio recordings stored as MP3 files or in another file format. The creator syndicates the recording via the Internet, and the listener plays it using a digital music player on a computer or a mobile device, such as an iPod or a Zune. Though the term *podcasting* combines *iPod* and *broadcasting*, you don't need a portable MP3 player to create or distribute the audio files. Coley produces most of the class's podcasts with just a computer, a microphone, Internet access, and free audio-mixing software such as Audacity or Apple's GarageBand. Teachers can even burn the audio files onto CDs so that students who lack iPods or computers at home have access to the material.

When used educationally, podcasts can empower students and teachers to become content producers rather than content consumers, and they can give them audiences beyond the classroom. Student-created podcasts reinforce course concepts, develop writing skills, hone speaking ability, and even help parents stay current on classroom activities.

"It gives them a sense of purpose, rather than seeming like just another academic exercise," says Dan Schmit, creator and host of the online community KidCast: Podcasting in the Classroom. "You give them a sense of mission for their work and give them all these authentic experiences that build their confidence for the future."

Story Time

Schmit says that the best student-created podcasts go beyond isolated episodes to engage in sustained academic conversations. They are focused on a real audience and explore grade-appropriate questions that are both interesting to students and important for them to understand. KidCast award winners such as Radio WillowWeb, from Willowdale Elementary School, in Omaha, Nebraska, illustrate this point. "It's not about the technology so much," Schmit says. "Podcasting is much more about inquiry, analysis, and articulation."

It's also about oral-presentation skills and storytelling technique—finding the characters, conflict, and resolution that help clarify a topic for the audience. "If a podcast feels like someone is just reading to me, it's not as engaging as when it feels like the students are having a conversation with me," Schmit says. "It's sort of like an extra step that we don't usually get to do in the language arts. Here, they are listening to themselves. Even in speech class, students read their work but don't hear it, because they are in the moment."

Speaking about course content also moves students away from copy-and-paste research. "You get kids to massage the content in a way that really makes it their own," Schmit points out. "The ability to tell a compelling story is going to be one of the most important twenty-first-century skills that we can give students."

The Next Frontier

In 1995, educator David Warlick created Landmarks for Schools to help teachers navigate the wilderness of online educational content. The Internet has grown exponentially in the years since, but he's still erecting guideposts to show teachers the way to valuable resources via his podcast Connect Learning, his site The Education Podcast Network, and his blog 2¢ Worth.

Looking ahead, Warlick expects communication and the selling of ideas to take on larger significance in the work world. This trend, he says, "requires that teachers and students learn to be information artisans—people who can creatively and artistically reshape information and raw material into compelling information products."

Those information products may take the form of blogs, podcasts, video games, or virtual worlds—whatever medium is best suited to the learning objectives. School facilities and assessment methods will have to change to embrace the shift, though. Warlick envisions libraries evolving into digital workshops where students produce multimedia content. In turn, new rubrics will emerge to evaluate students' multimedia work.

Still, Warlick reminds teachers that the exchange of ideas—not technology—is the point, and production—not memorization—is the proof of knowledge. "We're in the classroom to teach them not how to podcast, but how to communicate, and communicate compellingly," he says.

Connect to the many hyperlinks in the online article by accessing it at the Edutopia Web site (http://ww.w.edutopia.org/podcasting-student-broadcasts).

Suggested Readings

Buck, F. (2007). Saving time and paper with basic technology. *Principal, 96*(3),18–21.

Echlin, H. (2007, September). Digital Discussion: Take Your Class to the Internet. Retrieved on April 29, 2009 at the *Edutopia Magazine* Web site: http://www.edutopia.org/digital-discussion-take-your-class-to-internet

Mills, C. K. (2007). Building curriculum with digital materials. *Principal, 86*(3), 26–28.

Richardson, D., & Manabelli, R. (Jan./Feb. 2007). The read/write Web: New tools for a new generation of technology. *Principal, 86*(3), 12–17.

Smart, M. P. (2008, October 8). In one ear: iTunes U puts iPods to good use. Retrieved April 29, 2009, from the *Edutopia Magazine* Web site: http://www.edutopia.org/itunes-u-professional-development

eLearning and Virtual Schooling

From the most prestigious universities to the humblest of community colleges and high schools, more and more learning institutions now offer *eLearning* (the twenty-first-century version of *distance learning*—learning that takes place when the instructor and student are separated by space and/or time). eLearning takes place in the form of webcourses, telecourses, interactive video conferencing courses, and multimedia courses (which include—in addition to those delivery methods just mentioned—e-mail, discussion boards, videotapes, online chat, and streaming media).

In 2008, The U.S. Department of Education reported that during the 2006–07 academic year, 61% of 2- and 4-year degree-granting institutions offered online courses, 35% reported hybrid-blended courses, and 26% reported other types of college-level credit-granting distance education courses (NCES, 2009a). According to the Sloan Consortium (2009), the overall number of K–12 students engaged in online courses in 2007–2008 is estimated at 1,030,000. This represents a 47% increase since 2005–2006. Some states offer educational telecommunication networks available at multiple sites, such as university, community college, state agency or state/private alliance locations (see, e.g., METNET, n.d.).

New applications are constantly being found for eLearning. Research has even been done regarding distance learning for deaf elementary and high school students through videoconferencing, which facilitates visual communication through American Sign Language (ASL) (Parton, 2004; Lehman & Conceição, 2001). Distance learning is also increasingly being made available to students with disabilities.

Even a visit to the library (now more appropriately called a media center) takes on new meaning in the digital age with the advent of cyberlibraries. (Both Yahoo (http://dir.yahoo.com/Reference/Libraries) and Google (http://www.goodle.com/Top/Reference/Libraries) provide virtually unlimited electronic access to information about any topic imaginable. Just visiting the Library of Congress Web site alone (http://www.loc.gov) gives you access to a searchable database of millions of records—books, serials, computer files, manuscripts, cartographic materials, music, sound recordings, visual materials, and more. A site called Online Libraries (www.freality.com/libraries.htm) puts several search options at your fingertips (e.g., Questia Online Library, Smithsonian Institution Libraries) as well as encyclopedias, translation dictionaries, thesaurus, and quotations.

Virtual Field Trips and WebQuests

In the early days of the Internet, *virtual field trips* promised to take students to exotic places without having to worry about a travel budget. However, some were more entertaining than educational, and others were merely hypertext window dressing for lecture outlines. But with twenty-first-century technology, the highly interactive Web sites for many field trips feature "engaging storytelling, vibrant art, and curricula tied to the national standards" (Platoni, 2008). Examples of a few well-conceptualized virtual field trips follow.

- *Colonial Williamsburg*
  (www.history.org/trips)
  This site features several electronic field trips correlated to American history standards. Besides colonial history, these field trips involve stories from the 17th through 19th centuries, including Native American and African-American history.

- *Leonardo's Workshop*
  (http://www.alifetimeofcolor.com/play/Leonardo/index.html)
  This award-winning, graphic-rich field trip allows kids to jump into a time machine and travel back to Leonardo da Vinci's workshop in 1505. In the engaging mouse-click fashion of the best PC adventure games, students

explore the workshop to solve a mystery, learning about the renaissance and linear-perspective drawing in the process.

- *National Geographic Xpeditions* (http://www.nationalgeographic.com/resources/ngo/education/xpeditions) These "expeditions" address all the U.S. National Geography Standards, the five geography skills, and the main geographic perspectives. Both younger and older Xpeditioners use geography to complete a variety of missions, with resources such as maps, games, stories, Web sites, and other interactive features to help them to complete their tasks and visit related annexes in "Xpedition Hall" once their mission is through.

Twenty-first century educators are taking advantage of an even more sophisticated outgrowth of the virtual field trip: the WebQuest. Many teachers have difficulty distinguishing between a virtual field trip and a WebQuest. Tom March (2003/2004) helps to clarify their function:

> A real WebQuest is a scaffolded learning structure that uses links to essential resources on the World Wide Web and an authentic task to motivate students' investigation of a central, open-ended question, development of individual expertise and participation in a final group process that attempts to transform newly acquired information into a more sophisticated understanding. The best WebQuests do this in a way that inspires students to see richer thematic relationship, facilitate a contribution to the real world of learning, and reflect on their own metacognitive processes.

One must actually visit these Web sites to appreciate their truly interactive nature, involving students' decision making and creativity, not just passive absorption of information. A few examples follow.

- *Blue Zones Quest*. Why do people in some parts of the world live much longer than others? This highly interactive and motivating "sort of real-time design-your-own adventure requires students to vote online for nearly every move a team of doctors and demographers makes as it investigates the longest-lived populations on the planet" (Platoni, 2008).
- *GoNorth!* "An exhilarating combination of high-tech wizardry and true outdoor adventure" offering students "a virtual seat on a real-life around-the pole journey by dogsled" (Platoni, 2008).
- *A WebQuest Series on creating nonviolent schools* (http://www.kn.pacbell.com/wired/nonviolence/index.html). A series of activities designed to explore issues related to school safety, some to help questers learn new information, some to help them understand what they feel about these issues, and others to encourage discussion and problem solving. After getting an overview, questers can choose appropriate activities for their learning goals.

Christine Sleeter (2002) comments that teachers can design various multicultural curricula WebQuests: "For example, what was it like for poor Irish in this country? What would women of the past think about today's woman? If Helen Keller were living today, how might she experience the world?"

Impact on Learners

As we have seen, many benefits can be gained from the use of information technology in both basic and advanced skills.

> Today, students use multimedia to learn interactively and work on class projects. They use the Internet to do research, to engage in projects, and to communicate. The new technologies allow students to have more control over their own learning, to think analytically and critically, and to work collaboratively. This constructivist approach is one effort at educational reform made easier by technology, and perhaps even driven by it. (Stockard, 2001, pp. 212–213)

One of the reasons that technology impacts the ways in which we learn is that it also impacts the ways in which we think. Although our ability to think about our own thinking sets us apart from other animals, generally we are not very aware of how we are thinking (Costa, 2008). The very nature of Internet and Web technology requires changes in the ways learners think. Historically, curricula have been designed sequentially. For example, history courses have used time lines to align events chronologically to facilitate their recall; science content has been presented to show natural sequences (for example, the water cycle: rain, run-off, evaporation, condensation); and in English classes students have been taught to write phrases, clauses, simple sentences, compound sentences, paragraphs, and themes, with each skill depending on mastery of the ones preceding it. Each of these approaches is a linear process that facilitates recall. Cognitive mapping has been used to show the mental processes involved in learning. Often, the cognitive maps follow a general linear direction with only minor branching from the main path.

The nature of *hypertext* (computer-generated text linking one document to another), however, is not linear, and natural patterns are not necessarily present on the Web. Searches for information on the Internet can bounce in all directions as students use a hit-or-miss approach to surfing the seamless Web. Students who are new to the Internet may sometimes need guidance to narrow their searches, much as students of a half-century ago needed help from librarians when they walked into the library for the first time and felt overwhelmed by the ocean of information that surrounded them.

Being a knowledgeable and capable researcher online benefits teachers just as much as it does students, for both are learners (see the following section). Systems for simplifying searches have been developed (and are continually being refined), just as the Dewey Decimal System was developed to help twentieth-century learners simplify their searches. For example, in 2004 the search engine Google began working with academic publishers to offer Google Scholar, a search service that provides access to all kinds of scholarly materials. The service (http://scholar.google.com) allows users to search for "scholarly literature including peer-reviewed papers, theses, books, preprints, abstracts and technical reports from all broad areas of research" (Albanese, 2004). Today, there are entire courses devoted entirely on how to do research on the Internet, and many textbooks from various disciplines feature prominent sections on that topic.

In the past, when the use of the Internet in schools was new, teachers may have needed to adjust the time expectations they held for students and may have

Box 2.4 Technological Literacy: Students Mentoring Teachers and Classmates

In the twenty-first century, virtually every public school offers access to the Internet. According to the National Center for Education Statistics (2006), public schools have made consistent progress in expanding classroom Internet access. In 2005, 94% of public school instructional rooms had Internet access, compared with 3% in 1994 (NCES, 2006). However, the mere presence of the Internet does not mean that it is being used effectively for the maximum benefit of students.

In 2004, a NetDay study (see box 2.5) reported that 87% of students ranked themselves as intermediate to expert-level users of the Internet, and one-third ranked their teachers as beginners. They felt that teachers needlessly and counterproductively restricted the time and nature of their Internet access at school. *The Digital Disconnect: The Widening Gap between Internet-Savvy Students and their Schools* (Levin & Arafeh, 2002) documents the substantial disconnect between how students use the Internet *for* school (at home) and the ways they are allowed to use the Internet *at* school. Internet-savvy students are coming to school with different expectations, different skills, and access to different resources, and teachers and administrators would be wise to realize this fact in a proactive manner.

Some teachers may feel intimidated just from knowing that some of their students' technology knowledge and skills dwarf their own levels of competence. While some teachers try to limit tech-savvy students in an attempt to reduce the very real differences between the experienced users and their less tech-savvy peers (Levin & Arafeh, 2002), other teachers try to take advantage of the extra "something" evidenced by savvy students by asking them to share their skills and knowledge with classmates. As Prensky (2008, p. 45) explains,

> Once we [learn to] let students (particularly in a group) take the lead on technology projects, teachers tend to see better results. As students share works in progress with the class for critical evaluations from both teacher and students, the teachers takes on the valuable roles of explainer, content provider, meaning maker, and evaluator/coach.

In a blog entry, Tuttle (2007) made the suggestion that students could be trained directly to help teachers use technology. Other teachers who have had positive experiences with this situation commented:

> Once you've got past the fear of "being found out," it's a great experience—there's a real sense of sharing development in the classroom.... [W]hen teachers do not have an "I'm perfect and all knowing" attitude, the classroom becomes a very different place. They learn from the students and the students learn from them. Students engaged in and producing high-quality standards-based work through technology is a wonderful picture.

Creative school systems have turned this situation into a twenty-first-century learning opportunity by establishing programs like MOUSE that organize and train student-led squads to provide much of the technical support in their schools (Partnership for 21st Century Skills, 2009b).

> MOUSE is a nonprofit organization that creates technology-based opportunities that motivate underserved students to succeed in today's information society. MOUSE's three main programs are *MOUSE Squad*, a student-driven tech support helpdesk program addressing the technology needs of elementary, middle and high schools; *MOUSE Corps*, a youth development program designed to support the growth of leadership and career readiness for students through advanced training/professional internships, college-bound workshops, and experimental learning projects; and

TechSource, a research and policy initiative providing information and leadership around critical education and technology issues with the ultimate goal of increasing the quality and pervasiveness of effective technology usage in public schools (www.mouse.org).

When given the opportunity, in addition to augmenting their technical skills tech-savvy students also hone other critical workforce skills like teamwork, project planning, and time management (Partnership for 21st Century Skills, 2009b).

needed to devise methods to reduce the levels of frustration felt by students who spent long periods of time searching for information online without getting any human feedback and as a result feeling unsure of their progress. On the other hand, in the twenty-first-century classroom,

> students, who often know more about technology than the teacher [see box 2.4 on the following page], are able to assist the teacher with a lesson. Since this type of instructional approach and the technologies involved are recent developments, it is hard to gauge their educational effects. Still, an increasing body of evidence as presented by Bialo and Sivin-Kachala (1996), for example, suggest positive results. (Stockard, 2001, p. 212)

The process of thinking about one's own thinking is called *metacognition.* When students are aware of their own thinking patterns, they can develop independent use of effective learning strategies (Swartz, 2008). Metacognition may be combined with journal keeping or blogging to enable students to trace their search methods and develop individual strategies that work for them. Such data could become useful in grouping students with similar learning approaches. Teachers may have to adjust their roles to spend more time working with small groups of students who share common interests, backgrounds, and talents.

In order for them to use the Internet appropriately and effectively, it is also important to help students realize that not all online sources of information are accurate or trustworthy. Caught up in the excitement of the wide vista of information available to them, today's learners may be unaware that they need to develop the skepticism of a scientist when using the Internet. Furthermore, they must be taught how to evaluate the material they read from the Internet (Richardson & Mancabelli, 2007). Alastair Smith offers a comprehensive list of articles and discussions on evaluating information sources (http://www.vuw.ac.nz/staff/alastair_smith/EVALN/EVALN.HTM).

Impact on Teachers and Curriculum Planners

> I think the teachers could use technology better by learning more about it. I think if they learn more about it they could help the students better and help them do projects and stories.
>
> —*National Education Technology Plan,* comment from a young student

The flood of new technology makes it critical that educators stay up-to-date on the latest developments. Teachers increasingly use the Internet and other learning technologies on a daily basis as essential learning tools, both for their students and for themselves. A growing number of reports from organizations such as the Learning and Skills Development Agency (LSDA) evidence the rapid spread of information and learning technology as having a positive impact on both teachers and students (PublicTechnology.net, 2005). A multitude of projects and programs have sprung up to help teachers use learning technologies, investigating and piloting new techniques and resources. Teacher education programs from various educational institutions are now available on the Web, in both streaming and interactive video.

Desired learner outcomes should determine how technology is used (Brown, 2004). For example, according to DeRoma and Nida (2004), "If the teacher adopts a learner-centered philosophy, respect for learner experience and interest in technology should be reflected in classroom teaching practices" (p. 37). Teachers need time in their hectic lives to plan effective strategies to incorporate technology into their curricula (Moody & Kindel, 2004).

Before the full potential of computer-based technology can be realized, curricula must change to alter teachers' perceptions. In 1991, Geisert and Dunn (1991, p. 223) reported, "Some teachers still acknowledge having computer phobia and remain apprehensive about using computers as either an instructional or management tool." This problem has lessened dramatically over the past few decades, and there are fewer and fewer twenty-first-century holdouts. According to the LSDA report (Publictechnology.net, 2005):

> Technology is being used by the majority of staff in teaching and lesson preparation. Nearly three-quarters of staff in the survey were using word-processing to produce classroom notes or printed handouts. PowerPoint was also heavily used. . . . Beyond the classroom, a third of all staff said they used technology constantly in lesson preparation at home and over half used it for lesson preparation in their office. In this day and age, prospective teachers know the mandatory nature of computer literacy.

Armstrong et al. (2009) remind educators that there is an organization whose primary mission is to increase the emphasis on technology in schools—the International Society for Technology in Education (ISTE), and suggest that you compare your state's technology standards with the national education technology standards (NETS) of ISTE. Visit the ISTE Web site (http:// www.iste.org) to access the ISTE 2008 standards for teachers, as well as the 2007 standards for students. As you examine the standards, notice that the overwhelming emphasis is not on improving technology but rather on improving the ways in which teachers and students *use* technology. As of this writing, ISTE had begun survey research regarding a draft of new NETS for Administrators. To keep updated on NETS efforts, visit www.iste.org/nets-refresh.

Parental Involvement

Parental involvement has a powerful positive influence on learning. The 2001 No Child Left Behind legislation requires that federally sponsored programs give parents more feedback on their children's education and provides parents more options. Ninety-seven percent of the public believe there should be even more involvement on the part of parents (Rose & Gallup, 2004).

Although technology is a powerful tool, it should not be thought of as something special or separate but rather as one of several tools to use to achieve the school's goals (Mills, 2007). For example, at the end of the twentieth century the favorite and most effective means of involving parents were newsletters and open houses. Message boards, listservs, newsgroups, and forums can do anything a traditional newsletter could do, and do it much faster. In addition, computer communication can individualize interactions with parents. Individual academic computer files can be established, containing such items as individual education plans (IEPs), digital portfolios, and academic contracts involving parents, making communication much more immediate and continuous. Because messages to parents are accessible on their home computers, parents have 24-hour access, which sometimes frees them from having to leave work or domestic obligations in the home to make school visits. Such approaches seem particularly attractive to many schools where attendance at open houses has been declining over the past few decades.

Changes in technology also require a reexamination of the role parents play in their children's education. In the past, beyond their role in providing students encouragement to do their homework assignments, parents were virtually shut out of their children's school-time learning process. Now many parents—especially those who are computer-savvy—have an unprecedented ability to directly assist students with their homework. How and how much these parents can and should contribute are questions that need to be explored, now that they have 24–7 access to their children's assignments.

Box 2.5 User Surveys: Transforming Education and Training through Advanced Technologies

In October–November 2004, NetDay sponsored its first "Speak-Up Day for Students," facilitated by the nonprofit group, Project Tomorrow (http://www.tomorrow.org/).Online questionnaires asked K–12 students across the country about their use of technology. More than 160,000 students participated in answering questions. The NetDay questionnaires included an open-ended question to which students were encouraged to supply a short reply:

Today, you and your fellow students are important users of technology. In the future, you will be the inventors of new technologies. What would you like to see invented that you think will help kids learn in the future?

More than 55,000 students offered a meaningful answer to this question. The U.S. Commerce Department reviewed 8,000 of these answers to probe for common themes and interests among students about how they would use technology for learning. The resulting analysis, *Visions 2020.2: Student views on transforming education and training through advanced technologies,* explored the answers to this and many other intriguing questions concerning technology as seen through the eyes of today's students. To read this report, visit http://www.ed.gov/about/offices/list/os/technology/plan/2004/site/documents/visions_20202.pdf.

The latest version of this survey was conducted in 2008, and a new report titled *Learning in the 21st Century: 2009 Trends Update* was released in 2009 that included teachers, parents, and administrators as well as students. This report is available at http://www.tomorrow.org/speakup/learning21Report_2009_Update.html.

Once a school has a Web site or has connected to a "school content provider," parent chat rooms and bulletin boards can easily be implemented. A Web site also can be used to provide homework help. Some schools are exploring the use of video conferencing and streamed (stored for viewing at home) videos to promote parent understanding and involvement in student learning (Starr, 2005).

According to Cearley and Bennett (2008), "Despite assumptions to the contrary, the use of technology in schools to engage parents in students' education can be a highly effective tool—even with language differences, lower education levels, inflexible work schedules, and socioeconomic disparities." They discuss the efforts of two southern California schools that use technology to promote parental involvement. E-newsletters allow the school to determine which topics are most interesting to the parents, based on the links that the parents click on. With this information, the school can tailor the newsletter to feature topics that parents are most interested in. Online real-time videos of students on campus were effective in engaging parents and highly accessible to all levels of technological proficiency. One school had originally posted cameras on certain sections of the campus as a way of improving security. However, the school eventually realized that the cameras provided an opportunity to help parents feel more connected to the school.

In an increasing number of cases, parents are actually allowed a voice in planning their children's curriculum. They brainstorm with teachers to come up with a curriculum that is meaningful both academically and personally. (To read the intriguing details of one school's successful involvement campaign, see p. 251.)

Education Technology: Implications for the Future

How can technology best be used to promote learning? Although educators realize that technology has a powerful potential to enhance learning, it is still not entirely understood how technology should best be used in schools—and perhaps it will never be entirely understood, in part because of its rapidly evolving nature, A final caveat comes from Will Richardson (2008).

> At this moment, there are no easy answers for educators; most of the school districts I visit still have not begun to contextualize or embrace these shifts. Instead, . . . many of our students continue to explore the potentials and pitfalls of instant communication with little guidance from their teachers. The technologies we block in their classrooms flourish in their bedrooms. Students are growing networks without us. . . . At school, we disconnect them not only from the technology but also from their passion and those who share it. . . . In our zeal to hold on to the old structures of teaching and learning and to protect students at all costs, we are not just leaving them ill prepared for the future, we are also missing an enormous opportunity for ourselves as learners. Regardless of the limits of technology or the culture of fear in our workplaces, almost every teacher I meet now has the ability to tap into these shifts in their personal practice should they choose to. . . .

Yet it is not the intention of this chapter—although enthusiastically promoting education technology—to portray technology as the answer to all of our educational needs. On the contrary, some educators believe that the educational community should take a closer look at the limitations of technology (Carraher, 2003; Nicaise and Barnes, 1996), For example: What influence does technology have on interpersonal relationships? Pepi and Scheurman (1996, pp. 229–236) asked the following questions that reveal some relevant concerns:

> Just what do computers offer that those of us involved in elementary and secondary education really need? Are past, current, and anticipated uses of technology consistent with contemporary theories of learning? Is technology an effective catalyst for educational reform? Is using computers synonymous with good teaching? Does technology promote critical thinking? Does technology build cooperation? Is the appeal to a future dominated by computer technology a sufficient reason to give computer technology prominence in the public schools? How much information can we tolerate?

In our role as curriculum planners we will become increasingly challenged by the task of making sure that both teachers and students understand the limitations of technology as well as the benefits.

> Technology is an extremely valuable addition to the educator's toolbox. However, it does not replace traditional media or methods of education. There is still a role for the lecture or seminar, and for the chalkboard or whiteboard. The printed page remains the best way of absorbing dense academic detail. Situations can never replace the benefits of working with real objects. There is no direct substitute for the smell of the chemistry lab, and few of us would wish to be treated by a doctor whose only experience was with virtual patients.
>
> Technology does not remove the need for work on the part of the learner. It is still not possible to download knowledge directly to the brain. Indeed, the learner-centered learning offered by technology means learners have to take greater responsibility for their progress, though that progress should be of a higher quality. . . . Finally, technology can never replace the human element. The role of instructor is changed (i.e., from "sage on the stage" to "guide on the side") but not removed. Learners still benefit hugely from interaction with instructors and fellow students, whether that interaction occurs physically or virtually (Educational Technology, 2009).

Conclusion

Following is a summary of some of the advances made and concerns raised about the topics discussed in this chapter.

Advances	***Concerns***
• NCLB is aimed at helping at-risk students.	• Most factors that put children at risk are beyond educators' control.
• NCLB requires schools to engage parents in their children's learning activities.	• One of every school's central missions should be to prepare students to respect, embrace, and defend democracy and liberty.

- Contemporary teachers recognize the need for curricula that address the affective and social needs of students.
- NCLB requires attention to schools in impoverished communities.
- NCLB requires the same expectations for all students including poor students, minority group members, and non-native English speaking students.
- Metacognitive strategies are being used in today's classrooms.
- Technology has opened up a vast realm of opportunity.
- The integration of technology in the classroom has been shown to improve student motivation and achievement.
- Parental involvement in their children's education has been proved to improve student learning, and technology has provided new and exciting ways of involving parents.
- The child poverty rate in the United States is among the highest in developed nations.
- The expectations held for students in schools with high minority enrollments are lower than for other students.
- We need to make certain that technology is used to create the kinds of teachers, curricula, and social climate that will bring constructivism into our classrooms.
- Close attention must be paid to possible disadvantages and shortcomings inherent in technology as well as to its merits.

Every school has the potential to become a microcosm of the best features of the larger community of which it is a part. Like the community, the school has its own culture, which must be considered when curricula are developed. The curriculum developer must remember that the school is a creation of the community and is supported by the community, which means that the curriculum must serve the needs of the community. Curriculum developers must also serve the needs of the students. Closing the achievement gap remains a most difficult challenge. With the breakdown of the traditional family and the increase in poverty and diversity, this job has become more challenging.

Forces are continuously at work in the schools and outside the schools. Some forces create pressure for change, while others press to maintain the status quo. Through the years, the textbook has been the major curriculum determiner, although it has many severe limitations. Recently, education reform laws have been a dominant force, introducing strategies that involve both parents and teachers and requiring teachers to use materials validated by research. Teachers and other curriculum developers must take the responsibility for examining local reform practices and for protecting the interests of their students.

Teachers recognize the need to promote cultural diversity, and education reform programs are pressing for educators to enhance students' appreciation of diversity. In democracies, people value diversity and individuals are encouraged to express dissent. The expression of individuality enhances feelings of self-worth, and this ultimately promotes success and increased productivity for the individual, ultimately serving the entire society. Everyone in society suffers when some of its members do not reach their maximum potential. High but realistic expectations for all students can enhance academic achievement and can eventually increase productivity and satisfaction in the workplace.

The potential for computer technology to enhance academic growth is unlimited, yet this potential will not be realized unless certain conditions occur. All teachers must embrace this technology and develop a high level of technological literacy, and also ensure that all their students share this literacy. To promote higher-level thinking, teachers must give their students access to quality software that can help them achieve at all levels of the cognitive taxonomy and also help them develop in the affective domain.

Because computers offer teachers the potential to improve learning in the classroom and at home, teachers will need to reexamine how students learn and what role parents play in their children's learning. NCLB recognizes that maximum academic attainment requires parental involvement. Teachers now have access to electronic tools to draw parents into the academic lives of their children.

The Internet puts a world of information at the fingertips of teachers and students alike. eLearning has rapidly expanded opportunities for teaching and learning across distances.

Constructivists can use technology to help students develop in-depth understanding and tie newly acquired information to their existing knowledge base. However, if it is to be effective, connections must be made between the use of technology in the schools and its use in the community. By bringing business leaders and other leaders of different ethnic backgrounds from the local community into the schools to show how the use of computers has improved their business or institution, teachers can enhance appreciation for diversity while reaching their technology goals.

Teachers can also give authentic, practical, real-world computer assignments in their classes. To promote cultural diversity, teachers can use the Internet as a tool to pair students with classmates of other cultural backgrounds, not only within their own school, but also with neighboring schools, schools across the state and nation, and schools in other nations throughout the world.

Computers offer teachers a vast array of teaching assistance. Lesson plans in all fields, including interdisciplinary lesson plans, are available online. Through weblogs, listservs and chat rooms, teachers can share their lesson plans with other teachers around the country and the world. Teachers can also use these media to discuss their teaching experiences, share their successes, constructively analyze their failures, and mentor beginning teachers.

Educational technology and its partner, technological literacy, present one of the greatest opportunities in the twenty-first century for curriculum planners, administrators, teachers, and students. The complexity and vastness of education-related technologies also represent one of the greatest of challenges to curriculum planners in the new millennium.

Additional Learning Opportunities

1. Why does a curriculum developer need to be familiar with a school's culture?
2. Should the fact that the community owns the schools give local citizens the right to dictate to the schools? If so, what types of issues should the community dictate, and what types should it not dictate?
3. In your opinion, what is the most important thing a school can do to develop good citizens?
4. What do you believe is the strongest force acting on school curricula? Explain your answer.
5. Should curriculum development courses focus on education reform? Why or why not?
6. Does tradition have both a positive and a negative effect on the schools? How?
7. In what ways have teachers' technological needs expanded? How effectively are their needs being met?
8. Explain the importance of technological literacy to (a) teachers and (b) students. Should both be given equal priority in schools? Explain your answer.
9. Which do you feel should be given top priority: teachers' technological development, or students'? Or are they both equally important? Explain your answer.
10. Describe one area in which educators' multicultural efforts are lacking and recommend ways to improve them.
11. How can the curriculum developer adjust the curriculum to better meet the needs of children living in poverty?
12. What uncertainties do you have about making computer assignments? What conditions are necessary in order for your to reduce your uncertainty?
13. How have education reform programs empowered teachers and parents to significantly change the schools?
14. If your school could influence the community to change in any way you wished, what change would you desire most? Explain your answer.
15. If your school were a person, what do you think he or she would be feeling?
16. What does it mean to think of your school as a school as opposed to a training site or a factory?
17. How has technology changed parents' roles in their children's education?
18. How has the Internet impacted traditional linear thinking patterns? How can teachers help their students focus their Internet searches?
19. How can technology be used to enhance student motivation?

SUGGESTED ACTIVITIES

1. Examine the course syllabi from all the courses you have taken, looking for multicultural objectives. Make a list of these objectives. Place an *X* by each objective you believe would be appropriate for future classes you will teach.
2. Study your school's community and make a list of multicultural resources. Include such items as field trips and guest speakers.
3. Research the literature for as many definitions as you can find for cultural pluralism, cultural diversity, and multicultural education. Using these definitions, write your own definition for each of these terms.
4. Interview a professor of education technology at your college. Make a list of the computer skills currently required for all undergraduate students in teacher education. Make a second list with additional requirements that you feel are necessary for a teacher to perform effectively in today's classroom. Compare the two lists and discuss the nature of, and problems associated with, the discrepancies.
5. Interview two history teachers, asking them how they think the school can best develop citizenship in their students.
6. Select the method you prefer—for example, lecture, inquiry, discussion, simulation, or case study—and write an activity for your students to perform with the goal of developing good citizenship traits.
7. Develop a project to assign to your students to help them become more sensitive to world problems.
8. Write a computer-based assignment on a multicultural problem in an urban setting.
9. Write a computer-based assignment that links your discipline to at least three other disciplines.
10. Choose a current reform practice at a local school and evaluate it in terms of constructivist theory.

chapter three

HISTORICAL AND PHILOSOPHICAL FOUNDATIONS OF CURRICULUM

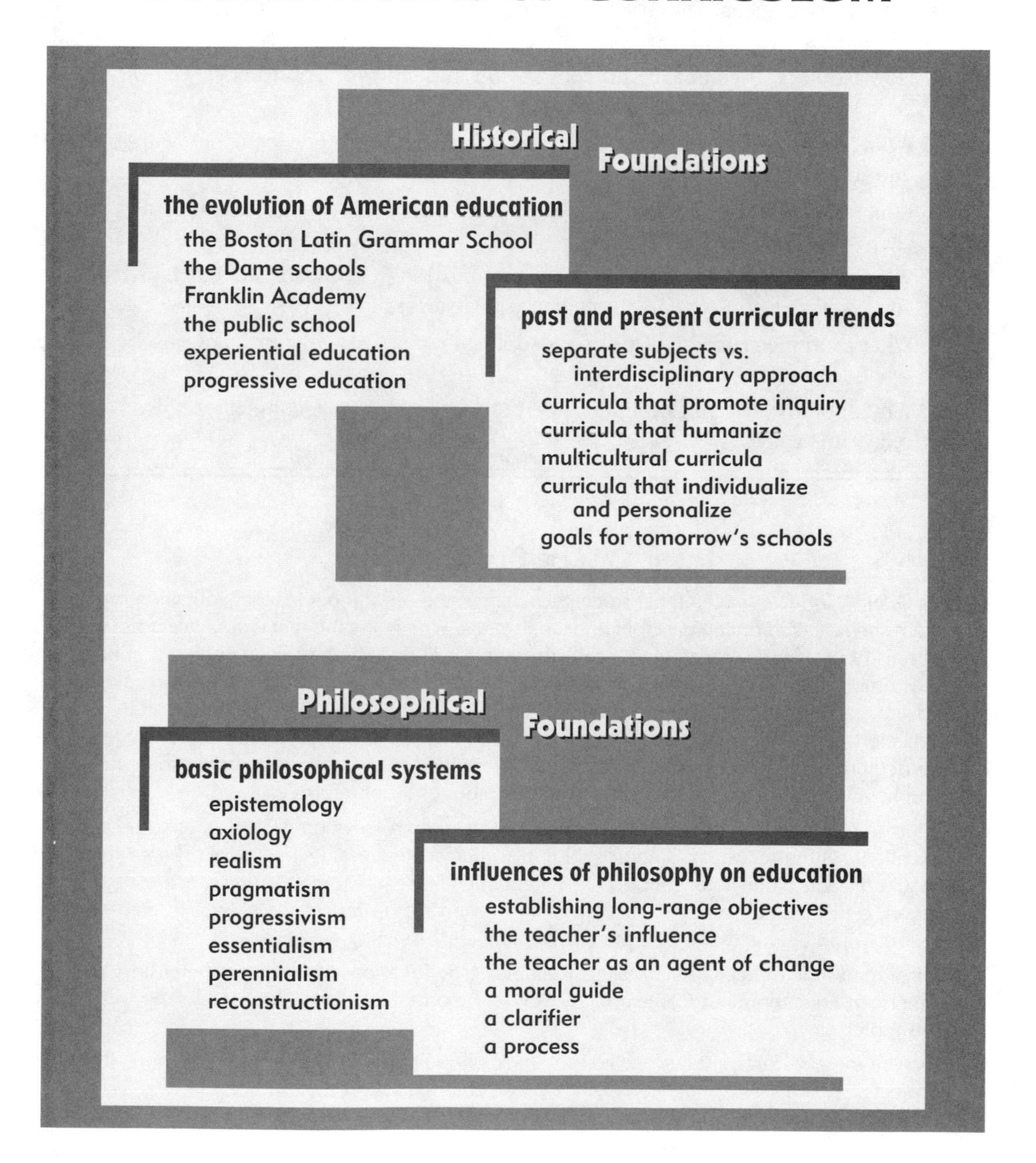

Focus Questions

1. How are the Cardinal Principles of Secondary Education relevant for today's schools?
2. How does colonial legislation affect today's schools?
3. What evidence can you give of the Progressive Education Movement in today's curricula?
4. How would you compare and contrast the influence of John Locke and John Dewey on today's curriculum?
5. What are three qualities in contemporary society that you consider valuable and three that you consider detrimental?
6. What role must the curriculum play in ensuring that the needs in multicultural classrooms are met?
7. Why are philosophers short on answers and long on questions, and how can you use this knowledge to strengthen your leadership?
8. What examples can you give of philosophical constructs in your fellow teachers' reactions to education reform?
9. Why should curricula be inquiry driven, and how can technology be used to reach this goal?

The Case of Diane Worley

As Diane Worley completed her student teaching semester and her teacher education program she reflected on the past four and a half years, which she thought would take forever to finish but which surprisingly passed very swiftly. At first she had been confused about the rumble over school reform in her state, but now she was glad that she had taken advantage of every opportunity to learn all she could about these activities. Having accepted her first teaching assignment and having enrolled in her first graduate class, a curriculum development course, Diane was determined to use both her school experience and her curriculum course to continue learning about school reform.

Education 501, Foundations and Principles of Curriculum Development, proved to be an excellent setting in which Diane could pursue her newest professional goal. The course required each student to conduct an independent research project, prepare a written report, and make an oral presentation of this report to the rest of the class. The written report would be due two weeks prior to the final class meeting.

Diane had little difficulty in choosing her topic, "The Relationship Between the History of American Education and Contemporary School Reform." Her professor readily approved this topic.

As with most research studies, the first and most difficult task for Diane was delineating the project so that it was manageable. Diane considered the following issues:

- *The effect of American legislation on school reform.* This would involve making a survey of such legislation as the Old Deluder Satan Act, the Kalamazoo case, and the

Northwest Ordinance, examining the goals of these laws, and comparing these goals to the goals of current school reform.

- *The effect that textbooks have had on the curricula in American schools throughout their history and the effect they are now having in current reform efforts.* This would include reviewing such books as the Bible, the McGuffey readers, required classical literature, and the contemporary textbooks that Diane would use in her classes during her first year of teaching.
- *The Relationship between the Cardinal Principles of Secondary Education and NCLB.*
- *The relationship between the goals of the Progressive Education Movement and those of contemporary school reform.*
- *The implications of the recommendations made at the Woods Hole Conference on current reform goals.*
- *The causes for the development of the junior high school and middle school and a comparison of these causes with the current school reform efforts.*
- *A comparison of the current priorities of middle-level education and NCLB.*
- *A survey of the major curriculum changes over the past 250 years and a comparison of these trends with the goals of current school reform.*

Diane found that just reflecting on these issues and the simple act of making the list were both stimulating. She imagined the many charts she could use to visually show relationships in new and interesting ways. This project would enable her to make a unique contribution to education reform in her school while equipping her with some of the tools needed to implement education reform.

Within a few days, Diane had settled into her new school environment. She enjoyed each part of her new world. Naturally, this included the lunch period and breaks spent in the lounge, which provided about the only opportunities she had throughout the day to socialize with her fellow teachers. The lounge was especially interesting because of the differences she could see among her coworkers. Although she expected to see more agreement among professional teachers than she had seen among her fellow college students, such was not the case. In fact, compared to her college peers, these teachers seemed to have even more pronounced differences of opinion. But what she liked most was that her new peers seemed free to express their views without fear of pressure to agree with their colleagues or without feeling that they needed their colleagues to agree with them.

Diane also enjoyed being treated as a professional. Her principal and the administrative staff treated her the same as they treated teachers who had taught for many years. "What a contrast," she thought, "from the way I was treated as an undergraduate student." It was surprising to realize the degree to which others' perceptions of her had changed in only a few weeks.

To Diane, the best part of her new teaching career was the relationship she had with her students; nothing equaled the joy she felt from the meeting of minds engaged in purposeful learning. Soon though, Diane was to learn that not everyone shared her love of the pursuit of knowledge. Or perhaps the problem was that her love of her chosen methods of inquiry was grossly misunderstood.

The challenge came early in the first grading period when Diane introduced the term *concept*. Since some students seemed a little confused, Diane decided to give some examples. She carefully lifted her desk chair and placed it on the center of her desk. She began the inquiry by asking the students to name the object on the desk. Although several of the older students seemed embarrassed about responding, everyone eventually said it was a chair. Then she asked the students how they knew it was a chair. The students began naming its parts: "It's a chair because it has a seat, four legs, and a back." "What would it be if these parts were disassembled?" Diane asked. After a lengthy discussion, the students concluded that it would no longer be a chair but just a collection of chair parts. "Then, a chair is more than something physical?" Diane concluded, with a questioning tone. The students agreed. Diane felt that she was really getting the idea of a concept over to these students; however, the district instructional supervisor happened to pass by Diane's classroom. Seeing the chair on the desk, the supervisor decided to pause long enough to see what was going on. The supervisor, Ms. Sterling-Austin, was more than intrigued by this novel approach. In fact, after the lesson, she questioned this teaching style very rigorously.

• • •

Many teachers have lost the passion for teaching that Diane feels. Negative reports, articles, and radio and television programs on education reform have caused many contemporary teachers to feel underappreciated. An awareness of the history of American schools and an ability to apply history and philosophy to curriculum development should help readers assess local reform practices.

PART I: HISTORICAL FOUNDATIONS

Our contemporary schools are a composite of all the large and small events that have occurred since the Europeans first began migrating to this country in the early seventeenth century. To understand our schools and the meaning of curriculum we must also understand the major events that have shaped them through the years. Following is a discussion of some of these defining events.

The Evolution of American Education

Certainly one of the most colorful characters in history was England's King Henry VIII (1491–1547), noted for his political cunning, lust, bad temper, and selfishness—among other qualities. When the Roman Catholic Church refused to sanctify Henry's marriage to Anne Boleyn, he established his own church, the Church of England, which today is still the major denomination in England.

The Migrations

When James I became king in 1603, he made life difficult for certain Protestant churches. After resisting his pressures for seventeen years, one Protestant group went to Holland. Meeting even greater opposition there, they soon left for America. By this time a second group of Protestants had left England for America, and by 1630 both groups had arrived in the area that was to be named Massachusetts.

Contrary to popular belief, these people, known as the Puritans, were not seeking religious freedom for *all*—they were seeking religious freedom for the Puritans. According to their strict laws, the role of the church was to interpret the will of God, and the role of the state was to enforce it.

Early Schools

For the Puritans, the church building commonly served also as the courthouse where civil laws were made and offenders were tried and sentenced. Since the civil law and the church were inseparable and since obedience to God required a knowledge of His laws, an institution was needed to guarantee that each citizen possessed this required knowledge. Thus began the evolution of the school in America. The settlers had a strong sense that democracy requires an educated populace (Bellamy & Goodlad, 2008).

The Latin Grammar School

In 1635 the first Latin grammar school, forerunner of our modern schools, appeared (Armstrong et al., 2009). Designed after the English schools, the goal of Latin grammar schools was to prepare select young men for entrance to an elite college that opened in 1636 in Massachusetts. Among the Puritan immigrants were more than a hundred graduates of Oxford and Cambridge universities. Steeped in a tradition that prized quality education, these highly educated settlers were determined to provide equally excellent educational opportunities for their sons. Thus, the General Court of Massachusetts appropriated approximately $1,000 for a new college.

Soon afterward, a young minister who was dying of tuberculosis willed his 400 books and half of his estate (worth almost $2,000—quite a large sum for that time) to the new college. This gift by John Harvard prompted the renaming of the institution to Harvard College.

The Dame Schools

By 1642 every home was required to teach reading, Puritanism, and the laws of the colony (Armstrong et al., 2009). Thus, the first American "public schools" were not really schools at all, at least not in the sense of having a schoolhouse with professional teachers. These schools were actually in citizens' homes. Some wealthy citizens met the requirements of the law by hiring English tutors and transporting them to America to work. But since this option was unaffordable for most people, many of the early settlers got together and designated one of the women to teach the neighborhood children. Because household help was expensive and the teachers' pay was meager or nothing at all, these "dames" often taught the children at the kitchen table while also preparing the family meals—thus the names *dame school* and *kitchen school*. The curriculum for these schools often consisted of no more than a few simple laws of the colony, a few Biblical rhymes, and some Biblical readings. Inspectors visited each house to ensure that this teaching was being done. Because this system was costly and ineffective, it was soon replaced by the public school system.

The main motivation for the Puritans' long, expensive, and dangerous journey to the New World was their desire to build a new community in which to worship God. Worried that the devil was constantly engaged in efforts to take advantage of their children's ignorance and mislead them, the Puritans wasted little time before passing a law to help their children escape the devil's snares. The law, called the *Old Deluder Satan Act*, passed in 1647, required Massachusetts towns to erect and maintain schools. Communities of 50 or more families had to teach reading and writing; those with 100 or more families had to establish a Latin grammar school and hire a teacher. The curriculum of this school was highly classical and dominated by Latin and Greek.

The Franklin Academy

The eighteenth century was characterized by expansion; surveyors were needed to build roads, navigators were needed for the expanding trade industry, mathematicians were needed for growing businesses, and so on. Soon a need developed for a very different type of school, one with a less classical and more practical curriculum. Benjamin Franklin responded to this need in 1751 by opening the *Franklin Academy* in Philadelphia. In many ways the academy was the very opposite of the Latin grammar school: the academy was both secular and practical, offering subjects such as mathematics, astronomy, surveying, bookkeeping, and navigation. Because of its practical emphasis, by the end of the Revolutionary War, schools modeled on the Franklin Academy had replaced the Latin grammar school as the most common type of secondary school. The content, strengths, and weaknesses of the three types of early schools are summarized in table 3.1.

Table 3.1 Curricula of Early Schools

	Dame School	Latin Grammar School	Franklin Academy
Content	Puritanism, colonial law, reading	Latin, Greek, religion	Astronomy, bookkeeping, mathematics, navigation, surveying
Outstanding Strength	The only school available	Availability	Practicality
Outstanding Weakness	Teachers were not trained professionals	Impractical curriculum	Charged tuition

The Public School

The Franklin Academy's practical curriculum enabled it to replace the Latin grammar school (Armstrong et al., 2009), but it had one weakness—it was private, and many parents could not afford its tuition. The Revolutionary War kindled a spirit of freedom and caused citizens to realize the value of education to a democratic society. Thomas Jefferson eloquently expressed this idea when he declared, "If a nation expects to be ignorant and free in a state of civilization it expects what never was and what never will be." In 1779, Jefferson proposed three years of free public education to all citizens of Virginia. Unfortunately, however, another 42 years passed before the Boston School Committee established the country's first public high school in 1821. The *Boston English Classical School*, later named the Boston English High School, was developed to prepare youth for employment. For many of its students, it served as an entry to the university. Since early high schools served these two distinctly different purposes, the curricula in individual schools varied greatly; most were very pragmatic, but some, located in college communities, were highly classical.

By 1860, half of the nation's children were in school. The commitment of the government to education was reconfirmed by the *Northwest Ordinance of 1787*, which reserved a parcel of land in every township to be sold to finance public education. Further support came in 1874 in the *Kalamazoo case*, which gave citizens in every town the right to levy taxes to support their secondary schools.

Goals for the Early Elementary School

Since the time of the establishment of the forerunners to modern elementary schools, the curriculum has been continually expanding. The first *Latin grammar schools* had the single purpose of preparing elite young men for Harvard and the ministry, and the dame schools continued this religious emphasis, but their curricula broadened to include colonial law and reading. These changes were not as bold as they might sound, since the colonial law and God's word were one and the same, and since the reason for adding reading was to prepare youths to read the Bible.

Goals for the Early High School

The last quarter of the nineteenth century set some definite trends that are still prevalent in high school education. The enrollment in these once small schools began to grow. Teachers and administrators joined to form the first unified coalition of organized educators, the National Education Association (NEA). The NEA assumed leadership in determining the goals for the early high schools, and in 1892 its Committee of Ten stated that the purpose of the school was to prepare students for life, yet recommended that all students be taught the college preparatory subjects. Three years later the NEA reinforced the college preparatory goal with its Committee on College Entrance Requirements. During this same quarter century, regional associations were formed to inspect and accredit high schools.

The new century brought further clarification of the goals of the high school. In 1918 the NEA's Commission on the Reorganization of Secondary Education listed the following seven principles, formally known as the *Cardinal Principles of Secondary Education*, as the main goals for both secondary and elementary schools:

1. health,
2. command of fundamental processes (development of basic skills),
3. worthy home membership,
4. vocational efficiency,
5. citizenship,
6. worthy use of leisure time, and
7. ethical character.

Many educators consider this list of broad goals for high schools as the most important aims ever set forth for American education. The goals, in fact, apply to both elementary and secondary schools. While the list contains only seven entries, the breadth and nature of the goals have caused them to remain relevant even though society has constantly changed.

Past and Present Curricular Trends

In the twentieth and twenty-first centuries, curriculum has moved in new directions and espoused new ideologies, including experiential education, progressive education, interdisciplinary curricula, inquiry-based learning, humanizing the curriculum, and multicultural curriculum. These developments are discussed below.

Experiential Education

According to the Association for Experiential Education (http:// www.aee.org), *experiential education* is a philosophy and methodology in which educators purposefully engage with learners in direct experience and focused reflection in order to increase knowledge, develop skills, and clarify values. Although experiential education has become quite popular in the late twentieth and early twenty-first centuries, school curricula have not always reflected such practices. Following is a discussion of the development of experiential education in this country.

From the beginning of public schools in America until 1875 (about 250 years), school curricula have been largely determined by one type of textbook or another. Initially, the main texts were the Bible and the *hornbook*, a slate with a sheet of parchment or paper, used in the dame schools, covered with hornlike (or bonelike) material to protect the paper from becoming soiled, so it could be used repeatedly.

In the 1690s the first basal reader, the *New England Primer*, was published. It, too, was a blend of religion and morals. Rhymes, called *catechisms*, were used to teach religious doctrine and language skills. In 1782 Noah Webster's book, known as the *Blue Back Speller*, was published, adding spelling to the curriculum. During the next 60 years, 24 million copies of the speller were sold. The intentions of the book were to provide moral and nonsectarian religious guidance, to provide valuable knowledge, and to motivate the students' interest.

During these first 250 years, instruction centered on recitation. Students studied, memorized, and recited their lessons until the material was committed to memory; those who failed received corporal punishment. In 1875 this method was openly challenged by Colonel Francis Parker, who had been orphaned at the age of 8 and apprenticed to a farmer until the age of 21. Parker had discovered that life on the farm was very educational, but he had found school to be so hateful and unbearable that he attended it only about eight weeks every year. Instead of turning his back on education, however, Parker decided to try to improve it. He believed that if education could be acquired pleasantly in the fields, woodlands, and pastures, it could also be enjoyed in the schools. His dream was to become a great teacher; little did he know that the fulfillment of his dream would result in a revolution of American education.

In 1875 this huge, bearded man was elected as superintendent of schools in Quincy, Massachusetts, a suburb of Boston. Parker transformed the teacher-centered classrooms into learner-centered, experience-based, problem-centered classrooms. Parker established teachers' meetings where he gave to his 40 teachers not advice and knowledge but questions and demonstrations. He did not tell them how to teach; he showed them. He gave them not only a technique but also a spirit; he made them want to put life into their curriculum. To create a natural learning environment, Parker substituted games and puzzles for recitation and rote memorization. In the lower grades he instituted singing, playing, reading, counting objects, writing, and drawing. Above all, he wanted the experiences at his schools to be happy ones. Reversing the traditional teaching process, which began with rules and definitions, he gave students real-life problems that made them seek out the rules or generalizations.

This system, which became known as the *Quincy System*, gained national attention. In his own words Parker told how enthusiastic the community had become over its schools: "Throughout the centuries of Quincy's history, its people have ever manifested a deep interest in education, and I believe that I am right when I say that at no time in the past has this interest been greater than it is in the first year of the new century [of Independence]" (Campbell, 1967, p. 83).

The Quincy System was the forerunner of other innovative experiments in education, including the Gary Plan, the Dalton Plan, and the Winnetka Plan. The *Gary Plan* was developed by William A. Wirt, the superintendent of schools in Gary, Indiana, where the elementary and high schools were designed as miniature communities. Unlike the other schools that had self-contained classrooms, the Gary Plan was open; students moved freely from one place to another throughout the day in platoons. Like Parker's system, this system was experiential and student-centered. The *Dalton Plan*, developed in Dalton, Massachusetts, in 1919, was significant in that it was a highly individualized program. Using contracts, students followed their own program. This plan involved students and teachers in the development of curricula. The *Winnetka Plan*, developed in 1919 by Carleton Washburne, superintendent of schools at Winnetka, Illinois, was also a highly individualized program. Stressing self-expression and creativity, it even used self-instructional materials to teach the fundamentals. The features of these experiential student-centered curricula are shown in table 3.2.

Table 3.2 Early Twentieth-Century Student-Centered Curricula

Quincy System	Gary Plan	Dalton Plan	Winnetka Plan
Games and puzzles	Miniature communities	Student contracts	Self-instructional materials
Student and teacher involvement in planning	Platoons	Student and teacher involvement in planning	Self-expression and creativity

These programs were important in two ways: First, they changed the way Americans thought about education, which no longer had to be textbook oriented and dominated by recitation. Students could become the center of the learning experience, and school could be enjoyed, since student activity was not stifled but encouraged. The belief of seventeenth-century philosopher John Locke—that experience is the basis of all understanding—was finally being implemented. Second, these programs were important because they led to several national movements in education, including progressive education, interdisciplinary education, and curricula that humanize and personalize the classrooms. The successful service-learning programs found throughout the country are examples of Locke's experience-based (or experiential) programs (Billig & Waterman, 2003). (For an example of experiential curriculum in action, see chapter 4.)

Progressive Education

The experience-based movement that Francis Parker began in 1875 moved vigorously into the twentieth century. Before his death in 1902, Parker took a position as head of a normal school in Chicago, which later merged with the University of Chicago, where John Dewey was head of the philosophy and psychology department from 1894 to 1904. Dewey established a school on the university's campus to serve as an experimental laboratory to study education processes. This laboratory school was like any other school except that it was accessible to the university professors and students to conduct on-site research on teaching practices. Within a few years, almost every state in the nation had at least one university laboratory school.

Fifty years later, most of these laboratory schools were still operating, but recently most of them have eliminated the high school grades. As the century ended, all but about one hundred of the laboratory schools had closed. Ironically, many of the surviving schools are now playing a major role in education reform by being forerunners in implementing school reform in their states, by serving as professional development schools, and by acting as role models through implementing education reform practices.

During the first quarter of the twentieth century, true concern for the student was evident. The *Progressive Education Movement* was child-centered as opposed to subject-centered. Though often confused with permissive education, the Progressive Education Movement did not espouse permissiveness. The concept of progressivism is much more akin to pragmatism, for during this era secondary school curricula became much more practical, offering agriculture, home economics, and other vocational subjects.

Progressivism meant more than practicality; it also meant that students helped plan the curriculum and sometimes selected their own individualized learning activities. The arts, sports, and extracurricular activities were added to the school program. Progressive educators' belief in the democratic process led them to involve parents, students, and teachers. For 50 years the progressive trend was well accepted by students, who perceived the curriculum as highly relevant. From 1933 to 1941 the Progressive Education Association sponsored the *Eight-Year Study*, a survey of the effects of such a general education on learners. Conducted by Harvard University, the study followed students of 30 experimental high schools through high school and college. The graduates of the experimental school equaled their counterparts in the attainment of subject matter, and they outperformed them in attainment of academic honors and grades. Furthermore, students who had had freedom of choice in their curricula proved to be significantly superior in intellectual curiosity, creativity, drive, leadership, and extraclass activities. They also proved to be more objective and more aware of world events. Unfortunately, because of timing alone, the results of the Eight-Year Study were lost in history; they were made public just as the country plunged into World War II. (For further discussion on the history of learner-centered education, see the themed issue of the journal *Education*, Fall 2003, vol. 124, issue no. 1.)

Separate Subjects vs. Interdisciplinary Approach

By the middle of the twentieth century, the question of how content should be structured had become a hot issue. The Progressive Movement had blended the various disciplines in the belief that more understanding would result. For example, the *core curriculum* had become very popular: a core of common experiences was believed to be essential for all students, and some of these experiences were interdisciplinary. But interdisciplinary movements were criticized severely by educators such as Arthur E. Bestor, who believed that they had weakened the curricula. Bestor and others criticized schools severely for this "anti-intellectualism."

But Bestor and his colleagues were wrong. Three waves of education reform covering more than 60 years have proved that students achieve more and are better able to apply their knowledge when they experience collaboratively planned and taught interdisciplinary curricula. The Progressive Movement of the early 1940s was first to convincingly demonstrate the superiority of interdisciplinary curricula. The reform programs of the late 1950s, 1960s, and 1970s reaffirmed this belief, and *A Nation at Risk* provoked reform of the 1980s and 1990s that rekindled the use of interdisciplinary curricula.

The 1960s saw a veritable "alphabet soup" of programs that often integrated two or more disciplines in an attempt to help students learn to inquire and discover relationships. Some of the more popular programs were the SMSG (Science-Mathematics Study Group), ESCP (Earth Science Curriculum Project), BSCS (Biological Sciences Curriculum Study), PSSC (Physical Science Study Committee), and ISCS (Intermediate Science Curriculum Study). Another contribution was Benjamin Bloom's *Taxonomy of Educational Objectives*, which enabled teachers to build learning experiences on increasingly higher levels of the thought processes. With advances in technology came another reason for structuring learning experiences: Students needed to be stimulated to think through processes and to establish relationships themselves—not just to remember facts but to *use* those facts to solve problems.

Although there was a resurgence of interdisciplinary curricula during the last half of the twentieth century, many teachers have found it difficult to fully collaborate with their colleagues, yet dialogue is essential (Boles & Troen, 2007). Most interdisciplinary teams operate as multidisciplinary teams, with each teacher on the team responsible for his or her own content area. Schools must be cultures for thinking, and through collaboration, teachers sharpen their thinking skills by making their thoughts visible (Ritchart & Perkins, 2008). Even when efforts are made to integrate the disciplines (as in team teaching), some teachers have a way of resisting changes that they perceive might weaken teaching in their discipline. Often they insist on teaching only their own discipline, in which they find familiarity and comfort (Boles & Troen, 2007). Perhaps this fear and discomfort might be alleviated by allowing ample time for teaching teams to collaborate. Kretovics and colleagues (2004) emphasized the importance for teachers who serve on teams to have adequate planning time.

Curricula that Promote Inquiry

John Dewey's educational reform led to the first inquiry-based learning methods in the United States, with his child-centered learning based on real-world experiences. In the 1950s, urged on by such critics as California Superintendent of Education Max Rafferty and U.S. Navy Admiral Hyman Rickover, the American public reexamined its schools. There was a general attitude of disappointment, culminating in the Russians' successful launch of the world's first satellite in 1957 and giving the American public the desperate feeling that they had been "beaten" academically by Russian mathematicians and scientists. The educational establishment became particularly interested in helping students become creative problem solvers. Harvard University's president, James B. Conant, had already been insisting that the secondary school curricula should be more rigorous. He urged that stronger minimum requirements be made of all students and that even more requirements be made for the academically gifted.

As a result, a special committee convened in Woods Hole, Massachusetts, in 1959 to design a better system for educating America's youth. The 35 leaders in education, government, industry, and science concluded that education should be built around broad theories and concepts. The following year, Woods Hole committee member Jerome S. Bruner reported the general conclusions of the study in his book, *The Process of Education* (1960). Bruner believed that any subject can be taught effectively in some intellectually honest form to any child.

In 1961 the Educational Policies Commission published a position paper suggesting that students needed to develop "ten rational powers"—recalling and imagining; classifying and generalizing; comparing and evaluating; analyzing and synthesizing; and deducing and inferring. These also happen to be some of the

FYI Developing a Sense of History

Thomas Oldenski • University of Dayton

Many teachers have little appreciation for educational foundations such as history, sociology, and philosophy of education, since these courses did not focus on the *how* of teaching or other practical dimensions of teaching. Usually such courses were considered as required courses for completing a degree in education.

To help teachers develop a sense of the interaction of these three aspects of foundations of education, my teachers work in groups of three to five. The groups do some historical and sociological reflecting on a decade-by-decade basis about what was happening in society and what was happening in schools during these time periods. The groups create two respective lists on these topics, beginning with the decade when they were in elementary school and ending with the present decade. Using the information they compile, the groups attempt to identify the relationship between society and schools. This exercise helps teachers become aware of their own history of education and how it influences their teaching and attitudes about schooling. The discussion can be extended to consider which philosophy of education and learning theories seem to be dominant in any given decade.

fundamentals of inquiry learning. The "alphabet soup" curricula mentioned above represented an attempt to turn science education into hands-on involvement with a focus on developing reasoning abilities, but in the end they fell short of becoming truly inquiry-based learning. However, this and other programs brought significant change in the ways that textbooks were developed, giving more consideration to ways of actively involving students in the learning process.

Armstrong et al. (2009) point out that the new technology offers teachers unprecedented opportunities to promote inquiry. Specifically, the Internet provides an avenue to an unlimited variety of information (Richardson & Mancabelli, 2007). By giving inquiry-based assignments, teachers can capitalize on their students' different learning styles. As you continue to study curriculum planning, think about ways you can use inquiry in your school to make learning more personal, more meaningful, and more enjoyable for your students (Eisner, 2004). The inquiry-based learning model is discussed in chapter 10.

Curricula that Humanize

An important goal of today's schools is to humanize the school environment. The country's first high schools were typically one-room buildings designed to accommodate at most a few dozen students, but during the early 1950s there was a national trend to consolidate small schools. This resulted in larger and larger schools, until today a school of 2,000, 3,000, or 4,000 students is common. The advantage is that a greater diversity of subjects is possible; the disadvantage is the resulting impersonal, dehumanizing environment. Humanizing curricula and caring teachers let students know they are valued. When students feel valued by their teachers, they are more willing to work harder at their assignments and comply with classroom rules.

Humanizing the curriculum goes hand in hand with embracing multiculturalism. Darder, Baltodano, and Torres (2008) emphasize how important it is for teachers and administrators to recognize the varied and valuable life experiences and knowledge that culturally diverse students bring into the classroom.

> Meaningful teacher-student interaction humaniz[es] instruction by expanding the horizons through which students demonstrate human qualities, dreams, desires, and capacities that closed-ended tests and instruction never capture. (p. 425)

Multicultural Curricula

In the early 1960s the views of Herbert Kohl provided the impetus for the development of the Open School Movement in the United States. His deep commitment to community interactions and his tremendous faith in students set a significant example for the practice of teaching diverse students from working-class populations (Darder, Baltodano, & Torres, 2003). In the decades that followed, acceptance of diversity and multiculturalism gained wider recognition among educators. Today's American society is likely more multilingual, multiethnic, and multicultural than any other nation in the world (Talleyrand & Kitsantas, 2003). It has been reported that the United States is comprised of at least 276 ethnic groups, including 170 Native American ethnic groups (Gollnick & Chinn, 2002).

Beginning teachers are often nervous or concerned about facing multicultural classes without the skills to help students of varied backgrounds meet their needs. Teachers can be taught valuable inquiry skills that can improve their ability to reach all students, including those of other cultures. Training in inquiry also helps teachers learn how to look at the world from multiple perspectives and to use this knowledge to reach diverse students. Researchers are trying to determine the most effective ways to teach in multicultural settings and to design curricula that promote an appreciation for diversity. The area of concern is expanding to include groups that have traditionally been ignored, even when attention was given to other minority groups. For example, one group that has long been overlooked is multiracial children. According to Bonnie Azab Powell (2008), multiracial children are a fast-growing segment of U.S. schoolchildren. Donna Jackson Nakazawa (2004) says that multiracial kids are caught between not existing at all—with outdated forms that require them to check only one box for their identity—and existing so far outside the perceived norm that people can't pass them by without commenting on their appearance. If no one talks about it, that means it's a secret, and children think secrets are bad. They feel something is wrong with them. Powell (2008) gives one example from Nakazawa of how teachers can help:

> Instead of shushing the first grader who says, "Hey, you must be adopted!" to a dark-skinned child with a white parent, a teacher might say, "It sounds like you think moms and dads have to match. But you don't have to look alike to be a family."

Nakazawa recommends drawing family trees, with parents' help, or identifying the place(s) where their relatives came from on a world map, as ways of helping children feel proud of their heritage (Powell, 2008).

One organization, The National Center for Culturally Responsive Educational Systems (NCCRESt) is funded by the U.S. Department of Education to close the achievement gap between diverse students and to reduce inappropriate referrals to special education. NCCRESt works with state and local systems to address ingrained school practices that contribute to perpetuating disparities in access to learning. For more information, visit their Web site (http://www.nccrest.org).

Box 3.1 Curriculum Guidelines for Multicultural Education

The National Council for the Social Studies (NCSS) has created curriculum guidelines for multicultural education, which are summarized below.

1. Ethnic and cultural diversity should permeate the total school environment.
2. School policies and procedures should foster positive multicultural interactions and understandings among students, teachers, and the support staff.
3. A school's staff should reflect the ethnic and cultural diversity within the United States.
4. Schools should have systematic, comprehensive, mandatory, and continuing staff development programs.
5. The curriculum should reflect the cultural learning styles and characteristics of the students within the school community.

6. The multicultural curriculum should provide students with continuous opportunities to develop a better sense of self.
7. The curriculum should help students understand the totality of the experiences of ethnic and cultural groups in the United States.
8. The multicultural curriculum should help students understand that a conflict between ideals and realities always exists in human societies.
9. The multicultural curriculum should explore and clarify ethnic and cultural alternatives and options in the United States.
10. The multicultural curriculum should promote values, attitudes, and behaviors that support ethnic pluralism and cultural diversity as well as build and support the nation-state and the nation's shared national culture. *E pluribus unum* should be the goal of the schools and the nation.
11. The multicultural curriculum should help students develop their decision-making abilities, social participation skills, and sense of political efficacy as necessary bases for effective citizenship in a pluralistic democratic nation.
12. The multicultural curriculum should help students develop the skills necessary for effective interpersonal, interethnic, and intercultural group interactions.
13. The multicultural curriculum should be comprehensive in scope and sequence, should present holistic views of ethnic and cultural groups, and should be an integral part of the total school curriculum.
14. The multicultural curriculum should include the continuous study of the cultures, historical experiences, social realities, and existential conditions of ethnic and cultural groups, including a variety of racial compositions.
15. Interdisciplinary and multidisciplinary approaches should be used in designing and implementing the multicultural curriculum.
16. The multicultural curriculum should use comparative approaches in the study of ethnic and cultural groups.
17. The multicultural curriculum should help students to view and interpret events, situations, and conflict from diverse ethnic and cultural perspectives and points of view.
18. The multicultural curriculum should conceptualize and describe the development of the United States as a multidirectional society.
19. Schools should provide opportunities for students to participate in the aesthetic experiences of various ethnic and cultural groups.
20. The multicultural curriculum should provide opportunities for students to study ethnic group languages as legitimate communication systems and help them develop full literacy in at least two languages.
21. The multicultural curriculum should make maximum use of experiential learning, especially local community resources.
22. The assessment procedures used with students should reflect their ethnic and cultural experiences.
23. Schools should conduct ongoing, systematic evaluations of the goals, methods, and instructional materials used in teaching about ethnic and cultural diversity.

For a downloadable multicultural education program evaluation checklist, visit the following Web site: http://www.muskegon-isd.k12.mi/us/downloads/services/curriculum-checklinst.pdf

Effective management of multiculturalism will require each administrator and each faculty member to invent curriculum and instructional approaches to meet the needs of the unique student body at each school and the needs of each unique classroom. Student involvement in the development of multicultural curricula, individualization, and personalization is indispensable.

Curricula that Individualize and Personalize

The 1960s saw much attention being placed on individualizing the curriculum, and some very good programs were developed. Individualized Guided Education (IGE), a program developed in Wisconsin, and Individually Prescribed Instruction (IPI), developed at the University of Pittsburgh, are two of the most successful. The competency-based movement of the 1970s introduced individualization into American schools at all levels, elementary through university. Competency-based programs have made significant contributions to individualizing education but, ironically and often justifiably, have been labeled "dehumanizing." It is becoming increasingly obvious that mere individualization is not enough. Our huge contemporary schools with their complicated schedules (many running on double shifts) need more. They need ways of personalizing all aspects of the schooling process. "Settings for effective learning nurture students emotionally and psychologically, as well as cognitively" (Nasir, 2008, p. 532). A curriculum grounded in the lives of students would enable them to more easily learn meaningful content and skills and to focus on their own needs and the needs of their communities.

To achieve academic success in the twenty-first century, schools must address students' social needs (Jensen, 2008). While the public and legislatures may mandate evaluation only in academic areas, success there can come only if the young adolescents we teach are socially and emotionally healthy. Linda Searby (2010) reports positive results from a project in which she picked out five teachers a week and held meaningful meetings with each individual teacher, using spreadsheets to keep track of each meeting, and giving positive feedback to each. Teachers can do the same with their students. (See also chapter 2 on the social foundations of curriculum.)

Increasingly, schools are providing students with opportunities for social and emotional learning. One approach to helping students cope with their personal and social problems is by offering conflict resolution experiences in their curricula that permit students to role-play their problems.

Goals for Tomorrow's Schools

A recent national poll (Rose & Gallup, 2007) reported that only 2% of the public opposes the heavy emphasis of today's curricula on science and mathematics. How can anyone know what needs the future will bring and what goals future schools will have? The task is not as impossible as it sounds; in fact, there are some clear goals. As far back as 1977, the late Dr. Harold Shane set forth goals that he called "the new basics" for our secondary schools. These goals include the need to (1) learn how to live with uncertainty, complexity, and change; (2) develop the ability to anticipate; (3) adapt to new structures, new constraints, and new situations without emotional drain and emotional collisions; (4) learn how to learn—that is, learn how to search out contradictions in one's values and understandings; (5) see relationships and be able to sort and weigh them; (6) understand the facts of life (realities) and become aware of alternatives; (7) learn to analyze the consequences of one's choices; (8) learn how to make choices; and (9) learn how to work together to get things done. For example, young people must learn how to reach compromises and how to accept compromises with honor. You may wish to compare Shane's goals with more recently stated goals for global education. For example, Marcelo Suarez-Orozco and Carolyn Sattin (2007) list essential goals for today's students as critical-thinking skills, language skills, collaborative skills, and technology skills.

Certainly, the "new basics" for the twenty-first century must include appreciating multiculturalism, including the study of foreign languages. It is advantageous for many of today's students to have competence in second and even third languages, with Chinese and Arabic becoming increasingly common in high schools (Aratani, 2006). The importance of arts education has also been reaffirmed (Smith, 2009; Camilleri, 2007; Reeves, 2008; U.S. Department of Education, 2004), in addition to learning about metacognition and reaching a greater depth of understanding of the core subjects.

Perhaps at no time in history have more criticisms been leveled toward goals and standards than are currently being aimed at the No Child Left Behind Act. Because the law holds schools and teachers accountable for equal progress from students with disabilities, students from impoverished homes, and students whose families speak a non-English first language, educators feel that the goals set forth in this law are impossible to reach.

PART II: PHILOSOPHICAL FOUNDATIONS

Having reviewed the development of American schools, let us now examine the philosophical beliefs that undergird these schools' curricula.

When Pythagoras (we are told) was asked what he meant by calling himself a philosopher, he replied as follows:

> Men enter their lives somewhat like the crowd meets at the festival. Some come to sell their merchandise, that is, to make money; some come to display their physical force in order to become famous; while there is a third group of men who only come to admire the beautiful works of art as well as the fine performances and speeches. In a similar way we meet each other in this life of ours; it is as if each of us were coming from afar, bringing along his own conception of life. Some desire nothing except money; some only strive for fame; while a few wish nothing except to watch or to contemplate the most beautiful things. But what are the most beautiful things? Certainly the universe as a whole and the order according to which the heavenly bodies move around are beautiful. But their beauty is merely a participation in the beauty of the first being which can only be reached by thought. Those who contemplate this first being [which Pythagoras seems to have described as the number and the pro-

> portion constituting the nature of all things] are the philosophers, the "lovers of wisdom." For *wisdom* [italics added] is the knowledge of things beautiful, first, divine, pure, and eternal. (Lobkowicz, 1967, pp. 5–6)

The Oxford English Dictionary defines *philosophy* as "the love, study, and pursuit of wisdom, or of knowledge of things and their causes, whether theoretical or practical." Regardless of the source of the definition, philosophy always involves thinking and is not limited to any subject. It usually is concerned with asking questions that are general and difficult, such as: What is the purpose of life? What is good? What is truth?

According to A. C. Ornstein and colleagues (2003, p. 5), "Education is growth and the focal point for the individual as well as society; it is a never-ending process of life, and the more refined the guiding philosophy the better the quality of the educational process." Philosophy can also be applied to various disciplines or to specific areas of thought. For example, natural philosophy is what we know as *science*. Philosophy can also be applied to the study of education; thus, the school of educational philosophy or philosophy of education.

McTighe and Thomas (2003) said, "Essential questions that human beings perennially ask about the world and themselves . . . should be the primary goals of teaching and learning" (p. 52). Is the primary purpose of schools to serve students, or is it to serve society? Should thc curriculum be content centered or learner centered? Which is more important, subject content or student activities? Which is more important, the mastery of content or the mastery of skills? Should the curriculum be controlled by the federal government? By state governments? By local communities? Which is more important, intellectual development or social development? Where do educators go to find answers to such questions? They must eventually turn to their basic beliefs, or their philosophies.

Knowing their personal philosophies empowers educators. Following is a look at several philosophical systems. An understanding of these systems will help you find answers to these and other seemingly impossible-to-answer questions.

Basic Philosophical Systems

For over twenty-two centuries, philosophers have grappled with questions such as the ones mentioned. These efforts have led to the formulation of several basic philosophical systems, including epistemology, axiology, realism, pragmatism, essentialism, perennialism, progressivism, and reconstructionism.

Philosophies can be distinguished from one another according to the major questions that philosophy poses. *Major* is emphasized here because no question is beyond the realm of philosophy. Examples of major questions are: What is real? (metaphysics) What is true? What is the nature of knowledge? (epistemology) What is good? (axiology).

Epistemology

Epistemology is the branch of philosophy that seeks the truth about the *nature of knowledge*. Epistemologists might ask whether each discipline has its own unique structure, and if so, whether it should be taught or explored in unique ways. A central purpose of the Woods Hole Conference, discussed earlier, was to identify the special structures of disciplines, particularly the sciences, mathematics, and foreign languages.

Epistemologists might ask educators whether one method of learning is better than another. Are teaching and learning methods situation specific? Is the scientific method superior to others? Educators who think so are likely to include more of the hard sciences in the curriculum; those who accept other learning processes are apt to include more of the humanities in the curriculum. Is giving students information inferior or superior to helping them discover it? Is insight better than inquiry? Is knowing *more* or *less* important than learning? How teachers answer these questions inevitably affects the kinds of curricula they establish in their classrooms.

Epistemology and the Themes

While the role of epistemologists is not to dictate or to recommend one learning theory over another, they would be pleased that this book recommends an eclectic approach (*eclecticism* incorporates ideas from several learning theories) to studying and applying learning theory, and they would also be pleased that one of the major themes of this book (constructivism) is a study of how students learn.

An education reform practice that is currently growing in popularity is the study of the disciplines to determine whether each discipline holds its own secret, a best method for studying it. Epistemologists would advise curriculum developers to keep this question at the forefront when participating in local school reform.

These questions can also serve teachers as they make decisions about how much and in what ways they will use technology in their classrooms. Do some subjects, more than others, lend themselves to being studied through the use of technology? Should technology be used to advance higher-level thinking to a greater degree in some subjects than in others? Does the integration of some subjects enhance the use of technology?

Axiology

Axiology is the school of philosophy that deals with values and ethics, raising such questions as: What is good? What is valuable? What is right? What is wrong? Is pleasure-seeking wrong? Asking such axiological questions helps teachers understand the role of ethics and values in the curriculum. This chapter mentioned the role that religion played in colonial curricula. Although the church has been legally separated from state-supported schools, some contemporary educators and citizens at large still believe that the study of morality is as important now as it was in colonial America—maybe more important.

Axiology and the Themes

Axiologists would not tell us what values the curriculum should promote, but they would remind us to think about this role of the curriculum. What effect, if any, does dispensing condoms in high school have on student values? Should the curriculum be changed to promote school safety? If so, how?

Realism

Proponents of *realism* believe that humans should seek the truth. They believe in rational explanations, and they believe that the scientific method should be used to discover the rationality of the universe. Formalized during the sixteenth and seventeenth centuries by the English philosopher Francis Bacon, the *scientific method* consists of the following steps:

1. Define the problem.
2. Formulate a hypothesis.
3. Gather data.
4. Interpret the data.
5. Use reason to draw a conclusion.
6. Test your conclusion.

To the realist, the truth is to be limited to that which can be tested and proved empirically (using the five senses). John Dewey (1939, p. 111) said that the "scientific method is the only authentic means at our command for getting at the significance of our everyday experiences of the world in which we live."

Some important contributors to realism include Aristotle (384–322 BC), St. Thomas Aquinas (1225–1274), Francis Bacon (1561–1626), John Locke (1632–1704), Johann F. Herbert (1776–1841), and Alfred North Whitehead (1861–1947).

Realism and the Themes

The realist is likely to believe that the sciences and mathematics should dominate the curriculum. Certainly, such thinking is common among contemporary education reformers. They also believe that students should be taught to use logic and the scientific method. Unlike the rationalists, such as René Descartes (1596–1650), who believe that all things in the universe are interconnected (see Spielvogel, 2006), the realists believe that these subjects should remain separated, as opposed to being part of interdisciplinary programs. The realist searches for the natural order in all things, including content generalizations such as concepts, principles, axioms, and theorems.

Another popular education reform practice is to implement authentic curricula. Proponents of realism would argue that our schools should build the curriculum around real-life problems. Authentic curricula and experiential learning go hand in hand. The current emphasis on integrated curriculum, conceptual themes, and problem solving reflect this philosophy. Critics would argue that teachers just don't have time to assign problems and wait for students to discover the answers. These teachers will say that they barely have time to cover the necessary content, even when using the most expedient instructional strategies.

Pragmatism

The philosophical structure called *pragmatism* had its origin in the sixteenth and seventeenth centuries. Its major contributors include the English philosopher Francis Bacon (1561–1626) and the German philosopher Immanuel Kant (1724–1804), who coined the term *pragmatism* (which means practicality). Pragmatists ask the questions: What is it good for? How can it be applied? Although pragmatism began in Europe, its growth has been led by American philosophers such as Charles Pierce (1839–1914), William James (1842–1910), and John Dewey (1859–1952).

Unlike the realists, pragmatists do not seek universal truths. Rather, they view the world as a world of change. English poet John Wilmont expresses a pragmatist's view of the world: "'Tis nature's way to change. Constancy alone is strange." Since the world is ever-changing, humans must constantly examine their own desires. Information that is useful to help people reach their desires is valuable.

To the pragmatist, the role of education is to help students learn how to discover themselves, and the best way to do this is through direct experience. This means the curriculum should be learner-centered and experience-based, full of problem-solving activities. This type of curriculum dominated education in the Progressive Era.

Pragmatism and the Themes

Since the development of the Franklin Academy, the curricula in American schools have been heavily influenced by pragmatism. Contemporary education reform practices are rich with pragmatism as well. For example, many education programs stress authentic activities, that is, hands-on activities that cause students to apply theory and knowledge to solve real-life problems. The discovery learning practices, which characterize many of today's education programs, are endorsed by pragmatists.

Constructivism is based on the premise that it is better to understand a little than to recall a lot without understanding it. This, too, is a pragmatist belief. The methods used by constructivist teachers are encouraged by pragmatists. Indeed, pragmatists believe changing and improving are natural processes.

Progressivism

Progressivism is the branch of philosophy that views knowledge as tentative and ever-changing. Progressivists view students as central to the learning process. Learning should be interesting and fun, and it can be if it centers on students' interests. Students have a natural curiosity that makes learning natural if students see the need for the subjects they are studying.

Progressivism is the work of John Dewey, who believed in putting the students at the center of the learning process by involving them in the selection of content and learning activities. Dewey also believed it absolutely essential to teach democratic values and build a sense of civic responsibility in each student.

Progressivism and the Themes

Progressivists believe that the teacher's role is to introduce problems and guide students in finding solutions, thereby creating their own understanding. Dewey's work, along with Russian sociologist Lev Vygotsky and Swiss psychologist Jean Piaget, gave us the form of education known as progressivism.

Progressivism parallels and serves the multicultural theme of this book in that it endorses hands-on involvement of all students. Direct involvement engages students of all backgrounds, overcoming some of the barriers that minority students and students of non-English first languages face in their daily lives.

FYI Group Moves

Lynn Varner • Delta State University

Often, when students are working in small groups of four or five, I will use this system to move the groups around and to get them to share their ideas. To form the original groups, I number around the room from one to five (prevents those sitting together who are already friends from being in the same group); it is important that they remember their numbers. After a portion of the time has elapsed (e.g., if they have a case study with five questions to answer, I'd do this after the first or second question), I ask all the threes to move one group to the right. The person who moves is responsible for explaining what his or her last group thought about the question. Then we go on to the next question; this time I'll ask all the twos to move one group to the left and explain their last group's answer to that question. This approach has several benefits. The groups change so they don't stagnate; if there is one student in a group who is difficult (e.g., too talkative, way off track) no one has to be with that person for too long. It saves time when the class is large and it would take too much time for the entire class to share their thoughts.

Essentialism

In rebuttal to the Progressive Education Movement, William Bagley organized a new philosophical structure called *essentialism*. Bagley believed that the purpose of schools is to stabilize society by teaching knowledge that is essential. This would require mastery of subjects such as reading, writing, arithmetic, history, and English, which are essential to prepare students for productive lives. The essentialists would agree with Descartes, who was first to say that understanding (and teaching) all subjects should be organized from the simple to the complex and from the concrete to the abstract.

Clearly, the curriculum for essentialists has no room for frills or individualizing or for nonessential, "popular" courses. Academic rigor must be the standard for all if the essential intellectual and practical goals are to be reached.

Essentialism and the Themes

Essentialists support such contemporary programs as school-to-work and service learning so long as they are subject-based. They are concerned that the trend toward using multidisciplinary approaches will weaken the disciplines. They have little concern for programs that attempt to meet individual needs, such as multiple intelligences and styles matching. Diversity is of little consequence to essentialists. Computer use, for example, is only supported when it is in the service of mastering the essential subjects.

Perennialism

Perennialism emphasizes knowledge that has endured through the years. Americans Robert Hutchins and Mortimer Adler introduced perennialism during the twentieth century. Perennial subjects include classical literature, philosophy, science, history, and the fine arts. The goal of the perennialist is to develop and challenge the intellect—to prepare students for life by teaching them to think. The perennial curriculum emphasizes the humanities and the "three Rs."

Opponents of perennialism would argue that the actual purpose of schools in general is to teach students to think. The perennialists agree but believe the best way to achieve this lofty goal is through studying a combination of classical subjects (including the humanities and the fine arts) and the basics.

Some critics of perennialism argue that students cannot be prepared for the changing world by studying age-old subjects. Many parents believe the main purpose of education is to prepare students to get well-paying jobs. These parents won't settle for their children just gaining knowledge; that might be nice, but it isn't as important as knowing how to earn a living.

Herein lies a natural conflict between perennialist teachers and parents who hold a more conservative "earn a living" attitude. In college most teachers learn to appreciate the arts and literature. They may want more for their students than the parents want.

Perennialism and the Themes

Today's education reform issues include practices that perennialists endorse. For example, they support contemporary critics' cries for more science and mathematics. It is much easier, however, to identity reform movements that the perennialists view as frills, such as constructivism and metacognition. Perennialists clearly favor the classical curriculum that characterized our first schools over these contemporary programs. Computers are fine so long as they help students master the essential subjects. Using computers for drill and practice would be fine with perennialists, and this is the very use of computers that some contemporary educators oppose.

Diversity is not a major concern for perennialists because they believe that the classical subjects are good for everyone.

Reconstructionism

Like pragmatism and perennialism, *reconstructionism* is considered an American structure. Reconstructionists believe that the schools should be reconstructed to remove from our society such cultural crises as poverty, racism, ignorance, and war.

Reconstructionists are quick to remind us that most teachers come from middle-class families and therefore have a propensity to protect the society they have always known. Reconstructionists say that because of their middle-class backgrounds, most teachers don't know about poverty and unemployment.

Reconstructionist-based curricula focus on the major problems of society and prepare students to make critical analyses. Emphasis is placed on the behavioral sciences, and students are taught to influence the community. Some major contributors to reconstructionism include Plato (427–347 BC), St. Augustine (354–430), John Dewey (1859–1952), George Counts (1889–1974), and Theodore Brameld (1904–1987).

Reconstructionists believe that teachers should raise the consciousness of students (Armstrong et al., 2009) and that society has traveled too far down its misguided path to be corrected by tinkering; correcting its problems will require major reform. Reconstructionists believe that the role of the school is to empower citizens with the capacity to ensure that democratic principles will be followed, bringing equity to all areas of society.

Reconstructionists believe that a major responsibility of the schools is to teach students to analyze and question practices that they perceive as unfair to individuals or groups, and that perhaps schools' foremost responsibility is to motivate students to take action to correct inequities.

George S. Counts and Harold Rugg were major leaders in the development and growth of reconstructionism. In his book *Dare the Schools Build a New Social Order?* Counts (1932) answered his question with a resounding yes.

Reconstructionists have always been concerned with the mission of the school's curriculum, which, to them, is clear: to redesign a society that has become inequitable. Modern reconstructionists are keenly focused on NCLB and on the direction of education reform programs. Students, they believe, should be given social problems to analyze and correct. Some contemporary topics that concern constructionists are AIDS, pollution, immorality, inhumanity, world hunger, crime, and war. These topics are especially important because they are worldwide; reconstructionists believe that the curriculum should cover global problems.

Reconstructionists believe that the curriculum should enlighten students politically. They would quickly recognize and take action to correct any perceived failure of educators to promote the cause and value of education to the masses.

The reconstructionist philosophy, which is deeply concerned with social welfare and espouses action to improve the community and society, should not be confused with *revolutionism*, which holds that the only way to improve society is to destroy the existing system. The concept of reconstruction has appealed to a wide range of personalities and fostered a number of subphilosophies. For example, some educators and philosophers consider Francis Parker and John Dewey as superb exemplars of reconstructionism while others, for example, George S. Counts, perceived them and other progressivists as failures. Viewing progressive educators as weak and ineffective, Counts (1932, p. 259) called on progressive education to:

> [F]ace squarely and courageously every social issue, come to grips with life in all of its stark reality, establish an organic relation with the community, develop a realistic and comprehensive theory of welfare, fashion a compelling and challenging vision of human destiny, and become somewhat less frightened than it is today at the bogeys of imposition and indoctrination. In a word, Progressive Education cannot build its program out of the interests of children: it cannot place its trust in a child-centered school.

Obviously, Counts was more radical in his beliefs and the ways he communicated them than were the progressivists.

Reconstructionism and the Themes

Many local education reform movements are headed by committees of noneducators who believe there is a need for people like themselves who can take an objective look at education (a task they believe is impossible for teachers because teachers are too close to the process to be objective) and plan strategies to adjust education to make it serve society's greatest needs. Equity is an important goal of reconstructionists; therefore, diversity becomes a major goal for the schools.

During the twenty-first century, every school in the United States continues to be affected by education reform. Most schools are contributing to the reform movement in some ways, but the nature of reform from one school to another differs immensely. Some faculties embrace reform, viewing it as an opportunity to improve education for their students; other see it as an imposition on their time and energy. Because reform is being forced rapidly by outside change agents, many highly professional, energetic, and dedicated teachers find it impossible to avoid feeling imposed upon by state and local reform programs.

The varying cultures in the surrounding communities partially explain the differences in the ways members of various faculties feel. The local school administration's philosophy and policies can also be strong forces shaping the ways faculty members feel and react to reform policies.

Box 3.2 Applied Philosophy of Education

Dr. Jonathan Dolhenty, president of the Center for Applied Philosophy, believes that reconstructionism is an offshoot of experimentalism, and realism an offshoot of essentialism. In his view:

- Realists tend to view learners as sense mechanisms, the teachers as demonstrators, the curriculum as the subject matter of the physical world (emphasizing mathematics, science, etc.), the teaching method as mastering facts and information, and the social policy of the school as transmitting the settled knowledge of Western civilization. When it comes to specific methods of teaching, the realist tends to favor demonstration and recitation. As for character education, realists prefer training in rules of conduct and tend to promote the disciplining of behavior to reason.
- Perennialists, who can be either secularly or theistically inclined, tend to view learners as rational and spiritual beings, teachers as mental disciplinarians (and sometimes as spiritual leaders), the curriculum as the subject matter of the intellect and spirit (mathematics, languages, logic, Great Books, Dogma, etc.), the teaching method as training the intellect, and the social policy as transmitting the great ideas (sometimes religious as well as secular) of Western civilization. Regarding specific teaching methods, perennialists like the lecture, controlled discussion, and formal drill.
- Reconstructionists tend to view learners as an experiencing organism, teachers as research-project directors, the curriculum as the subject matter of social experience (emphasizing social studies, projects, problems, etc.), the teaching method as problem-solving, and the social policy as teaching how to manage change, or as teaching how to reconstruct the social order. Reconstructionists favor the group problem-solving project methodology in their teaching methods. The reconstructionist insists on promoting character education by making group decisions in the light of the consequences of those decisions.

To discover more about the applied philosophy of education, read Dr. Dolhenty's article (http:// radicalacademy.com/philapplied2.htm).

Each school's faculty is made up of individuals, some of whom are reconstructionists and some of whom are not. Among those who are activists, each can be placed on a linear scale based on the intensity with which they share their beliefs. Some fall on the mild side with Dewey and Parker, while others belong on the strong side along with Counts. As each of us looks at the school with which we are most familiar, it is easy to identify the extremists, but sometimes it is not so easy to know where others stand who may covertly express their philosophies.

Some individuals may question the value of studying philosophies in a curriculum course. We must remember to think of philosophies not merely as statements in dusty books but rather as the beliefs of people we know. If we can consider the tremendous influence that some of our fellow teachers have in every meeting in which they engage, from planning for an accreditation visit to deciding how to use this year's in-service planning days, then perhaps we can see that our individual and collective philosophies determine how we behave in regard to all issues. Our philosophies determine how we feel about issues and about other people. In no other philosophical structure is this more obvious than it is in reconstructionism.

Philosophy is often viewed by students as a dry study of words and ideas detached from the real world of today. The following case study shows how powerfully teachers' philosophies affect the curriculum as well as their own teaching. As you read this case study, think about your own philosophy and how you stand on the issues faced by this teacher. When you finish the case, pay particular attention to the questions that follow; they will help you align your philosophy with that of your school and state.

case study

PHILOSOPHIES IN CONFLICT

Allen R. Warner
University of Houston

Background

Many educators consider educational philosophy to be an arcane study of ideas that are not very important in the day-to-day functioning of schools. The wise curriculum worker knows, though, that a working knowledge of differing schools of educational philosophy can be extremely useful in moving groups of people through the curriculum planning process. Often what appears to be a minor disagreement about terms in a curriculum meeting unfolds into major differences between deep-seated and strongly held beliefs of members of the group, frequently rooted in differing philosophies.

This case study explores philosophic differences between essentialist state policies and the more progressivist views of an individual teacher. *Essentialism* is the position that the primary purpose of schools should be to transmit selected elements of culture to the next generation. Associated with essentialism is the concept of mastery learning (often associated with Benjamin Bloom), assuring that every learner is brought to some minimum common level of achievement. *Progressivism*, on the other hand, views the primary purpose of schools to be the development of each individual child—a philosophy commonly identified with writers like Rousseau and Dewey.

In this case study, only the state is given its correct name. The teacher and her school are identified by pseudonyms to protect confidentiality.

The Teacher

Maria is in her fifteenth year of teaching at Antelope Bayou Elementary. Like many of her students she grew up poor, the child of Mexican immigrants. Her first language, and the one spoken at home with her family, was Spanish. Although she faced pressures at home to forego further education, go to work, get married, and have a family at a young age, she persevered. She worked her way through college, and she thinks back with joy at the pride of her immigrant parents when she graduated from college, the first in her family to do so.

Maria prepared herself to teach young children because that is where she saw the greatest need, and she subsequently obtained her bilingual teaching endorsement. Passing the Texas Oral Proficiency Test was not easy, even though Spanish was her first language. The dialectic Spanish with which she was reared is not the Spanish in which she had to show proficiency to qualify for her endorsement. But again, she persevered.

Maria enjoys teaching kindergarten and first grade because she likes to concentrate on the child as a person, an individual she can help to develop. Although subject matter is important to Maria, the person takes first precedence. She takes joy in watching her young charges learn new things, in watching each of them grow personally. She spends endless hours before and after school planning and coming up with new ideas, and she meets with other teachers to compare student work and discuss ideas to help each of her students grow. She tries to contact parents of students who have special challenges, but many of those parents can't afford a telephone. So she spends more time trying to make home visits on weekends. That's hard to do when an appointment can't be made by phone. Notes have to be sent home asking when a visit might be made, and sometimes the only times available are on weekends because of the working schedules of those parents.

Things are different now from the time Maria first joined Antelope Bayou as a new teacher fifteen years ago. At that time, there were statewide tests but the stakes weren't so high. Promotion from grade to grade was not so dependent on test scores. The professional recommendation of the teacher played a larger role in promotion or retention. Back then, local newspapers did not publish an annual pullout special section entitled, "How Did Your School Do?" that reports the statewide test results and state ratings of every school building in the fifty-four school districts in the Houston metropolitan area.

Student needs are also changing. Maria's preparation in bilingual education emphasized using the structure of the native language to help students acquire English skills. More and more, though, she is seeing students enter her school whose parents cannot read and write their native language. They are, to use a technical term, *preliterate* in their native language—and, with increased immigration from Central and South America, that native language may not be Spanish. In short, some students have no native language structure to use. New methods have to be developed.

Although many things were different then, Maria feels that some things have gotten better. Because students at her school have greater challenges, her school district provides more funds to the school, based on recommendations of the school's site-based decision-making team. Maria has been elected to serve on that team from time to time. She also works with colleagues to develop proposals for funding from foundations, including a foundation implemented within the district, to assist them in helping their students.

But there are so many tests, and so much time and energy is spent on them! When the time for annual testing approaches, teachers wear identical t-shirts urging their students to do well. Classroom time is taken to practice test-taking skills. Maria agonizes with her students who do not pass on the first try and must be retested. They struggle so hard, and some cry from the pressure.

"Can I keep doing this?" Maria thinks. "How do I help all my students develop when so much time and energy must be spent on those with the greatest needs—those most likely to fail the tests?" There are special programs for those with demonstrated high academic ability and potential, and special programs for those identified with diagnosed learning problems. However, the majority of Maria's students fall in the middle, and she still wants to help each of them develop special talents to become their best.

The State

Texas is generally recognized as having the most rigorous state accountability system in the nation. For more than two decades since the publication of *A Nation at Risk* (1983), policy makers have instituted statewide statements of curriculum outcomes collectively known as the Texas Essential Knowledge and Skills, or TEKS. The very name evokes the dominant philosophy: essentialism. The TEKS articulate those selected elements of the culture that are to be passed on from one generation to the next. They are the bases from which statewide examinations are developed, including examinations for the licensure of educators. They form the specifications for the statewide adoption of instructional materials such as textbooks and instructional software. Statewide tests based on the TEKS are developed, implemented, and changed every decade or so as new needs arise. And the TEKS form the basis for the statewide Professional Development Assessment System (PDAS) used to assess the instructional performance of working teachers and to provide direction for personal professional development.

Schools whose students fail to measure up to state minimum standards on a consistent basis must be addressed by the local school district, and districts that chronically fail to adequately serve their students up to state standards can ultimately be disbanded and absorbed into adjacent, more successful districts. This last drastic measure has occurred twice since 1999, most recently in May of 2005 (Texas Education Agency Press Release, May 3, 2005).

The idea of *curriculum alignment* is a topic of substantial writing by many authors in the recent past. Curriculum alignment, which is addressed later in chapter 9 of this text, deals with the degree to which the formal curriculum (what we want to be learned), is actually implemented in the classroom (instruction) and is formally assessed (evaluation). That is, do curriculum, instruction, and evaluation have some reasonably linear relationship with one another?

Too often curriculum plans are developed away from the school setting. When provided with plans, such experienced teachers often put them in a drawer because they feel they have a better sense of what their students need and feel no sense of ownership for the plans provided. Program evaluation often consists of nationally standardized tests that may have little to do with what was *intended* to be taught, or what was *actually* taught in the classroom. In this sort of scenario, curriculum alignment is nonexistent.

Texas policies certainly ensure curriculum alignment. But is that enough?

The Texas Business and Education Coalition (TBEC) is a group of educators and business people who have come together since 1989 to press for statewide policies that make sense to all concerned. From alignment of the curriculum to state policies, to classroom application, to evaluation, TBEC presses for policies that require school systems to distribute funds from district coffers to individual schools and also require each school to establish a site-based decision-making team consisting of parents, teachers, and local community representatives to advise the school's professionals on how best to use those resources to address local needs.

The School

Antelope Bayou Elementary School serves a "suburban" clientele that is geographically located outside the inner city of Houston, but the almost 700 students who attend the school have high needs. Eighty percent are Latino/Latina. Eighty-seven percent meet federal poverty guidelines to qualify for free or reduced lunch, and sixty percent have limited proficiency in English. The neighborhood around the school has all of the problems that would normally be described as "urban" but which are more often associated with socioeconomic level: crime, drugs, gangs, and occasional violent acts.

Antelope Bayou parents care deeply about their children. While unemployment is always a problem, a greater challenge is that many parents work two jobs. Because both jobs are likely to be low-paying, parents are working far more hours than the standard 40-hour work week and are not often available to help in the school or to help children at home. Many of the children are "latch-key"—coming to school with a key to the house or apartment, because when they return there will be no one home until a parent returns from work. These are children of the working poor.

Even if the time were available, many of these parents lack the skills to substantially help their children at home. Children with limited English proficiency come from families where English is not the primary language. Children of the working poor are members of families where skill levels and educational levels are low. It's not that parents don't want to help their children. They just don't know how. They may not be able to read to their children because of personal illiteracy. Many parents did not succeed in school and may not value education. The professionals at Antelope Bayou, however, manage to do rather remarkable things with these students, primarily because of leadership and an experienced, stable, and dedicated staff.

Results posted on Texas Education Agency's Web site for the 2003–04 school year (the most recent data available at this writing) show that more than 90% of third graders at Antelope Bayou passed the Texas Assessment of Knowledge and Skills (TAKS) test in reading and in mathematics. Writing tests are added at the fourth-grade level, and again more than 90% passed. At the fifth-grade level, though, challenges become evident and reading scores fall as the tests become more difficult and older students transfer into the school lacking requisite knowledge and skills. Science has been a recent addition to the state's testing program in fifth grade. Because science was not tested in the previous examinations, it was not a priority for either curriculum development or for instructional improvement. Because science is being added to third-grade examinations, it has now become a school priority.

A major problem faced by many schools with demographic challenges similar to those of Antelope Bayou is a transient teaching force of fairly new and/or unqualified teachers who try to get a few years experience so that they can then transfer to a less stressful setting. At Antelope Bayou, though, the average teacher has ten years experience. New teachers are carefully integrated into teams to help students learn.

The staff and leadership are also entrepreneurial. They look for funds outside the school to support things that they want to do, things they believe will help their children learn. One grant several years ago allowed a number of teachers to be trained in the techniques of Critical Friends Groups (CFG), a system designed to foster teachers working together in mutual support settings (Houston A+ Challenge, online). Once funding expired, Antelope Bayou's teachers chose to continue their CFG groups and to prepare new teachers joining the school in CFG techniques.

In addition, the school enjoys a partnership with selected universities as a professional development school. The staff and leadership say that this helps them "cherry-pick" top prospective teachers, who they then encourage to join them on completion of their preparation programs. It also brings them continuous opportunities for professional development in the form of the new strategies implemented by prospective teachers, and new ideas from university faculty who work with them.

Issues for Further Reflection and Application

1. Have you tried to write your own philosophy of education? With which of the schools of philosophy do you tend to identify? Are you an essentialist, or a progressivist? Do you detect a touch reconstructionism in your thinking?
2. Does your school, and perhaps your district, have a formal statement of philosophy? Have you read it? Do you use it? Is it reflected in the district's and school's programs?
3. Have you encountered challenges dealing with others whose educational philosophy differs from yours?
4. What appears to be the educational philosophy reflected by policies in your state? How about those in your district and school?
5. Maria's story reflects what social psychologists call *role conflict*. Personally, she tends to identify with progressivist ideas of promoting personal development, helping each person become the best (s)he can become. By virtue of her work, though, she finds herself in an essentialist system. Have you experienced role conflict? Do you know others who have?

References

"Chronic low performance causes commissioner to annex Mirando City ISD to neighbor," (May 3, 2005). Texas Education Agency press release available online at http://www.tea.state.tx.us/press/mirandopr5051.html

Houston A+ Challenge, *Critical Friends Groups*. Available online at http://www.houstonaplus.org/criticalfriends.htm

National Commission on Excellence in Education (1983). *A Nation at Risk: The Imperative for Educational Reform.* Available online at http://www.ed.gov/pubs/NatAtRisk/index.html

Texas Business and Education Coalition, available online at http://www.tbec.org

Texas Education Agency, available online at http://www.tea.state.tx.us

Texas Essential Knowledge and Skills, available online at http://www.tea.state.tx.us/teks

Influences of Philosophy on Education

It is common knowledge that teachers' philosophies have a powerful effect on the curriculum, and on their own teaching as well. Now let's examine the influence philosophy has on specific areas of education.

Establishing Long-Range Objectives

The philosophy of education is concerned with abstract and difficult questions such as: What are the purposes of education? Familiarity with the philosophy of education helps in the establishment of long-range objectives.

An analogy may help to explain this major function of the philosophy of education. A traveler had been lost for several hours. After escaping from a series of traffic jams which had left him feeling quite exasperated, he finally found the open road. As he continued driving happily and rapidly, a passenger asked if he weren't still lost. "Well, yes," he replied, "as a matter of fact I am, but we are making excellent time, aren't we?"

Without any long-range goals, educators can make good time and yet be lost. Curriculum developers must know what to teach and what effects they want schooling to have on students. They must know what they would have students become. For these answers, curriculum developers must turn to the philosopher; for the philosopher will force them to formulate a system of values and decide which values are more important than others. Armed with a system of values, curriculum developers can then adjust teaching methodology and curriculum in accordance with their ultimate educational objectives. As one philosopher, Herbert Spencer (1861), said, "In determining a curriculum, our first step must be to classify, in order of their importance, the leading kinds of activity which constitute human life."

Since the value systems of no two people are the same, there will always be conflict. Our values are continually changing, and we must continually readjust our school programs to align them with our current value system.

The Teacher's Influence

The second contribution that philosophy makes to education occurs through the influence of the teacher. Thought inevitably leads to action; the way teachers think inevitably influences the way they act. It follows that the way teachers act influences student behavior (Epstein, 2008). Since "modeling is an ongoing and pervasive component of teachers' classroom functioning" (Good & Brophy, 2008, p. 77), the frequency with which teachers' actions impact the behavior of students is great.

Our values and our views of the totality of existence affect our relationships with others. If teachers have good rapport with their students, the teachers' own beliefs and value system will affect those of the pupils. Moreover, teachers' power to influence is not limited to mainstream students. In fact, teachers have even more power to influence members of minority cultures. Singham (2003) reported that both mainstream teachers and minority teachers have more influence over minority students than they have over mainstream students. In fact, 81% of black female students and 62% of black male students want to please the teacher more than they want to please a parent. The comparable figures for white females and white males are 28% and 32%, respectively.

Teachers often find themselves in a seemingly impossible position when trying to teach about such controversial issues as abortion, drug use, and war. Students are notoriously curious about, and will inevitably ask questions to learn, their teachers' points of view. If teachers reveal their opinions, many students will accept them without questioning their validity. This is perhaps the worst thing that could happen because it prevents the students from engaging in the process of reasoning.

Ideally, the teacher's desire for students to engage in this reasoning process will eclipse the desire to have pupils accept the teacher's views. However, this does not suggest that teachers should have no influence on the students. It does suggest that teachers have a particular type of responsibility, that of encouraging students to think independently rather than blindly accepting the opinions of others.

> In more recent years the community at large has sometimes blamed the schools for such *value*-laden social ills as environmental pollution, exhaustion of natural resources, and economic recession. Teachers often question whether they have a right to purposely try to influence the values of students. It must be noted that teachers cannot avoid affecting students' values. All teachers should attempt to promote such values as honesty, fairness, and good citizenship. On the other hand, teachers should avoid trying to impose their own religious, political, and cultural or ethnic values on their students. (Henson, 2010, p. 224)

The Teacher as an Agent of Change

What role does the philosophy of education play in *changing* education? All significant change requires a philosophy. Some philosophers view philosophy as a theoretical activity that follows its own disciplinary rules and is not in itself practical or reforming. If you accept this point of view, you must believe that it is not the purpose of the philosophy of education to change education. However, it is essential that the person who philosophizes about education cares intensely about the practice and improvement of education. Notice that the word improvement implies change. Although philosophers are unlikely to suggest specific changes needed in our schools, they are likely to affect teachers so that the teachers will be stimulated to make changes, the need of which the philosopher may be quite unaware.

Regarding the role that the philosophy of education plays in changes, some things are clear:

1. Philosophy is a belief system, and what teachers believe is important (Bintz & Dillard, 2007).
2. The philosophy of education does contribute to change, but only when such change is needed.
3. Such contributions may be more indirect than direct.
4. The types of change caused by the philosopher deal with the important values of life and, therefore, are likely to be monumental.

Currently, an urgent need exists for educators to look at the whole education process in totally new ways, to explore the subconscious part of behavior, and to consider the basic overall changes in society when designing school curricula. This seems to illustrate the type of change that the philosopher is likely to stimulate—major change brought about indirectly as a result of the philosopher's help in sorting out the more valuable things in life.

A Moral Guide

Should our curriculum teach ethics? If so, what role does philosophy play in moral education? If we believe that no knowledge exists merely for its own sake, and all knowledge must in some way affect conduct, the answer to these questions is that teachers cannot avoid teaching ethics. This issue is vital, because education in any society serves to help initiate its young into its culture, and certainly the moral beliefs are a large part of any culture.

But educators must do more than just hand down the ethics of former generations to newer generations. As our culture changes, so do our moral standards. In ancient Greek, heritage meant "process"; later it meant "content." Now it means the whole intellectual, moral, and cultural setting into which we are born.

By *ethical and moral foundations* we refer to how our society answers the basic question of whether there are relationships that are right and relationships that are wrong. The answer is not clear. In the Western world there are two opposing positions: the Christian tradition, which believes in absolute right and wrong; and the Greek view that humans, through their own reasoning, make their own

---

Box 3.3 Philosophy with Children

The clarifying effect of philosophy not only influences teachers but also has an impact on students.

> Children think constantly, and reflect on their thoughts. They acquire knowledge and try to use what they know. And they want their experience to be meaningful: to be valuable, interesting, just and beautiful. Philosophy offers children the chance to explore ordinary but puzzling concepts, to improve their thinking, to make more sense of their world, and to discover for themselves what is to be valued and cherished in that world. (IAPC mission statement, n.d.)

Two major organizations promote philosophical inquiry among children.

- *The Institute for the Advancement of Philosophy for Children*
  http://www.cehs.montclair.edu/academic/iapc
  Ann Margaret Sharp (2002), a prominent and often-quoted member of IAPC, believes that philosophy, through education, is able to change the emotional and intellectual dispositions of children "to prepare the next generation to think and act differently in their daily lives in light of new, broader and more satisfying conceptions of existence." According to Sharp, education is transformed into a sort of laboratory that can bring about "a change in consciousness in which philosophical procedures, ideals and dispositions can become concrete and tested in practice."
- *The International Council of Philosophical Inquiry with Children*
  http://www.simnet.is/heimspekiskolinn/icpic.html
  This organization, with over 60 member nations, is concerned with both curriculum and education reform. It aims to expose children to philosophical inquiry within the context of a classroom community from the time they can use language. In such an educational setting, children not only learn the procedures of communal inquiry but become proficient at inquiring into the central and controversial concepts of their life experience.

morals. This places teachers in a difficult position. How can they transmit such conflicting information to students?

As previously noted, some educators believe that education must strive to enable pupils to think for themselves and make up their own minds. Most modern educators would agree that the curriculum must respect students' intellectual integrity and promote their capacity for independent judgment.

With respect to the moral role of philosophy in education, we can state that: (1) education has a moral responsibility to its pupils, (2) teachers should teach the morals of the society to their pupils, and (3) teachers must not impose their beliefs on their pupils but must encourage them to apply their own intellectual ability to reason out their own modes of behavior.

A Clarifier

Philosophy has yet another role in education: to help clarify concepts such as *cause, self, mind,* and *good*. By doing this, philosophers will inevitably help to clarify the relationships of these abstractions to each other, which will lead to the informed analysis of current educational theories.

A Process

The preceding paragraphs have presented philosophy as a thinking process for answering the most abstract, the most general, and certainly the most difficult types of questions. Immanuel Kant (1724–1804) told his pupils, "You will not learn from me philosophy, but how to philosophize, not to repeat, but how to think. Think for yourselves, inquire for yourselves, stand on your own feet." An important role of educational philosophy is to make us aware of the need for asking questions.

Ron Wolk (2004) says that the reason that American schools rank with those schools in third-world nations is because we ask the wrong questions. Instead of asking, "How can we raise test scores?" we should be asking, "What do we want every child to achieve?" and "How can we prepare every child for a rapidly changing world?"

Conclusion

Following is a summary of some of the advances made and concerns raised about the topics discussed in this chapter.

Advances

- Interdisciplinary curricula are experiencing a resurgence in today's schools.
- New technology offers unprecedented opportunities to promote inquiry.
- Teachers have special powers to influence minority-group members.

Concerns

- Successful use of interdisciplinary curricula requires special training.
- Emphasis on standards militates against the use of problem solving and other methods that promote creativity.

- By getting educators to ask questions, philosophy serves as a guide to developing the schools.
- Through planning and dialoguing, interdisciplinary teaching leads to the building of learning communities.
- Meeting the needs of students in minority and low-income schools is a perennial challenge.
- Emphasis on high-stakes tests robs teachers of planning time.

Formal education in America began in the homes, where the teaching of reading, Puritanism, and colonial law was required. In 1635 the forerunners of our current high schools appeared; similar to the English schools, they were designed to prepare the elite for the university. Because their curricula were dominated by classical Latin and Greek, they were called Latin grammar schools. Because of their impracticality, they soon gave way to very pragmatic curricula based on the Franklin Academy, founded in 1750. These schools were private, and many people could not afford them. The first public high schools, called the Boston English High Schools, appeared in 1821. The schools varied. Some were very pragmatic, but some were just the opposite.

In 1918 the NEA appointed a commission to identify the goals of secondary schools. Their findings, called the Cardinal Principles of Secondary Education, are equally applicable today. The twentieth century ushered in the Progressive Education Movement, which emphasized the practical, child-centered curriculum for 50 years until it gave way to a subject-centered curriculum. This conservative, subject-centered curriculum yielded to a process-centered curriculum.

All teachers have philosophies, and their personal philosophies inevitably affect their teaching behavior. By examining their beliefs, teachers and other curriculum developers can use these beliefs to design curricula to achieve their overall aims. An awareness of all of the major philosophical structures empowers teachers to use their preferred structures to design curricula. Employing the original philosophy of John Locke, who espoused experience-based, learner-centered curricula, Colonel Francis Parker was the first administrator to involve teachers and students in curriculum development.

Many philosophical structures have certain concepts in common, but in other respects, they differ totally. An awareness of the similarities and differences of these philosophies is essential if teachers are to maximize their contributions to education reform in their schools.

As noted throughout the chapter, each of these philosophical structures has particular potential for serving the schools' constructivist and multicultural goals, helping all students achieve their potential and succeed as capable learners and worthy individuals.

Additional Learning Opportunities

1. Why should the textbook be one of several curriculum determiners?
2. Why did the Boston Latin Grammar Schools become obsolete?
3. Why did the Franklin Academy lose popularity?

4. What is the significance of the dame schools?
5. What qualities of the Cardinal Principles have made them endure?
6. Why has the textbook been the single greatest curriculum determiner throughout the history of American schools?
7. What is the significance of such curricula as the Quincy System, the Gary Plan, the Dalton Plan, and the Winnetka Plan? How does each relate to constructivist theory?
8. If Progressive Education Movement curricula were so successful, why did this era end?
9. What is meant by the statement, "Effective management of multiculturalism will require each faculty and each faculty member to invent curriculum to meet the needs of each student body"? What is the school leader's role?
10. What is the significance of the Old Deluder Satan Act?
11. Suppose you could use only two of the philosophical structures introduced in this chapter. On which two structures would you base your curriculum? Why?
12. How does philosophy give direction without dictating directions? (Hint: At this moment, how is the author of this book influencing or directing your thinking?)
13. Why must education work to stabilize society and also work to change society?
14. Why do teachers have no alternative but to affect the values and morals of their students?

SUGGESTED ACTIVITIES

1. Name one goal or aim that you feel is of utmost importance to today's schools. Explain how you can work toward achieving that goal.
2. Make a list of the legislated reform elements in your district. This may require interviews with some of your education professors and/or a visit to your library's reference room and government documents department.
3. Interview three teachers and ask each to identify strengths and weaknesses in local school reform. Make a chart showing these strengths and the weaknesses.
4. Interview one or more education professors and ask them what changes education reform has stimulated in the classes they teach.
5. How would you explain the continued relevance of the Cardinal Principles of Secondary Education?
6. Compare and contrast the Cardinal Principles and NCLB.
7. Examine the legislation mentioned in this chapter, and list one purpose for each law. Tell how effectively you think current school curricula meet each purpose.

8. Make a list of the major concepts presented in this chapter.
9. Research the topics of values and morality in education.
10. For the school with which you are most familiar, describe features in that school's curriculum that reflect various philosophical structures introduced in this chapter.
11. Read the book *Summerhill* by A. S. Neill, and write a brief paper describing the philosophy upon which that school operates.
12. Read the book *Émile* by Jean Jacques Rousseau, and write a paper describing Rousseau's philosophy as it is expressed in the book.
13. List a school's three most important purposes, and describe at least one student activity you might assign to achieve each purpose.
14. Disregarding your physical appearance, identify your most pronounced personal strength and your most important weakness. Explain how you can modify or shape your curricula to capitalize on this strength and compensate for this weakness.

chapter four

Concepts, Theories, and Models

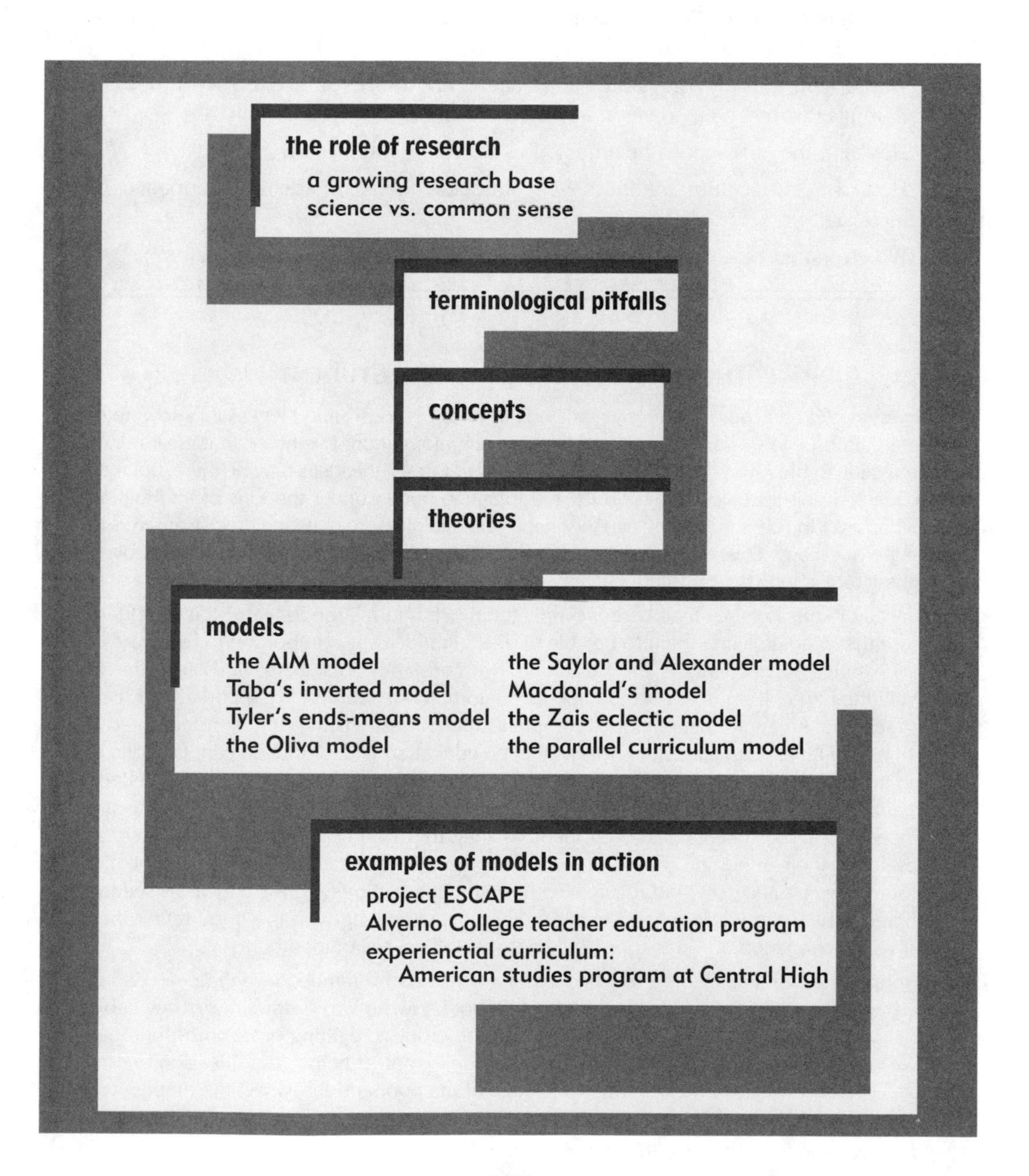

Focus Questions

1. Why should educators look at the past in order to build the future? How can curriculum developers use this principle to solve social problems such as meeting the needs of minority students?
2. How has the No Child Left Behind Act stimulated the use of research or data collection?
3. Would you classify the statement "There are more differences within than among cultures" as a concept, a theory, or a model?
4. How can the curriculum be adjusted to stimulate intellectual curiosity?
5. How can curriculum planners help students focus on ideas as opposed to facts?
6. Which model best supports the goal of meeting the needs of all students?

The Case of a Disappointed Student

Next semester I will be a senior; my grade point average is 3.73—and I feel as if I know nothing. In almost every class I attend, I get nothing but information. I've heard that great minds discuss ideas, but my college classes are like petrified forests: the ideas may be there, but they are viewed only as objects of curiosity, too long ago buried under the tons of information built up over the centuries. Long ago the simple-minded pleasure of giving precise answers to precise questions replaced the hard work of intellectual endeavor. This didn't happen overnight; it took a long time, and now here we are, in the petrified forest of education.

Why can't educators see that there is simply too much information to learn? It is important to use the mind. It is important to be able to deal with ideas. It is important to be aware of the changing world. Here is the frustration: we constantly look backwards in order to invent the future. It is not that we do not need information, but must we spend all our lives just accumulating information? I believe intellectual curiosity is the only constant in education, and unless that curiosity is awakened, no education will, or indeed can, take place. And this awakening does not come from gathering information; ideas awaken the intellect. I realize that *ideas* is an abstract term. That is precisely why it is so important. Ideas are concepts, and as students deal with them, as they try to bring them to concreteness, as they focus their minds on them, they are truly becoming educated. Again, I grant that information is a necessity, but it is gained throughout a lifetime. Unless educators see the difference between wisdom and knowledge and begin dealing with the mind rather than just with information, the classroom will continue to be a sea of mediocrity.

In trying to get an education, I feel like a non-swimmer who jumped into the deep end of the pool. The problem is that my instructors do not know how to swim either. They know all about the right strokes; they know all about the proper breathing procedures; but they have never been in the pool. It isn't that they don't want to help—they just don't know how. The best they can do is stand at the edge of the pool and throw me the empty container that used to hold the life preserver.

I don't want to just criticize—this is a plea. One day soon, I will be a teacher. What am I to do? I can't go back, since I am already in the water. I can't go forward, because I cannot swim. There is only one answer: I must learn to swim—even if only enough to stay afloat. I dare not struggle back to the edge; if I do, I will only become one of the nameless faces that throw out the empty containers.

• • •

As you read this bored and disappointed student's view of contemporary education, you may have found issues that were overstated and perhaps others that were totally inaccurate, but you should recognize the truth in the student's concern for the shallowness that characterizes what goes on in many classrooms. How do you know that your students need to learn how to think? When asking this question of teachers of all grade levels in countries all over the world, Arthur Costa (2008, p. 20) reported that teachers have given remarkably similar descriptions of their students' thinking:

- *They just blurt out their answers. I wish they would think before they respond.*
- *They depend on me for their answers. I wish they would think for themselves.*
- *They give up so easily on difficult tasks. I'd like them to hang in there.*
- *They can't seem to work in groups. They must learn to cooperate and work together.*
- *They don't apply their knowledge. I want them to use what they know in other situations.*
- *They are afraid to take risks. I'd like them to* be more creative, more adventuresome.

This chapter examines these problems and discusses ways that teachers and other curriculum developers can put meaning into education.

> No man claiming to be practically versed in a science can disdain its theory without exposing himself as an ignoramus in his field.
>
> —Immanuel Kant

The Role of Research

This chapter focuses on concepts, theories, and models. Constructivists emphasize the importance of using concepts to build the curriculum for each course. Theories are important because they expand concepts into broader themes. Models are important because they provide examples that can be followed. While it is not important to try to understand all of the relationships among concepts, theories, and models, educators should understand that the main power of each is its generalizability, a quality that is important to all curriculum planning because it increases applicability while encouraging the curriculum developer's creativity.

In defining *professionalism*, Armstrong et al. (2009) remind their readers that professionals share common values and ethical standards. Research is another characteristic commonly used to identify professions. Yet educational psychologists and other educators have reported that generally teachers have not used research to guide their practice, and they often overestimate the value of personal experience. Traditionally, educators have learned to manage classrooms from each other, and the focus is on practice rather than theory. When classroom management is taught in this way, teachers run the risk of making the same mistakes without realizing why. But research has its limits. As Ferrero (2005, p. 426) has reminded us, "Research tells us almost nothing about what to teach and why to teach it." It won't remove all our doubts, and professionalism always involves risk-taking (Martinez, 2006).

A Growing Research Base

Until recently, teachers had both an excuse and a reason for ignoring the research: Very little research on teaching was available. The scattered studies were isolated, and they provided only microscopic glimpses of segments of the educational process. But during the second half of the twentieth century, research on teaching increased rapidly. With a newly acquired *knowledge base* (research-derived knowledge that supports the practice of a profession), educators can more effectively use the data to make instruction-related decisions.

During the last two decades of the twentieth century we learned a great deal about instruction in American schools. Sophisticated observational research yielded more knowledge about schooling than had been previously obtained. In the twenty-first century an extensive quantitative and qualitative research database exists to help educators understand classroom problems and make decisions about instructional issues. The NCLB legislation encourages teachers to use research by requiring them to use scientifically researched data to support their chosen teaching strategies and student activities.

One promising development that has been focusing teachers on schoolwide curriculum and giving teachers a renewed interest in curriculum research and development is teacher participation in action research projects (discussed further in chapter 8). Such research appeals to twenty-first-century education reformers because it is authentic; it focuses on real-life problems and is aimed at improving current conditions. Teachers like the pragmatic quality of action research, as Gilbert and Smith (2003) explain: "Because action research is pragmatic and goal-oriented, it encourages a mix of theory and practice (*praxis*)" (p. 81).

The involvement of teachers in research ranges from micro (classroom level) projects to macro (schoolwide) restructuring projects. Action research projects usually involve more than one teacher, may or may not involve university staff members, and usually begin with the perception of a gap between the current state of affairs and a more desirable state.

Students also should be involved in research. Armstrong et al. (2009) remind us that "helping learners to become more sophisticated thinkers has been an aim of education" (p. 351). It's a disservice to students to expect them to express opinions on matters they have not researched. Reform programs of the late twentieth and early twenty-first centuries are bringing teachers out of their classrooms and involving them with the rest of the school's curriculum planning, and this broader involvement has led to an increased use of research by teachers. The comprehensive school reform programs generally include more research-based practices than the curriculum-focused programs. Ironically (and unfortunately), education reformers have neglected to continue researching the most important variable of all, which is the amount of learning associated with these various programs.

FYI Start a Wiki

Thelma Roberson • University of Southern Mississippi

A wiki is a Web-based collection created, edited, and added to by its members. Wikis are great tools for engaging teachers in ongoing professional learning and collaboration. School leaders can create and post induction and professional development materials, including PowerPoints, videos, handouts, handbooks, and blogs. Teachers can engage in professional conversations about teaching and learning and can share resources while creating their own lesson plans and educational materials.

Efforts to provide face-to-face opportunities for professional development and collaboration are often limited by time constraints, scheduling conflicts, and budgets. The asynchronous nature and low cost of wikis make them viable solutions to these problems. To learn more about wikis, read "Wiki Wisdom: Lessons for Educators" at http://www.edweek.org/dd/articles/2007/09/12/02wiki.h01.html.

Science versus Common Sense

Some educators reject research because they tend to rely on a *commonsense approach*, but common sense isn't reliable. For example, when inexperienced drivers enter a foggy area, they almost invariably turn their lights on high beam. Common sense has told them that the high beams will help them see better, but in this instance they don't. In fact, because of increased reflection, the high beams can be blinding to the driver. To use another driving example, when a car skids, common sense tells the driver to turn the wheel in the direction opposite to the skidding, but doing so intensifies the problem.

Readers who have taken a physics course may remember the problem that involves simultaneously shooting a rifle horizontally and dropping a bullet vertically. The problem is to determine which bullet will hit the ground first. Common sense says the dropped bullet will hit the ground first because the distance it travels is so much shorter. In fact, the two bullets land simultaneously. A basic principle of gravitation says that free-falling bodies travel at a velocity of 96 ft/sec^2, regardless of their horizontal speeds.

Kerlinger (1973, pp. 3–5) used the work of Whitehead (1911) and Conant (1951) to show that, although science can be misleading, it differs from common sense in important ways:

> Whitehead has pointed out that in creative thought common sense is a bad master. "Its sole criterion for judgment is that the new ideas shall look like the old ones." This is well said. Common sense may often be a bad master for the evaluation of knowledge. . . .
>
> Science and common sense differ sharply in [several] ways. . . . First, the uses of conceptual schemes and theoretical structures are strikingly different. While the man in the street uses "theories" and concepts, he ordinarily does so in a loose fashion. He often blindly accepts fanciful explanations of natural and

> human phenomena. . . . The scientist, on the other hand, systematically builds his theoretical structures, tests them for internal consistency, and subjects aspects of them to empirical test. . . . Second, the scientist systematically and empirically tests his theories and hypotheses. The man in the street tests his "hypotheses" too, but he tests them in what might be called a selective fashion. He often "selects" evidence simply because it is consistent with his hypothesis. . . . [The scientist] insists upon systematic, controlled, and empirical testing of these relations. A third difference lies in the notion of control. . . . The scientist tries systematically to rule out variables that are possible "causes" of the effects he is studying other than the variables that he has hypothesized to be the "causes." [The layman] tends to accept those explanations that are in accord with his preconceptions and biases. . . .
>
> A final difference between common sense and science lies in different explanations of observed phenomena The scientist, when attempting to explain the relations among observed phenomena, carefully rules out what have been called "metaphysical explanations." A *metaphysical explanation* [italics added] is simply a proposition that cannot be tested.

According to Ozmon and Craver (2008, pp. 269–270), teachers historically have treated information in the same manner as that of the man on the street:

> Teachers constantly call for practical solutions to educational problems. But this concern with "practicality" is itself open to analytic inquiry: just what does "practical" mean in this instance? Often, the "practical" teacher wants a technique, a gimmick, to apply to and solve a problem. It is reasonable, however, to observe that such "practical" solutions are often theoretical in the worst sense. Techniques are sometimes used indiscriminately. They are applied generally and universally in situations for which they were not designed; however, they are deemed "practical" because their mechanics are known and they are capable of being acted upon.

Terminological Pitfalls

Chapter 1 discussed some criticisms of current education reform practices. Paramount among these practices are the overreliance on achievement test scores and the careless use of terminology. Ozmon and Craver (2008, p. 270) explain the danger in the overuse and misuse of the word *practical*:

> "Achievement" is a talisman by which many educators swear, and the worth of any educational activity is judged on students' achievement scores. "Achievement" in such instances is usually understood to be a "practical" outcome of one's education, but such emphasis may serve to retard one's education if the meaning of achievement is vague and unclear. Suppose one wants to learn how to play the piano, and the educator says that the "practical" approach is to proceed by achievement in learning to play scales. Such a method may result in the student's learning to play scales but not in developing [an] ability to play the piano or in sustaining [the student's] interest. We may pose the question: how "practical" is this approach?

Criticism of theory is not new. Practitioners have always been critical, especially when the theory doesn't work when applied to practice. Over two centuries ago Kant (1793/1974, p. 41) had a good response to the critics of his day: "Thus, when the theory did not work too well in practice, the fault lay not in the theory, but rather in there not being enough theory which a man should have learned from experience." Remember, too, that having critics is an important part of society's checks and balances (Jensen, 2008).

Recall the student's plea at the beginning of this chapter. Too often, educators attend to the specifics at the cost of ignoring the meanings that these specifics could have, if students are prepared to make generalizations and apply these generalizations to their own lives and to the world around them. Learning without application tends to be useless. For learning to have value, students must be able to transfer the knowledge they acquire in school to the world beyond the classroom.

Words seem to be a common trap for educators and students alike. Too often, the aim is "achievement," but when measured by pencil-and-paper tests, that achievement amounts to no more than memorizing words or facts. To get beyond these facts, teachers need three tools: (1) concepts, (2) theories, and (3) models.

Concepts

A concept is a major idea with a recurring quality that gives the concept a very special power, *generalizability*. The recurring quality may be a physical property such as the four legs and flat surface that recur among tables, or the recurring pattern could be in other properties such as *utility*, which recurs in the case of all tools. Or the recurring quality can be an *abstraction* (something that is not concrete, i.e., a theoretical construct), as reflected in such feelings as love, hate, doubt, or curiosity. Discovering concepts establishes students to connect with the curriculum (Tomlinson & Doubet, 2005).

A study group comparing procedures in U.S. mathematics with procedures used in higher-achieving countries (TIMSS, 2003) said, ". . . teachers in the higher-achieving countries attended more to the *conceptual* [italics added] development of mathematics than teachers in the U.S." (p. 773). The power of the concept in learning must never be underestimated. Einstein (1951, p. 7) said that it is the very essence of all thinking:

> What precisely is "thinking"? When at the reception of sense-impressions, memory-pictures emerge, that is not yet "thinking." And when such pictures form series, each member of which calls forth another, this too is not yet "thinking." When, however, a certain picture turns up in many series, then—precisely through such return—it becomes an ordering element for such series, in that it connects series which in themselves are unconnected. Such an element becomes an instrument, a concept. I think that the transition from free association or "dreaming" to thinking is characterized by the more or less dominating role which the "concept" plays in it.

Ward (1969, p. 423) described the concept's special power of generalization:

> You enter the old kitchen, in which there is a blazing hearthfire complete with bubbling, boiling teakettle. Oh, it's always there anyway; you've seen it before.

> Besides, your mind is on something else. Your quaint kitchen is pretty well tuned out by you, or you only perceive it at the (blob) level. Wait, something focuses your attention on the event system that is the boiling kettle. You've noticed. Now you are beginning to operate. You've noticed something, and something is happening. The lid jumps up and down. You wonder why. Ah, cause, the why sets you to scrutinizing relationships. First you attend, focus, observe, isolate. Next, you want the cause of something. Establishing tentative cause gets you to infer a low-level generalization. "That lid will move because steam is pushing it up and down. If that particular kettle is put on that fire and it boils, then its lid will jump up and down" is a relatively low level of abstraction because the particulars of the scene are still involved. The next level of abstraction, of generalization, will take you to a point of thinking, "When a kettle is placed on a fire, the water will boil and cause a loose lid to move."

This illustrates how concepts can be discovered and formulated by students. Some of the current education reform programs stress the significance of identifying major concepts in each discipline. In contrast, other programs (particularly those that are authentic and performance-based) stress method to the degree that content is downplayed, the argument being that if the process is right the content will come automatically (Tomlinson & Doubet, 2005). These reformers argue that education is an emotional, learn-from-the-gut experience.

Most contemporary reformers embrace the teaching/learning style reflected in the teakettle scenario, the discovery method. Constructivists argue that direct involvement in identifying concepts enables students to tie the major content generalizations in the lesson to previous understanding.

Noting that 40% of high school graduates reported key gaps in their preparation, Mel Levine (2007) listed two dozen tools that students need. The number-one item on this list is *forming, grasping, and applying concepts*. Boix-Mansilla and Gardner (2008) caution teachers to slow down and give students time to explore each concept.

Students are usually unaware of the major concepts in each lesson, and, furthermore, there is evidence that teachers are aware of this oversight but are unwilling to make the adjustments needed to correct this flaw. Because students tend to deal with concepts in isolation, the teacher's job of getting the students to see the relationships among concepts may be made easier by explaining the tentative nature of concepts. The boundaries of all concepts are tentative. Even all disciplinary boundaries are tentative. Authentic problem solving, a popular technique found in today's education reform programs, can be a useful strategy for teaching concepts.

TMISS videos showed Japanese students using inquiry activities to discover concepts on their own. These periods of inductive inquiry were preceded and followed by discussions that helped them link the activities to the concepts. Czech Republic students presented their work publicly throughout their lessons. Most U.S. lessons lack these opportunities to connect the lesson activities with major lesson concepts (Roth & Garnier, 2007).

JoAnn Susko (2010) uses what she calls *exit cards* to ensure that her students understand important concepts in each daily lesson. At the end of each lesson, students tell what they have learned, raise any remaining questions, and suggest ways to apply the day's lesson to real-life situations.

Theories

Once students understand concepts, these concepts can be assembled to form even more powerful mental tools: theories and models. Kerlinger (1973, p. 9) gives the following definition:

> A theory is a set of interrelated constructs (concepts), definitions, and propositions that present a systematic view of phenomena by specifying relations among variables, with the purpose of explaining and predicting the phenomena.

Without theory, we are left with a bag of tricks.

Philosophy can help the educator use theories. An educator can begin by formulating a theory of education. Although many educators have tried unsuccessfully to formulate such a theory, this poor record should not preclude teachers from writing their own philosophies of education. On the contrary, curriculum coursework should prepare teachers to formulate their own theories and philosophies about education. All teachers must take time to reflect and reinvent. Systematic and ongoing inquiry must be a routine part of our roles as teachers and learners.

John Dewey explored the relationship between philosophy and educational theory in 1916. According to Ozmon and Craver (1999) Dewey believed that the theory of education is a set of "generalizations" and "abstractions" about education. Although many people probably think that abstraction is useless when dealing with practical matters, Dewey maintained that it can serve a very useful purpose. Things are generalized so they may have broader application. A theory of education contains generalizations that are applicable to many situations. Philosopher Alfred North Whitehead (1911) emphasized the importance of generalization. He saw the purpose of public schools as that of preparing students to apply knowledge to solve life's problems. To Whitehead, the way this is done is through generalization.

Who Theorizes, and What Theories Do

To many, the term *theory* may conjure up images of scientists working in laboratories. In addition, people tend to believe that theories, when followed precisely, will lead to the correct solution. These common views of theory aren't entirely accurate. First, scientists are not the only people who theorize; theorizing occurs outside the laboratory setting, too. At one time or another, all of us have used theories. Experienced teachers frequently change methods for achieving a particular goal, hoping the new method will work better than the old one(s). Although such behavior may not occur at a sophisticated level, these teachers are theorizing and building theories (Ozmon & Craver, 2008). We also theorize outside the classroom. Each time we buy a new automobile or dishwasher, for example, we theorize about its future performance and its durability. Finally, theories do not always produce correct answers, and they never tell us what we should do. Although some theories have predictive powers and can tell us what will very likely happen if we do this or that, the decision to choose one alternative over another is ours. So the role of the theory is not to guide our behavior; rather, it is to help guide our thinking. More accurately, theory is one of several forces that work together to guide our thinking. For example, our emotions and our value systems also play important roles in our decisions to behave in certain ways.

Theories are never final, because science is fluid in nature. The more we learn, the more we are able to learn. Learning is like stepping on a rock to see farther, then stepping on another, larger rock, and then another. Using another simile, learning is like the work of an astronomer. Each time a more powerful telescope is invented, our knowledge of the universe expands, and often our theories must be changed to accommodate our new understandings.

To be useful, an educational theory doesn't have to be proved. Some theories are used to predict; others are used to explain. What theory provides is order and intelligibility out of miscellaneous and unrelated profusion of phenomena. Applied to curriculum development, theories cannot tell teachers and other curriculum developers to develop curricula in a particular way. But theory can guide the curriculum developer's thinking, which can indirectly improve curriculum design.

Another misconception is that theories are complicated, esoteric, and pedantic in nature. Obviously, theories cannot be of value if they are obscure. Ozmon and Craver (1999, p. 10) advise:

> If a theory does not help us communicate in a better or more advantageous way, criticize our assumptions and actions, gain perspective, seek out new possibilities, order and direct practice, then we had better let it go or revise it in new directions.

Following are sample theories from the four major content areas.

1. *Science*: The total amount of energy is not affected by energy transformation.
2. *English*: Effective writing is a function of clear, concise sentences.
3. *Social Studies*: Attitudes are a function of group affiliation.
4. *Mathematics*: In a right triangle the square of the hypotenuse is equal to the sum of the squares of the other two sides.

Some of these theories are familiar because we memorized them in high school. We still use them, but perhaps only rarely (e.g., the Pythagorean theorem). Other theories guide our daily thinking. Using a theory requires awareness and understanding, not memorization. As you continue reading this book, your goal should be to understand and recall the relationships among the curriculum development theories.

Ensuring that the major concepts and theories in each discipline become the focus of the curriculum requires a carefully planned schoolwide strategy. These major content generalizations should rest on a solid foundation that includes results of the latest research, matching teaching/learning styles, local and state guidelines or benchmarks, and the learned societies' guidelines.

The following case study shows how teachers can personalize the curriculum and make it more meaningful to students by using a problem-oriented approach. This case study is so recent that as of this writing its effectiveness has yet to be determined. As you read it, consider whether you would be willing to experiment as this teacher has and, if so, how you might tweak the program to increase its effectiveness.

case study

Selecting Activities to Personalize the Curriculum

Judy D. Butler
University of West Georgia

Background

We the People . . . Project Citizen (referred to here as *Project Citizen*) is a middle-school civic education program designed to develop interest in public policy making and to develop the ability to participate competently and responsibly in state and local government. It is also available at the high school level.

The program is administered by the Center for Civic Education, in cooperation with the National Conference of State Legislatures. In *Project Citizen*, students tackle a problem in the world that they identify as truly theirs (e.g., in their school, their community, or their neighborhood). Perhaps they do not like the graffiti that decorates the walls of their bathrooms, or they notice that their school has rules that clearly deny them due process. Maybe they have noticed a particularly dangerous crossroads that could use a stoplight, crossing guards, or speed bumps. Perhaps they decide, as a class, that the water problem in their city is reaching a critical stage and an awareness campaign is warranted. Whatever their concern, a teacher gives groups of students the opportunity to make that concern known to their class in a public forum. The discussion of possible problems to tackle is often done in cooperative learning groups. After the class selects a problem that it wants to tackle, the work begins.

The next step is to postulate solutions. In small groups, students brainstorm ideas on possible ways to approach their problem. Competing proposals for solving the problem are put forth. Students may also think of individuals—a mayor, or groups of adults such as civil engineers—on whom they might call to assist them in their quest to effect a change in a particular public policy.

The merits of competing proposals are considered. Different groups in the classroom may bring in testimonials or suggestions from people in authority. Eventually, however, the class must reach consensus. The class must decide on one solution on which to focus.

Next, an action plan, including a time line for implementation, is outlined. This may culminate in a presentation before a city board or school board, where students respectfully make their point about the problem they have identified and offer a plan of action that is reasonable and well-outlined. The presentation may also be done in a "mock" forum in their classroom with parents or community members role playing the parts of people in authority.

All along the way, students keep a notebook (e.g., portfolio) of copies of letters they write, transcriptions or records from interviews they conduct, and research—the statistical data they gather on the problem—so that they will have a record of their efforts to change public policy. After the project is over, regardless of success or failure, reflection is important. Students should be allowed to ponder how they might have done things differently or to analyze and celebrate their successes.

The principle steps of *Project Citizen* enable students to practice being good citizens through an active campaign to make a difference in their community by

1. identifying a problem,
2. formulating possible solutions,
3. adopting one action plan,

4. implementing that plan, and
5. evaluating or reflecting upon the process.

The Teacher

The educator in this study was in her fourth year of teaching. She was working on her master's degree at a nearby university and learned about *Project Citizen* from one of her professors. Wanting to invigorate her classes and bring some excitement to the study of state and local issues, she decided to use the *Project Citizen* curriculum.

The Community

The community is a small town (approximately 25,000 people) 20 miles outside a large metropolitan area in the southeastern portion of the country. The entire region is experiencing a time of great growth, and the town is within one of the fastest-growing counties in the United States. The county is still predominantly lower-middle class, but the demographics are changing as new subdivisions spring up. New businesses and small industries are being drawn to the county.

The School

The school is one of six middle schools (grades 6–8) in the county. The school serves 950 students, with a professional staff of 60 and an auxiliary staff of 15. Forty-seven percent of the teachers have advanced degrees. Fifty-nine percent of the student population is Caucasian; 33% is African-American; and 8% is from Hispanic, Asian, or other ethnic groups. Students with learning disabilities, emotional/behavioral disorders, mild learning handicaps, and speech/language needs make up 10.6% of the student population. The students routinely score well on state-mandated tests.

The Case

Students in the eighth-grade class saw many problems in their local community, from teen pregnancy to dislike of the school cafeteria food. Many students who played in the sports programs sponsored by the county parks and recreation commission were disturbed that the parks were in disrepair. This became their focus for *Project Citizen*. The seats of swings hung broken and the ballparks were missing bases. Trash was not regularly collected. Many of the problems they identified could result in injury, especially to small children.

Upon investigating, the students learned that the parks and recreation commission no longer directly cared for the parks. The maintenance of the parks had been outsourced to a professionally contracted company. The question that immediately emerged was where the money was going, since it obviously was not being spent on the upkeep of the parks.

After pursuing several options, the students decided that the best way to approach the problem was to attempt to testify before the commission. While the teacher made efforts to get the students on the agenda of a commission meeting, the students worked on a presentation. They took pictures of the broken playground apparatus and interviewed a lawyer about what might happen if a child were hurt on one of the broken pieces of equipment. Parents became interested in the project and helped the students determine what funds would be required to bring the parks up to speed.

Near the end of the year, the students were asked to write reflections about their experiences. They indicated that they now realized that, even though they were adolescents, they could, when they united their efforts, get the adult world to listen to them. They were surprised to learn that a government agency could pay someone to work for them yet have no apparent oversight over the work. They learned that citizens cannot always get to speak to their elected officials when they would like.

The students were not successful at getting to speak before the parks and recreation commission during their eighth-grade year. However, when they were being recognized for their work at a school board meeting, a parks and recreation commissioner heard their story. During their ninth-grade year, they had the opportunity to speak before the commission. It remains to be seen if their work will bear fruit.

Issues for Further Reflection and Application

1. In the days of high-stakes testing, is there room in the curriculum for community based learning?
2. What are characteristics of teachers who have the ability to step out of traditional classroom roles to try programs such as this one?
3. How does a community-based program such as the one described here benefit or hinder specific populations of students?
4. There is a focus on developing young citizens in this program. How can this be defended as a worthy goal of curriculum in a middle school?
5. How can teachers be more proactive in assisting students in understanding the concept of community?

Suggested Reading

Jensen, E. P. (2008). A fresh look at brain-based education. *Phi Delta Kappan, 89*(6), 409–417.
Murdock, S. (2007). *IQ: A smart history of a failed idea*. Hoboken, NJ: John Wiley.
Sagor, A. (2008). All our students thinking. *Educational Leadership, 65* (6), 26–31.

To learn more about *Project Citizen*, or other civic education programs, as well as service learning programs, consider exploring the activities of the organizations listed below:

- The American Bar Association (http://www.abanet.org/publiced) has for over 30 years provided materials for teachers that relate to teaching students about the law. In addition, at this site there are lesson plans and information about celebrating Law Day.
- The Center for Civic Education (http://www.civiced.org/) has sponsored civic education programs for thirty years. They also oversaw the writing of the civics and government standards and are quite active in over fifty emerging democracies around the world. They work with the National Conference of State Legislatures to deliver the *Project Citizen* program to all fifty states, U.S. territories, and countries around the world.
- CIVINET (http://www.civinet.org/) is a Web site devoted to all who have interest in teaching and learning about civics. It includes connections to teachers in the emerging democracies, for those who might wish to set up communication between their class and a class abroad.
- Constitutional Rights Foundation (http://www.crf-usa.org/) develops, produces, and distributes programs and materials to teachers, students, and public-minded citizens all across the nation.

Models

The third special tool that educators need is models. Significant change always requires a model, which we can define as a set of logical relationships, either qualitative or quantitative, that will link together the relevant features of the reality. Functionally, models are used to represent events and event interactions in a highly compact and illustrative manner.

It should be noted that a model is not reality. Rather, like a painting or a story, it is a visual or written description of someone's perception of reality. It is said that, during an exhibition of Matisse's works, a woman criticized one of the drawings, saying, "The hand doesn't look like a hand." Matisse replied, "It's not, madam. It's a drawing of a hand." Like theories, models help their authors explain various related concepts and the relationships among the various parts of the models. Models help us organize what we already know, help us see new relationships, and keep us from being dazzled by the full-blown complexity of the subject. Rather than a picture of reality, a model is intended to be a tool for thinking.

Because variation is needed in all education systems, even the best model should vary from place to place and from time to time. Like theories, models are imperfect. As more knowledge is gained about what a model portrays, the model becomes weaker, projecting a less complete image and requiring modification from time to time. Currently, there is no adequate theory of education. Because curriculum theory is a subtheory of educational theory and curriculum models represent curriculum theory, it follows, then, that no curriculum model can be perfect; and no curriculum theory can be totally adequate until a satisfactory theory of education has been developed. Meanwhile, teachers and other curriculum workers will continue to benefit from learning all they can about a variety of curriculum models. Following are some models, with strengths and weaknesses noted. As noted earlier in this chapter, education reformers have increased the use of research; however, they have failed to study the most important variable of all, the effects of each program on student learning.

The AIM Model

The AIM model is simple and clear. It begins with objectives and moves in the single direction shown by the arrows (see figure 4.1). It includes both student activities and teacher activities, but it offers no foundation elements and no philosophy statement.

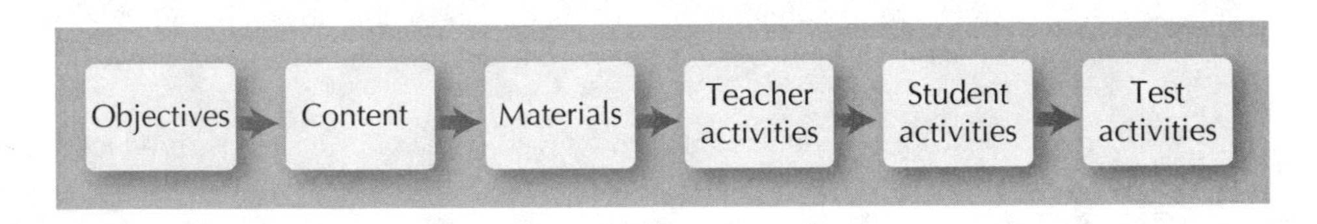

Figure 4.1 The AIM Curriculum Model

Taba's Inverted Model

Taba's approach to curriculum development is referred to as an inverted model because it begins in the classroom with the teacher, as contrasted with other models which begin in the district office, in state department offices, or in federal offices. *Taba's inverted model* has eight steps. Step 1 is diagnosing needs, using a needs assessment tool. Step 2 is formulating specific objectives, including concepts and attitudes to be learned, ways of thinking to be enforced, and habits and skills to be mastered. Step 3 is selecting content by carefully choosing topics, and writing a rationale to support each choice.

Teachers should be careful to select content and activities that parallel students' developmental levels. Table 4.1 shows the psychological stages in Piaget's developmental hierarchy reached by the majority of students at each age. However, teachers teaching for understanding do well to bear in mind factors like complexity of activities and content—but without rigid conceptions of what students can and cannot learn at certain ages.

Table 4.1 Percentage of Individuals in Piagetian Stages

Age (Years)	Preoperational	Concrete Onset	Concrete Mature	Formal Onset	Formal Mature
7	35	55	10		
8	25	55	20		
9	15	55	30		
10	12	52	35	1	
11	6	49	40	5	
12	5	32	51	12	
13	2	34	44	14	6
14	1	32	43	15	9
15	1	14	53	19	13
16	1	15	54	17	13
17	3	19	47	19	12
18	1	15	50	15	19

From G. P. Stefanich (1990, November), Cycles of cognition. *Middle School Journal, 22*(2), p. 49. Used with permission from National Middle School Association.

Step 4 is organizing the content, beginning with the simple topics on the list, exploring them in greater depth, and moving to the more difficult topics, noting the essential learner activities. (The idea is to also peek at the generalizations to be developed instead of just listing the generalizations for students.) Steps 5 and 6 are selecting and organizing experiences, ensuring that each activity has a definite function, and looking again at the developmental level of the students. What kinds of activities are needed by a given age group to develop the understandings sought? These steps include *multipurpose activities* that can help students achieve more than one objective. The activities must be ordered to make continuous and accumulative learning possible by connecting new information to previous experiences. Involvement in activities can help students see the relevance and meaning in the content they are studying. Because tasks help students to implement knowledge in genuine ways, they may also help students become aware of the relevancy and meaningfulness of what they are learning.

Step 7 is evaluating the unit continuously, noting the students' likes, and Step 8 is checking for balance and sequence, ensuring that the activities provide opportunities to learn how to generalize, that the content sequence flows, that there is balance between written and oral work and research and analysis, that different forms of expression are possible, and that the organization is open-ended, allowing students to open up and talk.

Taba's model has several unique strengths. Its inverted dimension involves teachers in its development, which gives them a level of commitment and ownership not common to other models and which prepares teachers to implement the model. Its unit base ties curriculum to instruction. Since "curriculum" is often interpreted to mean a document, as separate from instruction, too often curriculum development is thought of as disconnected from teaching. By bringing together curriculum and instruction, the model ties theory to practice.

Tyler's Ends-Means Model

Tyler's ends-means model introduced a revolutionary idea to curriculum planning. According to Tyler, the curriculum developer should start by deciding what purposes the curriculum is to have and then plan accordingly. Today this approach seems embarrassingly simple, but it was revolutionary at the time, since no curriculum developer had ever presented such a model. See figure 4.2 for a summary of Tyler's model. Tyler suggested that several ends, which he called goals, educational objectives, and purposes, be identified by examining five elements: the learners, life in the community, subject matter, philosophy, and psychology.

Figure 4.2 Tyler's Ends-Means Model

The Student as a Source

Tyler believed that a broad and comprehensive analysis of the student should be made. The curriculum developer should determine the learner's needs and wants, since that information can help educators in motivating the student to learn. The students' abilities must also be considered.

Society as a Source

Tyler believed that the process of generalizing was central to all learning. Because the learner needs to understand the environment, interacting with others is essential. This makes the local community and society at large the students' learning laboratory. By studying the community and the society, the student can find problems to solve and ways of solving them.

Subject Matter as a Source

Tyler was heavily influenced by John Dewey, who stressed learning by doing. He was also influenced by Jerome Bruner, who wrote about the structure of knowledge. They said (and Tyler agreed) that, to master a subject, one must understand its underlying structure.

Philosophy as a Source

According to Tyler, sound curriculum development begins with sound thinking, and sound thinking begins by formulating a philosophy. He believed it is necessary to define a school's philosophy. If Tyler were to lead others in curriculum development, he would insist that teachers spell out both their own individual philosophies and that of their school. In this respect, Tyler's model reflects the realization that to understand others, you must first understand yourself. To serve others you must understand both the serving agency (the school) and yourself.

Psychology as a Source

Tyler believed that effective curriculum development requires understanding the learners' levels of development and the nature of the learning process. This understanding helps to refine the list of objectives. Curriculum workers should use philosophy and psychology as "screens," filtering out objectives that are beyond students' capacity to attain and those that run counter to the faculty's philosophy (Oliva, 2009).

Aligning content with expectations reflects the constructivist philosophy. Tyler's philosophy involved beginning with what we want the students to know and be able to do, and then designing the content and activities accordingly. Might we say that teachers should begin designing every lesson by examining their own philosophies? Each of us can use our unique philosophy and expectations to design goals, content, and activities.

The Oliva Models

Oliva first introduced a curriculum development model in 1976 (see figure 4.3). In 1992 he expanded this model, as shown in figure 4.4. His intention was to develop a model for curriculum development that was simple, comprehensive, and systematic.

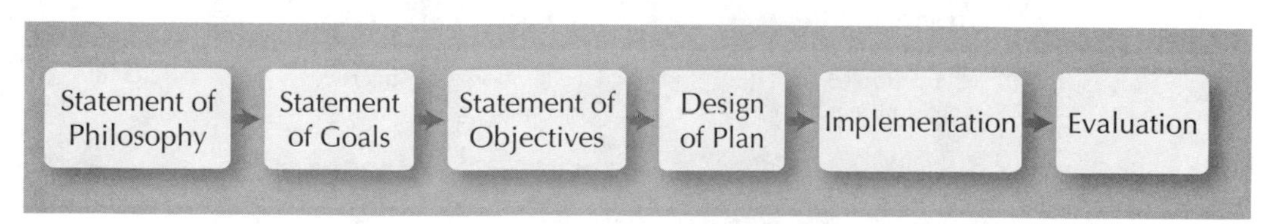

From Peter F. Oliva, *Developing the Curriculum*, 3/E. Published by Allyn & Bacon, Boston, MA. Copyright © 1992 by Pearson Education. Reprinted by permission of the publisher.

Figure 4.3 Oliva's 1976 Model for Curriculum Development

The Twelve Components

Figure 4.4 shows a comprehensive, step-by-step process that takes the curriculum planner from the sources of the curriculum to evaluation. In the figure, the squares represent planning phases; the circles, operational phases. The process starts with component I, at which time the curriculum developers state the aims of education and their philosophical and psychological principles. These aims are based on beliefs about the needs of our society and the needs of individuals living in our society. This component incorporates concepts similar to Tyler's use of philosophy and psychology as "screens."

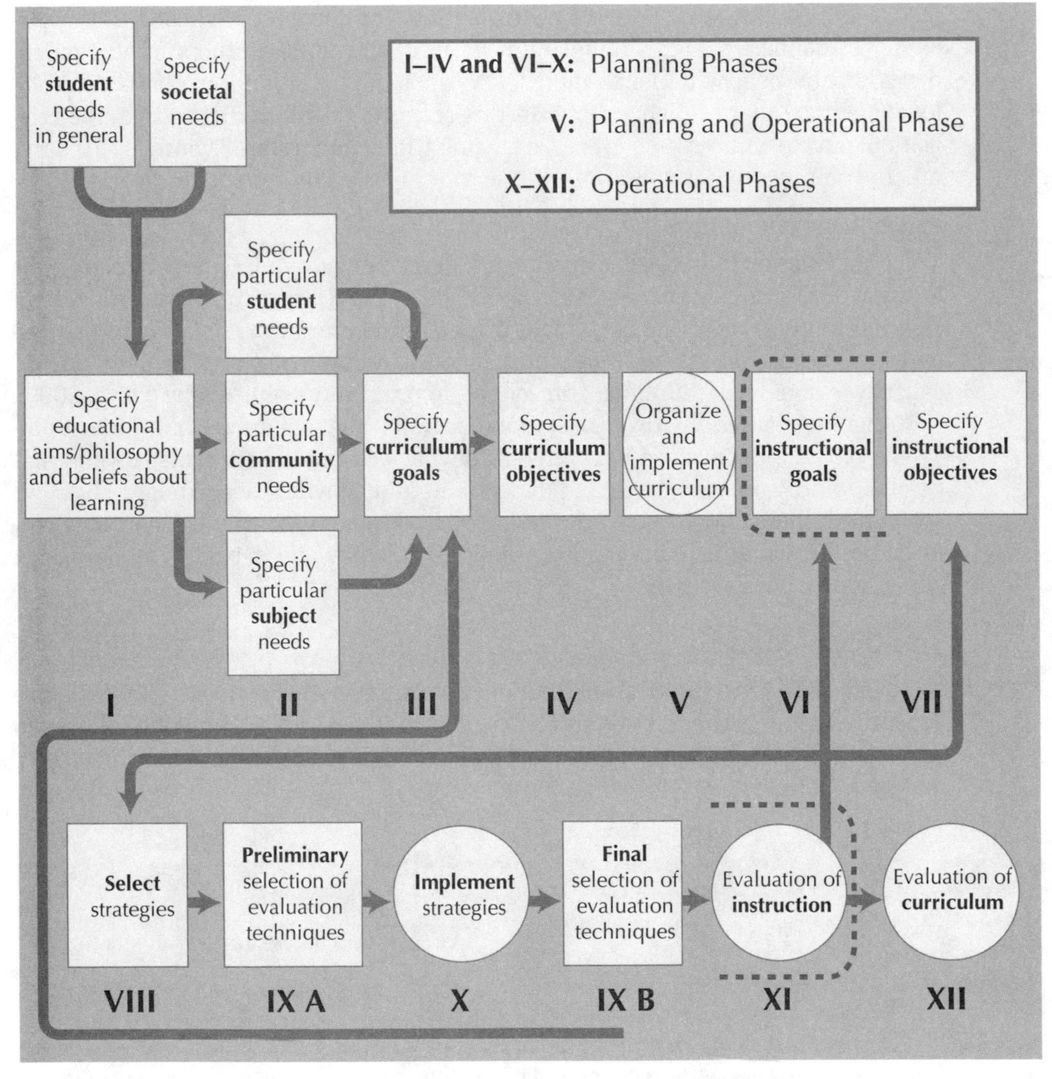

From Peter F. Oliva, *Developing the Curriculum*, 3/E. Published by Allyn & Bacon, Boston, MA. Copyright © 1992 by Pearson Education. Reprinted by permission of the publisher.

Figure 4.4 Oliva's 1992 Model for Curriculum Development

Component II requires an analysis of the needs of the community in which the school is located, the needs of students served in that community, and the exigencies of the subject matter that will be taught in the given school. Sources of the curriculum are seen as cutting across components I and II. Whereas component I treats the needs of students and society in a more general sense, component II introduces the concepts of needs of particular students in particular localities, because the needs of students in particular communities are not always the same as the general needs of students throughout our society.

Components III and IV call for specifying curricular goals and objectives based on the aims, beliefs, and needs specified in components I and II. A distinction that will be clarified later with examples is made between goals and objectives. The tasks of component V are to organize and implement the curriculum and to formulate and establish the structure by which the curriculum will be organized.

In components VI and VII an increasing level of specification is sought. Instructional goals and objectives are stated for each level and subject. A distinction between goals and objectives is visually portrayed.

After specifying instructional objectives, the curriculum worker moves to component VIII and chooses instructional strategies for use with students in the classroom. Simultaneously, the curriculum worker initiates the preliminary selection of evaluation techniques, phase A of component IX. At this stage, the curriculum planner thinks ahead and begins to consider ways to assess student achievement. The implementation of instructional strategies—component X—follows.

After the students have been provided appropriate opportunities to learn (component X), the planner returns to the problem of selecting techniques for evaluating student achievement and instructor effectiveness. Component IX, then, is divided into two phases: the first precedes the implementation of instruction (IX A), and the second follows the implementation (IX B). The instructional phase (component X) provides the planner with the opportunity to refine, add to, and complete the selection of means to evaluate pupil performance.

Evaluation of instruction is carried out during component XI. Component XII completes the cycle, with evaluation not of the student or the teacher but rather of the curricular program. In this model, components I to IV and VI to IX are planning phases, whereas components X to XII are operational phases. Component V is both a planning and an operational phase.

Like some other models, this model combines a scheme for curriculum development (components I to V and XII) and a design for instruction (components VI to XI).

The feedback lines that cycle back from the evaluation of the curriculum to the curriculum goals and from the evaluation of instruction to the instructional goals are important features of the model. These lines indicate the necessity of continuous revision of the components of their respective subcycles.

Use of the Model

The model can be used in a variety of ways. First, it offers a process for the complete development of a school's curriculum. By following the model, the faculty of each special area, for example, language arts, can fashion a plan for the curriculum of that area and design ways in which it will be carried out through instruction. Or the faculty can develop schoolwide, interdisciplinary programs that cut across areas of specialization such as career education, guidance, and extra-class activities.

Second, a faculty can focus on the curricular components of the model (components I to V and XII) to make programmatic decisions. Third, a faculty can concentrate on the instructional components (VI to XI).

Summary of the Oliva Model

A particular strength of the Oliva model is its inclusion of foundations. The original model requires a statement of philosophy, which is extremely important and, unfortunately, is not common among curriculum documents. Oliva's revised model includes societal and student needs, which are also invaluable parts of curriculum models.

The Saylor and Alexander Model

Saylor and Alexander (1966) introduced a curriculum model that has very strong foundations (see figure 4.5). This model was designed to suggest a process for selecting learner activities. A special strength of this model is its comprehensiveness. In a sense, it connects the curriculum with instruction by showing that teaching methods and strategies result from the curriculum plan. Another major strength of the model is that all steps in its suggested curriculum development process are grounded in social, philosophical, and psychological foundations.

Macdonald's Model

Macdonald (Macdonald & Leeper, 1965) perceived teaching as a personality system (the teacher) acting in a professional role and learning as a personality system (the student) performing task-related (learning) behaviors. He defined instruction as the social system within which formal teaching and learning take place, and curriculum as the social system that eventuates in a plan of instruction. Macdonald used a Venn diagram (see figure 4.6 on p. 148) to illustrate the model's parts and their relationships. He defined the intersecting parts of the diagram as follows:

V. Concomitant learning

VI. Behavior modification through teacher feedback

VII. In-service experiences

VIII. Supervision experiences

IX. Pupil-teacher planning experiences

X. Pupil-teacher planning experiences

A strength of Macdonald's model is in its presentation of the relationships among the model's various elements. Such relationships are essential if curriculum is a structural series of intended learning outcomes, as he perceived.

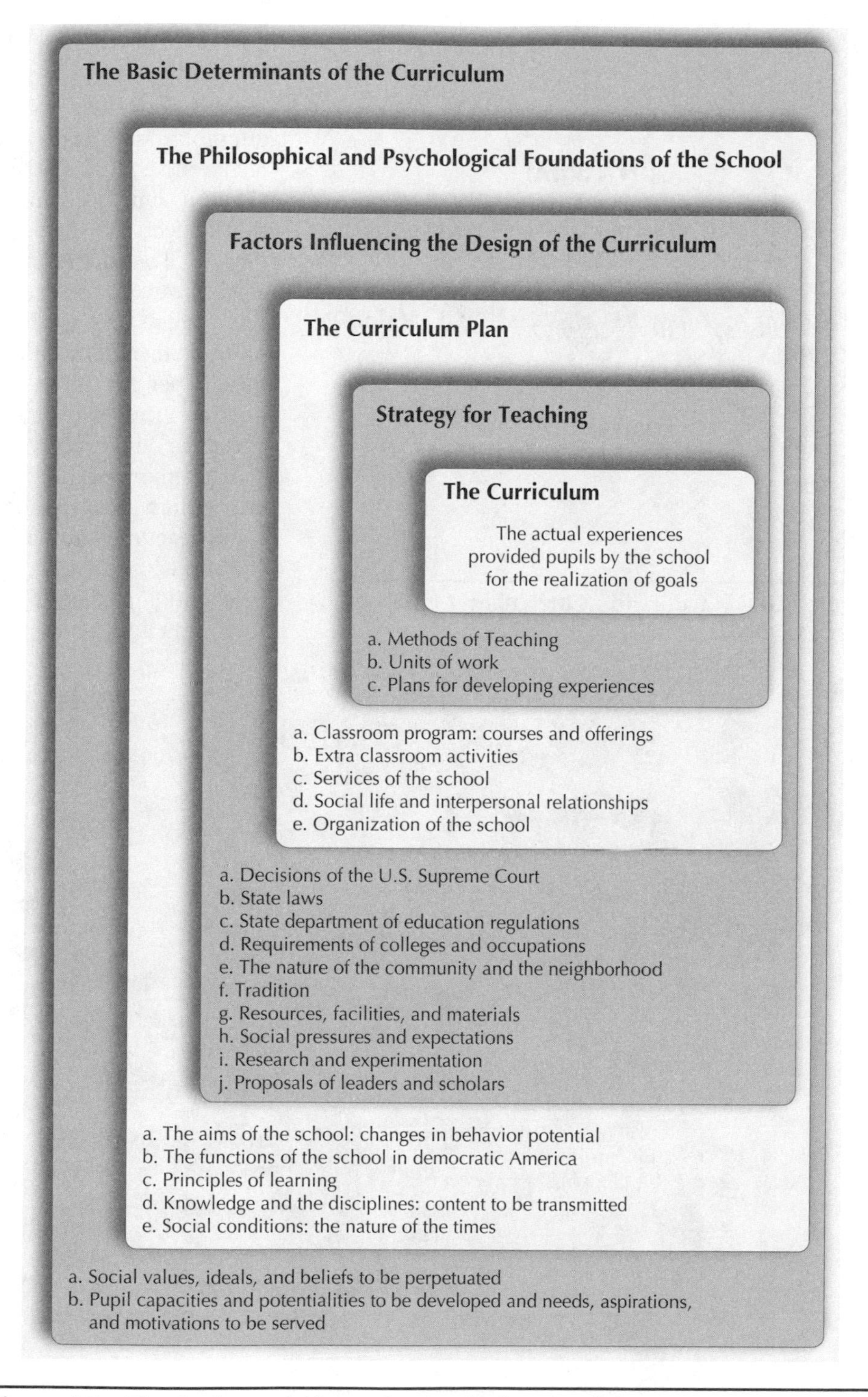

Figure 4.5 The Saylor and Alexander Curriculum Model

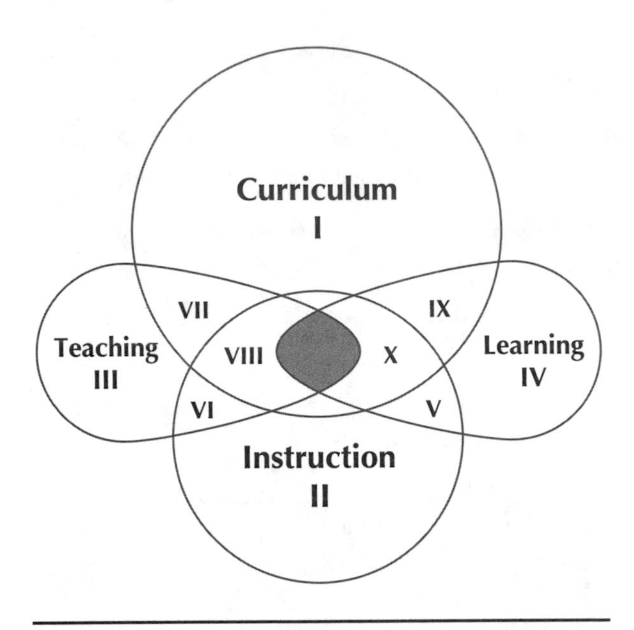

Figure 4.6 Macdonald's Curriculum Model

The Zais Eclectic Model

Figure 4.7 is a simple eclectic model developed by Zais that attempts to portray in static terms the components of the curriculum and the principal forces that affect its substance and design. The model is not concerned with processes of curriculum construction, development, or implementation—or even with design per se. Its purpose is to portray graphically the principal variables, and their relationships, that planners need to consider in curriculum construction.

The curriculum is shown in the model as a somewhat formless entity girdled by a double line. This indicates that, although

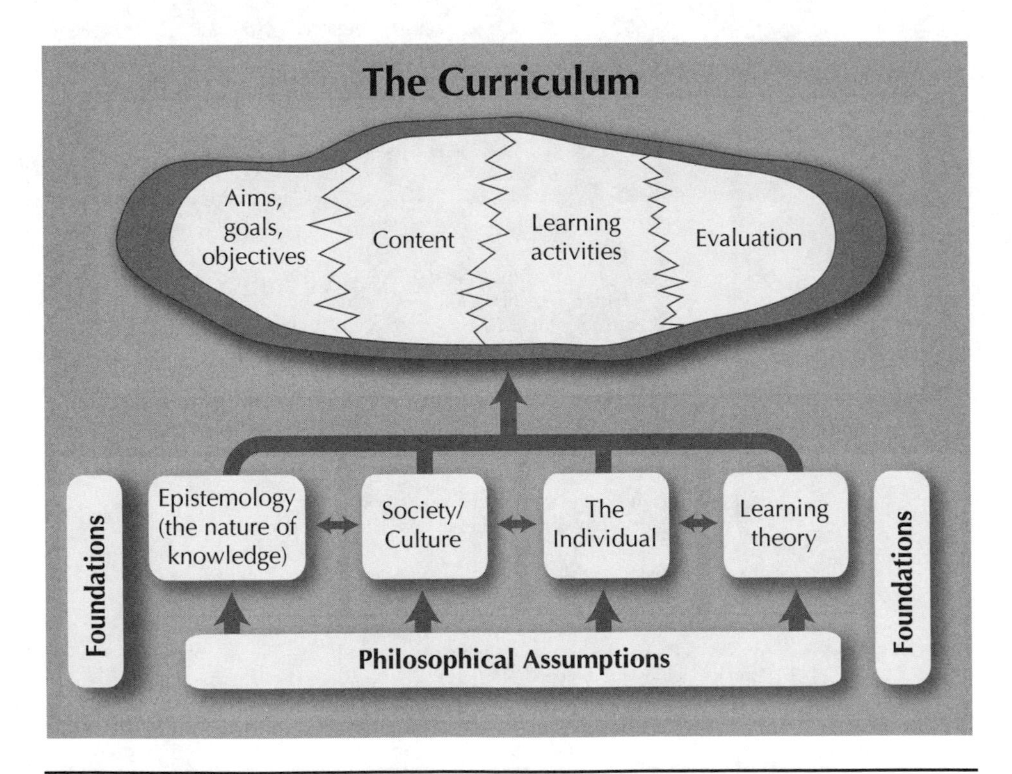

Figure 4.7 The Zais Model of the Curriculum and Its Foundations

the boundaries of the curriculum (as we currently understand them) are somewhat ill-defined, it is essentially an integrated entity. Within the double line the components that make up the curriculum (aims/goals/objectives, content, learning activities, and evaluation) are separated by jagged lines. This is meant to emphasize the relatedness of each component to all the others and to suggest that, as in a jigsaw puzzle, all the pieces should fit precisely to produce a coherent picture.

The four foundation blocks to the curriculum (below the "formless entity") indicate the influence of curriculum foundations on the content and organization of *curriculum components* (i.e., the curriculum design). In other words, we might say that the foundation blocks represent the soil and climate which determine the nature of the curriculum "plant." Each foundation block is joined to the others by double-headed arrows, suggesting the interrelatedness of all the areas. Although intimately connected, the foundation blocks do not, as do the curriculum components, form a unified whole. Undergirding the four foundation blocks is the broad area of philosophical assumptions. This aspect of the model indicates that, consciously or unconsciously, basic philosophical assumptions influence value judgments made about the foundations.

The Zais eclectic model, dealing only with the static nature of a portion of the curriculum enterprise, is quite modest. Yet it is highly significant because it addresses what is probably the most crucial of curriculum issues: the nature of the curriculum and the forces that determine its content and organization. It is interesting to note in this regard that far more attention has been paid in the literature to prescribing processes of curriculum development and change than to developing an understanding of the bases and nature of the curriculum itself. This typically American emphasis on activity and "how to do it," however, does not seem to have borne much fruit. Experience shows that in spite of a surplus of instruction and of activity in the processes of curriculum improvement and change, the curriculum remains controlled for the most part by the forces and events of historical accident, to say nothing of the influences of fashion and fad. In short, superficial understanding has apparently generated superficial strategies that get superficial results.

The Parallel Curriculum Model

According to Tomlinson and her colleagues (2002), curriculum should:

- guide students in mastering key information, ideas, and the fundamental skills of the disciplines
- help students grapple with complex and ambiguous issues and problems
- move students from novice toward expert levels of performance in the disciplines
- provide students opportunities for original work in the disciplines
- help students encounter, accept, and ultimately embrace challenge in learning
- prepare students for a world in which knowledge expands and changes at a dizzying pace
- help students determine constants in the past and in themselves while helping them prepare for a changing world

- help students develop a sense of themselves as well as of their possibilities in the world in which they live
- be compelling and satisfying enough to encourage students to persist in developing their capacities (p. 3)

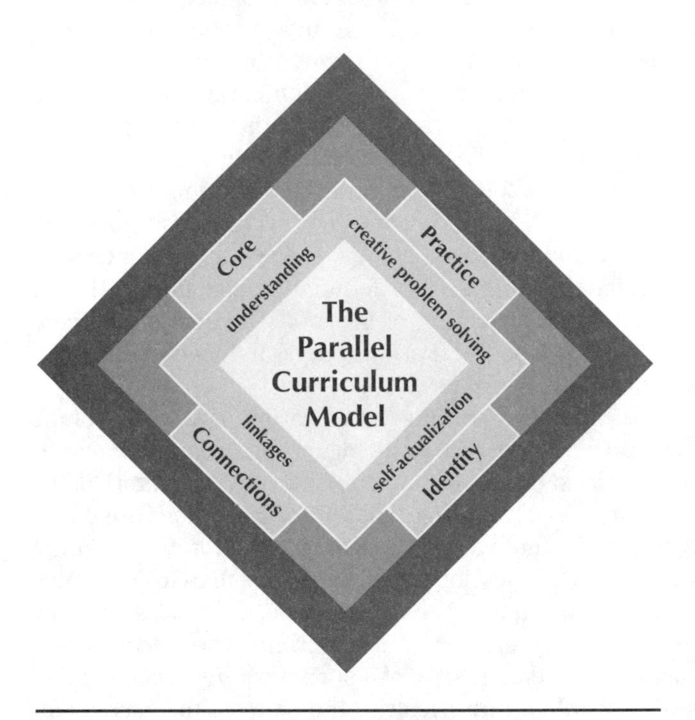

Figure 4.8 The Parallel Curriculum Model

Further, intelligence is conceived and expressed somewhat differently in different cultures. Therefore, educators should be aware of varied cultural conceptions and expressions of intelligence and should design learning opportunities that both honor diverse perspectives and develop multiple manifestations of intelligence (Tomlinson et al., p. 4). Proponents of the *parallel curriculum model* believe it possible to meet all these criteria, and more.

Tomlinson and her colleagues (2002) compare student perceptions about their learning experiences to the old fable about seven blind men who encountered an elephant: Because each man felt a different part of the beast, none was able to figure out its true nature. Similarly, "students learn only bits and pieces of the curriculum over time, never seeing, let alone understanding, the larger whole that is mankind's accumulated knowledge." Tomlinson et al. (2002) posit the following scenario:

> What if we were able to design curriculum in a multifaceted way to ensure that all learners understand (1) the nature of knowledge, (2) the connections that link mankind's knowledge, (3) the methodology of the practitioner who creates knowledge, and (4) the "fit" between the learner's values and goals and those that characterize practicing professionals? How would classrooms be different if the focus of curriculum was *qualitatively differentiated curriculum* that prompts learners not only to accumulate information, but also to experience the power of knowledge and their potential role within it?

The National Association for Gifted Children (NAGC) released the parallel curriculum model, suggesting that all learners should have the opportunity to "experience the elephant" and benefit from seeing the whole. The NAGC (2005) defines the parallel curriculum model as "an integrated framework and set of procedures for designing rigorous and highly motivating curriculum that attends to important student differences."

The model centers on four parallels: the core curriculum, the curriculum of connections, the curriculum of practice, and the curriculum of identity. The model's four parallels serve as

> . . . unique polishing tools to reveal the brilliance in each young person. The *Core* fosters deep understanding in a discipline, while *Connections* elicit the metaphoric thinking required to span the breadth of man's knowledge. *Practice* advances the methodological skills required to contribute in a field, and *Identity* cultivates the attitudes, values, and life outlook that are prerequisites to self-actualization in a field. (Purcell et al., 2002)

For a fascinating case study about how one teacher developed expertise in using the four parallels over several years, see the Purcell et al. (2002) article, "The Parallel Curriculum Model (PCM): The Whole Story."

Examples of Models in Action

Although we may have a tendency to think of models as programs on paper, we should realize that many versions and modifications of models are lived out in all ongoing programs. Following is a discussion of some excellent programs that put models into action, including: Project ESCAPE, the Alverno Program, and the American Studies Experiential Education Program.

Project ESCAPE

Although much disagreement on the pros and cons of education reform can be found among educators at all levels, most educators agree that there is always room for improving school programs. Constant improvement depends on a steady flow of credible ideas and innovations and a central power that wants and promotes change. Since part of the responsibility for introducing effective innovations must be borne by teacher education programs, the continuous flow of elementary and secondary school curriculum innovations requires an equally continuous flow of innovations among teacher education programs. In other words, our teacher education institutions must be wellsprings of curriculum improvement. A program that reflects much of the current thinking among both educators and layperson critics is described below.

With its origins as a normal school, the School of Education at Indiana State University has a history of developing innovative programs and offering them as models to other teacher preparation programs throughout the nation. One such program is called Project ESCAPE, an acronym for Elementary and Secondary Cooperative Approach to Performance Education. This program was created to provide an alternative to those education students who prefer classroom-based programs over traditional university-based programs.

A major difference between this program and traditional teacher education programs is its competency base, but perhaps its most profound difference is that all of the competencies are developed in elementary and secondary classrooms instead of in traditional teacher education courses.

The program began with the identification of 25 elementary master teachers and 25 secondary master teachers, selected by their principals. These teachers examined their own classes and identified the one major area of teacher skills that would profit most from improvement. Then each teacher was given the sample learning module shown in box 4.1 and asked to develop a learning module. The only restrictions were that the module should be highly tactile, visual, and activity-based and should not require extensive reading.

Box 4.1 Sample Learning Module: Spelling Words with *ie* and *ei*

Objectives

The purpose of this module is to focus attention on commonly misspelled ie/ei words. Completion of the following specific objective is required for satisfactory demonstration of this competency.

Spell correctly 100% of the words in the list containing the *ie/ei* element.

Rationale

To be considered an educated person, a student must spell correctly. This judgment may be illogical, but it is inescapable. Of course, spelling itself is essential to good writing.

Module Guide

1. Read the objectives and the rationale.
2. Take the preassessment. If you score 100%, you have completed the module.
3. Do the instructional activities.
4. Take the post-assessment.

Preassessment

Ask someone to dictate to you the words listed in the post-assessment. Try to write them correctly. If you score 100%, you have completed the module.

Instructional Activities

1. Memorize the following rhyme:
   I before e
   except after c
   or when sounded like a
   as in neighbor or weigh
2. Memorize the following exceptions to the rhyme:
   a. leisure c. seize e. their
   b. neither d. weird

Post-assessment

Have someone dictate the following list to you. Try to spell the words correctly. A score of 100% is required for completion of the module.

a. achieve e. ceiling i. freight m. seize
b. apiece f. conceited j. heinous n. their
c. belief g. deceived k. neighbor o. veil
d. neither h. received 1. reign p. weigh

Remediation

If you have scored less than 100% on the post-assessment, repeat the instructional activities with the help of your module resource person.

Once developed, each module was assessed to determine the approximate number of hours required to complete it. These contact hours were divided by 15 to arrive at a comparative number of semester credit hours. For example, a module that required 45 hours to complete was assigned 3 credit hours. The lengths of those 48 ESCAPE modules ranged from 0.5 credit hours to 3.5 credit hours. Each module was supported by a rationale designed to inform students of the benefits it offers, to encourage students to choose the module. A sample rationale statement is shown in box 4.2.

Box 4.2 Sample Rationale Statement

When teachers begin to plan for the learning activities of their pupils, they assume roles of decision makers as to what and how curriculum content is to be taught, as well as to what activities and behaviors will be engaged in by the pupils and teachers. These decisions cannot be guided by their preferences alone. There are certain rules and regulations that are imposed by the state, the school corporation, and the local school that limit their complete autonomy in these matters. To ensure secure legal positions in their classrooms, the teachers must have a knowledge of these rules and regulations and must work within the framework imposed by these regulations.

Today, teachers are being held accountable for the educational decisions that they make. More and more teachers are having to defend their actions in court. There are at least three reasons why this is true: the decline in reliance on the doctrine of "sovereign immunity" of school districts, students' increasing knowledge of these legal rights coupled with changing attitudes toward teachers and schools, and the decline of the acceptance of *in loco parentis* as a legal theory.

It is well worth noting that much of the court litigation resulting in severe penalties for the teacher might have been avoided had the teacher had knowledge of the law. Often teachers are not aware of their legal responsibilities and limitations.

As shown in figure 4.9 (on the following page), each module is accompanied by a flowchart to help guide the student. Each module has a self-evaluation and a preassessment (which is the same as the post-assessment). If a student passes the preassessment, the student receives credit and is not required to complete the module (see table 4.2 on pp. 154–155).

A list of the 48 different modules is given in box 4.3 (pp. 156–157). Some modules focus on skills and content that are considered indispensable for all teachers; these modules are required of all students. Other modules are optional, and individual students must choose from among the optional modules to obtain enough credits to fulfill their state's teacher certification requirements.

A final note of interest to curriculum workers is the module evaluation instrument (see table 4.2). Particular attention should be paid to the fact that this instrument is not designed to measure student performance; its purpose is to provide ongoing quality control for the module.

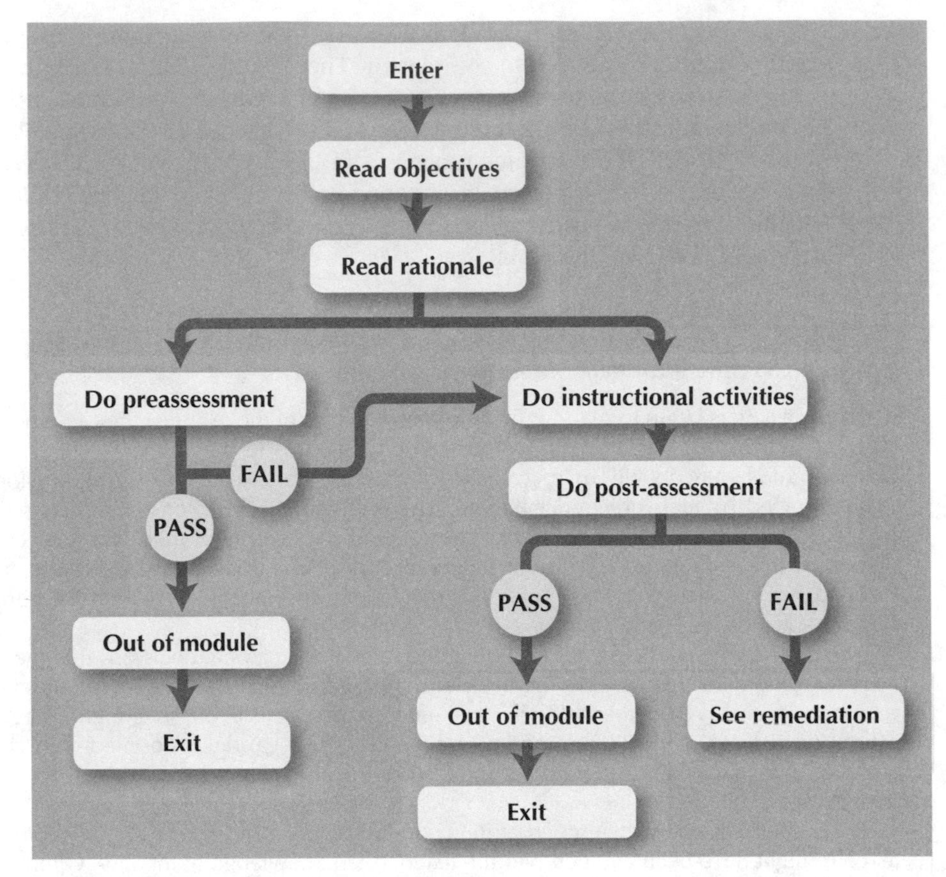

From *A module on modules.* Terre Haute, IN: Vigo County School Systems/Indiana State University. Used with permission.

Figure 4.9 Module Guide for Students

Table 4.2 Module Evaluation Instrument

	Unsatisfactory (0 points)	Satisfactory (1 point)	Very Satisfactory (2 points)	Not Applicable
1. Was the format easily read?	______	______	______	______
2. Were the objectives stated in behavioral terms?	______	______	______	______
3. During the initial introduction of the lesson, was adequate attention given to the review of facts and concepts learned in the previous lesson?	______	______	______	______

	Unsatisfactory (0 points)	Satisfactory (1 point)	Very Satisfactory (2 points)	Not Applicable
4. Were key questions listed in order to determine the pupil's comprehension and application of the concept reviewed?	______	______	______	______
5. Were the concepts, facts, or examples relating to the achievement of the objectives listed?	______	______	______	______
6. Was the step-by-step development of the lesson clearly outlined?				
7. Was a variety of activities provided to meet individual differences in needs, interests, and abilities of the pupils?	______	______	______	______
8. Were the pupils' learning activities meaningful enough to be conducive to achieving the objectives?	______	______	______	______
9. Was the summary complete enough to ensure a basis for the next lesson?	______	______	______	______
10. Were provisions made for flexibility?	______	______	______	______

Alverno College

Another innovative teacher education program is located in Milwaukee, Wisconsin. Like Project ESCAPE, the Alverno College program is outcomes based and performance based. Box 4.5 (on pp. 158–160) shows the general abilities required of Alverno students and their respective levels of mastery.

Students learn more when they use assessments to evaluate their own learning, and they have greater feelings of efficacy about their academic abilities (Stiggins, 2008). An important feature of the Alverno program is continuous self-assessment. Many contemporary K–12 education reform programs require students to assess their own progress. Another important feature of the Alverno program is the recognition that students can achieve at various levels of mastery. As Alverno students increase their levels of mastery, they earn more units of credits. All students are required to earn high levels of mastery in some areas of performance.

Experiential Curriculum: American Studies Program at Central High

One of the most promising yet underused types of curricula that is equally attractive to all subject areas and all grade levels is *experiential curriculum*. Students enjoy experiential programs because of the opportunities they give students

Box 4.3 ESCAPE Modules

I. Organizing and Teaching Subject Matter
   A. Planning
      101—Curriculum—fitting the curriculum of a subject or grade level into the total academic program
      102—Planning and Teaching a Unit—developing, executing, and evaluating plans with a central theme
      103—A Daily Lesson Plan—developing, executing, and evaluating a daily lesson plan
      104—Conference Planning—familiarizing the student (teacher) with procedures and organization of conference planning for an entire class
   B. Techniques for Teaching Subject Matter
      111—Principles of Reinforcement—identifying and applying various reinforcement methods in the classroom
      112—Asking Questions—asking higher-order questions
      113—A Module on Modules—identifying parts of a module

II. Human Dynamics of Teaching
   A. Teacher–Pupil Interaction
      201—Motivation—using Maslow's Hierarchy of Human Basic Needs to assist motivational learning activities
      202—Consistency—demonstrating use of consistency with pupils in and out of the classroom
      203—Classroom Management—demonstrating skills and techniques utilizing the democratic process in the classroom
      204—Reinforcement Techniques in Written Work—using written reinforcement techniques on written work
      205—Handling Discipline Problems Objectively—recognizing and handling discipline problems
      206—Humor in Education—demonstrating a sense of humor in the classroom
   B. Diagnosing Classroom Climate
      211—The Sociogram: Social Isolates—using the sociogram to identify social isolates and prescribing a suitable remedy
      212—Learning Difficulties—diagnosing learning difficulties and prescribing appropriate teaching–learning strategies
      213—Children's Misbehavior Goals—identifying and dealing with children's misbehavior goals as described by Adler
   C. Teacher–Pupil Relationships
      221—Empathetic Responses—aiding in developing empathetic responses
      222—Group Structure and Dynamics—reviewing group processes and their effects upon dynamics and task achievement
      223—Attitude Feedback—measuring and finding a means to a positive attitude
      224—Value Clarification—defining values and related behavioral problems
      225—Recognizing Enthusiasm—identifying verbal and nonverbal behaviors which demonstrate enthusiastic teaching and assessing the consequences of those behaviors

III. Developing Teaching Skills
   A. Technical Skills of Teaching
      301—Handwriting—demonstrating the ability to form letters according to the curriculum guide of the student's (teacher's) school
      302—Use of Instructional Media—developing and executing an instructional presentation demonstrating the proper operational techniques of audiovisual media
      303—Plan Book–Grade Book: Development and Utilization—developing and using a plan book and a grade book to meet the needs of a student's (teacher's) teaching situation
      304—Utilizing and Supplementing Cumulative Records—familiarizing the student (teacher) with ten pupils through cumulative records, observations, and interviews
      305—Parent Conferences—conducting a parent-teacher conference
      306—Field Trips—planning and/or executing a field trip

B. Varied Approaches to Teaching
 311—Individualizing Instruction—demonstrating techniques of individualizing instruction
 312—Guided Discovery—using the guided discovery technique
 313—Problem Solving—using the problem-solving technique
 314—Performance-Based Education in the Classroom—preparing and implementing a performance-based lesson plan identifying specified skills or competencies
 315—Creativity—describing and demonstrating the humanistic teaching technique of creativity
 316—Individual Needs—using activities for meeting individual performance levels

C. Verbal Communication in Teaching
 321—Enunciation—focusing attention on and corrective measures for commonly mispronounced words
 322—Communicating on the Pupil's Level—restating a school directive at the pupil's level of understanding
 323—Voice Simulation—using voice simulations in storytelling, story reading, and role playing
 324—Listening Skills—using listening variables and reacting to pupil comments to facilitate better pupil understanding
 325—Lecture and Demonstration—describing and practicing lecture and demonstration techniques

IV. Professional Responsibilities

A. Policies and Regulations for the Classroom
 401—Rules and Regulations—familiarizing the student (teacher) with state and local regulations, requirements, and curriculum policies
 402—Emergency Preparedness—demonstrating knowledge of and developing a plan for federal, state, and local Emergency Preparedness Plans
 403—School Policy—demonstrating knowledge of local policies and procedures as presented in policy handbooks
 404—Good Health—demonstrating the importance of a working knowledge of health factors in education

B. Professional Contributions of the Classroom Teacher
 411—Professional Organizations—learning about professional educational organizations
 412—Code of Ethics—demonstrating a knowledge of ethical behavior
 413—Legal Responsibility of the Teacher—demonstrating legal responsibility
 414—School Communication and the Community—demonstrating the ability to communicate with the community through various media
 415—Co-Curricular Activities—identifying common problems of and participating in activities not part of the regular academic program
 416—Professional Growth—demonstrating a knowledge of professionalism, an awareness of impedances to it, opportunities and resources for growth, and professional responsibilities

Box 4.4 Competencies Printout Used in Interviews

The purpose of this printout is to attest to the fact that [*name of student*] has demonstrated a mastery level of competence in the following teaching behaviors:

In the area of PLANNING, [*name of student*] has demonstrated a mastery level of expertise in [for students who completed Module 101] fitting the curriculum of a subject or grade level into the total academic program; [for students who completed Module 102] developing, executing, and evaluating plans with a central theme; [for students who completed Module 103] developing, executing, and evaluating a daily lesson plan; and [for students who completed Module 104] planning and organizing a conference planning session for an entire class.

In the area of TEACHING STRATEGIES, [*name of student*] has demonstrated a high level of competence in . . .

Box 4.5 Alverno College Ability-Based Learning Program*

Abilities and Developments

1. Communication: Speaking, Writing, Listening, Reading, Quantitative Literacy, Computer Literacy

Beginning Levels: Uses self assessment to identify and evaluate communication performance
Level 1—Recognizes own strengths and weaknesses in different modes of communication
Level 2—Recognizes the processes involved in each mode of communication and the interactions among them

Intermediate Levels: Communicates using discipline concepts and frameworks with growing understanding
Level 3—Uses communication processes purposefully to make meaning in different disciplinary contexts
Level 4—Connects discrete modes of communication and integrates them effectively within the frameworks of a discipline

Advanced Levels in Areas of Specialization: Performs clearly and sensitively in increasingly more creative and engaging presentations
Level 5—Selects, adapts, and combines communication strategies in relation to disciplinary/professional frameworks and theories
Level 6—Uses strategies, theories, and technologies that reflect engagement in a discipline or profession

2. **Analysis**

Beginning Levels: Observes individual parts of phenomena and their relationships to one another
Level 1—Observes accurately
Level 2—Draws reasonable inferences from observations

Intermediate Levels: Uses disciplinary concepts and frameworks with growing understanding
Level 3—Perceives and makes relationships
Level 4—Analyzes structure and organization

Advanced Levels in Areas of Specialization: Consciously and purposefully applies disciplinary frameworks to analyze complex phenomena
Level 5—Refines understanding of frameworks and identifies criteria for determining what frameworks are suitable for explaining a phenomenon
Level 6—Applies frameworks from major and minor discipline independently to analyze complex issues

3. **Problem Solving**

Beginning Levels: Articulates problem solving process and understands how a discipline framework is used to solve a problem
Level 1—Articulates problem solving process by making explicit the steps taken to approach a problem
Level 2—Practices using elements of disciplinary problem solving processes to approach problems

Intermediate Levels: Takes thoughtful responsibility for process and proposed solutions to problems
Level 3—Performs all phases or steps within a disciplinary problem solving process, including evaluation and real or simulated implementation
Level 4—Independently analyzes, selects, uses, and evaluates various approaches to develop solutions

Advanced Levels in Areas of Specialization: Uses problem solving strategies in a wide variety of professional situations
Level 5—Demonstrates capacity to transfer understanding of group processes into effective performance in collaborative problem solving
Level 6—Applies methods and frameworks of profession/discipline(s): integrating them with personal values and perspectives; adapting them to the specific field setting; demonstrating independence and creativity in structuring and carrying out problem solving activities

*Alverno faculty are constantly engaged in refining and extending their understanding of the abilities and their developmental levels. If you are interested in further refinements, please contact the Alverno College Institute.

4. Valuing in Decision-Making

Beginning Levels: Explores the valuing process

Level 1—Identifies own and others' values and some key emotions they evoke

Level 2—Connects own values to behavior and articulates the cognitive and spiritual dimensions of this process

Intermediate Levels: More precisely analyzes the role of groups, cultures, and societies in the construction of values and their expression in moral systems or ethical frameworks

Level 3—Analyzes reciprocal relationship between own values and their social contexts and explores how that relationship plays out

Level 4—Uses the perspectives and concepts of particular disciplines to inform moral judgments and decisions

Advanced Levels in Areas of Specialization: Explores and applies value systems and ethical codes at the heart of the field

Level 5—Uses valuing frameworks of a major field of study or profession to engage significant issues in personal, professional, and civic contexts

Level 6—Consistently examines and cultivates own value systems in order to take initiative as a responsible self in the world

Developmental Levels

5. Social Interaction

Beginning Levels: Learns frameworks and self assessment skills to support interpersonal and task-oriented group interactions

Level 1—Recognizes analytic frameworks as an avenue to becoming aware of own behaviors in interactions and to participating fully in those interactions

Level 2—Gains insight into the affective and practical ramifications of interactions in their social and cultural context

Intermediate Levels: Uses analytic frameworks and self awareness to engage with others in increasingly effective interaction across a range of situations

Level 3—Increases effectiveness in group and interpersonal interaction based on careful analysis and awareness of self and others in social and cultural contexts

Level 4—Displays and continues to practice increasingly effective interactions in group and interpersonal situations reflecting cognitive understanding of social and cultural contexts and awareness of affective components of own and others' behavior

Advanced Levels in Areas of Specialization: Integrates discipline-specific frameworks with social interaction models to function effectively with diverse stakeholders in professional roles

Level 5—Consistently and with increasing autonomy demonstrates effective professional interaction using multiple disciplinary frameworks to interpret behavior and monitor own interaction choices

Level 6—Uses leadership abilities to facilitate achievement of professional goals in effective interpersonal and group interactions

6. Developing a Global Perspective

Beginning Levels: Identifies what shapes own opinions and judgments with regard to global issues, as well as the extent to which these opinions and judgments reflect multiple perspectives

Level 1—Assesses own knowledge and skills with regard to ability to think about and act on global concerns

Level 2—Examines the complex relationships that make up global issues

Intermediate Levels: Incorporates response to multiple perspectives and uses frameworks from disciplines to reflect on own judgments about issues

Level 3—Uses disciplinary concepts and frameworks to gather information to explore possible responses to global issues

Level 4—Uses frameworks from a variety of disciplines to clarify and articulate own informed judgment on the issues

(continued)

Advanced Levels in Areas of Specialization: Refines general abilities by integrating them with frameworks and concerns of major areas of study to further develop own global perspective

Level 5—Uses theory to generate pragmatic approaches to specific global issues

Level 6—Creatively and independently proposes theoretical and pragmatic approaches to specific global concerns

7. Effective Citizenship

Beginning Levels: Identifies significant community issues and assesses ability to act on them

Level 1—Develops self assessment skills and begins to identify frameworks to describe community experience

Level 2—Uses discipline concepts to describe what makes an issue an issue and to develop skills necessary to gather information, make sound judgments, and participate in the decision making process

Intermediate Levels: Works within both organizational and community contexts to apply developing citizenship skills

Level 3—Learns how to "read an organization" in terms of how individuals work with others to achieve common goals

Level 4—Develops both a strategy for action and criteria for evaluating the effectiveness of plans

Advanced Levels in Areas of Specialization: Takes a leadership role in addressing organizational and community issues

Level 5—Works effectively in the civic or professional realm and works effectively with others to develop their ability to participate

Level 6—Tests developing theory, anticipating problems that are likely to emerge, and devising ways to deal with them

8. Aesthetic Engagement

Beginning Levels: Develops an openness to the arts

Level 1—Makes informed artistic and interpretive choices

Level 2—Articulates rationale for artistic choices and interpretations

Intermediate Levels: Refines artistic and interpretive choices by integrating own aesthetic experiences with a broader context of disciplinary theory and cultural and social awareness

Level 3—Revises choices by integrating disciplinary contexts

Level 4—Develops awareness of creative and interpretive processes

Advanced Levels in Areas of Specialization: Creates works of art and/or interpretive strategies and theories that synthesize personal preferences and disciplinary concepts

Level 5—Develops and expresses personal aesthetic vision

Level 6—Integrates aesthetic vision into academic, professional, and personal life

From Alverno College Faculty (1972/2005), *Ability-based learning program*. Reprinted with permission of the Alverno College Institute, Milwaukee, Wisconsin.

to be involved in "real-life" activities. This type of curriculum is a favorite of the medical profession, for obvious reasons. However, experiential curricula can be created for a surprisingly wide range of programs. Teachers appreciate experiential programs for their power to motivate students. Following is a description of a successful experientially based program.

What can a school do to generate enthusiasm among students for nonbasic courses? In the American Studies Program at Central High School in Tuscaloosa, Alabama, students look forward to going to jail.*

*This program description first appeared in J. Ingram, K. T. Henson, & A. Crew (1984, December), American studies at Central High. *Phi Delta Kappan*, 66(4), 296–297.

The American Studies Program was conceived in response to a federal court ruling that achieved racial desegregation by pairing two recently built segregated high schools. Although this measure eliminated segregation in the schools, many people felt that it did so at the expense of the students' community identity. And many students did indeed respond negatively to the ruling. The level of participation in school activities decreased, while absenteeism soared.

A committee of teachers, administrators, and faculty members from the University of Alabama concluded that participation in community life would diminish feelings of alienation among the students. The American Studies Program they designed is housed in the Old Jail, which is located in Tuscaloosa's historical district. The program provides students with a sense of community, gives them a reason to explore their different heritages, involves them in preservation of the area's history, and requires them to participate in the political life of the city.

The program began in 1980 with 145 juniors and seniors and has continued to grow. The staff consists of a director and three teachers who team-teach in a four-hour block each morning. The students return to the main campus for classes each afternoon.

Flexible scheduling allows students to attend town meetings, seminars, and labs and to participate in extended field trips. Films, lectures, and performances in the program are followed by seminars attended by 25 to 30 students. The labs are designed to focus on the skills in reading, writing, speaking, and problem solving that are required for specific tasks.

The courses for the juniors—American history, American literature, writing, and environmental science—emphasize historical preservation. The students are encouraged to familiarize themselves with the many resources available through the University of Alabama and the local junior college and from the citizens of Tuscaloosa. Some students research local history using genealogies, oral histories, and data from their own archeological survey. Another group forms the staff of *Timepiece*, a student publication that features project-related articles, interviews, family stories, and local tall tales.

Students also visit Tanglewood, a 480-acre plantation donated to the university in 1949. The mansion, built in 1858, contains documents dating back as far as 1819 that provide fascinating insights into the history of a southern family. The original land grant, signed by President Martin Van Buren, hangs on one wall beside two original bills of sale for slaves. Students camp out on the grounds of the estate, using only equipment that would have been available in the mid-nineteenth century. Such activities encourage cooperation and a sense of community among the students.

The seniors' course of study is broader. It revolves around participation in the national political process. Students form their own government and explore such themes as the struggle to survive (frontier and wilderness), the struggle to cooperate (the formation of government, with emphasis on the executive branch), the struggle to create (the legislative branch), and the struggle to justify (the judicial branch).

Significant contemporary events are used as peak experiences in the curriculum. Local, state, and national elections provide students with a variety of opportunities through which they can investigate the American political process. Some students volunteer to work in the campaign headquarters of the political party or candidate of their choice. Candidates and their campaign organizers visit the classroom and describe the electoral process to the seniors. Appropriate literature, such as Robert Penn Warren's *All the King's Men*, helps to relate classroom work to field study.

The seniors also study and employ propaganda techniques in a mock debate and election. They learn to analyze the arguments offered on opposing sides of controversial issues and to write position papers on the issues. As a community service, on the day after an election, students collect every visible campaign poster within the city limits. The culminating experience of the senior semester is an extended field trip to Washington, DC.

The American Studies Program offers many important advantages. Perhaps the most important is that it provides an opportunity for personal growth. Students learn to look at experiences as multifaceted, to make judgments from a broader base, and to bring their own heritage into clearer focus. For many, this method of perceiving experience and making judgments will become a habit. The experiential nature of the program necessitates firsthand learning by the students. Because they are given tasks that require cooperation, they have developed a sense of community by the end of the semester. At the same time, their personal investment in these tasks motivates students to improve their basic skills in reading, writing, speaking, and problem solving.

Thanks to its popularity and record of success, the American Studies Program has become a permanent part of the Tuscaloosa curriculum. An officer of the Southeastern American Studies Association described Tuscaloosa's program as "the most extensive and challenging application of American Studies in the high school that has ever been attempted anywhere in the country." The team of American Studies teachers at Central High School has found the experience both time- and energy-consuming but professionally fulfilling. The students, too, have found that the program requires extra time and effort, but there is general agreement among all the participants that the quality of the experience makes it worthwhile.

Some Final Suggestions

Before studying these models, you were advised to keep in mind each model's potential to affect student learning. To a large degree, the outcome will depend on the effectiveness of the communications among all parties involved in the model's implementation. Here are three final suggestions about using models. First, use them. Second, be fluid with their use. Third, and perhaps the best advice of all to those who work with curricula, continuously revise and reinvent the models you use.

As seen in earlier chapters, there is currently a strong perceived need to personalize curricula. Consider the effects that performance-based programs such as Project ESCAPE and the Alverno program have on personalizing student experiences.

Conclusion

Following is a summary of some of the advances made and concerns raised about the topics discussed in this chapter.

Advances

- Action research encourages a mix of theory and practice.
- Teachers are using a variety of methods to meet students' different learning styles.
- NCLB requires teachers to provide data to support their chosen teaching strategies.
- Helping students become more sophisticated thinkers is an important goal of educators.

Concerns

- Traditionally, teachers have tended to perceive research as impractical, using the methods that their own teachers used.
- Models are not being fully used to improve our schools, yet, significant change always requires a model.
- Teachers have been reluctant to embrace research.
- Students in high-achieving countries spend more time developing concepts than in lower-achieving countries.

According to the literature, most teachers teach the ways they were taught, ignoring the research. But during the past two decades, a strong knowledge base on teaching has been developed.

Teachers rely on common sense, but common sense is not always reliable. Science has given us a more reliable system that includes concepts, theories, and models.

Many current education reformers are constructivists. Both the focus on major content generalizations (concepts) and the use of activities that let students discover these concepts are qualities of constructivists.

Currently, there is no complete, perfect theory of education, but there are opportunities to contribute to the development of such a theory. Don't wait for new theories to be proven beyond a reasonable doubt. Many theories that shed light on our understanding and provide direction will never be proved beyond a reasonable doubt, but that does not justify our not knowing and using them (Jensen, 2008).

Teachers often criticize theory, saying that it is unrelated to practice. Actually, theory is not supposed to dictate practice. The role of theory is to guide our thinking. Thus, without telling us what to do, theory—plus several other factors, including our emotions and our value systems—determines our behavior.

There are two types of models: descriptive and predictive. Descriptive models explain the relationships among their parts. Predictive models help us predict future consequences. Two of the most influential curriculum models are Tyler's ends-means model and Taba's inverted model. Tyler's model proposes that we begin curriculum development by identifying desired outcomes and designing the curriculum accordingly. Taba's model is called an inverted model because, unlike traditional models which were developed at the district, state, and federal levels, it begins in the classroom with teachers. Because of this, teachers are more effective in implementing the new curriculum.

The value of any model or theory hinges on the degree to which its users understand the purpose of models and theories and the users' willingness to revise the model or theory as their local community, school, and students change. Confidence in models and theories and the skills required to use them effectively require a climate that makes teachers feel comfortable enough to put aside their dependence on the security of having the sole purpose of helping students remember facts. Put simply, effective use of theories and models requires a climate that encourages experimentation and tolerates errors.

Future teachers can expect increased diversity at their schools. It is imperative that these themes are remembered and that the welfare of all students remains paramount when all types of educational decisions are made.

Additional Learning Opportunities

1. Why is just teaching concepts inadequate?
2. What is the purpose of models?
3. What is the relationship between concepts and theories? Between theories and models?
4. In what ways can the scientific method be superior to common sense at times?
5. What evidence can you offer to show that current education reformers have used research? Have ignored research?
6. How can the interdisciplinary approach to multicultural education be defended?

This chapter began with a statement describing a student's pessimism and anxiety about a career in teaching. This chapter dealt in part with the role that generalizing plays in learning. The following questions are intended to help you make some generalizations about the important relationships between the student's comments and the chapter content.

7. The student's plea for meaning that goes beyond the accumulation of disjointed facts contains a powerful sentence: "To me, intellectual curiosity is the only constant in education." What does this statement mean?
8. What is the real difference between wisdom and knowledge?
9. What is the essence of this student's plea?
10. Are contemporary educators addressing this student's concern?
11. How can this student's claim that educators look at the past to build the future be applied to our school's failure to address growing social problems, such as the needs of minority students?
12. How can teachers help students focus on ideas as opposed to facts?
13. What can teachers and other curriculum developers do to respond to the growing body of information?

Suggested Activities

1. Select two curriculum models and contrast them.
2. Explain why all curriculum developers need to begin by stating their educational philosophies.
3. Contrast the Taba model with other models. List at least two unique strengths of each model.
4. Explain what is unique about the Tyler ends-means model.
5. Describe your strongest-held belief about: (a) the nature of youth, (b) the role of the school in social development, and (c) the nature of learning.
6. Remembering the goal of meeting the needs of all students, design a curriculum model that represents your own unique philosophical, social, and psychological beliefs.
7. Describe the biggest change that has occurred in society during your lifetime, and explain how that change has or should have influenced school curricula.
8. Choose an approach used in the American Studies Program and use it to bring reform to your local school.

chapter five

Designing and Organizing Curricula

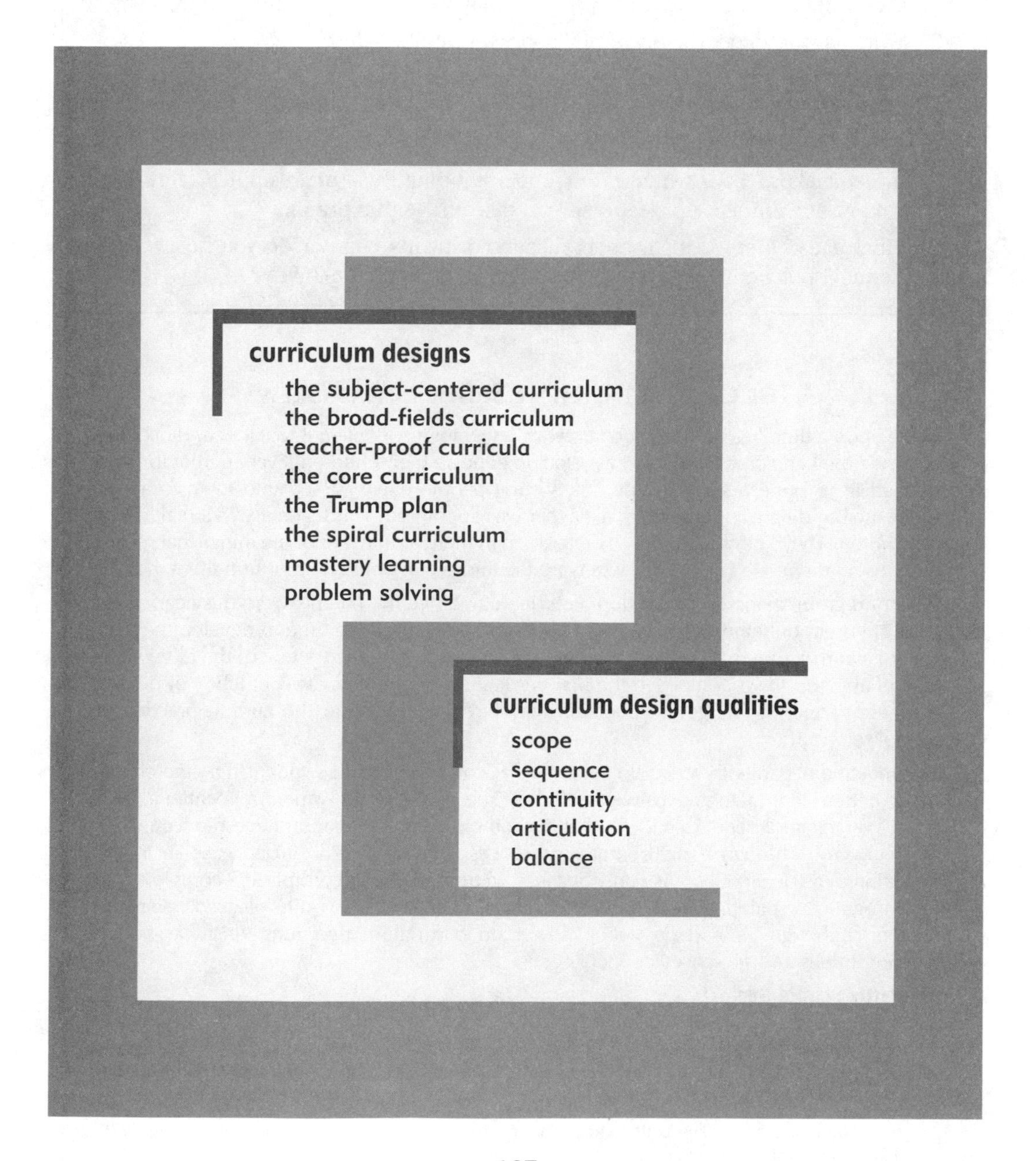

Focus Questions

1. What effect do constructivist strategies such as problem solving and storytelling have on minority students?
2. What is the relationship between making connections and academic success? What roles should curriculum planning play with forming connections?
3. Which is worse: poor sequence or poor continuity? Why?
4. What are the major arguments for and against core curricula?
5. Which curriculum design is most popular in your school(s)? Why?
6. Do you think the American culture has any qualities that cause teachers to implement practices without fully understanding their philosophies? How can you provide influence or leadership to discourage this practice?
7. Which curriculum design model discussed in this chapter do you believe has the most potential for improving learning for all students? Why?

THE CASE OF THE LITTLE SCHOOL THAT GREW*

Once upon a time in a land not too far away, a few townspeople got together and decided that the time had come to develop a system to educate their children. Every parent in town pitched in to build a schoolhouse; many rural people even walked into town to assist. Once the building was completed, a teacher was appointed. This teacher was a real leader of children. They knew he was really interested in them and aware of the things that meant the most to them. He knew that these were the things that could help or hurt them most.

A second group gathered to develop a curriculum. Since the parents were busy caring for their children, only the people without children could spare the time to develop the new school's curriculum, so a few merchants, a few craftspeople, and a few of the elite, well-to-do fathers in town comprised the first curriculum committee. (This practice of putting business people in charge of education may have given rise to the current practice in school reform.)

The meeting began with a decision about what courses should be taught. The merchants made certain that mathematics was included. The craftspeople wanted a vocational program to teach adolescents a trade so that the common eight-year apprenticeship would not be necessary. Through a rigid bargaining process, the well-to-do group gave in to the inclusion of a vocational course only because, in turn, they were promised a complete fine arts program of painting, sculpture, and music. Everyone was quite pleased, even the teacher, although he had no voting power on curriculum decisions (this was before teacher unions and site-based councils).

The Little School Begins

The first day of school proved to be typical of many days that followed. With only one room in the schoolhouse, the older children helped the younger ones with their lessons. The teacher understood that self-fulfillment comes most easily through helping others. Per-

*From the author's article, The Little School That Grew, *Journal of Teacher Education*, Spring 1975, *26*(1), 55–59. Permission granted by Sage Publications.

haps the ease with which these youngsters of varying ages and ethnic backgrounds got along could be attributed to the teacher, who seemed to care immensely for each child.

At the back of the room on a large table were glasses of watercolors, a large pork-and-beans can full of brushes, and a stack of white paper. This was the art "program." No class hour was set aside for art. As the children finished their lessons, they were free to go to the back of the room and try out their skills. In fact, there was no planned instruction in art. The teacher was available when a child asked for help, but even then, little instruction was provided; mostly the child got encouragement. The room was encircled with paintings attached to a line by clothespins. On any day, a production from each child was displayed, representing as many subjects as there were students.

As you may have suspected, the physical education program was not well organized. At recess, the children went to the ball field for a game of shove-up, a game the teacher knew was remarkable because no side choosing is necessary—no child has to suffer being chosen last. Each player has an equal opportunity to play each position. Most important, each child can experience success and failure without disappointing teammates, since when someone strikes out, only that one child is out. This vigorous game was always enjoyed by all.

The noon hour was a daily highlight. Paper sacks blossomed to give forth smells of sandwiches made from home-cured ham or sausage. Exchanges of sandwiches were common, since most kids brought two identical sandwiches and welcomed the variety. But taste was not as important as was the opportunity to enjoy the food as the children sat beneath a large oak (some had favorite seats up in the tree where they enjoyed their noon meal). On hot days, the cool, shady cement doorstop of the schoolhouse always attracted a few diners.

For many years, the little school continued to offer these uniquely human activities, and everyone assumed that the school's first teacher was doing a fine job and that it was a fine little school, until a certain event changed their minds.

Change Comes to the Little School

While visiting the adjacent community, a school board member found a larger, more sophisticated school with many fine qualities not found in the little school. When the board member returned, a board meeting was immediately called and the other members were informed of the many good qualities of the newer, larger school. When it was mentioned that School X had a lunchroom, someone asked, "Why can't our school have a lunchroom?" When the board was informed that the uniformity and structure in School X's curriculum was made possible by multiple classrooms and a bell system, someone asked, "Why can't our school have separate classrooms and a bell system?" Each time an advantage was noted at School X, the notation was followed by the question, "Why can't our school have that?"

Immediate plans were begun to implement these innovations. A larger two-story schoolhouse was constructed. An electric bell system made possible the dividing of the curriculum into many subject units and the development of grades and grade levels. Content specialist teachers were hired. The students readily accepted change, for it meant freshness—a way to escape the present school program. From listening to their parents, they had learned that their school curriculum had gradually become dull, routine, and traditional.

The first year, the new curriculum seemed an overwhelming success. The students were getting expert instruction and were motivated by a real sense of competition. Class times were regulated by a bell system, and a new lunchroom provided a hot lunch for each student.

But as time passed, these innovations brought some unforeseeable changes. The grouping based on age, grade, and ability level caused the more capable students to develop an attitude of superiority, and they had little tolerance for slower learners. The slower students knew they had been singled out as "average" (meaning below average) or low achievers. In other words, they had been labeled "failures."

A real difference could be seen in the way students moved about. Children who had once gaily skipped off to recess or leisurely wandered at will to the back of the room to paint pictures were now literally running from room to room. When the bell system was installed, five minutes was allotted between periods. Later this was decreased to three minutes, then two.

Thirty minutes was provided for lunch. The lunch period bell sent each student running at top speed. The lucky few who captured positions at the head of the line were too excited to eat; the slower runners found themselves with only five to ten minutes to bolt down their food. The time of day that had once meant complete relaxation had now disappeared.

Inside the classrooms, the new teachers presented eloquent lectures and held all students accountable for attaining set objectives, each having a minimum acceptable level of performance and specific conditions under which it was to be demonstrated. Each art student was carefully instructed on matters of content and technique. No longer could they waste time dabbling in watercolors, creating meaningless paintings that were often crude and ugly.

On the playgrounds, a highly structured and competitive program was installed for those students who excelled in physical skills and endurance.

The little school had come a long way. Its administrators and faculty were proud. Parents knew from hearing teachers' comments that it must be one of the most progressive and innovative schools because its curriculum had been completely restructured to meet the demands of the times. Student complaints reinforced the faith in the new curriculum, because everyone knows that kids never like anything that is good for them.

• • •

Remember that curriculum changes are made every day and that teachers are involved in the decisions to change and how to change. This chapter will review some of the basic curriculum designs that have become standard over the years, and it will also introduce curriculum dimensions that provide ways of examining the curriculum, such as scope, sequence, articulation, and balance. Think critically about your own philosophy of education, the major purposes of schools, and the major flaws and shortcomings in today's curricula. As a curriculum planner who will be involved in schoolwide planning, you can significantly influence the quality of your school. This chapter will provide some of the concepts that you will need to achieve this goal.

Curriculum Designs

Through the years, curricula have been tailored, modified, and shaped to fit the needs of a changing society. The curriculum for the first American schools was simple and straightforward because the purpose of those first schools was simple and straightforward—to prepare students for admission to Harvard College, a school of divinity.

But during the last half of the twentieth century, different demands were placed on the schools. Each added purpose has required an adjustment to the curriculum. It bears repeating that significant change in any organization requires a design. John Dewey (1916, p. 409) expressed the need for continuous curriculum design when he said that democracy has to be born anew in each generation, and education is its midwife.

Almost a century has passed since Dewey made this statement, and educators are still worried that

> A good deal of the typical curriculum does not connect—not to practical applications, personal insights, or much of anything. It's not the kind of knowledge that would connect, nor is it taught in a way that would help learners make connections. (Dewey, 1916, p. 24)

FYI Making Connections

Victoria Robinson • University of Northern Iowa

In order to maximize student learning, teachers must connect what to teach, how to teach it, why to teach it, and how to assess what students learned. Too often these four aspects fail to be explicitly linked.

Students are asked to create a mini unit and then explain how "what is taught, how it is taught, why it is taught, and how it is assessed" are connected. Before submitting this assignment, students meet in groups of four to review and discuss one another's mini units and how the four elements are connected.

Pennsylvania teacher of the year Howard Selekman (1999, p. 59) says, "Teachers seek to establish any connections, connections that are meaningful to us and our students." Some of the connections that are necessary for maximum academic success are connections among students, connections between the teacher and students, connections between the content and the students (Good & Brophy, 2008), connections among important concepts within the discipline, and connections with major concepts in other disciplines. Decreasing the use of textbooks in favor of using more storytelling can strengthen connections. Questioning can be used in conjunction with storytelling to activate student background knowledge (Abell, 2007).

The curriculum designs that teachers choose determine to a large degree how well students tie the major concepts they study to other concepts. As mentioned earlier, students in countries like Singapore that score highest in the TIMSS international science and mathematics exams spend more classroom time making such connections (CCSSO, 2008).

This chapter chronicles some of the most important curriculum designs. As you examine each of the following designs, consider the amount of time it might provide for students to make essential connections. These designs are grouped according to the age level of the students they serve (elementary, junior high or middle level, and high school) and according to patterns that recur among them. Within each level, the major curriculum designs are discussed. These are shown

Table 5.1 Common Curriculum Designs at Various Grade Levels

Level	Common Curriculum Designs
Elementary	Graded Open education Nongraded Cooperative learning Integrated
Junior High	Graded Core curriculum Open education Cooperative learning Integrated
Middle School	Graded Nongraded Open education Cooperative learning Integrated
High School	Graded Subject matter Broad fields Alternative Cooperative learning Integrated

in table 5.1. For certain, many of these divisions are not as distinct and separate as table 5.1 might suggest. For example, it is common for a school at any level to have a combination of several designs. But separating the designs enables us to discuss and understand the unique needs and characteristics of each design.

Since schools typically start at the kindergarten level and go through grade 12, several patterns are common. Originally, the schools were designed for age 6 through about age 15. Later, as the school curriculum was extended to grade 12, the schools were divided into two areas: elementary (grades 1–6) and secondary (grades 7–12). But at the secondary school the development range was too broad. Some students hadn't reached puberty; others were young adults. For this reason and for administrative convenience, the junior high school was formed. This became the 6–3–3 curriculum design.

As more knowledge about the effects of maturity on student behavior became available, it became apparent that the preadolescent age group was very different from the younger and older students. Educators also learned that American youth were aging socially at a more rapid pace than their predecessors had. It was decided that a special school was needed for this age group; it became known as the middle school. The ages represented in middle schools vary; the most common are ages 11 to 14 or 15. The curricula for the systems that have these schools are 5–3–4 or 4–4–4. Since the kindergarten is common among curricula today, the patterns are often represented by K–5–3–4 or K–4–4–4. Table 5.2 shows the changes in grade groupings through the years.

Table 5.2 Changes in Grade Groupings

Years	Grade Levels Represented		
1835–1847	Nongraded		
1848–1909	1–12		
1910–1950	1–6–6		
1951–Present	K–6,	7–9,	10–12
	K–5,	6–8,	9–12
	K–5,	6–9,	10–12
	K–4,	5–8,	9–12

Although the number of curriculum designs that can be used at each level is almost unlimited, each design is associated more with some levels than with others. Some of the more popular curriculum designs that have had an impact on the schools at various times include subject-centered, broad-fields, core, Trump Plan, spiral, mastery learning, and problem solving.

The Subject-Centered Curriculum

The first curricula of the Latin grammar schools were composed of religion, Latin, and Greek. Thus, the first American school curriculum design was the subject-centered design. Subject-centered implies more than just that the curriculum is built around one or more subjects. Throughout our schools' history, subject-centered curricula have been complemented by a particular teaching style, the lecture. The objective of *subject-centered curricula* is to learn the subject—that is, the content.

The subject-centered curriculum is the oldest curriculum design in the world. It isn't surprising to learn, therefore, that subject-centered curricula are surrounded by tradition (Armstrong et al., 2009). In fact, the subject-centered content itself is traditional content—that is, content that over the years has been accepted.

As mentioned earlier, the major delivery system for subject-centered curricula is the lecture, itself the most traditional teaching method. Even the objective of subject-centered curricula is the traditionally accepted goal of accumulation of information.

Strengths

The subject-centered curriculum design has several features that cause proponents to favor it. The continued use of this design through the years means that people are familiar with it and comfortable using it. Furthermore, its long-term use gives a sense of "tried and proven," or, "It was good enough for me; therefore, I trust it for my children."

A more tangible quality of the subject-centered curriculum is its tight organization. The content is rigidly sequenced. When using this design, teachers can (and almost always do) follow the sequence of the textbook. This facilitates the task of keeping track of where each lesson ends and where the next one begins. This tight organization helps the teacher avoid accidental duplication of content and makes the testing simple. Easy design of tests was mentioned earlier as a strength of the textbook. Since the subject-centered design is characterized by use of textbooks; it benefits from the strengths and suffers from the weaknesses of textbooks.

The tightly organized subject-centered curriculum is easy to implement. Courses can be added to or deleted from a school's program (or even added to or deleted from a student's individual curriculum). Thus, transferring from one school to another, and even from one state to another, is easy. This advantage is realized by high school students who go on to colleges out of state. Of course, for transfer students the college may stipulate a particular additional course or courses.

Still another advantage of the subject-centered curriculum design is its efficiency. The well-organized, compact curriculum enables students to cover a lot of content in a short time. Lorin Anderson (2009) reminds us that covering a lot of content in a short time may actually be a disadvantage, because moving through lessons at a rapid pace can be frustrating to teachers and students and may deny students the opportunity to reflect and test their ideas. The ability to move rapidly through subject-centered curricula becomes clear when contrasted with an inquiry curriculum (which requires students to discover relationships for themselves before they learn them), with case studies (which require students to sift relevant information from irrelevant information), with simulations and games (which are student-paced), with mastery learning (which permits students to remediate and recycle), or with the discussion method (which also requires much more time to cover the material).

Weaknesses

Among the limitations of the subject-centered curriculum are its failure to consider the unique needs and interests of students and its detachment from contemporary events in the world. Marion Brady (2008) says, "To move beyond rote memorization and use a full range of thinking skills, students need to tackle issues straight out of the complex world in which they live." Perhaps the most severe criticism against the subject-centered curriculum is the effect it has on learners. Although it is satisfying to the teacher, the subject-centered design is a poor motivator for students. Interestingly, the lecture is favored by poorer students because it places less classroom responsibility on learners. Too often, the goal is to be able to recall information rather than to attempt to understand it. Subject-matter learning merely increases students' information base; it does not prepare them by disciplining their minds to think like the experts in the disciplines (Boix-Mansilla & Gardner, 2008).

Success in reaching the underachievers requires special effort from the teacher. O'Neal, Earley, and Snider (1991, p. 122) explain:

> Research indicates that while many underachieving students have poorer auditory and visual skills, their kinesthetic and tactile capabilities are high. Implications are that teachers may need to use a greater variety of instructional methods.

Geisert and Dunn (1991, p. 223) say that "difficult material needs to be introduced through each student's strongest perceptual modality (preferred learning style) and then reinforced through supplementary modalities." Obviously, the

FYI Covering Material

Donna McCaw • Western Illinois University

Do you want to improve student achievement? *Try NOT to use the word "cover."*

As the size of the curriculum continues to expand, most of us just try to *cover* the material—to get through the text. Unconsciously, we know that we are not spending sufficient time to have actually taught the material to our students. Then, when a colleague states," I don't understand it, I started fractions this morning and they looked at me as if I were speaking French," we immediately respond with, "I don't understand why, I covered that last year." Think about how often (or how seldom) you state that you taught something—anything. Because we have students that go through 13 grades of having material "covered," why would we be surprised that they have learned so little?

Trying to get control of the curriculum can be an almost impossible task, but I have found that by asking myself on a daily basis if I have taught anything on a particular day, I have given myself permission to "do less" better. No more skimming the surface at the speed of "covering."

subject-centered curriculum design makes comparatively little use of such necessary reinforcement.

The subject-centered curriculum can be effective when used by those teachers who are willing to alter their teaching styles and lower the level of instruction to the point at which the student can become a successful learner. But to assume that teachers will make this change is perhaps a mistake. Marshall (1991) explains teachers' reluctance to leave the security of the subject-centered curriculum. To meet the learning needs of today's diverse classrooms, teachers "must come to recognize, respect, and support the learning differences of students. If students do not learn the way we teach them, then we must teach them the way they learn" (p. 226).

The Broad-Fields Curriculum

Realizing that the neat containers (called *subjects*) that had been designed to hold and dispense knowledge had limitations, educators decided to enlarge the containers. The result was referred to as the *broad-fields curriculum*.

An important goal of this design, devised around the turn of the twentieth century, was to reduce the propensity that students in subject-centered curricula had for memorizing fragmented facts. The broad-fields curriculum would solve this problem by broadening such subjects as history, geography, and civics into a curriculum category—social studies. Instead of studying reading, writing, literature, and speech, students would study language arts. Instead of taking physics and chemistry, students would take physical science. Instead of taking botany, anatomy, physiology, and zoology or biology, students would take biological science. These larger categories (biological sciences, earth sciences, and physical sciences) were expanded to form general science.

Unfortunately, the broad-fields curriculum design has not always been effective. A major cause for its shortcomings is the way the curriculum has been delivered. For example, some teachers ignored the broad content generalizations that the creators of this design sought to help students develop. Other teachers taught the generalizations, but as facts to be memorized; and this won't achieve the goal of having students understand the generalizations: "Instruction must focus on the use of the concepts (content generalizations) and the context in which they occur in order to ascertain their practical connections."

Furthermore, success in teacher-centered classrooms requires good note taking, and under the best conditions only 52% of the major ideas are captured in students' notes (Maddox & Hoole, 1975). When recording lectures, students focus more on specific, less important points while missing the more important general understandings. King (1990, p. 131) reported:

> Researchers have found that when students take notes during a lecture they are far more likely to record bits and pieces of the lecture verbatim or simply paraphrase information rather than organize the lecture material into some sort of conceptual framework or relate the new information to what they already know.

Because the lecture affords teachers the opportunity to demonstrate their expertise, many teachers depart on an ego trip, leaving the confused students behind. This practice leads to failure: To be successful we teachers must be prepared to lower the level of instruction to the point where each student becomes a successful learner.

The broad-fields curriculum was an attempt to use an integration of traditional subjects to help students develop broad understanding in all areas. This curriculum design has survived for well over half a century and enjoyed a resurgence during the early 1960s, stimulated by the cold war political climate and the Woods Hole Conference. J. S. Bruner chaired this conference and proposed the use of integrated themes. His words were misinterpreted (see Orlich, 2000), having an even greater effect on the rapid development of this integrated theme approach. Fortunately, the revival addressed the delivery system that had caused much failure when the broad-fields design was first implemented. Content generalizations such as concepts, principles, and themes were the organizing elements that were coupled with inquiry and discovery learning methods in the 1960s designs.

Teacher-Proof Curricula

The dependence of this curriculum design on its delivery system for success reflects the inextricable and interdependent relationship between curriculum and instruction in general. The dependence on the teacher for the success of this curriculum can be generalized to all curricula. Eisner (1985, p. 195) explains:

> When the curriculum development movement got underway in the early 1960s, there was talk about the desirability of creating "teacher proof" curricula. That aspiration has, through the years, given way to the more realistic view that teachers are not mere tubes for curriculum developers. Teachers cannot and should not be bypassed.

As Darling-Hammond (1996, p. 5) explains, "Educational reform was 'teacher proofed' with hundreds of pieces of legislation and thousands of discrete regulations prescribing what educators should do." This is most unfortunate because today's teachers are highly educated adults with the potential for creating meaningful learning environments that address the needs of every student.

Educators are concerned that many highly competent teachers often lack the opportunities necessary for their expertise and talents to be fully employed. Both teachers' expertise and parents' skills are being underused, and without the positive involvement of parents, most changes are short-lived. Fortunately, today's trend is away from "teacher-proof" curricula. The No Child Left Behind Act gives local educators added flexibility. Districts may use up to 50% of the funds they receive from the state to increase teacher quality, improve technology, provide safe and drug-free schools, and establish innovative programs to promote student achievement.

The No Child Left Behind Act requires school districts to close the gap between the performance levels of mainstream students and minority students. The following case study shows how one university is partnering with local schools to achieve this goal. The teacher in this case study uses concept maps to help ELL students master content concepts while also mastering the English language.

case study

Using Concept Mapping for Collaborative Curriculum Design

Jaime Curts
University of Texas–Pan American

This case study began as collaborative effort to use bilingual concept mapping as a metacognitive tool for planning and assessing the mathematical knowledge of a group of migrant students learning mathematics in English as a second language. These students had limited or interrupted schooling in their first language.

Background

The study took place in a middle school situated in Starr County, a predominantly Mexican-American community situated along the south Texas-Mexico border (The Rio Grande River) and one of the nation's poorest regions in the United States. Starr County median household income is only $19,127, which is less than half the median household income in the state of Texas and the nation. Most of the population speaks Spanish, 38% of the total population are children under 18 years of age (93% of whom speak Spanish), and from this total percentage of children, 49% speak English "very well," 36% speak it "well," 12% "not well," and 2% "not at all."

The School

"La Grulla Middle School" (GMS) (not its real name) is situated in the city of La Grulla, Texas, a small community in eastern Starr County that was founded around 1870. The community adopted its name after a migratory bird (the crane, or *grulla* in Spanish) that once migrated in large quantities around the town. It is one of three middle schools in the Rio Grande City Consolidated Independent School, and during the 2006–2007 academic year the school registered 751 students in grades six through eight, all being of Latino/Mexican-American heritage.

To understand the framework of our case, it is important to mention that staff and faculty at GMS are committed to improve performance and provide quality educational opportunities that enable all children to reach their fullest potential. Their logo, T.E.A.M. (Together Everyone Accomplishes More), reflects the philosophy of how curriculum is planned, implemented, and assessed with input from teachers, staff members, parents, and members of the community. Because one of their main goals is to increase all students' academic performance in mathematics, the planning, delivery, and evaluation of instruction is strictly aligned to the Texas Assessment Knowledge and Skills (TAKS) objectives and the state mandated curriculum, the Texas Essential Knowledge and Skills. The school has emphasized the use of cooperative learning and higher-order thinking skills to develop collaborative student participation in problem solving. Writing and visual learning have become an integral part of learning mathematics. The use of concept mapping and physical and virtual manipulatives supports and enhances learners' language comprehension of mathematical vocabulary and increases understanding of math-related concepts.

The Case

The study presented here was part of a research project I conducted to assess the effect of bilingual concept mapping (BCM) on middle-school limited-English-proficient (LEP) students' achievement in mathematics. BCM intervention was part of a Gear-Up Initiative implemented in a predominantly Hispanic middle school in South Texas with a high number of LEP students. Little is known about the effective use of bilingual concept maps with English language learner (ELL) students.

Our case begins when I was invited to work with and monitor several in-service mathematics teachers who had recently graduated from the University of Texas–Pan American and were working with LEP students. The school's LEP population is 42%, although 99% of the total population is considered economically disadvantaged.

During my first observation in a sixth-grade LEP classroom, we worked with several recently migrated children from Mexico to discuss the concept of *circle*. We explained to the children that during the week they would learn several basic properties of circles, and from these properties they would discover "a magic number." "On March 14," I said, "mathematicians celebrate *Pi Day* and we will celebrate too." I also mentioned to the class that at the end of the unit they would use their knowledge about circles to study and determine satellites' spinning velocity around the world. (Their teacher, Mr. Cruz, assigned time for them to go to the library to research satellites.)

We began with a focus question, drawing a circle on the chalkboard and then asking students to identify circular objects around the classroom or to recall objects from outside school or home that had a circular shape. We initially wanted students to get the idea that *round = circle shaped.* We instructed them to work collaboratively in groups, by hearing, identifying, discussing, and writing in Spanish the definition of target words related to circular objects. As with other learners, I was aware that meaningful learning takes place when students' prior academic knowledge occurs first in their native or first language, providing the opportunity to focus on the comprehension of key words and/or concepts within their linguistic comfort zone. (At a later stage, students selected words and wrote them in both Spanish and English on 3 × 5 cards accompanied by a drawing, a picture, or a clip-art image on the back of the cards. We also encouraged the use of bilingual dictionaries to nurture them in their efforts to be familiar with new English vocabulary.)

We organized the groups (four children per team; each member of a team identified with the number 1, 2, 3, or 4), provided sets of adhesive notes and easel pads, and explained—both in English and Spanish—the protocol of how they would work collaboratively. Mr. Cruz explained, "Each member of the team, starting with number 1, should come up with a Spanish word for something that has a circular shape, write it on a sticky note, and post it on the easel paper pad." They followed this procedure three more times (for the students identified as 2, 3, and 4). Each group gathered a total of 12 words, and once the members finished, they were to use their Spanish-English Dictionary to look *only for the English spelling* of each word, writing it down on a sticky note and posting it on the easel pad next to its Spanish counterpart.

It is important to point out that the use of dictionaries was not the only word-learning strategy employed in Mr. Cruz's class. We discussed gradually moving beyond the definition of vocabulary words into a deeper understanding of mathematics concepts through a consecutive array of dynamic strategies (building conceptual and factual understanding through oral, writing, visual, and kinesthetic explanations of word origins). We required students to discover, compare, and discuss the meaning, properties, and relationships of mathematical concepts and ideas. We're convinced that students benefit from using concept mapping as a tool to support their understanding of meaningful relationships.

Once we finished explaining the team strategy, words popped out immediately in Spanish: *tortilla* [flat, thin, round cornmeal or wheat cake], *aréte* [earring], *plato* [plate], *maceta* [flowerpot], *taza* [cup], *ojo* [eye], *pulsera* [bracelet], a *la rueda de San Miguel* [game, song, Wheel of Saint Michael], *sol* [sun], *rueda de bicicleta* [bicycle wheel], and *anillo* [ring], were some of the words students identified as "circle-shaped" objects. Once each team gathered 12 words and posted them using sticky notes on the easel paper pad, we asked the students to draw visual models to compare and contrast their circle-shaped objects (using their prior knowledge of concepts like point, length, line segment, vertices, angle, shape, plane, polygon, and measure).

Next we showed students how to put a circle inside a square so that it touches the sides of the square. (The diameter of the circle is identical to the width of the square.) As a follow-up activity, students drew a square (marking the vertices as A, B, C, and D) outside any of their circle-shaped objects that they had already drawn. We planned this activity as a means to "discover the concept of center" and scaffold by drawing a line from a corner of the square (point A) to the edge of the circle (E) and repeat the same from B to F. The resulting lines, A to E, and B to F, are at 45 degrees to the sides of the square and the intersection of these lines define the center of a circle. (See figure 1.)

We instructed students to draw lines through the center of a circle and measure its length, to illustrate that a circle is a simple geometrical shape consisting of points on a plane (flat surface) and that a circle is a shape with all points the same distance from its center.

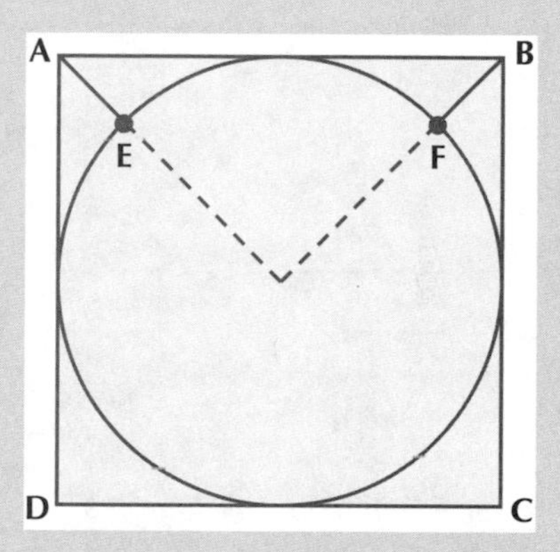

Figure 1 Discovering the concept of *center*

Next we had students focus on two specific distances: (a) the distance around the circles they had drawn, and (b) the distance that crosses a circle through the center. We asked the students to select and label three different-sized circles as circles 1, 2, and 3. Once the circles were identified, the students labeled and measured the distance around the circle as C (Curved line that goes around the circle) and the distance across the circle through the center as D (for Diameter). After receiving training in measuring and simple data-collection techniques, students created a table in an electronic spreadsheet with the following information: Circle #, distance C measure (centimeters), distance D measure (centimeters).

After students finished inputting the data into the spreadsheet, we asked them to add an additional column labeled "Magic Number" and to perform a calculation defined as "Column "C divided by Column D." In this manner, students learned that the ratio of the circumference of a circle to the diameter is π (the irrational number known as Pi) as they deduced the measures of segments in circles. We relied on students' prior knowledge and allowed them to connect new information *at their own developmental level* as they brainstormed new ideas individually and in cooperative groups. We focused on having the students understand basic properties of circles and to discover why the ratio of the circumference to the diameter of any circle is a constant (Pi).

Finally, we instructed students to prepare a vocabulary list (Spanish and English) and to prepare a hierarchical concept map with circle as the basic concept. When creating the concept map, students were to seek the answer to the following question: *What are the relationships among concepts associated with circles?* Students were organized in teams and instructed to follow the same collaborative rules (every member having an opportunity to spell out a word related to the focus question and to write it on the sticky note and post it on the easel paper pad). This activity would be repeated three times until they gathered 12 major concepts. Students could use all the words they knew in Spanish and English in their concept map, as long it was done collaboratively with each team member contributing to the vocabulary terms.

Illustrated below in figure 2 is one of the hierarchical bilingual concepts maps that Mr. Cruz and I used to prepare our curriculum lesson on the topic of *circle*. We used this "expert" map as a metacognitive tool, comparing it to students' bilingual maps and measuring their conceptual understanding and meaningful learning.

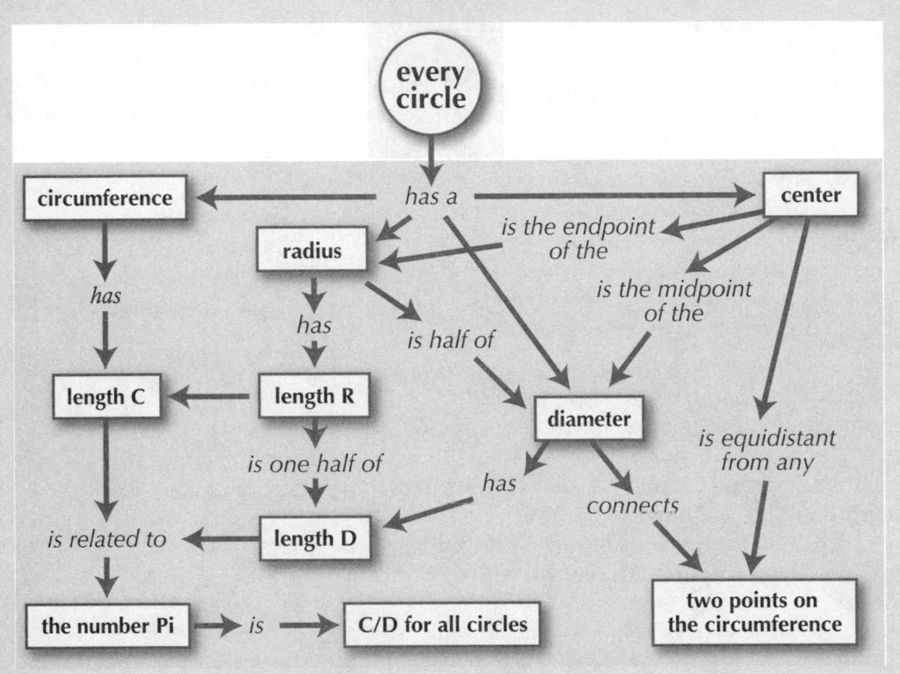

Figure 2 Expert concept map used for planning the curriculum unit, "What is a circle?"

This research project continues to examine the use of bilingual concept maps, and I believe it will allow us to understand how to integrate students' primary language into concept-mapping tasks. I strongly believe that allowing students to support their ideas by using their primary language will increase their long-term memory and cognitive lexical development in both languages.

Issues for Further Reflection and Application

1. This project focused on the potential of concept maps to help students grasp mathematical concepts. Why do you think this worked so well? Consider the location, students, and other factors.
2. What barriers account for the previous learning problems these students have experienced?
3. Do you believe concept mapping would be more, less, or equally effective if used with mainstream students? Explain your answer.
4. Why do you think this lesson is built around a phrase such as "magic number" instead of simply calling it a lesson on Pi?
5. Can you think of other metacognitive approaches that would be effective for designing curriculum for ELL students?

Following is a discussion of several types of curricula, including the core curriculum, the Trump Plan, the spiral curriculum, mastery learning, and problem solving. As you read about each of these curriculum designs, consider its unique opportunities for enhancing students' self-concepts and remember that designs that meet legislators' needs don't always meet students' needs.

The Core Curriculum

Near the turn of the century, some innovative curriculum directors such as Francis Parker (discussed in chapter 3) began searching for a way to escape the fragmentation that characterized the traditional (subject-centered) curricula. The result was a design called the *core curriculum*. The theory behind the development of this approach begins with the realization that some content is indispensable for all students. This content would become the core. See figure 5.1.

Around the core are a number of spokes that represent academic discipline courses (A), pre-professional courses (P), special-interest courses (S), and vocational courses (V).

The core curriculum has a dimension of versatility that makes it attractive to advocates of a variety of philosophies. For example, core curricula are character-

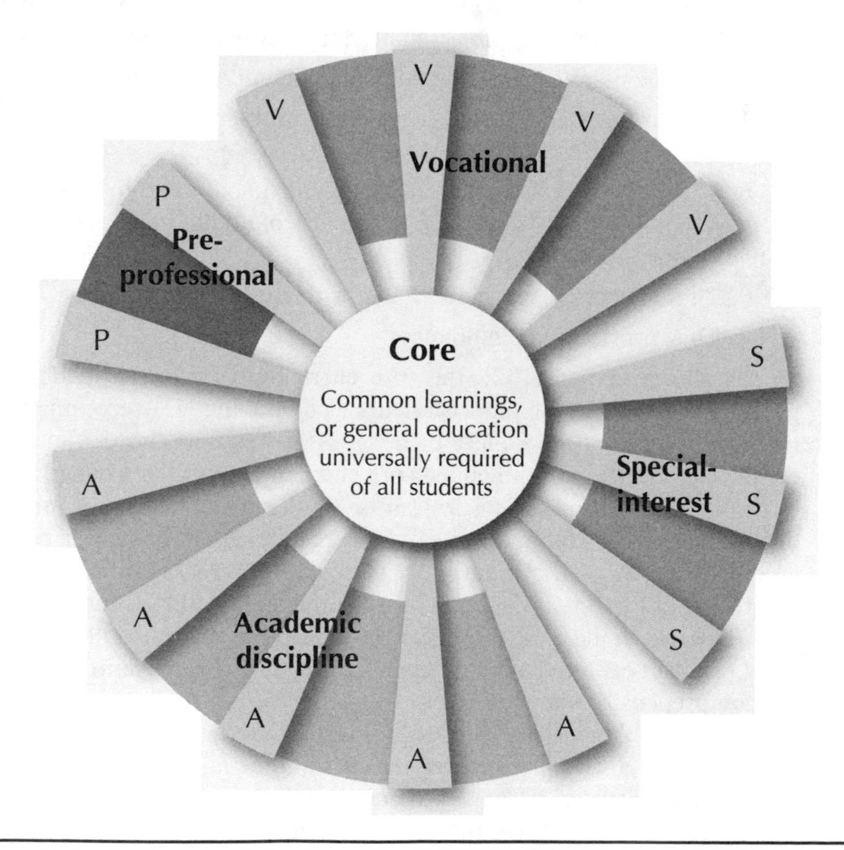

Figure 5.1 Structure of the Core Curriculum Design

ized by high expectations for students, frequent high-quality academic interactions among teachers and students, and direct instruction (Wang, Haertel, & Walberg, 1998). Essentialists can use the core to ensure coverage of the essential subjects. At the other extreme, the progressive educator can assign both content and activities to ensure that individual students' needs are met. In between, the pragmatists can use the core to ensure the coverage of practical curricula. However, the core curriculum is not effective in meeting employers' expectations.

Zais (1976, p. 423) identified six types of curricula as core curricula: (1) the separate subjects core, (2) the correlated core, (3) the fused core, (4) the activity/experiences core, (5) the areas-of-living core, and (6) the social problems core.

The core curriculum represented the second attempt to integrate learning. Contemporary, real-life problems were used for organizing the curricula. Typically, core programs are organized into blocks of time, often two or three successive periods, during which the teacher or a team of teachers integrates two or more subjects or disciplines. According to the National Center for Education Statistics (2002), the core curriculum consists of 4 years of English and 3 years each of social studies, science, and mathematics. Oliva (2009, p. 249) lists seven characteristics of core curricula:

1. They constitute a portion of the curriculum that is required of all students.
2. They unify or fuse subject matter, usually English and social studies.
3. Their content centers on problems that cut across the disciplines.
4. The primary method of learning is problem solving using all applicable subject matter.
5. They are organized into blocks of time, usually two to three periods under a "core" teacher (with the possible use of additional teachers and others as resource persons).
6. They encourage teachers to plan with students.
7. They provide pupil guidance.

As shown in figure 5.2, the core curriculum of American high schools has proven successful in the past. Students who take the ACT-recommended core curriculum in high school achieve higher ACT scores than those who don't; and students who take the recommended core curriculum enroll in college at a higher rate than those who do not—regardless of gender, family income, and racial/ethnic background (ACT, 2006). However, the core curriculum has never been universally accepted. As with other innovative curricula, the success of the core curriculum, regardless of the version used, hinges on the ability and willingness of teachers to make it work. In the past, most American teachers have been ill-prepared to implement problem-centered approaches or to integrate subjects and activities to achieve the comprehensive understandings sought by the core curricularists, because most teachers were themselves educated in textbook-oriented, subject-centered curricula. Proponents of the core curriculum say that it presents information in integrated form by cutting across the disciplines and centering on real-life issues.

However, critics attack the core curriculum, saying that it ignores the fundamentals (Ornstein & Hunkins, 2004, p. 264). The core curriculum no longer can

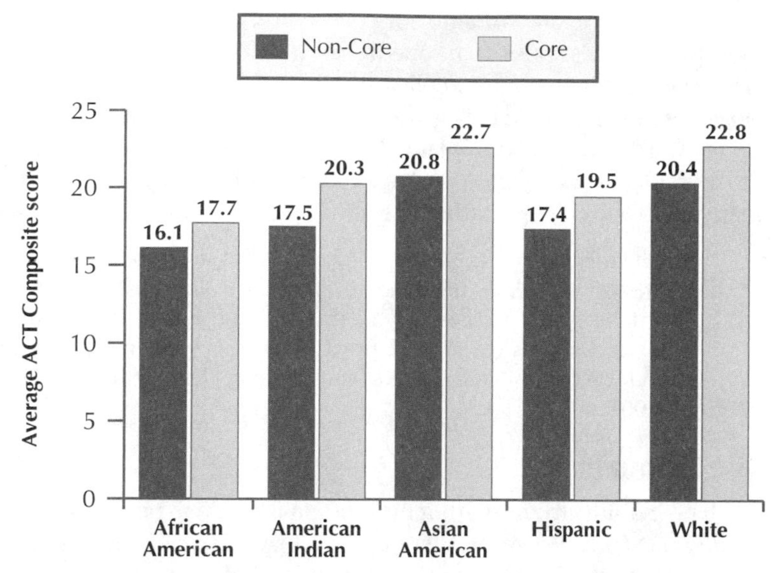

For all racial/ethnic groups, students who take the core curriculum score between 1.6 and 2.8 points higher on the ACT Composite than those who do not take the core.

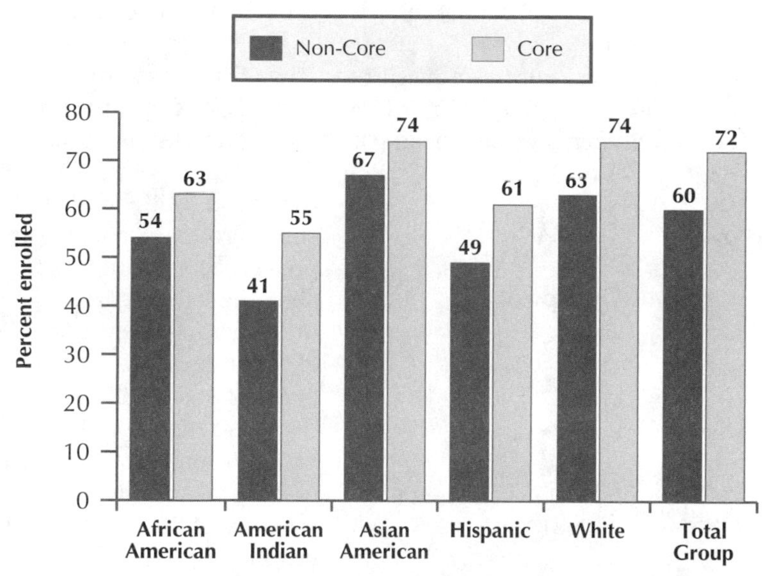

Students who take core curriculum are more likely than those who do not take the core to enroll in college in the fall following graduation (72% vs. 60% for the total group).

From ACT, *College readiness* (http://www.act.org/research/policymakers/pdf/core_curriculum.pdf).

Figure 5.2 Benefits of a High School Core Curriculum

be trusted to prepare students for college. In 2007, of the 1.3 million students who took the ACT test, less than one in four (23%) scored high enough to be considered ready for introductory college work. Only 14% scored high enough to be considered ready for basic college mathematics courses. The students who scored the lowest were those who took only the required core courses. In comparison, 40% of those students who also took trigonometry scored high enough to be considered ready for basic college mathematics ACT's CEO Richard L. Ferguson commented,

> Too often core courses in our high schools fail to teach students the essential knowledge and skills they need to succeed in first-year college courses. We must take the steps necessary to ensure that the core courses offered in our high schools are rigorous and provide students with the essential skills they need to succeed in college-credit courses after they graduate. (Education Portal, 2007)

The Trump Plan

The inability to meet students' personal needs is perhaps the most destructive quality of NCLB. However, there is good news. By looking to the past, we can discover one of the best personalized curriculum models ever developed, a model that has been successfully field tested for more than 50 years. This model is called the Trump Plan, and Keefe and Amenta (2005) give the following testimonial to its developer: "Future historians of American education may well recognize J. Lloyd Trump as the pivotal school reform figure of the second half of the twentieth century" (p. 538).

The *Trump Plan* (introduced more than 50 years ago) recommended placing students in small groups (15 or fewer students) and in large groups of 100 to 300 students. Students would spend part of each day in small groups and part of each day in large groups. They would spend the remainder of the day studying alone or in small groups according to each student's preference. Trump had definite ideas about how much time should be allotted to these arrangements: small-group activity, 20%; large-group activity, 40%; and independent study, 40%.

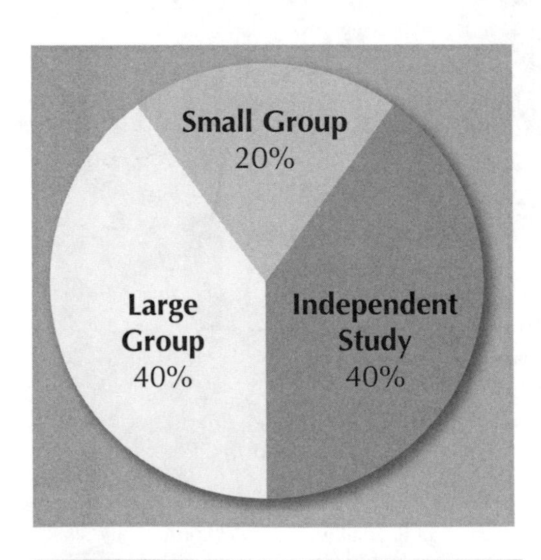

Figure 5.3 The Trump Plan Time Allotments

A strength of the Trump Plan is its variety—something for everyone. Evidence of this model is seen in our nation's schools. At the beginning of the twenty-first century nearly 100% of teachers used whole-group instruction at least once a week, over 90% worked with individuals at least once a week, and at least 80% used small groups at least once a week (Meek, 1998). Furthermore, this plan specified a variety of teacher or discussion leader activities and a variety of media for the large groups. Small-group work provided a variety of activities involving all students. Independent study time also afforded students a high level of involvement while performing laboratory experiments, problem solving, reading, listening to tapes, or pursuing a variety of creative activities. The ability that this curriculum design provides for meeting the unique needs of diverse students has extended its use in schools at a time when education reformers are dedicated to ensuring that each student can and will learn.

One feature of the Trump Plan is variable scheduling, not only during the school day but throughout the year. Another feature was year-round instruction. The January 23, 1993, *Richmond Register* daily newspaper carried an article headed "Ft. Knox pupils begin year-round school." The article noted that "year-round school is practiced in over 2000 school districts in the United States and it's growing rapidly."

In an era of unprecedented pressure to prepare students to score well on education reform-initiated exams, some may consider the Trump Plan dated, but a study of America's teachers (Meek, 1998, p. 15) revealed several facts that validate this model for use in the twenty-first century:

- Nearly 100% of teachers reported using whole-group instruction at least once a week.
- More than 90% of all teachers reported working with individual students at least once a week.
- Eighty percent of teachers report working with small groups at least once a week.

The Spiral Curriculum

Throughout the twentieth century, proponents of *connectionism* insisted that learning occurs in steps, each part building on simpler content learned earlier. Recognizing the constructivist viewpoint that each part of the content should be tied to prior learning, the *spiral curriculum* takes connectionism one step further: It recommends that the same topics be returned to the curriculum at a later date, sometimes at a higher grade level. Having gained in maturity and in the accumulation of prerequisite knowledge, students will be able to develop understandings that were beyond their capacity when simpler elements of the topic were introduced earlier.

The repetitive nature of the spiral curriculum is viewed by some as a strength and by others as a weakness. Some who view this design positively use professional journal reading and other strategies to purposefully "spiral" the curriculum, helping students see relationships among concepts in the curriculum (Watson, Beliveau, & Nelsen, 2004). Some contemporary educators attribute the success of Asian students at least in part to the fact that, unlike American students who confront the same material repeatedly, Asian curricula address each topic at only one level, providing time needed to pursue each topic in depth. This concern is supported by the TIMSS Video Mathematics Research Group (2003), which reported that students in countries that score the highest on mathematics spend more time making connections but less time repeating material from year to year.

Mastery Learning

In 1963 an article in the *Teachers College Record* (Carroll, 1963) described a curriculum designed to ensure that all students could succeed. Rejecting the work of E. L. Thorndike, which correlated students' success with their IQ, Carroll said that all students could learn if certain curricular and instructional adjustments were made.

This new program, called *mastery learning*, would first incorporate flexible time, as much as each individual needed. Second, students who failed to master the content and objectives on the first attempt could recycle without penalty. Remediation using a variety of different learning styles would be provided between testing cycles. Formative evaluation, not the traditional summative evaluation, would dominate. *Formative evaluation* is given in small steps throughout the teaching unit. It can help teachers identify gaps and know when certain concepts need to be retaught (Fisher et al., 2007/2008). Its purpose is to promote learning by using test scores to improve both instruction and the curriculum. Formative test scores are never used to determine grades.

As to letter grades, which most schools require, mastery learning typically uses As, Bs, and Is; there are no Cs, Ds, or Fs. Students who score below the level set for mastery (usually 80%) must remediate and recycle.

Like all other curriculum designs, mastery learning succeeds or fails depending on its application. Cunningham (1991, p. 84) explains:

> There are two essential elements of the mastery learning process. The first is an extremely close congruence between the material being taught, the teaching strategies employed, and the content measured. The second essential element is the provision of formative assessment, opportunities for students followed by feedback, corrective and enrichment activities.

There are basically two types of mastery learning: (1) teacher-paced and group-based, and (2) student-paced and individual-based (Block & Henson, 1986). Most mastery learning programs are student paced (the students set their own pace), and most are individual based (individual students pursue the content independently). This quality enables students to tie new information to previously learned knowledge and, in this sense, reflects the constructivist theory. Obviously, modern reformers who are committed to meeting the diverse needs of all students and those who adhere to the constructivist approach to learning find mastery learning appealing. Though mixed, the results of studies of the effects of mastery learning programs are encouraging. The first studies (Bloom, Hastings, & Madaus, 1981) found that at least 95% of all high school students could master all school objectives. Burns (1979) reviewed 157 such studies. Although in one-third of his studies (47) no differences in achievement were found, in two-thirds of the studies (107) mastery learning students significantly outscored their traditionally taught counterparts. In only 3 of the 157 studies did mastery learning students achieve less than their counterparts. Burns' review covered 3,000 schools and spanned over 15 years.

School systems must recognize that traditional methods of teaching and learning are unsuccessful for many students. Mastery learning is an alternative to the unsuccessful traditional methods of teaching and learning. A change from traditional curriculum and instruction models and adoption of a new method will require major restructuring of how the schools are organized and how teachers are prepared and empowered. School systems have the task of defining success, determining what it requires to be successful in the twenty-first century, and then evaluating research, outcomes, and discussions of which method would best meet each individual's needs.

Guskey and Gates (1986) reviewed 25 studies of group-based and teacher-paced mastery learning programs in elementary schools and secondary schools. In all 25 studies, the students in mastery learning groups outlearned their counterparts.

Problem Solving

The problem-solving curriculum became popular during the Progressive Education Era (from about 1925 to 1945) because of the emphasis during that time on learner-centered curricula. What better way to involve students and provide a means for connecting new information to prior understanding than to give them problems to solve? Problem solving received a rebirth in the 1960s, when the cold war was at its peak and the *Sputnik* scare gripped the psyche of America. Realizing that American students were long on facts and short on the ability to apply these facts, curriculum designs cast the new interdisciplinary curriculum in the form of problems.

These new programs were identified by acronyms and titles, many of which reflected their developers. For example, Harvard had its Project Physics, and Boulder, Colorado, had its Earth Science Curriculum Project (ESCP). There was a Science and Mathematics Study Group (SMSG). These curricula were three-dimensional.

Typical of laboratory schools and other innovative schools during this era, the P. K. Younge Laboratory School at the University of Florida was equipped with a room full of objects, including a set of scales, tension springs, a toy truck, an inclined plane, and dozens of other gadgets. This was the hardware required to implement one of the new problem-solving curricula. By requiring students to use this hands-on equipment to solve problems, these curricula forced students to apply their acquired knowledge.

Problem solving is still a valued curriculum design because many people maintain that this skill is a necessity for coping in the future. Students need opportunities to solve problems that are authentic—problems that involve real-life issues. Since real-life issues are by nature transdisciplinary, attention to them integrates the curriculum in natural ways. For problem solving to be effective, the problem-solving scenario must spring from genuine student learning objectives.

The need for curricula to be offered in a risk-free environment has been mentioned throughout this book. The amount of time teachers give students to spend on each problem is equally critical. A recent study reported that, on average, Japanese students spend three times as long on each mathematics problem as their U.S. counterparts (TIMSS, 2003). At no place is this need greater than in a problem-solving classroom.

Providing students with opportunities to solve problems can make the difference between their dealing with the content superficially and their developing in-depth understanding of the content and learning how to apply it to solve authentic problems (Armstrong et al., 2009). By solving a variety of problems, students deepen their understanding, and they begin to abstract the concepts and refine the techniques needed to apply to the complex original problem. We cannot expect children to maximize retention and generalization of information presented to them at school under conditions of high pressure, low relevance, and great challenge.

Today, educators' heavy emphasis on constructivism has again rekindled the passion that educators have for problem solving. The need to connect to previous understanding and learn in depth continues to make problem solving popular in American schools. Students need to develop disciplined minds, and teachers need to know how to nurture disciplined minds. Cindy Reed (2010) recommends having students identify and draw metaphors. This lets the teachers and students see what the students are thinking. Veronica Boix-Mansilla and Howard Gardner (2008) suggest that in-depth learning can be reached by spending considerable time on fewer topics, encouraging students to examine every topic from multiple perspectives. The deeper knowledge a learner has, the more analytical, experimental, and creative the learner's thought processes are.

Since each curriculum design has a unique combination of strengths and weaknesses, curriculum developers who are aware of these designs can match them with the needs of their schools. For example, the many schools that are now being required by reform practices to implement integrated thematic units can benefit from the broad-fields design. Schools seeking ways to improve educational opportunities for minority students may choose to implement mastery learning, because it gives students the time they need to master each concept and because it provides students with opportunities to remediate and recycle without penalty. Multicultural classes may choose the Trump Plan or problem-solving curricula because they provide students with opportunities to participate in cooperative group projects.

Curriculum Design Qualities

None of these curriculum designs is unique. Rather, each design shares some common qualities. Examples of features include: scope, sequence, continuity, articulation, and balance.

Scope

Curriculum scope refers to the breadth of the curriculum at any level or at any given time. For example, the breadth of eighth-grade science refers to the variety of science topics covered during the eighth grade. Because scope concerns only one point in time, it is called a *horizontal dimension*. Many contemporary educators are concerned that the scope of today's curriculum has been dangerously narrowed by NCLB. For example, Berliner and Nichols (2007) say, "The narrowing of the curriculum to just what is tested shows a huge increase in time spent on test preparation instead of genuine instruction. We are turning America into a nation of test-takers, abandoning our heritage as a nation of thinkers, dreamers, and doers" (p. 3).

Sequence

Curriculum sequence is concerned with the order of topics over time. For example, in biology, students might study the cell and then tissue, organs, and systems. Because it examines the curriculum over a period of time, curriculum sequence is called a *vertical dimension*.

Mary Culver shares an activity that she uses to engage her students in sequencing the curriculum and aligning the content with the required standards.

FYI Chunking Content to Meet the Standards

Mary Culver • Northern Arizona University

To develop the fundamental skill of "chunking out" a course, my class plays this game using a super simple set of state standards for a nonadvanced course (no AP Calculus!). I've cut these standards into individual slips of paper containing one goal or performance objective on each with no "coding" included. Working in groups of four, students are asked to "chunk" the set of standards into "organized" piles based on some "logic" that works for them. When everything has been grouped together in sets, students are asked to place each group in logical progression.

Here's the kicker, though: They do this in total silence! Groups have to work collaboratively to "chunk" their course by passing slips to their peers if they feel it may fit better with their pile. When they agree that their group has logically grouped "chunks" of the course in an effective order, they all raise their hands. As I review their "course" they can explain why they have certain goals or POs grouped together and what determined the sequencing order. Their final step in this exercise is to "estimate" the time necessary to complete each "chunk" of instruction and calibrate that with a school calendar (They need to chat about that step!).

Continuity

Continuity refers to the smoothness or the absence of disruptions in the curriculum over time. A curriculum that has good sequence but also has disruptions lacks continuity. For example, as shown in table 5.3, curriculum A has good sequence and good continuity. Curriculum B has good sequence but lacks continuity. Curriculum C has poor sequence. Also, even though no topics are missing, the lack of order creates disruptions; therefore, curriculum C lacks continuity. So, sequence without continuity is possible, but continuity without sequence is not.

Table 5.3 Sequence versus Continuity

Curriculum A	Curriculum B	Curriculum C
H	H	H
G	G	G
F		F
E	E	E
D	D	C
C		D
B	B	B
A	A	A

When the sequence does not reflect the cumulative nature of (the subject), the resulting sequence of topics becomes nothing more than a meaningless list of items that students memorize but soon forget.

Articulation

Articulation refers to the smooth flow of the curriculum in both dimensions, vertical and horizontal. Vertical articulation is called continuity. Its horizontal counterpart has no name, since *scope* implies only one point in time rather than a flow.

Balance

Another important curriculum feature is *balance*. Frequently, the layperson speaks of a "well-rounded education," implying that an individual is getting (or a school program is offering) a curriculum with balance between the arts and sciences or between college prep subjects and vocational subjects. No Child Left Behind may be having a negative impact on curriculum balance. A major study released by the Center on Education Policy in March of 2006 showed that since the advent of NCLB, 71% of the elementary schools in the study had decreased the time devoted to subjects other than language arts and mathematics—or had eliminated some of these subjects—in order to make more time for instruction in the tested subjcct areas (Center on Education Policy, 2006).

The Role of Emotions in Learning

Now, let's reflect on the confluency concept and what the brain research discoveries (LeDoux, 1996; Wolfe & Brandt, 1998) say about the role emotions play in learning. How can curriculum planners use this information to improve the curriculum's balance? One way to ensure a balance between the cognitive and the affective role in each lesson is to plan activities that you know most students will enjoy. Some clues as to how this can be achieved may be found in the words of some former teachers of the year who give testimony to the importance of the joy in learning (Henson & Eller, 1999):

- According to Duane Obermier, former Nebraska teacher of the year, "I believe that working and learning at school can and should be fun. I joke and laugh freely with my students."
- Cynthia Lancaster, former Washington State teacher of the year, tells beginning teachers that setting clear behavior roles early in the year is a good way to provide an atmosphere that allows the teacher and students to have fun.
- Susan Lloyd, former Alabama teacher of the year, suggests that the best experience a teacher can plan is the joy of learning, and says that in planning for this to happen in her classes, she spends most of her time learning, attending lectures, reading, and discussing current issues. She uses "fascinating facts and thought-provoking questions" to kick-start their brains.
- Marilyn Grondel, former Utah teacher of the year, says, "I believe that wonder and joy are always in the attic of one's mind." She shares a few of techniques she uses to bring joy into her classes. First, she looks to the community. Since her school is in a rural setting, she uses stories of horses

to get students' attention. Next, she models: When she has reading class, for instance, she takes her turn and reads and writes along with the students. She also brings in community leaders for career day. Finally, she shares her techniques with fellow teachers: "A successful teacher becomes more successful by dialoguing with colleagues and sharing ideas and materials."

A tool called curriculum mapping can be used to monitor the curriculum for balance. For further information, see chapter 9.

A Final Note

Some of these programs are more student focused than others. This author believes the goal of all curriculum designs should be to keep the focus on the students. Kowal (1991, p. 269) has reminded curriculum designers that keeping the student as the center of attention does not imply that students should always get what they want. Student wants and student needs may be two entirely different things:

> The task is not to design a . . . program based on who yells the loudest or the longest or to use compromise as a rationale for curriculum design. The basis of an appropriate rationale is centered on the student; how students can be best prepared for a future, which is at any given time unknown.

Designing curricula to meet the future needs of students is an ongoing challenge that educators must meet. Most schools use modifications of several of the curriculum designs discussed in this chapter. In fact, because of the effect of the culture of the school and the culture of the local community, all curriculum designs must be modified so that they can adapt to the unique characteristics and needs of each particular school.

Conclusion

Following is a summary of some of the advances made and concerns raised about the topics discussed in this chapter.

Advances

- The curricula in our schools are successful in teaching reasoning abilities.
- The spiral curriculum can be used to help students build connections between concepts.
- Curriculum mapping can be used to monitor curricula for balance.

Concerns

- To be successful, problem solving must spring from students' interests.
- Recent research has shown that our curricula must strengthen connections between concepts and disciplines.
- Curricula need more relevance and less pressure.

The subject-centered curriculum is the oldest curriculum design. Teachers like it because it employs textbooks and the lecture method. The textbook provides specific, tightly organized content, enabling teachers to show off their expertise. Students like subject-centered curricula because of the specific content and tight organization and because they can remain passive while in the classroom.

Near the turn of the twentieth century, educators became concerned that subject-centered curricula led only to the memorization of disjointed facts and bits of information. As a result, this curriculum was replaced in many schools by broad-fields curricula, which integrated the subjects to produce broader understanding.

By the 1920s the educators of the Progressive Era wanted curricula that would enable them to serve each individual student's needs. They devised the core curriculum to achieve this goal. Other groups used it to achieve other goals. The many variations of core curricula had two things in common: (1) a common core of content required of everyone, and (2) a combination of content and activities used to meet particular goals.

Many modern education reformers believe that the subject-centered curriculum approach restricts learning. Thus, multidisciplinary curricula have regained popularity in schools throughout the country. Current reformers who push to have all children succeed like the individual emphasis given by the broad-fields and multidisciplinary approaches introduced by progressive educators. During the late 1950s, the Trump Plan was developed. This design was different from existing designs because it focused on grouping. Students were required to spend 40% of their time in large groups, 20% in small groups, and the remaining 40% in independent study or in small groups if they preferred.

Like the core curriculum, the Trump Plan had strength in its variety, with variation in methods, materials, and even in the length of the school day and the school year, including year-round curricula. Its emphasis on individual and small-group work appeals to current educators. Eighty percent of today's teachers use small-group assignments weekly, and 90% work with individual students weekly.

The spiral curriculum is built on two psychological foundations: connectionism and constructivism. It also employs developmentalism, recognizing that students are not ready to study certain concepts until they reach the required level of development and until they have had the necessary experiences.

Mastery learning is a curriculum design that purports to offer the opportunity for all students to succeed by giving individual students all the time they need to master the objectives, by affording them opportunities to remediate and recycle without penalty, and by using formative evaluation (which is given during instruction), not to assign grades but to improve learning by improving the curriculum and instruction. Obviously, this dedication to meeting the diverse needs of all students appeals to those contemporary educators who are dedicated to meeting the needs of students from all cultural backgrounds.

The problem-solving curriculum has long been a favorite design for educators who espouse learner-centered education. The cold-war-era launching of *Sputnik* created an atmosphere of panic and competition that gave problem-centered curricula a boost. It was hoped that, by discovering the answers to problems, students would more thoroughly understand the broader content generalizations required to master a discipline. In the twenty-first century, the problem-solving curriculum has received a renewed level of interest in American schools because it enables students to learn the topics at a greater depth and affords them opportunities to link new information with prior understanding.

Most mastery learning programs are individually based, making them attractive to teachers who are dedicated to meeting the needs of diverse groups of students.

Although these curriculum designs are all different, they all have certain features in common, such as scope (breadth), sequence, continuity, articulation, and balance. Success with any of these designs depends on teachers understanding the underpinning philosophies and on the quality of instruction used with the designs.

Additional Learning Opportunities

1. What qualities in the Little School That Grew are examples of constructivist theory?
2. Can you identify any practices in contemporary education reform that parallel the forces that caused the Little School to lose some of its valuable qualities?
3. What curriculum designs were reflected in the curriculum of the Little School before and after its changes?
4. Can you think of ways to make the changes the Little School made and yet avoid the losses that it suffered?
5. To what extent is formative evaluation (compared to summative evaluation) used in your school? Why do you think this is so?
6. What kinds of balance do you think your own college curriculum should strive to maintain? Examples: humanities versus sciences, general studies versus major subjects.
7. Do you believe it is important for teachers to understand a program's underlying philosophy? Why or why not?
8. Do the current education reform practices in your school have sound philosophical and theoretical bases? Explain your answer.
9. What is the best way you know to make school enjoyable to all students?

Suggested Activities

1. Select a curriculum design from this chapter and research (a) its philosophical and psychological bases, and (b) its degree of success as reported in the research and other literature.
2. Examine your own school (or visit a local school) and see what evidence you can find for each of these designs. Don't be surprised if you learn that the school uses a combination of several designs rather than a single "pure" design.
3. Get a copy of your state's curriculum guide from your library or from a local school counselor. Choose a discipline and grade level. For your chosen discipline and grade level, describe the program in your state's curriculum guide in terms of (a) how the content is sequenced, (b) the scope of the content, and (c) the balance between the sciences and the arts and between required subjects and electives.

4. The success of any curriculum design depends on the teacher's ability to implement the design. Select a design and describe how you could help teachers prepare to use it successfully to meet the needs of all students.
5. Make a list of the reform elements under way in your district. Now compare the curriculum designs in this chapter with the items in your list. What designs offer the best opportunities to meet some of the local reform goals?
6. Examine your school's curriculum plan and identify signs of constructivist theory.

AIMS, GOALS, AND OBJECTIVES

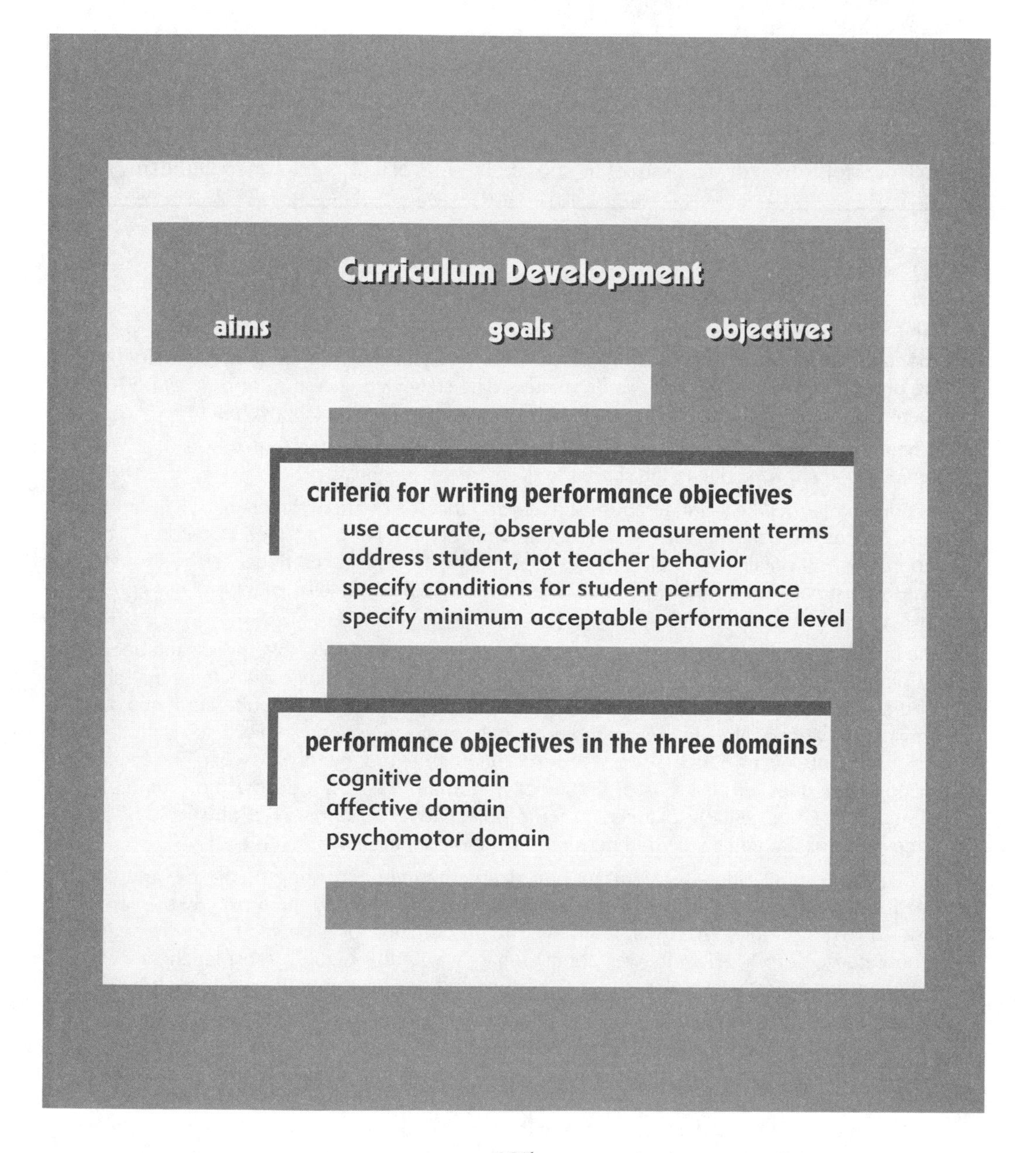

Focus Questions

1. How can curriculum planners use performance objectives to reach multicultural goals?
2. How can tests be used to raise students' levels of thinking?
3. How do aims, goals, and objectives relate to constructivist theory?
4. What implications does education reformers' emphasis on academic accountability have for teachers' competence in writing aims and goals?
5. How can curriculum planners use objectives in a positive way to support education reform?
6. How would you draw a model to show your interpretation of constructivism?

The Case of San Sona Elementary School

San Sona Elementary School has the reputation of being one of the most innovative, experimental, and advanced schools in its district. The many oil wells in the area make financing one of the least of the principal's worries. The state's education reform program has been pressing all of the schools to increase their students' level of achievement.

When Sondra Bell became principal last year, she promised the board members that with their support she would lead the school to even greater heights.

As Sondra planned her annual report, she realized that the board members had lived up to their part of the bargain, but she wondered whether they felt as positive about her. The report was to contain two parts, "In Retrospect" and "In Prospect." Because she thought that the first part was a little weak, Sondra decided to compensate by planning an impressive "In Prospect" section.

She began by spelling out her objectives for the coming year. Could she impress the board by planning everything for the coming year around the performance objectives that she would set for the students? This seemed like a logical approach, so she pulled out a taxonomy of educational objectives from the notes in her curriculum course. For each daily lesson, she wrote an objective at each level of the cognitive domain. But when she began writing objectives for all levels of the affective domain, her task became more difficult. Although she had initially planned to write objectives that represented all levels of all three domains, Sondra gave up in despair long before the task was completed.

Rather than admit failure, Sondra appointed a committee consisting of the department heads and one or two members of each department. She assigned them exactly the same task—to write sample objectives at all levels in all domains for each subject in the entire school curriculum. The faculty was not at all happy with this request. Most teachers were already using objectives in planning their lessons, but they thought this was going too far.

Sondra heard some of the teachers' complaints so often that she almost suspected a conspiracy. Most teachers insisted that the implementation of the education reform practices had already made their workload almost impossible. Sondra supposed they were telling the truth, because a new performance evaluation system required all teachers to develop portfolios for all their students and forbade the use of paper tests. In addition, soon all tests would have to be aligned with the state's 150 new valued outcomes. As Sondra reflected, she realized that, indeed, the new education reform requirements were truly overloading her faculty.

Another complaint that was voiced daily questioned the value of stating everything in terms of objectives. Some teachers speculated that it was just another policy imposed on them from the outside and written by nonteachers who had little or no experience in writing objectives for classroom use. Other teachers said that they thought that trying to write everything in terms of objectives would restrict classroom activities and make lessons seem overstructured or prefabricated. Some said that the use of objectives would lead to totally depersonalized teaching.

As Sondra considered these complaints, she wondered whether there might be a more acceptable way to convince the faculty to use objectives with all lessons.

• • •

This vignette shows what can and often does happen when administrators lack an awareness of the damaging effect that objectives can have on teachers. But this does not have to be the case. On the contrary, when correctly used, objectives can raise the performance of teachers, students, and schools. As you read this chapter, make mental notes of the many positive uses of objectives, and challenge yourself to think of additional ways you can and will use aims, goals, and objectives.

The Aims, Goals, and Objectives of Curriculum Development

Curriculum developers at all levels share some common roles. Today, as never before, reform programs hold teachers, instructional supervisors, administrators, and curriculum specialists responsible for student achievement. Although most of the reform reports speak of "quality," an amorphous term, quality is not the ends—it is the means. The primary objective of the current education restructuring movement is to improve learning, but without a systematic, intensive, and long-term professional development design, restructuring does not necessarily lead to instructional change.

Terms such as *performance evaluation*, *alternative assessment*, and *valued outcomes* reflect the determination of education reformers to hold educators responsible for ensuring that their students are making satisfactory academic progress. Teachers are caught between two very different mandates and are working to make both the trip (education) and the destination (improved test scores) happen.

Curriculum alignment, another popular term, is one more reminder that educators have the responsibility of ensuring the academic success of their students. Curriculum alignment means adjusting the planned curriculum so that the taught curriculum will parallel the tested curriculum. Although some critics caution that politicians often use curriculum alignment as a lever to cause schools to invoke the politicians' goals, Guskey (2003) points out that curriculum concepts, skills, and criteria need to align with the teacher's instructional activities and, ideally, with state or district standards.

Outcomes-based education (OBE) is defining clearly what students are to learn (desired outcomes), measuring their progress in terms of actual achievement, meeting their needs through various teaching strategies, and giving them enough time and help to meet their potential. Although critics have challenged the effectiveness of OBE, Connecticut—the first state to adopt statewide goals—has experienced increases in the percentage of students graduating and the percentage of students going to college as well as a higher average in reading and math scores. Unfortunately, as discussed in chapter 9, the OBE concept evokes resentment among many.

Ideally, curriculum development should begin by examining the desired outcomes, including aims, goals, and objectives. Such formative assessment is discussed in chapter 9. The purpose is simply to know what the curriculum, and hence the instruction that follows, is trying to achieve. Many states are developing new tests that all schools within the state must administer periodically. Obviously, curriculum developers should examine these desired outcomes and design the curriculum accordingly.

Teachers must also involve students and parents in reshaping the curriculum. According to Bunting (2007, p. 41), "Talk among teachers almost always can be turned to benefit." Ironically, however, while NCLB has encouraged teachers to involve parents and other community members, teachers are finding less time to collaborate even among themselves (Hanson & Moir, 2008).

One of the most disabling traditions in America (and, in fact, in world education) is the self-contained classroom. Teachers work by themselves and are insulated from intervention by the four walls of their room and the tradition of being fully in charge. A successful teacher does not keep ideas and materials secret but becomes more successful by dialoguing with colleagues and sharing ideas and materials. Current reform seems to demand a holistic approach. Such an approach is *systemic reform*, a term that means everyone working together to change the entire school (Armstrong et al., 2009). Increased accountability requires a cooperative approach to curriculum development. Subject-matter teachers should meet at regular intervals to discuss and plan curriculum and to develop sound strategies designed to achieve quality standards. Curriculum planning requires teachers to be collaborative inquirers (Bintz & Dillard, 2007).

Curriculum developers need to differentiate among the aims, goals, and objectives used to express desired outcomes. The statement made earlier—that ideally, curriculum development should begin by examining the desired outcomes—begins with an important conditional word, *ideally*. As practitioners very well know, most curriculum development doesn't occur under ideal conditions. While recognizing the ideal can help one to grasp an understanding of the curriculum development process, most curriculum developers find themselves revising existing curricula, which may be far from ideal.

Before you begin reading about aims, goals, and objectives, take a moment to reflect on the fact that a culture of high expectations for students, teachers, administrators, and parents has been found to be a hallmark of high-achieving schools (Thompson, 2008). Students take their teachers' high expectations to heart and try to live up to them. Robert Walker's (2008) analysis of the top 12 characteristics of effective teachers as seen by students found that one of the most important was students' perception of high expectations held by their teachers. Walker concluded that the most effective teachers hold high expectations, set no limits on students,

FYI Shared Planning Period

Holly L. Kunert • Tarleton State University

One of the most important things that every campus seems to really benefit from is shared planning periods. While research indicates that having a shared planning period is helpful for aligning curriculum, I have found it to be very helpful for several additional reasons. To begin, having a shared planning period seems to help faculty to develop shared interests and congeniality with each other within their departments, especially in larger schools. It also is extremely beneficially to have a common area to go to each day or week to allow curriculum and instruction to be better aligned, as there is not need to "make time" to facilitate that task. Finally, as an administrator, it is a wonderful opportunity to stay abreast of the curriculum that is being used with students, and it allows faculty to see a friendly, administrative presence that is nonthreatening, communicative, and helpful. It has been my experience that a daily (or even weekly) meeting of faculty within a department for a shared planning period helps morale, perceptions of administrative support, and organization of lesson planning.

consistently challenge their students to do their best, and build students' confidence, teaching them to believe in themselves. Make an effort to keep this in mind when you consider the aims, goals, and objectives you will set for your students.

Aims

Of the different types of educational expectations, aims are the most general. When developing curriculum, educators should include aims that relate to what students can and will do outside the school when they have more choices of behavior (Eisner, 2001). *Educational aims* are lifetime aspirations that provide long-term directions for students, encompassing nearly every aspect of human experience. Most aims are written for groups rather than individuals. Two important aims are that all students will become critical thinkers and lifelong learners (Noddings, 2008). Other good examples of educational aims are those expectations found in the Cardinal Principles of Secondary Education discussed in chapter 3: health, development of moral character, worthy home membership, citizenship, worthy use of leisure time, vocational efficiency, and development of the fundamental processes.

Like a cross-country road map, aims help us guide our lives in general, desirable directions. Aims can never be fully attained. For example, one aim might be to design and maintain a curriculum that promotes multiculturalism. Another aim could be to construct and use a curriculum that exhibits constructivist learning theory. Neither of these aims can ever be fully met, because there will always be room for improvement.

Goals

Because goal identification should involve students and parents, it essentially is a lengthy process. Like aims, *educational goals* are also expectations for groups, and they may take weeks, months, or even years to attain. By definition, goals differ from aims in that goals are attainable, even though many go unattained. A particular high school may have as one of its goals that the mean achievement scores for all classes tested in the next year will equal to or exceed their counterparts' scores on this year's tests. Because they are group-oriented, the successful attainment of goals does not require every student to succeed.

Because group projects can contribute to students' social growth, which is often one of a school's aims, students should be involved in setting goals. Such involvement can also enhance multicultural goal attainment. Student involvement should occur early, on the very first day of class, as students and teachers get acquainted and share their hopes for the coming year.

An example of a multicultural goal might be to have all students working cooperatively on small-group assignments with all their classmates by the end of the first grading period. A constructivist goal might be to have all students put in writing, by the end of the first week of school, their individual perception of how they learn best, naming at least three conditions that they find supportive. One goal might be to have every student end each unit wanting to know more. Another goal would be to have all students end the year feeling more capable than when they began (Sagor, 2008).

Objectives

To avoid confusion, this book will use the term *objectives* to refer to what is expected of students on a daily basis. We could also call these *performance objectives*, since each objective refers to the ability of students to perform selected tasks in one or more specific ways.

Performance assessment is not always easy, but it is important, and experts in the field of educational measurement continue to wrestle with how to make performance assessment valid and reliable, not to mention honest and fair. Clear expectations are a prerequisite for maximum learning in any class (Roberts, 2008) and are especially critical for at-risk students.

Returning to the road-map analogy, objectives are like statewide maps in that they chart the course for each day. Many educators have insisted that all worthwhile expectations that schools hold for students should be stated in objectives. This author disagrees and maintains that some of the most valuable services provided by schools, some of the most important effects of schools and teachers, may never be stated in terms of objectives. For example, by definition objectives must be measurable, but how can you measure the growth of a student's self-concept or appreciation for learning?

Attempts to state all of a school's business in terms of objectives have been made, and they have failed. One teacher education faculty attempted this feat and produced over 2,500 objectives to be met by each student majoring in teacher education. The cause of this problem is not the objectives but rather their misuse. Such findings do not negate the importance of appropriately used objectives. Objectives clarify the expectations teachers hold for student performance. When objectives are used, there are no unexpected or surprise results since both parties have agreed upon the end product. When students know the expected outcomes, they usually become more involved in their assignments. Because performance objectives are the most specific of all expressions of education expectations, they must be written with great precision and detail. The following sections introduce techniques for writing performance objectives.

Criteria for Writing Performance Objectives

The exact steps that teachers use when writing objectives may vary according to the preferences of their administrators and according to the content being studied. Most authorities appear to agree that all statements of performance objectives must meet at least three criteria, as follows:

1. Objectives must be stated in terms of expected student behavior (not teacher behavior).
2. Objectives must specify the conditions under which the students are expected to perform.
3. Objectives must specify the minimum acceptable level of performance.

Stating objectives in terms of expected student behavior rather than teacher behavior is important because all lessons are developed for students. For each student the success of each lesson depends on appropriate student involvement. For example, rather than saying, "The teacher will teach verb conjugation," the objective would read, "Students will conjugate verbs."

Reform efforts are bringing pressures on educators from many directions. The emphasis is usually on test scores, pressuring teachers to raise the scores of their students. But educators must remember that schools exist for students, not educators, pressure groups, or parents.

To be more precise, the school exists to change the behavior of students—mentally, physically, socially, emotionally, and even morally. When teachers state all objectives in terms of desired student performance and use specifics that are observable and measurable, they and their students more clearly understand what is expected and the degree to which these expectations are being met. The lists of terms in table 6.1 show types of verbs that describe specific, observable, and measurable actions (see the *Yes* column) and those that are too general and vague to be accurately observed and measured (see the *No* column).

Table 6.1 Performance Objective Terms

Yes (specific and measurable)	No (vague and not measurable)
build	appreciate
classify	consider
contrast	desire
demonstrate	feel
distinguish	find interesting
evaluate	have insight into
identify	know
interpret	learn
label	like to
list	love to
match	really like to
measure	recognize
name	remember
remove	see that
select	think
state	understand
write	want to

Because students can grasp only a limited number of major ideas in a period of 45 or 50 minutes, the daily lesson plan for a given period should contain only four or five major ideas. Suppose an English teacher wants to teach composition writing. That teacher could select four or five of the most important ideas about capturing and holding the reader's attention. These would become the content for the first day's lesson in a unit titled "Composition Writing." Suppose the teacher determines that five ideas are essential to capturing the reader's attention and that, once captured, four ideas are essential to holding it. If so, the teacher could plan one lesson on how to capture the reader's attention and a subsequent lesson on how to hold the reader's attention.

Since objectives should be written in terms of desired student behavior, the emphasis should not be "Today I'll teach" but "As a result of the lesson, each student will. . . ." Teachers should also state the conditions under which the students are expected to perform ("When given a list containing vertebrates and invertebrates, . . ."). Teachers should also state the expected level of performance ("with 80% accuracy" or "without error"), and they should avoid using verbs that cannot be observed or measured, such as *appreciate*, *learn*, *know*, and *understand* (see table 6.1). Such general verbs should be replaced with specific, action-oriented verbs such as *identify*, *list*, *explain*, *name*, *describe*, and *compare*.

Performance Objectives in the Three Domains

Some education aims and goals deal with thinking (for example, command of the fundamental processes), others involve attitudes (for example, development of moral character), and still others focus on physical skills (for example, competency in art, music, and sports). Many educators say that teachers should write performance objectives in each of these domains (cognitive, affective, and psychomotor) for each class. Although this may not always be practical or sensible, perhaps you will agree that teachers should be able to do this and should also be able to write objectives at varying levels of difficulty in each domain.

Writing Objectives in the Cognitive Domain

The first real systematic approach to helping teachers write objectives at specified levels came in 1956, when Benjamin S. Bloom and a group of students at the University of Chicago developed an *educational taxonomy* of objectives in the *cognitive domain* that included the following six levels (Bloom, 1956):

Level 1: Knowledge
Level 2: Comprehension
Level 3: Application
Level 4: Analysis
Level 5: Synthesis
Level 6: Evaluation

This taxonomy is a useful tool for thinking and talking about what is happening and what is not happening in students' heads (Brady, 2008). As Woolfolk Hoy and Hoy (2009) have noted, "Using taxonomies of objectives inspires planning (p. 192).

Involving students in tasks that require them to operate at these different levels requires the ability to write objectives for each level.

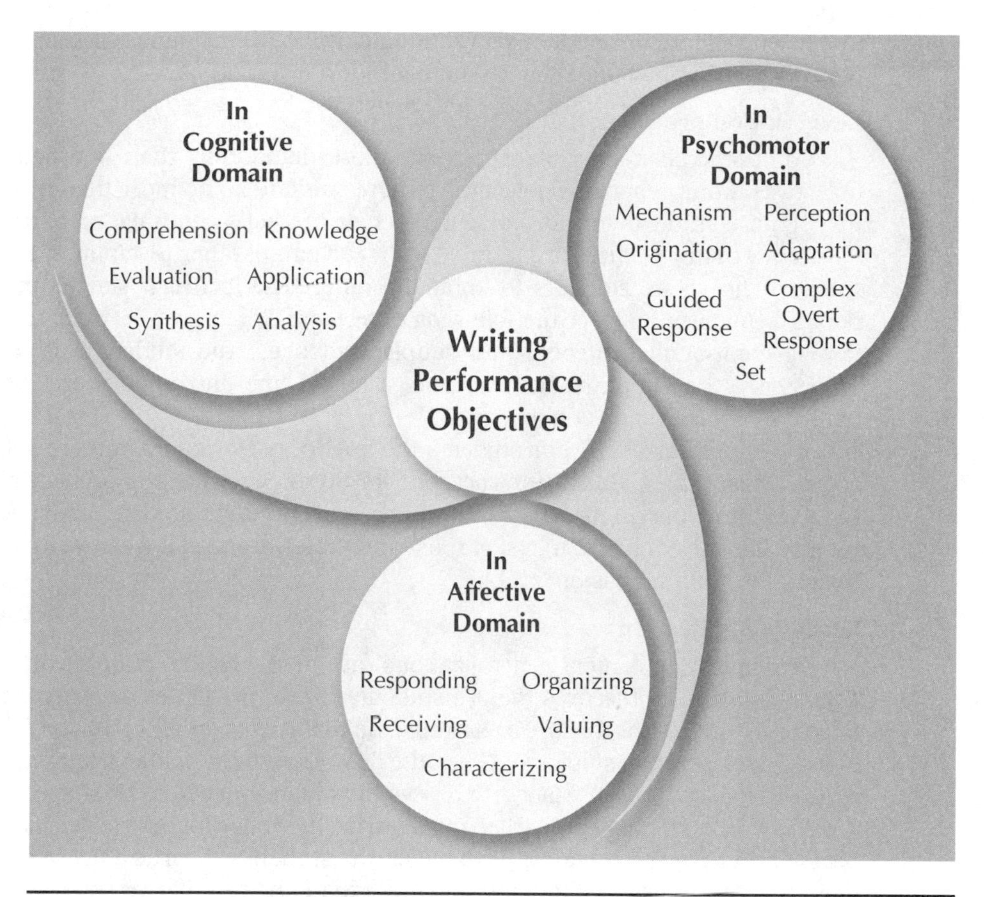

Figure 6.1 Writing Performance Objectives

Level 1: Knowledge

Mastery of facts and concepts is a prerequisite for performing higher mental operations. For example, many mathematics problems require students to multiply. Learning the multiplication tables can probably best be done by simple rote memorization. Objectives that focus on memorization are the easiest to write. Unfortunately, fifty years have passed since this taxonomy was developed and yet "recall seems to play as important a role in instruction as ever" (Brady, 2008, p. 66). Many lessons fail to go beyond this most elementary level. Some assignments or tasks at the knowledge level are essential, but they should not dominate the curriculum.

An example of a *knowledge-level objective* would be: "When given a list of 10 adjectives, 10 verbs, and 10 adverbs, the student will correctly identify 8 of the 10 adverbs and 8 of the 10 adjectives." This objective begins with a statement of the conditions under which students are expected to perform the task ("When given . . .), and it is written in terms of desired student performance ("the student will . . .). In addition, the objective contains an action-oriented verb that can be observed and measured ("identify"), and it ends with a statement of the minimum acceptable level of performance ("8 of the 10").

Level 2: Comprehension

Comprehension-level objectives are more demanding than knowledge-level objectives. Comprehension objectives require students to do more than memorize; they require students to translate, interpret, or predict a continuation of trends.

Today many teachers are teaming with teachers of other disciplines. A history teacher who wants students to know the differences between simple and compound sentences may set the following objective: "When given a paragraph containing compound sentences and simple sentences, the student will correctly underscore the simple sentences using a single line and underscore the compound sentences using double lines."

You should also tell your students the level of performance you are willing to accept. Must it be 100%? Is 90% acceptable? 80%? Since the comprehension level requires students to translate, interpret, and predict, student activities that require the use of charts, maps, graphs, and tables are useful when writing objectives at the comprehension level.

Level 3: Application

Principles (or content generalizations) are at the center of *application-level objectives*. These objectives require students to use principles or generalizations to solve a concrete problem. For example, an art teacher might write the following objective for painting students: "Given the definition of the golden triangle, the student will use the golden triangle to assess the balance of colors or shapes used in a picture." Or an English teacher might write the following objective: "Given the beats and measures in iambic pentameter, the student will write a five-verse poem in iambic pentameter without missing more than one beat per verse."

A professor at St. John's University who teaches a writing-for-publication class to doctoral students requires each student to prepare an article for one journal and then rewrite it to make it suitable for another journal. This is an excellent example of the use of an application-level objective.

Level 4: Analysis

Analysis-level objectives also require students to work with principles, concepts, and broad generalizations. In this case, students are required to break down the concepts and principles in order to better understand them, and to do this they must understand not only the content but also its structural form.

For example, a government teacher might write the following objective for a class that is studying how a bill becomes a law: "Given a particular law, students will trace its development from the time it was first introduced as a bill, listing every major step without missing any." A teacher of auto mechanics might write the following objective for a group of students who have been studying the electrical system in an automobile: "Starting with the positive battery terminal, the student will trace the electric current throughout the automobile until it returns to the negative battery terminal, stating what happens in the coil, alternator, distributor, and condenser without getting more than one of these steps out of sequence."

A biology teacher might ask students to trace the human circulatory system in a similar manner.

Level 5: Synthesis

Unlike analysis objectives, which require students to take principles apart, synthesis requires students to take several parts of something and put them together to make a whole. *Synthesis-level objectives* are more demanding because they require students to form a new whole, requiring students to think in new ways and to be creative. For example, a science teacher might require students to design a toy machine that could climb a set of stairs. Because of their divergent and creative nature, synthesis-level questions are difficult to write. Generally, practice is a prerequisite to competence in writing objectives at this level.

Today's students, the world over, need higher-order cognitive skills (Suarez-Orozco, 2007). Writing higher-level objectives can safeguard against shallow teachers using shallow lessons that produce shallow learning. The need for teachers to be able to write higher-level objectives is great. Over three centuries ago, René Descartes (see Spielvogel, 2006) advised us to divide anything we couldn't understand into parts and arrange them from simple to complex. As we lead students to higher-level thinking, we must realize that: (1) Without objectives, classroom thinking will remain dominated by rote memorizing, (2) Higher-level thinking cannot be demanded, and (3) We must help students attain it by nurturing them through a series of successfully more advanced learning tasks until the they reach the desired level of performance.

Level 6: Evaluation

The evaluation level is the highest level in Bloom's cognitive domain. *Evaluation-level objectives* require students to make judgments based on definite criteria, not just opinions. Evaluation-level objectives contain various combinations of elements of the first five levels of objective types.

A speech teacher might use the following objective with students who are studying diplomatic and persuasive techniques: "While viewing a video recording of a public figure's two most recent public addresses, each student will rate the speeches in terms of tact and persuasion, pinpointing in each address at least three areas of strength and three areas of weakness." Or a physical education instructor who is teaching bowling may want to write an objective that involves evaluating a participant's starting position, delivery, and follow-through.

The ability to write objectives at each cognitive level is crucial, since this is the only way to be sure that students will learn to develop intellectual skills at each level. Because this is the most important work a teacher does to effect learning, teachers must be able to state objectives clearly.

Not all educators agree that such distinct steps parallel the actual development of youths. As early as the mid-1980s, educators have been warned to raise the level of thinking in their classrooms. In his book, *A Place Called School*, John Goodlad (1984) said:

> Only rarely did we find evidence to suggest instruction [in reading and math] likely to go much beyond merely possession of information to a level of under-

> standing its implications and either applying it or exploring its possible applications. Nor did we see activities likely to arouse students' curiosity or to involve them in seeking a solution to some problem not already laid bare by teachers or textbook. . . . And it appears that this preoccupation with the lower intellectual processes pervades social studies and science as well. An analysis of topics studied and materials used gives not an impression of students studying human adaptations and exploration, but of facts to be learned. (p. 236)

When people are given a specific objective, they will often reach that objective at the expense of the overall purpose (that) that objective was established to attain. This negative effect is known as *goal displacement.*

If students are to reach the upper levels of the taxonomy it will be the result of purposeful planning by the teacher, yet teachers often hold expectations that are beyond students' levels of development. As you already know, success is more likely to come when the entire school and community are involved early and often.

The success of any new program depends on the factional interactions of the players. Following is a case with plenty of subgroups, each with its own agenda. As you read this case, consider the future role for which you are currently preparing and, if confronted with these events, the reactions you might have. Think also about any proactive measures you might take to help a faculty avoid some of these problems.

case study

"TOGETHER WE ARE BETTER"

Judith Patterson, Kennesaw State University
Barbara Vella, Vickery Creek Middle School
Tak Cheung Chan, Kennesaw State University

Background Information

This case represents a common problem in schools where some faculty members have been teaching the same grade level in the same school for a number of years. As years go by, without some kind of change, teachers of long standing may become settled and stagnant without new ideas. There is less willingness to embrace opportunities that, although they are aimed at improving the achievement of students, are perceived as unnecessary, burdensome, and perhaps threatening. "The status quo is the way to go" could be the slogan for these particular teachers. One of the kindergarten teachers wants to ensure that all her students are achieving to their maximum by introducing a remedial approach to assist the strugglers and offering to examine the effectiveness of the entire kindergarten curriculum. What can a relatively new, enthusiastic teacher do to initiate a change in the classrooms that will increase student achievement? As the school curriculum and instructional leader, what can a school principal offer to help? How does the principal determine whether the change proposal is the right thing to do? Can individual teachers make a change without getting the consent of their colleagues? How does the change initiative tie in with the mission of the school? Principals can take a leadership role to help resolve some of these curriculum and instructional issues.

The Community

Holmes County School District is a medium-size, rapidly growing school district. With a student enrollment of 32,000, the district continues to grow with an average of 2,000 students a year. Because Holmes County has a lot of undeveloped land and good resources plus an admirable state highway system, it is attractive to many small and mid-size industries establishing regional bases of their businesses. Furthermore, the county has a strong tax base providing stable support of its educational needs. Development of new industries in Holmes County has brought in young populations seeking opportunities for career growth. Despite its rapid development, the county prides itself on maintaining a "small town" feel. It has distinct areas of "new and old" communities. Citizens in the newer communities are generally more highly educated, with above average incomes. Setting excellence as the standard, Holmes County School District believes that students must be challenged with high quality work every single day. Its caring schools offer the type of personalized education that residents are seeking for their children. Much of the school district budget is allocated for its nationally recognized technology support for education. Academic class sizes in the district schools are among the lowest in the state. Student standardized test scores of Holmes County School District are among the highest in the state and its schools have received numerous state and national recognitions.

The School

Located in the town of Stillwater, a newer community of Holmes County, Villa Elementary School was constructed in 1976 with a new classroom addition in 2002. The playground was renovated in 2001 with assistance from its business partner, Super Target. The school has a student enrollment of 727 with 89% Caucasian, 7.5% Hispanic, 2.5% African American and 1% Asian. Approximately 16% of the students receive free or reduced price lunch. Since its establishment, the school has set its mission statement as *"Quality learning and superior performance for all,"* which is a direct reflection of the school district's goal for academic excellence. The school motto, "Together, We Are Better," can be seen in every school hallway, promoting a climate of collaboration and achievement. Teachers in Villa Elementary School believe in instructional technology. Interactive White Boards are used daily in every classroom along with desktop computers, offering every child twenty-first-century learning experiences. Various research-based instructional techniques are used to meet the needs of all students, and success is celebrated daily.

The Principal

Mr. Edwin Truitt, the principal of Villa Elementary School, was an elementary teacher for 15 years before he was appointed assistant principal of a rural elementary school where he stayed for 3 years. Now in his second year as school principal in Villa Elementary School, Mr. Truitt is known for his effort in promoting student success through different collaborative channels. He establishes excellent relationships with parents and key community members in support of student learning experiences. Internally, he believes in a bottom-to-top management philosophy, which some faculty dislike as reactive leadership. However, he is respected by many teachers as a site-based school administrator.

The Kindergarten Teacher for Change

Mrs. Barbara Bagwell has 25 years of teaching experience in elementary and middle school. When she came to this state, she wanted to focus on her area of expertise: the teaching of reading and writing. She is now in her third year as one of the 8 kindergarten teachers in Villa Elementary School. Because of her previous out-of-state kindergarten experiences, she also serves as grade chair this year and works with the Leadership Team. Mrs. Bagwell has repeatedly sought to draw other kindergarten teachers into discussions about the students' achievements, not just "your" students and "my students," but "all of our students." She has pushed the idea that the kindergarten teachers are responsible for all kindergartners.

Two years ago she began to have conversations with other kindergarten teachers about the number of students retained in kindergarten each year. In their meetings, she initiated conversations in which she and her kindergarten team members reflected on the strengths and weakness of each "struggling" student and what kind of remediation each of their teachers provide. She also questioned the activities of the existing kindergarten program to determine whether it was providing sufficient challenge to kindergarteners.

Before bringing the topic to her teammates, she had often asked herself: How can I ensure that my students are being challenged throughout the year and are achieving to their utmost potential? Would it be possible to rearrange the schedule so we could provide the additional support to our strugglers? Is there a way to offer remediation to the two or three students in every class who fall so far behind the rest of the class? Would such a plan help more strugglers succeed and move on to first grade? Could the kindergarten program be entirely re-examined to provide systematic differentiation in reading and writing?

Mrs. Bagwell proposed to the other teachers that a remediation time for students is an important first step to helping the "strugglers." She suggests that a 45-minute pull-out time in early morning would be a significant way to take the strugglers to very small groups with intervention strategies to begin remediation. To maximize this window of learning opportunity, teachers would have to agree to reschedule their mornings in order to create a forty-five minute block of time every day from which struggling learners would be pulled for extra help specific to their needs. During the pull-out time, the strugglers would go to the assigned paraprofessional for remediation. While the strugglers are gone, each teacher would be responsible for creating practice or enrichment activities for the rest of the class so that new or critical instruction would not occur while the strugglers were in remediation.

Mrs. Bagwell recognized that many members of the learning community did not feel "safe" and therefore, were resistant to change. Because they felt their professional abilities were being called into question, some teachers felt vulnerable to criticism, even if it was constructive. These teachers felt very ill at ease with Mrs. Bagwell's proposal.

The Other Kindergarten Teachers

There are seven other kindergarten teachers, each assigned a full-time paraprofessional. They are all a part of the learning community, although three of them are reluctant members. When the learning community began, teachers were asked to reflect on their teaching styles and strategies. Several teachers were uncomfortable examining their own pedagogy and class scheduling and were much less committed to helping ALL kindergartners—not just those in their classes.

One of the kindergarten teachers, Stacey Reeves, is working on her master's degree in early childhood education. She is so absorbed in her graduate work that she often does not meet the expectations of the other team members. She doesn't want to change her morning schedule because she is accustomed to using the 45-minute time slot (when her paraprofessional would be pulled) in the teachers' workroom to copy materials for her graduate course work.

Mildred Tarpley is the most experienced teacher on the kindergarten team. She is in her twenty-eighth year of teaching and is eager to retire as soon as possible. Mrs. Tarpley is the most outspoken critic of any change in the schedule and sees no reason why she should be concerned about any kindergartners other than her own. She is blunt in her criticisms, not only of proposed curriculum changes but of her co-workers as well. Convinced that due to her years of experience she should be considered the expert, she resents the efforts of Mrs. Bagwell and others.

Another kindergarten teacher, Teresa Stafford, is a "career changer" and this is her second year of teaching. She is extremely motivated and loves her job as a kindergarten teacher. She is anxious to do whatever she can to advance the achievement of all the kindergartners, and her paraprofessional is very committed, too. Mrs. Stafford is so enthusiastic that sometimes the other teachers are overwhelmed by her enthusiasm. Because this is only her second year, Mrs. Tarpley, the most experienced teacher, is especially bossy toward her and tries to suppress her interests and enthusiasm with caustic comments.

The Paraprofessionals

The eight paraprofessionals are as diverse as the teachers. Some have been working at Villa Elementary for ten or more years and have lived in Holmes County all their lives. They know many of the students and their parents. It could be said that they have a vested interest in the school and protecting its culture. They are happy with things the way they are. In some cases, their support of the school, though well intentioned, is counterproductive, because it rests in maintaining the status quo.

One of the paraprofessionals, Mrs. Wright, has been at Villa Elementary for twenty-one years. She has outlasted five principals and has been there longer than most of the faculty. She is the great-granddaughter of Conrad Villa, whose family donated the property on which the school was built and for whom it was named. She is a prominent member of the "old" Stillwater community and represents a body of citizens who are unhappy with the influx of wealthy, demanding newcomers. She sees changes in school and community as a threat to the lifestyle associated with the rural roots with which her family is connected. Although Mrs. Wright is a respected paraprofessional, she is resistant to the idea of learning communities and does not want to change anything in her work schedule or responsibilities.

Another paraprofessional, Mrs. Allgood, is highly respected among the kindergarten teachers, but she is undergoing an extremely difficult divorce. Previously she had been among the helpful and successful paraprofessionals, but now she is distracted and emotionally distraught over her personal situation. While she has always been dependable, co-operative and creative, she is now frequently absent, subject to crying episodes, and has become increasingly short tempered with the children.

A third paraprofessional, Mrs. Vane, has been at Villa Elementary for three years. She previously worked as a day-care provider but found that working for the public school system was more lucrative. The school calendar, the salary, and the benefits were better than those she had as a day-care provider. However, she feels that she is overqualified for her job as a paraprofessional, and the kindergarten teacher with whom she is assigned, Patience McGarity, often becomes exasperated with Mrs. Vane's "know it all" attitude. Ms. McGarity is challenged with keeping Mrs. Vane on track and doing what she is supposed to do.

The Case

The proposed change in the kindergarten schedule was not well received by most of the teachers. They considered their own schedules as "sacred" and did not want to rearrange their classroom schedules to accommodate a morning pull-out group of students from across the kindergarten for remedial work. They said that their paraprofessionals would be unavailable to take care of the "housekeeping duties" that usually occur first thing, such as attendance, lunch count, collecting notes from home, and homework.

In curriculum issues, Mrs. Bagwell has always compared the Villa Elementary kindergarten program with other out-of-state programs. She complained that the Villa Elementary program confines kindergartners to too much indoor center-to-center activities. As a great advocate of outdoor learning activities to enrich kindergartners' school experiences, Mrs.

Bagwell presented a proposal of kindergarten program revision to include over 30% of the learning activities outside the kindergarten classrooms. Since this revolutionary proposal would require all kindergarten teachers to completely reorganize their class activities, Mrs. Bagwell met with strong opposition from many teachers who do not want any change or simply have no time to do the planning for change.

Another proposed change by Mrs. Bagwell was the kindergartners' exposure to technology experiences. In lieu of the 30-minute elective activities on computer program use, Mrs. Bagwell proposed to change it to a 60-minute mandatory activity to allow students to be acquainted with basic technology skills and to enjoy the fun of computer technology. Some of the kindergarten teachers and paraprofessionals who are not proficient in the use of instructional technology spoke strongly against it.

In particular, Mrs. Tarpley delivered an especially outspoken criticism of the plan, and tried to get other teachers and paraprofessionals to resist any changes without her approval. On one occasion, Mrs. Tarpley told the other kindergarten teachers that the existing program had been successfully implemented in Villa Elementary for years. Parents seemed to like the program even though it retained some students from moving on to Grade 1. She said that retention is pretty normal for kindergartners who are not quite ready to continue and said there was not much to worry about.

At the same time, Mrs. Wright, the paraprofessional, expressed her negative feeling about the proposed changes of the kindergarten program in front of Mr. Truitt, the school principal, who was dismayed that Mrs. Bagwell had not brought the proposed changes to his attention. Even though Mr. Truitt was willing to consider the possibility of the proposed changes, he was uncomfortable that Mrs. Bagwell had not discussed them with him before bringing up the proposal to her fellow colleagues.

One afternoon, Mr. Truitt received a phone call from Mrs. Black, an angry parent of a child in the kindergarten program. She was totally upset with proposals about kindergarten program changes without even involving parents. She was opposed to any remedial work to push her child forward, no matter how gentle the pressure. As for the issue of increased hours of technology instruction, her opinion was that it would end up killing children's technology interest at an early age. She threatened that if these proposed program changes did not stop, she would bring it to the attention of the school superintendent and the school board. Mrs. Black said that all of her information came from her good friend, Mrs. Vane, the paraprofessional. Mrs. Black further stated that Mrs. Vane has been working with children for a long time and has seen educational "frills and trends" come and go. Mrs. Vane advised her that nothing beats the old curriculum, and she encouraged Mrs. Black to call the principal and complain.

The next day, Mr. Truitt told Mrs. Bagwell about the phone call from the unhappy parent and expressed great concern about her proposed changes. He asked that she schedule some time to further discuss the issue with him.

Issues for Further Reflection and Application

Case Analysis

1. What is the rationale behind Mrs. Bagwell's proposal to change in the kindergarten program at Villa Elementary School?
2. What is the procedure of proposing a program change in school? Has Mrs. Bagwell followed the procedure?
3. In the assessment of climate for change, has Mrs. Bagwell brought up the proposed kindergarten changes at the appropriate time?

4. Is Mrs. Bagwell's proposal for program change in line with the school mission statement, "*Quality learning and superior performance for all*" and the school motto, "Together, We Are Better"? What is missing in her proposed program for change?
5. How should teachers react to proposed changes in a school climate that calls for collaboration for student success?
6. Should teachers frequently be challenged with new initiatives to re-examine the program quality to which they long adhere?
7. What are the roles of parents in school curriculum? Should parents have a say in what programs are offered to their children in school?
8. Are school curricula pretty much decided at the state/district level? Do teachers have the right to propose changes to existing school curricula?
9. If curriculum changes can be made, should it occur at the grade level, principal's level, or the district level?
10. What are the roles and responsibilities of school principals as curriculum and instructional leaders?
11. What would you do to handle this proposal for kindergarten program changes if you were Mr. Truitt, the school principal?
12. What, if anything, should Mr. Truitt do about Mrs. Vane's encouraging the parent to call and complain?
13. Should Mr. Truitt speak to Mrs. Tarpley about her stance on the changes in the kindergarten program? Why or why not?

Class Activities

1. On behalf of Mr. Truitt, draft a memo to all faculty members of Villa Elementary School outlining the procedures involved in proposing program changes.
2. Compose a letter from Mrs. Black to the school superintendent, stating her position of opposing the proposed kindergarten program changes.
3. As a district early childhood program supervisor, you are invited to study the proposal of kindergarten program changes by Mrs. Bagwell. What criteria would you use to judge whether the proposed changes are acceptable?
4. If Mr. Truitt is to discuss the proposed program changes in the next kindergarten grade-level meeting, what would you suggest he should say in the best interests of the school and the children? Draft an agenda of his discussion.
5. Draft a speech for Mrs. Bagwell in defense of her proposed kindergarten program changes for delivery to the Villa Elementary School Curriculum Committee.

Writing Objectives in the Affective Domain

As addressed in chapter 3, teachers have no choice but to affect students' values, and teachers are responsible for teaching certain values such as honesty and citizenship. An important role of the school and the teacher in the realm of values is to help students become aware of their own values, to question these values, and to discover the basis for those values, be they factual and logical or prejudiced and illogical.

David Krathwohl and his colleagues (1964) developed a system known as the *affective domain* to categorize values. The outcome was the following hierarchy of objectives in the affective domain: level 1: receiving; level 2: responding; level 3: valuing; level 4: organizing; and level 5: characterizing.

Level 1: Receiving

This level refers to students' awareness of new information or experiences. Students receive information in varying degrees. In a single class, some may not receive the information at all, while others attend or receive at a low level of awareness, and still others are very selective, paying attention only to the things that are most meaningful to them. Of course, students can be encouraged and taught to develop their attention skills.

Level 2: Responding

At the *responding* level, students react to whatever has attracted their attention. This requires physical, active behavior. Some responses may be overt or purposeful behaviors, as contrasted to the simple, automatic responses. A student who becomes involved at the responding level might, at the teacher's instruction or even voluntarily, go to the library and research the issue further, or the student may choose to obey the rules set forth in the class.

Level 3: Valuing

A *value* is demonstrated when someone prizes a behavior enough to be willing to perform it even in the face of alternatives. A value is not necessarily reflected when a person reacts without having had time to think. In other words, if people really value a behavior they are likely to perform it repeatedly, regardless of the results it may bring.

For example, a mathematics teacher whose students are learning to use simulation games might write the following valuing objective: "When given free time next week at the end of each period to read, play simulation games, talk to friends, or sleep, each student will choose to play simulation games at least two out of the five days." Note that the objective asks students to choose a certain behavior individually of their own free will and to repeat that choice. Also notice that there are other alternatives from which to choose.

Level 4: Organizing

The *organization* level of behavior requires individuals to bring together different values to build a value system. Whenever there is conflict between two or more of their values, they must resolve the conflict. For example, elementary through high school students constantly encounter conflicting expectations of friends and parents. As students mature, their behavior should be influenced less by the expectations of the people they are with at the moment; they should learn to combine the two different sets of values with their own existing beliefs and knowledge about themselves. They will respond to the orderly composite of the combined values, developing their own value systems. At this level students may change their behavior or defend it. For example, a teacher might assign students to defend opposing positions on a controversial issue. By defending both sides, each student will, in effect, compare the two points of view and may even devise a compromise between the two extremes.

A teacher of a class in U.S. government might introduce a hypothetical bill and have students form two teams, one composed of those who favor the bill and one composed of those who oppose it. The objective might read: "After having had the opportunity to support the bill, and the opportunity to try to defeat it, the students will consider all the information and write a statement that expresses their feelings for and against the bill. Given the opportunity, the students will choose to modify the bill to make it reflect their own value systems."

Level 5: Characterizing

At the *characterization* level, students have already developed their own value systems. Their consistent behavior is predictable. At this level, students also demonstrate a degree of individuality and self-reliance.

An example of an objective written at the characterization level is: "Each student will bring one newspaper article or news report to class and explain at least two ways in which the article caused the student to change his or her mind from a previously held position on a controversial issue." Does this objective prove that the student has really changed values? What if the student just *says* that the change has occurred? At the moment the student may believe this, but what about a week from now or a year from now? This objective could be rewritten so that this doubt would be removed or reduced, should the teacher wish to do so.

Writing Objectives in the Psychomotor Domain

The *psychomotor domain* involves the development of physical skills that require coordination of mind and body. This domain has always been especially relevant to such courses as physical education, art, drama, music, and vocational courses; the current emphasis on interdisciplinary, integrated curricula and performance evaluation makes the psychomotor domain particularly relevant.

Although this domain was the last to have a taxonomy developed for it, at least two scales have now been developed. The following taxonomy is based on a scale developed by E. J. Simpson (1972): level 1: perception; level 2: set; level 3: guided response; level 4: mechanism; level 5: complex overt response; level 6: adaptation; and level 7: origination.

Level 1: Perception

Purposeful motor activity begins in the brain, where received phenomena act as guides to motor activity. The performer must first become aware of a stimulus, pick up on cues for action, and then act upon these cues. For example, a writer discovers that she is separating her subjects and verbs with too much descriptive material, thus diluting the impact of her themes. Or a baseball batter notices himself flinching and taking short steps away from the plate when striking, causing him to miss the ball. A piano student may learn that he is failing to maintain a steady tempo when playing quietly.

A sample objective at the perception level would be: "Following a demonstration, a geometry student who has been confusing the *x* and *y* axes in plotting graphs will recognize that the *x* axis always runs horizontally and the *y* axis always runs vertically."

Critical analysis and reflection play important roles in our behavior. Notice that even this first level in the psychomotor domain requires self-analysis and reflection. Patricia Hoehner offers a tip to help teachers improve their students' reflection skills.

FYI Replicating Research

Patricia Hoehner • University of Nebraska at Kearney

The value of our leadership as educators is based on the value of our thinking. To be skilled in thinking we need to be skilled in asking the difficult questions. Coupled with the importance of implementing research into the classroom, I challenged my students to replicate the research on an article titled *Research: Self-discipline may trump IQ when it comes to school success*, and ask the question, Why? The students were to address the following issues in their schools, which ranged from urban to rural.

Demographics: Size of school, poverty, ELL, and number of eighth graders in the school
Merit Roll: Define your highest honor roll only (grade range) and number of eighth graders on honor/merit roll.
Standardized Test/IQ Test: Identify your standardized test (number of eighth graders who had a total score of 95 or higher) and identify your IQ test (number of eighth graders who scored at 120 or above).
High Ability Learners Program: Identify program offerings and procedures.

The students learned the importance of keeping abreast of current publications and the analysis of data. This miniature study addressed research skills, current trends in curriculum, collaboration, and most important, reflection.

Level 2: Set

In the psychomotor domain, *set* refers to an individual's readiness to act. It includes mental, physical, and emotional *readiness*. For example, a high diver is always seen pausing before a dive to get a psychological, emotional, and physical set. Emotionally she must feel confident about her ability to make a safe and accurate dive. Although she may have performed the same dive hundreds of times, she still takes the time to think through the sequence of steps before each dive. Physically, she must ready her muscles in order to respond quickly and accurately. On a less dramatic scale, a student preparing to take notes or do a writing assignment may be seen flexing his fingers or rubbing his eyes—in short, getting set to perform at his best.

An example of a psychomotor objective at this level for piano students is: "Upon the signal 'ready,' each student will assume proper posture and place all fingers in the correct keyboard position." Is there a minimum level of performance specified in this objective?

Level 3: Guided Response

Once the students perceive the need to act and ready themselves to act, they may find that whenever the act involves complex skills they will need guidance through their first few responses. For example, students in the photography club may need oral guidance as they process their first negatives.

An example of an objective to enhance the development of these skills would be: "When given step-by-step directions in the darkroom, each student will open the film cylinder, remove the film, and, without touching the surface of the film, wind the film on a spool so that the surface of each round does not touch previous rounds."

Level 4: Mechanism

This level involves performing an act somewhat automatically without having to pause to think through each separate step. For example, the photography teacher might want students eventually to be able to perform the entire sequence of development operations while simultaneously counting the number of seconds required to wait following each step. Or a chemistry teacher might write the following objective at the mechanism level: "Given a series of compounds to analyze, the student will operate the electron microscope without having to pause even once to think about the sequence involved in mounting the slide, focusing the projector, and changing the lens size."

Level 5: Complex Overt Response

The level of complex overt response is an extension of the previous level, but it involves more complicated tasks. For example, a driver education teacher may write an objective at this level such as: "When given an unexpected and abrupt command to stop, the student will immediately respond by checking in the rearview mirror, applying the correct amount of pressure to the brakes, giving the correct signal, and gradually pulling off the road."

Level 6: Adaptation

At this level the student is required to adjust performance as different situations dictate. For example, to allow for an icy surface, the driver would adjust her brake pressure and steer into a skid if needed. Or a cook would adjust the cooking time when changing from an electric stove to a gas stove. A boxer would alter his style to adjust for a left-handed opponent.

An example of a psychomotor objective at the adaptation level is: "When dancing the tango, the student will insert the fan at three appropriate places."

Level 7: Origination

At the origination level, the highest level of the psychomotor domain, the student creates new movement patterns to fit the particular situation. For example, the cook adds his own touch of genius, and the pianist alters her style or the music itself.

An art teacher might write the following objective: "Given a mixture of powders and compounds of varying textures, the student will use these to accentuate the feeling he is trying to communicate in an oil painting."

As seen in this chapter, clearly worded objectives are essential in all classes to clarify teacher expectations.

Conclusion

Following is a summary of some of the advances made and concerns raised about the topics discussed in this chapter.

Advances

- Throughout the country, education reform efforts are increasing the level of accountability of teachers, administrators, and other curriculum developers, making them responsible for the academic success of their students.
- By learning to write aims, goals, and objectives, educators are improving the level at which they support the reform efforts in their state.
- Expertise in writing aims is empowering teachers to become involved at a higher level in setting their school's mission.

Concerns

- Not everyone supports the use of objectives. Some critics believe that some of the most important functions of schools cannot be expressed in terms of objectives; others say that setting objectives lowers students' levels of aspiration; still others question the traditionally held belief that the levels of the taxonomies must be taught in sequence.
- Expectations must not be considered only as expectations others hold for us. Rather, these aims, goals, and objectives are powerful tools that we can use to help all students overcome adversity and succeed academically and socially, tools we can use to meet the multicultural and constuctivist goals endorsed by this text.

The production of aims, goals, and objectives supports the constructivist approach to education because, by nature, constructivism is criterion referenced. Constructivist teachers consider objectives to be essential in order to attain their more theoretical aims and goals.

Objectives should always be expressed in terms of individual student performance, and they should always specify the conditions under which the student must perform and the minimal acceptable level of performance. Objectives should use only verbs that are observable and measurable. Writing aims, goals, and objectives also serves other education reform goals, including curriculum alignment, cooperative learning, and restructuring.

ADDITIONAL LEARNING OPPORTUNITIES

1. What implications does education reformers' increased emphasis on academic accountability have for teachers' competence in writing aims and goals?
2. If education aims can never be reached, then why are they needed?
3. Which are the most essential in meeting all students' needs: affective objectives or cognitive objectives?

4. Why should teachers involve students in planning, and how can they do so?
5. Do you believe that educators have gone too far in using objectives? If so, what are some effective teacher responses to the requirement that every class should have objectives?
6. Why should teachers include affective and psychomotor objectives in their curricula?

Suggested Activities

1. Select an education video, DVD, or book and write one aim, two goals, and five objectives for the lesson accompanying this medium.
2. What one thing would you most like to change in the world? Write one objective in each of the domains that would help make this change.
3. Check the personal philosophy statement you wrote while studying chapter 3, or write a statement of your beliefs about the main purpose of schools. Based on this statement, write one affective goal. Next, write at least two affective objectives to help your students reach this goal.
4. Make a list of observable, measurable verbs to use when writing objectives.
5. Examine the example psychomotor objective at the end of the section entitled "level 2: set." Can you rewrite this objective to assess behavior in a more meaningful way? Taking a moment to think about this objective, list two ways you could establish minimum levels of performance. Does either of your objectives explain what is meant by "correct posture" or "correct keyboard position"? Do both of your suggested changes help make the act measurable?
6. Suppose you are teaching the circulatory system to a biology class. Write an objective that will measure whether students understand the sequence in which the blood travels throughout the body. (*Hint:* You may want to designate one of the heart's chambers as a beginning point.) Check your objective to see whether it includes the designated criteria: Is it written in terms of expected student performance? If so, underscore the part of the objective that identifies both the performer and the performance. Does the verb you used express action? Can it be observed or measured? Does your statement of conditions accurately describe the conditions under which you expect the student to perform? Circle it. Did you begin the objective with a statement such as "Given . . ." or "When given . . ."? (This is an easy way to be sure you have included a statement of conditions in each objective.) Is your statement very general, such as "When given a test" or "Following a lesson"? Can you make it more specific? Can you think of a way to alter the task, making it easier to perform, simply by changing the conditions? Finally, examine your objective to see whether it includes a statement of the minimum acceptable level of performance. Does it tell the student exactly how accurately the task must be performed before it will be acceptable? Does it contain a percentage or fraction, such

as "with 80% accuracy" or "four out of five times"? Can you think of other ways to express your concept of the minimum acceptable level of performance without using percentages or fractions?

By now you probably would like to start over and rewrite your original objective, improving each part. Do so. Then examine your evaluation-level objective. Does it require that the judgment be based on supportive data or on internal or external standards?

7. Because of the lack of emphasis on concepts and the lack of opportunities to develop concepts, principles, and other content generalizations in schoolwork, American students often fall short in their ability to grasp the structure of the disciplines. Suppose you are an art teacher. In your class, you have studied such concepts as cubism (using cubes to form objects) and pointillism (using points to form shapes). Can you write an objective at the synthesis level? (*Hint:* You might begin by identifying a particular effect, feeling, or mood that you would like your students to achieve through the use of cubism and pointillism.) One example of such an objective might be: "Based on examples of cubism in Picasso's paintings and pointillism in some of Renoir's paintings, the student will combine these two techniques (adding a personal technique if desired) to express at least three of the following feelings: happiness, surprise, sadness, anger, love." At the synthesis level, the objective should provide enough structure to make the assignment meaningful and yet allow students enough freedom to put themselves into the work.
8. Write a multicultural aim and then write three or four goals to help students pursue that aim.
9. Make a list of verbs that describe constructivist behaviors.
10. Explain the relationship between outcome-based education and education reform.

chapter seven

Selecting Content and Activities

the importance of content and activities selection
- the comprehensive high school
- arenas and actors in curriculum planning

problems in content and activities selection
- pressure groups
- an increasing knowledge base
- overreliance on textbooks
- personal preference

content selection
- national goals
- the nature of knowledge
- society's needs
- learners' needs
- human development
- personalizing the curriculum
- at-risk students and gifted students

activities selection
- the knowledge base
- problem solving
- internationalization and global awareness
- a call for increased flexibility
- teacher empowerment
- student empowerment
- building self-confident and security
- tables of specifications

Focus Questions

1. What is the difference between content and knowledge, and how can curriculum planners use this understanding?
2. How is education reform in your school affecting students' appreciation for diversity?
3. How should your knowledge of constructivism affect your selection of content and activities?
4. How would you justify the use of problem solving, even though content and class time may be sacrificed as a result?
5. How would you defend the inclusion of multicultural content in the curriculum?
6. How does knowledge about other cultures affect appreciation for diversity?
7. How can curriculum planners prevent the information explosion from making the curriculum shallow?
8. How can tables of specification help you to cover the most important aspects of content and activities in the curriculum?

THE CASE OF BUILDING BRIDGES TO REFORM*

Wednesday is a special day at Model Laboratory School in Richmond, Kentucky. Walk the halls, and you will see a bustle of educational activity indicating that something exciting is going on. A group of students sits on the floor in a classroom working on a weather map that shows lows, highs, and fronts. But upon closer inspection you will realize that all the words on the map are in Spanish and that this is a Spanish class for young children. In the cafeteria, students are participating in a simulation that challenges them to consider the relationships between power and authority in a democratic society. In one of the school's three computer labs, other students are learning the intricacies of Microsoft Word. In the chemistry classroom, teachers playing the roles of pharmacists, clerks, and sales representatives in a simulation are questioned by students using forensic chemistry to sort out facts in a "murder case." The two school administrators, the librarian, the gifted coordinator, and the two counselors are teaching today. A local college dean and a mystery writer from the college's English department are team-teaching a writing-for-publication class to high school sophomores, juniors, and seniors.

What's happening at Model Laboratory School is one attempt to reform a school program at the grassroots level. The impetus for the Wednesday activities was provided by the passage of a reform act known as the Kentucky Education Reform Act (KERA). The state's Supreme Court declared the state's entire public school system unconstitutional, based on a case claiming that the state's educational funding was insufficient and that the funds were being distributed unfairly among the school districts. The result was the passage of legislation that created a new way to fund and run schools, different ways to measure student progress, and different techniques for teaching kids.

*Appreciation is given to Dr. Bruce Bonar, the former director of Model Laboratory School, for providing the information for this case.

With a proclivity toward experimentation, the Model Lab teachers were inclined to embrace the school-reform movement. As members of an institution whose aims are to test and disseminate innovative projects, the faculty at Model jumped onto the reform bandwagon with vigor. The laboratory school formed a site-based council during the first year after KERA was passed, and it began the first nongraded primary program in the area. As part of a grant, a writing resource teacher worked with faculty to facilitate the writing process in all subjects, the goal being to train all faculty to teach writing.

The faculty received enormous amounts of training both within and outside the school building. The primary teachers attended a total of 80 workshops in preparation for teaching nongraded classes. All faculty were trained in performance-based instruction and academic theme building. Other teachers and administrators attended meetings on portfolio construction in math and language arts, assessment, and technology. All teachers and administrators attended a five-day curriculum alignment workshop.

After receiving this extensive reform training, the laboratory school teachers searched for ways to put the training into practice. During the early days of reform, there were no KERA reform models in Kentucky schools, and it seemed as if every few days a new element (or required practice) in the reform law would appear. Implementing Kentucky education reform during its development was characterized by one educator as "building an airplane while you're flying it."

Despite the demands of KERA and the extensive training of the faculty, the structure of the high school and middle school remained unchanged. Teachers began to develop event and portfolio tasks that demonstrate student competency in learning, either individually or within a group. Some teachers joined with colleagues to teach integrated units and tasks. Still, the reform attempts remained sporadic, with some teachers more readily aligning their classes with the KERA curriculum elements while others remained tied to more traditional educational practices.

The state education-reform legislation encouraged the development of alternative curricula. The Wednesday classes were designed to meet this need. The new curriculum, called the *alternative schedule*, caused everyone at this school to focus on reform. This program has given teachers an almost threat-free environment in which to try new curricula, experiment with reform, and cover topics inadequately covered in the traditional curriculum.

The decision to implement the alternative schedule was made by the teachers and endorsed by the school's site-based decision-making council. The program requires teachers to construct courses that run for nine consecutive Wednesdays, with some classes meeting for one hour and others meeting for two consecutive hours. The courses are designed to fulfill at least one of four reform criteria:

1. Meet the needs of students who work at different learning rates (the reform act states that *all* children can and will learn).
2. Integrate learning experiences with the real world.
3. Demonstrate performance-based learning and evaluation.
4. Increase social awareness and cooperative behavior.

Teachers submitted proposals that were reviewed by faculty and evaluated based on the efficacy of the offering and its match to the criteria. Parents assist teachers in some classes; in others, parents teach and faculty serve as supervisors. Courses are designed in two-hour blocks for high school students. Middle school students take classes that last for one hour, except for those students taking high school offerings.

Working with administrators, teachers use student choices and faculty recommendations to set up class schedules. Students needing remediation and those needing accelerated curricula are assigned the same offerings, particularly labs in math, social studies, and language arts. Students receive most, but not all, the classes they request. In the middle school, students have fewer choices, and some of the younger children are required to take certain classes in math. The Wednesday schedule is shown in box 7.1.

Box 7.1 Courses Offered in the Wednesday Alternative Curriculum at Model Laboratory School

Block A

APPLIED PROBLEM SOLVING:

The students will have the opportunity to use many types of media and machine or processes to solve problems by designing and building a prototype.

DATABASES AND SPREADSHEETS:

This course will explore uses of databases and spreadsheets. Students will create, edit, and update data and investigate given sets of data for research and finance problem. FIND OUT WHY DATABASES AND SPREADSHEETS SPARKED THE PC REVOLUTION!

HISTORICAL RESEARCH:

Students will explore a topic of history, using secondary and primary resources. Students will produce a product depicting some aspect of the topic. WHAT DO YOU KNOW ABOUT LIFE ON THE FRONTIER IN MADISON COUNTY 200 YEARS AGO?

THE INKWELL:

This is a practical, hands-on course in the production of a student magazine. Students will write, select, edit, and use desktop publishing technology, including the scanning of images and artwork.

Block B

AMERICAN STUDIES LAB:

Offers opportunity for study in topics of interest in American culture, whether historical, literary, or pop. A variety of interests and purposes will be tolerated and encouraged. Students requiring additional time and/or guided practice in reading, note taking, or communicating may be assigned to laboratory on a contract basis, with improved performance keyed to grades in regular classes.

ATHLETIC TRAINING:

Students will be familiarized with trainer's techniques for prevention of sports injuries and will have the opportunity to learn basic equipment, safety tips, and taping procedures. Students will study topics related to elite athletes and athletic performance.

CHORUS:

Students will learn and perform choral music with a concert October 15th at 7:30 PM in Edwards Auditorium. EVERYONE JOIN! EVERYONE ATTEND!

CREATIVE FOODS:

This course includes the study of planning, preparing, serving, and eating regional and foreign foods, for occasions such as holidays, receptions, and company meals. A $20 fee will be required to cover the cost of foods. WHERE ELSE CAN YOU GET 8 OR 9 MEALS FOR $20!

Block C

ACADEMIC TEAM:

Think you're smart? Wish you were? Or just want to sit around and watch a bunch of people who are? Take Academic Team and you will have time to study areas of strength or weakness, to develop the all-important coordination of your right hand (beep, beep!), and to interact with some of Model's most interesting people.

ART APPRECIATION & STUDIO WORK:

FEE: $6.

Students will explore a different type of art each week. Learn about famous artists and different cultures and then create an art project that uses similar ideas, materials, and techniques.

DIPLOMACY:

Diplomacy is a role-playing board game of skill and cunning in which chance plays no part. Game recreates events in pre–WWI Europe. Tests ability to plan a campaign and outwit one's fellow in negotiation. Students of Macchiavelli's *Prince* should enjoy this game! Only 18 high school students can participate in teams of three.

Block A

LAB SKILLS:

Required of all freshman science students and all new sophomores. Students will learn and practice skills required for success in labs in earth science, biology, chemistry, and physics.

MATHEMATICS LABORATORY:

Students will be allowed extra computer time and assistance in exploring mathematics and computer topics of interest. Students experiencing difficulty in math classes may be placed into the lab with contract tying improved performance back to the classroom grade.

MOCK TRIAL, AN INTRODUCTION:

Students will receive an in-depth introduction to the mock trial and will participate as attorneys or witnesses in several "class" mock trials. Interested students will be encouraged to try out for Model's immensely successful Mock Trial Team. Not open to students who took this class last year.

THE OBSERVER:

Monthly newspaper—work with everyone/every aspect of the school! Must be able to sell ads, write articles, do layouts, take and print pictures, and meet deadlines.

RED, YELLOW, BLACK, AND WHITE: EXPLORING CULTURAL DIVERSITY:

This class will explore the cultural diversity of the United States and the world through a variety of experiences. Students will read both fiction and nonfiction, view films/movies, participate in role-playing games, meet guest speakers from diverse cultures, and visit the displays of the Cultural Festival at EKU.

Block B

"HERSTORY"—WOMEN IN HISTORY:

It is said that "The hand that rocks the cradle rules the world!" Join Herstory and examine the impact the hands of women have had throughout history.

INSTRUMENTAL MUSIC:

If you never started on a band instrument but would like to, or you started and dropped but would like to try again, or scheduling kept you out of Band, or you are in Band and would like to learn a different instrument, this course is for you! Course teaches basics of instrument and music reading, enabling students to develop skills leading to performance with the Band. *REQUIRED: You must have your own band instrument to use!*

MATHEMATICS LABORATORY:

Students will be allowed extra computer time and assistance in exploring mathematics and computer topics of interest. Students experiencing difficulty in math classes may be placed into the lab with contracts keying improved performance back to the classroom grade.

SEIKO YOUTH CHALLENGE:

Would you like to solve a real environmental problem in our community? In this class we will form teams who will then identify, investigate, and prepare a solution to be entered into the Seiko Youth Challenge competition.

Block C

FROM EXECUTIONS TO EXPLORATIONS—MEDIEVAL AND RENAISSANCE WORLD:

Is it better to be beheaded with a sword or an axe? Did Robin Hood fear the Black Death? Did knights wear clothing under their armor? Can you turn other metals into gold? Were damsels really in distress? What would have happened if Columbus had stopped and asked for directions? The answers to these and other exciting questions will be explored by students through films, readings, guest speakers, music, discussions, projects, role-playing, and games. Activities will culminate with a schoolwide Renaissance fair.

INTRODUCTION TO MICROSOFT WORD:

This word processing course will meet in the high school computer lab and will teach beginning or advanced students how to create letters and other personal-use documents using Microsoft Word.

LIGHTS, CAMERA, ACTION—BEGINNING VIDEO PRODUCTION:

The students will be actively involved in the proper usage of the camcorder and will plan and produce a video.

PUBLIC SERVICE COOPERATIVE:

Students will be placed in a public work setting, attend seminars, and participate in field trips to increase social awareness and allow career exploration through interaction with the public. Students should increase their understanding of the importance of community service and of the diversity of the community.

(continued)

Block A

SOCIAL STUDIES—CAFETERIA STYLE!

Students will be free to select from a variety of experiences in the rich world of social studies. CAMPAIGN '08 students will study and debate the issues Americans *should* be talking about and have the opportunity to get involved in the election. Students interested in Kentucky's *only* Bicentennial will be able to study issues of local or statewide interest. Students will be encouraged to produce scholarship-winning products for the Kentucky Junior Academy of History.

WEIGHT TRAINING:

An introduction to and application of weight training principles. AVOID HEART ATTACKS! GET YOUR IRON THE SAFE WAY—PUMP IT!

AMATEUR RADIO:

Operate Model's Amateur Radio Station. Current equipment puts us on 80, 40, 20, 15, and 10 meters, capable of 180 watts CW or SSB, and 150 watts AM phone. We plan to expand to 160 meters and into VHF range as equipment and antennas become available. Must have valid amateur radio license on file with Mr. Stephens and be checked out on equipment.

All Blocks **All Day**

Block B

SPEECH LEAGUE:

This class will offer students the opportunity to explore their public speaking and dramatic talents by participating in the Kentucky High School Speech League. Students may choose from a variety of categories, such as Oratory, Debate, Extemporaneous Speaking, Radio Broadcasting, Duo Interpretation, Dramatic and Humorous Interpretation, Storytelling, Poetry, Prose, etc. This offering will require students to participate in two Speech League competitions at a small entry fee.

WEIGHT TRAINING:

An introduction to and application of weight training principles. GIVE YOUR BODY A WEIGHT BREAK! TAKE YOUR IRON THE HEALTHY WAY—PUMP IT!

WRITER'S WORKSHOP:

Students will increase their writing skills in a broad range of areas, from writing mechanically correct, killer themes to creative writing.

Block C

TEST PREPARATION—THE PSAT:

Students will have pre- and post-assessments with the PSAT. Use of test scores, strategies for testing, and content area review will be the major focus of the course. *Recommended for all juniors and those sophomores planning to take the PSAT this year.*

WINDOWS ON ARCHAEOLOGY:

During these nine weeks, students will examine the basic tools and techniques of field archaeology, including the study of rock formations, artifacts, fossils, carbon dating, statistical methods of "dig" site identification, and layout of a "dig" site. Students will participate in a "dig" at an artificially "salted" site. They will have field trips to the Universities of Kentucky and Cincinnati, where they will see museums and archaeology departments. This project, partially funded by a grant from GTE, will offer students exciting, in-depth exploration of archaeology and will develop skills and attitudes crucial to success in science in today's world.

THE EXEMPLAR:

This course is for the yearbook staff, which will have the practical experience of designing and producing another outstanding, award winning annual for the school. Students will write copy, work on layouts, use computer equipment, and meet deadlines—all valuable experiences today.

Evaluations were carried out after the first year of the Wednesday classes. More than 90% of the students enthusiastically endorsed the project. Only 3 of the school's 25 faculty members opposed the alternative schedule. Many parents commented positively about the mini-courses, stating that children seemed more enthusiastic about school on Wednesday.

School attendance records indicated that on the average, 98% of the students came to school on Wednesdays as compared to the overall 95% daily rate. Teachers reported that students seemed to be more productive on Fridays while the alternative schedule was in place, perhaps because of the variety they experienced in their weekly schedule.

• • •

The alternative schedule is an attempt by one school to cope with the demands of local school change. Whether this program remains intact and becomes institutionalized or whether the ideas in the alternative schedule become incorporated into a larger and more comprehensive restructuring of the school remains to be seen. As you read this chapter, consider how much education reform requirements in all states are demanding educators to upgrade their content and activities-selection skills.

The Importance of Content and Activities Selection

Almost 150 years ago, at the beginning of the Civil War, British educator Herbert Spencer (1861) posed the simple yet profound and enduring question, "What knowledge is of most worth?" Before Spencer's question can be answered, other questions must be asked: "Of most worth for what? Of most worth for whom?" We can begin to find the answers to these questions by examining the purposes of our schools. Although by their very nature these questions are philosophical, they have highly practical implications. Selecting content and activities is a responsibility shared by all teachers. Since different individuals and groups hold different opinions regarding the purposes of schools, the job of selecting content and activities is not simple. Before reviewing the purposes of schools, let's look at some current practices that contribute to the complexity of content and activities selection.

Curriculum development, if it is effective at all, is an ongoing activity—every day throughout the year. This constant demand for updating requires teachers and other curricularists to stay on top of the job, yet the lag in curriculum development and lag in funding continues. At a time when political leaders—from the local level to the president of the United States—are pressing for education reform, the importance of selecting the most appropriate content for K–12 classrooms cannot be overstressed.

The Comprehensive High School

One of the most far-reaching efforts to ensure that schools develop the full potential of their students occurred in the late 1950s when James Conant, who had been a chemistry professor and later was president of Harvard University, began openly expressing his dissatisfaction with the American high school. Through his contributions as a chemist, writer, researcher, and president of Harvard, Conant had earned the respect of the public at large and especially the scientific community. He was commissioned by the Carnegie Corporation to write *The American High School* (1959), a report designed to strengthen the education of all students. The comprehensive high school that was first recommended in 1918 by the NEA Commission on the Reorganization of Secondary Education (publishers of the Cardinal Principles of Secondary Education), had come under major attack.

Conant defended the concept of large, comprehensive schools with core curricula but recommended that the schools offer vocational and pre-college programs along with a strong general studies program. The report was highly prescriptive, requiring of all students four years of English, three or four years of social studies, one year of math, and one year of science. A heavier curriculum was prescribed for gifted students (*curriculum compacting*). The report recommended both *heterogeneous groupings* (as in homerooms, where high- and low-ability students are grouped together) and *ability groupings*. It also set a minimum number of hours of homework. To achieve currency and to respond to the nation's needs, he recommended requiring all seniors to take a course on American problems. Conant's critics questioned that a single course could achieve so much, especially since a large portion of students dropped out before reaching the senior year. However, Conant's recommendations were widely adopted, reaffirming the credibility of the comprehensive school and the *Carnegie unit* (120 clock hours of instruction).

Parkay, Hass, and Anctil (2010) say that the comprehensive high school has proven inadequate for the program of education many of today's students need. "Some observers believe that attempts to develop comprehensive high school curricula that address the needs of all middle adolescents have resulted in curricula that lack coherence. High schools tend to try to teach 'too much' to students. As a result, high school curricula focus more on *covering content* than on *developing understanding*" (p. 521). Others now agree that today's schools must go beyond the Carnegie units, stop awarding credits for seat time, and focus on the skills required in today's workforce, including skills in oral and written communication, time management, critical thinking, problem solving, personal accountability, and the ability to work with others (DiMartino & Castaneda, 2007). In 2005, New Hampshire became the first state to eliminate the Carnegie unit. However, this does not imply that grouping students in no longer valued. As Julia Roberts (2008, p. 505) has noted, "When the goal is to ensure that all young people are making continuous progress, grouping and regrouping of students becomes the norm."

It is worth mentioning here, however, that some educators are convinced that large schools are often organized to maintain control rather than to promote learning. The most current school of thought is that *smaller is better*. "Smallness is a quality common to almost all successful schools" (Meier, 2004, p. 291). Smaller schools are generally safer, more effective, more inviting, and higher-achieving schools (Gootman, 2008; Kinnaman, 2007; Kretovics, Farber, & Armaline, 2004).

Arenas and Actors in Curriculum Planning

Curriculum planning occurs at several levels, including the classroom, school, school district, region, state, nation, and world. Each level has its own set of actors (see figure 7.1). Following is a discussion of each of these levels, each with its own actors and their means of influencing the curriculum.

Classroom

Teachers have always played an important role in the shaping of classroom-level curricula. As the type of curriculum itself has shifted (for example, from con-

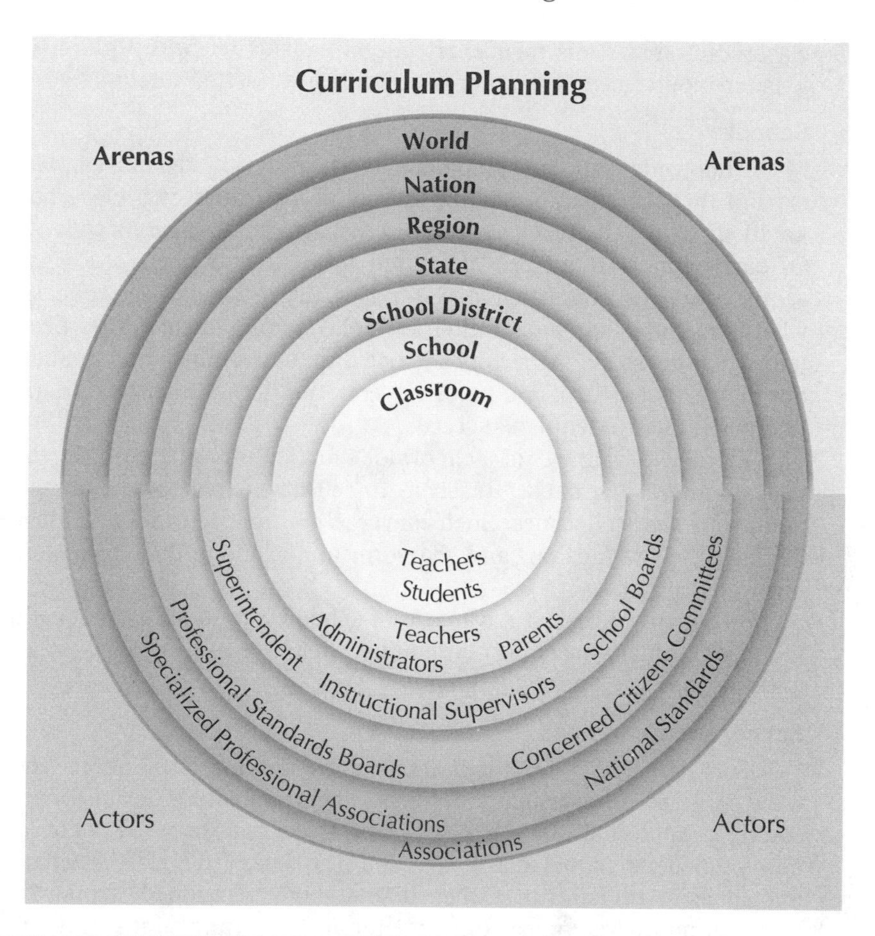

Figure 7.1 Arenas and Actors in Curriculum Planning

tent centered to student centered and vice versa) and the nature of the teacher's role has changed, teachers' influence has remained significant, both overtly and covertly. For example, in most schools teachers are permitted to add their own objectives, content, and activities to their syllabi (overt influence), and the way teachers behave can also heavily influence the curriculum (covert influence).

An advantage of classroom-level curriculum planning is the significant influence of teachers, since teachers largely determine the amount of learning that occurs. When teachers are more directly involved, their commitment level increases, and improved clarity often results. Classroom planning that also involves students can create a sense of community. As Berman (2003) has pointed out, "Studies of social development show that creating a sense of community in classrooms and schools has a powerful impact on adolescents' social development" (p. 36). (For an in-depth discussion on creating learning communities, see Henson, 2010.) Classroom-level curriculum planning also has limitations, however. Teachers whose involvement with the curriculum is limited to their own classrooms may focus their curricula on instruction, with little or no thought to long-term outcomes or to other parts of their students' curricula.

School

Schoolwide curriculum planning has several advantages. When teachers expand their curriculum planning arena beyond their own classrooms, students are likely to benefit. Teachers must increase their interactions with other teachers. Of particular value is their increased awareness of their students' curriculum scope, sequence, and articulation—that is, they are no longer concerned only with what happens to students in their own classrooms. Instead they become committed to helping shape the school's curriculum to promote student success throughout their school years, and in all subjects, and it is the particulars of each school that permit its students to succeed.

Another advantage of schoolwide curriculum planning is that increased teacher interaction causes teachers to reflect on their own practices and share them with their colleagues. Such conversation can occur at the dialogue level, producing collective meaning and shared meaning, and at the discussion level, which involves decisions.

Perhaps the greatest advantage of schoolwide planning is its contribution to the formation of a learning community, where all professionals at a school work together to create understanding.

School District

During the early twentieth century, the nation's population grew until there were so many schools that state department educators began to worry that they could not control all the schools in their respective states. This concern led to the development of school districts. Thus, the school district is actually a tool for management or control, rather than a body developed primarily to conduct research and development on curriculum design and/or instruction. School districts were created not to help schools improve but to require them to maintain a desired level of quality.

School districts differ greatly from state to state. Traditionally, the size and number of districts within states were determined by the size and number of counties. Often, each county had one school district office. As town populations grew, many towns began forming their own school districts. Thus, a county might have a district office to serve rural students, and one or more towns within the county would have their own district offices. In many instances the influence of population growth on the decision to form town or city school districts was secondary to the residents' desire to have their own football or basketball district.

Mentioning the influence of sports on school districts does not imply that there is a total lack of concern in these districts for the improvement of the quality of education; however, it does say that in some locations concern for quality education is shared with, and in some instances is overshadowed by, other concerns.

The key players at the district level are the superintendent and the school board (often called the board of education or board of trustees). Superintendents may be either elected by popular vote or appointed by the school board. In either instance, they are accountable to the school board. Some school boards give their superintendent a budget and almost total latitude to use it as she or he sees fit; other school boards are much more restrictive. Curriculum planning is one of several roles of most district boards. Other roles include providing necessary finances and faculties, ensuring that schools meet state mandates, and curtailing drug abuse.

Other important players at the district level include such experts as psychologists, psychometrists, special educators, curriculum developers, and instructional supervisors (Oliva & Pawlas, 2007). The curriculum developer and instructional supervisor are the most influential with regard to improving the schools' curricula. Traditionally, teachers held periodic, districtwide in-service meetings to address curriculum and instructional concerns. In recent years, in many districts the district expert has moved the in-service support to the school campuses, recognizing the advantages that schoolwide collaborative planning has over planning at other levels.

Region

Several states have chosen to create regional education offices. The reasons for this choice may differ from one state to another; often it results from a concern over disparity of financial funds for schooling among schools and districts. Put simply, some geographic areas are so poor that they need help to provide quality education to their children. Other states are so populous or so large geographically that they become extremely awkward to manage.

Regional centers are sometimes referred to as "services centers" because they provide a range of services to their members. Some states require all schools or school districts to hold membership in a regional center, while other states (e.g., Indiana) make the choice optional. The services provided by regional centers are varied. Some centers provide staff development, which helps large states such as Alaska or Texas that would find it time consuming and expensive to either send consultants or transport teachers across the state for faculty development.

The recent expansion of the use of technology has made regional centers even more advantageous for purposes of staff development. Equally important, regional centers have a history of providing help with purchasing to their members. Acting as a co-op, the centers can save their members a lot of money by setting up bidding among competing companies. For example, the state of Kentucky directs each district to hold membership in a regional co-op, which may be operated by the state department, a higher education institution, or a private (commercial) organization. These regional co-ops provide both faculty development services and purchasing.

Regional education systems are usually run by school boards made up of superintendents of the districts that hold membership in the regional system.

State

The U.S. Constitution gave the states power to run their schools. Beginning in the 1980s and continuing to the present, an increased emphasis on accountability has intensified the role the states play in controlling such issues as the curriculum and testing to ensure that all schools provide quality education for all students.

Traditionally, states have exerted control of curricula through such efforts as setting certification standards for teachers, administrators, counselors, and other professional educators. The goal of educating all children, first emphasized during the 1980s and 1990s, increased the production of personalized curricula through the use of individualized education programs (IEPs).

As expectations for schools grew, the 1990s also brought an increase in the number of educational professional standards boards whose job was to ensure the upgrading of elementary and secondary education. Some states identified master teachers (often called distinguished educators) who were assigned to help faltering schools improve their curricula and instruction. The No Child Left Behind legislation gives the states the latitude to target up to 50% of federal non-Title I dollars to programs that will have the most positive academic impact on their students.

Nation

Although the amount of financial support for education coming from the national level traditionally has been small (below 10%), this amount has been large enough to heavily influence the curriculum at most schools. The 1990s brought an increased emphasis on national curriculum standards (discussed further in chapter 11). Federal legislation has always emphasized those values that are paramount at the time. The 1960s and 1970s brought a deluge of prepackaged programs developed by federally funded regional research and development programs; the 1970s and 1980s brought an emphasis on bilingual curricula and also brought a swing in emphasis to more traditional or basic curricula. The 1990s witnessed a shift toward educating all students, including minorities and special students. Paradoxically, as the 1980s and 1990s brought these increased federal interests, the Reagan administration also made a commitment to decreased federal intervention in education. Whenever national security seems threatened or when the national economy falls behind that of any of the world's other leading nations, a clamor for increased federal control develops, and vice versa; therefore, the role of federal influence on curricula waxes and wanes.

Traditionally, the level of federal support has always seemed to lag far behind federal control. This unfortunate trend finally seemed to be broken with the passing of the NCLB legislation, which provides unprecedented fiscal support to ensure that its goals are met. Providing literally billions of dollars, NCLB provides the most fiscal support for schools of any legislation ever written. Unfortunately, the demands for services set forth in the legislation are so great that even the billions of dollars appropriated are in many cases woefully inadequate. For example, as discussed earlier in this chapter, the Title I portion of this act is severely underfunded; the cost of implementing the act is so great that some states and many districts find it beyond their means. Yet, at the time of this NCLB legislation, it is interesting to note that the public was so concerned over the schools that they favored continued high use of testing. Now examples of student work are preferred as a measure of academic progress by 32% as compared to only 21% preference for using test scores (Bushaw & Gallup, 2008). Even with the huge funding that this act provided, three years after the act was passed the public still considered lack of finances as the greatest problem facing the nation's schools (Rose & Gallup, 2004). In the twenty-first century, during a time of recession compared in magnitude to the Great Depression, newly elected president Barack Obama promised that education reform would remain one of the top priorities of his administration.

Another major player in national influence on schools is the group of organizations known as *specialized professional associations*, for example, the National Council for the Teachers of English (http://www.ncte.org), the National Council for the Teaching of Mathematics (http://www.nctm.org), and the National Science Teachers Association (http://www.nsta.org). As the 1990s came to an end, each of these organizations was exerting a major influence on school curricula through its recently developed minimum standards. To see the latest twenty-first century developments, visit the organizations' Web sites.

Although the idea of national standards continued to grow throughout the twentieth century, and such lists eventually became a reality, the use of national standards continues to be controversial. Some opponents object on a constitutional basis for, indeed, the use of national standards takes the right to control education away from the state and local governments. Other objectors point to a flaw in the use of minimum standards, doubting the assumption that setting minimums can and will force higher levels of performance on students.

Increased retention seldom increases learner success. On the contrary; Many studies over the past two decades have found that retaining students contributes to academic failure and behavioral difficulties rather than to success in school. Jane David (2008), director of the Bay Area Research Group in Palo Alto, California, says that "Although individual studies can be found to support any conclusion, overall the preponderance of evidence argues that students who repeat a grade are no better off, and are sometimes worse off, than if they had been promoted" (p. 84).

World

Although the national or federal level is often considered the highest level of influence on the curriculum, some individuals and organizations are committed to making worldwide improvements to curricula. As Armstrong et al. (2009) have noted, we educators need to understand the nature of external pressures exerted to influence the curriculum. For example, such organizations as the Fulbright Association and the Peace Corps are dedicated to improving relationships of people of all nations throughout the world. These associations sponsor international exchanges of teachers and support travel for educators who are committed to improving international relations and raising teaching standards.

In addition, such groups as the Association for Supervision and Curriculum Development, Kappa Delta Pi, and Phi Delta Kappa International are committed to the improvement of relations among cultures. These organizations hold conferences and host speakers to achieve this goal, and they use their professional journals to promote multiculturalism.

Problems in Content and Activities Selection

Several forces can affect the selection of content and activities, some exerting more influence than others. Some of the forces that exert the most influence include pressure groups, overreliance on textbooks, personal preferences, national goals, learners' needs, and the need to improve society. Following is a discussion of these influences.

Pressure Groups

At each level, from the classroom to the world, there are pressure groups committed to influencing the curriculum. Some pressure groups are loosely organized and work informally to shape the curriculum. Others are highly organized groups with carefully outlined strategies. These groups often use mass media such as television, radio, and newspapers to publicize their views and increase their influence through ads and editorials. They may also carefully plan to get on the program agendas of educational boards. Particularly at the state and higher levels, pressure groups often target legislators, governors, and other politicians in an attempt to alter laws.

Nowhere and at no time has the work of pressure groups been more prevalent than at the present in education reform. Curriculum debates are often the most impassioned to be found anywhere in society. Every state has a number of pressure groups, some with little power and some with enormous influence. In many states, pressure groups exert a major impact at the state level through media ads, the presence of pressure groups at state meetings, memberships on statewide committees, and through their individual and collective influence on legislators.

Collectively, the influence of pressure groups on the curriculum is powerful. The efforts of some pressure groups support those of others, although some pressure groups work to suppress or overcome the pressure of other groups. As shown in box 7.2, the actual curricula in the classroom is the product of all these pressures and the expectations and plans of educators.

Unfortunately, education today suffers from an undue responsiveness to private interest groups rather than a focus on the idea of the public good. "A democracy of consumers focused on their private interests ceases to be a democracy" (Barber, 2004).

Box 7.2 Pressures Help Shape the Actual Curriculum

pressures at the school level — pressures at the state level

Formal Aims ⟶ Goals ⟶ Objectives = The Actual or Living Curriculum

pressures throughout the region — pressures throughout the district — worldwide pressure groups

An Increasing Knowledge Base

A major problem that has persisted through the years and has accelerated in recent years is the increasing amount of information from which curriculum developers must choose. The so-called "knowledge explosion" militates the lack of a rational system for selecting content and activities. Instead of just covering information, today's students need to understand the content.

Overreliance on Textbooks

As mentioned earlier, the number-one day-to-day influence on curriculum throughout the history of our schools has been the textbook. Applebee, Langer, and Mullis (1987, p. 2) reviewed the results of several studies on the extent to which textbooks shape the curriculum: "Numerous studies report that textbooks structure from 75 to 90% of classroom instruction." Marsh and Willis (2003) reported that teachers spend an estimated 90% of their teaching time teaching from their textbooks (p. 338). Indeed, some researchers have concluded that in many schools a single textbook constitutes the entire curriculum (Daniels & Zemelman, 2003/2004).

This reliance on the textbook would be more acceptable if textbook writers and publishers used a logical system to select content, but they do not. Consequently, the content in textbooks is usually a hodgepodge of topics. Daniels and Zemelman (2003/2004) have said, "Today's textbooks cover too many topics without developing any of them well. Central concepts are not covered in enough depth to give students a chance to truly understand them" (p. 37).

Recall seems to dominate in education as much today as ever before (Brady, 2008). With reference to the constant addition of content to textbooks, Tyson and Woodward (1989, p. 15) stated, "It is not surprising then, that American textbooks have become compendiums of topics, none of which are treated in depth." Excessive content coverage can lead to shallow coverage and more; it can also diminish student interest.

Another problem with letting the textbook determine the curriculum is the failure of textbooks to cover *pertinent concepts*, that is, material whose understanding is a prerequisite to understanding the discipline being studied. Still another serious problem is the failure of textbooks to promote higher levels of thinking and understanding. Most textbooks are written at the recall level. Brady (2008) says that "Conventional textbooks are all but useless for teaching higher-order thinking because they present the final conclusion of other people's thought processes. The opportunities for complete thinking have been squeezed out of them" (p. 66).

Personal Preference

Another variable that affects, indeed often dictates, content selection is personal preference. A team of researchers (see Berliner, 1984, p. 53) reported that an elementary teacher who enjoyed teaching science spent 28 times as much time teaching science as a fellow teacher who said that she did *not* enjoy teaching science.

Since the search for the best content and activities for curricula of any era must be ongoing, consequently the search for the best *system* of selecting content and activities must never stop. It is clear that such determiners as the textbooks and personal preference fall short in the search for an answer to Spencer's question, "What knowledge is of most worth?"

FYI Using Blackboard to Discuss Current Curriculum Topics

Marjorie C. Ringler • East Carolina University

My students work in groups on a current curriculum topic. Each group develops a brochure or informational flyer to summarize the topic and share helpful resources for instructional leaders. The document is typically developed with the help of a publishing software (e.g., Microsoft Publisher) and then saved as a PDF file (see cutepdf.com, where you can download a free trial version of Windows software that facilitates advanced control over PDF document output).

The brochure or flyers are posted as separate forums for discussion on the Blackboard discussion board. The use of Blackboard technology allows for the extensive curriculum content to be presented in condensed sections, or forums. Students access the site via the Internet and participate in online discussions on the topic of the forum. In addition, because students have time to read and think through their responses before typing them onto the discussion board, the quality of feedback is typically in-depth and thoughtful. Students appreciate this asynchronous communication style, which provides meaningful learning experiences. Many students print the informational flyers and brochures they have created and share them with their instructional leaders at their current jobs.

In any era, a search for the best content should include, at a minimum, a consideration of (1) the known information (i.e., the body of knowledge the curriculum developer has available); (2) society's needs (including current trends and perceived future needs); (3) the needs and interests of learners; and (4) the state of human development (what has social worth).

Content Selection

There are five important factors in the selection process for the best content: the national goals of education reform, the nature of knowledge or information, the needs of society, student needs, and human development. After taking these factors into consideration, curriculum planners can take the extra step of personalizing the curriculum for unique individuals (e.g., gifted students or at-risk students). Now let's examine each of these factors.

National Goals

Since curriculum development is a continuing process, and since the purposes of schools change, the selection of content should begin by considering the existing aims and goals (e.g., the Cardinal Principles of Secondary Education mentioned in chapters 3 and 6). The importance of these goals for today's schools has already been discussed.

Toward the end of the twentieth century, the Goals 2000 became the ideal. However, something more was clearly needed, and in 2001 George W. Bush responded with proposed legislation that was to become the No Child Left Behind Act. The NCLB legislation has the strongest set of goals ever set in this country for elementary and secondary students—all of which are subsets of the one major goal: bringing the achievement level of students in poor schools up to the level experienced by students in other schools. While this law has created strong discomfort levels for many teachers, and it arguably misses the most important goal of taking all students to their highest possible motivation levels (Eisner, 2004), the funding behind this legislation is undoubtedly having a major impact on both teachers and students. Teachers are challenged to meet NCLB achievement goals (referred to by detractors as "teaching to the test") while at the same time choosing curriculum content and activities that foster problem solving, creativity, teamwork, decision making, and independent thinking.

The Nature of Knowledge

Many criticisms are heard today about the schools' failure to teach students how to master the subjects they study. Nationally normed standardized tests show that an alarming number of students fail to develop a clear understanding of the content they encounter in their classrooms.

Because the subject-centered design has dominated the curricula in American schools throughout their existence, concern for content mastery has always been present. Initially, there was little question of what content was most important. The Puritans created the schools to teach the laws of the colony (which the Puritans defined as God's laws), which were determined by the Scriptures. This curriculum quickly gave way to the practical curriculum of the Franklin Academy. The English secondary schools' curricula seemed to take over and serve the schools for many decades. In fact, in more modern times little formal attention was given to content prior to the 1960s.

In subject-centered curricula, content plays a dominant role. First, information, often in the form of seemingly unrelated facts, is selected for inclusion in the curriculum. Once selected, this information becomes curriculum content. *Content* is defined as the information selected to be part of a curriculum. The aim is for this content to become knowledge. *Knowledge* is defined as the content that students have connected to their previous experiences. The relationship between information, content, and knowledge is shown in figure 7.2 (on the following page). Although the differences between these three terms (information, content, and knowledge) may appear slight, their effects on students make the difference between memorizing and understanding.

Constructivists (e.g., King & Rosenshine, 1993) stressed the importance of students being able to relate newly acquired information to previously acquired understanding:

> When presented with new information, individuals use their existing knowledge and prior knowledge to help make sense of the new material. Effective teaching is aided by the constructivist practice of helping students learn by building connections between prior knowledge and new ideas. These claims are supported by comparing U.S. students' standardized test scores with the performance of their Asian counterparts. (p. 127)

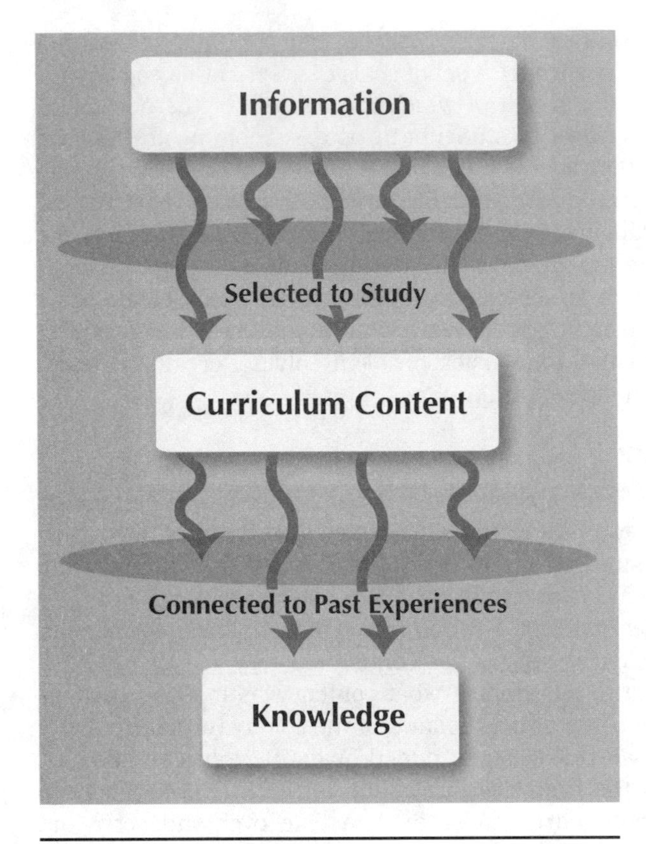

Figure 7.2 The Relationship between Information, Content, and Knowledge

Recall the highly acclaimed 2007 TIMSS study (CCSSO, 2008), which reported that the high-performing Asian students spend far more time making connections among major concepts than U.S. students do.

Teachers generally recognize the importance of students learning the main concepts in each lesson, yet Perkins and Blythe (1994, p. 4) reported that students do not do so:

> Teachers were all too aware that their students often did not understand key concepts nearly as well as they might. Research affirms this perception. A number of studies have documented students' misconceptions about key ideas in mathematics and the sciences, their parochial views of history, their tendency to reduce complex literary works to stereotypes, and so on.

This concern was further expressed by Boix-Mansilla and Gardner (2008, p. 16), who said, "Subject-matter learning may temporarily increase students' information base, but it leaves them unprepared to shed light on issues that are even slightly novel. A different kind of instruction is in order, one that seeks to discipline the mind."

Society's Needs

Since the time of the development of the English classical school, curriculum content received little attention. In fact, throughout our nation's history, unfortunately, the schools have for the most part been taken for granted. In the early 1980s, it became obvious that the nation's dominant position in world productivity was being seriously threatened. For the first time, it was recognized that other nations could mass-produce higher-quality automobiles and equally good electronics at prices that were competitive in the national and international markets. The writers of many education reform reports perceived this situation as a national emergency, and the schools were to be held accountable for putting the nation in jeopardy. Consequently, the education reform movement exemplified society's perceptions of its needs. John Dewey believed that each generation brings on a new culture. If this is so, then with each new generation a new curriculum must be developed to serve the unique needs of that new culture.

Learners' Needs

To understand the needs of learners, curriculum developers can begin by examining their most basic beliefs about the youths they know. Although this list is far from exclusive, the following questions might be asked. By nature, are young people:

- social?
- curious?
- self-centered?
- active?
- passive?
- competitive?
- cooperative?

These traits can be studied merely by observing the behavior of a group of young people. If left to choose, will most young people work with others or will they work alone? Do most have more questions than answers? Although most young people are social, are they not also self-centered? Do they not perceive the world as revolving around them and their wants? As they mature, many young people are taught by their parents or peers to be more considerate of others. Are not young people both cooperative and competitive? These paradoxes (social, yet self-centered; cooperative, yet competitive) allow for curriculum developers to choose. For example, suppose that a teacher believes that young people are basically social but then notices that the behavior of a group of children contradicts this assumption. The curriculum must be adjusted to correct this behavior.

Among learners' needs is the need to explore their interests. Rousseau's book *Émile* stressed the need to give students complete freedom. This meant that they could study what they pleased. A. S. Neil (1960) described his school, *Summerhill*, as giving students the freedom to study what they wished and the freedom to attend only the classes that interested them. The Progressive Education Movement gave students choice of content. Contemporary curriculum leaders stress the need to involve students in the selection of content. Teachers and other curricularists must remember to look for content that students will find interesting. Almost all subject matter, no matter how dull, mundane, or prosaic it may seem at first, has latent intrinsic appeals that our most effective teachers have learned how to reveal to students.

Some teachers make special efforts to meet the social needs of all their students. They choose multicultural texts to send positive messages to all students. When their students view films and tapes, these teachers mention cultures—especially those cultures represented in their classes—that are not represented in these media.

Human Development

For many decades, America's dream has been for each generation to surpass the accomplishments and status of its parents (Armstrong et al., 2009). This requires fully developing the talents of all its young people. Thus, some content should (must) be selected on the basis of its potential for helping improve the quality of thinking and the quality of behavior of humankind. The definition of philosophy as the "pursuit of wisdom" (see chapter 3), coupled with the definition of wisdom as the "knowledge of things beautiful, first, divine, pure, and eternal," seems to guarantee a place in the curriculum for the study of philosophy, values, and the arts.

Personalizing the Curriculum

This book embraces and endorses the development of classrooms in which everyone cares about the feelings of others. Because of their home and neighborhood environments, many students may experience cultural shock in such a classroom. Initially, some students may resist such personalized environments, in the same way some students are ashamed of earning good grades. Nevertheless, most people want others to respect and care for them. Educational environments that stress student interest, personal choice, firsthand experience, thoughtfulness, and humanness need to be encouraged.

Unfortunately, many young people grow up on the streets or in homes where the first and only rule is survival. In such environments, youths appear to have no choice but to be tough, if, indeed, they are to survive. But, given a choice, many—perhaps all—of these youngsters would prefer a safer climate such as that offered by the schools.

Weiss and Pasley (2004, p. 28) have said, "Teachers need a vision of effective instruction to guide the design and implementation of their lessons." They go on to explain that what teachers really need to do is find ways to personalize their curriculum: "Teachers need to know how students typically think about particular concepts, how to determine what a particular student or group of students thinks about those ideas, and how to help students deepen their understanding" (p. 28). As Keefe and Amenta (2005, p. 541) have said, "The idea that the teacher must be an advisor and know each child's capabilities is widely replicated by today's reform models."

This personal approach includes respecting students' perspectives. Showing respect requires being a good listener, and being a good listener requires the ability to hear both what the speaker is saying and the feelings being expressed (Kladifko, 2010). The process of allowing students to build, express, and defend their own interpretations has become a valued goal of text discussions.

Some programs individualize curricula for students. These programs may personalize or depersonalize the curriculum, depending on the circumstances. Kohl (1998, p. 12) explained the difference between individualized education and personalized education:

> Individualized learning programs are often a series of tracks for children—suggesting that they all are trying to get to the same place but at different speeds—whereas in personalized learning the goals may be the same, but the paths may be different. In personalized learning there's a personal relationship between

FYI Split-Screen Feedback Method

Robert C. Morris and Dawn Putney • University of West Georgia

Feedback has always been an important aid for improving the quality of teaching and subsequent student learning. However, we often don't take advantage of one of our most important sources of information—our students. Teachers often assume that everything is fine in our classrooms, especially if we hear no complaints or see no apparent problems. However, operating under such an assumption puts the quality of both teaching and learning at risk.

Using simple techniques, teachers can solicit student feedback that can easily help them become more effective facilitators of learning. Successful application of these techniques only requires teachers to consider the following:

- Commit to sharing feedback results with your students. This does not mean that you pledge to follow their suggestions, only that you will share results with them.
- Prepare to receive student feedback that may be critical of your actions. Recognize that such feedback represents honest student perceptions and is not meant as a personal attack.
- Acknowledge the validity of their views and consider changes you can make based on their comments. For it to be meaningful, students must see some changes resulting from their feedback.

When you are ready to solicit student feedback, you may want to try a simple pro-and-con survey called the split-screen method. This approach is particularly useful when implementing a new teaching method or learning activity. Have your students draw a horizontal line across the middle of a piece of paper. Above the line, have them list one or more positive comments about the class, activity, or teacher being evaluated. Below the line, have them list their negative comments. Make students aware that their comments will be kept anonymous. Later, categorize and summarize their written comments for a class discussion.

> teacher and child. As a teacher you respect the unique way a child perceives the world and, accordingly, shape the way a child is going to learn. And you respect the learner as a person who is connected to a family, the world, and larger things in life.

It is interesting to note that at a time when many reformers compare our schools unfavorably with Asian schools because of differences in standardized test scores in mathematics and foreign languages, Japanese elementary teachers rank students' personal growth and fulfillment as a top education priority, self-understanding and human-relations skills as the second-highest priority, and academic excellence is ranked seventh.

Nowhere in the accountability-based, content-focused education reform reports is anyone likely to find suggestions for developing personalized curricula; yet for proactive teachers the opportunity is there. The Ohio Center for Essential School Reform (Hoffman & Levak, 2003, p. 30) offers five areas in which schools can focus their personalization efforts: know our students better, trust our students more, empower our students in authentic ways, connect our students in meaningful ways, and honor all students in varied systems of recognition and reward.

At-Risk Students and Gifted Students

One condition of modern society with which future curricula must deal in order to remove a major learning barrier is the growing number of at-risk students, most of whom come from impoverished backgrounds. More than one student in ten needs special help to achieve (Potter, Carruthers, & Green, 2002). At-risk students are more likely than average students to drop out of school. According to the Children's Defense Fund (2008), 1 in 15 teens age 16 to 19 is a dropout in the United States. (Recall in chapter 1 the list of social disadvantages that impede impoverished student learning.)

According to Dallmann-Jones (2002),

> National At-Risk Education Network (NAREN) research reveals that if an at-risk curriculum is to be effective it must shape itself to the student. . . . Each student has different individual needs, problems, and a personal life journey. A personalized curriculum holistically recognizes that one cannot separate academics from personal issues and is structured to deliberately and definitively address issues interfering with achievement and success in all facets of a student's life.

School can be a refuge for many at-risk children because it provides them needed stability; these youths know that the schools and teachers can be counted on. If students obey the policies, they can expect to get along fine. If they put forth the required effort, chances are good that they will succeed in the school environment. This is far from the case in other aspects of their lives. Also, unlike the families of a large percentage of today's youth, the school is not going to fall apart; it is not subject to divorce. By realizing what this comforting quality of consistency means to children from broken families, schools can provide structure and stability and maintain a foundation that's not going to unravel, unlike many of the families in poverty-stricken communities.

Six of the nation's largest cities have created special charter schools in order to improve learning opportunities for at-risk students (Robelen, 2007). Unlike the competitive, norm-referenced systems used in many traditional schools, a system using clear, criterion-based objectives that specify definite results of specific behaviors instills a sense of security in students. A curriculum that supports reasonably high expectations of all students communicates that the school has confidence in students' capabilities. Teachers who consistently communicate their concern for and confidence in the ability of all students to learn are empowered to motivate at-risk students.

The arts have also been shown to have a stabilizing influence on at-risk students, and on gifted students as well (see chapter 9 in Henson, 2010). The National Association for Gifted and Talented Children (nagc.org) reports that approximately three million children are considered to be gifted, which is 6% of the entire student population in America. For a more detailed discussion about gifted students (who also benefit from personalized instruction), see chapter 11 of this book.

Activities Selection

For the sake of simplicity, the first part of this chapter was limited to a discussion of the importance of content and the need for curriculum developers to use a logical strategy to select the best content for their schools. In reality, of course, to separate content from the activities that students need in order to master this content is to take a superficial approach. If educators accept John Locke's concept of *tabula rasa* (that everyone is born with a blank mind and the only way to put anything on it is through experience) or John Dewey's philosophy of "learning by doing," then they also accept the fact that content and activities are inseparable.

The process of content selection, then, is meaningless unless it includes the selection of activities through which that content can become meaningful. To be meaningful, educational activities must be accompanied by or followed with opportunities to reflect on each activity. As Boix-Mansilla and Gardner (2008, p.17) explain, "All disciplines embody distinct ways of thinking about the world." Students should also be given opportunities to connect service learning activities to the real world. Yet, educators often focus on content while ignoring activities. For example, although the textbook remains the dominant curriculum determiner and although many studies have analyzed textbook content, too few studies analyze the uses that teachers make of textbooks. Educators need to conduct more investigations on both planned teacher activities and student activities. Such investigations should include determining which instructional methods are best suited to specific disciplines.

Consider, for example, the kind of activities that can be used to help students appreciate diversity. By assigning group projects, teachers can let students experience other cultures firsthand. For example, groups of students from varied cultures could be assigned to examine newspapers, textbooks, video recordings, computer software, and other materials for possible use in their classroom.

Another approach to appreciating diversity is through conversation. Most people lack the communication skills needed to hold such directed conversations, however. As new content and activities are selected and disciplines are integrated to strengthen the curriculum, a key to success is collaboration.

The following case study is an excellent example of a program designed to help graduate students improve their communication skills while preparing undergraduates for their future profession.

case study

BUILDING CAPACITY THROUGH COLLABORATION

Pat Casey and Karen Dunlap
Texas Woman's University

The Nature of the Project

This project represents an effort to create a partnership between two previously disconnected programs within the College of Education at Texas Woman's University. This collaborative venture was developed to improve the quality of education for both aspiring teachers and aspiring educational leaders. Each semester, prospective principals who were graduate students in educational administration presented professional development sessions to pre-service teachers who were students in the university teacher-preparation program. Following these sessions, a study was conducted to determine the effectiveness of the project.

The educational administration students enhanced their professional development presentation and group-dynamics skills by developing and conducting interactive workshop sessions/seminars for the pre-service teachers on effective classroom management, instructional planning, and the adaptation of instruction for diverse populations. At the same time, the pre-service teachers were given the opportunity to learn about core teaching behaviors and interact with master teachers in a collegial environment that encouraged the mutual sharing of ideas and open dialogue (Dunlap & Casey, 2007).

Mounting evidence demonstrates that an individual teacher's effectiveness significantly impacts student achievement. Traditionally, a teacher who has received a license to teach is considered to be ready for practice. Still, new teachers do have identifiable needs for emotional and professional support, and the "sink or swim" process of transition to the classroom adds to existing problems with new teacher attrition and erects barriers to the effectiveness of the new teachers.

For the aspiring principals, the project engaged them in meaningful activities to enhance their understanding of the critical skills associated with professional development as conceptualized in the Interstate School Leaders Licensure Consortium (ISLLC) Standards. For the pre-service teachers, the professional development sessions focused on three INTASC standards of practice known to be critical and challenging for novice educators.

Given that principals and teachers are most successful when they work together, and with meaningful collaboration as a primary goal, the principal purpose of the professional development project was to provide authentic learning experiences for aspiring teachers and aspiring administrators. Furthermore, collaboration and collegial interaction are critical needs of new teachers, and many teachers find that they need more support, encouragement and direction than they receive at the school. Moreover, such interaction can be satisfying and rewarding, "deepen learning" and provide "interpersonal support and synergy" (National Staff Development Council, 2001, p. 26). Thus, teacher preparation programs need to offer professional development opportunities provided by experienced, practicing educators that enable pre-service teachers to begin forming these much needed collegial relationships.

New teachers are often unprepared for certain actualities of classroom life. The process of acculturation—socialization into the profession—takes place after they leave the preparation program and actually begin teaching. Further, the sociological setting varies between schools, and beginning teachers are expected to apply general knowledge from preparation programs to diverse school settings and diverse student populations. Therefore, the professional development sessions for the pre-service teachers that were developed and presented by the aspiring leaders focused on three standards of practice that are known to be most critical and challenging for the novice educators: (1) lesson planning, (2) adapting instruction for diverse learners, and (3) classroom management (Council of Chief State School Officers, 2008; Interstate New Teacher Assessment & Support Consortium, 1992).

The Focus of the Project

New teachers struggle with pedagogical strategies for instructing and assessing students. In today's diversified classrooms, teachers are called upon to meet a myriad of student needs by addressing as many learning styles as possible within any given lesson in an effort to ensure student success. No longer is one instructional approach acceptable for all students. For a novice teacher who may likely be functioning primarily in survival mode, such differentiation to meet individual students' needs may be a daunting task.

Effective teachers realize that there is no single instructional strategy that will be successful with diverse learners. One frequently mentioned barrier to new teacher success is the lack of time management/ lesson organization skills, suggesting that new teachers spend more time and have more difficulty planning instruction. Additionally, new teachers often express a desire to learn instructional strategies that address the needs of students at various points along the academic continuum.

For decades, new teachers also have struggled with classroom management. The ability to maintain discipline or classroom control is a critical factor in determining new teachers' success in the classroom. Indeed, decisions classroom teachers make regarding classroom practices may either facilitate student progress or impede it.

These identified needs were to be addressed in four professional-development sessions (one day for each of four semesters), with the goal of creatively collaborating to solve any existing problems and determining ways of proactively addressing issues before they become new problems

Project Goals and Outcomes

This project had two goals. First, the project was organized to address known needs of aspiring teachers and administrators and to develop the necessary knowledge and skills to improve their professional practice of teaching and leadership. However, the project itself was limited in scope, and the evaluation did not aspire to assess the lofty goals of the participants' improvement in the areas of practice. Nonetheless, this evaluation did address the second goal, which was to incorporate more practical, field-based learning experiences and enhance pre-service training for the students. Thus, the evaluation of this project sought (1) to document whether the project could make a difference, and (2) to improve the project's effectiveness.

Participants

The target population for the study was undergraduate and graduate students who were pre-service teachers and graduate students enrolled in an educational administration program. During each semester, the pre-service students were invited to participate in a collaborative professional development workshop wherein the graduate, educational administration students presented training for the pre-service teachers.

Methodology

For the aspiring administrators, the practice planning and presenting professional development was intended to contribute not only to their knowledge and understanding of professional development, but also to their level of confidence. For the aspiring teachers, the seminars were intended to contribute to their knowledge and understanding of teaching practice and also to build confidence. Consequently, a combination of quantitative and qualitative methodology was employed.

Data from two sources were used to evaluate the effectiveness of the professional development. The primary source of data was an online survey containing both closed-ended, quantitative-type questions and open-ended, qualitative-type questions. Unsolicited written reflections from some of the participants were also used as a secondary source of data.

Professional development sessions were held on one day in each of four semesters. On a workshop day, topics were presented in concurrent, one-hour sessions. The graduate students in educational administration worked in groups to prepare and present a session on one of the topics. The graduate students presented their topics three times, to three different groups of attendees. The attendees were assigned to three different topic sessions.

Following each of the workshop sessions, the presenters and attendees were invited to participate in an online survey about their experience. A total of 67 presenters and 177 attendees responded to these surveys. Finally, survey data and written feedback from the four workshop days were combined to obtain a deeper understanding of the participants' perceptions.

Following the conclusion of all the professional development sessions, study participants were invited to participate in a final evaluation survey. The anonymous survey consisted of a two-part questionnaire designed to gather both participant demographic information and their perceptions of the professional-development workshop. The questionnaire used both seven-point Likert-type questions and open-ended questions. Filling out the questionnaire took approximately 20 minutes of participants' time.

Findings for Prospective Teachers

Pre-service participants were asked if the INTASC-focused presentations highlighted skills that they thought were essential to their success as future teachers. All participants (100%) indicated that they "learned something they did not know," "would use what was learned about the topic," "were given multiple opportunities to interact/question the presenters," and "would recommend this experience to someone else."

The themes and patterns emerging from the responses to the open-ended questions and the reflective commentaries identified and described factors of the program that contributed to participant satisfaction and identified areas that needed improvement. From these data, the following themes were identified.

- First, the aspiring teachers were overwhelmingly satisfied with the sessions they attended, commenting that everyone did an excellent job and that they ranked the workshop as "one of the best!!!!"
- Second, regarding the organization of the workshop sessions, the participants regularly mentioned organizational/structural factors of time, handouts, and activities. Respondents repeatedly reported that they would have liked more time to participate in the workshop and in some cases felt that they would have benefited from more handouts.
- A third salient theme that emerged from the responses was that respondents valued the fact that the presenters were practicing, experienced classroom teachers. They made comments such as, "I hear so much about teacher burnout, and it was good to see teachers who still care and are enthusiastic about teaching. I hope my mentor teacher shares the same beliefs and drive as some of the presenters." They agreed that the content/material provided in the sessions was significant and appropriate.

Finally, the prospective teachers responded that they had learned a great deal of useful content in the three targeted areas of differentiated instruction, classroom management, and lesson planning. They repeatedly commented about "real-world applications" of things they were learning about in theory/classes.

Findings for the Presenters

Like the aspiring teachers, the prospective administrators were very satisfied with their experience. From the presenters' responses, the following themes were identified.

- First, the aspiring administrators overwhelmingly confirmed their satisfaction with the experience they had in planning and presenting workshops.
- Second, similar to the prospective teachers, the aspiring administrators referred regularly to organizational/structural factors of time, and the size/makeup of their groups and activities. They felt they needed more time to adequately present their informa-

tion. Overall, however, most of them commented that it was not only a great experience for everyone involved, but also that having the opportunity to present the same topic three times gave them a great opportunity to practice with different audiences and refine their presentation skills.

- Third, many of the administrators group said that they wished they had been able to participate in this type of experience before they began teaching, referring specifically to the content of the sessions.
- Finally, some of the educational administration students reported that this was their first experience presenting to adults and felt that, as a result of their experience in this program, they would feel more comfortable in the future when addressing other teachers in faculty meetings or presenting in-service training for other teachers.

Discussion

The quantitative data were very one-sided—describing participants' satisfaction with the workshop sessions regardless of their role as presenter or participant. The themes and patterns that emerged from the qualitative data were also very one-sided but did contribute to a richer description of significant factors.

Overall, the findings of this study were very positive and consistent. The responses of all participants confirmed that they were very satisfied with their experiences. With the quantitative data being so one-sided, the qualitative data became even more important to our understanding. More important, the qualitative data contributed to our identification, description, and understanding of some areas for improvement.

Issues for Further Application and Reflection

1. Only in recent years have educators have embraced qualitative research on a large scale. Does this case study suggest a possible cause for this change in practice?
2. The stated goals for this program were the attainment of the knowledge and skills needed for both (a) instructional improvement and (b) improved administration. For which of these two goals do you think the program was more successful?
3. One of the stated achievements of this program was changes in attitude. How important do you consider this achievement in comparison with the goals listed in #2 above?
4. This was a highly successful program. Can you offer a suggestion for making it even more successful?

References

Council of Chief State School Officers. (2008). *Educational leadership policy standards: ISLLC 2008 as adopted by the National Policy Board for Educational Administration.* Washington DC: Author. Retrieved on July 6, 2008, from http://www.ccsso.org/publications/index.cfm

Dunlap, K., & Casey, P. (2007, Winter). Collaborative professional development project. *Academic Exchange Quarterly, 11*(4).

Interstate New Teacher Assessment & Support Consortium. (1992). *Model standards for beginning teacher licensing, assessment and development: A resource for state dialogue.* Washington DC: Council of Chief State School Officers. Retrieved on April 14, 2009, from http://www.ccsso.org/content/pdfs/corestrd.pdf

The National Staff Development Council. (2001). *Standards for staff development: Advancing student learning through staff development.* Oxford, OH: Author.

The Knowledge Base

Within the past few years, researchers have collected more information about effective teaching than had been accumulated over the previous two centuries. This fact alone demands that, when selecting teacher activities and learner activities, teachers make full use of the existing knowledge base, keep abreast of the findings reported monthly in professional journals, and whenever possible contribute to the knowledge base. However, caution should be used to avoid the temptation to overgeneralize data and draw unfounded conclusions. Although teachers should be encouraged to use the knowledge base when selecting teacher activities and learner activities, they should proceed with caution. This caveat equally applies to teacher education programs. To be capable of achieving the desired balance—that is, to select and use valid research without imbuing the findings with unwarranted substance—requires knowledge of and skills in using research. Teacher education programs, undergraduate and especially graduate, should include research across the curriculum. Without a research component, the potential for in-service faculty development programs to help teachers build the necessary research skills—indeed, the potential of a single research course to achieve this goal—is extremely limited.

Problem Solving

Since the Woods Hole Conference in 1959 (discussed in chapter 3), problem solving has been emphasized in curricula in both elementary and secondary schools. Its heavy emphasis in the early 1960s was predicated on its effectiveness in helping students understand the content they studied.

Unlike taking nationally standardized achievement tests, "which are designed from the get-go to yield comparative scores" (Popham, 2005, p. 92), when students solve problems in a cooperative manner additional benefits accrue: They can achieve several goals simultaneously. Cooperation leads to increased and deeper understanding (O'Donnell & Dansereau, 1993). After studying the cognitive effects of guided cooperative questioning, King and Rosenshine (1993, p. 143) reported that "children at fifth-grade level can be trained to use the highly elaborated question stems to generate thought-provoking questions about material presented in classroom lessons."

Since many problem-solving situations are open ended, students learn from dealing with them that knowledge seeking does not stop with a single answer. Often one answer may lead to additional questions. And students need to know that understanding is never complete. It is a sometimes-nonlinear process where the learner moves gradually toward greater understanding.

Some teachers have mistakenly thought that effective use of activities requires choosing one activity to help students meet one objective; they have assumed that there should be a separate activity for each objective in their curriculum. But this is not so: Carefully designed, a *multipurpose activity* can serve several objectives. Group problem solving has something for everybody and can motivate different students in many different ways. While solving group problems, students can learn about teamwork, leadership, the subject-matter area of the problem, and problem solving itself.

> Problem-based learning is presented as a way of challenging students to become deeply involved in a quest for knowledge—a search for answers to their own questions, not just answers to questions posed by a textbook or a teacher. Identifying problematic situations within the curriculum, posing questions, researching, and reporting depend on and foster a community of inquiry. In such a community, participants feel free to pose tough questions, learn from and build upon each other's questions, are open to different points of view, listen to and respect each other's ideas, and can work collaboratively toward reasonable conclusion. (Barell, 2007, p. 3)

In summary, problem solving is a strategy that offers tomorrow's citizens opportunities to prepare for the type of lifestyle that will require critical thinking and problem-solving abilities. According to Alvarez (1993, p. 13), "If we expect critical thinking to take place, we need to provide students with problem-solving lessons in meaningful learning contexts." Alvarez suggests that one viable context in which students can develop critical thinking skills is the case study method: "Self-selected cases spurred curiosity and invited students to initiate critical and imaginative thinking" (p. 14). Cases provide an open invitation to generalize, and they allow students to be creative and imaginative. Case studies involve collaboration, which is essential to the development of creative thinking.

Internationalization and Global Awareness

You will recall that a high level of panic was apparent in the education reform reports of the 1980s and 1990s. Setting the pattern, the title of the report, *A Nation at Risk*, suggested a crisis, speaking of "a rising tide of mediocrity." That concern over the ability of U.S. citizens to compete internationally suggests how important it is for American students to be knowledgeable about the world at large. Over half of the public (57%) believes schools should spend more time than they do now learning about other nations and the way other people of the world live (Rose & Gallup, 2007).

If a school's curriculum is to serve society by providing leadership, it must incorporate technological developments and international trends and must include content and activities to prepare the current generation of youth for their contemporary and future roles in the community and in the world. Civic values must be extended to include concern for the world, and students must develop concern for human rights and respect for other cultures (Stewart, 2007b). Our students need deeper knowledge than traditionally provided through fun, food, and festivals; they need to understand trends in trade, economy, and cultural concerns.

To survive, all societies depend on the cooperation of the rest of the world. As this interdependency increases, another responsibility of the curriculum is to recognize, and help others recognize, the importance of global awareness. We must make sure we recognize the vital role of education in helping members of all societies understand and discharge their global responsibilities.

Selecting activities that promote global awareness can help prepare students to make better decisions about world issues. This goes beyond deluging children with international art projects and festivals. Students need to work with people from different countries, in different languages, in the realms of business, politics, and human understanding. As future global citizens, they will need to forge relationships and solve problems across borders of race, culture, and geography. In addition to knowledge, the traits of compassion, acceptance, and a sense of responsibility to the world are essential for global citizenship (Rubenstein, 2006).

Below is a list of Web sites related to global learning.

- *National Geographic Society's My Wonderful World*
  www.mywonderfulworld.org
- *International Education & Resource Network*
  www.learn.org
- *Asia Society's K–12 Initiative*
  www.internationaled.org
- *Global SchoolNet Foundation*
  www.globalschoolnet.org
- *Thinkquest International*
  www.thinkquest.org

Box 7.3 United National Educational, Scientific and Cultural Organization

Globalization and Higher Education—an "expert meeting" addressing the impact of globalization, quality assurance, accreditation, and the recognition of qualifications in higher education—was organized by the Division of Higher Education at UNESCO in 2001. This meeting's goal was "to establish an international forum for dialogue among nation-states, the private sector, traditional and nontraditional higher education institutions, and students."

In 2003, The Conference on Globalization and Higher Education, also organized by UNESCO, explored the challenges facing institutions and national higher education systems in an increasingly globalized environment. Debates at this conference centered on stakeholder responses to the pressures of an emerging knowledge society—how policy makers and higher education institutions can develop a common platform on policy guidelines, frameworks, and instruments. In 2005 UNESCO organized the "United Nations Decade of Education for Sustainable Development (ESD) (2005–2014), with a commitment to education that empowers people to change their lifestyles. Five years into the endeavor, one of the goals of the 2009 Bonn Conference was to reorient curricula to address sustainability issues through policy. The Bonn Declaration recognized that the knowledge, technology, and skills already exist to turn around unsustainable development models.

Further information about these meetings and about current global education efforts can be found on UNESCO's Web site (http://portal.unesco/org).

Education Reform's Impact on Content and Activities Selection

Throughout the country, education reform is causing educators to alter the selection of curriculum content and activities. For example, the No Child Left Behind Act requires teachers to defend their selection of teaching strategies and learning activities by providing data that ensure that these strategies and activities actually enhance learning.

The *official curriculum* is the planned curriculum. That the curriculum will be altered significantly is fact; *how* curricula will be altered depends in large part on teachers. The point here is that teachers need not, and indeed must not, wait to see how tomorrow's content and activities will look; rather, responsible teachers must take a proactive stance to shape the new curricula by choosing the content and activities students need in the twenty-first century. Recognizing the need for ongoing improvement does not imply that all change or all reform is good, however. Rather than blindly accepting all reform as improvement, teachers should continually evaluate the worth of new as well as old practices.

A Call for Increased Flexibility

Taking a proactive role will require teachers to think and even feel in different ways. The time is ripe for contemporary teachers to ask what they want of tomorrow's schools. Although the *Tylerian curriculum model* (also known as *ends–means planning*, discussed in chapter 4) is sometimes criticized, it is an excellent beginning. The reform reports call for more science and mathematics and for students to develop the ability to apply their knowledge in their adult lives. These reports call for American students to be able to achieve the highest scores on national achievement tests and to outperform their counterparts internationally. Although these goals may have merit, teachers must look beyond them, for, by themselves, the goals do not address the need to prepare students for the future.

Specifically, the new century requires high levels of flexibility—in thinking, in accepting the differences between people, in accepting the ideas of others, and in relating to errors (that is, accepting mistakes as a part of the learning process). As role models, teachers must excel in their flexibility, and curricula must be designed to nurture these flexible behaviors. The flexibility that educators need to meet the needs of all students is essential in the selection of both content and activities.

Risk taking must be supported and rewarded, and different routes to each learning destination must be recognized. Teachers must look to each student's unique needs to determine which route is best. They will consider different cognitive styles and modality preferences. They will design activities that appeal to both left- and right-brain learners. They will also vary the pace at which they drive students toward the learning objectives.

Flexibility must go even further: Teachers who use authoritarian methods must learn to relinquish some of their authority; they must learn how to feel comfortable in letting students set some of their own objectives, knowing that these will vary among different students and knowing that many mistakes will be made.

The expansion of flexibility must be a personal goal of experienced and new teachers alike, and a curriculum goal for students. Piaget wrote about the inseparable connection between the cognitive self and the emotional self. If students become emotionally involved from being allowed the flexibility to select the content and activities in their classrooms, their cognitive abilities will benefit.

Teacher Empowerment

Teacher empowerment is another term associated with education reform. Teacher empowerment is more than a fad of current education reform, and its purpose goes beyond securing higher pay and better working conditions for teachers. By controlling their teaching behavior, teachers are the most powerful influence on students' learning and can serve as curriculum leaders. Teacher empowerment is also valuable because it expands teachers' professional arenas and allows them to extend their leadership skills beyond the walls of the classroom.

Current education reform efforts emphasize the need to empower teachers. Exacerbated by the No Child Left Behind demands, however, teacher burnout continues to be a major problem (Richards, 2007). Teacher burnout robs teachers of their feelings of empowerment, yet most educators believe that teacher empowerment is indispensable to meaningful reform. Teacher empowerment can be further enhanced when teachers increase their involvement in planning and developing the school's curriculum. Teachers who traditionally have remained in self-contained classrooms must assume a larger role in the entire operation of the school if, indeed, education reform efforts are to succeed.

In this context it is virtually impossible to distinguish between curriculum content and curriculum activities. Teacher empowerment requires an understanding of one's own philosophy of education (Ferrero, 2005) and the ability to select both content and activities to promote the empowerment of students. Shen (1998, p. 36) studied teacher empowerment practices and concluded, "Despite today's rhetoric of teacher empowerment and decentralization, empowerment thus far appears to have gone to principals." However, in the twenty-first century we have made great strides in empowering teachers. Teaching is also about strengthening, invigorating, and empowering others. As Joanne Rooney (2007, p. 87) has said, "To truly empower teachers we must move the responsibility for professional growth from our desks to theirs."

Student Empowerment

Like teachers, if students are to become creators of knowledge, they must be empowered to take risks. Constructivist teachers collaborate with their colleagues to create classroom environments where students can hypothesize without fear of being ridiculed. In such classrooms students learn to view mistakes as doorsteps to success. Constructivist teachers recognize that they must not let tradition dictate the selection of content and activities. Problem solving is a timely process, but the benefits justify the extra time that must be allotted for this purpose. As Opportunities for reflection and collaboration arise when teachers work together with worthy standards that encourage students to pose and solve problems. Schools need classrooms with dialogues (National Service Learning Clearinghouse, 2008) and continuous, deep conversations. Student empowerment also requires a safe climate, providing a learning community where students and teachers can work together to create understanding.

Parent Empowerment

For almost two centuries American parents were purposefully kept from "interfering" with decisions related to curriculum and instruction, but this tendency to keep parents at arm's length began to change in the late twentieth century, when the effective schools research discovered that involving parents in academic matters can produce remarkable levels of student achievement. American schools might take a cue from a school in London, where teachers initiate a two-way dialogue with parents about the curriculum and experience remarkable results.

> Teachers invite parents into the school for a meeting twice a year. They explain the topics coming up and ask the parents for any useful information and input. The parents work in small groups to make a concept map of each topic, brainstorming ideas around the central theme, thinking about what their children already know and what they would be interested in knowing, and suggesting different activities. A teacher commented, "The concept maps help to demonstrate to parents how we teach thinking to pupils, rather than just facts."
>
> By taking on parents' suggestions, the school now offers a curriculum that truly reflects the needs and interests of the children. The dynamics of the school have also changed. Parents no longer feel that teachers are superior, and the teachers talk positively about empowering parents to make an effective contribution. School now has a place in family life for both parents and children. Parents are engaged and interested in what their children are learning and leave the planning sessions buzzing with excitement. The ideas they suggest tend to be hands-on and interactive, often involving objects that their children bring in from home. As a result, the children feel represented and valued, and levels of engagement in lessons have improved considerably. The teachers have noticed a difference in their own work as well. Their discussions with parents are inspiring them to leave behind traditional topics and lessons and to focus on things that are more relevant to the children. (Qualifications and Curriculum Authority, n.d.)

Building Self-Confidence and Security

The best confidence builder is acceptance, and self-acceptance is best achieved through success. Too often, education reformers and reform policies have unintentionally and unknowingly sent the message to teachers that their prior efforts have been futile. For example, consider what happens when, without their involvement in and input into the decisions to alter the curriculum, teachers are told to replace existing practices with new ones. A common perception of this directive is that someone—usually an outsider who knows little about the characteristics and needs of students and the community—has decided that the current practices are all wrong, which is interpreted to mean that teachers have failed. The harm that this conclusion causes can easily be avoided by involving teachers in decisions to change and by letting teachers know that reform can occur by building on the existing curriculum; indeed, destroying or replacing an existing curriculum is seldom, if ever, necessary or desirable.

For example, during a workshop designed to help teachers develop an integrated curriculum, one teacher was overheard saying, "When we collapsed four subjects to form a central integrated theme and we designed 120-minute periods, some of the teachers insisted on having 30 minutes to devote exclusively to their discipline." Although success with integrated programs requires teachers to give up the idea of having time exclusively for their discipline, reprimanding a teacher who balks at this would gain nothing. A far better approach would be to compliment such teachers on their level of dedication to their discipline and explain that although they will be required to forgo spending their time exclusively on their discipline, they will not have to give up their level of commitment to their subject.

Because constructivism involves problem solving, which requires more time than direct methods of instruction, students in constructivist classes may spend time on fewer types of activities—but they explore them in greater depth. Block scheduling is useful in constructivist classrooms because it gives teachers the opportunity to blend two or more disciplines. Integrated themes open up a curriculum, giving students freedom to head in many directions and take many risks as they search for answers.

Both teachers and students need confidence-building activities. Students need the self-confidence required to live in a future that will place new demands on all citizens, prominent among them the ability to deal with uncertainty. Education is about learning how to deal with uncertainty and ambiguity.

Feeling uncertain is being in a zone of high discomfort. As seen in chapter 2, in the past schools have been bastions of tradition, protecting teachers from the unknown. Like other adults, many teachers fear uncertainty because when they went to school, they were punished for making errors. Of course, the "commonsense" conclusion is that the best way to avoid errors is to avoid experimenting with new approaches. This condition can be rectified for both the teachers and their students by curricula that make mistakes acceptable. The best way to drive out fear of the unknown is to make the unknown familiar. In the classroom this means taking risks, making mistakes, and using mistakes to learn instead of hiding from them.

Another way to help teachers approach reform with confidence is to assure them that they have the time needed to implement it. Unfortunately, the tone of urgency expressed in some of the reform reports has intensified teachers' anxieties; yet curricularists know that significant educational change comes slowly. A timetable can be used to assure teachers that they are making progress at a rate that is both reasonable and acceptable. The curriculum should offer an effective route whereby students can succeed, and self-esteem should come from self-improvement rather than from self-concept development programs that rely on telling students that they are important.

By planning activities to help their students increase their self-esteem, teachers can enhance their own self-concepts, and by covering all the reform practices endorsed by their district, teachers can feel more comfortable about education reform. Following is a description of a system teachers can use to ensure that they are achieving local education reform expectations.

Tables of Specification

Because curriculum development is a complex process, and because it is rapidly becoming more complex (through the pressure of education reform), including the most important content in the curriculum has become a formidable challenge. A system is needed to ensure that the most important content and activities are being covered so that the expectations of the curriculum are met. One such system is a *table of specifications*.

Tables of specifications vary, but their principle is constant. Each table uses a matrix, with the columns and lines labeled. Table 7.1 is a sample table of specifications designed to ensure that the local education reform practices are being covered in a teacher education curriculum.

In this example, the teacher education courses are listed horizontally across the top of the chart, and the reform elements are listed vertically at the left. The table of specifications can be used in two ways. First, the left side of the matrix can be used as a point of origin. For example, this approach would be used if you wanted to know how thoroughly a particular reform element is being covered. Or you might wish to know how comprehensive a particular course is in covering education reform. You can determine this by using the top as your point of origin; locate the course in question and move down the column to see how many reform elements are addressed in this course. This particular matrix goes further: a 1-to-3 numbering system is assigned to show the depth to which a particular reform element is covered. Coverage at level 1 is an introduction; level 3 is mastery; level 2 is between introduction and mastery.

Table 7.1 Table of Specifications for Educational Reform

	Courses in the Program Area											
KERA Topics	*ELE 361*	*ELE 262*	*ELE 445*	*ELE 446*	*ELE 490*	*ELE 491*	*ELE 492*	*ELE 493*	*ELE 499*	*ELE 530*	*ELE 541*	*ELE 551*
1. Curriculum goals	2	2	1	2	1	3	3	2	3	2	1	2
2. Performance-based student assessment	1	2	0	2	2	3	1	2	2	1	2	1
3. Nongraded primary	2	1	0	2	3	3	1	2	2	2	1	1
4. Site-based decision making	1	0	1	1	1	2	1	1	1	0	1	0
5. Instructional uses of technology	1	0	1	1	1	3	2	1	2	0	1	1
6. Research-based instructional practices	3	1	1	2	3	1	3	2	2	2	1	3
7. Extended school program	0	0	0	2	1	0	0	0	1	1	1	0
8. Motivating students of diverse cultures	3	1	1	1	1	1	2	2	3	3	2	3
9. School finance	0	0	0	0	0	0	1	0	1	0	0	0

Rating scale: 1—awareness of topic; 2—topic is reinforced; 3—mastery of topic is achieved.

On a smaller scale, a table of specifications can be designed for each course. Across the top you can list the objectives you want students to master. The first column can list the content generalizations (concepts) needed to achieve these objectives. Once the top row and the first column are filled in, you can use the chart to check each objective to determine whether the content needed to achieve the objective is covered. Table 7.2 is a sample table of specifications for a high school class in world history.

Table 7.2 Table of Specifications to Ensure Content Coverage for All Objectives

Content Generalizations	*Obj. 16*	*Obj. 17*	*Obj. 18*	*Obj. 19*	*Obj. 20*	*Obj. 21*	*Obj. 22*	*Obj. 23*	*Obj. 24*	*Obj. 25*	*Obj. 26*	*Obj. 27*
1. Concept of power and authority and law and order												
2. Generalizations on social orders of feudal classes												
3. Little representation of lower classes												
4. Foundations of democracy laid in medieval period, quality of life and secularism increased		✓		✓	✓						✓	✓
5. Value of art created by many great artists during this period		✓	✓	✓	✓		✓		✓	✓	✓	✓
6. Even though centuries pass, life remains the same	✓	✓			✓	✓		✓	✓	✓	✓	✓
7. Past contributions relate to total picture of history		✓	✓	✓	✓	✓	✓			✓	✓	✓

Similar tables of specification can be developed to ensure coverage in the affective and psychomotor domains. An advantage of tables of specification is that they can be used to ensure coverage of objectives at varying levels of the three domains of the educational taxonomies. See table 7.3, a table of specifications for an art class.

Still another use of the table of specifications is to ensure that a curriculum contains activities covering each major concept or objective. List the objectives or concepts on one axis and the activities on the other. When the table is used for this purpose, one activity should correspond to each objective or concept, although the same activity may be assigned to more than one objective or concept. For example, table 7.4 (on p. 256) shows a table of specifications for a grade 4–6 unit on

Table 7.3 Table of Specifications to Ensure Coverage of All Levels of the Three Domains

Domains

The levels of each domain are arranged in a hierarchy from left to right at the top. Each level assumes inclusion of lower levels. The highest targeted level is checked.	*Cognitive*						*Affective*					*Psychomotor*						
	Knowledge	Comprehension	Application	Analysis	Synthesis	Evaluation	Receiving	Responding	Valuing	Organization	Characterization	Reception	Set	Guided Response	Mechanism	Comp. Overt Resp.	Adaption	Origination
1. Name materials	✓													✓				
2. Select materials		✓						✓						✓				
3. Identify terms	✓							✓						✓				
4. Spell terms			✓					✓							✓			
5. Name design element	✓							✓						✓				
6. Name design principle	✓							✓						✓				
7. Identify design element				✓				✓						✓				
8. Identify comprehension principle					✓				✓						✓			
9. Identify comprehension areas				✓				✓						✓				
10. Identify comprehension in pictures				✓				✓						✓				
11. Mix colors: hue			✓						✓						✓			
12. Create: tint, shade					✓					✓								✓
13. Create: mood					✓					✓								✓
14. Create: design element					✓					✓								✓
15. Compare pictures				✓					✓					✓				
16. Compare sculpture, pictures				✓					✓					✓				
17. Use technique			✓					✓							✓			
18. "Wait turn"				✓				✓						✓				
19. Choose for group				✓						✓						✓		
20. Properly use material and equipment			✓		✓			✓								✓		
21. Construct 3-D objects				✓						✓								✓
22. Store materials				✓				✓								✓		
23. Store equipment								✓								✓		
24. Share with instructor								✓						✓				
25. Share with group								✓						✓				
26. Share with the class								✓						✓				
27. Display, classroom						✓				✓								
28. Display, other						✓				✓								
29. Prepare display			✓						✓							✓		
30. Select group				✓						✓				✓				
31. Show followership				✓						✓				✓				
32. Show leadership						✓								✓				
33. Accept others' work						✓					✓	✓						
34. Evaluate products						✓				✓						✓		
35. Evaluate process						✓				✓						✓		
36. Work alone, cooperate		✓						✓						✓				
37. Cooperate in group		✓						✓						✓				
38. Adapt techniques						✓				✓							✓	

weather. Major concepts are expressed in 1 to 3 words so that they will fit in the table. Whenever possible, concept statements should be kept to simple sentences.

The number of ways teachers can use tables of specifications is limited only by teachers' imaginations. Certainly, discovering creative applications of this instrument to solve contemporary problems epitomizes the exhilarating nature of curriculum improvement and the challenges that face today's teachers. As teachers' roles in curriculum development grow, so will the need to be skilled in discovering new ways to use this and other versatile instruments.

Table 7.4 Table of Specifications for a Unit on Weather

	Goals								
Objectives	1. Processes	2. Knowledge	3. Curiosity	4. Independence	5. Group participation	6. Communication	7. Economics	8. Culture	9. Reduce fear
1. Apply symbols	✓	✓							
2. Identify terms		✓							
3. Write paragraph		✓		✓					✓
4. Record weather	✓	✓		✓					
5. List effects							✓		
6. Identify clouds	✓	✓		✓		✓			
7. Design mural					✓				
8. Research climate				✓			✓	✓	
9. Complete activity	✓	✓	✓	✓					
10. Apply symbols	✓	✓							✓
11. Complete evaluation	✓			✓					
12. Resupply center				✓	✓				
13. Perform in grade					✓				
14. Label measurements	✓	✓							
15. Interview				✓		✓		✓	
16. Record forecasts			✓			✓			
17. List machines	✓								
18. Construct instructions	✓			✓	✓	✓			
19. Write questions			✓						
20. List rules									✓
21. List services							✓		✓
22. List variables							✓		
23. Make graph	✓	✓							
24. Make puppets				✓		✓			
25. Write letter	✓		✓	✓					✓
26. Write story			✓	✓		✓			✓
27. Create game				✓	✓				
28. Write review		✓	✓						✓
29. Develop problem	✓				✓				
30. Construct satellite		✓			✓	✓			

Conclusion

Following is a summary of some of the advances made and concerns raised about the topics discussed in this chapter.

Advances

- A sense of community in classrooms and schools has a powerful impact on students' social development.
- NCLB offers the largest funding opportunity to elementary and secondary schools in decades.
- Expanding teachers' work arenas leads to increased student benefits.
- NCLB gives schools latitude to target up to half the non-Title I funds to their programs that impact learning most.
- Parents are becoming involved in curriculum development at unprecedented levels.
- Education reform offers unique opportunities for both teachers and students to build their self-confidence.

Concerns

- Teachers need time to develop a sense of community.
- Since NCLB was passed, over half of the nation's schools have received less money.
- Increased student success depends on the particulars of each school.
- The public sees lack of finances as schools' number-one problem.
- Textbooks cover too many topics, too lightly.
- Curriculum planners must find a way to improve the retention rate of at-risk students.

We know that contemporary constructivist educators believe that a major role of the curriculum is to help students make meaning out of newly acquired information. Achieving this goal requires the ability on the part of teachers to make careful selections of content and activities. Yet, in the past, most teachers have not selected content and activities logically. The textbook, a very poor source for determining content, remains the dominant curriculum determiner, followed closely by another equally poor curriculum determiner, personal choice.

Constructivists believe that the only way to make sense of newly acquired information is by integrating it into previously acquired understandings. This requires using concepts and themes and selecting appropriate student activities to enable students to use the new information.

The curriculum should serve the student and the society. Content selection should use human development (improving society through the improvement of individuals) in the selection of content. Multipurpose activities serve a multiple number of objectives. Problem solving is an excellent form of multipurpose activity, since the future will require individuals to solve more problems. Current world events, current education reform goals, and the future welfare of students should govern the selection of content and activities. Many contemporary educators are convinced that less is more, preferring schools to cover fewer topics but in greater depth (a practice that characterizes Asian curricula).

Curricularists are encouraged to use a criterion-referenced approach—that is, to first select the desired outcomes and then select the appropriate content needed to achieve these outcomes. These outcomes must include the desire for all students, regardless of their ethnic background, to succeed to their maximum capacity. Curricularists are reminded of the need to use their judgment and weigh the relative importance of content against its contributions to the aims, goals, and objectives of the school and the classroom.

As our society becomes increasingly diverse, we must not exempt students whom we might consider less capable or under special challenges from meeting class expectations. Rather, we must attend workshops and read professional literature to continue discovering ways of helping all students reach national, regional, and local standards and goals. Attaining this goal of including all students when making decisions about the curriculum will require taking risks; therefore, we must create a climate where experimentation is valued and mistakes are expected and accepted as necessary steps to growth.

Additional Learning Opportunities

1. Which of the four major factors—society's needs, knowledge, student needs, or human development—do you think is most important to curriculum development? Explain your answer.
2. Which should receive more emphasis in curriculum development, the present or the future? Explain your answer.
3. How would you explain the sentence, "In selecting content, more is less"?
4. How can activities be used to meet the needs of minority students?

Suggested Activities

1. Research the topic "human development." Begin by finding three definitions of this term, and then write your own definition. Next, make a list of actions you can take to help achieve this goal as you plan curricula.
2. Choose one lesson that you enjoy teaching. List and describe one activity that you might include in that lesson to address human development.
3. Write a one- or two-page statement describing your beliefs about the nature of youth. Include your perceptions of young peoples' nature to be (a) curious or apathetic, (b) active or passive, (c) cooperative or competitive, (d) self-centered or social, and (e) honest or dishonest.
4. With regard to John Dewey's admonition to redesign our curricula to fit the rebirth of a new culture with each generation, make a list of important factors in the lives of contemporary youth that are unique to this generation.
5. Develop a system that you can use to gather information about student preferences.
6. Examine a state study guide or your state's reform program. Then select two or three goals and develop a multipurpose activity to serve the goals.

7. Develop a group assignment whose goal is to increase appreciation for diversity. *Hint*: Critique curriculum materials regarding their portrayal of minorities.
8. Develop an activity that will enable students to use their previous multicultural experiences as building blocks to gain an even greater appreciation for diversity.

chapter eight

HELPING PEOPLE CHANGE

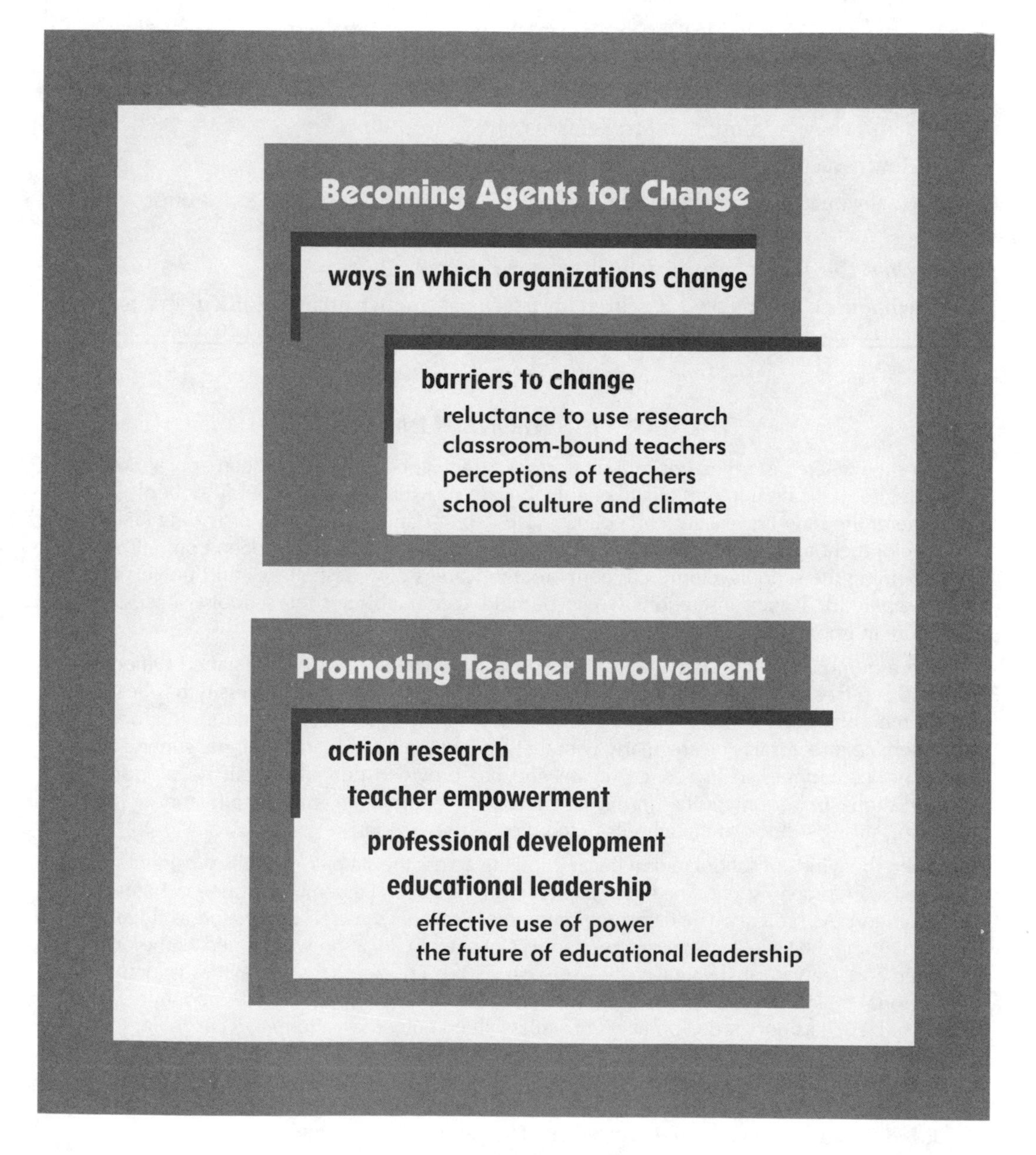

Focus Questions

1. How has the curriculum role of the educational leader changed in recent years?
2. Why do teachers need to conduct research? What are some of the benefits involved?
3. What are some reasons for the increased need for teacher involvement in schoolwide curriculum matters?
4. What effect has education reform had on teacher involvement in schoolwide matters?
5. What effect does teacher involvement in classroom assignments have on student behavior in multicultural classes?
6. How can education consortia contribute to school reform?
7. How would you justify teacher empowerment as a prerequisite to (a) improving a school's curriculum and (b) implementing education reform?
8. What role does power play in education reform?
9. What implications does research have for constructivism and multiculturalism?

The Case of Regional University

In a state where a storm of education reform was raging, no money had been appropriated for higher education institutions to enable them to provide help to the public schools, yet some of the state universities and colleges had a long-standing record of providing faculty development and other services to the schools. These educators had a deep commitment to helping the schools reform. Furthermore, the leaders at these colleges and universities anticipated that their institutions would be held accountable for the schools' success or failure in implementing the new laws.

Like a number of other state universities, Regional University has a fully staffed Office of Field Services and Professional Development. For 12 years Regional University has hosted the monthly meetings for about 40 public school superintendents. In addition, Regional's in-service director has met regularly with the superintendents and instructional supervisors in the 22 counties in its service region and has provided numerous staff development workshops. Other universities in the state have similar arrangements and a history of providing strong support to the schools in their respective regions.

When the winds of school reform began blowing across the state, Regional's president and its education dean spent time in the capitol with the general assembly at open debates on education. As radical change became imminent, Regional was self-designated as a leader in mapping the state's school reform, and its College of Education was named as the organizer and leader for the university. As soon as the education reform bill was drafted, Regional began holding trainer-of-trainer workshops on major reform issues contained in the bill, such as nongraded primary curricula, valued outcomes, alternative curricula, integrated curricula, portfolios, alternative assessment, performance evaluation, multicultural education, curriculum alignment, site-based decision making, educational technology, and research-based teaching. It was expected that as new reform elements were introduced, new workshops would be developed.

With the news that the state was appropriating additional funds to the public schools for education reform (increased dollars based on average daily attendance), but that no additional money would be provided to the universities, Regional University made the following proposal to the school districts in its service region.

Educational Excellence Laboratory
A Proposed Staff Development Consortium Proposal Abstract*

The State General Assembly, as a part of its education reform package, has identified staff development as a serious need in improving the state's public schools and has recommended that regional centers and consortia be established to address this need. In response to this recommendation, it is proposed that a staff development consortium, the Educational Excellence Laboratory, be established at Regional University. The Educational Excellence Laboratory would utilize the existing facilities and expertise of the university to provide effective staff development programs targeted to the identified needs of the participating school districts.

Statement of Need

1. Many state school districts lack the fiscal resources to provide staff development activities that have the necessary breadth and depth to effect change.
2. The districts lack a sufficient number of supervisory personnel necessary to plan and manage long-range staff development programs.
3. Many districts are in remote and isolated areas, far removed from access to exemplary programs. More programs, addressing area-wide concerns, need to be located in the various areas.
4. Assistance in the design, analysis, and application of school-based research, addressing local problems, is critical.

Regional's Role

Regional University has a definite role to play in this effort to enhance staff development activities in the public schools. An office to assist the schools in staff development already exists in the College of Education. The faculty members of the College of Education have close, trusting relationships with the teachers and administrators in the schools. Regional's leadership role in teacher education, both preservice and in-service, is recognized and accepted.

Goals

The Regional University Educational Excellence Laboratory will revitalize school districts in the consortium through programs designed to provide continuous in-depth professional development opportunities. Extensive assessment will determine local needs related to the recommended educational reforms. Utilizing the nursery through twelfth-grade laboratory school at Regional, along with on-site assistance, Regional will help local districts improve their staff development programs through:

1. *Staff development:* Continual training will be offered to effect positive school changes.
2. *Curriculum and instruction research:* This will focus on assessing local needs and on designing and conducting research related to effective instructional techniques and curricula.
3. *Technology services:* The future of education reform is related to the efforts of schools to use computers as instructional and administrative tools.
4. *Diagnostic, assessment, and assistance services:* Students placed at risk or with handicapping conditions are in need of diagnoses and assessments for individualized educational plans.

*Special thanks to Dr. William R. Thames for his development and leadership with the Education Excellence Consortium.

5. *Learning resource center:* Teachers need accessible locations where they can review materials, create instructional materials, and share ideas.
6. *Needs assessment and evaluation:* Continued progress in education requires assessing needs and evaluating expected outcomes in order to tailor the professional development program to the school level.
7. *Professional renewal opportunities:* Practicing teachers and administrators need opportunities for professional renewal which will motivate them and bring about their commitment to educational reform.

Organizational Structure

The proposed Educational Excellence Laboratory consortium would provide professional development services at several sites on the Regional campus and in the field. The consortium would be operated through the existing Office of Field Services and Professional Development located in the College of Education. This office has the responsibility for assisting the school districts in the planning, implementation, and delivery of quality staff development activities. The director of this office would serve as the director of the consortium under the guidance of a steering committee composed of representatives from participating school districts.

The Educational Excellence Laboratory consortium would have five sites, each with a distinct function in professional development. The sites and their functions would be as follows:

1. *Assessment and evaluation site:* Located in the College of Education's Office of Research and Planning, this site will conduct needs assessments, long-range planning, and program evaluation.
2. *Training sites:* Located at Regional's off-campus center and at the on-campus Sam Ervin Center, these sites will provide easy access for training that reflects the best practices and is responsive to participant needs.
3. *Demonstration site:* The laboratory school, located on Regional's campus, will serve as the demonstration site for innovative approaches to instruction and curriculum.
4. *Resource sites:* The off-campus facility and the Horns Library will provide instructional materials libraries for use by participating districts. Other sites to be utilized would be the Tri-Lakes Environmental Center, the Planetarium, the Department of Special Education (with its communication disorders laboratories), the College of Allied Health and Nursing, and the Department of Health Education.
5. *Research and development site:* Located within the laboratory school, this site will provide assistance in identifying the best developing instructional practices and assistance in conducting research with and disseminating results to participating school districts.

The establishment of the Regional University Educational Excellence Laboratory, as outlined above, would result in more effective professional development and improvement of instruction for school districts participating in the consortium.

Educational Excellence Laboratory Proposed Initial Funding

Funding for the initial activities of the consortium would be provided jointly by Regional University and the participating school districts. Regional University will seek outside funding for its initial share, and participating districts will match that amount dollar for dollar. The exact amount required from each participating district will depend upon the amount of outside funding secured by Regional and the number of school districts participating in the consortium.

Funding for the continuing operation of the consortium would come from the monies provided to the districts through the reform package in the following manner:

Year 1	$1 per child
Year 2	$5 per child
Year 3–5	$25 per child

Twenty-one school districts joined the new consortium, each agreeing to pay a fee based on the number of students in its region. After two years, the consortium expanded its services to include purchasing goods (food, instructional supplies, and cleaning materials). During the following year, purchases of goods exceeded $2 million, saving the districts thousands of dollars.

During the second half of the consortium's third year (June through December) 598 reform workshops were provided to 15,990 teachers. Most of the workshops were delivered on site in the local districts.

Questions on the Educational Excellence Laboratory Consortium

1. What responsibility do you believe the directors of such consortia have for determining the most critical needs of their clients?
2. How do you think consortia directors can learn what services a district needs most?
3. Most of the workshops given by this consortium were given on site in the respective school districts. How important is this? Explain your answer.
4. Each school district's membership cost is based on the number of its students. Why is this important?
5. How can a consortium afford services that a district cannot afford? After all, the consortium gets no funding beyond that given to the schools.

• • •

This vignette is a true story about one of the many innovative programs that are spin-offs of the NCLB legislation. The administrators and teachers who gave its workshops are to be commended for stepping up and supporting the local schools. But successful reform requires the work of all educators, K–university. Furthermore, successful reform requires people to change. As you read this chapter, think about your own relationships with colleagues and parents, and about how you can improve your ability to persuade others to step outside their comfort zones and contribute to reform.

Becoming Agents for Change

Improving schools involves changing the curriculum and changing the behavior of those who implement the curriculum. Making changes can be slow and awkward at first but the good news is that clearly, administrators and teachers can effectively be taught the issues and process involved in making changes. Historically, the appropriate leadership role in the schools has been that of ridding schools of their problems. Responsibility for providing this leadership belonged to the principal and the principal's assistant. Basically, the charge of these administrators was to fix or have fixed whatever went wrong, from leaky roofs to student behavior, and sometimes even teacher behavior.

These perceptions have changed. First, the charge no longer is to maintain the status quo. The academic expectations of all schools have been raised, making the curriculum the center of attention. Second, the administrator is very much in the center of efforts to improve curriculum and instruction. Third, the curriculum is being improved on a continuous, nonstop basis instead of waiting until "problems" are identified. Fourth, teachers are increasingly encouraged to take charge of their own professional development by becoming involved in action research.

Ways in Which Organizations Change

Many changes in today's schools have an impact beyond traditional classroom-level curriculum. In fact, the most common change today is to restructure the organization. Restructuring means comprehensive curriculum change to attain the school's mission. Education reform is a major catalyst for much of this change. Education reform and the process of change are intertwined: In fact, change is a prerequisite for meeting any of the elements of education reform. Because of this dependency on change, educators must learn more about the way organizations change and work together to overcome resistance to change.

Most of the changes that have occurred in the schools within the last few decades did not result from local initiation. The most important changes in our schools have been unplanned and have been stimulated by external forces such as federal laws. Kowalski (2002) devised a way to show some of the forces that lead to change and how most schools change. The left side of figure 8.1 lists the ways most schools have changed; the right side lists behaviors that are foreign to many of today's schools.

Although schools do not need outside forces to "fix" them, one of the most effective models for educational change is school–university partnerships employing simultaneous renewal. (For more on change through school–university partnerships, see Henson, 2010).

Organizations have a built-in resistance to change. Because of their fundamental nature, schools are especially resistant to change. Teachers are reluctant to get involved with prescribed changes, many of which are likely to be short-lived. As explained by Pat Goldys, Clare Kruft, and Patti Subrizi (2007), before accepting a change, teachers want to know if it will be worth their time, how much it will change what they're doing, and the impact it will have on students. In other words, they don't want to invest in reform that is ineffective or in reform practices that might not last.

Barriers to Change

Changing the behavior of organizations requires changing the behavior of individuals in the organizations. It is an accepted and well-documented fact that many teachers have *historically* avoided meaningful involvement in the organization in which they work. Therefore, changing the schools must begin with changing teacher behavior. Following are three of the biggest barriers accounting for teachers' resistance to change.

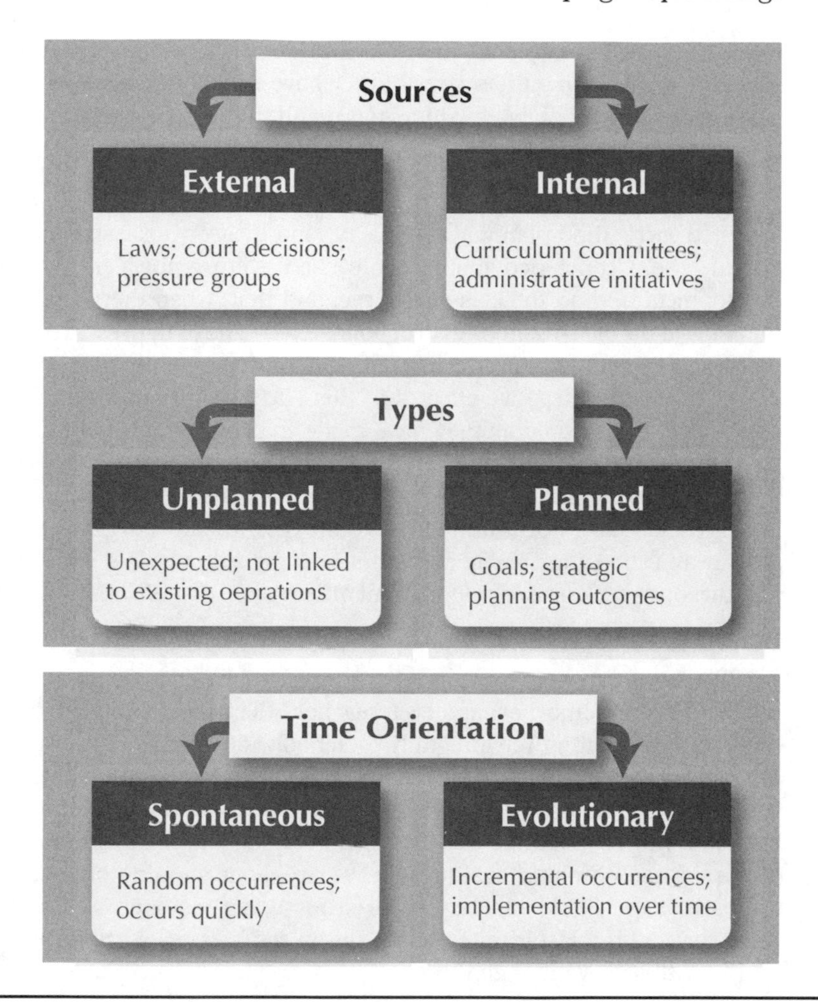

Figure 8.1 Conditions Leading to Education Change

Barrier 1: Reluctance to Use Research

Chapter 1 identified one of the major barriers that kept twentieth-century teachers from getting involved with organizational change: Prior to NCLB, most teachers had not been involved with research. If we can understand the reasons why teachers choose to ignore research, we may gain some insight as to how the problem could be corrected. An examination of these reasons suggests that teachers may have had little choice; many teachers have shunned research because they have not been trained to conduct and use it. The consequences of this lack of training are unfortunate. Consider, for example, the limits that teachers' failure to use research has placed on promoting such learning theories as constructivism.

But these circumstances are rapidly being transformed by reform legislation. For example, NCLB requires teachers to *cite data* to show that their chosen methodologies produce academic gains on required standardized tests. Teachers who regularly read professional journals and conduct action research studies have access to such data, and as a result they have a heightened awareness of the benefits and techniques of establishing and maintaining constructivist classrooms.

Barrier 2: Classroom-Bound Teachers

The inability to use research may also explain why twentieth-century teachers shunned curriculum planning at levels beyond their own classroom. Young (see Haberman, 1992) concluded that most teachers were ambivalent toward curriculum development beyond the classroom level and that, when they do develop curricula, they stay at the classroom or instructional level: "The data presented clearly indicates that teachers' primary interest was in translating curriculum into instruction" (p. 15).

Consider the negative effect that this classroom-bound tendency has had on any attempts that schools may have made to promote multiculturalism or to better serve challenged students. By merely translating the existing curriculum into instruction, teachers with challenged students and students of diverse cultural backgrounds have been limited by a "one-size-fits-all" curriculum. Teachers who stay away from other teachers cannot become role models who demonstrate the positive outcomes of working with members of other cultures.

Barrier 3: Perceptions of Teachers

Teachers' proclivity to avoid research and schoolwide involvement has caused other educators, and perhaps even teachers themselves, to view teachers as incapable of contributing meaningfully to schoolwide change. To a degree, this result has been a self-fulfilling (or—perhaps more accurately—a self-limiting) prophecy.

Although the evidence is convincing that teachers have preferred not to get involved with curriculum development outside their classrooms and that they have purposely avoided dealing with research, one should not conclude that teachers cannot or should not be prepared for using research and working with the total curriculum. Haberman (1992) discusses how teachers have been perceived and how this view must change:

> Another barrier to change in schools has been the perception that teachers are part of the existing problems and that any successful attempt to improve the schools must first be teacher-proof. . . . Classroom teachers must be viewed as part of the solution, never as the problem. (p. 17)

Perhaps teachers' reluctance to change can be attributed, at least in part, to the failure of schools to involve teachers in change. Barth (1990) vividly describes teachers' situation and the possible consequences of any attempts to get involved:

> The lives of teachers and principals . . . closely mirror the cultivation of mushrooms: You're kept in the dark most of the time, periodically you're covered with manure, and when you stick your head out it gets chopped off. (p. 513)

Apparently, major education reform is required to lessen the perceived risk of involvement and increase the awareness of the advantages that teachers and administrators can experience from change. The No Child Left Behind Act purports to give local educators responsibility and flexibility. As seen in chapter 4, districts may use up to 50% of the funds they receive from the state to increase teacher quality, improve technology, provide safe and drug-free schools, and establish innovative programs to promote student achievement. Although many forces work to impede change, other forces are at work to improve the schools. Often we must unlearn old ideas and practices to allow these positive forces to take effect.

Basom and Crandall (1991, pp. 74–75) have identified seven additional common barriers to change.

- A discontinuity of leadership deters change. (Many schools have frequent changes in personnel in key leadership positions.)
- Many educators view change as unmanageable. (Administrators and teachers do not believe they can bring about purposeful change.)
- Educators have not been properly prepared to deal with the complexity of restructuring schools. (Administrators and teachers know little about organizational behavior, conflict management, and other related topics.)
- In following a "top-down" approach to making decisions, educators have not relied on research and craft knowledge to inform their decisions. (Decision makers have not been required to justify their decisions.)
- Educators are conditioned and socialized by the format of schooling they experienced and understand. (They believe that school structure is not the problem.)
- There are conflicting visions of what schools should become. (Teachers and administrators cannot agree on what changes are needed or what goals should be established.)
- Time and resources have been insufficient. (Time and money are not available to conduct necessary staff development.)

As you read this list, perhaps you noticed that some barriers are conceptual, relating to traditional ideas about the schools and how improvement should occur

FYI Using Chairs to Sense Change

Larry Wilder • Wilder & Associates Management Consultants

Change is always difficult to envision. To make it more realistic for my students, I have all the chairs in the classroom facing in different directions when the students enter the room. None of the chairs face toward the front of the room where I usually "lecture" about change. One entire class period is conducted this way. I also assign their seating arrangement to break up the usual seating pattern, and students are instructed not to change their seats. This proves difficult for everyone in the class. The students usually find it funny, weird, disturbing, or confusing. Depending on the length of the class period, we discuss their thoughts and feelings about the "change" on that same day or during the next class session. We then relate their experiences, concerns, and ideas about change to other changes at their school or in their classroom. The students always find this exercise in change to be instructive and interesting.

(e.g., the top-down approach), while others are actual barriers (e.g., lack of funds, hopeless attitude). Some barriers result from the newness of restructuring, and these can be reduced as the knowledge base on restructuring grows. Twenty-first century educators should, by now, realize the importance of collecting data and writing cases that reflect the problems they face, and they should acknowledge the victories they have won in overcoming these barriers as they accept new challenges such as restructuring. For example, educational leaders (discussed later in this chapter) often need help in convincing their peers that their school really does have a problem, and leaders need the skills to guide their teachers to develop a clear mission and goals.

The Role of School Culture and Climate

Anyone who has worked with schools knows that each school has its own culture, its own ethos. Schools are like homes: Some make you feel welcome; others don't. Some schools send a message that they are exciting places to be. Some schools are threatening; others offer security. Some are as dead as a petrified forest; others are like a freeway during rush hour—people have places to go, and they are eager to get there. The idea of a school having an ethos, being distinct from other schools, and subjecting all aspects of school life to this quality is powerful. Kowalski and Reitzug (1993, p. 311) explain the interactions among these factors.

> There are three common perspectives of how change occurs in organizations. The first is a technical view erected on an assumption that increased knowledge and technical assistance produce change. This approach assumes rationality and focuses on the nature of the innovation (e.g., a new program). The second perspective accounts for power and influence that may be used by groups and individuals to support or ward off change. The focus is political behavior, and attention is given to both the innovation and the context of the organization. The third perspective looks at the shared values, beliefs, and norms of the organization. It is identified as the cultural perspective and emphasizes the importance of organizational context. After more than ten years of attempted reform, educators and the general public are recognizing the limitations of the first two approaches. Hence, more recent reform efforts have focused largely on the third category. More precisely, second wave change efforts are inquiring about the ways in which culture produces barriers that prevent change.
>
> Imagine a situation in which a third-grade teacher is considering whether to administer corporal punishment to a disruptive student. What factors affect the decision? First, the teacher's behavior is influenced by personal values, experiences, and beliefs regarding the moral and practical dimensions of hitting a child. Additionally, the teacher hopefully considers whether corporal punishment is acceptable professionally and legally. The third, and often most influential, component is the teacher's perception of what the school expects from him or her. In other words, the teacher considers the school's norms. Do other teachers use corporal punishment? Does the principal advocate it? In some combination, the teacher weighs personal considerations (e.g., personal beliefs, motivations), legal and professional dimensions, and school-specific norms. Thus, even though the teacher may reject the use of corporal punish-

ment, both personally and professionally, the act still may be carried out because of social pressures maintained by the school.

Educating teachers to become empirical collaborators requires changing today's school culture (Boles & Troen, 2007).

> Effective educational leaders . . . have a major responsibility of ensuring that the proper climate is created within their schools and district so that, whenever inevitable change arrives, teachers, staffs, students, parents, and community members will not view it as some fundamental threat to the way things "should be" in schools. The way in which the leader can move her or his school in that direction involves the creating of an ongoing climate where discussions of new ideas and practices are the rule, not the exception. (Daresh, 2007, pp. 192–193)

Good principals use three building blocks of transformational leadership: (1) a clear and unified focus, (2) a cultural perspective, and (3) a constant push for improvement. By involving students in curriculum planning, teachers can improve the culture of their classrooms.

A school's culture can facilitate or impede change. William Phillips (2010) suggests using "e-walks" to facilitate this community-building process. Using a handheld electronic device, he notes the number of students off task, evidence of a clear learning objective, higher-order critical thinking, on-task discussion, and noninstructional student discussions. He presents these data on a grid and lets the teachers control their solutions. Dean Halverson (2010) takes University of Western Illinois educational leadership students on similar walk-throughs. He doesn't allow note taking until the visits are over. According to Halverson, student evaluations indicate that this is one of the best learning experiences in the entire leadership program.

Promoting Teacher Involvement

Staying in the classroom and attending only to instruction and other "classroom matters" seemed appropriate until states and school districts began gathering research data on effective schools. These data indicated that transforming ineffective schools into effective schools requires teacher involvement with the total school, especially with curriculum matters. Haberman (1992, p. 14) explained:

> Recently, more attention has been given to the concept of the teacher as a professional with specialized knowledge and a pragmatic approach to curriculum planning that is derived from classroom experience. At the classroom level, the teacher would carry out action research to provide knowledge about the needs of students and their relationship to the curriculum.

Contemporary educators have several reasons for insisting that teachers should be involved in changing the curriculum at levels beyond their own classroom. We now realize that improving schools requires more than just changing the curriculum; it also requires changing people, which is neither simple nor easy:

> It is humbling to realize how little each generation learns from the experience of its equally earnest forebears about just how crude a tool curriculum change is for transforming student knowledge and behavior. (Cuban, 1993, p. 192)

When teachers who are directly involved in curriculum development tend to shift their teaching style from prescriptive to interactive, their interactions with students allows them to more effectively evaluate their students' needs. In turn, the improved teacher–student relationships will result in increased student achievement. Thus, curriculum development becomes curriculum renewal as the chain of communication from student to teacher to curriculum committee becomes a continuous cycle of analysis and problem solving.

When teachers are encouraged to become involved and to contribute to curriculum improvement at levels beyond the classroom, they influence the degree to which their peers accept change. It is not surprising that teachers are willing to follow the lead of their peers rather than mandates imposed by outsiders. Ambrosie and Hanley (1991, p. 78) discovered that when change comes from the central office, teachers react positively 38% of the time; when the impetus for change comes from other teachers they react positively 86% of the time. When former principal Joanne Rooney (2007) involved her faculty with curriculum improvement, the results were staggering: "The teachers enjoyed as well as wrestled with the intention of creating learning communities, but true connections emerged as we wrestled with issues that confronted us" (p. 88).

Ways of Motivating Teachers

We've established that teachers should and must be more involved in curriculum than they have in the past. But, while all teacher and student involvement in curriculum renewal are good, some types of involvement are more beneficial than others. Perhaps the most important way teachers can be involved in curriculum renewal is at its offset or during the planning stage. In the environment of this early stage, all teachers are allowed to provide input, giving them a sense of ownership. As improvements are made, all persons who work on curricula have responsibility for communicating the new curriculum to their peers and to the community at large.

Persuading teachers to expand their levels of involvement in curriculum matters will require special incentives, and although more money may contribute to this persuasion, financial incentives are not always the strongest motivator. Wright (1985) found that the most frequently identified incentives that motivate teacher involvement are intrinsic rewards, such as increased self-confidence, a sense of achievement or challenge, or the opportunity to develop new skills. Perhaps the number-one motivator for teachers' involvement in curriculum development is their desire for personal involvement in decision making.

Psychologist Frederick Herzberg (Herzberg, Mausner, & Snyderman, 1959) uses the diagram in figure 8.2 (*two-factor motivation theory*) to show the relationships between factors that prevent workers from being dissatisfied and factors that motivate individuals to do their best. According to Herzberg's model, to increase satisfaction on the job, the organization should be concerned with the nature of the work itself—the opportunities it presents for gaining status,

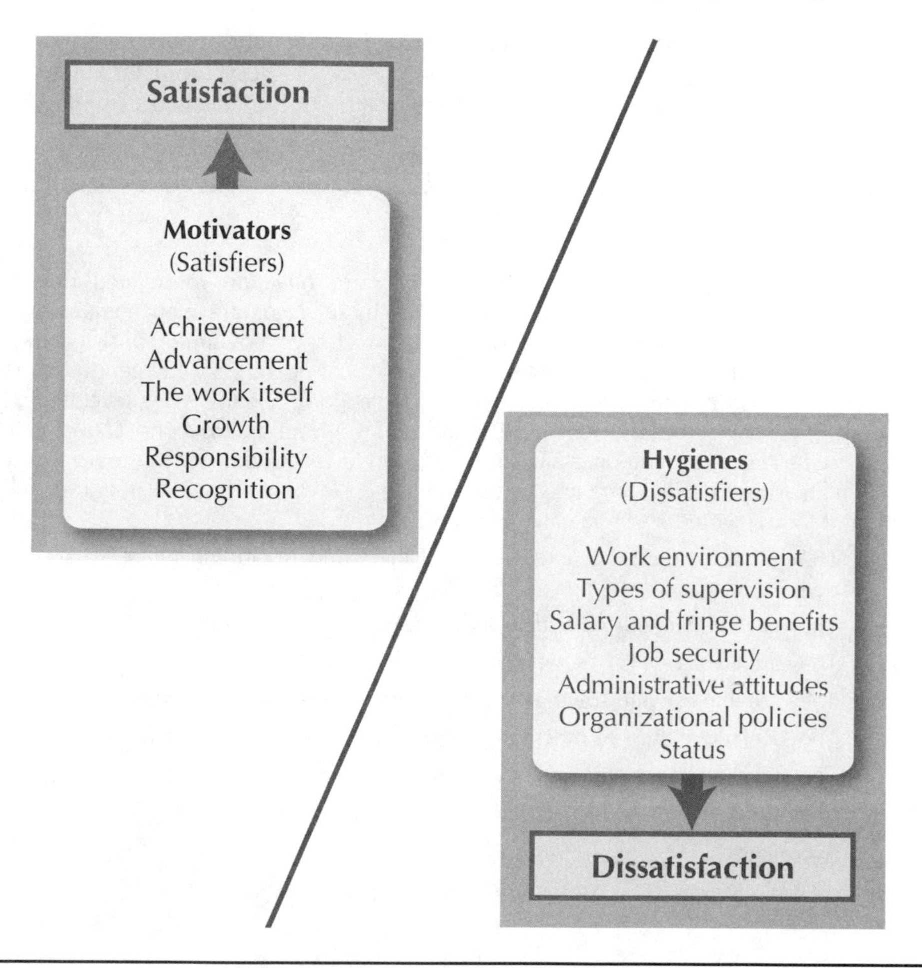

Figure 8.2 Model of Herzberg et al. Two-Factor Motivation Theory

assuming responsibility, and for achieving self-realization. Herzberg made us aware that those things that satisfy and those that motivate are often different, and the removal of the dissatisfiers, though necessary, does not automatically bring about motivation. To reduce dissatisfaction, then the organization must focus on the job environment—policies, procedures, supervision, and working conditions. If an organization is equally concerned with both (as is usually the case), then managers must give attention to both sets of job factors. Notice that many of Herzberg's motivators are intrinsic.

Seeing that intrinsic motivators are influential on teachers' involvement in curriculum development, within or outside their schools, should not be surprising. *Maslow's hierarchy of needs* (see box 8.1 on the following page) clearly explains the force of such motivation.

Through a series of teacher interviews, Young (1985) learned that lack of compensation for extra time spent working on committees and the absence of released time deterred teachers from considering involvement in curriculum development. Supporting these types of staff development is very important. Given support, teachers will become more involved in curriculum decision making, which will

Box 8.1 Maslow's Hierarchy of Needs

Abraham Maslow (1943), in his theory of human motivation, formulated a hierarchy of human needs. This theory contends that as the basic needs are met, humans experience higher-level needs. Maslow's hierarchy is often depicted as a pyramid consisting of five levels, or needs. The bottom level represents physiological needs (e.g., hunger, thirst). The next level up consists of safety needs (i.e., security, protection). The following level depicts social needs (love, or a sense of belonging. The second level from the top consists of esteem needs (e.g., self-esteem, recognition, status). Only after all lower-level needs in the pyramid are met will higher-level needs come into focus. The highest level is self-actualization or self-fulfillment. Maslow writes of self-actualizing people that:

- They embrace the facts and realities of the world (including themselves) rather than denying or avoiding them.
- They are spontaneous with ideas and actions.
- They are creative.
- They are interested in solving problems—often the problems of others.
- They feel a closeness to other people and appreciate life in general.
- They have a self-created system of morality.
- They judge others objectively rather than with prejudice.

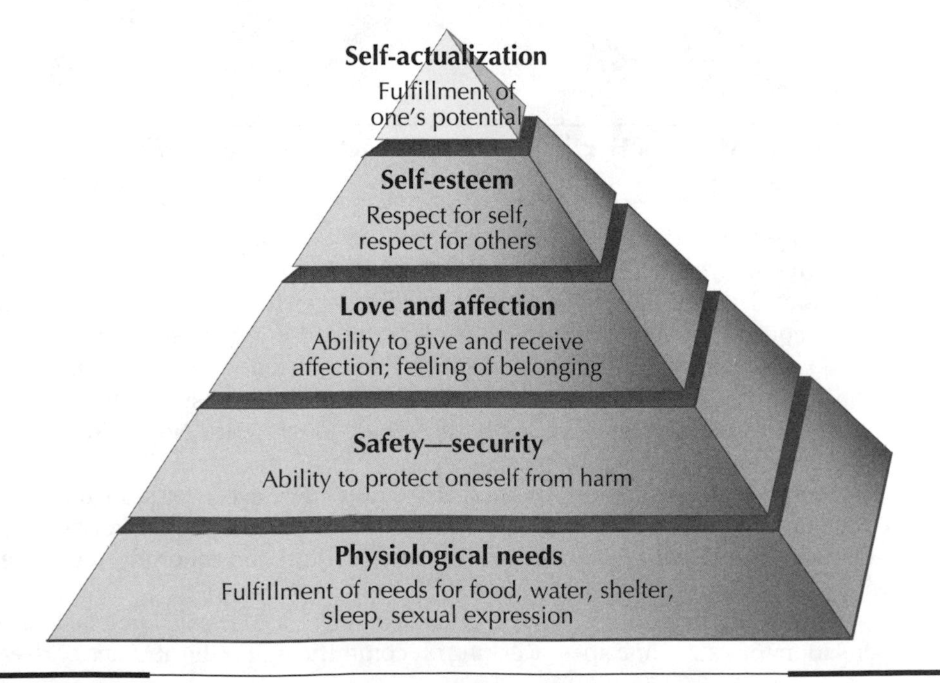

require significantly more curriculum development skills and knowledge than they typically now have. Supervisors should work to get their teachers time off to compensate for the time they use on their own to achieve faculty development goals. This practice lets teachers know that their administrators really do consider faculty development important.

A major factor that inhibits many teachers from becoming more involved in curriculum planning is their uncertainty about what activities and behaviors are appropriate for teachers. Obviously, as the teacher's role rapidly changes, the array of appropriate teacher activities increases. Fortunately the twentieth-century practice of individualistic teacher behavior is giving way to collaborative behavior.

Schwahn and Spady (1998, pp. 45–47) offer the following rules for effecting change:

1. People don't change unless they share a compelling reason.
2. People don't change unless they have ownership in the change.
3. People don't change unless their leaders model that they are serious about the change.
4. People are unlikely to change unless they have a concrete picture of what the change will look like for them personally.
5. People can't make a change—or make it last—unless they receive organizational support for the change.

These suggestions can and should be used daily by all educators to make improvements more effective and enjoyable. Only then will the levels of teachers' and students' resistance be lowered.

Action Research

From its inception until the mid-twentieth century, the American school was the hub of all sorts of community activities. Cake walks and fish fries were common means of raising money for the schools, to be given to the teachers for the purpose of buying supplies to help develop the curriculum. In rural areas, the school building was the meetinghouse for the vocational associations (the Farm Bureau, Future Farmers of America, Future Homemakers of America, and 4-H Clubs), and in town the schoolhouse was used by civic groups. In both rural and urban settings, schools have served as polling places. A special meeting at school brought in not only mom and dad but the entire extended family including the grandparents, uncles, aunts, and cousins. Involvement of parents and other community members increased a school's academic gains.

But increased urbanization, school growth and consolidation, and forced busing destroyed the concept of the school as the hub of the community. Federal and state curriculum mandates reshaped the curricula. In the one-room schoolhouse of the past, teachers were in charge of the entire curriculum. By the early 1960s, however, prefabricated curricula were being manufactured at research and development centers and sent to the schools. The results of these changes were (1) a diminishing *level of teacher responsibility* for curriculum development, and (2) a reduction in the *range of teacher involvement* in curriculum development, from schoolwide control to projects that are limited to their own classrooms. Removing teachers from the center of schoolwide curriculum development isolated them from research activities, kept them from seeing the need to verify their practices, and hindered them from participating in schoolwide decisions.

On the positive side, teacher involvement with research is growing. To expand this trend, teacher educators must educate pre-service teachers to consult and conduct research relevant to the issues they wish to address and the goals they hope to achieve (Goldys, Kruft, & Subrizi, 2007). A review of the literature shows that as early as 1908, concrete efforts were being made to involve classroom teachers in research (Lowery, 1908; Henson, 1996). The purpose of this early research by teachers was to develop curricula (McKernan, 1988), and this purpose remained constant throughout the twentieth century, although a new term, *action research*, has become popular in recent years (see box 8.2).

Action research (or *research-based teaching*) encourages a mix of theory and practice (Gilbert & Smith, 2003). McCutcheon and Jung (1990, p. 144) define

FYI Action Research: A Six-Step Model

Robert C. Morris and Dawn Putney • University of West Georgia

Research often seems far removed from the classroom. However, as one develops as a teacher, the need for a systematic method to check how well an approach or technique works and why it works makes action research an invaluable tool. It is the "missing link" between the world of research and the world of the classroom. Teachers need tools to do their own research, solve their own practical problems, and improve their teaching. What is research, after all? It is the systematic collection and analysis of the information needed to answer specific questions.

Using action research in your classroom is easy, especially with this six-step model:

1. *Identify the problem.* State it as a question to be answered.
2. *Consider data-collection possibilities.* Data will be collected through a variety of sources, such as evaluated group projects, student diaries (in which they reflect on the process being examined), the teacher's reflective diary, and an objective test taken individually.
3. *Data collection.* Select items to be analyzed.
4. *Data analysis.* Evaluate group work, compare objective test results and achievement results from sources where students were not in a tested group, read student diaries to find recurring thoughts or themes, and read and analyze the teacher's diary.
5. *Reporting results.* Discuss results with appropriate parties.
6. *Take action.* Make a decision on whether, when, and with what topics to use any insights gained. Also, consider how to improve the action research process for the next evaluation activity.

Repeat steps 3 and 4, using different data-collecting methods as needed. Systematically collected data help determine the action teachers take. This kind of research activity lends support to that "gut instinct" teachers often have when trying out a new idea.

Box 8.2 Action Research

According to *Action Research International*, action research can be defined as a family of research methodologies which pursue action (or change) and research (or understanding) at the same time. It does so by

- using a cyclic or spiral process which alternates between action and critical reflection, and
- in the later cycles, continuously refining methods, data, and interpretation in the light of the understanding developed in the earlier cycles.

It is thus an *emergent* process which takes shape as understanding increases; it is an *iterative* process which converges toward a better understanding of what happens. In most of its forms it is also participative (among other reasons, change is usually easier to achieve when those affected by the change are involved) and qualitative (Dick, 1999).

Educational action research . . . is empowering, enabling teachers to critique the curriculum structures which shape their practices and the power to negotiate change within the system that maintains them (Waters-Adams, 2006). Teachers who engage in action research validate the importance of the work teachers do and helps them to

- become more confident about their ability to promote student learning,
- become more proactive in dealing with difficult situations arising in their teaching,
- acquire habits and skills of inquiry used beyond the research experience to analyze their teaching, and
- develop or rekindle an excitement about teaching (*Teacher Magazine*, 2009).

Several journals are published on action research, a few of which are specifically education oriented. Visit their Web sites for further information.

Action Research
http://arj.sagepub.com/

Action Research International
http://www.scu.edu.au/schools/gcm/ar/ari/arihome.html

Educational Action Research
http://www.tandf.co.uk/journals/titles/09650792.asp

Action Research Electronic Reader
http://www.scu.edu.au/schools/gcm/ar/arr/arow/default.html

AR Expeditions (Action Research Journal)
http://www.montana.edu/arexpeditions/index.php

action research as "inquiry teachers undertake to understand and improve their own practice." When conducting action research, teachers may work alone or collaborate with others. Accordingly, a good way to get teachers involved in action research is to begin informally, asking them to select areas for informal study. Then schedule a room and time for meetings and put a teacher in charge (Bunting, 2007).

This enduring involvement by some teachers in research should not be interpreted to mean that all or even most teachers have been conducting research. On the contrary, as previously mentioned, most teachers have purposefully avoided research, and for a number of reasons. For example, teachers often perceive research topics as too theoretical and too abstract. This perception may result, at least in part, from the different natures of the teacher's world and the researcher's world. Cuban (1992) contrasted the two worlds, saying that the teacher's world is characterized by action and concrete facts, whereas researchers deal with abstractions and theory. Teachers want concrete answers to questions such as, "What should I do?" while researchers are comfortable exploring possibilities.

When teachers do become involved with research, several significant gains are realized. For example, their own teaching often improves. As teachers involve themselves with research, their style shifts from prescriptive to interactive. Through involvement with research, teachers experience a renewed desire to stay current. As teachers become researchers they become learners. Action research sharpens teacher perceptions, stimulates collaborative discussion, and stimulates questioning.

After teachers involve themselves in conducting research, they become more critical, questioning their own beliefs and the assertions of others. Involvement with research also makes teachers more reflective (Darling-Hammond & Baratz-Snowden, 2007), a critical trait for contemporary teachers (Bintz & Dillard, 2007). When they conduct their own studies, teachers begin to generate knowledge about teaching, learning, and schooling. When this happens, they become more critical of both university-based research and standard school practices. They find that they are able to challenge taken-for-granted assumptions about theory and practice.

Improved teacher attitude is another benefit that arises from teacher involvement with research, and one common result of improved attitude is increased teacher effectiveness. When teachers first begin action research projects they often feel anxious and hostile, but they emerge feeling positive about what they learn from the experience and proud of their newly found identities as teacher–researchers.

Gregory Gibbs (2010) is a big proponent of using real data to teach his students the methods of action research. He says that this process often helps districts come up with answers to nagging questions.

Teacher Empowerment

As discussed in chapter 7, an important dimension in many contemporary educational reform efforts is *teacher empowerment*. According to Carson (1990, p. 167), "Action research has been seen as a way of giving teaching back to teachers." Education literature often reports on how involvement in action research increases teachers' self-development (Bernauer, 1999). As Tripp (1990, p. 165) says, "Action research enables teachers both to formulate and act upon their own concerns, thereby personally and professionally developing themselves within and through their practice."

Action research brings both perceptual and phenomenological benefits to teachers. First, involvement in research makes teachers more aware. One way to think about perceptual benefits is to consider what happens to teachers' perceptions when they are *not* involved in ongoing research. Sanger (1990, p. 175) has said that "as teachers, we gather to ourselves that which confirms our deepest underlying prejudices and attitudes." Involvement in action research can move teachers beyond their perceptions, clarifying their understandings and feelings about themselves and how they relate to their work. It can help teachers understand and accept that, although they often pretend to have all of the answers needed in their daily work, they never really do. Each of us interprets the world about us in unique ways. Involvement in research can help us view our professional role open-mindedly. As Carson (1990, p. 172) explains, "This requires an openness to our own experience and the experience of others, putting aside dogmatic arguments and preconceived opinions."

Increased understanding about ourselves in relation to the world around us opens the path to clearer, more honest relationships with others. Because most current action research projects are collaborative efforts, all participants will benefit. According to McElroy (1990, p. 209), "Being authentic (or real), for example, in our relationship with another is at the heart of collaborative action research, and is at the heart of a matter of ethics." He reports that his collaborative research efforts have caused him to replace his concern for self with a greater connection, a freedom to experience more authentically. "This ego-less[ness] is not weakening; rather, it provides a feeling of strength, of standing firmly on a formless, shifting ground" (p. 209).

As faculties throughout the country are being "forced" to implement education reform, it is evident to the outside observer that egos are threatened. Much, if not most, resistance comes from teachers who feel threatened by the forced changes. When told that we must change, we infer that we have been doing something wrong; the message is that our performance is unacceptable. Few forces can combat the level of resistance that follows when individuals are told, either overtly or covertly, that they are unworthy. If, indeed, involvement in collaborative action research can free teachers from some of their need to protect their egos, then it may be paving the road to progress for school reform. (For a more complete discussion on teachers as researchers, see Henson, 1996.)

Like theory, research and development are not linear, problem–answer processes. Since the goal is often to change the infrastructure of the school's curriculum, and since lasting change is a slow process, action research requires patience and commitment. Sanger, an action research trainer (1990, p. 175), says,

> The deepest and least changeable levels seem to accrete slowly through experience. Rather like a coral reef, "significant" bits are drawn down from the surface of daily events and settle and fuse with deeper layers. They add to and complement what is already there.

Evidence exists that involvement with research prepares teachers for future change by making them more flexible and accepting of change. According to Bennett (1993, p. 69), "As teachers gained experience and success with research, their attitude toward research greatly improved. Teacher-researchers viewed themselves as being more open to change."

New ways to involve teachers in action research are continually being sought. Often we hear teachers say they would be eager to get involved in schoolwide planning if only they had time. In fact, teachers everywhere are struggling with heavy workloads. The following case study shows how a good organizer can help busy colleagues find the time and energy required to make significant changes in the school curriculum.

case study

Collaborating for Change

Stephen D. Lapan and Patricia A. Hays
Northern Arizona University

Background Information

Change is an issue teachers must face from the day they enter a teacher training program until the day of their retirement. Change comes in many forms, from curriculum reform to state competency mandates to changes in personnel. Very often in the education world, change is imposed on, rather than initiated by, classroom teachers. The result is generally a reluctance to embrace change and the change process. Acceptance and support at the classroom and building levels come much more easily when the agents of change are classroom teachers.

To participate in a training project funded by a Jacob Javits grant,* fifteen potential change agents arrived in the summer on the campus of Northern Arizona University (NAU). The goal of the training project was to prepare teams of classroom teachers to develop and implement programs of gifted education for underrepresented populations in the school. Schools had been approached by NAU project directors earlier in the year with specific focus on sites that served a large number of ethnic minority students.

These teacher teams faced ten weeks of intensive training that included practice in teaching methods, lesson and unit development, and analysis of their own teaching. They would be expected to learn how to identify underserved minority gifted youth and to develop a faculty collaboration plan to implement upon their return to school in the fall.

The stories of the 15 participants during the course of training and school-year implementation are as unique as the school sites they represented. Levels of success were varied as well. One particularly successful site was an elementary school in southwest Arizona, an oasis in the middle of the desert regions near the border of Mexico. This is that school's story.

The Community

The community has a population approaching 55,000, a medium-sized city by Arizona standards. Agriculture, through irrigation of the desert, is a part of the lifeblood of the economy. A significant number of Mexican families, representing more than 33% of the community's population (all Hispanics represented nearly 36%) were drawn to the city, either due to the proximity of its location or the job opportunities that beckoned. The community struggled with providing the best educational programs possible for these students; a disproportionately high dropout rate of Hispanic students was an indicator that much more needed to be done.

The School

The K–6 elementary school site that was selected as part of the training project was a relatively new building in a growing section of the city. Socioeconomic diversity was apparent as one drove around the neighborhood. The staff, including the principal, was primarily female, with several teachers at each grade level. An absence of diversity on the staff was quite obvious when compared with diversity in the student population; only one of 40 staff members was Hispanic while the school had a 52% Hispanic enrollment. The presence of bilingual office staff was a positive factor, not only in terms of translating communications

*The project reported in this case study was supported under the Javits Act Program (Grant No. R206A90087) as administered by the Office of Educational Research and Improvement, U.S. Department of Education. Professors Lapan and Hays directed this NAU project.

but also serving somewhat in the role of "liaisons" between the school and the Spanish-speaking community.

The school offered a gifted education program that was similar to many across the state. State-mandated intelligence and achievement tests were used as criteria for placement, and the program focused on acceleration and enrichment. Very few minority students had been identified for this program.

The Players

The key players in the NAU project training were Melinda, a fifth-grade teacher, Bart, a sixth-grade teacher, and Kelly, the school principal. Melinda had not been teaching long, but her classroom was very well organized. Bart had taught at the school for a few years and was known for his success with challenging students. It was no surprise to walk in his classroom and find a large number of boys (and a few girls) who had the potential to be very disruptive. Bart's laid-back, carefree attitude was in direct contrast to Melinda's stoic approach to teaching.

Kelly had been the building administrator for a few years and steered her faculty and staff smoothly and efficiently. You knew where you stood with Kelly, and she ran the school's business with fair yet demanding expectations. Kelly was a natural administrator. She was a "no-nonsense" kind of decision maker when situations called for a "the buck stops here" kind of solution. Kelly also was an innovative instructional leader; she recognized many needs not being met in her school and explored creative ways to meet those needs under the funding constraints of the district.

The Case: Part One—The Training

Melinda and Bart arrived on campus at Northern Arizona University in June along with the other project participants from across the state. The two teachers spent the first few days attending intensive full-day sessions that provided experiences in knowledge acquisition, reflective thinking, self-evaluation, critical thinking, and collaboration. As the training progressed, Melinda seemed to be quieter, more serious, and more efficient. Bart became far more outgoing in his behavior.

Early in the training, teams from each of the project sites were prepared for the curriculum and program planning that would take place as the training progressed. A site plan was to be developed, in collaboration with the building administrator, for a gifted education delivery model that would identify and provide programming for underrepresented populations at each school. These site plans were highly specific to the needs of the school community and culture.

Melinda and Bart were very effective in developing their site plan. Having full support and continuous communication with Kelly, they designed a plan that would focus on identifying students with potential in the areas of leadership and creativity. They both saw this as a program needed by the students with whom they worked. They determined that the most effective initial implementation of their design would be in two stages. Initially, they would go into classrooms at their assigned teaching levels (Melinda at fifth grade, Bart at sixth grade) and teach whole-class lessons designed to tap the creative and leadership talents of students. Together with the regular classroom teacher, they would begin collecting data to help them determine which students might benefit from a gifted program focusing on leadership and creativity.

Phase two of their program implementation would be to jointly select students who had demonstrated potential in either the leadership or creativity areas and meet with the identified students on a regular basis by pulling them out of classes at scheduled times, Bart working with sixth graders and Melinda with fifth graders. With the help of teaching colleagues, they would identify students from all of the classrooms (including their own) who were not currently a part of the traditional gifted program.

The Case: Part Two—Fall Semester

Sometimes agents of change may make sacrifices for the sake of an innovation. Such was the case with Melinda and Bart. They, as well as Principal Kelly, knew they had a very good plan, but they wondered how there would be time to implement it. They all knew, after ten weeks of reflection, that this was something the students would benefit from, and they were committed to making it work. So, together, they sat down to look at the dreaded "master schedule."

What resulted from hours of reconfiguring was a give-and-take outcome: Melinda and Bart would give of their talents to students and staff and take from their individual schedules a portion of the all-too-few planning times they were allotted. Kelly mapped out the most advantageous times for each to do so, and the first major logistical obstacle had been overcome. They hoped that the rest of the staff, recognizing the efforts being made by Melinda and Bart, would be supportive of whatever scheduling changes needed to be made that would affect them.

In August, the first order of business was an optional in-service orientation with teachers whose students might be selected for participation in the program. An information session was held early one morning during "prep" week, with Melinda, Bart, and an NAU project staff member presenting an overview of the year ahead.

Initially, the school site team had planned to ease into implementation, starting out with demonstration lessons in classrooms. Once again, the teachers on the team were charting unfamiliar territory. The idea of peer modeling is not new, but it was new in their building. The demonstration lessons would have a variety of targeted outcomes. Bart and Melinda would provide teachers with lesson models that would foster creative responses from students in the regular classroom setting. It was hoped that teachers would be motivated to incorporate similar types of lessons into their daily teaching. A direct outcome of the lessons would be opportunities for Bart and Melinda to interact with students and list those students who might benefit from inclusion in the alternative gifted program.

Although the original intent of the demonstration lessons had been broader, Bart and Melinda chose to focus on the use of the lessons as a means of identifying gifted students. The classroom teachers for the most part shared this goal. In addition, a sixth-grade teacher saw the lessons as a means of expanding her students' reasoning and their ability to perceive things differently than they might in a typical classroom. The lessons were viewed more as expanding students' minds than as teaching definite skills. A fifth-grade teacher, having experienced the lessons, recognized Melinda and Bart's new expertise in identifying the creative talent. She also recognized her own limitations and was very pleased that the two were able to share this expertise with her.

The Case: Part Three—Spring Semester

When the second semester began, it was time to initiate the planned pull-out program. This would be a real test of collaboration, support, and teamwork for Melinda and Bart. They planned on meeting with the newly identified students on a weekly basis. As the semester progressed, a few more students were identified, and students were involved in a number of projects in the pull-out program that tapped both their creative potential and their leadership skills. Students shared their enthusiasm for being in the program with classmates and classroom teachers. They said they enjoyed the chance to use their imaginations, and some said that their enthusiasm for being involved with the program had extended to their families. One student stated that when he talked about the program, his parents would "stop what they were doing and listen to me." He added that his parents contributed ideas related to specific projects on which he was working in the program.

Not only was the impact of the new program being felt at the building level, but Bart and Melinda's work was being recognized throughout the district. They had met with the director of gifted programs in the district early in the second semester to update her on progress. The director had then contacted Bart and Melinda a few times, including requests for conference presentations, and she appeared to want both teachers to stay actively involved in gifted education at the district level.

As the school year drew to a close, both teachers finished up projects not only in the pull-out program but in their own classrooms as well. As the three team members—the principal, the fifth-grade teacher, and the sixth-grade teacher—looked back at the year that had gone by so quickly, they began to reflect on the changes that had taken place.

Throughout the school year, and particularly during the second semester, Melinda and Bart worked closely together. Initially they had planned how the implementation would take place and prepared demonstration lessons. As the year progressed, their collaborative effort grew as they focused on identifying students for the program, developing activities for the pull-out sessions, and providing in-service programs and consulting for staff and district personnel. You might be curious to know how the two teachers viewed such a close partnership, since more often than not teachers perform their daily teaching duties in the isolation of a self-contained classroom. Looking back at the year, Melinda and Bart had only positive remarks to make about their year-long collaboration.

One indication that this was a successful collaboration was the impact the two teachers, with the support and guidance of the principal, had at the building level. Principal Kelly noted the positive effects the implementation had on her school community:

> I think it's been very creative, very beneficial to the students. It's created a lot of parent interest, and I think the neatest thing I've seen happen is the interest the other teachers now have in developing upper-level thinking skills. . . . I think the teachers were excited to know that Melinda and Bart were willing to come into their rooms and actually model lessons.

Beyond the immediate changes they saw in the students and in their teaching, Bart and Melinda saw changes in their roles at the building level, too, identifying kids that could "get lost in the cracks and maybe not even finish high school" and recognizing and valuing their talents might have long-range effects. They also saw the program's impact on the teachers, many of whom were rethinking what "giftedness" meant. Both teachers saw themselves being recognized as leaders in the building and in the district. The opportunities to serve as in-service presenters were new to each of them, but they quickly grew comfortable with the new roles.

The Case: Part Four—The Epilogue

This program was implemented during the academic year 1991–1992. So what does it prove? What does something that happened almost two decades ago, in some unknown place, have to do with education reform now?

If nothing else, perhaps the reader of this success story can see that more is happening in the public schools than what is often so negatively portrayed in the media. Perhaps you can see a bit of yourself in Melinda, Bart, or Kelly. Maybe someone reading this will think back on a situation or setting very similar to the one presented. Perhaps that reader can make a difference too.

This case is not a story of great political changes or sweeping educational reform. This isn't a story that will someday become a blockbuster movie or a best seller. This is a testimonial to the hard work of a trio of everyday educators who, with some training and support, demonstrated how positive change can happen by using collaboration with colleagues and a school principal.

Issues for Further Reflection and Application

1. What are the advantages and disadvantages of working with no-nonsense, linear thinkers when changes are being made?
2. Change often brings varying degrees of discomfort, if not downright pain, to people having to adjust to new circumstances. Can innovators be conditioned to accept and overcome the discomfort that change brings?
3. What role does flexibility play in change leadership?
4. What steps can agents of change take to ensure that students will not feel left out or ignored?

Suggested Readings

Bintz, W. P., & Dillard, J. (2007). Teachers as reflective practitioners: Examining teacher stories of curricular change in a 4th-grade classroom. *Reading Horizons, 47*(3), 203–227.

Boles, K. C., & Troen, V. (2007). How to improve professional practice. *Principal, 87*(2), 50–53.

Fisher, D., Grant, M., Frey, N., & Johnson, C. (2007/2008). Taking formative assessment schoolwide. *Educational Leadership, 65*(4), 64–69.

Hanson, S., & Moir, E. (2008). Beyond mentoring: Influencing the professional practice and careers of experienced teachers. *Phi Delta Kappan, 89*(6), 453–459.

This experience shows that collaboration is based on trust, openness, and flexibility. At different phases of the project, the authors explain how they altered their plans at the last moment, adjusting their approach to make the students more comfortable. This flexibility is characteristic of successful teachers in multicultural classrooms and of teachers in constructivist classrooms. When plans are altered based on need, one might conclude that the planning was wasted time, but such a conclusion overlooks the purpose of planning. Good planning helps teachers organize the lessons in their minds. Once the organization is made, teachers are freed from the intense fear that can result from not knowing what to do. Good planning doesn't close the door on alternatives. On the contrary, it empowers the teacher to pursue them in different directions.

Such flexibility is essential in constructivist classes, for a common characteristic of teacher behavior and one of the most frequently made mistakes of constructivist teachers is a tendency to rush students. Problem solving takes time, much more time than more direct instructional methods. Making errors and exploring alternative solutions take time, but making errors is an essential part of the learning process in problem-solving, constructivist classes. Flexibility is equally important in diverse classrooms, where teachers must be devoted to the concept that all students can and will learn. Flexibility is an essential quality for anyone attempting to help people change, whether students or teachers.

Professional Development

Teacher research occurs in many different ways. One variable among organizational structures of research activities is the teacher's role, which can range from that of a passive assistant to that of an independent researcher or a full partner in school–university research.

Some teachers find research threatening, others enjoy it; therefore, success in promoting teacher research depends on the selection of appropriate teachers—that is, teachers who possess the desire and qualities conducive to conducting research. Teachers who try out a new method in their classroom and compare its results with previously used methods are engaging in action research (Oliva & Pawlas, 2007). An obviously necessary quality for successfully using action research is curiosity; teacher researchers must have questions for which they want answers—questions about their own teaching.

Another quality that facilitates the conducting of research is the habit of constant reading. Teacher researchers must read professional journals in their fields. All teachers can benefit by keeping up with the professional literature. This practice is essential because regular reading of the professional literature keeps teachers current in their field and reflects an attitude of intellectual flexibility.

An analysis of the benefits teachers derive from being involved with research found that most of the benefits are realized only when teachers are involved at the highest level. This type of involvement occurs only when teachers identify a problem that is important to them. As Chattin-McNichols and Loeffler (1989, p. 21) explain, identifying an important problem is easy:

> Classroom teachers are faced, on a daily basis, with questions that puzzle and concern them in their interactions with children. Many of these questions provide appropriate material for microresearch projects for teachers to carry out in their classrooms.

Once a problem is selected for study, the investigator must define the problem. Part of this identification might include establishing a baseline. A baseline or benchmark level provides a starting place for measuring improvement. A baseline can be established by using a pretest or simply by gathering data.

Once the baseline is established, the investigating teacher(s) should implement the change strategies and then follow up by testing to determine the amount of progress. Full teacher involvement is essential in every stage of the research. Maria Cardelle-Elawar (1993) developed the model for initiating teacher research on which figure 8.3 (on the following page) is based.

There is evidence that teacher-facilitated staff development models do give schools a better return on investment than traditional models. According to Nancy Fichtman Dana (in Rebora, 2009), research is starting to show that job-embedded methods such as action-research projects are more likely to result in changes in the classroom.

> Part of the reason for this is simply that teachers often have a better grasp than outside consultants or remote district officials of the kind of knowledge and

> training they and their colleagues need to help their students. . . . Many observers also believe that, because it is closely connected to teachers' day-to-day work, teacher-led training is more likely to embody the hallmarks of high-quality professional development—feedback and follow-up, connection to practical classroom issues, and teacher engagement and reflection on practice.

Several professional organizations—especially state education association chapters—are dedicated to helping teachers become empowered and prepared to

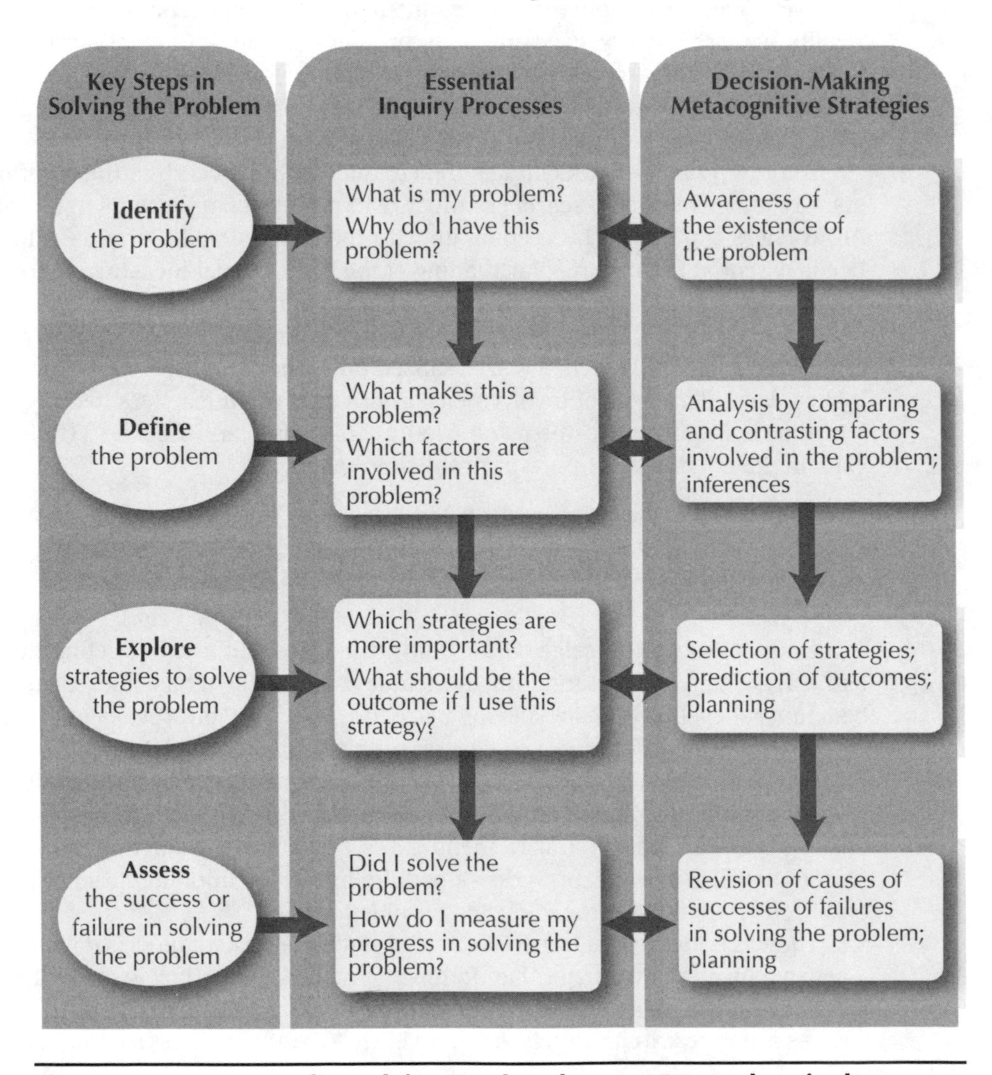

Figure 8.3 A Strategy for Helping Teachers become Researchers in the Classroom

assume greater curriculum leadership roles. Many workshops are required to prepare in-service teachers and administrators for the reform challenges in their state, but even the best workshops are no better than the degree to which the objectives, content, and skills they cover match the needs of the teachers and administrators who attend the workshops. One organizational structure used to assume this match is the consortium.

An *educational consortium* is a formal coalition of two or more school districts designed to aid them in achieving common goals. Educational consortia work much like traditional agricultural and vocational education cooperatives. Member school districts pool their resources to purchase services that no district could afford by itself.

The concept of faculty development has taken a dramatic turn. One-day workshops have not been very effective overall and have, therefore, given way to continuous involvement of teachers in their own disciplines. Willis (2002) says that to be effective, *professional development* must:

- be school-based,
- be ongoing,
- be collaborative,
- provide feedback to participants, and
- allow participants to analyze their own practice, use reflection, use group process, and use coaching with follow-up.

Faculty development must be "rooted in the needs of students, teachers, and community and based upon the most advanced knowledge and skill available. Claudia Whitley (Mayo & Whitley, 2004) is a middle-school principal in Nacogdoches, Texas, who uses a constructivist approach to professional development. Ms. Whitley has discovered a way to give her teachers voice and ownership: She lets each teacher select a strand and work with colleagues who share this interest. Each member applies a technique in class and reports the results at the following faculty meeting. Teacher learning communities put teachers in charge of their own professional development, enabling any school to use formative assessment to produce unprecedented improvements in school achievement (William, 2007).

Several suggestions have been given for encouraging educators to get involved with research. Studies are needed to discover new and better methods of preparing others to introduce positive change into our schools. Mayo and Whitley recognize this need:

> Research studies that inquire into the nature of professional development and its relationship to student learning are needed to increase our understanding of how successful change can occur within the context of the larger social and political agendas of educational reform. (p. 52)

Box 8.3 National Board for Professional Teaching Standards

The National Board for Professional Teaching Standards (NBPTS) is a 63-member board of teachers, administrators, and other citizens (mostly teachers) developed in 1987 to identify the standards teachers need to fulfill the following propositions:

1. Teachers are committed to students and their learning.
2. Teachers know the subjects they teach and how to teach those subjects to students.
3. Teachers are responsible for managing and monitoring students' learning.
4. Teachers think systematically about their practice and learn from experience.
5. Teachers are members of learning communities.

More than 100,000 teachers have become nationally certificated. The standards set by this board are very high, and most teachers who meet these standards have to work hard to prepare for the required examination. By paying a fee, individual teachers can apply for state-issued NBPTS certification. While NBPTS certification is far more rigorous than state-level certification, it does not replace state credentials or licenses (Armstrong et al., 2009). However, teachers who meet these standards have increased confidence, enhanced teaching skills, clearer focus on student outcomes, and a greater commitment to professional growth. Portfolio development is an important part of this program. Additional information about NBPTS can be found at the their Web site (http://www.nbpts.org).

Educational Leadership

This chapter has stressed the need to examine the teacher's work environment and to provide fiscal and physical support to curriculum leaders and their colleagues, as they work together to improve the curriculum. This kind of support is essential for effective leadership, but success requires more. Curriculum leaders must be motivated to achieve beyond their previous levels. Remember John Dewey's human development goal: that each culture would be elevated above its previous culture through the development of individuals. In other words, as essential as the tools needed to do the job are, success requires more: Teachers must be motivated to want to exceed the accomplishments made by the previous generation.

Staff development makes specific demands of its leaders. When those demands are not met, problems arise. Reporting on a study by the Southern Education Consortium, Purvis and Boren (1991, p. 21) identified three major problems related to staff development: "(1) Incentives for attendance are lacking, (2) programs are not related to teachers' needs and interests, and (3) staff development programs are not well organized and thought out carefully enough." Regarding the roles and responsibilities of staff development, Myrick and Jones (1991, pp. 3–6) suggested that leaders must

- be aware of new practices in curriculum and instruction,
- help develop a vision for their school,
- communicate the school's or department's mission and goals,

- be team members,
- secure financing,
- conduct assessments,
- value growth,
- earn trust,
- remain open-minded, and
- recognize contributions by others.

Interestingly, some of these responsibilities seem to apply to *educational leadership*, not just to staff development. Clearly, the education reform reports have changed the role of educational leaders quite dramatically, making it broader and increasing their management responsibilities (Daresh, 2007). Education reform has pressed for participation in management as a means of empowering teachers because, as indicated earlier, there is evidence that successful involvement of teachers in managing the schools is essential to maximum educational improvement (Ackerman & Mackenzie, 2006).

Poplin (1992) discusses this shift in the role of educational leaders, making several points that deserve repeating. First, the role of educational leaders has, indeed, changed, becoming much broader. Because of school-based management, the teacher must be prepared to manage a broad spectrum of the school's busi-

Box 8.4 Educational Leadership Resources

Educational Leadership

An online journal published by the Association for Supervision and Curriculum Development (ASCD), the journal is described as "a journal for educators, by educators." Published eight times each year, September through May, with a combined December/January issue. Free to all ASCD members; subscriptions and individual issues are also available for sale.

Academy of Educational Leadership Journal

http://www.alliedacademies.org/public/Journals/JournalDetails.aspx?jid=5

Published twice annually by the Allied Academies (with an independent editorial board), the journal's self-described mission is "to expand the boundaries of the literature by supporting the exchange of ideas and insights which further the understanding of education."

IEL Leadership Connections

http://www.iel.org/news/newsletter/index.html

Published by the Institute for Educational Leadership, this free bi-monthly e-newsletter focuses on leadership for education.

Education Leadership Toolkit

http://www.nsba.org/sbot/toolkit/

A free, online technology resource from the National School Boards Foundation (NSBA), implemented by NSBA's Institute for the Transfer of Technology to Education. Described as "a collection of tips and pointers, articles, case studies, and other resources for education leaders addressing issues around technology and education." Included in the toolkit is a section on curriculum and assessment.

ness, including financial and curriculum decisions, heretofore outside the teacher's purview. Second, today's leaders must provide a climate that lets teachers expand their horizons (Danielson, 2007). Third, the contemporary leader must help teachers develop skills they can use to evaluate their own performance. Fourth, today's leader must protect teachers' time (Kretovics et al., 2004). (This translates into providing released time from regular assignments.) In short, today's leader is a highly skilled manager, able to provide latitude, freedom, support, and encouragement for teachers to grow and become less dependent on their leadership.

Teachers can become leaders through the use of self-analyzing strategies including journal keeping, asking for constructive criticism from their peers, and using action research. All curriculum leaders, including department and grade-level chairs, need these types of skills. It is a long-standing axiom that good leaders are good agents for change. For many leaders, the greatest challenge may be to bring about the changes in attitude that will be required to provide leadership or management while working alongside other teachers.

Good leaders recognize that if schools are to remain functional in a rapidly changing community they must grow and develop, just as individuals grow and develop (Oliva & Pawlas, 2007). Good leaders are dreamers, yet they also have the capacity to go beyond their own dreams and help teachers exceed the leader's imagination. Good leaders may have very different styles, but they also have some qualities in common. Good leaders never quit asking questions about practices that affect learning, and they give their teachers latitude and meaningful personal support. Allan Glatthorn (2004, pp. 67–69) gives some good advice regarding leadership tasks for curriculum development at the school level. First, it's important to develop a culture that supports curriculum work. This means nurturing the values and norms of collegiality, teamwork, and continuous improvement. Leaders should encourage teachers to value their expanded responsibilities in contributing to curriculum development. It's also important to provide support for curriculum work. Encourage teachers to take risks, reducing the pressure of teacher evaluation during early implementation of new practices, and encouraging teachers to identify related problems. Teachers should be allowed quality time for developing curriculum units and learning materials. Work with teachers to plan and implement the staff development needed to ensure curriculum alignment and support implementation. Assess whether the hidden curriculum is congruent with the espoused values of the administrators and teachers.

John Daresh (2007) comments that educational leaders must think about the specific actions they should take concerning the issues of "what shall be taught and how it shall be taught" (p. 281). All designated curriculum directors, principals, vice principals, department and grade-level chairs, and individuals designated or elected to effect changes in the curricula at some point must deal with diversity among their team members, the teachers. The emerging natural leaders who stand like the U.S. Marines, ready to go into action at any moment, are an asset to any organization, but their value is defined by the support they receive from the established leaders. But *naysayers*, who have perhaps the clearest vision of their role in life—to share their cynicism, doubts, and complaints with anyone who will listen—have the power to sabotage almost any operation, if they are neglected by the school's leaders. The contributions of the members of the critical mass, who absorb conflicting messages from the other groups as they wait to do what they must, will be determined by the leadership they receive. Left alone, the majority will do little or nothing; correctly motivated, they often surprise even themselves with their contributions.

No leader knows exactly how much time and energy to assign to these different groups, but experienced leaders know that because the naysayers are the loudest they often get the most attention. The "squeaky wheel" syndrome often forces leaders to focus their attention, and to use most of their time and resources to try to redirect, appease, or subdue this group. This is usually a mistake, since this group can seldom be redirected or subdued.

Although the naysayers seem aggressive, and aggressiveness suggests self-confidence, they may actually be suffering from low self-esteem. Perhaps the best way to help individuals improve their self-esteem is to direct them to goal-oriented activity that is linked to some social or positive purpose. Although this approach sounds logical and simple, building self-esteem is not easy and many self-esteem programs are ineffective. Self-assessment programs offer more promise if they lead students to understand what success looks like (Chappuis, 2009).

Effective Use of Power

Leaders have several types of power at their disposal. By being aware of the sources of power, leaders can often increase their power and improve the ways they use it. Steers, Ungson, and Mowday (1985) identified five types of leadership power: (1) reward power, (2) punishment power, (3) legitimate power, (4) expert power, and (5) referent power.

Reward power and *punishment power* are often combined and collectively called *coercive power*. Reward power is the more appropriate power to wield when dealing with professionals. Merit pay is an example of thc use of reward power. NCLB and many current state school reform programs are using punishment power to increase academic achievement. Baselines for performance are established for each school. If the achievement scores fall significantly below the baseline, the school may be put on warning or probation and given a designated time to raise its achievement scores to an acceptable level. If the school fails, a variety of punishments may be implemented, including removal of the local governing body. In other words, the local administrators may be fired.

NCLB and current education reform programs are also using reward power. These same programs may set levels above the baseline at which the local school can earn a specified number of dollars for each point achieved above the baseline. In some instances, this money can even be used as bonus pay for teachers.

Legitimate power is power sanctioned by an organization. For example, the chair of the high school science department has power simply because of holding this position.

Educational leaders rely heavily on *expert power*, derived from having special knowledge and skills, and *referent power*, which comes from the ability to get others to identify with their leader and imitate their leader. As teachers themselves become empowered and educational leaders become better managers, referent power grows increasingly indispensable for educational leaders.

Expert power, too, is indispensable for educational leaders. But the type of expertise required of educational leaders has changed. More than ever before, this expertise comes not so much from acquired cognitive knowledge as it does from growth in the affective domain. Future educational leaders will have to be experts in coping with the unknown. Much security is relinquished as fellow teachers are placed in leadership roles. A power shift occurs when *site-based decision-making* teams (often called school councils) take on problems and make decisions that a single individual (for example, the principal or superintendent) lacks the expertise to handle.

Another type of expertise that is quickly becoming indispensable for the educational leader is consensus development. No longer can the leader make unilateral choices; rather, a leader must lead the team to consensus. Skilled leaders can motivate team members to reconcile individual disagreements in order to gain consensus. Douglas DeWitt (2010) suggests that an effective way to improve teacher relationships is to redirect the focus of any disagreement to what is best for our students. Interestingly, as a local decision-making team perfects its consensus-building skill, the team also gains power. Steers, Ungson, and Mowday (1985, p. 436) acknowledged this type of power: "In general, the more cohesion and homogeneity a group or collection of groups has on a particular issue, the greater its influence." For tips on resolving within-group conflict and building collaboration, see Harris (2010).

Of the various types of power, several are derived from the organization and some are inherent in the leader. True leaders always depend on expert, referent, and consensus-building power. Steers, Ungson, and Mowday (1985, p. 307) stated that "Leadership exists when subordinates *voluntarily* comply because of something the leader has done."

The Future of Educational Leadership

Predicting the future is always risky, but leaders have the responsibility to do just that. The risk can be reduced by gathering as much information as possible and using that information in their predictions. Notice that the task is to predict the future of educational leadership, not to predict what type of leadership the future will bring. There is a subtle but powerful difference between the two concepts. The latter assumes that educational leaders will exist in some form; the former makes no such assumption.

There is reason to consider the possibility that educational leadership is becoming moribund, and education reform is the likeliest culprit. Holzman (1992, p. 36) asks, "Are we sure that leadership itself and the cult of personal leadership are not in large measure the problem with public education in the United States today?" There has been a radical shift in the role of the leader, away from leadership as we have known it. Sergiovanni and Staratt (2002) blame leadership for standing in the way of an exploration of alternative ways to run the schools. They also point out that leadership is something that someone does to others, whereas the greatest improvement in our schools and teachers is likely to come from within—from the teachers. Although they never say it, they "lead" their readers to suspect, if not conclude, that leadership also hampers professionalism. They say that both professionalism and leadership are frequently prescribed as cures for school problems, but in many ways the two concepts are antithetical. The more professionalism is emphasized, the less leadership is needed. The more leadership is emphasized, the less likely it is the professionalism will develop. "American education has long labored under the mistake notion that leadership was something for administrators to exercise, not teachers" (Sergiovanni & Staratt, 2002, p. 148). Their message is that supervisory leadership as we have known it will become less and less important and will be replaced by self management as teachers, themselves, exercise more and more leadership.

The National Center for Educational Achievement (NCEA) offers an interactive portfolio of best practices that can be used to help schools change. According to the NCEA Web site,

> Ongoing study helps us continually refine our understanding of these broad principles of best practice. Built upon, and continually informed by, student in consistently higher-performing schools, the framework provides an organizational schema to examine the practices of those school systems, as compared to average-performing ones. More than 500 schools from 20 states have been studied.

Donald Wise (2010) explains how this framework can be used in a work session with administrators and teachers. Visit http://www.just4kids.org/en/research_policy/best_practices/framework.cfm to use the interactive framework.

Conclusion

Following is a summary of some of the advances made and concerns raised about the topics discussed in this chapter.

Advances

- NCLB requires teachers to cite data to defend their selection of instructional methods.
- Faculty development that is rooted in the needs of students, teachers, and community can enhance learning.
- Teachers can become leaders through use of self-analyzing strategies.
- Teachers can improve the culture of their classrooms by involving students in curriculum planning.
- The most effective model for school improvement is action research, including school–university partnerships.

Concerns

- Many teachers are not conversant with research on teaching.
- Research is needed to discover relationships between faculty development and learning.
- Teachers must be given time to plan cooperatively.
- Teachers sometimes cooperate to block improvements.
- Teachers are reluctant to get involved with prescribed changes.

The role of educational leaders is changing dramatically and rapidly. In the past, these leaders served as reactive curriculum troubleshooters who located and fixed problems. Today, curriculum development is a continuing, proactive process that doesn't require the occurrence of problems to get attention. Education reform has brought curriculum development to the center of attention. Effective schools balance top-down and bottom-up reform (Fullan, 1999) and empower their teachers to manage both types.

Traditionally, most teachers have handicapped themselves by avoiding involvement with research and with the rest of the school outside their classroom. However, to bring student performance to the levels called for in the reform reports, teachers must become involved with the total curriculum.

Successful teacher involvement in restructuring will require teachers to develop skills in research, in curriculum development, and in working cooperatively with other teachers, administrators, and parents. Leaders must help and by managing teams of teachers as they work on the curriculum. Such successful management will require skilled use of power, especially expert power and referent power. As teachers become empowered, educational leaders will no longer be able to depend on traditional types of powers (legitimate and coercive) but will be required to become more proficient in developing and using referent power.

Another responsibility of contemporary and future leaders is to determine the needs of individuals and faculties and to arrange for staff development opportunities to address these needs. One method that has proven effective is the consortium.

In the future, educational leaders may no longer be as much in demand as they have been in the past. If the term *leader* continues to be used in this context, the "leaders" will have to be adept in management skills and will have to trust their colleagues to set goals and make all types of important decisions.

This chapter has endorsed collaboration and flexibility, two qualities that constructivist teachers in diverse settings can use to help all students succeed. The chapter has also stressed organization. Future educators will experience an increased need to be able to develop organized strategies to meet the increasing academic and social needs of their increasingly diverse classes. Remember the constructivist and multicultural themes of this book as you examine the following questions, and consider the potential that such concepts as research and student empowerment have for helping students reach these goals.

Additional Learning Opportunities

1. How are educational research and education reform related?
2. Why have teachers avoided research in the past?
3. Why does education reform require teachers to expand their horizons?
4. What are some intrinsic motivators that can be used to help teachers become involved in improving their schools?
5. How can educational leaders ensure that staff development workshops will match the teachers' needs?
6. What are some responsibilities of staff development leaders?

7. How have the education reform reports altered the role of educational leaders?
8. Why is teacher empowerment a major goal of education reform?
9. How does Herzberg's two-factor theory relate to educational leadership?
10. What types of power do educational leaders need most? Explain your answer.
11. Why must educational leaders change their perception of their need for security?
12. How does individuals' reluctance to change affect their cultural perceptions?
13. How should research help teachers develop and maintain multicultural and constructivist classrooms?

SUGGESTED ACTIVITIES

1. Curriculum change has become a continuous process. Develop a calendar you can use to help fellow teachers make curriculum improvements throughout the year. Designate times for: (1) developing a needs assessment, (2) conducting a needs assessment, (3) setting goals, (4) planning workshops, (5) advertising workshops, and (6) giving the workshops.
2. The success of an educational consortium depends on a match between the staff development offered and the needs and desires of its members. Design a system that will communicate the relevance of programs offered throughout the year and that will show the relationships between the goals of the workshops and the needs of the consortium members.
3. As leaders prepare for their new roles as managers, their success requires good human-relations skills. Choose a current education reform practice and prepare a presentation to use during an open house to convince parents of the importance of this reform element.
4. Design an assignment that permits your students to "show off" the multicultural progress of their class.
5. Create an assignment that requires students to research and list strengths of the various cultures represented in your classroom.
6. Research the topic "constructivism" and plan a lesson that uses several constructivist principles.

chapter nine

EVALUATING INSTRUCTION AND THE CURRICULUM

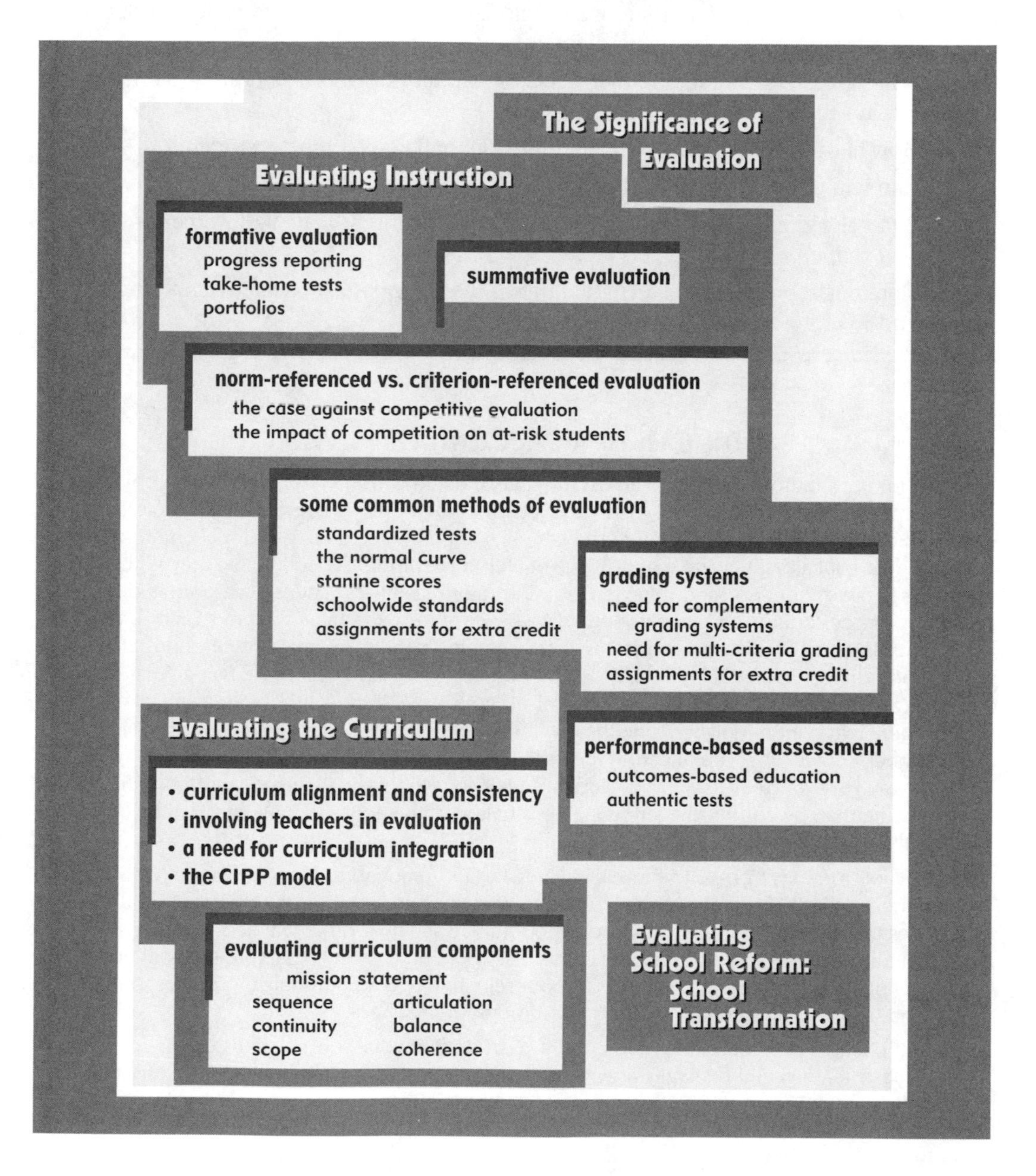

Focus Questions

1. What impact does education reform have on curriculum evaluation?
2. What is the role of curriculum alignment in education reform?
3. What is progress reporting, and should it be used in the schools? Why or why not?
4. How would you differentiate norm-referenced evaluation from criterion-referenced evaluation in elementary and secondary schools?
5. What are the differences in the effects of competition and cooperation on mainstream cultures?
6. How should the mission statement for a school affect minority students?
7. Can you describe two ways that curriculum balance should be evaluated?
8. What are the proper relationships among curriculum articulation, continuity, and scope?
9. How might you evaluate a curriculum to determine its constructivist strengths and weaknesses?

The Case of an Accreditation Visit

By Sunday afternoon, cars from across the state and a few from out of state begin converging at a local motel. The next three days will be grueling for these university professors, public school administrators, and teachers. As a regional accrediting team, each morning these 12 educators will arrive by 7:30 AM at Hillsboro Middle School, where they will visit classes, study records, and interview administrators, teachers, counselors, and students. Even the custodians and lunchroom workers will not escape their scrutiny. Each day, at about 4:00 PM, the team members will reassemble in their designated workroom at the school, drive back to their motel, have an hour for dinner, and begin discussing what they saw and making plans for the next day. If all goes well, they will be able to retire each evening by about midnight. If not, they will work until 2 or 3 o'clock in the morning. Each member knows what lies ahead. If they are lucky, there will be some good humor along the way. But the real reward for working these long hours without pay will come from knowing that, by conducting a thorough evaluation of the entire school, they will be helping this school improve itself.

The next two days prove to be both successful and enjoyable. Team members who are teachers spend several hours in classrooms watching teachers in their respective disciplines teach. Teachers rarely have an opportunity to see how other teachers organize their curricula and manage their lessons, so this classroom time is one of the professional benefits of participating on such a team. The counselor and two administrators on the team also spend time with their counterparts at Hillsboro Middle School.

But the classroom and office visits are only part of the overall observations of this school. As these team members walk down the halls, and even during lunch, they constantly observe the teachers and students. Several team members notice that the school's faculty had practically no minority members. The minority student representation at Hillsboro is also extremely low, and this, too, concerns some of the team members.

Because of their hectic schedule, Wednesday comes faster than the team thought possible and the visit is complete, except for the detailed written report that the chair must prepare and mail to the principal. As the team anticipated, the work was hard, but they did enjoy some humorous moments. Mr. Sims, a team member, is a veteran superintendent who is proud of his school district and likes to talk about his schools. But during their initial meeting, the team chair had made a rule that any members who talked about their own professional experiences would have to put a quarter in the kitty. At the end of the visit, the money would be used to buy refreshments for the group to enjoy while celebrating the completion of the evaluation.

Each time Mr. Sims started to talk about his schools, he was interrupted and reminded to put a quarter in the pot. At one meeting, after he had deposited three quarters, he became so frustrated that he raised his hand to silence everyone, reached into his wallet, took out a $10 bill, and, dropping it into the kitty, said, "Now all of you are going to shut up until I finish my story." And they did! After that, Mr. Sims received a lot of respect.

Accreditation visits can have some surprises. On this visit, the surprise came early. Sunday evening was special because the administrators and the school board had an opportunity to express their appreciation to the team members for giving their time and energy to the important goal of helping the school improve. The dinner itself was very nice, but it was the entertainment that surprised the team members most. First, they were surprised to be entertained by an orchestra. Even more surprising was the fact that the school's students were the orchestra musicians. None of the evaluators had ever known of a middle school that had an orchestra, and these youngsters had performed like professional musicians.

Accreditation visits usually reveal some weaknesses, too, and this visit was no exception. Apart from the lack of minority representation, the greatest disappointment was with th
science department. More accurately, it was the absence of a science department, si
there was none. Actually, the entire three grades offered only one course in scienc
that course wasn't required of all students. This meant that some graduates of th
entered high school having had no science in their program. On the positive sid
look revealed that the school's outstanding music curriculum was complem
superb art curriculum. In summary, the school had an outstanding fine arts
the expense of having no science program.

One of the team members, a professor of curriculum and instruction, w
of coordinating the part of the report that focused on the school's i
She referred to her notes as she described her impressions of the En

> The English curriculum has a purposeful sequence. Withi
> leads to the next, and each year builds on the preceding y
>
> Within and between years, the content is continuous an
> say that the English curriculum has excellent sequenc
>
> I do question the scope of this curriculum. It seems
> that there is more literature than composition. I w
> used to raise the achievement test scores. As y
> near the top on the state achievement test sc
>
> As for the social studies curriculum, it see
> scope and good sequence. Nothing ma
> the same. I did see one thing that bothe
> For example, I didn't find any trace of ma
> vice versa. I wonder why the math departm

address social problems. I didn't see much in the way of writing assignments being required outside the English Department. Thus, I would say that the curriculum lacks integration. I believe that many of these shortcomings could be overcome if the school's curriculum had a more contemporary focus. More topics such as urban living and cultural pluralism are needed.

I also examined the testing program. The curriculum content and the tests are aligned with the state's valued outcomes. In other words, the taught curriculum is tied to the tested curriculum. I'm sure this contributes to the success the students have on the state's achievement tests.

When all reports are completed, the team chair will have the responsibility of writing the summary report. This task will require checking the individual reports to determine whether any elements are missing from the major curriculum. He will then consolidate the reports and add his own observations on the major components of the curriculum.

• • •

Accrediting teams such as the one that visited Hillsboro Middle School provide a significant service to schools by evaluating their curriculum and instruction. But schools cannot rely on the work of others whose visits are separated by long periods of time. The school's curriculum and instruction must be continuously evaluated from the inside. As you read this chapter, you will want to learn all you can about curriculum and instruction evaluation processes—gathering information and skills that you can use to prepare teachers to take responsibility for evaluating and improving their school's curriculum and instruction.

The Significance of Evaluation

Historically, teachers have been responsible for using *evaluation* and *measurement* (the nonqualitative part of evaluation) in their classes to assess the outcomes of their instruction; however, most teacher preparation programs have not required a course designed to prepare them for this important task. Furthermore, when a course in evaluation is required, the emphasis is invariably on standardized tests. In reality, teachers spend much more of their planning time and classroom teaching time preparing, administering, and scoring tests they create themselves than they spend on standardized tests. This statement is not intended to downplay the need teachers have for understanding standardized tests but, rather, to point out a serious failure in most teacher education curricula to prepare teachers to develop, administer, and score teacher-made tests.

Armstrong and colleagues (2009) encourage teachers to use essay tests to meet
udents' background characteristics. Teachers who give regular quizzes have higher
ademic performance in their classes. Weekly quizzes have more power than home-
k assignments to increase learning. The assessments best suited to guide
rovements in student learning are the quizzes, tests, writing assignments, and
assessments that teachers administer on a regular basis in their classrooms.
second major curriculum shortcoming in many teacher education programs is
ure to offer instruction on testing, measurement, and evaluation. At both the
nd the K–12 levels, the overwhelming emphasis has been placed on summa-
ation while ignoring formative evaluation (discussed later in this chapter).

A third concern, which makes evaluation more significant than ever as a topic for teachers and all curriculum workers to study, is the emphasis that education reform is placing on evaluation and the manner in which it is being used to determine progress in education reform.

All of these concerns focus on instruction and learning. As mentioned in earlier chapters, historically (perhaps through no fault of their own) teachers have limited their involvement in the schools to their own classrooms, and they have limited their attention to that part of the education process with which they are most comfortable—instruction. Administrators have accepted this limitation of teacher involvement and, in fact, have often promoted it. Given the history of teachers' isolation within their own classroom, it is not surprising that they have not been involved in curriculum evaluation. Yet, as pointed out in chapter 1, maximum success with education reform will require teachers to become intensely involved with the total school program, including its evaluation. Teachers have a special need to be involved with the whole school curriculum. Oliva (2009, p. 413) addresses this need:

> [M]ost valuative studies must be and are conducted by the local curriculum planners and the teachers. The shortage of trained personnel and the costs of employing specialists are prohibitive for many school systems. Even in large systems that employ curriculum evaluators, many curriculum evaluation tasks are performed by teachers and curriculum planners.
>
> Only when teachers are involved in designing the curriculum are they capable of implementing it, and only when they are involved with developing the curriculum are they committed to working to make it succeed. Reconstructionists are calling for teachers to become intensely involved in redesigning the entire school structure. But successful contribution to the restructuring of school programs will require skills that most teachers currently lack. Central to these necessary skills is the ability to evaluate the school's curriculum.

The first part of this chapter examines the roles of testing, measurement, and evaluation in instruction. The second part examines the role that evaluation must play in curriculum. Finally, we examine several models for evaluating the curriculum.

Evaluating Instruction

Assessment should always be tied to the needs of students. The most significant evaluation of student achievement should be the extent to which they want to know more and their ability to do so. Unfortunately, today's high-stakes testing programs seem to ignore student needs in favor of serving the needs of politicians. Parents and teachers should be careful not to perpetuate this mistake.

Formative Evaluation

Assessment can take place *after* a student has been taught (*summative assessment*), or *while* a student is being taught (*formative assessment*, the topic of this section) Just how much can formative assessment improve students' aim? A great deal, if we can believe the composite findings in five reviews of a total of

4,000 research studies finding that when correctly used, formative assessments can double the speed of student learning (William, 2007/2008).

Initiated by Carroll (1963) and promoted by Bloom, Hastings, and Madaus (1971), and Block, Efthim, and Burns (1989), *formative evaluation* is now receiving a resurgence of attention, stimulated by the current education reform efforts. Unlike its counterpart, *summative evaluation*, which is used to determine grades and to differentiate between passing students and failing students, formative evaluation has one ultimate purpose—to promote learning. It achieves this goal through improving study habits, instruction, and the curriculum.

The purpose of this type of assessment is to improve the teacher's performance, with the ultimate goal of improving student learning. "Assessment drives instruction" (Sternberg, 2007/2008). Formative evaluation enables teachers to monitor their instruction and keep it on course (Oliva, 2009). In other words, formative evaluation can be used throughout the period of instruction to determine whether progress is being made regarding the aims, goals, and objectives discussed in chapter 6. Summative evaluation can then determine whether these aims, goals, and objectives have been met (figure 9.1).

Formative assessments—ongoing assessments designed to make students' thinking visible to both students and teachers—are essential for guiding instruction and helping both teachers and students monitor progress. In addition, if any student cannot learn excellently from the original instruction, this can be accomplished with one or more correctives. Since it is intended to identify exactly where, in a unit of instruction, a student is experiencing difficulty, formative evaluation is *criterion referenced*—meaning that each student is assessed according to his or her mastery of a particular set of learning tasks or objectives.

A key element of formative assessment is feedback (Andrade, 2007/2008). When giving feedback, teachers should be positive yet specific, pointing out both errors and strengths in students' work (Brookhart, 2007/2008). Feedback is so important because, as students often need a chance to test their knowledge without penalty, through feedback they will know how to adjust their study techniques, and their teachers can determine whether their instructional techniques need adjusting.

Tests can become strong clarifiers of teacher expectations, thereby guiding students toward expected outcomes. Although most teachers agree that going over

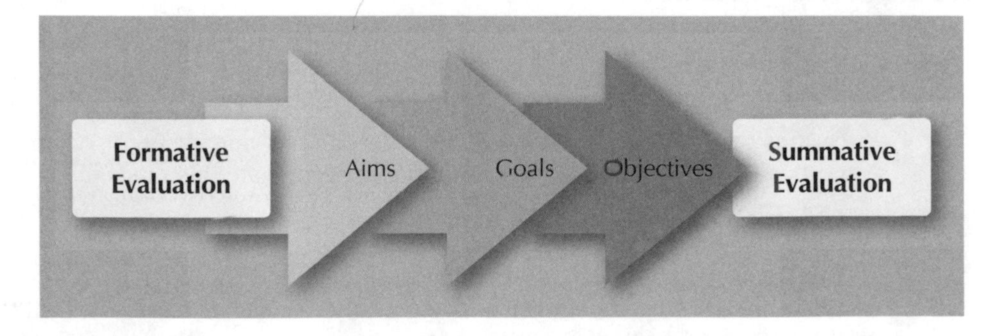

Figure 9.1 Formative and Summative Evaluation

test answers in class can help some students learn more about the material, they are aware that this approach is not likely to result in total mastery of the material. In essence, formative evaluation works because it enables teachers to better serve learners, and this is the ultimate test of any education reform practice: When assessment is used to control outcomes rather than to identify needs and when test results, rather than learning, become the goal, the education system serves the controller, not the learner. Given the enormous pressure placed on today's teachers to boost their students' scores on external exams, teachers understandably tend to give less attention to their own assignments. That's a mistake, if the teachers' tests are instructionally useful.

Students, however, do not usually see the potential that tests have for promoting learning. At least this is what is suggested by their behavior after they complete a test. After a test is finished, it is time to shut down the schema. Teachers are sometimes frustrated over the lack of interest students have in reviewing their tests. A much more systematic use of evaluation is needed, one that will separate evaluation from grading, a system that is aimed only at promoting learning.

When using tests for formative purposes, teachers should

- avoid recording individual scores;
- be concerned only with whether the student has mastered the material at an acceptable level;
- involve each student in keeping a continuing record of individual progress;
- avoid mentioning grades;
- assume that, when properly motivated, all students can master the material;
- avoid pushing students so hard that they become confused and discouraged; and
- reassure students that these test results will not count toward their grades.

Progress Reporting

Letter grades are being replaced with *progress reports*, a type of formative evaluation that can be far more revealing than traditional grades. This is a good change. Progress reporting is a viable alternative because it imparts information about what is being taught, alternative activities the student has completed, and how each student is coping with the course. No individual letter grade can do this. Direct conferences supplement narrative reports, and a portfolio of student work is much more revealing and reliable than a letter grade.

Another advantage of progress reporting is its ongoing nature. Unlike traditional exams that give only one-time results, ongoing testing produces a much more comprehensive view of student progress, which often varies continuously. It should include talking to students frequently about their learning (Brookhart, 2007/2008).

Take-Home Tests

Another example of formative evaluation is the use of *take-home tests*. This type of test gives students access to more information sources and provides students with more time to internalize that information. Take-home tests can provide an answer for teachers who wish to evaluate student progress with longer and more complex problem situations.

Portfolios

A *portfolio* is a collection of tangible products that provides evidence of a student's efforts, progress, and achievements (Woolfolk Hoy & Hoy, 2009). This type of formative assessment is also a collection of information about a teacher's practice. Of course, good portfolios also reflect student behavior. Believing that there are advantages in involving students in their own ongoing evaluation, many teachers are now using portfolios in their classes. In fact, by 1998, half of America's teachers had begun using portfolios in their classes. The success of portfolios is contingent upon establishing the purpose of the portfolios when they are assigned. Teachers by themselves and teachers and learners together must explicitly define purposes of the portfolio so that learners know what is expected of them before they begin developing their evidence file. From the beginning, students must know whether their portfolio is an instructional tool or an assessment tool.

Portfolios can often include more information about a child's learning than either a traditional, graded report card or a nongraded, narrative report. Many schools allow students to write their own self-appraisal, causing them to reflect on their own learning. Portfolios also have the power to motivate students, and portfolio development shifts the ownership of learning to students. They should include writing-across-the-curriculum projects. If students are not regularly writing across a variety of topics and in a variety of styles for diverse purposes, then promoting self-evaluation has limited value.

The use of portfolios embraces the idea that students' judgment should be sought and used in determining their grades. A couple of relevant questions commonly asked about student portfolios are, "How do you believe the quality of your present work compares with your previous work?" and "Do you believe this sample of your work represents the best you can do?" This approach requires that the teacher know each student, not merely as a recognizable face but as a developing, growing person.

Portfolios function much as a commercial artist's portfolio that shows the artist's skills in several related areas. The portfolio requirements shown in box 9.1 are typical in that they cover a variety of skills such as writing, artwork, and oral performance. Requiring such a variety of products is a common strength of portfolios. Since a portfolio is part of a student's curriculum, this quality makes this portfolio a good example of curriculum alignment.

Another example of a portfolio is shown in box 9.2 (on p. 306), an oral history project for ninth graders designed by Albin Moser at Hope High School, Providence, Rhode Island. This project has two outstanding strengths: It requires the student both to reflect and to be creative.

As stated earlier, most portfolios require a variety of products from the students, and this is considered a strength. Not all portfolios are multidisciplinary, however. Some portfolios focus only on an activity required to develop a particular skill. For example, Abruscato (1993) describes a portfolio used in Vermont schools in grades 4 and 8 that is designed to enhance the development of writing

Box 9.1 A Sample Portfolio

The Rite of Passage Experience (R.O.P.E.) at Walden III, Racine, Wisconsin*

All seniors must complete a portfolio, a study project on U.S. history, and 15 oral and written presentations before a R.O.P.E. committee composed of staff, students, and an outside adult. Nine of the presentations are based on the materials in the portfolio and the project; the remaining six are developed for presentation before the committee. All seniors must enroll in a yearlong course designed to help them meet these requirements.

The eight-part *portfolio*, developed in the first semester, is intended to be "a reflection and analysis of the senior's own life and times." The requirements include:

- a written autobiography
- a reflection on work (including a resume)
- an essay on ethics
- a written summary of coursework in science
- an artistic product or a written report on art (including an essay on artistic standards used in judging artwork)

The *project* is a research paper on a topic of the student's choosing in American history. The student is orally questioned on the paper in the presentations before the committee during the second semester.

The *presentations* include oral tests on the previous work, as well as six additional presentations on the essential subject areas and "personal proficiency" (life skills, setting and realizing personal goals, etc.). The presentations before the committee usually last an hour, with most students averaging about 6 separate appearances to complete all 15 presentations.

A diploma is awarded to those students passing 12 of the 15 presentations and meeting district requirements in math, government, reading, and English.

Note: This summary is paraphrased from both the R.O.P.E. Student Handbook and an earlier draft of Archbald and Newmann's (1988) *Beyond Standardized Testing*.

*From G. Wiggins (1989, April). Teaching to the authentic test. *Educational Leadership, 46*(7) pp. 4–47.

skills (see box 9.3 on the following page). Effectiveness in the use of portfolios requires continuous reflection by their owners.

In summary, the real value in formative testing of any type is to improve real-time teaching and learning (Chappuis & Chappuis, 2007/2008). Do not miss any opportunity to include assignments that require students to write about their learning, causing them to reflect on what they have learned and what they still find confusing (Brookhart, 2007/2008).

Summative Evaluation

You will recall that summative evaluation occurs *after* instruction. A good way to start planning summative evaluation is to involve students. One use of summative evaluation is to determine whether a teacher meets minimal accountability standards. Summative evaluation can also measure student performance to determine such major decisions as grades, passing, and failing.

Box 9.2 An Oral History Project for Ninth-Graders*

To the student:

You must complete an oral history based on interviews and written sources and then present your findings orally in class. The choice of subject matter is up to you. Some examples of possible topics include: your family, running a small business, substance abuse, a labor union, teenage parents, and recent immigrants.

Create three workable hypotheses based on your preliminary investigations and four questions you will ask to test out each hypothesis.

Criteria for Evaluation of Oral History Project

To the teacher:

Did the student investigate three hypotheses?
Did the student describe at least one change over time?
Did the student demonstrate that he or she had done background research?
Were the four people selected for the interviews appropriate sources?
Did the student prepare at least four questions in advance, related to each hypothesis?
Were those questions leading or biased?
Were follow-up questions asked where possible, based on answers?
Did the student note important differences between "fact" and "opinion" in answers?
Did the student use evidence to prove the ultimate best hypothesis?
Did the student exhibit organization in writing and presentation to class?

Note: This example is courtesy of Albin Moser, Hope High School, Providence, Rhode Island. To help your teachers give their students an appreciation of the past, see Roy Rosenzweig's *Everyone a Historian* at http://www.chnm.gmu.edu/survey/index.html

*From G. Wiggins (1989, April). Teaching to the authentic test. *Educational Leadership*, p. 44.

Box 9.3 The Writing Portfolio

The writing portfolio used in Vermont schools in grades 4 and 8 includes two types of products: (1) a collection of six pieces of writing done by the student during the academic year; and (2) a "uniform writing assessment," a formal writing assignment that is given by all teachers to all students in the grade level.

Examining a student's writing portfolio reveals the following:

1. a table of contents
2. a "best piece"
3. a letter
4. a poem, short story, play, or personal narrative
5. a personal response to a cultural, media, or sports exhibit or event or to a book, current issue, math problem, or scientific phenomenon
6. one prose piece from any curriculum area other than English or language arts (for fourth graders) and three prose pieces from any curriculum area other than English or language arts (for eighth graders)
7. the piece produced in response to the uniform writing assessment, as well as related outlines, drafts, etc.

Because teachers have used tests almost exclusively for the purpose of determining student grades, it might be assumed that, with all that practice, teachers are systematic in the way they convert raw scores into letter grades. But this is not so; most teachers have never even been taught how to make a good test (Oldenski, 2010). Each teacher seems to have an individual system, and many teachers use a different system from one grading period to the next. Why? Because most teachers never find a system with which they are satisfied. There is no single system that is right for evaluating all classes. An awareness of the strengths and weaknesses of various grading systems empowers teachers to choose wisely.

Norm-Referenced versus Criterion-Referenced Evaluation

Evaluation systems that force a student to compete with other students are called *norm-referenced*, and those that do not require interstudent competition but instead are based on a set of standards of mastery are called *criterion-referenced.* As a rule, formative assessments are criterion-referenced, while summative assessments are norm-oriented. This is important because traditionally, by using norm-referenced evaluation, our schools have required students to compete with their classmates. Many teachers believe that competition among students is necessary for motivation, but classroom competition is often damaging, especially when the competition is excessive and when students of unequal abilities are forced to compete. Without realizing it, parents and teachers set up situations guaranteeing that children will feel defeated and inept. But evaluation should be for the purpose of promoting further learning, and therefore it should always be a positive, supportive experience.

The Case against Competitive Evaluation

Researchers and educators have discovered much evidencc that grading in the high school should be an individual concern exclusively involving the teacher and the student. Criterion-referenced tests (which do not force competition among students) contribute more to student progress than do norm-referenced tests. Once it was thought that competition for grades was necessary because it motivated students to do their best. This may be true for students who have the most ability, but forcing the less capable students to compete with their more academically capable classmates can discourage those who are less capable, causing them to concentrate on their inadequacies. Competition can also be bad for more capable students in that it can cause them to have a superior attitude toward their less capable classmates. Teachers can reduce these problems by refraining from making test scores and grades public.

Many contemporary educators believe that grades should reflect a student's effort—that no one should receive an A without really trying, and that no students who are exerting themselves to their full potential should receive an F. These teachers hold that the purpose of grading is not to acknowledge high ability levels and not to punish those who do not have high ability; rather, each grade should reflect the degree of progress a student makes relative to that student's ability. Consider the following report (Brogdon, 1993, p. 76):

> An accrediting team member reports being approached by a student named Darlene. "Is it fair for them to keep my diploma?" she asked, fighting back the tears. She talked about kids who fought and sassed the teachers, who cut class and took dope, who acted up and interfered with instruction, lazy kids who refused to do homework. After each example, she would say, "I didn't do that; I did what they told me to do." Three times during our conversation she sobbed, "I know I'm in special education and we're slow. But I tried hard and did my work. I didn't cause trouble. . . ."
>
> Darlene's counselor supported her: "She tried so hard and worked so hard; she came early and stayed late on test days." Near the end of the conversation, the counselor talked about Darlene's strengths. "She knew how to get along with people. Her clothes were always clean and ironed, and that's impressive, especially for a student as poor as Darlene. (She lived in a run-down mobile home with her mother and several brothers and sisters.) The kindergarten teachers who supervised her in the program loved her. She would have a diploma and a job if it weren't for that stupid test."
>
> Although she started school at age 7 and repeated the first grade, Darlene made good grades in every subject, except social studies, throughout elementary and middle school. Her high school grades were low average.
>
> The counselor reminded her colleagues of a similar student who now holds a responsible position with a national firm. "Like Darlene, Suzanne, too, could barely read, but she worked hard and she got along. She got the opportunity to work there because she got a diploma. Suzanne probably couldn't read above the 4th grade level, but she has kept a job because of other traits—being responsible, courteous, dependable, and hardworking."

To realize how far we have come with testing, contrast Darlene's case with the type of teacher certification evaluations that were conducted a century earlier (Huggest & Stinnett, 1958, p. 416):

> Grandfather was on the school board in the little rural community in which he lived. He and another board member had in mind a young man named Matthew as a teacher in their school. Matthew had little "book larnin." He attended church regularly and his character seemed to be quite satisfactory. So far as was known he did not use intoxicating beverages. . . . But he had only attended and finished the local one-room school. The certification law at that time stated that all candidates must be examined in respect to character, ability to teach, and soundness of knowledge of the subject taught. . . . Matthew was examined by Grandfather—who commanded him to open his mouth. . . . Grandfather peered inside the tobacco-stained cavity and then ran his fingers over the blackened teeth. Grandfather said to the other member of the board . . . "Write Matthew out a certificate to teach. . . . I find him sound in every way."

The Impact of Competition on At-Risk Students

At-risk students are those millions of students in elementary, middle, and secondary schools whose likelihood of dropping out of school is higher than average. These students exhibit several risk factors that include

- living with only one parent,
- being a child of a single parent,

- having parents who failed to complete high school,
- living in a low-income household,
- living in high-growth states,
- having poorly developed academic skills,
- having low self-esteem, and
- speaking English as a second language.

The need for continuous curriculum evaluation has already been emphasized. Because local communities and the American society change continually, teachers and the curricularists must align the curricula with the environment and with the school's mission. For example, the curricula and practices at many schools do not make a connection between the classroom and students' lives in their homes and communities. The result of this mismatch is known as *cognitive dissonance*. Failure to tie school experiences to nonschool experiences causes dissonance, which is counterproductive to achieving instructional goals and social goals. Cognitive achievement is made more difficult for students from different cultures who face incongruence between their school lives and home lives.

Competition also impedes the attainment of current multicultural goals because much of the personal/cultural knowledge that students from diverse cultural groups bring to the classroom is inconsistent with school knowledge and with the teacher's personal cultural knowledge. Many minority students are more likely to experience academic success in cooperative rather than in competitive learning environments.

To succeed, students of many different backgrounds must figure out the rules of the school's culture. This means that at-risk students need clear objectives. James Popham (2007/2008) says, "You are dealing with disadvantaged learners, and these are the very students who most need to feel good about themselves and schooling" (p. 88). Without a curriculum that provides assistance, many minority students will not be able to cross the bridge to academic success. Continuous curriculum evaluation is needed to ensure that this assistance is provided.

Some Common Methods of Evaluation

Standardized testing, the normal distribution curve, stanine scores, and schoolwide standards are some ways that schools use to measure the progress of their students. Although stanine scores hold some promise, most of the other methods have disadvantages. One common problem is competitiveness. Each of these evaluation tools is discussed below.

Standardized Tests

As we are all well aware, education reform has increased the use of standardized testing. *Standardized tests* are based on norms derived from the average scores of thousands of students who have taken the test. Usually these scores come from students throughout the nation, so each student's performance is compared with those of thousands of other students.

Standardized tests are usually employed to measure or grade a school's curriculum. Seeking to make teachers more accountable, state officials have forced schools to give standardized tests to students to measure both student success and teacher success. On one hand, standardized tests provide a means of comparing local performance with state and national means; on the other, standardized tests may unintentionally shape a school's curriculum—and not always in a positive manner. Most educators think that several other factors should also be major influences in shaping the curriculum.

Misuse of standardized test scores has always been a problem. The common practice of states using the same standardized test to improve instruction and to force educators to be accountable is a mistake. Unless teachers and other curriculum directors work to prevent such misuse, education reformers' emphasis on increased accountability, as measured by standardized tests, will intensify this problem.

The Normal Curve

A second use of tests that requires students to compete with one another is the *normal curve* (also called the *normal probability curve* or the *probability curve*). The curve could just as well be called the *natural curve* or the *chance curve*, because it reflects natural or chance distribution. This distribution is shown in figure 9.2.

The normal learning curve is divided into equal segments. The vertical line through the center (the mean) represents the average of a whole population. Each vertical line to the right of the mean represents one average (or standard) unit of deviation above the mean. Each vertical line to the left of the mean represents one standard unit of deviation below the mean. As the figure shows, about 34% of the population is within one standard deviation unit above the mean, and about 34% of the population is within the one standard deviation unit below the mean. Only about 14% of the population is in the second deviation range above the mean, and about 14% is in the second deviation range below the mean. A very small portion of the population (approximately 2.3%) deviates enough from the mean to fall within the third unit of deviation above the mean; an equal portion deviates three standard units below the mean.

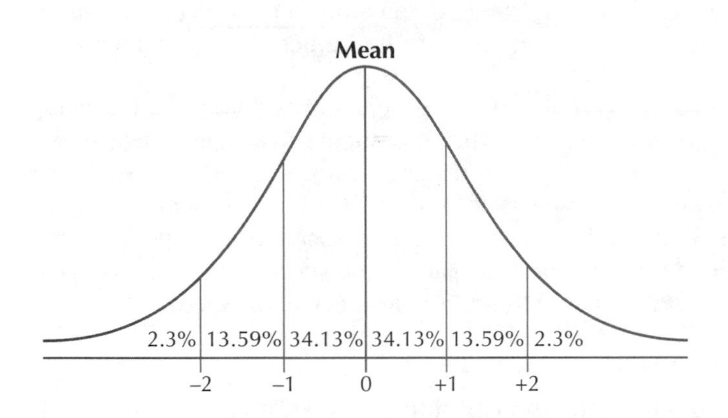

Figure 9.2 Normal Distribution Curve

Teachers who use the normal curve to assign grades in a school classroom make several bold assumptions. First, like other evaluation schemes based on competition among students, the normal curve rests on the assumption that the level of a particular student's performance compared with the average performance of a group of students (usually the student's classmates) is important. Second, use of the normal curve assumes that all students have an equal opportunity to succeed—as though all have equal study opportunities, equal encouragement and help from home, and equal potential, which is extremely unlikely. Third, the use of the normal curve assumes that the number of students used as a norm is large enough to reflect the characteristics of all students at a particular grade level. Unless the class size exceeds 100 students, this is a bold assumption indeed. The use of the normal curve assumes that 68% of the students will earn Cs, 13.5% will earn Bs and another 13.5% Ds, and that 2.5% will earn As and 2.5% will fail. Its use is appropriate only to the degree to which these percentages actually reflect the subjects' distribution.

Box 9.4 shows how standardized test scores can have a very high error rate, using an example of standard error in the field of geology.

Stanine Scores

Stanine (from standard nine) *scores* are derived by using the normal distribution curve to group test scores into nine categories. This modification of the normal curve eliminates the As, Bs, Cs, Ds, and Fs. An advantage of stanine scores is that they remove the stigma associated with letter grades. Another advantage stanine scores have over the normal curve is the use of nine categories instead of the normal curve's five categories, giving the teacher more groups in which to place projects that must be subjectively evaluated. Stanines may become more useful as education reform programs press for the use of more self-evaluation instruments (such as portfolios) and for other qualitative evaluative instruments.

Box 9.4 A Very Standard Error

Let's Ponder

The following passage illustrates the magnitude of the standard of error in geology and demonstrates why standardized test scores often have an equally alarming high standard error.[1] Read the passage, then think about this as you respond to the questions below.

> My friend is a geologist. We were in his backyard, expressing awe at the majesty of the Rocky Mountains. The monstrous, flat, sloping rocks that are the hallmark of Boulder, Colorado, were the subject of our conversation.
>
> "Do you know how old those rocks are?" my friend inquired.
>
> "I have no idea at all," I replied.
>
> "They are about four hundred million years old," he said, "give or take a hundred million years."

1. Do you think the general public is aware of the large standard of error common to many standardized test scores? What evidence can you offer to support your answer?
2. What do educators do that suggests that they do not consider the fallibility of standardized test scores?
3. Realizing that standardized tests frequently have large margins of error, how do you think this should affect a teacher's use of standardized test scores? Explain your answer.

[1] J. Frymier (1979). On the way to the Forum: It's a very standard error. *Educational Forum, 36*, 388–391.

Schoolwide Standards

Even more popular than the normal curve is the practice of schools setting their own standards. Most teachers are undoubtedly familiar with the system shown in box 9.5.

Box 9.5 Traditional Grading Scale

Score		Grade
90% and above	=	A
80–89%	=	B
70–79%	=	C
60–69%	=	D
Below 60%	=	F (Failure)

This type of evaluation makes an important and often false assumption: that the level of difficulty of the test fits the abilities of the students exactly. Student teachers usually realize this error as they begin marking their first set of papers, discovering that most of their students have failed the test. Although the exact percentage used to define the boundaries of each grade may vary from school to school, the system remains a common method of evaluation.

Grading Systems

Since most teachers have considerable latitude in choosing whatever criteria they use to assess grades, all grading, including criterion-referenced systems, is essentially subjective. One question should preface all gradc assignments: What grade will be the best for this student? The answer will be determined, at least in part, by each individual student's ability and by the level to which the student applies this ability. To assign a grade that is higher than deserved is certainly not good for the student, nor is assigning a grade lower than the student has earned.

Obviously, each teacher's philosophy on grading shapes the teacher's choice of grading systems, but having a philosophy of grading is not enough. Teachers must base their choice of a grading system on the information they have at hand, and although this choice significantly shapes the teacher's instructional program, it is seldom appreciated. The best grading practices provide accurate feedback designed to improve student performance (Reeves, 2008). Grading is a sensitive area, one in which the teacher can feel uncomfortably exposed and can be subject to powerful pressures to make decisions that are in conflict with the educator's professional judgment.

A Need for Complementary Grading Systems

A strength of many education reform programs is the fact that they require a combination of types of measurements of student performance. There is no one way to teach every child and there is no one set of standards by which all children can be measured. Performance evaluation and progress grades can be blended. For example, a school that officially rewards improvement by using progress grades along with performance grades can expect fewer of its male students to eventually drop out.

Too often teachers rely on test scores alone to determine student grades. But there is strength in using a variety of criteria to assign grades. The more diverse and imaginative the evaluation activities used by the teacher, the more all-encom-

FYI Blind Grading

Lynn Varner • Delta State University

I choose to have my students submit all of their work with an ID number instead of a name. This way I do not succumb to the "Halo" or the "Pitchfork" Effect, in which the subsequent review of work is biased by the quality of the students' previous work. It sometimes takes a few tries to get them to believe and understand that I really do not want their names on anything they turn in. Eventually, they all come to appreciate and, I believe, trust that I do not tie the names to the papers until after all have been graded. This, along with using a good rubric, has really helped me minimize bias in my grading.

passing and valid the evaluation is likely to be. Including both norm-referenced and criterion-referenced assessments will reduce the chance of students receiving unfair grades.

Ideally, teachers have a variety of activities upon which to base each grade. For example, there may be class projects, presentations, classwork, homework, and tests (Reeves, 2008). Some examples of student performance that could be used to assess the grade at the end of a six-week grading period include:

- six weekly tests
- one final exam
- one term paper
- one oral presentation or term project
- one group project
- thirty homework assignments
- twenty classroom assignments

In order to arrive at a single grade for the six-week period, the teacher can assign equal or varying values to each item on this list. Consideration should be given to the amount of time the student has spent on each activity. Ranking these elements according to the time invested in each, as shown in box 9.6, may simplify this process.

The activities in box 9.6 required 49 hours of student time. To simplify the process, an additional hour of credit can be added to represent class-

Box 9.6 Grade Relative to Time

Activity	Time Required
Homework 30 × 40 minutes	20 hours
Classwork 20 × 30 minutes	10 hours
Group project	6 hours
Six weekly tests at 50 minutes	5 hours
One term paper	4 hours
Oral presentation of project (including preparation)	3 hours
One final exam	1 hour

Box 9.7 Relative Weights of Grade Determiners

Activity	Percentage of Grade
Homework	40
Classwork	20
Group project	12
Weekly tests	10
Term paper	8
Oral presentation	6
Final exam	2
Classroom participation	2

room participation. With a total of 50 hours, each hour spent in an activity could account for 2% of the grade. Thus the percentage assigned to each activity could be as shown in box 9.7.

Suppose the teacher of the class represented in box 9.7 is not happy to have the final exam count only 2% against 20% for classwork. This is no problem—the distribution can be changed (10% to the final exam and 12% to classwork or 5% and 17%, and so on).

The distribution will not be identical from one teacher to another. This does not matter, so long as each grade is based on the chosen system. Criteria other than the time spent on each activity may also be considered when determining the value of each activity, for example, the degree of emphasis given to each topic in class and the degree to which the student has cooperated with other students.

Traditionally, most schools have required students to earn a designated percentage of the possible points to receive an A, B, C, or D. Contemporary educators question this rigid approach, wondering whether such systems will meet the needs of future citizens. Traditional evaluation is not likely to provide the clarity and focus students need.

A Need for Multi-Criteria Grading

Although some reform programs are strengthened by the use of nontraditional evaluations, a major weakness in other education reform programs is their exclusive use of standardized test scores to hold teachers and administrators accountable for student performance. No test has the ability to accurately measure student progress in all desired learner outcomes.

Although the terms *grading* and *testing* are often used synonymously, this is a mistake. Most teachers believe that a student's grade should reflect more than test scores. No test reveals all there is to know about the learner, and no test should be used as an exclusive measure for any student's capacity. Because no single test can measure all a student knows about any topic, and some things other than the acquisition of knowledge are important in school, a variety of measurements is needed. For example, teachers are responsible for seeing that each student develops certain behavioral patterns and attitudes, such as honesty, promptness with assignments, the ability to work with others, and respect for others. Therefore, each of these traits should be reflected in a student's grade. Evaluation of these qualities is essentially subjective, and to avoid becoming prejudiced teachers should decide at the beginning of the year just how much weight these parts of the total evaluation have and take care not to depart from the guidelines they set.

Grades should represent all the major activities in which a student engages while in the classroom. Daily work and term projects may, and perhaps should, carry as much weight toward the final grade for the term as do the tests. The use of several tests (weekly or biweekly), daily assignments, term projects, and daily discussions provides more satisfactory material on which to base the final grade. Good philosophy limits competition and substitutes direct conferences and written evaluations for formal grading systems.

Assignments for Extra Credit

To challenge the most capable students, some teachers include a bonus question on every major test. This is fine, if those who do not choose to answer this question and those who answer it incorrectly are not penalized. Some teachers offer extra credit to students who attend special sessions and complete extra assignments in areas in which they are having difficulties. This practice can also be helpful in motivating students.

When a student asks for an assignment for extra credit at the end of the grading period, however, the student may be less interested in learning than in raising a grade. The student may really be asking, "Will you extend an assignment that failed to motivate me the first time I was confronted with it so that my grade can be elevated?" Sometimes such requests prompt teachers to assign additional problems that the student already knows how to work, or to assign the task of copying hundreds of words from an encyclopedia, library book, or magazine without requiring the student to understand or use the content. This practice is most undesirable, for it encourages some students to procrastinate until the last minute and then subject themselves to X amount of punishment rather than attaining X amount of understanding. Students may also associate the undesirable assignment with the subject and learn to dislike the subject that produced the meaningless assignment.

Decisions on whether to honor students' requests to do extra work for credit should be based on the probability that the student will learn from the task. Savvy

FYI Correcting Tests

Lynn Varner • Delta State University

For short-answer tests like multiple-choice, after the tests have been graded and returned, I often have students find the correct answer in the text. They submit the correct answer, the page number where they found it, and an explanation of why it is the correct answer. I then give them half a point (or some small amount of credit) toward their grade for each answer they find. This moves me closer to my goal of everyone knowing and understanding the material. Those who missed more have more to correct, but they also are able to get more credit. I have found that this helps to increase performance on cumulative examinations, even though the questions are not the same as they were on the previous tests.

teachers may ask the students what type of assignment they propose to do and what they expect to learn from it. If the students can convince their teacher that they can and will learn as a result of the task, the assignment may be warranted.

Performance-Based Assessment

Few innovations in evaluation have caught on as quickly as performance-based assessment. However, there is no unanimity of agreement on its definition. *Performance-based assessment* requires students to create an answer or a product. It is not a new idea. Historically, good teachers have used performance assessment to monitor the progress of their students. Education reformers of the 1990s placed much confidence in performance-based assessment as a means of motivating teachers and students to increase the level of academic attainment. The current enthusiasm for performance assessment reflects a hope that it can drive school reform and improvements in student performance, particularly complex thinking skills. Performance assessments also give a more complete picture of a student's learning over a period of time.

Performance-based assessment exists in many forms. It can require verbal performance (e.g., a voice music major's recital or an oral dissertation defense), writing (e.g., an essay exam), or manipulative skills (e.g., a science laboratory assignment). Performance evaluation is best understood as a continuum of formats that range from the simplest student-constructed response to comprehensive demonstrations or collections of large bodies of work over time.

Another form of performance-based assessment is exhibitions between students or between groups of students. For example, a simulation baseball game can be used in any subject at any grade level.

Performance-based assessment can be defended by the fact that it requires students to go beyond simple recall of knowledge, requiring them to use the newly acquired knowledge. At a higher level, performance-based assessment can provide opportunities and motivation for students to transform meaning. The value of performance-based assessment goes further: Authentic, performance-based assessments can actually drive instructional improvements. This approach is called *measurement-driven instruction* (MDI).

Offering such meaningful advantages as it does, one might think that performance-based assessment would be universally accepted, but it is not. Because performance-based assessment sparks competition, it also sparks controversy, and not everyone favors it; however testing at close and regular intervals is important. The assessment best suited to guide improvements in student learning are the quizzes, tests, writing assignments, and other assessments that teachers administer on a regular basis in their classrooms.

Outcomes-Based Education

No reform practice has drawn more controversy than *outcomes-based education* (or OBE, first discussed in chapter 6). Although to most educators it means simply that educational planning should begin by determining the desired outcomes and should end by having students perform the activities needed to achieve those outcomes, not all people see it so simply. Outcomes-based education is a student-centered, results-oriented design based on the belief that all individuals can learn. However, OBE opponents are concerned that the approach may be lowering the standards for good students. To a degree, OBE may be allowing our best and brightest future teachers to go unchallenged, drifting aimlessly from one undemanding task to the next. But the OBE controversy itself is confusing because the term means different things to different people. The disagreement is not so much over whether to target outcomes as it is over what outcomes we should have.

The concern about the shortcomings of OBE includes not only the fear of failing to challenge students' intellect, as measured by standardized education reform tests, but also the fear of failing to challenge students' creativity. Likewise, teachers' creativity is a human resource that some people fear is being taken from teachers by reformers' testing programs. We must remember that in classrooms throughout the country there are highly educated adults with the potential for creating meaningful learning environments that address the needs of every student. They should be supported and empowered so they can introduce practices that meet the needs of their very singular classroom communities.

Recognizing the need for highly competent teachers, the NCLB legislation provides Title II funds for recruiting and preparing highly qualified teachers and principals. To qualify for professional development support, the district must involve teachers in selecting scientifically-based professional development activities.

Although adding clarity (and therefore meaning) to our teaching is very important, it is just one advantage of using OBE. One common argument for increased use is that in many cases it provides information about students' abilities to analyze and apply information—their ability to think. With the recent emphasis on promoting higher-order thinking, this goal itself is enough to garner the support of many for OBE.

Authentic Tests

Tests designed to cause students to develop those skills measured by standardized tests are called *authentic tests*. Assessment is authentic when it focuses on real performance and mastery of a field of knowledge. Authentic tests get their name from the fact that they test for valuable understanding and that the test activities themselves are valuable. Whether these assessments are called *authentic, alternative*, or *performance,* their common denominator is that they call on students to apply their thinking and reasoning skills to generate often elaborate responses to the problems put before them. Another way to view authentic assessment is "in the context of its application to everyday life." Authentic tests can increase both teacher and student creativity by bringing integrity to learning and are flexible enough to encourage teacher and student activity. Successful authentic testing requires teachers to (1) begin planning by examining the types of skills they wish their students to have, (2) design their tests to meet these aims, and (3) teach accordingly. Authentic assessment doesn't require a major, large-scale curriculum overhaul. For example, a few New Hampshire schools are reducing the number of required Carnegie units, redirecting their instructional time toward more authentic instruction and assessment (DiMartino & Castaneda, 2007).

case study

Integrating and Assessing Critical Thinking across the Curriculum

Janet Moss and Christy L. Faison
Rowan University

Background Information

A small northeastern state attempted to address the challenge of providing a thorough and efficient education for all children while allowing the many independent school districts to maintain local control. Educators from around the state joined with education department officials to develop content standards that would be applied to grades K–12 in all districts. This comprehensive curriculum guide was meant to serve as a source of expectations for individual districts to follow at all grade levels, not as a state-mandated curriculum. In addition to content-specific standards, the state developed five cross-content standards, one of which was "the ability to learn, to reason, to think creatively, to make decisions, and to solve problems." (This standard is the focus of this case study.) To evaluate the attainment of these expectations, the state also developed a series of required assessments to be given at the fourth, eighth, and eleventh-grade levels. Classroom teachers, principals, and curriculum specialists all over the state are now having lively discussions about classroom instruction and how to assess student learning in light of the implementation of these new standards. This case study gives you the opportunity to "eavesdrop" on one such discussion and, like the teachers, debate relevant issues with regard to the use and evaluation of statewide standards.

The Community

The case study takes place in a large suburban district recognized for its educational excellence. The district has experienced rapid growth in the past five years. Due to a very supportive community, the district has been able to match this growth with additional classroom space and personnel. The residents of the district are predominantly professionals who commute to nearby urban areas to work. Many residents are also employed by a local university. The average household income is approximately $55,000. Housing costs range from $60,000 to close to $1,000,000. The population is 48,000, and about 12% of the residents are members of minority groups.

The School

This discussion of standards takes place at a local elementary school (grades 1–5) within the district, which has an enrollment of approximately 600 students. English is the primary language in 95% of the homes. The school enjoys high attendance and low mobility rates. Twenty-seven percent of the faculty hold graduate degrees. Information regarding previous testing at the fourth-grade level is not available due to the newness of the assessment requirement. The school has a dynamic principal known for her instructional leadership, an active site-based council which makes school-level decisions, and a district supervisor of curriculum who is readily available to the teachers.

The Case

Once the state-initiated standards became official, a great deal of focus was placed on understanding them in their entirety as well as at each specific grade level in many districts throughout the state. As a result, numerous in-service sessions, curriculum meetings, and faculty meetings were spent attempting to coordinate efforts for addressing and assessing the standards at the classroom level. To support teachers in this endeavor, state frameworks were created to assist in implementing the standards in each subject area. Not surprisingly, one focus of discussion among teachers throughout the state was the changes in the tests at the fourth, eighth, and eleventh-grade levels as well.

Even though teachers began integrating the subject-specific standards into their thought processes regarding planning and teaching, what seemed to be left out of the initial discourse were the five standards that were to be addressed across all subject areas and at all grade levels. At our chosen school, a third-grade teacher and a fourth-grade teacher were discussing these cross-disciplinary standards to identify what their two grades were covering in relation to the expectations for these standards. The district curriculum supervisor was in the building that day, and she joined in on the discussion. They concluded that this discourse should occur among all faculty members.

After consultation with the principal, an ad hoc committee was formed with one staff member from each grade level (first through fifth) and one representative from among the special area teachers. The principal agreed to sit in on these meetings as a participant rather than its organizer or leader. She believed that the group's potential for success was much greater because the group was started by teachers and run by teachers. The fourth-grade teacher volunteered to organize the meetings; her motivation came in part from her concern that state testing based on the new standards would have a major impact at her grade level. The following description summarizes the first four meetings of this group.

The committee quickly realized that meeting the standards to be addressed in all disciplines and across all grade levels would require a schoolwide effort. They decided to begin with the standard that addressed critical thinking, decision making, and problem solving. They spent the first session discussing the stated expectations of students, sharing examples of critical thinking and creative thinking activities already a part of teaching and learning in various classrooms. Two points emerged. The first was that teachers were already providing instruction across the grade levels in higher-level thinking exercises, but rarely in any uniform manner. The second was that this group should identify a focus of specific topics for future meetings. They generated the following list for discussion at future meetings, knowing that as they progressed, other topics and tangents might seem appropriate to add to the list:

1. What is involved in critical and creative thinking? Do these terms have the same meaning in all subject areas?
2. How should we teach and reinforce critical and creative thinking? Should they be covered at a separate time of the day or integrated into existing instruction?
3. How will we assess whether our students are becoming better thinkers?
4 How will we communicate these efforts to parents?
5. How should our efforts to promote critical and creative thinking be related to state tests?

At the second meeting, the group had a lively discussion about critical and creative thinking. One person saw the two types of thinking as opposites; another believed individuals tend to be better at one than the other. A teacher who did a lot of interdisciplinary instruction with a focus on science found that the state expectations for critical and creative thinking paralleled the scientific method. Another teacher utilized the same steps in teaching her students creative problem solving. The group brainstormed a list of skills associated with critical and creative thinking and came up with over 25 skills. Topping the list were comparing and contrasting, finding similarities and differences, sequencing, classifying, predicting and hypothesizing, seeing things from multiple perspectives, identifying unique alternatives, observing and analyzing, interpreting data, weighing alternatives, making analogies, and making inferences. Everyone agreed that effective decision making and problem solving were broader goals for all students.

Prior to the next meeting, committee members met with other teachers at their grade levels and discussed how to address the teaching of critical and creative thinking. The committee unanimously agreed that teaching specific skills related to effective thinking was important and that decision making and problem solving should be incorporated into every subject whenever appropriate. They also agreed that these skills should be taught within the context of already existing curriculum, not during a separate block of time. The teachers thought it essential for all teachers to help students see how the thinking skills taught in one subject were applicable to others. For example, when a lesson focused on a particular thinking skill or strategy such as comparing and contrasting climates in different regions of the country, teachers would encourage students to reflect on examples of comparing and contrasting earlier in the year in social studies, in another subject, or perhaps in a prior year.

The third-grade teacher suggested that teachers at each grade level brainstorm examples of lessons where they teach or reinforce the major thinking skills that were identified at the first meeting. She thought it would be interesting to see how teachers at lower and higher grade levels address the same skills she teaches. The fifth-grade teacher added that it would be beneficial to hear about specific assignments at different grade levels that included these skills. The first-grade teacher suggested that, at a future meeting, teachers bring in samples of student work that demonstrate effective thinking skills. The members of the committee agreed that a sharing session would be scheduled a month later and be open to all teachers of the school. Perhaps the next step would be to create a matrix of skills introduced and applied throughout the grade levels.

At the next committee meeting the teachers present began discussing how to assess students in the area of critical thinking and problem solving. They knew that this would be just the beginning of discussing this subject. Their prior year's in-service workshops on alternative and authentic assessment would certainly be of value here. The second-grade teacher, who was new to the school that year, mentioned that the sharing session with samples of student work was extremely valuable to him in his understanding of the many dimensions of thinking skills as well as serving as a wealth of creative curriculum ideas. A discussion followed in which committee members debated the value of assessing students on specific thinking skills or on their overall skill in decision making and problem solving. One teacher believed that some of her students were more successful at certain thinking skills in some subjects than in others. She saw this as an opportunity to help her students apply their successes in subjects that they found more challenging, but she wondered how their assessments should address this. Would they assess students' application of thinking skills in specific subject areas or across the curriculum? One teacher thought that it would be interesting to see if there would be a discrepancy in skill level across the curriculum with regard to thinking skills. Another teacher who had been using portfolios in her classroom for a number of years described how this would be a natural method for assessing students' growth in specific thinking skills as well as decision making and problem solving. A second-year teacher asked if she should begin writing specific assessments regarding thinking as she created new lessons that involved a focus on thinking skills. That led to a discussion on formative and summative assessment and what their overall goals were at this time. The committee agreed that they should continue to explore the variety of assessment options available to them and to generate a list to be discussed and prioritized at the next meeting. At that time, the teachers would also discuss piloting different assessment strategies according to grade level or their areas of interest.

Issues for Further Reflection and Application

You have now been appointed to be a member of this committee. Your charge is to respond to the following questions and to be prepared to participate in the next committee meeting.

1. List at least ten strategies you could utilize to assess aspects of critical thinking. Which do you believe would be the easiest to implement? Which do you believe would be the most complex? Why?
2. Since the teachers are revising their instruction in response to the new statewide standards and assessments, does this infer that they are "teaching to the test"? If so, is this a positive or a negative aspect of statewide educational reform?
3. Given the fact that letter grades are used on report cards, how will teachers be able to communicate to parents the emphasis on and assessment of critical thinking?
4. Would you prefer to be on a grade-level team or an interest-based team to develop critical thinking assessments? Why? What would be the advantages and disadvantages of each?
5. How might this case differ if the discussion occurred among middle school teachers? High school teachers?

Suggested Readings

Brady, M. (2008). Cover the material—or teach students to think? *Educational Leadership* *65*(5), 64–67.

Costa, A. L. (2008). The thought-filled curriculum. *Educational Leadership, 65*(5), 20–25.

David, J. I. (2008). What research says about grade retention. *Educational Leadership, 65*(6), 83–84.

Fisher, D., Grant, M., Frey, N., & Johnson, C. (2007/2008). Taking formative assessment schoolwide. *Educational Leadership, 65*(4), 64–69.

Jensen, E. P. (2008). A fresh look at brain-based education. *Phi Delta Kappan, 89*(6), 409–417.

Murdock, S. (2007). *IQ: A smart history of a failed idea.* Hoboken, NJ: John Wiley.

Popham, W. J. (2007/2008). What's "valid?" *Educational Leadership, 65*(5), 78–79.

Roberts, J. (2008). Talent development: A must for a promising future. *Phi Delta Kappan, 89*(7), 501–506.

The case study above concerns standards that cut across subjects and grade levels. As mentioned in chapter 7, integrated themes facilitate constructivist lessons. This faculty believes that the most effective arena for such changes is the entire school. *Effective schools* research supports this theory. Other factors in this case reflect the current understanding of practices that will best promote multiculturalism and constructivist themes. These teachers acknowledged that they were already teaching creative thinking and critical thinking, although not in a uniform way.

Likewise, most schools already use constructivist and multicultural practices. Currently there is a reluctance among many education reform groups, particularly at the state level and particularly among pressure groups, to acknowledge the many good practices that are already in place in schools throughout the country. This reluctance is caused, at least in part, by a feeling that the reform group will not receive full credit for a school's improvement if people recognize that some of the practices were already being used. But teachers and administrators must receive credit for success at their schools. The need to give students and teachers credit for progress is even greater in diverse classrooms, where expectations in the homes and throughout the community can differ significantly from those at school.

Evaluating the Curriculum

Curriculum evaluation involves the procedures for evaluating student outcomes and the curriculum plan. Evaluative data become the basis for decision making and further planning. In the past, evaluation was often delegated to supervisors or outside consultants and the results to administrators who may or may not have communicated the findings to teachers, parents, or the community (Lunenberg & Ornstein, 2004). In the twenty-first century, however, teachers play an active part in evaluating their curriculum. As they become involved in research, their findings give them a unique opportunity to judge the alignment, consistency, and integration of the curriculum in their schools.

Curriculum evaluation also must include assessing the degree and quality of parent involvement (Blendinger, 2010). Today's teachers have a unique opportunity to work together with parents in shaping the curriculum. (See p. 251 for an intriguing account of the positive effects of parental involvement in their children's curriculum.)

Curriculum Alignment and Consistency

Curriculum evaluations should be comprehensive and consistent. Unfortunately, many widely used programs are not being evaluated consistently and comprehensively. In addition to meeting the demands that education reform reports

FYI Creating Improved Test Questions

John Dellegrato • PaTTAN (Pennsylvania Training & Technical Assistance Network)

This is an in-class team assignment. Each team must complete specific assessment items to correlate directly with the reading and writing standards and benchmarks in the following areas:

a. enhanced multiple-choice items
b. essay items—restricted and open ended
c. performance items—to include five-item checklist
d. document-based or visual interpretation items

1. The task will *not* include true-false, fill-in-the-blank, yes-no, or short-answer items (one or two sentences).
2. The task is to be completed during class time.
3. The task is to be collated by one group member and submitted electronically at the end of the course.
4. The actual number of items in each area is to be determined during the first class meeting.
5. The template is to be developed during the first class meeting.

have made with regard to increased ongoing evaluation of the entire school program, evaluating the curriculum provides needed direction, security, and feedback for teachers. Consider, for example, the concept of *curriculum alignment*. Reporting on effective practices used by a dozen education reform programs, Wang, Haertel, and Walberg (1998) noted that all of these programs maximized the use of curriculum and assessment alignment. A faculty that is unaware of this concept is unlikely to align the taught curriculum with the tested curriculum and even more unlikely to try to align the implied curriculum with the taught and tested curricula. If caught teaching test items, these teachers are inclined to invent explanations or excuses to justify this practice.

After visiting the world's leading school system (Singapore), the Council of Chief State School Officers issued a report recommending that U.S. schools follow the model set by Singapore and "Establish or update mechanisms to regularly review and streamline your curriculum" (CCSSO, 2008, p. 10) and reconfirmed the need for frequent, well-planned curriculum audits. Administrators must audit the curriculum by meeting with teacher teams to review which standards were covered (Schmoker, 2007).

Aligning curricula with standards is a better use of time than preparing students to take tests (Anderson, 2009). In Singapore's education system, all crucial aspects of the system—teaching, leadership, curriculum/instruction, testing—are aligned in a comprehensive vision (CCSSO, 2008). When teachers understand the proper relationships among curricula, they are apt to feel good about their efforts and to derive a sense of security from knowing that they are doing what they should be doing.

Involving Teachers in Curriculum Evaluation

While it is clear that teacher involvement increased toward the end of the twentieth century (Latham, 1998), there is evidence that more involvement in curriculum decisions is needed. As education reform and its required restructuring increases, the need for teachers to become involved in evaluating the school's curriculum will continue to increase. Involving teachers in evaluating the curriculum requires early and continuous involvement. To understand the relationships among such curriculum components as philosophy, aims, goals, objectives, content, teacher activities, student activities, and evaluation, teachers must be involved in writing the school's mission statement and in writing their department or grade-level goals, so that they can see how the components are interrelated and understand the basis on which all curriculum decisions are made (i.e., the school's philosophy).

Needless to say, historically most teachers have not been involved continuously with shaping the school's written philosophy. Nor have teachers been involved continuously in relating their grade-level objectives to the objectives in their subjects at the grade levels that immediately precede and follow their own grade level. Although this book has reported on teachers' failure to use research in the past and their failure to use the knowledge base on testing and evaluation, this is not an attempt to engage in teacher bashing. Such practice for its own sake would prevent the success of education reform efforts the book promotes. Teacher education programs must share any blame directed at teachers, for they have failed to prepare teachers to conduct research and thus fail to provide an adequate knowledge base on evaluation and testing. The point of mentioning these shortcomings again is to stress the critical need for teachers to develop curriculum evaluation skills.

A Need for Curriculum Integration

Teachers' inability to expand their understanding of the curriculum either vertically (to grades above or below their own) or horizontally (to other subjects) without working with other teachers at these levels is obvious. This process is discussed further in chapter 11, but it must be understood that although effective curriculum evaluation begins in the classroom, it must spread throughout the school. Curriculum evaluation cannot occur in isolated classrooms. Each individual teacher's curriculum must *always* be assessed in relation to the school's overall mission. Developing a mission statement, as discussed earlier in this book, is a major undertaking in itself. Weller, Hartley, and Brown (1994, p. 298) explain: "Developing vision, that seemingly mystical and sometimes elusive concept, is the most important element in making any organization highly effective in promoting quality products."

The CIPP Model

One of the most popular curriculum evaluation models developed in recent years is the *CIPP model* shown in figure 9.3. (CIPP is an acronym for *context*, *input*, *process*, and *product*.) A Phi Delta Kappa committee chaired by Daniel Stufflebeam developed this comprehensive model. Context evaluation involves defining the environment of the curriculum. This part of the model is similar to the concept that Beauchamp (1981) called the *curriculum arena* in his curriculum theory model. It includes a needs assessment. The input part of the CIPP model involves determining appropriate and available resources to use to attain the objectives. Process evaluation is an ongoing monitoring of the evaluation to detect flaws. This information is used to revise the model. The evaluation stage refers to assessing the product to determine whether to continue the use of the model.

Evaluating Curriculum Components

Another way to evaluate a curriculum is to examine each of its components, beginning with the institution's mission statement (see box 9.8 on p. 326).

The Mission Statement

Perhaps the most underappreciated and certainly the most underused curriculum component is the *mission statement*, which reflects the institution's philosophy. The mission statement serves as a rudder to steer the ongoing curriculum. Usually dusted off and tinkered with only at those periods just preceding an accreditation visit, the school's written philosophy is then quickly put back on the

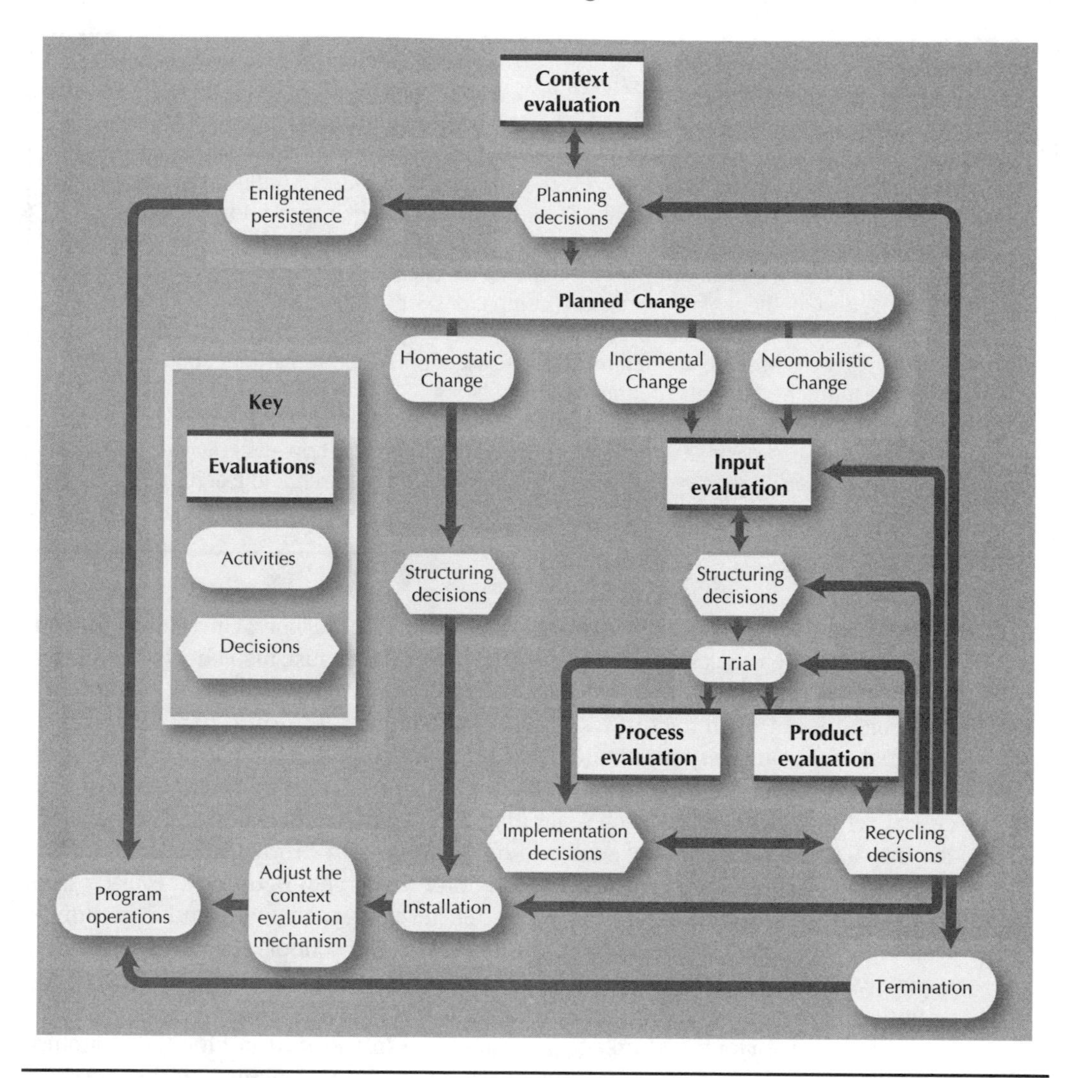

Figure 9.3 CIPP Model

shelf and thought of only as a document. As Schwahn and Spady (1998, p. 47) have reminded us, "Planning, compelling purposes, and inspiring visions mean nothing until something different and better happens for children."

A school's philosophy, as stated in its mission statement, should give rise to the curriculum's aims (remember the Cardinal Principles) and goals (remember No Child Left Behind). In most states, reform efforts are strong enough to require an evaluation and revision, if necessary, of a school's philosophy. Interestingly, the philosophy affects all components, and these components have an impact on the philosophy.

Curriculum evaluation is multidirectional. In figure 9.3, the lines with arrows on both ends show an energy flow in both directions; consequently, the element on

Box 9.8 University Mission Statement

Eastern Kentucky University shall serve as a residential, regional university offering a broad range of traditional programs to the people of central, eastern, and southeastern Kentucky. Recognizing the needs of its region, the University should provide programs at the associate and baccalaureate degree levels, especially programs of a technological nature.

Subject to demonstrated need, selected master's degree programs should be offered, as well as the specialist programs in education. The elimination of duplicative or nonproductive programs is desirable, while development of new programs compatible with this mission is appropriate.

The University should continue to meet the needs in teacher education in its primary service region and should provide applied research, service, and continuing education programs directly related to the needs of its primary service region.

Because of the University's proximity to other higher education and post-secondary institutions, it should foster close working relationships and develop articulation agreements with those institutions. The University should develop cooperative applied research and teaching programs using resources such as Maywoods and Lilley Cornett Woods and Pilot Knob Sanctuary.

each end of the arrow affects and is affected by its counterpart. Curriculum evaluation, then, is not a simple, one-way, linear process. The figure also shows an uninterrupted circular flow, representing the continuous nature of curriculum evaluation.

The amount of impact of each part of the curriculum on other parts can be minimal, or it can be monumental. For example, consider the effect that one part of society, such as the economy, has had on today's curricula. The success of education reform practices in each state hinges on that state's economy. Or consider the impact that a federal law such as Public Law 94-142 (now P.L. 101-476, *Education for All Handicapped Children*) has had on the curriculum in every school in the country. Influenced by the economic level in each state and community, technology is having varying degrees of impact on the schools. Innovative teaching practices and their accompanying philosophies (such as mastery learning or the nongraded primary program) can reshape an entire curriculum.

Several major curriculum components were introduced in chapter 5, including curriculum sequence, continuity, scope, articulation, balance, and coherence. Now let's return to these components to examine the role that each plays in curriculum evaluation.

Curriculum Sequence

The curriculum *sequence*, the order in which objectives, content, and activities are presented, can significantly determine the level of difficulty or ease with which students can comprehend the content. The attainment of some objectives would be impossible without first attaining some prerequisite objectives. Parallel sequence among schools prevents disruptions for students who move from one district to another. The children of migrant farm workers exemplify the need for consistency in sequence. When curriculum sequence is disrupted, continuity cannot be maintained. Lack of sequence can also cause unintentional redundancy and omission.

FYI A Curriculum Timeline Tune-Up

Carol Ritter • Sam Houston State University

Many states provide the entire yearly curriculum to the schools and school districts. However, it is up to these districts and schools to break down the curriculum into logical, teachable skills that can be mastered by their students and to choose when each topic will be taught. Just as our cars need tune-ups to run properly and not leave us stranded on the highway, our written curriculum should be tuned up yearly to ensure student success.

The Curriculum Timeline Tune-Up (CTT) uses test data to determine when the curriculum should be taught throughout the school year. It should begin each year as soon as the assessment scores are returned. The total scores of all students in each grade and subject should be analyzed. The state assessment should be examined and the curriculum skills that were tested should be identified and organized into mastered skills and skills in need of improvement. The written curriculum timeline should then be changed yearly to better meet the needs of these students. This is a simple process of looking at when the skills were taught during the previous year and then changing the curriculum timeline for those skills in need of improvement. For example, if students in the district did well on a curriculum target, that target should be kept in the same place and time in the curriculum's timeline. However, if students did poorly on another target, then it should be taught at a different time spot during the following school year.

The time frame to teach, and for students to master, several curriculum targets should be broken down into time frames of two or three weeks. Teachers then know exactly the amount of time they have for their students to master this section of the curriculum. While they can review during the year, they must go on to the next two-week window in order for all essential knowledge and skills to be taught before the test. Some curriculum should be taught several times during the year, not just right before the test is given.

This avoids having some topics covered after the test. (Students were not taught the curriculum until after the test had been administered, but they were held responsible for the content on the test!) Complete this process yearly and scores will improve.

Curriculum Continuity

Continuity is the absence of disruptions in the curriculum. As noted in chapters 5 and 7, learning is strengthened when connections are made (Hewett, 2004; TIMSS, 2003). Failure to maintain continuity contributes to learning difficulty. To illustrate the need for continuity, consider the difficulty in remembering the following letters: NISEYLANNAPV. These letters lack continuity because they also lack sequence. There are two reasons why a curriculum lacks continuity: either it lacks sequence or it has gaps. The letters in our example lack sequence. Ordered correctly, they are much easier to remember: PENNSYLVANIA.

Curriculum Scope

Curriculum evaluations should also examine the curriculum's *scope*, which refers to its breadth; it is a horizontal dimension or a snapshot of the curriculum.

For example, one might wish to examine the number of subjects a middle school curriculum offers at the eighth-grade level. Or when helping a high school student plan his or her curriculum for the senior year, the counselor might examine the number of subjects the student would have on Tuesday. Curriculum evaluation should consider, in addition to the number of subjects in a curriculum, the variety or breadth of content that each offers.

Curriculum Articulation

Curriculum developers want to be sure that each part of the curriculum fits the other parts. This "smoothness" quality is called *articulation*. When evaluating the curriculum for its articulation, the curriculum developer examines both the vertical dimension (through the grades) and also the horizontal dimensions (across the grades).

Curriculum Balance

One of the most important characteristics of any curriculum is *balance*. The balance of a curriculum should be examined from several perspectives. Since most schools have some graduates who enter the world of work, care should be taken to offer a balance between college preparation courses and vocational or business courses. College entrance examinations measure both quantitative and qualitative abilities, so care should also be taken to offer a balance between quantitative subjects such as mathematics and the hard sciences and qualitative subjects such as English, social studies, and the fine arts. Since good health requires exercise, each curriculum should offer some types of physical education.

Even within the disciplines, care should be taken to offer a balance of subjects. For example, the hard sciences curriculum is often expected to offer some physics, chemistry, biology, and earth science. A junior-high earth science curriculum might be evaluated to ensure that it contains some geology, oceanography, meteorology, astronomy, and physical geography. Although some education reform programs are stressing the need to integrate the curriculum, increased integration of the disciplines will not negate the importance of balance among the subjects offered.

Curriculum balance is equally important to each student's individual curriculum. The need for a "well-rounded" education reflects a history of concern for curriculum balance.

Chapter 7 described a teacher who taught 28 times as much science as a colleague who did not feel comfortable with science. The education reform reports have consistently recommended more science and mathematics for public school curricula. Perhaps the imbalance of these subjects from one classroom to another will be rectified by their recommendations; however, most reform reports have consistently ignored the fine arts. Contemporary teachers and other curriculum directors have a shared responsibility for protecting these subjects and thus contributing to the maintenance of balance in the curriculum.

Curriculum mapping, a procedure for collecting data about the operational curriculum in a school and in a district about the instruction that students are experiencing (Perkins-Gough, 2004, p. 12), can help to create and maintain curriculum balance.

Curriculum Coherence

A common flaw in curricula is the failure to connect or relate the components to each other. As stated earlier, the aims must flow from the philosophy or mission statements, and goals must flow from the aims. Such relationships among the curriculum components is called *coherence*. Achieving coherence requires collaboration among teachers (Clark, 2004).

An example that illustrates the common lack of coherence occurred in a college that offered a course in music appreciation. Some students elected the course because they wanted to increase their understanding and appreciation of classical music; others elected it because of its reputation for awarding an easy A. The word spread about the course's reputation for being easy, and adjustments were made to the course. Rigid, objective, pencil-paper exams were administered. Dissatisfied and discouraged with their first scores, some students dropped the course. Of those who remained, few students earned an A. Ironically, most students exited the course having developed a disdain for classical music.

FYI Paraphrasing: Let's Do It Right!

Jane Irons • Lamar University

In addition to avoiding plagiarism, when done correctly paraphrasing broadens your view of a subject and brings interest to the unknown. A paraphrase converts a source's words into about the same number of your own words. I use the following process to teach paraphrasing:

1. Read the source several times.
2. Outline the passage.
3. Rearrange your outline.
4. Write your paraphrase.
5. Read your paraphrase carefully—you should have about the same number of your own words as those included by the source.
6. Add the appropriate citation.

Evaluating School Reform

School reform (or education reform) inevitably involves changing the curriculum, for by doing so reformers can shape the nature of schools and, indeed, of entire communities. Cuban (1993, p. 183) explained the impact that curriculum change can have on society at large: "To change the curriculum is to fiddle with important values in American culture."

The primary tool for evaluating school reform has been and continues to be standardized exams. Forty percent of the public supports the current amount of standardized testing (up 11% from the prior year), 43% say there is too much testing, and 15% say there is too little testing (Rose & Gallup, 2007). By 2008, those corresponding numbers were 37% and 23%, indicating that more citizens are beginning to favor extensive testing (Bushaw & Gallup, 2008). But parents are far less supportive, with 4 out of 10 saying there is too much testing and only 1 out of 10 saying there is too little testing. About two-thirds (66%) of the public choose to continue reforming within the schools. (For a suggested activity to help teachers sort out the good and bad reform and build a vision for their school, see Robinson, 2010.)

School Transformation

Education reform is not easy, yet it can start at the top, at the bottom, or wherever someone has the energy and commitment to work to make it happen. The type of reform required to transform many schools into highly performing institutions is systemic reform, which Armstrong and colleagues (2009) define as "the belief that significant improvement requires simultaneous change in all parts of the system" (p. 378). Another good definition of systematic reform is *everybody changing everything.* According to Schlechty (1990, p. 8), "Change can be most effectively implemented when those whose energy, commitment, and goodwill are needed to support the change believe in, understand, and support the change."

True education reform requires effecting substantial changes in the schools, and evaluation is needed to determine when schools need change. Evaluation is essential to avoid the dead-end trap of rhetoric that characterizes so much of today's "reform." It is also needed because transformation itself is often part of the rhetoric and, when applied to schools, its meaning is unclear.

School transformation involves more than changing the curriculum. Goodman (1992) says that school transformation is partly ethereal, referring to its temporary nature and also to its emotional or attitudinal quality. Like curriculum itself, *school transformation* should be defined at each school. Following are some questions that can be used to determine whether your school has been transformed.

- What kinds of questions do we want our students to ask?
- What kinds of attitudes do we want our students to have?
- What are the desired values that our faculty agrees should be promoted at our school?
- What is the teacher's role in promoting attitudes?
- How can we help our students develop the sense of efficacy required for success?
- How does our faculty define true success?
- What is the future of our culture, and how can our curricula be adjusted to prepare students for the future?
- What barriers do our schools present to minority students, and what adjustments are needed to help them cope with these barriers?

- What types of desirable and undesirable attitudes, beliefs, and behaviors does our evaluation system reward?
- What kinds of real passions should our school promote, and how can we adjust the curriculum to promote them?
- What kinds of values does our school's hidden curriculum promote?
- What currently unused resources does our community have that can be tapped to achieve our school's major goals?
- What evidence of constructivism can be seen in our school's curriculum plan?

Paul Gorski (2009) identifies six stages of multicultural school transformation (see box 9.9).

Box 9.9 Stages of Multicultural School Transformation

Status Quo

Traditional educational practices are maintained with no critique of existing inequities in any aspect of the school or the education system. Curricula, pedagogies, counseling practices, and all other aspects of education continue to reflect primarily white, male, upper-middle class, Christian, and other privileged perspectives and approaches.

Heroes and Holidays (Food, Festivals, & Fun)

Small changes to curricula or classroom materials focus exclusively on surface-level cultural traits, often based on generalizations or stereotypes. Multicultural education is practiced as an international food fair or a celebration of a particular representative of a group. Students make headdresses or tomahawks to learn about Native American culture. Teachers purchase and display a poster of a famous woman or African American figure (usually during the paralleling history "month").

Intercultural Teaching and Learning (Cultural Dictionary)

Teachers study the customs and behaviors of the cultures from which their students come in an attempt to better understand how they should treat those students. They may have a handbook that describes how they should relate to African-American students, Latino students, Asian American students, Native American students, and other groups based on an interpretation of the traditions and communication styles of those particular groups.

Human Relations (Why-Can't-We-All-Just-Get-Along)

Members of the school community are encouraged to celebrate differences by making connections across various group identities. Teachers show an enthusiasm for learning about "other" cultures beyond the Intercultural Teaching and Learning approach, drawing on the personal experiences of students so that the students learn from each other. Diversity is seen as an asset that enriches the classroom experience.

Selective Multicultural Education (We Did Multicultural Education LAST Month)

Recognizing the inequities in various aspects of education and the need to address them, teachers and administrators initiate one-time or temporary programs. They might call together a town meeting to discuss racial conflict or hire a consultant to help teachers diversify curricula. They might create a program to encourage girls to pursue math and science interests. This approach is usually reactive—in response to a particular issue or critique that has become public.

(continued)

Transformative Multicultural Education (Social Justice and Equity Education)
All education practice begins with a determination to make all aspects of schools and schooling equitable and to ensure that all students have the opportunity to reach their full potential as learners. All educational practices that benefit whites, males, the upper-middle class, or any group to the detriment of other groups are transformed to ensure equity.

Another term that is closely related to transformation is *restructuring*. Schlechty (1990, p. xvi) defined restructuring as "altering systems of rules, roles, and relationships so that schools can serve existing purposes more effectively or serve new purposes altogether."

Measuring school transformation requires getting beyond surface answers. *Retreats* are a valuable transformation evaluation tool, because they offer opportunity to assess difficult-to-measure feelings and impressions. Retreats give teachers time to think deeply about important questions such as the purpose of school. For example, Goodman (1992) reported that, at the beginning of a two-day retreat, one fifth-grade teacher responded to the question "What is the purpose of the fifth-grade curriculum?" by saying that it was to prepare students for the sixth grade. At the end of the retreat, the same teacher said that the purpose of the fifth-grade curriculum was to prepare students to live in a democracy.

Conclusion

Following is a summary of some of the advances made and concerns raised about the topics discussed in this chapter.

Advances

- When used correctly and consistently, tests have the power to increase learning substantially.
- Used regularly, formative assessment can be a means of meeting the needs of minority-group members.
- When kept separate from accountability, standardized tests can be used to enhance instruction.
- Clear objectives can help teachers meet the needs of at-risk students.

Concerns

- Teachers have been slow to embrace formative testing.
- Many educators and education critics claim that the needs of minority students have largely gone unmet.
- Standardized tests often impede teachers' efforts to meet the needs of all students.
- No single method can help all students learn.

In the past, teacher education programs have neglected to prepare teachers to construct, administer, and score tests. Most programs that require a measurement or evaluation course offer a course that deals almost exclusively with standardized tests, ignoring teacher-made tests.

Education reform has stressed accountability as measured by student performance on standardized exams. Education reform is also stimulating the restructuring of the school's curriculum. Maximum success with this process requires teacher involvement in evaluating the total curriculum. Effective evaluation is continuous and comprehensive, covering all parts of the curriculum. Teachers have often been accused of teaching to the test. Today, teachers are taught to align the taught curriculum with the tested curriculum.

Historically, most tests used in elementary and secondary schools were summative tests administered at the end of the teaching unit. Today, teachers are learning that a far more powerful tool to promote learning is formative tests, which are administered prior to and throughout the unit and which can promote learning by improving instruction, study skills, and the curriculum.

Instead of using objective test scores exclusively as grade determiners, as has been a common practice, schools are being encouraged to use a combination of test scores and portfolios or other subjective criteria.

Curriculum evaluators should examine such qualities as articulation, balance, continuity, scope, and sequence; these must be tied to the school's philosophy or mission statement. The mission statement should produce the curriculum's aims, and the aims should produce the goals, which in turn produce the objectives. Unfortunately, the philosophy and mission statement have often been overlooked.

Teachers in multiculturally or socially or academically diverse classrooms must discover alternative ways to recognize achievement, both academic and social. The community at large may hold grades or scores on national or statewide exams as the ultimate purpose of schools; therefore, educators must relate the goals and objectives to the school's mission. They should periodically question the goals of the local, state, and national reformers.

Additional Learning Opportunities

1. Why must teachers become more knowledgeable of curriculum evaluation?
2. What relationship should exist between the curriculum and the school's testing program?
3. Why have teachers ignored formative evaluation, and why is this important?
4. Why is criterion-referenced evaluation more appropriate for use in elementary and secondary schools than norm-referenced evaluation?
5. What impact is education reform having on testing, and how should teachers respond?
6. What advantages do progressive reporting systems have over traditional testing?
7. Why do curriculum developers need evaluation models?
8. Indicate which of the following curriculum elements relate to the vertical curriculum and which elements relate to the horizontal curriculum: scope, sequence, articulation, continuity, balance, coherence.

9. What general advice would you give beginning college students to help them plan their curricula?
10. Why is continuous curriculum evaluation necessary?
11. Is it ever acceptable to sacrifice one discipline to achieve excellence in another? Why or why not?
12. If a school invested all its resources and time in academics at the expense of a physical education program, would that practice be more acceptable than Hillsboro Middle School's curriculum (see the opening vignette)?
13. When economic recessions occur, usually the first program to be eliminated is fine arts. Is this practice acceptable? Why or why not?
14. What do you suppose could have motivated the faculty members at Hillsboro to shape their curriculum as they did?
15. The current education reform programs are pressing for more math and science. What precautionary measures should school personnel take to ensure curriculum balance?
16. How does competition affect the attainment of multicultural goals?
17. What criteria can be used to evaluate a curriculum for its constructivist strengths and weaknesses?
18. Can the results of a norm-referenced test provide information about whether a student has mastered particular content? Why or why not?

Suggested Activities

1. Draw a diagram to show your own concept of the CIPP evaluation model and, for each part, write a descriptive paragraph.
2. Draw a chart to contrast formative and summative evaluation according to when they occur and according to their purpose.
3. Make your own portfolio. Include at least *five* of the following six items: (a) formative test, (b) summative test, (c) objectives, (d) essay test, (e) your philosophy of evaluation (how you believe it should and should not be used), and (f) a sample simulation you will use to teach a future lesson.
4. Identify the two curriculum elements that you believe are most important and write a paper giving the reasons for your choices. Explain how each element can be used to develop and maintain (a) a constructivist classroom, and (b) a multicultural classroom.
5. Identify the major strengths in your curriculum model and identify relationships among its parts.
6. Critique your school's curriculum and explain any recent effects of educational reform efforts on its multicultural goals.

chapter ten

PLANNING AND CONVERTING CURRICULUM INTO INSTRUCTION

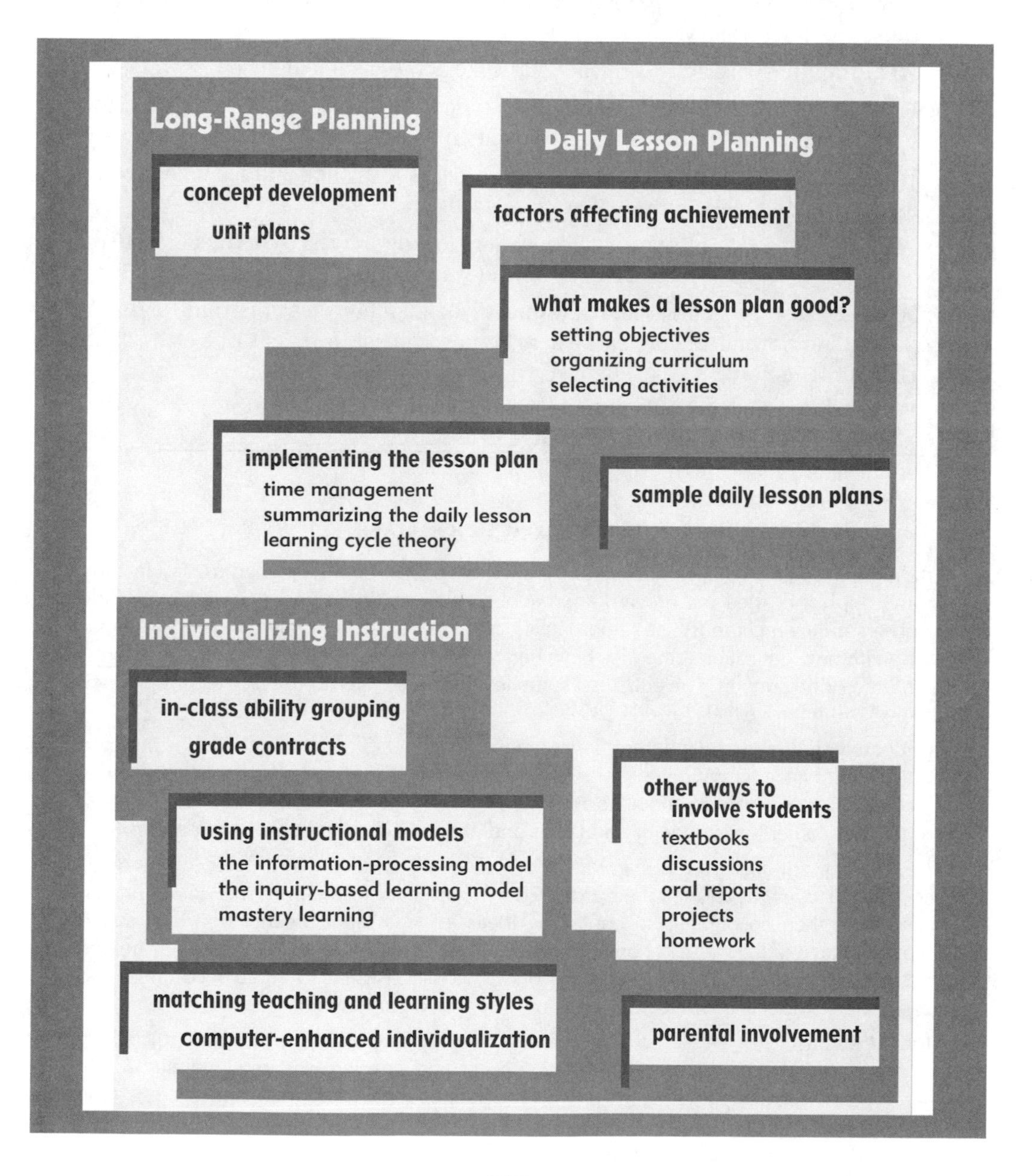

Focus Questions

1. How would you explain the relationship between curriculum and instruction?
2. How might you ensure that the major concepts in each lesson will be understood by all students?
3. How might you plan to prepare students to discover new concepts and relate those to existing knowledge?
4. What multipurpose activity might you use to achieve some daily objectives?
5. What difference do token rewards and student involvement have in promoting interaction among students from different cultures?
6. What are some guidelines for assigning students to groups and for using group assignments to meet individual student needs?
7. What are some elements you would include when developing a contract to be used with students whose needs differ significantly from those of their classmates?
8. What are some qualities and advantages of matching teaching and learning styles, and how might you use style matching to meet the needs of a class of at-risk students?
9. How have recent local reform practices reflected constructivist theory?

A Wichita School Case

Traditionally, many teachers throughout the country have been expected to stay in their rooms, apply the "tried and proven" approaches, and keep things under control. With little or no encouragement to try new approaches, many teachers who have chosen to experiment with new educational theories have had to do so in the isolation of their classrooms, with little or no support. Nevertheless, some teachers are eager to use any technique they believe will improve their lessons.

Fortunately, today most districts are encouraging teachers to experiment. Such is the case here in Wichita. One Wichita junior high school teacher attended a district in-service meeting where he learned about learning styles theory. He then invited a consultant from the teacher center to visit one of his classes and explain the concept to his students.

The teacher administered a learning-style preference questionnaire, and the students scored the survey, developed their profiles, and shared the results with the class. The students were then encouraged to contribute ideas for classroom organization that would take advantage of the variety of preferred learning modalities within the class. They helped set up areas where students could hold discussions and listen to audio recordings and areas where students could read or work on written assignments.

Student enthusiasm soon spread, and parents became interested, so at a parent meeting the teacher explained the learning-styles concept and how he was implementing it. He then administered the survey to the parents and helped them interpret the results regarding their own preferences. To demonstrate the use of styles management and thus earn potential support, the teacher began using the parents' learning styles when he conducted parent-teacher conferences.

The results of this experiment were very positive: Student–teacher shared planning increased, and tolerance for others' learning differences increased. Parent-teacher conferences became more effective, and soon other teachers began experimenting with the concept in their classrooms.

Because innovations often require additional facilities, materials, space, and program flexibility, success requires the support of administrators, teachers, students, and parents, all of whom must understand the importance of the change. A simple approach is first to inform others about the process and then to involve them with the innovation.

Districtwide implementation of an innovation shows support for the change; therefore, teachers who can persuade the district office to try a new approach are academically empowered. The teacher must establish the credibility of the proposed change. First, the teacher should provide evidence that the approach is effective. The literature can be used to show the success other teachers or districts have had with the innovation. Also, the teacher might ask permission to try the innovation at the classroom or department level, collecting test data to show whether the new approach is effective compared with the approach currently in use.

• • •

Experienced teachers know that many variables affect learning, including students' natural interests, skills, and aspirations. What captures one student's attention might not affect another, and further complicating the challenge, what appeals to one student today might miss the mark tomorrow. Some students learn best in the mornings; others learn best in the afternoons. Kahlil Gibran (1923) said of the teacher, "If he is indeed wise he does not bid you enter his house of wisdom, but rather leads you to the threshold of your own mind." The first step in meeting the needs of learners is to understand how they learn.

Strategies of Curriculum and Instruction

This book began by examining a variety of definitions of *curriculum*. Although the perceptions of curriculum are many and diverse, the ultimate purpose of curriculum is universally accepted: All curricula exist to provide the basis for effective instruction, that is, instruction that maximizes learning. To the degree that any curriculum succeeds in improving instruction and learning, that curriculum is successful; conversely, any curriculum that fails to improve learning cannot claim success. This interpretation of the role of the curriculum, predicated on the assumption that all children can learn, makes the curriculum accountable for the academic success of all students. An effective curriculum and effective instruction require effective planning.

Teachers are an often neglected group in the planning process. In addition to requiring pedagogical and content databases, maximum academic attainment requires providing teachers with time to collaboratively plan interdisciplinary curricula with their fellow educators. Most planning is done without the input of other teachers, but collaborative planning changes the way teachers view their subjects. The presence of a partner or other group members may cause each teacher to explain her ideas, elaborate on her thinking, or attempt to articulate misgivings, concerns, and hunches left unsaid or not pursued in solitary planning.

Another group to include in curriculum planning is parents, because of their vested interest in the schools and their ability to influence students positively. The recent popularity of school-based decision making has intensified the need to include parents in all aspects of schools, especially academics. Research has consistently indicated that parent and family involvement is critical to the academic success of many children. If parental involvement is to increase achievement, this involvement must occur during planning.

This chapter begins by examining long-term curriculum strategies, followed by daily lesson planning. The chapter ends with a discussion of ways to adjust the curriculum to meet individual student needs.

Long-Range Planning

Long-term or *long-range planning* is often a defining attribute that distinguishes between the approaches of novice teachers and those of more experienced teachers. Whereas experts are engaged in long-range planning, the novice's approach is more short-term in nature, focused on preparation.

The research indicates that when teachers increase their understanding of content and methodologies, student achievement also increases (Davis, 2010). Maximum academic attainment requires teachers who have both a firm grasp of their content areas and a repertory of effective teaching strategies. For example, planning is richer and more successful when it stretches both horizontally across the disciplines and vertically from week to week and month to month—even year to year. Some schools permit their teachers to follow their students from year to year. This process, called *looping*, is most common between grades eight and nine and then between grades nine and ten.

Concept Development

Recall from chapter 5 the highly acclaimed international study of mathematics teaching (CCSSO, 2008), which reported that the high-performing Asian students spent far more time making connections among major concepts than U.S. students do. Sometimes students need help in focusing on the major concepts in a lesson, and a badly crafted curriculum can cripple learning. The decline in performance on standardized tests may be the result of the way our students store information. To be able to use newly learned information, students must see how the new information relates to a larger whole as they learn it.

Just prior to or at the beginning of a lesson, teachers may ask questions, present a simple outline, or give students a few key words to help them focus on the major concepts. Such strategies, called *advance organizers*, can be an effective means of gaining student attention and directing it to the lesson. Armstrong and colleagues (2009) say that advance organizers help students sort out fragmented pieces of information and help students clarify the purpose of the lessons. Students who read and paraphrase an advance organizer prior to study are able to answer more lower-order and higher-order study questions than students who do not encounter the organizer.

When they begin with an advance organizer, teachers can take several actions to help students identify and become familiar with each lesson's (or unit's) major concepts. Whether a learning unit or lesson begins with a story or an assignment, the advance organizer can be used to help students focus on the major concepts. The advance organizer may be in the form of questions for students to listen and look for in the lesson. In a follow-up discussion, the teacher can ask students to tell what they observed. Then the students are asked for examples and nonexamples of the concepts. The procedure is as follows:

1. Present a nominal definition of a concept and give examples.
2. Emphasize the common attributes and ask students to name further attributes.
3. Ask students to generate examples.
4. Have students give totally opposite examples (nonexamples).
5. Have students name metaphors to compare and contrast with the original idea.
6. Have students review contexts in which the concept takes place.
7. Describe the overt application of the concept.
8. Identify factors in the environment that facilitate or hinder the application of the concept.
9. Formulate an operational definition involving the last steps of this process.
10. Discuss consequences in terms of viable solutions to a given problem.

Just understanding concepts is not enough: Instruction must focus on the use of the concepts and the context in which they occur in order to ascertain their practical connotations. Students must be given opportunities to reflect on and experiment with concepts (Stinchfield et al., 2007). Giving students this responsibility helps them develop their own conclusions. Concepts and principles in a discipline are not taught—they are learned, and they are not understood in isolation. Grasping what a concept or principle means depends in considerable part on recognizing how it functions within the discipline. This requires a sense of how the discipline works as a system of thought.

Science teachers in Australia and Japan carefully develop just one or two concepts during a lesson. Activities and discussions preceding the introduction of the major concepts provide a vehicle for discovering and understanding them. Mary Culver shares an activity (on the following page) that she uses to help her beginning teachers lead their students to discover the big ideas in their lessons.

One method that teachers can use to help students apply concepts is the *case study* (Levine, 2007), which enables students to separate relevant information from irrelevant information. In doing so, they can gain a clearer grasp of the concepts. The case-study method of teaching provides learners with opportunities to strengthen their critical thinking and to become more deeply engaged in their learning. This method, which presents students with either a real-life or a fictional situation, is a student-centered, problem-centered approach. Good cases always conclude with a problem to be solved by students and require them to sift through

FYI Ice Cream: Ah-ha or Uh-oh?

Mary Culver • Northern Arizona University

I've seen the same chemistry class experiment in two separate schools. Both teachers were excited about it, and both sets of students were really engaged and enjoying the lab. They were making ice cream in plastic bags and coffee cans. In one school, I asked the students what ice cream had to do with chemistry, and student after student told me about freezing point depression, sodium ions, endothermic processes, and so on. At the other school, the same question produced shrugged shoulders, don't know's, and "ice cream's good!"

What does all this have to do with curriculum? It's the "ah-ha!" moment—the event that students should have during an effective lesson, unit, and course. "Because I said to learn it" is not enough to motivate students to "get" the lesson. I share this scenario with my curriculum leadership students, and then "challenge" them to come up with an "ah-ha!" for their favorite lesson. This is assigned as homework. When we next meet, students present their favorite "ah-ha!" moments to the class. We conclude with discussion on the challenge of finding the "ah-ha" for one great lesson, and we brainstorm ideas for them to motivate teachers to find, create, and deliver the "ah-ha" for every lesson they teach.

irrelevant and relevant information to make judicious decisions. Once the relevant information is identified, students must organize it to give it new meaning (Henson, 2010).

The Unit Plan

Chapter 6 focused on setting appropriate aims, goals, and objectives, and chapter 7 focused on selecting the appropriate content and activities needed to reach those aims, goals, and objectives. To do so requires a long-term plan, or *unit plan*.

Unit planning should be a joint effort by the teacher and students, whose roles in curriculum planning are obviously different. Teachers' extensive study of their subjects gives them insights into what students need to know about the subject of the unit (which students by the very nature of their role cannot have).

Involving students in planning a unit can lead to more meaningful activities and to the forming of a cooperative social environment, enriching the quality of learning in the classroom. Student involvement helps avoid the sequential approach that often limits learning. Because the ordinary classroom does not provide this richness in learning and, in most instances, limits what the brain can do, students become habituated to this limited, sequential approach. Involving students can also increase their emotional commitment to the material, enhancing their learning of that material. If students are engaged in learning activities, as opposed to remaining passive, both sides of the brain will participate in the educational process regardless of the subject matter. Experiential curricula (discussed in chapter 4), the curricula that actively involve students, also have been found to motivate students to voluntarily associate with members of other cultures, whereas token reward systems have failed.

An important part of the teacher's role in planning a unit is to help students select activities necessary for learning the content. This does not mean that the teacher selects some of the activities and the students independently select other activities. When presenting the option of selecting class activities, teachers should have on hand a list of activities from which the class can choose and should permit students to add activities that are feasible, safe, and consistent with school policy. Student interest in a particular activity may in and of itself make that activity worthwhile by raising the level of motivation in the class.

Parts of the Unit Plan

The learning unit, or unit plan, is much more than an outline of the subject material to be explored within a certain topic. Although there are many variations, most unit plans contain a title, a statement of philosophy, the purposes/goals/objectives, and the content to be covered. Unit plans typically include teacher and student activities to enhance the attainment of the objectives, and a method of evaluating the degree of understanding developed while studying the unit (see figure 10.1). Learning units should include certain practical information, including the title, subject, grade level, and a list of resources—consultants, equipment, facilities, and supplies—needed to teach the unit, especially audiovisual aids. Learning units should also include a list of resource materials and people (consultants), and a bibliography or reference list that support the unit and can be used to pursue the topic further. Each unit should contain performance objectives that (1) are stated in terms of student behavior, (2) describe the conditions, and (3) specify the minimum acceptable level of performance.

Figure 10.1 Anatomy of a Learning Unit

A *statement of philosophy* is a declaration of a teacher's beliefs about such issues as the purposes of the school, the nature of youth, how youngsters learn, and the purposes of life in general. Because some teachers spend too little time reflecting on their beliefs about these all-important issues, the philosophy statement is perhaps the most neglected part of learning units. The first question teachers hear at the beginning of a new unit (or perhaps the question students most often ask themselves) is "Why do we have to study this stuff?" Only by thinking through these broad issues can teachers prepare to answer this question intelligently.

The *statement of purposes* is a list of general expectations the teacher has of the unit. For example, the general expectations of a tenth-grade unit in government may include an understanding of how a bill is introduced, increased tolerance of the opinions of others, or an appreciation of democracy as a type of government. Unlike the performance objectives used in daily planning, which are stated in specific, observable, and measurable terms, the purposes for a unit should be general.

The *selection of content* for any unit should be based on four broad considerations: (1) the significance of the content in attaining the purposes of the particular unit (in other words, it must be content that is necessary to master in order to reach the general objectives), (2) the importance of the content to society, and (3) the needs and interests of the learners. The NCLB legislation adds a fourth criterion for selecting activities: Teachers are now required to cite data to support or defend their chosen activities.

When *selecting activities*, teachers need not feel obligated to choose one activity for each objective, for some of the best activities serve multiple purposes and lead to the attainment of several objectives. For example, one activity for a senior English class might be to write a composition contrasting Shelley's poetry with that of Byron, which would provide students with opportunities for both gaining writing skills and sharpening concepts of an author's style by contrasting it with that of another author. Planning activities that have multiple objectives does not necessarily promote inefficiency. Each learning unit should include different types of measurement, such as written tests, oral tests, debates, term projects, homework assignments, classwork, and perhaps in-class performance or group discussions. This type of evaluation, which examines the quality of a product, is called *product evaluation*. Portfolios are increasingly popular for this purpose.

Another type of evaluation that can be applied to each learning unit is called *process evaluation*. This is a description of the effectiveness of the teaching of the unit. Process evaluation analyzes the various parts of the unit in isolation to determine whether the unit needs improvement. It also involves looking at all parts together to see how they relate to one another. Teachers should ask themselves such questions as: Is my philosophy sound? Does it convince these students that the unit is important? Are the purposes and objectives important? Am I being realistic in expecting students to achieve them in this length of time? Is the content in this unit sufficient to achieve the unit's stated purposes? Are the unit activities helpful in attaining these objectives? Is the evaluation fair to everyone? Does it discriminate between those who have met the objectives and those who have not?

Sample Unit Plans

Following are several sample unit plans. The title of each unit describes the unit; the statement of purpose or objectives describes a desired change in the students; and the evaluation is related to the objectives stated at the beginning of the unit.

The unit plan in box 10.1 was chosen for its brevity and simplicity. This does not make it a superior plan, but such brief units are often used. Perhaps the unit is too skimpy. What would you say about the format? Is the outline adequate? Figure 10.2 (on p. 344) shows the parts commonly found in a unit. Notice that some of the parts in figure 10.2 are not included in the sample unit given in box 10.1.

The meteorology unit has neither a statement of philosophy nor a statement of rationale to show the significance of the unit. Many educators feel that a statement

Box 10.1 Unit Plan—Meteorology

Meteorology Unit Plan: What Meteorology Means to You

I. Purpose

A. Knowledge: To understand—
1. The different types of weather
2. The principles of weather formation
3. The role of the weatherperson
4. The names and principles of commonly used weather instruments
5. Weather vocabulary

B. Attitudes: To appreciate—
1. The damage weather can do
2. The advantage of good weather
3. How weather affects our daily behavior
4. The rate of accuracy of weather predictions
5. The precision use of weather instruments
6. The fallacies of superstitions about the weather

C. Skills: To develop the ability to—
1. Read and interpret weather instruments
2. Read and interpret weather maps
3. Predict future weather

II. Daily Lessons

A. Definition of weather

B. Precipitation
1. The different types of precipitation
2. How each type of precipitation is formed

C. Reading the weather map

D. Reading weather instruments

E. Predicting weather

F. Effects of geographic location on weather

G. Effects of the earth's rotation on weather

H. Effects of the earth's tilting on weather

I. How to change weather that can hurt you

III. Materials

A. Weather reports from newspapers

B. Weather maps

C. Equipment for making fog: air pump, water, jar

D. Barometer, thermometer, anemometer, wind vane

E. Graph paper for each student

IV. Evaluation

Tests for each section of the unit: approximately one test per week's study of the topic

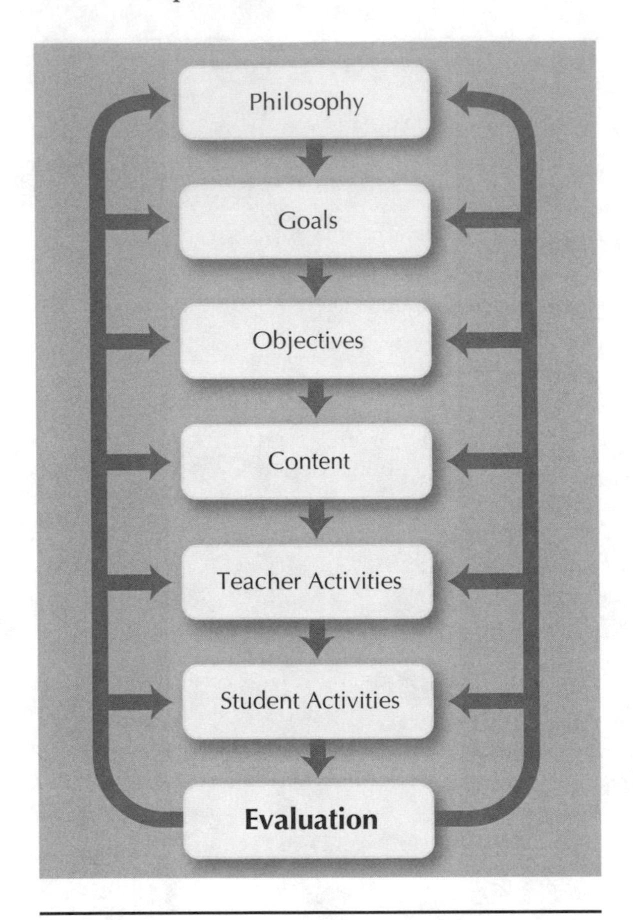

Figure 10.2 A Learning–Teaching Unit

of philosophy is needed to help teachers clarify their basic beliefs about life, school, adolescents, and how adolescents learn. Goals and objectives should coincide and should reflect the teacher's basic beliefs. Other educators prefer to have a statement of rationale instead of a statement of philosophy. By writing a *statement of rationale*, teachers justify the unit to themselves; then they can use the rationale to convince students that the unit is worth their time and energy.

The meteorology unit has no sections titled "Teacher Activities" or "Student Activities." This is unfortunate, because at the time of planning the unit the teacher should make decisions about activities, such as taking the class to a weather station and showing films on meteorology. The weather station may need advance notice, and for field trips students will have to identify in advance what information they will attempt to obtain during the visit. Films must be scheduled and ordered in advance so that they will be available when they are needed, and time will be required to preview them. You can probably identify other weaknesses in this unit plan.

Box 10.2 contains a sample chemistry unit designed for use in an eleventh-grade class. This more comprehensive plan has fewer weaknesses because it has most of the parts that educators consider essential to any unit. Examine its strengths and weaknesses. Pay particular attention to the unit's overall structure and organization, and you will probably be able to improve it.

Daily Lesson Planning

As essential as they are by themselves, aims and goals remain no more than elusive generalities. Making them attainable requires designing *daily lesson plans* that include general expectations (goals) that can also be translated into more specific terms. Each daily lesson plan should be developed to achieve a particular part of the unit—in fact, most units contain a series of daily lesson plans.

Box 10.2 Chemistry Unit

Chemistry Unit Plan: The Organization of Chemistry

I. Statement of Purpose: The chapters covered in this unit are designed to introduce the beginning chemistry student to the basic background and structural knowledge needed for further studies in chemistry. Topics include Atomic Theory and the Periodic Table.

II. Performance Objectives

A. Chapter I: Atomic Theory. The eleventh-grade general chemistry student will be able to—

Lesson 1

1. Define an atom correctly in a closed-book test.
2. Give the size of an atom in the unit posttest.
3. Identify the parts of an atom by name and describe them, given an unlabeled diagram of the atom. Four or five parts must be correctly labeled and described.
4. Match the mass of the parts of the atom to the correct path, given a list of masses.

Lesson 2

1. Define the atomic number of an atom.
2. Define the mass number of an atom in a closed-book test.
3. Utilize the concept of isotopes by correctly grouping given atoms into isotopic groups.
4. Apply the concept of energy level shells by designating the number of electrons in each shell, given an atomic number.

Lesson 3

1. Correctly define atomic mass in a closed-book test.
2. Define Avogadro's number in a closed-book test.
3. Apply the concept of a mole by the amount of a substance in a mole of a given substance.
4. Define the atomic weight of an atom in a closed-book test.
5. Apply the concept of atomic number, Avogadro's number, mole, and gram atomic weight in solving simple stoichiometric problems. Given the problem and required information, the student must solve for the asked-for information, correctly answering 80% of the problems to receive credit. (Partial credit given for correct setups.)

B. Chapter 2: Periodic Table. The eleventh-grade general chemistry student will be able to—

Lesson 1

1. List at least three of the four basic elements.
2. Identify the common elements by symbol. This will be shown by correctly giving the elements or symbol asked for in 15 of 18 questions in two in-class quizzes.

Let's Talk

Each performance objective should contain four parts. Check the above objectives against these criteria. It is as simple as A, B, C, D.

Audience:	The student should be the subject of each objective.
Behavior:	The student's behavior should be the verb of each objective.
Conditions:	The objective should describe the conditions under which the student is expected to perform.
Degree:	The degree or level of performance required of the students should be specified.

Lesson 2

1. Obtain atomic numbers of elements from the periodic table with an accuracy level of 80%.
2. Obtain the mass number of elements from the periodic table with an accuracy level of 80%.
3. Obtain a given element's electron configuration from the periodic table.

Lesson 3

1. Define periodic law.
2. Define "group of elements."
3. Define "period of elements."
4. Distinguish the characteristics of families of elements by matching the correct family with the given characteristic with a minimum accuracy level of 80%.
5. With 80% or above accuracy, match the correct family with the given element.

(continued)

III. Attitudinal Objective. The eleventh-grade general chemistry student will be able to participate in class discussions. This objective will be met when 80% of the class answers general questions, directed to the class as whole, during the course of the discussion.

Let's Talk
Following are lists of concepts and content generalizations under topics to be studied. A check to see whether students know these terms can help the teacher begin at the appropriate level. The second list—generalizations—is even more important. These are the major understandings that should come from the unit. Notice that they are essential for achieving the preceding objectives.

IV. Concept and Generalizations

A. Topic 1: Atomic Structure

Concepts	*Generalizations*
Atomic theory	Atomic theory has been developed to support observations.
Atom	Each subparticle composing the atom (electron, neutron, proton) has certain characteristics and is unique in energy levels or shells.
Proton	
Neutron	
Electron	Each atom has its electrons arranged.
Nucleus	
Element	
Mole	
Avogadro's number	
Angstrom A	

B. Topic 2: Arrangement of Electrons in Atoms

Concepts	*Generalizations*
Orbitals	Quantum numbers describe the orientation of an electron in an atom in terms of (a) distance from the nucleus; (b) shape; (c) position in space with respect to the three axes (x, y, z); and (d) direction of spin
Orbital notation	
Electron configuration notation	
Electron dot notation	

C. Topic 3: Periodic Table

Concepts	*Generalizations*
Periodic table	The periodic table organizes the elements; properties can be predicted from the element's positions. Elements with similar arrangements of outer shell electrons have similar properties.
Series (period)	
Group (family)	
Noble gas family	
Sodium family	
Calcium family	
Nitrogen family	
Oxygen family	

Because the teaching unit is usually content-oriented and may not specify the experiences needed for learning each day's lesson, daily strategies are required to help students move nearer to the unit goals. For most teachers, the daily lesson plan is the most organized approach. Like a map, the lesson plan gives direction to the lesson objectives. If the lesson begins to stray, the lesson plan brings it back on course. Staying on course is difficult without a lesson plan; however, despite the emphasis teacher education places on the ends-means approach, there is much evidence that many teachers, even experienced teachers, do not begin the planning process by determining objectives. Even when teachers modify their teaching approaches, they seldom consider the lesson objectives.

Factors Affecting Achievement

Several factors should be considered carefully in lesson planning because of their affect on student achievement. Instead of teaching the concepts needed to understand their subject, teachers of the same subject and grade level may cover very different materials. The amount of *engaged time* teachers spend on a topic or concept compared to the time that is allocated for the subject affects achievement. The disparity between schools in the allotted time in which students are engaged in their subjects is enormous.

Another factor that affects achievement is the time students spend identifying and developing particular concepts, as opposed to the time they spend just studying the concepts. As we have stressed throughout this book, compared to students in those countries that perform highest on standardized exams, our students tend to cover *more* concepts but spend less *time* on each concept. For example, a TIMSS video study found Australian and Japanese teachers teaching only one or two concepts per lesson (Roth & Garnier, 2007).

In the developmental portion of a lesson, students should spend time discussing such issues as why the concept is true, how skills or concepts are interrelated, and how to use broader relationships to estimate answers to problems. In other words, developmental time should put the important concepts and skills in a broader context in order to extend the students' understandings of those ideas.

Another variable that has been studied for over 50 years to determine its effect on achievement is class size. Although the research shows the positive effects of smaller classes to be minimal, the cumulative effect may be significant over time. One advantage of smaller classes is improved teacher morale. Additional research is needed to determine the effect of class size on the level of student participation, since participation directly correlates with achievement and since over the years the research results have been mixed.

Traditionally, clear concepts in each discipline, and effective models and strategies for teaching them, have not been available because they have not been identified. Methodological advances have outpaced conceptual advances, but there is hope, because more studies that identify important concepts in disciplines are being conducted today; and there is an increase in metacognitive studies, which will help determine more effective ways to teach students to analyze their individual conceptual development processes.

What Makes a Lesson Plan Good?

Lesson plans come in many sizes and varieties, and the length or style of a lesson plan does not make one plan better than another. A good lesson plan can be a comprehensive outline that is worded formally, neatly typed on bond paper, and enclosed in a plastic binder, or it can be a brief outline written in pencil on 3- by 5-inch cards. The styles of good lesson plans vary as much as their length. A good lesson plan contains material that will challenge and engage students throughout the class period with activities that involve every student, using a format the teacher can follow without having to stop the lesson to read it. Planning sufficient time for learning each concept allows students to engage in different kinds of learning experiences (TIMSS, 2003). By the same token, if a lesson is not capturing the students' attention, teachers should take short detours to pursue tangential topics that capture their attention.

Setting Objectives

Planning a daily lesson should begin with the teacher asking such questions as: In what ways do I want this lesson to change my students? What will they be able to do as a consequence of the lesson? When stated at the outset, these proposed behavioral changes can give direction to daily activities. Writing performance objectives was the focus of chapter 6.

Organizing Curriculum

Chapter 5 provided assistance in organizing material. Having decided what material to include in the lesson, the teacher must next decide on the sequence in which students will experience it. Sometimes the nature of the subject dictates the order of presentation, so the teacher should check the major ideas to be covered to determine whether there is a natural sequence. For example, a physical education teacher who wants to provide experiences that are essential for learning to drive a golf ball will think, "What ideas are important to understanding this process?" The answer is: "Addressing the ball, the backswing, the downswing, and the follow-through," which is a natural sequence. A lesson on how to bake a chiffon

FYI The Chalkboard, Dry-Erase Board, and Active Board

Robert C. Morris and Dawn Putney • University of West Georgia

Take a look at your classroom. Do posters, attendance sheets, job charts, and seasonal decorations cover a large portion of your chalkboard? Are bookshelves or computer tables blocking access to your chalkboards?

In an effort to integrate technology, many teachers are neglecting the chalkboard or its modern counterpart, the dry-erase board or active board. Don't hide these boards—they can be vital tools for learning. Teachers have learned that students gain confidence and skills by coming to the board each day. Handwriting is a skill that requires guidance and practice. When students complete handwriting worksheets at their desks, it is difficult for teachers to monitor the work and correct errors as they occur. The large surface of the chalk or dry-erase or active board offers room for students to practice lettering where teachers can easily observe and guide students' work.

As students solve math problems or write sentences on the chalkboard, teachers can give positive corrective feedback. Write lesson objectives, new vocabulary, page numbers, and other important class information on the board, as well, to focus students' attention and to remind them. Boards—whether they be chalk, dry-erase, or active boards—can provide yet another place where both students and teachers can communicate.

cake would follow the sequence of the recipe. A history teacher, too, would prepare many lessons involving historical events taught in chronological order.

If the four or five objectives of a day's lesson have no natural order, perhaps a particular sequence would make the lesson more easily understood. For instance, a chemistry teacher would probably not teach the formula of a compound until the students had learned to recognize the symbols of the elements contained in the compound.

Selecting Activities

Generally, more emphasis is placed on activities than on content, because today's educators recognize that classroom activities are major avenues for learning. For this reason, a lesson plan must describe those activities the teacher expects to use to teach the content. Because students learn more when they participate in lessons, each lesson plan should provide meaningful activities.

At this point the teacher should review the partially completed lesson plan. A statement of how the lesson should change the students—that is, the objectives of the lesson—has been made. Some major ideas to be developed have been selected and organized. The next step is to plan involvement by assigning a task that will require the students to use each of the major ideas in the lesson. Questions can be used as advanced organizers to focus students' attention on the lesson and improve student achievement.

The English teacher who is planning a lesson on "How to Capture the Reader's Attention" would assign tasks that make the students use what they have just learned. Presented with several compositions, the students could be asked to identify the principles of capturing the reader's attention each time they occur. Later in the class period, each student could write the lead paragraph of a composition, employing the techniques of capturing the reader's attention introduced earlier in the lesson.

The physical education teacher who wants to teach the correct procedure for driving a golf ball may demonstrate each step and ask students to identify mistakes that the teacher deliberately makes in each phase. Eventually, the students go through the process themselves, while other students critique. A vocational shop teacher would follow a similar process, as would math, science, history, English, music, and art teachers.

Each of these activities is an assigned task that requires students to do things they could not do correctly unless they understand the content taught in the earlier part of the lesson.

Alexandra Fahner-Vihtelic (2006) has identified 16 components to ensure successful lesson planning. A lesson that engages her students will

1. be well planned;
2. have all materials prepared in advance;
3. be interactive and hands-on;
4. appeal to students' interests;
5. include the use of visuals and manipulatives;
6. be challenging yet still allow students to succeed;

7. have age-appropriate objectives;
8. include positive motivation;
9. feature a "hook" to pique interest or to make the lesson personal;
10. use a variety of learning styles;
11. link to prior knowledge;
12. be taught enthusiastically;
13. have clear expectations set;
14. include sharing and/or closure;
15. allow for student reflection; and
16. include a variety of assessments.

Implementing the Lesson Plan

The results of any lesson are likely to be no better than the daily lesson plan, yet the lesson plan does not guarantee learning success. Even the best plans may need modification as the students interact with the materials and activities. Prolific planning may be counterproductive if the teacher becomes single-minded and does not adapt the lesson to the students' needs. As teachers develop planning skills, they should consider ways to alter their plans in case the plans are not effective with a particular group at a particular time.

Time Management

Although many educators recognize that the key to leading students to become capable thinkers is to provide them time to reflect on their learning, many teachers resist this practice because they are already expected to cover more content than they have time to cover. Almost inevitably, teachers' use of classroom time has been blamed for declining achievement in America's schools. Perhaps what teachers need is better time-management skills. Technology can help save both teacher time and learner time. By using a digital learning system, teachers can create a digital lesson and post it on the system for their students and fellow teachers to see, making it instantly available (Mills, 2007). Researchers now talk in terms of allotted time, engaged time, and academic learning time.

The well-planned assignment takes time to design. Benefits accrue not only for teachers themselves but also for students as they take on the responsibility and challenge of a well-planned assignment. Effective teachers can distinguish between important information and other information and can simplify these major concepts for their students; less effective teachers attempt to deal with more issues. Because beginning teachers often lack the ability to simplify and make sense of classroom events, the time spent identifying the major principles and concepts in a discipline will be a wise investment.

An important time-management skill is to learn to say no. If teachers are having trouble finding the time to plan effective lessons, when asked to fill in for a friend on a committee or assignment, they should say either "I'm sorry, but I'm tied up at that time," or negotiate: "I'll be happy to, if you will take my place selling football tickets Friday night." With practice, these strategies will become natural

FYI Time Management

Donna McCaw • Western Illinois University

When I give students a small-group or cooperative group activity to complete, I tell them the number of minutes they have to complete their work. The amount of time that I give is half of whatever I anticipate it will take to successfully complete the assignment. Due to the sense of urgency, this gets them immediately engaged.

For example, if the activity should take 15 minutes I tell them that they have 7 minutes to complete the task. At 7 minutes I check to see how many are done (no one ever is) and then I graciously grant them 5 more minutes, check again and then add additional time as needed. If I had told them, up front, that they had 15 minutes, the groups would chit-chat among themselves for 4–5 minutes. Only with prompting from me would they begin to profitably use their time.

and easy, and colleagues will learn to find an easier target elsewhere, thus leaving teachers with more time for lesson planning.

Summarizing the Daily Lesson

The lesson plan should end with a review of the main ideas covered in the lesson, but the summary should not include every detail, nor should it merely list the main parts of the lesson. A good way to summarize is by having students name analogies and metaphors, and compare and contrast these with the original idea. The review should show the relationships among the major ideas, tying together the parts of the lesson.

Returning to the earlier example, the physical education teacher planning a lesson on how to drive a golf ball would include in the review each of the major ideas—the address, the backswing, the downswing, and the follow-through—and go over the major issues related to each. The review would begin with the first idea—how to address the golf ball—and include the major points involved in the proper address as they were mentioned in the lesson. Likewise, an English lesson on "How to Capture the Reader's Attention" would include each point and its development.

While reviewing can help students make essential connections, this does not imply that the more time spent on a concept, the better. This is probably true *only* up to a point of diminishing returns. It is believed that a major, indeed if not *the* major, reason that U.S. students underperform their Asian counterparts is because U.S. students spend much more time repeating procedures they have already been taught (Gonzales, 2008).

Learning Cycle Theory

One instructional theory uses a learning-cycle approach to instruction to help students move through the levels of understanding in lessons. The *learning cycle theory* has three parts: exploration, concept introduction, and application. The hands-on introduction enables students to develop descriptive and qualitative understandings. The concept introduction stage lets them talk about their experiences, with the teacher or in cooperative learning groups, where the teacher guides the discussion. During the application phase, students are given assignments that let them apply the concepts in different ways.

Teachers should guard against making assumptions about what students know. They must provide a procedural structure that tells students in advance what they are going to do, what the key points are, and what they should know when the lesson is completed.

Sample Daily Lesson Plans

Boxes 10.3 and 10.4 show some sample daily lesson plans. They differ in style, but each contains a few major ideas and is arranged in a sequence that facilitates learning. Note that each major idea is followed by an assigned task that requires students to use the idea. Note also that each sample lesson ends with a review that ties together the major ideas in the lesson.

The best curriculum planning seldom occurs when teachers are isolated from their colleagues. The following case study by Resta, Nelson, and Huling describes a school that has been converted into a learning community. As you read this case, consider the type of leadership that is needed to energize a school community.

Box 10.3 Daily Lesson Plan—Business

I. ***Title of Lesson:*** How to Read and Analyze a Newspaper's Financial Page Effectively

II. ***Reason for Lesson:*** To show how a stock exchange allows people to put their capital to work whenever and however they choose

III. ***Points to be reviewed***
   A. What common stock is
   B. What common stock means to an issuing corporation
   C. What common stock ownership means to the investor
   D. Advantages and disadvantages of common stock

IV. ***Content and Activities***

Content	*Activity*
A breakdown of the different headings contained in the stock quotes.	Each student will be asked in advance of my explanation as to their meanings.
The prices will be analyzed as to what they actually mean.	Different prices will be put on the board with students giving the answer in dollars and cents.
Actual examples from a newspaper will be analyzed as to their meanings in relation to other stock quotes.	Each student will recite the quotes from a newspaper handout and will tell what they mean.

Summarizing the concepts:

V. ***Evaluation:*** A simple quiz on the material just covered and the review work will be given. A simulated paper quote will be provided to test whether they understand all the aspects of the heading and the prices contained in the quotes.

VI. ***Assignment:*** They will be given a project of keeping the daily price quotes of a particular stock, which will be turned in at the end of the week and evaluated. Each student will be assigned a different stock.

Box 10.4 Daily Lesson Plan—Speech

1. **Title:** "How to Use *Time* When Reading with Expression." Establish set by reading a poem ("Richard Cory") aloud as monotonously and ineffectively as possible, with no pauses or variation in speed.
2. **The essential concepts of time:** pause, rate, duration. Introduce these concepts (pause, rate, and duration) in that order because we go from time where no words are involved to time that involves several words, down to time that involves just one word.
3. (a) *Pause*—the pregnant space of time when no sound is uttered, the dramatic pause after a heavy statement—give an example; the anticipating pause—slight hesitation before key word, often used both in dramatic and comedy punch lines—give an example.

   (b) *Duration*—the amount of time spent on just one word. Used for emphasis and imagery. Show how one can stretch out a single word and how it highlights the meaning of a passage.
4. **Assignment:** Go around the room and have each one say, "Give me liberty, or give me death," using the three concepts of time for more expression.
5. **Summary:** Read the same poem ("Richard Cory") as in beginning, only read it well and with expression. Then ask class if they've heard it before. Tell and then show how important the proper use of those three concepts is for effective communication. In the second reading, demonstrate how those three concepts worked.

In The George Lucas Educational Foundation's *2009 Readers' Survey* (2008), educators voted for the best Web site from which to download free lesson plans. For a list of the winning Web sites and reviews of the material offered, visit http://www.edutopia.org/print.4072.

One measure of a successful unit plan is gauging the level of student engagement and enthusiasm. Susan Black (2003) provides this checklist for assessing engaged learning:

- Are students able to select resources and strategies thoughtfully and apply them to unfamiliar tasks?
- Are students excited about their learning and eager to spend extra time and effort?
- Are tasks complex and designed for students to stretch conceptually and take greater responsibility for learning?
- Do students have frequent opportunities to get to know and work with all students?
- Are groups formed for specific purposes, and are they re-formed as needs require?
- Do students have time to explore "uncharted territory?"

case study

Reenergizing a School in a High-Challenge Environment

Virginia Resta, Sarah Nelson, and Leslie Huling
Texas State University–San Marcos

Background Information

Demands for high academic standards coupled with high-stakes accountability systems make schools an increasingly stressful environment for teachers and administrators. Schools that serve large percentages of students who are Limited English Proficient or who are from poor socioeconomic backgrounds are high-challenge environments, and educators at these schools are especially susceptible to stress and burnout. Frequently such schools experience high rates of teacher turnover, which in turn compound the challenges faced by the educators and students whom they serve. Many such schools have found themselves in a downward spiral that is difficult to reverse. Yet, some high-challenge schools have avoided this fate and can serve as a model to other campuses aspiring to overcome the challenges they face. Analysis of these campuses and the strategies employed by those who lead them can provide a useful road map to other committed educators. It is in this spirit that we embark upon the journey to Houston Elementary in Austin, Texas.

The Community

In 1976, Houston Elementary School opened its doors to the children of Dove Springs, a new subdivision on the southeastern edge of Austin, Texas. Surrounded by pastures and void of commercial development, Dove Springs offered first-time home buyers the promise of country living in the city. The young professionals and military personnel who built homes in the community were strong supporters of public education. They eagerly sent their children to Houston Elementary and were actively involved in the life of the school. This strong parental support, coupled with a dedicated and experienced staff, quickly made Houston a vibrant place of learning.

By the early 1990s, the circumstances in Dove Springs had changed. The military base was shuttered. Many of the original residents had moved to other parts of the city. Rental property with absent landlords dominated the neighborhood, and the pastures that once lured people to the area became vacant lots strewn with litter. The lack of city services that was a purposeful part of the subdivision's design became barriers for the new families who often had no transportation and little money. More disturbingly, gangs moved into the neighborhood and the area became one of the highest crime zones in Austin.

Predictably, this dramatic transformation of the community had a significant impact on the school. As the neighborhood changed, the student population at Houston Elementary shifted from predominately white and middle class to 90% minority and poor with a 30% mobility rate. School personnel struggled to help families access health and social services that were not available in the neighborhood. Student achievement declined and discipline problems escalated. In response, many teachers who had been at the school since it opened transferred to other campuses. The novice teachers who took their place did not stay long. By 1990, up to one-third of the teachers were leaving the campus each year. These factors, coupled with the pressures of the state's high-stakes accountability system, created a highly stressful school climate.

In spite of the challenging circumstances, the staff of Houston Elementary was determined to reenergize the school so that Houston would once again be an inviting place to teach and learn. By working with partners across the community, they did just that.

The Case

Through collaborative leadership, Principal Sarah Nelson encouraged a proactive stance to the many challenges facing the faculty and staff at Houston Elementary. She worked with the faculty to identify aspects of the school that they felt were problematic, and together they sought solutions. Teachers were involved in deciding the needs of the school and in finding and implementing steps to address those needs. They quickly recognized that many of the challenges they faced required resources beyond what an already thinly stretched school budget could provide. They set to work on an aggressive agenda to find business, community, and university partners who could provide extra resources for the school. As each new partnership was added, the faculty and staff gained confidence in their ability to change the school in positive ways that improved the school for teachers and students alike. Following are examples of the types of partnerships that brought much needed resources to Houston Elementary.

- At the beginning of the effort to revitalize the school, the campus looked barren and somewhat neglected. Repeated efforts to beautify the campus through landscaping failed, because vandals would tear up gardens and steal newly planted trees. In 1997, Larry Schultz, a PK teacher, formed a partnership with Tree Folks, a nonprofit organization dedicated to improving the environment by planting trees in public areas. Each year for four years, Tree Folks donated between 12 and 15 trees to the campus. Larry got the entire school community engaged in this project. Each year, after new trees were planted, the school held a celebration during which the trees would be adopted by particular grade levels. As part of the science curriculum, the students were actively engaged in planting and caring for the trees during the school year. During the summer, families in the community took turns watering the trees to ensure they made it through the heat. Although a few trees have been lost to drought-related disease, only one has been lost to vandalism. After the campus had a sufficient number of trees, this project evolved into development of a butterfly garden complete with koi pond, crushed granite pathways, and a decorative iron fence to enclose it. Parents helped with this project by planting and weeding as well as raising money for the installation of the pond, pathways, and fence. The garden won a "Keep Austin Beautiful" youth project award.
- Pat Jones, first-grade teacher, had an interest in science and felt that the textbook-driven instruction did not fit with what she knew as best practice. She began investigating science programs and found one of the most outstanding programs, Full Option Science System (FOSS), a research-based science curriculum for grades K–8 developed at the Lawrence Hall of Science, University of California at Berkeley. (FOSS is also an ongoing research project dedicated to improving the learning and teaching of science.) During the summer, she went to UC Berkeley's Lawrence Hall of Science to receive training in the FOSS curriculum. While there, she developed a partnership that resulted in other Houston teachers receiving the training and Houston becoming a pilot site for the FOSS curriculum. This eventually led to Houston being the first elementary school in Austin ISD to have a science lab and to have several teachers who became national trainers for FOSS.
- Several teachers had young children. High-quality day care was not available close enough to campus to allow teachers sufficient time to drop off their children and get to school on time. The teachers decided to start a day-care facility on campus. Working with business partners, the teachers created a child development center of the highest quality. The center has been in operation since 1998 and is a strong factor in recruiting and retaining teachers.

- Patti Adams, a school nurse, was instrumental in getting the Skippy Mobile Health Clinic to select Houston as a regular service site. Because Patti worked so closely with the Houston families, she knew of the tremendous struggles they had in accessing health care. Patti brought the needs of the school to the attention of the Skippy staff and successfully lobbied to have Houston designated as a service site. Skippy offered families a wide range of health-care services (e.g., physicals, inoculations, prescriptions) on a sliding scale. This service was critical, because no health-care services were available in the neighborhood.
- Teachers were concerned that the needs of students from migrant families required attention beyond what the faculty was currently able to provide. They were able to establish a partnership with St. Edward's University. Through the partnership college students, themselves children of migrant workers, serve as mentors to the migrant students at Houston. The mentoring program was supported by a grant from Americorps to St. Edward's University.
- Houston hosted the first "Only the Best" staff development conference in 1997. The conference was started as a way to bring teachers from several campuses together to hear from national curriculum experts. The conference has evolved to include more than 350 teachers from five central Texas districts. Presentations became a mix of national experts and local educators. Publishers sponsor the conference by providing door prizes, providing speakers, and paying for a catered lunch.
- Working with various Even Start grants, Houston created a parent education program. The program included ESL, GED, and citizenship strands in addition to the required parenting workshops. One of the participants in this program completed the GED and ESL classes, then went on to earn certification, and is now a teacher at the school.
- Recognizing the many positive initiatives taking place at Houston Elementary, Texas State University College of Education invited Houston to host one of its field-based blocks for preparing undergraduate preservice teachers. The block integrates three teacher preparation courses that are taught by college professors on the school campus. Preservice teachers spend two full days per week on the school campus, half of the day in classrooms assisting teachers and half of the day in their college classes. The "block" emphasizes the reciprocal relationship between educational theory and classroom practice. Houston offered preservice teachers an opportunity to address their own cultural misconceptions, prejudices, and fears in the context of a culturally responsive faculty and staff who effectively support student learning in a diverse low-income community. The program has an ongoing positive effect on teachers at the school, as they feel recognized for the expertise they possess while deriving the satisfaction of making a positive contribution to the teaching profession by helping to prepare the next generation of teachers.
- In the past it was difficult to attract new teachers to the school and even more difficult to retain them beyond one year. Recognizing the instructional costs of teacher turnover and the need for intensive induction and mentoring support for beginning teachers, Houston was one of the first in Austin to partner with Texas State University to host the Teacher Fellows Program, an intensive induction and mentoring program for fully certified first-year teachers who are graduate students seeking masters degrees. The program provides an opportunity for veteran classroom teachers at the school, through a unique exchange of service agreements with the university, to have full-time release to serve as full-time mentors for three beginning teachers on their school campus. The selected veteran teachers participate in ongoing, weekly training

through a university-led mentor seminar program. Following their two-year assignment in the Teacher Fellows Program, the mentor teachers returned to the classroom full-time with renewed interest in best practices and with new insights into how to most effectively support their novice teacher colleagues. The new teachers who participate in the Teacher Fellows Program receive intensive on-site classroom assistance from their experienced mentors as well as support from their university professors. Teacher Fellows conduct action research projects in their classrooms as part of their graduate course. Their action research is shared with the faculty in proactive problem-solving strategies. The program has proven effective in enhancing retention of both novice teachers and veteran teachers, many of whom took on leadership roles at Houston Elementary and at the district level.

While there is no magic remedy or quick fix for changing high-challenge schools into stress-free schools with high test scores, Houston Elementary demonstrates that a collegial community of leaders, with high commitment to school improvement and openness to mutually beneficial partnerships, can bring about many successes. Following are a few examples of Houston's improvements.

- Houston boasts three national board-certified teachers.
- Houston is the host of an annual staff development conference featuring national experts, attended by teachers from five central Texas districts.
- Houston has one of the lowest teacher turnover rates in the district (< 9%).
- More fifth-grade students at Houston than any other school in the district were accepted into the middle school magnet program.
- Houston has hosted a field-based site for preservice teacher programs from three universities (University of Texas at Austin, St. Edward's University, and Texas State University–San Marcos).
- Counselors at Houston were recognized for creating a model comprehensive guidance program; they presented their program to counselors across the state.
- Houston teachers serve as district trainers for science, math, reading, and technology initiatives.
- The Houston school choir was invited to perform for the governor.
- Houston's approach to literacy was featured in a book on exemplary practices for urban education. (See O'Neal, S., Nelson, S., Gaines, L., & Valentino, A. [2004], Literacy learning for every child in an urban classroom: Can we raise scores and scholars? In D. Lapp, C. Block, E. Cooper, J. Flood, N. Roser, J. Tinajero (Eds.), *Teaching all the children: Strategies for developing literacy in an urban setting* [pp. 153–160]. New York: Guilford.)
- Houston's principal was invited to participate in the University of Pittsburgh Institute for Learning–Wallace *Reader's Digest* Principal Think Tank.
- The school was featured in SEDL publications. (Belt, L. [2002], One child at a time: The case for school-based mentoring. *Southwest Educational Development Laboratory News, 14*(1), 3–7; Trail, K. [2000], Taking the lead: The role of the principal in school reform. *CSRD Connections, 1*[4], 1–4.)

While many high-challenge schools have found themselves in a downward spiral that is difficult to reverse, Houston Elementary has avoided this fate and can serve as a model to other campuses facing similar challenges. Houston Elementary initiated partnerships with local businesses, community organizations, and universities that not only brought new and sorely needed resources but also reversed a negative trend and created a vibrant and high-quality school. It has not been an easy journey, but it has been a highly productive one that has reenergized the faculty, staff, students, and community. Analysis of schools like Houston Elementary and the strategies employed by those who lead them can provide a useful road map for other committed educators.

Issues for Further Reflection and Application

1. In what ways does this case illustrate the concept of shared leadership, and why is shared leadership important in energizing a campus?
2. What effect does an energized school community have on student achievement and well-being?
3. Is it important for a high-challenge school to focus on more than increased student achievement? Why or why not?
4. How can a school create synergy and momentum in the process of energizing itself?
5. What factors entice teachers to continue teaching at a high-challenge school?
6. How might the strategies employed in this case be applied to a middle school or high school setting?

Think of Your School

7. What endeavors at your school help energize the faculty?
8. If you were going to lead an effort to further energize your school, what would be the first steps you would take toward that goal?
9. At your school, which factors promote and which factors hinder attempts to energize the school?

Suggested Readings

Boix-Mansilla, V., & Gardner, H. (2008). Disciplining the mind. *Educational Leadership, 65*(5), 14–19.

Levine, M. (2007). The essential cognitive backpack. *Educational Leadership,64*(7), 15–22.

Noddings, N. (2008). Cultivating optimism in the classroom. *Educational Leadership, 65*(6), 26–31.

Roberts, J. (2008). Talent development: A must for a promising future. *Phi Delta Kappan, 89*(7), 501–506.

Suarez-Orozco, M. M., & Sattin, C. (2007). Wanted: Global citizens. *Educational Leadership, 64*(7), 58–62.

Individualizing Instruction

Without adequate planning, teachers can be overwhelmed by the challenge of designing instruction for students who have a broad range of abilities and levels of motivation. If students do not learn the way we teach them, then we must teach them the way they learn. Individualized instruction is based on the premise that each student is different and that each has unique learning needs that every teacher must make special efforts to meet; otherwise some students will become bored because they are inadequately challenged and others will become discouraged by expectations that are beyond their abilities.

Parents believe that individual attention to their children's needs leads to academic growth. This attention includes a combination of clear expectations, meaningful activities, and daily monitoring the lesson objectives while also monitoring student behavior. Lessons are enriched when teachers are flexible enough to take "side trips" when individual interest is shown by one or more students.

Following are some of the many approaches that schools and teachers use to individualize instruction.

In-Class Ability Grouping

A common approach to reducing the task of teaching 30 or so students of varying abilities and needs is to form subgroups of students who have abilities and interests in common. Simple arithmetic would suggest that dividing a class of 30 students into five groups of six students per group would reduce the range to which the instruction must be adapted to one-fifth the original range. Unfortunately, the results of ability grouping are not usually dramatically successful (Slavin, 2006), though ability grouping does tend to improve student learning. An analysis of more than 40 studies found that ability grouping makes a small contribution to the improvement of learning and a larger contribution toward improvement of student motivation (Julik, 1981). Grouping enhances long-term teacher-student relationships and higher academic achievement.

The effect of grouping largely depends on the type of grouping used. (Types of ability grouping are discussed later in this section.) Whichever method is used, positive results primarily depend on giving quality tasks that relate to students to the content being taught.

The effectiveness of ability grouping on learning also depends on the teacher's ability to adjust the instruction to each group. In general, less capable students need more concrete material and examples of ways to apply the newly learned concepts to real-world experiences, and more capable students need greater challenges, but challenges of different types. For example, rather than assigning a high-ability group of math students a much larger number of the same type of problems given to less capable groups, the teacher might assign this group more creative challenges that require divergent thinking. Advanced groups might even be assigned to develop problems instead of finding solutions, or to find a variety of solutions to a problem. Grouping should be flexible enough to allow peer groups to work together (Roberts, 2008).

The teacher using ability grouping should expect to spend more time with the less capable students, especially after the more capable groups get on task. Slower students may require more careful monitoring and guidance. When working in groups, higher-ability students tend either to dominate the group or to not participate in the group. Furthermore, low-ability students perform less well when placed with other low-ability students, probably partly because teachers usually spend less time with the less capable groups, who benefit most from having more time to respond (Good & Brophy, 2008). Many schools serving mainly non-English-speaking students offer less breadth and depth of content coverage, and students from affluent communities are more likely to be placed in high-ability classes, regardless of achievement scores (Neihart, 2007).

Although the use of higher-order questions is no substitute for mastering content (Armstrong et al., 2009), taking time to ask higher-order questions, encouraging students to ask each other questions, and giving students time and encouragement to reflect on their thinking are imperative. Involving wait time enables students to continue interacting with the content. Children's ability to move from the concrete to the symbolic level requires distancing themselves from the present. Higher-order questions can be used to make this necessary cognitive linking occur. Drawing can be used to help young children make this necessary time transition.

Students should be led to ask questions of themselves to ensure that they are comprehending the content at a sufficient depth. Mel Levine (2007) calls the process *comprehension monitoring*. He says that "High schools should stuff the curriculum with questions to activate their thinking" (p. 19).

Unintentional Differential Treatment

Ability grouping requires different treatment for different groups at different levels, but unintentional differential treatment must be avoided. For example, while it is realistic to expect high-ability students to cover more material more quickly than less capable groups, teachers often make unrealistically different demands of the groups. High-ability groups may be paced as much as 15 times faster than groups of lesser ability, increasing dramatically the difference in amounts of material covered by the two groups.

A major drawback of ability grouping is that it has been found to hamper minority students' literacy. According to Christy Lleras (2009), "From previous research, we know teachers group students not just on standardized test scores, but also on behavior, race, and class. So by using ability grouping, we're creating larger achievement gaps among minority students, which exacerbates inequality." Lleras said that lower-grouped students are much more likely to be assigned lesson plans that emphasize rote memorization and routinized kinds of thinking, while higher-grouped students are assigned more challenging lessons that develop reading comprehension skills. "If you set a high bar for students and you back it up with instructional quality, students learn," says Lleras. "If the materials and expectations are lower, then that's what you'll get."

Teachers tend to treat students for whom they hold low expectations in several different ways. For example, Good and Brophy (2008, p. 6) report that teachers will:

1. Wait less time for lows to answer questions.
2. Give lows the answer or call on someone else.
3. Provide inappropriate reinforcement.
4. Criticize lows more than highs for failure.
5. Praise lows less than highs for success.
6. Fail to give lows feedback on their public responses.
7. Interact with lows less and pay less attention to them overall.

8. Call on lows less often in class.
9. Ask for lower performance levels from lows.
10. Smile less, have less eye contact, have fewer attentive postures towards lows.

Teachers' tendency to treat low achievers differently without realizing they are doing so is a powerful message for teachers in diverse settings, because invariably this special treatment becomes a barrier to success for these students. The goal must be to always keep the standards high and find ways to help all students meet them. The danger of underestimating students' abilities is especially acute among English language learners (ELLs). During a 2008 symposium, parents expressed major concern over their children being "assigned to low-level classes that often limit their opportunities to excel and move into the main stream, even when their intelligence and work ethics are strong" (Christie, 2008, p. 469).

Differences in Evaluation

The teacher may find it desirable to devise nontraditional ways to evaluate advanced students, because objective tests may not measure the kinds of growth anticipated for these groups. Such methodology as oral discussions or one-on-one questioning may be needed to discover the depth of insights developed by advanced students and to detect progress made by students of limited ability. Term projects may be preferable to exams. For example, the teacher of a student who accepts responsibility for writing a computer program to analyze data on breeding plants may find that the resulting product—that is, the computer program—is itself the best measure of success for this assignment.

Precautions

Whenever students are grouped by ability, the teacher must take certain precautions. There is a certain prestige in being affiliated with the upper group(s), whereas a certain disgrace befalls students who are assigned to the lower group(s) (Pare, 2004). Attempts to disguise the ranking or ordering of groups usually fail. Indeed, students often know the level to which they are assigned even before their teachers know it. By making comments that allow comparisons among ability groups and allowing students to make judgmental or derogatory comments about another group, teachers may unwittingly contribute to the caste problem.

The high premium set on peer approval in schools can exacerbate the emotional damage caused by ability grouping. Also, higher-ability groups tend to become snobbish and condescending toward members of lower-ability groups.

An alternative to ability grouping is multi-age grouping. Multi-age classrooms enable students to make continuous progress instead of being promoted each year or waiting until next year to move forward in the curriculum (Protheroe, 2007).

Types of Ability Grouping

Different results are obtained from within-class ability grouping, cross-grade ability grouping, between-class ability grouping, and between-class grouping for particular subjects (e.g., reading or mathematics) (Westchester Institute for Human Services Research, 2002). Interclass grouping and intraclass grouping produce different types of competition. When grouped within the same class (*intr-*

aclass ability grouping), students are forced to compete with classmates, but when the grouping is done externally (*interclass ability grouping*) the competition is between two or more classes, causing students to cooperate while competing. Other schools choose *homogeneous ability grouping*. For example, five groups of students with similar abilities may be formed, producing five "tracks," each representing a different level of general ability.

For group work to be effective, groups must be assigned worthwhile tasks. Any worthwhile task must: be open-ended and require complex problem solving; provide students with multiple entry points and multiple opportunities to show intellectual competence; deal with discipline-based, intellectually important content; require positive interdependence as well as individual accountability; and include clear criteria for the evaluation of the group's product.

In some schools, ability grouping is done independently of teachers—standardized intelligence tests determine the placement of students in groups. Under these circumstances, teachers are still responsible for protecting the members of lower-ability groups from ridicule.

Grade Contracts

Grade contracting recognizes that students are more highly motivated by some topics than by others. It permits individuals to place more emphasis on certain topics, thus giving them a voice in their learning.

At the beginning of each unit of study, students are issued contracts. According to the student's ability and interest in the topic, the student agrees to perform a certain amount of work in order to earn a certain grade. A sample contract is shown in box 10.5. Contracts can also be used to provide students with opportunities to earn free time and other rewards.

Box 10.5 Student Contract for Art History

Grade	*Requirements*
A	Meet the requirements for the grade of B and visit a local art gallery. Sketch an example of a Gothic painting. Visit a house that features gothic-style carpentry work and sketch the house. Show at least three similarities in the two products.
B	Meet the requirements for the grade of C and name and draw an example of each of the major classes of columns used in buildings.
C	Meet the requirements for the grade of D and submit a notebook record of the major developments in art since 1900, naming at least six major painting styles and two authors of each style.
D	Attend class regularly and participate in all classroom activities.

I, ______________________, agree to work for the grade of _____ as described in this contract.
(Student's name) (specify grade)

Using Instructional Models

Another way to organize lessons is to use the formats provided by instructional models. An advantage to using models is that they have been tested and proved to be theoretically and practically sound. Examples include models for information processing, inquiry-based learning, direct instruction, scientific inquiry, concept attainment, and the Socratic method. Instructional models provide a convenient organizer for teaching the precepts of effective teaching or for teaching the steps of lesson planning. For the teacher in the classroom at any level, models of instruction can structure his or her decision making. For example, the teacher's choice of classroom questions, homework assignments, introductions to lessons, and so on are typically influenced by the instructional model being used as an organizer.

The Information-Processing Model

A popular contemporary way to examine and describe learning is by viewing it mechanically, as you might describe the process that computers use to store and retrieve information. Using the five senses to gather information (see figure 10.3), humans immediately decide which information to store. A perceptual screen is used to filter out unwanted information (see figure 10.4 on the following page).

Information that is going to be used immediately or in the near future is stored in short-term memory; the other information is stored in long-term memory. Students cannot possess information unless it is stored in a manner that allows them to make use of it. Stress is placed on the need for interconnections.

When introducing new information to students, advance organizers can be used to point students toward the most important information, thus affecting the information that is retained. Then, by relating this new information to previously acquired information, students can get meaning from new information that might otherwise be meaningless to them.

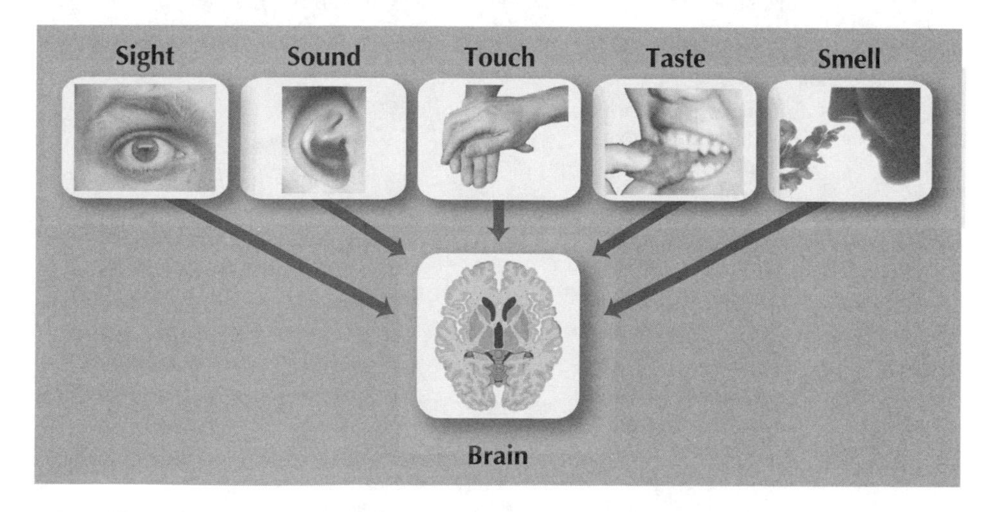

Figure 10.3 The Five Sensors Act as Receptors

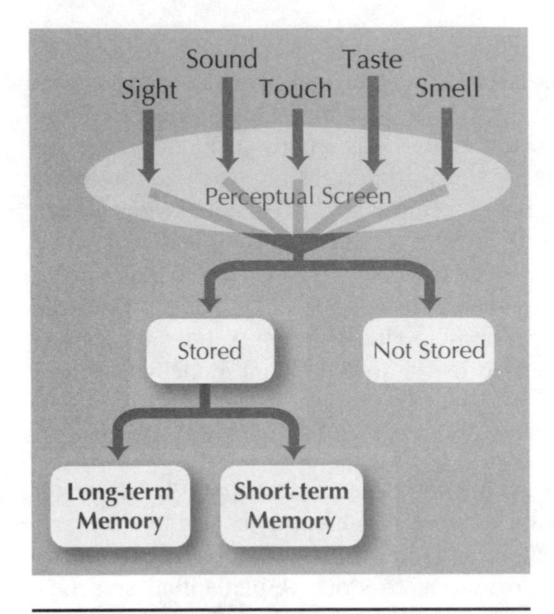

Figure 10.4 Information Is Stored in Either Short-Term or Long-Term Memory

The Inquiry-Based Learning Model

Three of the leading developers of constructivism (John Dewey, Jean Piaget, and Lev Vygotsky) used problem solving as their main teaching and learning strategy. Today, much attention is given to the development of in-depth learning and critical thinking. Problem solving is an ideal way to reach both of these goals. The inquiry-based learning model (figure 10.5) can be used to understand the problem-solving process.

This model is based on the scientific method of investigating phenomena in a structured and methodical way. It allows students to take charge of their learning, discovering meaning and relevance to information through a series of steps that lead to a conclusion or reflection on the newly attained knowledge. Teachers typically use guided inquiry to focus the learning experience and structure the inquiry around specific instructional goals. Critical thinking, creative thinking, and problem-solving abilities are all enhanced through inquiry-based learning.

According to Paula Sincero (2006),

> We learn best when we are at the center of our own learning. Inquiry-based learning is a learning process through questions generated from the interests, curiosities, and perspectives/experiences of the learner. When investigations

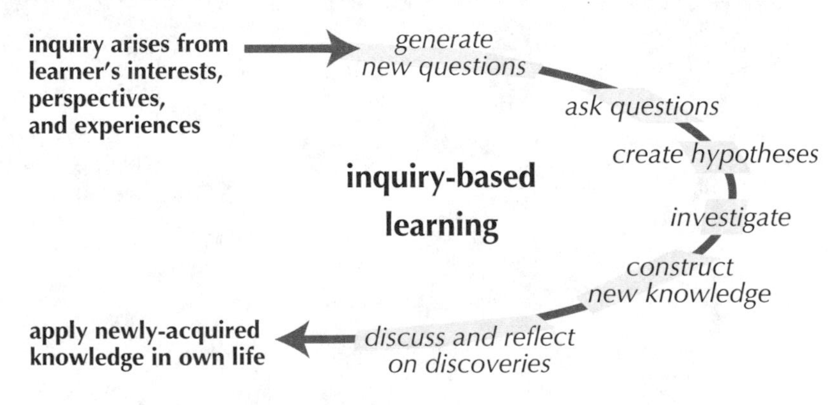

Adapted from Sincero (2006), What is inquiry based learning?

Figure 10.5 Inquiry-Based Learning

> grow from our own questions, curiosities, and experiences, learning is an organic and motivating process that is intrinsically enjoyable.

The Worksheet Library.com (2007) teaching tip on inquiry-based learning lists the main components of this model as

- a question(s) related to the topic of inquiry to be explored (problem statement),
- followed by an investigation and gathering of information related to the question (data collection),
- continuing with a discussion of findings (analysis),
- commencing with a reflection on what was learned (implications/conclusion).

The procedures for inquiry-based learning appear below.

1. The first step in any inquiry is the formulation of a question or set of questions related to the topic of inquiry. The question can be posed by the teacher or by the student(s). Sometimes the question is referred to as a hypothesis or a problem statement.
2. Once a question is posed, students are encouraged to investigate the topic by gathering information from sources that either are provided by the teacher or exist within learning resources or tools that are readily available to students.
3. When enough information related to the topic of inquiry is gathered, it is organized in categories or outlined by highlighting the important information relative to the topic. This helps students make connections with new learning and prior learning.
4. The information is discussed and analyzed for further understanding. The teacher can direct the discussion and highlight the implications that arise from the investigation and show how it relates to the solution of the problem.
5. Conclusions are made and related to the original question. Student reflections are encouraged and serve as a way to relate to the original inquiry and retrace the steps that led to the conclusion. This also serves to reinforce the model so that pupils can repeat the process in any problem-solving situation.

Mastery Learning

In 1963, J. B. Carroll, a professor at Harvard University, wrote an article titled "A Model of School Learning" in which he challenged the then-accepted belief that students' IQs are a major factor in determining academic success. Carroll hypothesized that if three conditions were met, at least 90 to 95% of all high school students could master class objectives. The three conditions were that: (1) each student must be given enough time to complete a task; (2) each student must be properly motivated (i.e., the subject matter must be presented in a manner compatible with the individual student's *learning style*); and (3) when students fail to learn, they must be given an opportunity to recycle (i.e., to have the subject matter retaught and to be retested) without penalty.

Using Carroll's model, Benjamin S. Bloom and his students at the University of Chicago developed an education system called *learning for mastery* (LFM) (see Block & Henson, 1986). This system is teacher paced and group based. In other words, the teacher leads the lessons and the class as a group follows. In contrast, most *mastery learning* programs are student paced (that is, the students set the pace) and individually based. Each student pursues learning individually, at that student's own preferred pace.

All mastery learning programs have several important characteristics in common. First, they provide students with different lengths of time to master each topic. Second, they give students opportunities to remediate or restudy material that proves difficult for them, and then to retest without penalty. Third, all mastery learning programs use formative evaluation—that is, evaluation designed to promote learning, not to be computed as part of the grading system. Short daily or weekly tests diagnose learning weaknesses and teaching weaknesses, and then teachers and learners adjust to improve learning. Finally, all mastery learning uses criterion-based evaluation. This means that the criteria essential for success are revealed before the study unit begins. (For further discussion of formative evaluation and criterion-referenced evaluation, see chapter 9.)

Finally, with mastery learning programs, as with all other programs, success depends on how it is used. There are two essential elements of the mastery learning process. The first is an extremely close congruence between the material being taught, the teaching strategies employed, and the content measured. The second essential element is the provision of formative assessment, opportunities for students followed by feedback, accompanied by corrective and enrichment activities.

Gentile and Lalley (2003) summarized the data from hundreds of studies and literature reviews and concluded that mastery learning improves performance on criterion-referenced tests. Among Gentile and Lalley's conclusions drawn from the summaries, Downey et al. (2009) list the following positive effects of mastery learning (pp. 157–158):

- Student achievement using a mastery learning model is superior to traditional teaching approaches.
- Students in mastery learning groups scored higher on retention tests after several weeks or months than did those in traditional teaching groups.
- Students taught in mastery learning are significantly more likely to self-report positive attitudes toward, liking for, and confidence in their ability in what has been taught as compared with transitional groups.
- Teachers exposed to and using mastery learning in their own classes altered their expectations, as well as their attributions, for student achievement and what causes it (higher student expectations).

But mastery learning is not without its critics. In a review of studies on mastery learning, Arlin (1984) reported some of the more popular criticisms. Some critics say the claim that mastery learning equalizes students' learning abilities is an overstatement. Some critics describe mastery learning as a "psychological trap" that does not have a proper conceptual base. Some critics even call mastery learning a "Robin Hood phenomenon" that takes from the advanced students and gives to the poor students. Arlin himself has argued that studies that find all students equally capable should be interpreted more cautiously.

Readers of professional journal articles must remember that any innovation may experience either astounding success or total failure, depending on the conditions of the moment. The old adage, "Never believe anything you hear, and believe only half of what you see," is good advice to remember as you interpret research findings; proceed with caution. Curricularists must also carefully examine the studies being reported; many are so flawed that Bracey (1993, p. 85) was prompted to write, "Far too many flawed studies are getting through the seams of peer review and into print. Mislabeled and misleading graphs and figures abound."

Matching Teaching Styles and Learning Styles

For more than three decades, educators have conducted research to discover how to teach students with diverse learning styles using complementary instructional strategies. Figure 10.6 (on the following page) shows five major categories of characteristics that affect learning: environmental, emotional, sociological, physiological, and psychological. While the effects of the environment on learning may be obvious, the other elements may affect learning without the teacher's being aware of it.

Research conducted with the Dunn and Dunn model represented in figure 10.6 at more than 115 institutions of higher education reported successful applications of their strategies for matching instructional approaches to students' learning-style strengths at the primary, elementary, secondary, and college levels (Dunn & Dunn, 1999). For example, a meta-analysis of 42 experimental studies conducted with this model at 13 universities revealed that students whose learning styles are accommodated would be expected to achieve 75% of a standard deviation higher than students who have not had their learning styles accommodated (Dunn, Griggs, Olson, Gorman, & Beasley, 1995). This indicates that matching students' learning-style preferences with educational interventions compatible with those preferences is beneficial to their academic achievement.

According to the Center for Research in Education (CRE), the 20-year period of extensive federal funding from 1970 to 1990 produced few programs that consistently resulted in statistically higher standardized achievement test scores for special education students (Alberg et al., 1992). Prominent among those few programs was the Dunn and Dunn model. The average students in the Dunn et al. (1995) meta-analysis revealed the largest effects.

Dunn, Dunn, and Perrin (1994) perceived knowledge of learning-style preferences as a tool teachers can use to design more effective instructional experiences. According to Dunn and Dunn (1999), difficult academic material needs to be introduced through each student's strongest perceptual modality, reinforced through his/her secondary or tertiary modality, and then applied by the student when creating an original resource that includes the information, such as a poem, a set of task cards or flip cards, a time line, or a kinesthetic floor game. Using these procedures, the Dunns developed guidelines (called Homework Disc prescriptions) for having students do their homework using their learning-style strengths. At almost every grade level, students have achieved statistically higher

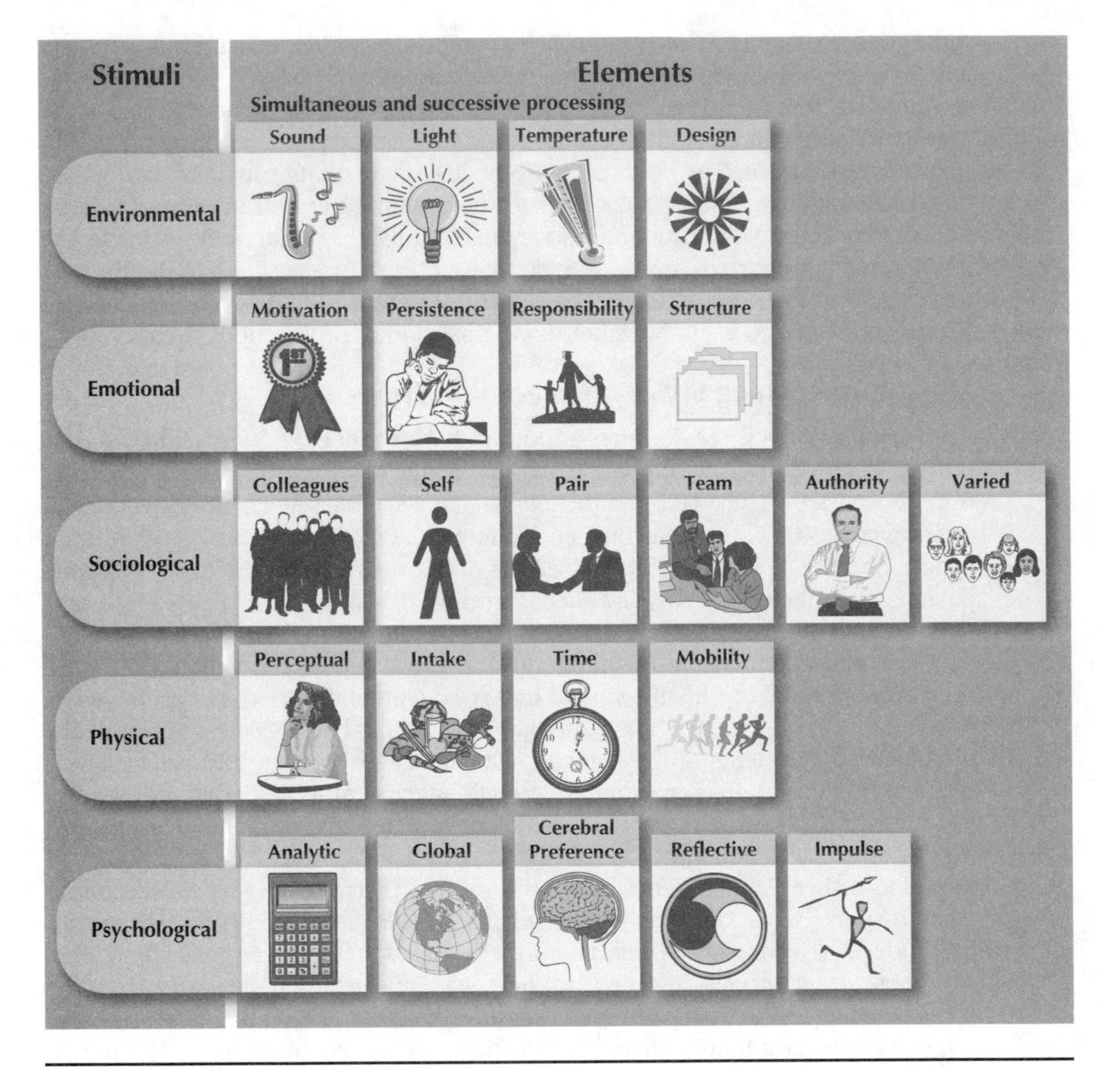

Figure 10.6 Diagnosing Learning Styles

achievement and attitude test scores by following those Homework Disc prescriptions (Dunn & Klavas, 1992). Studies show that such matching of learning style and instructional approach consistently increases academic achievement, improves attitudes toward school, and reduces discipline problems. This last finding is consistent with the often-heard statement that a well-planned lesson is the greatest deterrent to discipline problems.

Miller and Dunn (1997) tested the relative effects of traditional lectures, readings, and class discussions, versus the affects of programmed learning sequences (PLS) in book format, versus PLS using software on CD-ROM for thc computer on students in a college of allied health. All students were exposed to several topics through each treatment in varying sequences. Students whose learning styles were auditory, motivated, and authority-oriented performed statistically better with the traditional approach than with either the book PLS or the CD-ROM PLS. Fewer students performed better with the CD-ROM approach than with the PLS book format; some teachers complained about the technology noises in the computer lab and their inability to sit comfortably, eat, and work privately. Most students earned significantly higher test scores with the PLS book format, and those students were highly visual; preferred informal seating; liked learning alone in a softly lit, quiet environment; and preferred snacking while studying.

How to Match Styles

There are several ways to attain a match between teaching style and learning style. First, teachers can be matched with students who have similar personalities. Personality matches are said to produce more "manageable" classes and increase student satisfaction with classroom activities, but there have been mixed results with this method.

A second (and perhaps more practical) approach to matching is to have the teacher select teaching methods that correspond to student learning styles. To address students' preferred learning styles, teachers must possess a variety of teaching strategies and methods from which to choose. Working with at-risk students requires a particularly high level of skill and an even broader repertoire of strategies (Mathews, 2008). The teacher who discovers that a particular class of students responds favorably to simulations and not to lectures, for example, should use more simulations than lectures with that class. Watson et al. (2004) reported on the success of memory games to enhance vocabulary growth in both math and language arts classes, and Curts (2004) reminds educators that electronic simulations and games are especially appropriate because today's students have grown up playing video games. Another way to match methods with learning styles is to administer a learning-style inventory to the entire class, which usually results in a variety of preferences. The teacher can then group students according to their style preferences.

To provide students with opportunities to develop preferences, teachers may choose to expose students to a variety of styles. Teachers benefit from conducting self-evaluations of their instruction. JoAnn Susko (2010) at Rider University suggests that teachers keep a journal of the methods they use on their USB drives. This provides ready access to each method and it also lets teachers see their growth as they continuously expand their variety of methods and styles. Of course, this means each teacher must master a variety of teaching styles. Changing styles may be difficult for many teachers, however, because it requires a change of attitude. Marshall (1991, p. 226) explains:

> Consequently, for teachers to change their teaching styles, to understand and risk planning instruction on the basis of learning style patterns of students—and, therefore, to teach successfully a wider range of learners—[teachers] must come to recognize, respect, and support the learning differences of students.

Not everyone believes in the powers of matching teaching styles with learning styles. For example, consider the hypothetical statement in box 10.6 on the following page. Consider also the fact that the level of students' effort on a task affects success more than the type of instruction.

Box 10.6 The Matching Learning and Teaching Styles Movement

The movement to match learning styles with teaching styles is believed by some to be a fluke that several educators dreamed up to get attention. Little quality research had been conducted in this area, and some of the limited studies on matching styles found little or no difference in learning. Some studies suggest that teachers should expose students to several styles, but teachers naturally tend to alter their approaches according to students' responses. So, say its detractors, matching teaching and learning styles is nothing new—it's the same old wine in a new bottle. To quote Shakespeare, it's "much ado about nothing."

1. How consistent must research findings be to be considered conclusive? In other words, must all studies produce the same answer before the answer can be considered factual?
2. Choose one of your favorite teachers. Did this teacher use different teaching styles? If so, list three or four of this teacher's styles.
3. Do you have a single preferred style? To reach an intelligent answer to this question, draw a vertical line down the middle of a sheet of paper. On the left side, list variables that enhance learning for you. On the right side, list variables that impede learning for you.
4. Challenge or defend this statement: All teachers should purposely increase their repertoire of teaching styles.
5. Do you think teachers should spend more or less time developing new styles? Explain your answer.

Computer-Enhanced Individualization

Information technology offers teachers unprecedented opportunities to individualize instruction. Computers are powerful student motivators that can help students integrate learned factual knowledge and abstract concepts, leading to higher learning levels. Software is readily available that enables students to develop their creative potential—including software for students with disabilities and non-English-speaking students (e.g., LD Online). See chapter 4 for an in-depth discussion on computer applications in the classroom.

Former South Carolina teacher of the year Nancy Townsend (1999) advises educators to use technology when it works best with students and to continue learning new ways to meet students' cognitive needs. To be effective, Internet applications must use constructivist strategies. WebQuests, for example, use authentic tasks and open-ended questions that cause students to tie the new information they have accessed via the Internet to their prior understanding.

Once information is accessed, it must be transferred into meaningful knowledge by each student. For example, students can use the Internet to gather information about national events and then be required to apply the newly acquired information to solve a local problem. It is such metacognitive tasks that cause rich understanding to occur and can be further enriched by small-group discussions.

A Title II program called Enhancing Education through Technology (Ed Tech) requires: (1) improving student learning through the use of technology, (2) ensuring that all students are technologically literate, and (3) integrating technology and curriculum development to establish research-based instructional methods. (For further information on this program, visit the Web site at http:// www.ed.gov/programs/edtech/index.html.) Another related program, the Regional Technology in Education Consortia (R*TEC), helps state and local educational agencies, teachers, school library and media personnel, administrators, and other education entities successfully integrate technologies into kindergarten through twelfth grade (K–12) classrooms, library media centers, and other educational settings, including adult literacy centers. For more information, visit their Web site (http://www.rtec.org).

Other Ways to Involve Students

In addition to varying lesson plans and learning styles, a variety of learning avenues such as textbooks, discussions, field trips, oral reports, term projects, homework, and parental involvement is necessary. We now turn to the use of these approaches to individualized instruction and the teacher's role in each.

Textbooks

As discussed in chapter 7, throughout the history of education in the United States, one type of textbook or another has dominated the curriculum. At first, the textbook determined the content to be studied. Lectures followed by rote memorization and recitation often resulted in a boring, irrelevant curriculum. Some teachers still consider the textbook to be the major source of content, and although it is no longer the sole determiner of content, the textbook still plays an important role in today's planning. This is a concern because U.S. textbooks seldom put content and activities together in ways that develop major ideas (Roth & Garnier, 2007).

But textbooks can actually be used to promote student involvement. This requires the teacher to be proactive. Instead of letting the textbook lead the teacher and students in the selection of content and experiences, the teacher can take a proactive posture and lead the designing of the curriculum. For example, instead of following the textbook organization from chapter 1 to chapter 2, teachers can determine their own sequence of topics, or they may decide that some chapters are not worth including in the curriculum. Teachers are becoming increasingly competent in curriculum development, and more and more teachers are insisting on shaping the curricula in their classes as they see fit. Many reform programs provide teachers with curriculum frameworks (guidelines for selecting curriculum content and activities) and require teachers to design the curriculum.

Some teachers almost totally avoid using a textbook, substituting current problems, learning-activity packages, or learning units they have developed themselves. But herein lies a big problem. Some lessons are completely activity based with no content at all. Unlike educators in Australia and Japan, American teachers seldom use activities to help students develop content ideas. When they do introduce content, they often organize it in a set of discrete facts or algorithms and definitions rather than in a connected set of ideas (Roth & Garnier, 2007). Few teachers have total freedom to design their curricula. Concern that students may not "cover" all the content needed for the following year or for college is always present, and this concern is legitimate. School administrators must ensure that the total school curriculum does not have major content gaps. Many larger secondary schools hire a curriculum director, a curriculum supervisor, or an assistant principal who is directly responsible for this. Teachers should work with the curriculum leader and/or other teachers to avoid curriculum redundancy and gaps.

Discussions

Today's students want to be involved, and good discussions provide all participants opportunities to relate the topic to their own experiences. This sharing of various perspectives can enrich the knowledge and understanding of individual participants. Nicaise and Barnes (1996, p. 206) address the importance of providing students opportunities to discuss lessons:

> Discourse and dialogue are essential in learning. Discourse among students helps them construct hypotheses and tests them against what they believe to be reality; it helps people to view knowledge and information from multiple perspectives. Conceptual growth occurs when students and teachers share different viewpoints and understanding changes in response to new perspectives and experiences.

Grouping students according to their interest in the topic and letting students choose discussion topics can encourage total participation. Putting the reserved students together forces one or more of them to assume leadership, and placing aggressive students in the same group forces some of them to learn to yield the floor to others. Assigning roles, such as "discussion moderator" and "recorder," and then rotating the assignment of these roles, will prompt all group members to participate even further. Selecting topics that have answers, even though there may be multiple answers, and letting students know that a definite outcome of their discussions is expected can give students a sense of purpose and responsibility.

A student moderator's failure to keep group discussion progressing and on target can prompt teacher intervention, but too much interference will cause a group to become dependent on the teacher's leadership. The group moderator must not dominate the discussion; she or he must communicate that all serious comments are worth hearing. A free-flowing discussion provides a valuable opportunity to develop social skills, itself an important goal, and helps students identify with their peers. All adolescents need to belong, and all need positive recognition and approval from peers. Group discussions should help fill these needs.

The participants need to know that each person has a definite role in every discussion. First, each participant is obligated to read the assignment so the discussion will begin from a common base. Second, each person is responsible for contributing information to the discussion. Opinions and contributions of knowledge should be prized only when the participants can present evidence or facts to support them. Third, each participant is responsible for listening to others and, when possible, for referring to specific comments of others. This assures all participants that their comments are being considered.

In addition to keeping the environment informal, pleasant, and nonthreatening, the teacher is also a facilitator, helping students to locate appropriate resources and to plan and evaluate their discussion.

Oral Reports

Begin planning oral reports by first deciding each report's purpose. For example, oral reports can provide advanced students the opportunity to share their expertise, they can provide a group of students from diverse backgrounds the opportunity to learn to work together cooperatively, or they can give shy and insecure students experience in public speaking.

Assigning a report to punish misbehavior and/or to substitute for effective planning is unacceptable. Students will quickly connect the report with those purposes and will not expect any significant learning to result. Similar results occur when reports are used at the end of a grading period to give students an opportunity to improve their grades.

Always communicate to the class the primary purposes of the assignment and what is expected of them during the report. Should they take notes? Ask questions? Take issue with the speaker? Should they ask for clarification when they do not understand? Should they interrupt the speaker with comments or wait until the end of the presentation? Will they be held accountable on the next test for the information presented orally by their peers? By answering these questions before the report is delivered, teachers can draw each student into the oral presentations, maximizing interest and involvement.

As a precaution against students' taking reports too lightly, credit might be given for oral reports—and perhaps to the rest of the students for their responses. A positive reward system can let students earn credit for participation without penalizing those whose contributions are minimal.

The timing of oral reports can be critical, and care should be taken to avoid scheduling so many reports in succession that students are bored by the repetition. Because many secondary school students and some middle school students hold part-time jobs, and extracurricular activities consume much of their out-of-class time, class time should be allotted for preparing oral presentations. Giving students time to prepare and an opportunity to present the results of their assignments tells students that the presentations are worthwhile.

Projects

Whatever subject a teacher teaches, assigning projects offers several valuable options: long-term projects (which may last for a grading period or even a semester), short-term projects, group projects, and individual projects. Not all projects must end with an oral presentation; some may conclude with written reports or concrete products. Regardless of the product, students need opportunities to discuss their projects with their teachers and with each other (David, 2008), and to show their creations. For example, a science teacher might want to arrange a local science fair to display students' insect collections, or a music teacher may want to set up a student recital.

Homework

The purpose of homework is to prepare the student for the next lesson and/or reinforce concepts and skills learned in the previous lesson. Duke University researchers have reviewed more than 60 research studies on homework and concluded that homework does have a positive effect on student achievement when used correctly, but the effect varies dramatically with grade level (Cooper, 2006; Cooper, Robinson, & Patall, 2006). For high school students, homework has substantial positive effects. Junior high school students can benefit from homework, but only about half as much. For elementary school students, the effect of homework on achievement is negligible. The optimum amount of homework also varies with grade level. For elementary students, no amount of homework—large or small—affects achievement. For junior high school students, achievement continues to improve with more homework until assignments last between one and two hours a night. For high school students, the more homework, the better achievement—within reason, of course. Homework seems to be equally effective in all subjects. There are those, however, who don't necessarily believe that homework is innately good. Alfie Kohn (2007), for example, says that homework is rarely beneficial. More research needs to be done on this topic.

The purpose of each homework assignment should determine the teacher's behavior. Too often, homework is used erroneously—for practice. It should be used to develop higher-order thinking skills, involve and increase student motivation, and inform the teacher whether students are benefiting from the lessons, and it should not figure into students' grades (Mangione, 2008).

Box 10.7 offers suggestions that should help teachers design and implement a system for assigning homework.

Box 10.7 Homework Guidelines

Clarify the Assignment. Homework assignments must be clear. Assignments that involve problem solving can be clarified and simplified by giving students an opportunity to work at least one problem of each type in class before asking them to do problems at home.

Individualize Homework Assignments. Consider the abilities and needs of each student. Certain homework assignments for slower students will help them catch up with the rest of the class, while the more advanced students can explore areas of special interest to them in depth.

Make Homework Authentic. Homework assignments are more interesting when they are authentic. Students could be asked to respond to something that is on the evening news, in the newspaper, or on an educational television program.

Be Reasonable. Many secondary school students and some middle school students use after-school hours for part-time jobs on which their families depend for some essentials. For such students, homework assignments that require a few hours each evening are impossible to complete. Secondary school teachers must also remember that students have several other courses and may be receiving homework assignments in all of them. A good rule of thumb is 10 minutes of homework for each grade level (Cooper, 2006). Teachers who succumb to their temptation to assign far too much homework should know that some recent research studies report a negative correlation between the time students spend on homework and student achievement (Mangione, 2008).

Follow-Up. Spending time and energy on an assignment, only to have the teacher forget about it, can be disheartening. Teachers should schedule a follow-up at the time of the assignment. Regular follow-ups result in improved results: When students are held responsible for assigned work, they are more likely to do the work than when their efforts go unnoticed.

Parental Involvement

As noted in chapter 2, the NCLB legislation requires a higher rate of parent involvement in curriculum planning. NCLB also requires schools to keep parents involved in their children's performance and will provide parents opportunities to be involved in the shaping of their children's learning activities. The past decade has seen a definite trend toward increased parent involvement and an increasing desire among parents to have a greater role in controlling the future of their children's school.

Site-based decision making, a trend that is sweeping the country, offers much hope for garnering the support of family members. Most site-based teams include parents and are empowered to make decisions on curriculum, finance, and all other major school matters. Teachers are meeting with parents to collaborate on curriculum and are using technology to engage and inspire them to take an interest in their children's education (Boston Digital Bridge Foundation, 2006). Communicating with parents has become easier, quicker, and more effective because of the Internet. As just one example, blogs offer schools a means of communicating school news as fast as it happens (Buck, 2007).

Without question, the curriculum is being fundamentally reconstructed to respond to the diversity of this nation. As parents in poor communities become more involved, curricula are being reconstructed to meet the needs of students from all segments of society. The power of involving the community in schoolwork is illustrated in a study by Reinstein (1998), who reported that a program featuring someone in the community who used high-level math skills with practical applications did more to motivate students than any action the school could have taken.

Conclusion

Following is a summary of some of the advances made and concerns raised about the topics discussed in this chapter.

Advances

- Many teachers are using the case-study method to help students engage more deeply in their learning.
- Involving students in planning their curricula can enrich the social climate in the classroom, and NCLB requires increased student involvement in planning.
- Electronic simulations and games cause students to pursue concepts more deeply and draw relationships among concepts.

Concerns

- Our students cover too many topics, too lightly.
- Teachers need to learn effective methods of engaging students in planning.
- Our students perform less well than Asian students because our students study topics in isolation from other concepts, and they fail to see the connections between their classroom activities and the major concepts being stated.

- We now know better ways of using homework to effect learning, and parents continue to support the amount of homework given.
- Ability grouping can negatively impact minority students' literacy.

This chapter encourages the matching of styles in the classroom. There are a number of advantages to matching teaching and learning styles, but this method is not a solution for all education problems, and teachers should be aware of the limitations and criticisms of this movement.

The general approach of grouping may present overwhelming problems. Studies show that many teachers, especially novices, find it impossible to monitor different groups in classrooms (Good & Brophy, 2008). Studies show that if the major purpose of style grouping is to accommodate students, a degree of discomfort can be an asset in learning rather than a problem to be circumvented (Harvey, Hunt, & Schroder, 1963; Piaget, 1952).

Even the term *learning styles* is not clearly defined in the literature, and a clear definition in terms of student performance would be helpful. Learning style is not static, because learning itself is highly complex. Indeed, learning is such a broad activity that it cannot be contained within the cognitive domain. The study of the effects of matching learning and teaching styles is still in its infancy. The findings hold promise, but these studies and their claims should be read with a critical eye.

The information-processing model and the inquiry-based learning model are just two of the many instructional models instructors can choose to organize lessons. Inquiry-based learning allows students to take charge of their learning, discovering meaning and relevance to information through a series of steps that lead to a conclusion or reflection on the newly attained knowledge.

Mastery learning has proven both successful and controversial. Some of its major strengths for learners include unlimited time on each topic, opportunities to remediate without penalty, and the absence of grades. Unfortunately, each of these strengths can also cause major administrative headaches. Flexible time for individual students doesn't fit the school calendar, and many parents insist on receiving traditional A–F grade reports based on competition.

Individualized instruction can be facilitated and enhanced through information technology. An approach to individualizing learning which has been highly successful with many classes is grade contracts. Such successful approaches have some common elements. They spell out the expectations the teacher holds for students, and the teacher carefully monitors student behavior. Maximum success usually requires involving parents, and site-based decision-making teams are doing just that.

This chapter has introduced several curriculum structures that can be used to meet the multicultural goals of this text. Long-range planning, short-term planning, and individualizing instruction all contribute to the goal of helping each and every student succeed. Teachers who are empowered can, in turn, pass on this power to their students through helping them earn ownership of their education.

ADDITIONAL LEARNING OPPORTUNITIES

1. What is the difference between long-range planning and unit planning?
2. What are some ways that a constructivist perception should affect (a) long-term planning? (b) daily planning?
3. How can we minimize the stigma of students who are assigned to lower-level ability groups?
4. What are some advantages of mastery learning, and what is one planning step teachers can use to ensure that a lesson realizes each advantage?
5. What new reform practices in local schools enhance students' self-images?
6. How would you relate the terms *individualized instruction, ability grouping, mastery learning*, and *academic contracts* to each other?
7. Is the current reform practice of providing a curriculum framework to introduce students to activities adequate, or must teachers also lead students to identify major concepts within each discipline? Explain your answer.
8. How do curricula for non-English-speaking students differ from curricula for mainstream students?

SUGGESTED ACTIVITIES

1. Develop three separate ways of using advance organizers to introduce a lesson.
2. Develop a set of guidelines for teachers to use to involve all students in planning.
3. Describe the strengths and limitations of the sample daily lesson plans given in this chapter in meeting the needs of at-risk students. Tell how each plan may be adjusted to reach the needs of these students.
4. Make a chart showing some obstacles to implementing mastery learning in K–12 schools. Describe a planning adjustment that teachers and other curriculum developers can make to overcome each obstacle listed.
5. Draw a model to show your perception of the relationship between curriculum and instruction.
6. Develop a contract to be used in a class of students with diverse needs. Ensure that the conditions enable students to build on their previous experiences.
7. Choose a lesson plan and convert it into a mastery learning plan or an inquiry-based learning plan.
8. Make a list of positive multicultural features of recent reform practices in the schools in your area.
9. Having read pros and cons on the matching of teaching and learning styles, consider your own position. Some critics see the entire movement as a unilateral approach in which the teacher assesses the learning style of the student and prescribes or selects an acceptable teaching style to match the learner's style. Do you think the student should be involved in this selection? If so, identify some ways to make style matching a bilateral process.

chapter eleven

CURRENT AND FUTURE CURRICULUM TRENDS

Trends across the Disciplines

- safe schools
- home schooling
- multidisciplinary/ thematic approach
- reading and writing across the curriculum
- alternative assessment
  - performance assessment
  - authentic assessment
  - continuous assessment and progress reporting
  - self-assessment
- tenure and life certification
- gender equity
- geographic stereotyping
- students with special needs
- gifted students
- senior citizens
- magnet schools
- charter schools
- business–school partnership programs
- national standards
- increased parental involvement and control
- Interstate New Teacher Assessment and Support Consortium (INTASC)
- privatizing public schools
- the world of work
- global education
- vouchers and school choice
- cooperative learning
- multiple intelligences
- evaluating textbooks and ancillary materials
- increased and expanded use of technology

Trends within the Disciplines

- mathematics
- science
- language arts
- foreign languages
- English language arts
- fine arts
- social studies
  - history
  - geography
  - civics
- health and physical education

Focus Questions

1. How would you describe some impacts of assessment on school reform?
2. Using a definite knowledge base, how would you challenge or defend the tenure and lifelong certification issue?
3. What impacts are school-to-work programs having on today's curriculum?
4. What are some pros and cons of inclusion?
5. Which of the following topics have had the most impact on education today: multiple intelligences, magnet schools, or charter schools?
6. What are some guidelines advocates should use to evaluate textbooks for their contribution to ensure that the goals of (1) multiculturalism and (2) constructivist curriculum are met?
7. What are two trends in your subject area? Are they beneficial or detrimental?

The rapid rate at which education is changing demands that curriculum planners attempt to stay abreast of new changes and, furthermore, develop the ability to anticipate future changes. This chapter should enable the reader to review current major trends and identify emerging trends. The first part of the chapter focuses on trends across the disciplines, and the second part focuses on trends within the disciplines.

Trends across the Disciplines

Safe Schools

The twenty-first century began with the public expressing great concern over the need to provide children with *safe schools.* According to the National Center for Education Statistics' Indicators of School Crime and Safety (2007),

> Among youth ages 5–18, there were 17 school-associated violent deaths from July 1, 2005, through June 30, 2006 (14 homicides and 3 suicides). In 2005, among students ages 12–18, there were about 1.5 million victims of nonfatal crimes at school, including 868,100 thefts and 628,200 violent crimes (simple assault and serious violent crime). During the 2005–06 school year, 86% of public schools reported that at least one violent crime, theft, or other crime occurred at their school. In 2005, 8% of students in grades 9–12 reported being threatened or injured with a weapon in the previous 12 months, and 25% reported that drugs were made available to them on school property. In the same year, 28% of students ages 12–18 reported having been bullied at school during the previous 6 months.

In a Gallup Poll on children and violence (2009), 26% of interviewed parents said they feared for their children's safety at school (up 15% from 2008), and 10%

of schoolchildren expressed concern to their parents about feeling unsafe at their schools (up 2% from 2008). Fighting, violence, and gang activity in schools also are of great concern to most Americans. These conditions and the presence of drugs in schools ranked among the top concerns in this survey. These problems demand continuous attention. Some schools have formulated safety teams—composed of regular and special education teachers, personnel from related services, administrators, and parents—to ensure a consistent and individualized response to disruptive students.

Several state legislatures are providing major funding to support school safety centers, which will be prepared to work with schools to promote safety. Many states have written policy requiring schools to take steps to reduce bullying. But for decades a more common approach has been to increase the harshness of school policies, an approach which is not educationally based but rather is based on the use of force and punishment. In many urban schools police involvement is necessary, yet an overdependence on police intervention can have a variety of unintended negative consequences, including their failure to address the conditions of schools and the acts of educators that may increase school disruptions. Critics of such policies suggest that schools step up the use of democratic principles, which they say has always been more effective in reducing crime than the traditional punishment and constraint approach.

Efforts to reduce violence in schools are paying off. Although there is definite cause for concern, students are actually twice as safe in school as they are in the outside community (DeVoe et al., 2002).

The Office of Safe and Drug-Free Schools and Communities (OSDFS) funds programs that focus on improving discipline policies, security procedures, and crisis management. A newer feature of this program provides funds for schools to hire school safety program coordinators. For further information on OSDFS, visit their Web site (http://www.ed.gov/about/offices/list/osdfs/index.html). OSDFS also offers a list of "editor's picks" featuring links to safe and drug-free schools, online workshops, youth and school violence prevention resources, threat assessment in schools, readiness and emergency management for schools, school safety organizations, and many other education-related safety issues (http://www.ed.gov/admins/lead/safety/edpicks.jhtml?src=ep).

Self-Directed Learning

Self-directed learning is a process in which individuals take the initiative to diagnose their learning needs, formulate learning goals, identify resources for learning, select and implement learning strategies, and evaluate learning outcomes. According to Maurice Gibbons (2004), "Computers and the Internet are transforming education and provide an enormous resource for self-directed work" (p. 466).

Gibbons (2004) suggested a five-stage model for teachers to use to transform their classes from teacher-directed to student-directed:

1. *Incidental self-direction.* The teacher introduces self-direction in assignments.
2. *Independent thinking.* The teacher transforms the curriculum into questions for students to answer as a class, group, or individually.

3. *Self-managed learning.* The teacher creates guides that tell students how to achieve course outcomes, providing a support system.
4. *Self-planned learning.* The teacher shows students how to design their own plans for achieving course outcomes, negotiates their proposals with them, and coaches them to success.
5. *Self-directed learning.* The teacher leads students to analyze the situation, formulate their own goals, plan how to achieve them, take action, solve problems that arise, and demonstrate their achievement.

Changing from teacher-centered education to learner-centered education is perhaps the most promising hope for diminishing discipline problems. Put simply, the best preventative method is an effective lesson, one that meaningfully involves all students. Support for a learner-centered approach, issues of societal change, alternative pathways to teaching, and the historical context of educational practices is not something that will occur automatically. There must be a commitment to reflection, creating thinking-centered learning, and constantly assessing the quality of instructional programs (Laboard, 2003, p. 5).

Gibbons (2008) says that motivation is the key to successful self-directed learning. He recommends that teachers help students find and pursue a passion, and translate their interest into clear and compelling goals. Self-directed learners benefit from feedback from their teachers and discover the advantages of securing feedback for themselves. These students need to be challenged and should be taught to challenge themselves. They should be encouraged to identify their strengths and weaknesses, and to take full advantage of their strengths. Most important of all, Gibbons (2008) says to make sure every student experiences success. Teachers should help students set realistic goals and help them become competent in achieving them.

Home Schooling

In recent years many parents have chosen to educate their children at home, and the number that make this choice is growing annually. Approximately 345,000 children were home schooled in 1994, increasing to as many as 850,000 in 1999 (Cloud & Morse, 2001) and to 1.5 million by 2007 (Gaither, 2008). Families with low incomes and four or more children are the most likely to choose to home school their children. Home schooling has some clear advantages. The teacher, often a parent, is usually highly dedicated, and a growing number of home-schooling resources are available on the Internet (e.g., The National Independent Home Education Network [http://wnla.tripod.com/nationalindependenthomeeducationnetwork] and *Home Education Magazine* [http:// www.homeedmag.com]). Home-schooled children get plenty of attention, and the process is learner-centered. A major disadvantage of home schooling is the lack of opportunities for these students to socialize with peers, but creative parents can find healthy programs throughout their community for their home-schooled children.

Multidisciplinary/Thematic Approach

Elementary and secondary school curricula of the 1980s experienced a swing toward the use of themes that cut across the disciplines. This shift came more unintentionally than by design, as teachers searched for ways to make learning more authentic and move students up the learning hierarchies. As educators examined the schools of the early 1980s, they found that students were generally passive listeners, as many teachers taught from the text. Even activities-oriented classes often found students engaged physically without understanding or caring deeply about the exercises or the understanding these exercises were designed to promote.

To give assignments more meaning to students, teachers invited students to become involved in choosing problems—not from the textbook, not from a list of problems by the author at the end of the chapter, but real problems that exist in their communities. Few real problems exist within the boundaries of a single discipline; therefore, the move to make schooling more authentic automatically changed curricula, making it integrated and multidisciplinary.

Multidisciplinary education is supported by learning theory. As noted in chapter 1, constructivists say that grasping an in-depth understanding of a subject requires that the students themselves create understanding. Rather than being told about the relationships between bodies of knowledge, students must discover these relationships and must tie newly acquired information to their own previously acquired understanding. One key to an effective interdisciplinary unit is the degree of genuinely enthusiastic support it receives from the teachers involved. Teachers say that a key to success in multidisciplinary learning is choosing a theme that will excite all students. Controversial local problems allow the teacher and students to bring the community into the classroom.

Curriculum planners should understand that terms such as *interdisciplinary, multidisciplinary, integrated learning, authentic learning, problem-solving,* and *accelerated learning* tend to run together. A good program may, and indeed should, contain a mix of these characteristics and approaches. Across-the-curriculum programs do not guarantee in-depth learning, however. Boix-Mansilla and Gardner (2008) point out that in-depth learning can occur either within a discipline or across disciplines, but it is not likely to occur at all unless teachers understand that each discipline has become a discipline because it has its own preferred ways of organizing content. While much interdisciplinary work is vital and impressive, such results can occur only after teachers have mastered at least portions of their specific disciplines (Boix-Mansilla & Gardner, 2008).

As with teaching within the disciplines, teachers' success with multidisciplinary units hinges on their ability to help students understand the analytic styles and problem-solving approaches that work best within each discipline and across disciplines and craft these into their own personal learning methodologies. These are both areas whose surfaces have been barely scratched by research, and future curriculum planners should continue to strive to learn more about the key relationships within and across disciplines that lead to better understanding of how the content can best be understood. Teachers must remember that involvement in any curricular approaches, regardless of how highly touted the approach may be, does not diminish their responsibility to ensure that their students master those parts of a discipline essential to operating successfully in twenty-first-century society and those areas of a discipline needed to pursue further study in that discipline.

Reading and Writing across the Curriculum

Historically, curricula have been departmentalized into content areas or disciplines. In the twenty-first century, a strong push to integrate the disciplines is complemented by the practice of ensuring that students also read and write across the curriculum. Knowing that the more opportunities students have to write what they read, the more likely they are to comprehend the material, educators in the Southern Regional Education Board's highly successful High Schools That Work make reading and writing across the curriculum the norm for most of their courses. These students read the equivalent of 25 books each year across the curriculum, conduct research, and write papers on their findings (Bottoms, 2007).

At least two advantages can be derived from reading and writing across the curriculum. Obviously, reading strengthens students' understanding of the discipline being studied; understanding is enriched further when the subjects cross the discipline boundaries. Writing also offers an avenue for enriching understanding. Writing forces students to ascend the learning hierarchy, for having to write about a subject is an invitation to internalize otherwise possibly random-seeming information, making it personal and meaningful to the individual. Stephanie McConachie and colleagues (2006) say that "a new offshoot of reading and writing across the curriculum is disciplinary literacy, and that this new approach is based on the premise that students can develop deep understanding in a discipline only by using the same habits of reading, writing, and thinking as those used by experts in the discipline" (p. 8). Achieving this deep thinking demands the use of a variety of approaches including quick write (students have one minute to respond to a teacher prompt), structured note taking (students take notes on a form supplied by the teacher and end each section with a summary of the lesson), and learning logs (students respond to prompts designed to activate prior knowledge).

Writing across the curriculum is an excellent way to connect students to their subjects and to their school. Blum (2005) says that students are more likely to succeed when they feel connected to school. Teachers can provide students with meaningful learning experiences by assigning activities that connect to the world beyond the classroom, and writing across the curriculum is a natural means for achieving this goal.

Alternative Assessment

Assessment could well be called the paradox of education reform. Like Dickens's "age of enlightenment" and "season of hope," assessment offers unprecedented opportunity to improve schooling. Yet, also quoting Dickens, the ways that we have used assessment can cast us into a "season of darkness and an age of foolishness."

The significance of assessment to contemporary teachers is reflected in the amount of time they spend on it. Contemporary teachers spend as much as a third to half of their professional time on assessment-related activities, yet current teacher education programs are practically void in covering basic assessment techniques. In effect, we have used assessment almost exclusively as an indicator of success, even though it has the potential of being so much more—an instrument of improvement.

The educational critics of the late 1980s and 1990s were aware of the awesome power that assessment can have in shaping the curriculum. Critics often complain that the curriculum is test driven or that teachers teach to the test. *Alternative assessment* is a general term that refers to a variety of types of assessment designed to replace traditional testing, including performance assessment, authentic assessment, continuous assessment, progressive reporting, and self-assessment.

FYI Assessing Student Learning

Christopher R. Gareis • The College of William & Mary

In my experience as a former secondary school principal and in my current role working with school leaders, I have found that one of the most overlooked and undersupervised domains of teacher responsibilities is that of *assessing student learning.* In an era of accountability, a teacher's ability to create and use assessments in the classroom to support student learning should be of primary importance. With this in mind, I have developed a simple series of prompts that instructional leaders can use to sharply focus on classroom-based assessment in practical terms.

The term *assessment* as used here means any instrument, tool, activity, technique, or method that a teacher uses to gather information about the nature and degree of student learning—including something as formal as a paper-and-pencil unit test or as informal as monitoring students' oral responses during discussion. The prompts can be used in a variety of supervisory settings—for example, during a post-observation or pre-observation conference. They also can be used to frame your own focus as you observe a teacher's lesson or as you review a teacher's professional portfolio.

Finally, you may notice that several of these prompts could easily be characterized as *leading questions.* In other words, most of the prompts are worded in such a way as to make clear what is expected as *best practice.* In this way, expectations for professional practice in the domain of student assessment can be reinforced during the supervision process. The prompts appear below.

- How do you go about either creating or selecting the assessments you use in your class?
- At what points during a unit do you typically assess student learning, and how do your purposes change at these different points?
- How do you ensure that your assessments are reasonably valid (that is, they are indicative of the intended learning outcomes of the unit)?
- How do you ensure that your assessments are reasonably reliable (that is, they are relatively free from the influence of unintentional error in your construction)?
- What different types of assessments do you use in your class and why (e.g., select-response, open-response, and performance-based)?
- Describe how you provide feedback to students on assessments in order to support their learning.
- Give an example or two of instructional decisions you have made that were based on classroom assessment results.

Performance Assessment

Performance assessment is an attempt to escape the simple testing that required only the recalling of information, which was the most popular form of testing until the 1980s. *Performance assessment* requires instead that students use the information and knowledge they acquire. Because students must use this knowledge to solve problems, performance evaluation leads students to develop higher-order thinking skills.

Authentic Assessment

During the education reform movement of the late 1980s and early 1990s, the schools attributed students' failure to perform at least in part to a dysfunctional testing system. At that time, true-false, multiple choice, and fill-in-the-blank tests dominated elementary and secondary assessment. The curricula offered teachers very limited options for measuring those skills students needed to function in an information-based society. Students had trouble perceiving those tests as being related to real life.

Authentic assessment (discussed in chapter 9) is designed to measure students' ability to apply the knowledge they acquire to their real-life experiences. Armstrong et al. (2009, pp. 63–64) state, "Authentic assessment requires learners to demonstrate what they have learned in a way that has much in common with how a proficient adult might deal with the content that has been learned." Because authentic assessment deals with real-life problems, these tests prompt students to raise their thinking to higher levels. Authentic assessment uses a variety of instruments to assess student progress, including portfolios, exhibitions, performances, learning logs, and experiments as measures of student progress. Some educators fail to recognize that multiple-choice tests can be one of several methods of authentic testing, so long as they are not the only or dominant means (Popham, 2007/2008). Some opponents of authentic assessment question whether authentic learning can ever be measured accurately and argue persuasively that if it can be measured, it would require years.

Continuous Assessment and Progress Reporting

As the name implies, continuous assessment is ongoing. The term also implies that the assessments are related to one another, which makes sense: Just as students' education program should be a continuous effort (as opposed to sporadic, unrelated exercises and unrelated sessions), proponents of continuous assessment argue that the assessment program should be a *series* of assessments, each leading to the next.

A type of testing that is included in continuous assessment is formative evaluation. Discussed in chapter 9, *formative evaluation* is defined as "the designing and using of tests for only one specific purpose—to promote learning" (Henson, 2004). Formative evaluation consists of a series of short tests given at short intervals to provide students with ongoing feedback on their progress. Formative evaluation never affects students' grades. A second use of formative evaluation is to inform teachers about how effective their teaching and curriculum are, thereby helping teachers improve their instruction.

Progress reporting (also in chapter 9) is a term often used in conjunction with continuous assessment, and it refers to the popular practice of reporting student progress. On a continuing basis, student progress is systematically reported to the students themselves or to the students and their parents. Although progress reports can take various shapes, parents find written descriptions of student behavior to be the most useful.

Self-Assessment

Self-assessment is the practice of involving students with the assessment of their own work. It has the benefit of motivating students by promoting a sense of ownership over their education program. Fisher and colleagues (2007/2008) say that schoolwide formative assessment is at its best when rich instructional conversation among teachers drives the changes needed to reach group goals. Ironically, the national role that assessment plays in education reform involves the opposite: no willingness to involve local educators in the design of these tests or in deciding how they are to be used. This unwillingness to involve teachers results, at least in part, from the fact that today assessment is a billion-dollar business. Unfortunately, although schools and teachers are held accountable, the testing industry is not held accountable but is allowed to cloak itself in secrecy.

Self-assessment can be improved through the use of *rubrics*. Each rubric should set clear expectations, and teachers should give students opportunities to revise their work (Andrade 2007/2008). Tom Oldenski cautions that teachers often use rubrics without first testing them in relation to what is being expected of students. When aligned with the expectations that teachers hold for students, rubrics can bring their expectations for students closer to students' self-expectations.

FYI Creating Rubrics

Thomas Oldenski • University of Dayton

To assist teachers in creating rubrics and valuing the importance of testing and evaluating the rubric before it is use, the supervisor can provide a nonthreatening experience of creating and evaluating a rubric. I have utilized the following activity as part of staff-development programs and in my assessment courses. The task is to create a rubric for a chocolate chip cookie. This is done by small groups of teachers, usually three to four. The group chooses the criteria and the scale for evaluating the criteria. Each group shares their rubric. After this, each group is given the same several types (brands) of chocolate chip cookies (about 4 to 6) and uses their rubric to evaluate them. Each group then shares its experience of the process of creating and utilizing the rubric. Through this discussion, the strengths and weaknesses of the rubric are identified. Teachers realize that many times they create rubrics or use already-developed rubrics without ever testing or evaluating them in relation to what is being asked of the students in terms of work and performance.

Tenure and Life Certification

Of all the issues that face educators in the twenty-first century, probably none is more volatile than the issue of tenure. Some legislators are dedicating their full time and energy to crafting, introducing, and passing legislation in their state that would completely abolish teacher tenure. These legislators not only maintain that tenure does not serve education but that, indeed, it does just the opposite. They say that tenure protects incompetent teachers, making reform difficult or impossible. Whether these legislators really believe this or whether they are using this issue to garner votes is impossible to know.

Perhaps no other issue has the power to rally teachers and provoke strikes more than attempts to abolish tenure. Teachers often remind those who would rid their schools of tenure that tenure was created to protect competent teachers from the whims of administrators and pressure groups. They argue that such protection is essential if they are to experiment with new methods and openly exchange ideas and practices, in particular those ideas and practices needed to bring positive reform to their schools.

Even tenured teachers can be dismissed, but usually only for the following reasons (Armstrong et al., 2009).

1. *Incompetence.* Conditions that have been used to dismiss teachers for incompetence include lack of knowledge, failure to adapt to new teaching methods, violation of school rules, lack of cooperation, persistent negligence, lack of ability to impart knowledge, physical mistreatment of learners, and failure to maintain discipline. Failure to maintain discipline is one of the most common causes for dismissal actions filed against tenured teachers.
2. *Incapacity.* This standard includes any physical or mental condition that keeps a teacher from performing his or her assigned duties.
3. *Insubordination.* This is most commonly applied to teachers who stubbornly and willfully violate reasonable school rules and policies. Usually several insubordinate acts are required before dismissal can occur.
4. *Conduct.* This is a broad standard that can embrace behaviors as varied as insulting fellow teachers, espousing personal political causes in the classroom, taking time off without permission, and even shoplifting. Some specific instances where school districts have successfully dismissed teachers for inappropriate conduct have involved drinking to excess, serving alcohol to learners in the teacher's home, and telling wrestling team members to lie about their weight when registering for a tournament.
5. *Immorality.* The courts have consistently ruled that moral fitness is a standard that teachers must meet. Dismissal actions related to this category may include such things as criminal activity, sexual misconduct, drug use, and dishonesty.
6. *Other causes.* Many tenure laws provide for dismissal for a number of other reasons that include such things as intemperance, neglect of duty, cruelty, and willful misconduct.

Although there are varied reasons for firing teachers, their administrators must prove that a teacher has behaved in one or more of these specified ways. School districts can dismiss nontenured teachers much more easily than they can dismiss tenured teachers.

Ethnic Diversity

Historically, teachers have been poorly prepared to address the increasingly diverse nature of our society. Textbooks not only have failed to address this issue, but they have actually contributed to the problem by promoting unacceptable stereotypes and prejudices. Although for decades educators have known that a large number of nonmainstream Americans have experienced low academic achievement, they have chosen not to try to help these students because they have believed them less capable, a perception known as the "genetic deficit." By the 1960s, this view was replaced by a "cultural deficit" view, which was the belief that nonmainstream students perform poorly because they receive less intellectual stimulation at home than mainstream students receive.

These views have limited teachers' efforts to help all students achieve, and they have damaged the self-images of these students. The curriculum ought to describe ways different cultural groups have contributed to Western civilization. Immigrants are well represented in occupations that, while perhaps not requiring a higher education, require much skill (for example, chefs, tailors, and jewelers). When selecting textbooks and ancillary materials, teachers should choose those that represent nonmainstream persons positively.

Another major limiting factor for many nonmainstream students is the language barrier. An increasing number of students come from homes where English is not the primary spoken language. Studying in their primary language improves students' self-images and enhances their understanding of their own worth. In selecting textbooks and ancillary materials, teachers should consider the potential language barrier and avoid those texts and other materials that are poorly written and difficult to understand.

Fortunately, even with all the mistakes our nation has made in dealing with the needs of its people, in general Americans are now committed to serving the needs of all students. The American public believes that the achievement gaps that separate black and other minority students from the mainstream should be closed, and the public believes that the best ways to do this are to provide more instructional help for low-performing students, provide additional voluntary pre-school care, let parents enroll their children in any public school they choose, and give these parents financial support to cover or all tuition at private schools (Rose & Gallup, 2007). Unfortunately, there are major differences in achievement among students of different ethnic groups, and student dropout rates vary from group to group.

Stereotyping can be harmful. One way to get rid of stereotyping is to make students aware that the differences from one culture to another are exceeded by the differences among members of the same culture. Stereotyping can be further reduced by increasing cultural awareness in the classroom (Asher, 2007). For example, consider the common belief that white people are smarter than black people. Consider that this image may come from the fact that most white students start school at an earlier age (Milner, 2007).

Gender Equity

Age-old stereotypes about women have produced ongoing, negative impacts on their future. In the United States, boys historically were content with their culture's expectations for them as physically active and self-reliant. Girls, however, had to settle for the cultural expectations of them as obedient and affectionate. Could genetic-deficit theory explain females' overall lower performance in the hard sciences and mathematics? Our schools have been guilty of sustaining and even promoting these ideas. For example, girls generally have not been encouraged to take advanced mathematics. This pattern continues in college, where female achievement in mathematics and the sciences has lagged behind that of males (Armstrong et al., 2009).

In recent years, we have tried to give girls tougher subjects such as math and the sciences because it has been touted as politically correct. Perhaps this is not a good reason. Instead, perhaps when we increase the amount and difficulty of science and math for girls it should be done with an eye toward nurturing girls' unique strengths. For example, mathematics teachers could give girls assignments that require more writing, since girls' verbal scores on achievement tests are higher than boys' scores. Teachers of co-ed science and mathematics classes should use some strategies that acknowledge the strengths of students of each gender. Because the culture in any class is an important variable, this practice

FYI Using Diaries to Address Gender Bias

Victoria Robinson • University of Northern Iowa

To correct gender-biased classroom behavior, teachers need to be exposed to gender-equity issues. This activity can point them in the right direction.

I ask my students to close their eyes and imagine that they are sitting next to a babbling brook with the sun casting shadows through the trees. As the birds chirp and the wind rustles the tall grass, they pick up a diary and begin to read it. It is the story of their life, with rich description of daily routines, parental guidance, academic and extracurricular school experiences, fears, joys, and plans for the future. Everything in this diary reflects their life (same family, school, neighborhood, and so on) except for one detail: It tells their life story as it would have unfolded *had they been born the opposite gender*.

Still keeping their eyes closed, the students are asked to think about how the events in this diary might differ from those they have actually experienced. After three minutes of thinking time, students conduct a ten-minute walk-and-talk with a classmate, describing what they thought and felt as they considered how their life story might be different if born the opposite gender. Students reconvene and report their conversation to the large group. Issues of stereotyping, bias, and advantages/disadvantages of being either male or female come to light during this discussion.

could hold considerable promise for teaching math and science. Teachers at all levels, especially at the preschool and early elementary levels, should be careful to choose textbooks and other educational materials for their classes that portray females in roles that once were held only or mainly by males, and vice versa. Images of male and female secretaries, flight attendants, nurses, doctors, and law officers can help dispel the myth that these jobs are appropriate for members of only one gender. In addition, teachers should use this awareness when making role-playing assignments. When planning to use consultants, efforts should be made to use this opportunity to break gender stereotypes.

In the twentieth century, single-sex classrooms were created to promote the achievement of females. In 1995, only three public schools offered single-sex classes (Spielhagen, 2007), but by 2007, 51 schools had gone to single-sex classes throughout (Bauer, 2007).

Geographic Stereotyping

As a nation, we have held enduring stereotypes about people because of where they live. In the United States, Northerners and Southerners each have their specific prejudices against each other. Rural people have been thought of as "hayseeds," yet a substantial portion of today's farmers use advanced technology to run multimillion-dollar farms and ranches. People dwelling in the mountains are sometimes portrayed as ignorant and backward ("hillbillies"), yet improved communications, transportation, and technology have put many mountain people on the cutting edge of their businesses. Teachers should look for opportunities to debunk such stereotyping.

Students with Special Needs

The No Child Left Behind legislation requires school districts to describe how they will provide professional development to help teachers address students with special needs. One approach to helping these *special students* is by redesigning the curriculum to meet their needs. High expectations are needed for all students, including special students. If we accept the premise that all children can and will learn, then teachers and schools are responsible for accomplishing this objective. The following questions by Hoover (1990, pp. 410–411) can help ensure that this goal is reached:

1. *Content:* Does the student possess a sufficient reading level?
   a. Has the student demonstrated mastery of prerequisite skills?
   b. Does the student possess sufficient language abilities?
   c. Does the student possess appropriate prior experience?
2. *Instructional strategy:* Is the student motivated to learn through strategy?
   a. Does the strategy facilitate active participation?
   b. Is the strategy's effectiveness relative to content to be learned?
   c. In what conditions is the strategy effective/ineffective?

3. *Instructional setting:* Does the setting facilitate active participation?
   a. Is the student able to complete tasks in a selected setting?
   b. Is the student able to learn in a selected setting?
   c. Is the setting appropriate for the learning selected?
4. *Student behavior:* What types of behaviors are exhibited by the learner?
   a. Time on task?
   b. Attention to task?
   c. Self-control abilities?
   d. Time-management skills?
   e. What are the most appropriate behaviors exhibited in selecting a strategy?

The teacher can also help students with disabilities by choosing textbooks and other materials carefully. Once selected, the following strategies to enhance learning can be used with these materials:

1. Change the nature of the learning task from one that requires reading and written responses to one that requires listening with oral responses (for example, use a cassette tape/CD or a peer tutor).
2. Allow the student to demonstrate understanding through group projects or oral reports.
3. Allow the student to complete smaller amounts of material in a given time.
4. Have the student circle or underline the correct responses rather than write them.
5. Fasten the student's materials to the desk to help with coordination problems.
6. Provide extra drill-and-practice materials for those students who understand the material but need more time to master it.
7. Present information using graphs, illustrations, or diagrams.
8. Incorporate rhyming, rhythm, music, or movement into lessons.
9. Lessen distractions from other sources within the learning environment.

Another approach to helping special-needs students is through the use of technology, which can improve these students' achievement levels and attitudes. Some educators believe that the possibility for improvement through the use of *assistive technology* (designed especially to help students overcome their disabilities) will be so profound that it will require educators to rethink the scope of instructional opportunities for children with disabilities. Technology can be a great equalizer for individuals with disabilities that might prevent full participation in school, work, and the community. This is most evident in the case of students with mobility, hearing, or vision impairments but is also true for individuals with limitations in cognition and perception. Programs such as Technology and Augmentative Communication for Learning Enhancement (Curtis, 2008) use computer-enhanced learning tools such as speech-generation devices, motion-sensitive and breath-sensitive communication technology, and other cutting-edge techniques to ensure equal participation and inclusion in the classroom.

Inclusion

The opposite of the concept of ability grouping is the concept of *inclusion*. Inclusion differs from mainstreaming in that mainstreamed students spend only part of their days in regular classrooms, whereas students in inclusion curricula spend their entire day in regular classrooms. Mainstreamed students may not receive special services in the regular classroom, while students in inclusion curricula are given whatever special services they require within the regular classroom. Yet another important difference is that students who are challenged are welcomed and valued in the inclusive classroom (Armstrong et al., 2009).

Students with disabilities tend to achieve a modest to moderate amount more when placed in classrooms with nondisabled students. Learners with disabilities taught in inclusive classrooms have performed better on academic tests and have improved their social and communications skills. A report by the National Center for Educational Restructuring and Inclusion (Villa & Thousand, 2005) found that students placed in inclusion programs showed academic gains, improved standardized test scores, and reached IEP goals. These students also had fewer incomplete assignments, interacted more positively with peers, and positively increased their attitudes toward schooling (Weishaar et al., 2007).

Inclusion is a highly controversial issue across the country. The public does not support holding special education students to the same standards as all other students (Rose & Gallup, 2007) because they believe it is disruptive and it lowers the quality of education for nonchallenged students; yet inclusion is required by federal law. Undoubtedly, the controversy over this practice will continue. The 2001 No Child Left Behind legislation increased the emphasis on accountability for schools to ensure that all children were able to meet state standards for learning. School reform in special education paralleled, and was then dovetailed with, the NCLB.

> The 2004 Individuals with Disabilities Education Improvement Act [IDEA] contained many NCLB references, including the participation of children with disabilities in state and district assessment systems, goals for children with disabilities that reflected goals for all children, the flexible use of funds from the IDEA to carry out schoolwide programs under the NCLB, and a mandate that all personnel were adequately prepared to work with children, subject to the provisions in the NCLB. (Weishaar et al., 2007, p. 38)

Currently, federal law (NCLB) requires schools to offer disabled students the right to be educated with their nondisabled peers. School officials who remove disabled students from inclusive classrooms must be capable of proving that such placements benefit the disabled students. Real inclusion involves restructuring of a school's entire program and requires constant assessment of practices and results. More comprehensive research must be done as inclusion becomes more widespread. Constant reflection is necessary if we ever hope to be able to make clear determinations about which specific strategies will help children to become happy, contributing citizens. For further information, visit the Web sites in box 11.1

Box 11.1 Inclusion

- *Inclusion in Education: Issues and Resources*
  http://thechp.syr.edu/Inclusion_in_Education.html
  A vast and comprehensive database of excellent resources, including an annotated bibliography, selected readings, case studies, the latest research studies and legislation, links to other Web sites for inclusion-based organizations and projects, teaching and assessment advice for all age levels, resources for parents and families, and much, much more.
- *Electronic Journal for Inclusive Education*
  http://www.cehs.wright.edu/~prenick
  A peer reviewed electronic journal which deals with research concerning inclusive education with scholarly contributions from faculty and graduate students. The journal addresses inclusion issues at all levels of educational endeavors: research, administrative issues, classroom teaching, and exemplary university student work.

The following case features a highly effective teacher-made program designed to help regular students understand their autistic classmates. As you read it, think about its title: "Whom are we preparing for inclusion?"

case study

Whom Are We Preparing for Inclusion?

Ursula Pridgen Ricketts
Concordia University

Background

The current educational system leaves little time for the development of social skills, yet such skills are vital for learning achievement. Using special strategies to increase social opportunities between students with special needs and a broad base of peers could significantly benefit children who are differently able.

In planning for inclusion, the views of students are often overlooked. Most of the literature speaks to issues from the perspective of how to fit the special-needs children into the general education environment, rather than how to prepare the environment to include the special-needs children. Thinking about how education and training affect the acceptance and social interactions of students with special needs—specifically, children with autism—by their general education peers is an interesting and worthwhile exercise. Let's consider how to prepare the environment to include an autistic child.

The Community

In a middle school outside a large metropolitan city, a decision was made to take a reflective look at who was being prepared for inclusion. This school had thirty-two special education students, twenty of whom were in self-contained special education classrooms. Twelve of the students were being mainstreamed into the regular education classrooms. Eight of those participating in the regular education classroom were identified as having Autism Spectrum Disorder.

The school's current model failed to successfully promote academic competence in its special education students, while not hindering the academic success of the regular education students. It was determined that one source of the problem was the lack of social competence of the special-needs children. Autistic children in particular, as a result of their disorder, are not able to establish social competence. The demands placed on these children are enormous. Social competence is achieved by a person continually evaluating and instantaneously readjusting to situations. This skill of executing a variety of tasks and reading diverse social cues of other individuals is extremely difficult for an autistic child. Developing children are not always explicitly taught social norms. That understanding is gained automatically through their exposure and experiences. Social competence in autistic children can be acquired if they are provided with effective strategies and placed in an inclusive environment with the same consideration.

The Counselor/Case Manager

Ms. B, the counselor/case manager for the school, had been a part of the district for twelve years. Originally, Ms. B taught sixth- through eighth-grade social studies. Then she taught kindergarten for several years. Eventually Ms. B moved to first grade and began to loop through third grade for several years. Because she felt she was not meeting the needs of the students, Ms. B decided to return to school and complete the school counselor certification. Upon gaining certification, Ms. B. became a counselor/case manager within the district. She was frustrated with the concept of inclusion of special education children in its current state. This motivated her to think more consciously about how to maximize the experience for special-needs children.

While contemplating how to resolve her concerns, a parent approached her about an autistic child in her daughter's classroom. The parent said her daughter was afraid of the autistic child because the child stared and made inappropriate sounds, gestures, and responses in the classroom. The parent felt that this was a distraction to her child, and she was concerned about her daughter's academic success in the class. Ms. B attempted to explain that autism is a developmental disorder that impacts the way a child sees and interacts with the rest of the world. She explained that the disorder limits the child's ability to socially interact with others due to an abnormal functioning in communication skills, social skills, and the ability to reason. This, however, failed to ease the parent's concern; in fact it served to heighten her sense of angst.

As a result of that conversation, Ms. B began to realize that so much emphasis was placed on preparing the autistic child to join the regular education environment, along with provisions given to the regular education teacher, that no one bothered to think about the perspective of the regular education child. Ms. B wondered how to assist those children in handling the alteration of their sense of "normal." This sparked a thought of how to prepare the environment to truly include the special-needs child.

Ms. B decided to observe the situation more closely. She wanted to remain on the perimeter as much as possible to identify the underlying issues in order to determine how best to implement strategies to improve the situation for all. She noticed that the autistic students were not being accepted in unstructured and informal environments. All of the children, both the autistic and regular education children, ate at the same lunch tables and played on the same playgrounds, but the autistic children were not included in the conversations or games. Observations in a more structured environment, like the classroom, revealed the same situations. Both groups of children sat in the same class and participated in the experience of the same curriculum, but the autistic children remained alone and disconnected. Ms. B noticed that the common thread in both the structured and unstructured settings centered on socialization and interaction. This experience caused her to wonder how she could increase the social interactions between students with autism and those without.

The intriguing twist was that Ms. B wanted to directly impact the attitude of the regular education children. Recalling the story that the parent shared with her, she knew that those children did not understand the unfamiliar, which they needed to do in order for real change to occur. She also knew that if the autistic children were accepted socially, then the ability of all children would increase because there would be less distraction. Most of all, this would increase the motivation of the autistic children to learn. She set out to expand the regular education children's definition of "normal."

The Case

Along with teaching autistic children the strategies to enhance their social competency, Ms. B taught typically developing students about autism, empowering them to facilitate social interactions with the autistic children. She revisited the classification of autism. Children with the diagnosis typically have impairment in social interaction. They may have impairments in the use of nonverbal behaviors, fail to develop peer relationships, lack the spontaneity to engage in enjoyment, and lack emotional reciprocity. In addition, autistic children have impairments with communication, experiencing a delay in speech development, a lack of ability to initiate or sustain conversation with others, and repetitive use of language. The final symptom is stereotyped patterns of behavior that manifest with preoccupation, inflexibility to adhere to routines and rituals, repetitive motor mannerisms, and a persistent preoccupation with parts of objects.

Based on these classifications, Ms. B developed and implemented a process to prepare the environment to include the autistic children. The emphasis was on the regular education student. Ms. B spent forty-five minutes a session, on two different occasions, teaching the regular education students about Autism Spectrum Disorder. In the first session she began soliciting the opinions, attitudes, feelings, and knowledge of the regular education students about children with autism. The students were grouped in teams of three to complete a question sheet on autism. The students generated and shared their questions with Ms. B and with each other. She then shared information about how communication messages travel through the brain for both typical developing children and autistic children, pointing out that in autistic children pathways in the brain become confused and oftentimes the messages are lost. She shared the following ten facts about autism with the regular education children.

1. Children with autism need friends just like other children.
2. You cannot catch autism from another person.
3. Autism cannot be cured.
4. People born with autism will not outgrow the disorder (although they can learn ways to fit into the world around them).
5. People with autism can obtain jobs.
6. People with autism need others to be patient with them.
7. Some people with autism become upset when things change in their environment or schedule (and therefore, planning ahead of time is important).
8. People with autism are not all alike. (They have different behaviors, personalities, and needs.)
9. People with autism are able to learn.
10. More boys than girls have autism. (Autism usually is recognizable by the age of 3.)

Ms. B then showed the regular education children a video about an autistic child named Gordon, whose ultimate goal was to have friends.

At the next session, Ms. B sought to integrate the previous session's information. The focus of the session began with the communication system of the autistic children. Ms. B demonstrated how an autistic child (in the same grade level as her regular education students) communicates. Then she shared guidelines for how to be a friend to the autistic child. The regular education students discussed their current opinions, attitudes, feelings, and knowledge in comparison to those before the two sessions. Both she and her students recognized a noticeable improvement.

Ms. B had learned from a professional development experience that peer training can be a viable tool to increase interactions among children. Therefore, she asked the regular education students to be a part of a recess buddy group by being paired with an autistic child. The regular education students and the autistic children were paired together to be recess buddies based on similar interest and skill level. Ms. B determined how best to pair the students by engaging the autistic children in various games. While participating in these games many social communication skills were identified to assist the autistic children in initiating appropriate contact. The recess buddy partnership continued for five sessions.

Ms. B began to notice that the regular education children were able to prompt and engage the autistic students who, after repeated modeling, were able to communicate independently. The autistic students were observed having fun and reciprocating responses. Along with the regular education children, the autistic students were giving high fives, thumbs up, and laughing with each other. Ms. B also observed the regular education kids initiating indoor recess activities. During literacy center activities, all regular education students volunteered to include autistic students in their groups and worked with them. In addition, lunchtimes were more inclusive and engaging for both types of children. Prior to the education and training sessions for the regular education children, the general education teacher found it necessary to assign a child to partner with the autistic children. After the sessions, the students were volunteering or initiating contact on their own.

The general education teacher with whom Ms. B had worked for a long time always treated the autistic children like visitors to the class. After the education and training, the regular education teacher began to think of more creative ways to include the autistic children in the classroom and, most importantly, into the curriculum approach. That teacher requested that the program be provided for all grades in the school and the district.

This formula of education, training, and participation in the recess buddies groups was successful in increasing social interaction among general education peers and students with autism. Ms. B was eventually able to implement this program on a wider level within the school and in the district. She presents the program and the outcomes annually as a part of districtwide professional development. The greatest achievement was that the autistic children were no longer a distraction in the educational environment. Both the children with autism and the regular education students were engaged in meaningful ways that fostered and promoted academic success. This positive development served to unify a district torn apart by the entire concept of inclusion.

The most surprising outcome was experienced by the parent who started the entire inquiry. She returned to Ms. B and thanked her for listening and finding a way to help all the children. When her child became comfortable interacting with autistic children, the parent became more comfortable with the idea of her child being in a class with autistic children. She worked with Ms. B to create an education and training program for the parents of regular education children and the parents of autistic children.

Issues for Further Consideration

1. How can this program be expanded to include all special education children who are mainstreamed?
2. What current research-based strategies could enhance the effectiveness of this inclusion model?
3. How can additional underlying issues be explored and addressed?
4. How can the direct impact on student achievement be measured?
5. What community resources might be available to assist in further development of this inclusion model?
6. What additional support is needed to support the regular education teachers?

Suggested Reading

Lee, S., Odom, S., & Loftin, R. (2007). Social engagement with peers and stereotypic behavior of children with autism. *Journal of Positive Behavior Interventions, 9*, 67–79.

Miller, M. (2008). What do students think about inclusion? *Phi Delta Kappan, 89*(5), 389–391.

Owen-DeSchrywer, J., Carr, E., Cale, S., & Blakely-Smith, A. (2008). Promoting social interactions between students with Autism Spectrum Disorder and their peers in inclusive settings. *Focus on Autism and Other Developmental Disabilities, 23*, 15–28.

Sansosti, F., Powell-Smith, K., & Kincaid, D. (2004). A research synthesis of social story interventions for children with Autism Spectrum Disorders. *Focus on Autism and Other Developmental Disabilities, 19*, 194–204.

Gifted Students

Historically, little has been done to ensure that the needs of gifted students have been met. One popular approach to helping gifted students is through grouping, which can enable teachers to enrich the curriculum used with these students. Grouping can provide a special curriculum for gifted students, one they will not find boring. The Internet provides unlimited possibilities for connecting these students with problems that can even challenge their creativity and problem-solving skills.

The creative needs of these students can also be met through the fine arts (see Henson, 2010, chapter 9). They may benefit from opportunities to hold discussions with artists and opportunities to create their own projects. The alternative curriculum shown in chapter 7 (see box 7.1) offers a variety of classes that challenge students to use their creative abilities. Although such programs are motivating and fun, it is important that they be profoundly academically challenging if they are to be used by gifted students. Two curriculum models that have proved to engage and challenge gifted students are the parallel curriculum, discussed in chapter 4, and inquiry-based learning, discussed in chapter 10.

The University of Connecticut is home to the Neag Center for Gifted Education and Talent Development. Their studies focusing on meeting the needs of gifted and talented youth have received national and international attention for over 40 years. The earliest research emphasized studies related to creativity, assessment, identification, programming, and evaluation. Several studies conducted by their research team are considered seminal research that guides the design and development of programs and services to meet the needs of gifted and talented students. An interesting feature of their Web site is a special section for parents of gifted students. For further information, visit http://www.gifted.uconn.edu.

- For a wealth of information on curriculum design for gifted students, visit www.kidsource.com/kidsource/monthly/mon.gifted.web.010100.html
- A comprehensive list of Web sites on gifted students can be found at www.usd320.k12.ks.us/whs/lmc/gifted.html

Senior Citizens

Perhaps the most overlooked members of American society are its senior citizens. In most countries, the senior members of a society maintain high status because they are respected for their knowledge and wisdom. Even the most primitive societies have organized education systems that use senior citizens as teachers. Unfortunately, the United States has not yet recognized seniors' potential as a valuable educational resource.

Service learning programs offer teachers an excellent opportunity to bring students and senior citizens together. Projects can be planned that encourage senior citizens to share their wisdom with students at all grade levels. One effective vehicle that can be used to transfer knowledge and values is storytelling, through which senior citizens can share a wealth of knowledge about the values and lifestyles of earlier generations. Storytelling connects the cognitive side of learning with the emotions. Such knowledge can give youth a much-needed anchor for their own values and beliefs.

Senior citizens can serve as role models, participating in mentor programs to provide emotional support and guidance to students. Seniors can help with schoolwork, job-skill development, career planning, and many other challenges that face young people today. Nearly 40% of Americans over 60 years of age are now involved in some type of volunteer activity. Volunteers can serve as tutors or teacher aides, work in the library, or help with after-school activities. In one school, grandparents served on patrol and as school guards to help keep kids safe. For more information, visit the Partnership for Family Involvement in Education Web site (http://www.ed.gov/pubs/PFIE/community.html).

Magnet Schools

Magnet schools have a specialized theme—a curriculum that generally is not available in other schools in their community (e.g., an auto mechanics school in Indianapolis or a fine arts school in Houston). Most magnet schools are secondary schools, but some offer K–12 curricula. Students in schools located throughout the city can opt to spend part of their week in one of these magnet schools.

Overall, magnet schools have been successful in providing many students educational opportunities that they otherwise would not have had. In many communities, proponents claim that these schools enhance integration (Armstrong et al., 2009). However, these schools have not escaped criticism. Critics say that had the enormous amount of dollars required to build and operate these schools been instead spread out among the other schools in the district, then tremendous improvement could have been made in the other schools. Another major criticism of magnet schools is accessibility. Many magnet schools require students to furnish their own transportation, thus eliminating the possibility of attendance by many poorer students.

Charter Schools

Charter schools have been given special permission (usually for a period of five years) to experiment with unique curricula. For example, by law, schools with twenty or more students whose first language is not English are required to offer instruction in each non-English language for which there is a large enough population; however, a charter school located in an Hispanic community might receive permission to teach *only* in Spanish.

Success depends on the effectiveness of the authorizers, most of whom do not have to report to anyone. School boards are generally poor authorizers because they lack adequate infrastructure and they are often hampered by charter-averse individuals and interest groups (Palmer & Gau, 2005).

Most founders of these schools say their reason for wanting them is to match their vision. Families like them because of their small size, higher standards, educational philosophy, greater opportunity for parent involvement, and good teachers. Teachers like them because of their philosophy, their good reputations, their administrators, and their small classes. Teachers and administrators in charter schools enjoy an unusual scope of freedom with regard to teaching methodology, but they can lose their jobs if students fail to achieve.

A basic belief about charter schools is that a higher-quality education can be offered when the micro-management and bureaucracy that characterizes traditional public schools can be eliminated. It is not surprising to learn that most charter school members come from families who were dissatisfied with traditional schools. Perhaps it is also not surprising to learn that these customers want higher standards and a louder voice in the running of the school. Some may be surprised to learn that charter schools often attract low-income families and minority parents. For example, in Minnesota, most members of charter schools are from low-income groups and communities of color. Charter schools actually have a higher percentage of low-income and minority students than standard public schools.

The number of charter schools grew from one in 1992 to over 2,700 in 2003 (Metcalf et al., 2003). This suggested that many people were ready to change to a nontraditional system to educate their children. In 2007, the majority of citizens (60%) favored charter schools (Rose & Gallup, 2007). However, the following year, the public's support for charter schools dropped from 60% to 51% (Bushaw & Gallup, 2008).

Limitations of Charter Schools

If the sudden drop in support for charter schools leads you to suspect that they have limits, you are right. Students in charter schools perform no better than their counterparts in regular public schools. Ironically, students in charter schools are more segregated than students in public schools (Barton, 2007/2008).

Resistance to change has slowed the development of charter schools. Merrow (2008) gives testament to charter schools' resistance to experiment and become the laboratories for testing innovations: "Now 20 years old, the charter movement has never come close to achieving its original vision of being 'laboratories of innovation' for the rest of the system. Too many charters are revved-up versions of the existing system, public schools on steroids, instead of breaking the mold" (p.18).

Often, without discussion among the teachers, the school's principal or the superintendent makes the decisions that guide charter schools. Teachers, parents, and students are rarely involved in discussions of the direction of their school. Christensen, Aaron, and Clark (2005) have stated this problem succinctly, "Many charter schools, particularly those authorized by local school districts, have failed to deliver on their educational promises because they are not in fact fully autonomous organizations" (p. 550). Like all other curricula, those at charter schools have both advantages and limitations and, therefore, have both supporters and critics. At their best, these schools have stimulating curricula and enthusiastic teachers. Consider a fine-arts charter school in Houston that uses performing artists to teach. Where else could such teachers find a school that is dedicated to the arts alone? Where else could students find teachers who are professional artists?

Some states are proceeding slowly with legislation and are taking various precautions. Some critics worry that the charter school movement has a creaming effect, taking from the public schools their best teachers and their best students (Lacireno-Paquet & Holyoke, 2007). California has set a limit of no more than 100 charter schools for the state and no more than 10 for any district, and some states issue charters only to existing schools to prevent the use of funds to pay for new buildings. Recently, however, many state departments of education were found to be charter friendly or, at least, charter tolerant (Palmer & Gau, 2005).

According to Betts and Tang (2008), in the long run the success of the charter movement will depend on whether it is able to build on its successes and abandon its failures. To reinforce success and eliminate failure, we need to understand what explains these variations. A second generation of achievement research in these areas is urgently needed. We need to ask ourselves: What are the attributes of highly productive versus unproductive charter schools? What are more successful states and cities doing that others might replicate? What explains the apparent low performance of some charter high schools, and what can be done about it?

Business–School Partnership Programs

Business people have always taken an interest in schools because schools are vital to a prospering community, and their level of interest was further kindled by the education reform reports of the 1980s and 1990s. Partnerships are purposeful arrangements with other organizations that are fundament to the creation, survival, and growth of an individual organization. Many businesses have participated in adopt-a-school programs, taking special responsibility for helping a single school. This help has come in a variety of ways, including financial support, providing consultants to the schools, and providing students on-the-job experience to see whether they wish to pursue various careers. For example, The Ford Partnership for Advanced Studies has some 160 sites, and Project Lead the Way has pre-engineering programs in more than 1,000 high schools throughout the United States (Hoachlander, 2007). In New York, the Long Island Works Coalition (2003) established a business–school partnership to ensure a continuous supply of qualified workers who possess the knowledge required of their employees. In Wisconsin, the Milwaukee School District has modified the entire K–12 curriculum to prepare students to work in apprenticeship programs. In Alaska, some 70% of the Anchorage schools participate in about 200 partnerships with local businesses (Anchorage School District, 2002).

Like all partnerships, business–school partnerships must offer advantages to both partners if they are to succeed. For the participating students, these programs provide income, opportunities to explore careers, experience needed to develop expertise in the job role, and an inside track to a permanent job at a time when employment opportunities are becoming increasingly scarce. The participating business must also realize meaningful benefits. Partnerships with schools have become a politically correct practice. In addition to benefiting from positive publicity, a major enticement for many businesses to join partnership programs is the opportunity to train students, some of whom will become lifetime employees who have grown up in the culture of the company, taking on the characteristics of the successful supervisors/trainers who are role models for these future employees. Furthermore, positive shaping occurs to these supervisors as a consequence of their leadership roles, including improved management skills, greater enjoyment of their jobs (and hence better employee retention), and increased attention to improving the development of their own skills.

Partnerships have the power to bring dramatic improvement, but partnerships also can be used to promote self-serving interests, which can be damaging to students. To reduce the likelihood for such damage, the roles of both parties should be carefully delineated.

National Standards

During the 1980s and 1990s the public showed a renewed interest in and demand for schools and teachers to be held accountable for learning. For some people, such concerns are usually accompanied by the felt need to have *national standards*. Fifty percent of the public supports the idea of having one set of standards for all states, and the other 50% prefers that each state should have freedom to set its own standards (Bushaw & Gallup, 2008). Proponents say that without national standards, many states will not provide adequate education for their youth. Although supportive of national standards, the public is becoming disenchanted with the increasing reliance on standardized testing (Rose & Gallup, 2007). Those who oppose the movement, however, argue that the teaching and learning we all desire cannot be imposed by the state, and that such standards limit the learning of the best students by lowering the level of expectancy.

Standards hold student learning and demonstrations of work at a constant level. This leveling effect can be argued to be either good or bad. Perhaps a more important observation is that merely setting high standards will not improve student learning. It might be worth questioning the effectiveness of setting higher standards if students cannot now measure up to old, presumably less demanding standards. It can be argued that the search for a test (sometimes referred to as a silver bullet) that will avoid the difficulties posed by the norm-referenced tests that have dominated the last century keeps us tied to a false hope, however well intended.

Another argument against national standards is that they tend to stifle creativity among students and teachers, and that the encouragement and opportunity for students to be creative is important to the student and the nation. But the advocates for national standards argue that these standards are not dictates of specific student and teacher behavior, nor are they prescriptions for specific information to be dictated by the government. Standards are not a narrow description of information to be learned and skills to be performed under a particular set of conditions but rather are broad enough to be articulated with benchmarks.

Initially, the majority of citizens supported massive national testing, but that support has diminished and currently the population is divided, with four times as many saying there is too much testing as those who favor increasing it (Bushaw & Gallup, 2008). Most favor using a national test to determine whether students should graduate from high school. Furthermore, most Americans believe that our students are not the only ones who should be tested. Three-fourths of all citizens feel that teachers and administrators also should be required to take national standardized tests to ensure quality instruction (Bushaw & Gallup, 2008).

Quality education cannot be guaranteed by legislation, and this includes setting national standards. Some educators question whether externally mandated goals ever result in meaningful improvement, yet one thing is certain: Teachers must be involved early in goal development. Teachers may need help in wrestling with the standards issue. Perhaps the best approach is to step away and review the potentials and limitations of the standards and of how they are used. Box 11.2 has been developed to assist teachers who have responsibility for choosing whether their school will either create their own set of standards or adopt an existing set of standards.

Box 11.2 Guidelines for Adopting and Crafting Standards

We need standards that

- help ensure opportunities for all students to master the essentials.
- lead to objectives that are attainable by all students.
- define attainable essentials and help educators guide students in achieving them.

We don't need standards if

- better only means more.
- they do not represent what educators know is best practice.
- they are handed down from above (top-down) and teachers are not involved in setting them.
- they are specific dictates of content and classroom procedures.

Many states have taken the initiative to set their own standards. Most of these standards require higher levels of understanding. For example, in South Carolina's standards, two frequently used words that identify the lowest levels of Bloom's Taxonomy of Educational Objectives (*recall* and *recognize*) appear in fewer than 10% of the state standards (Anderson, 2009). As you continue to study the national standards movement, you will probably discover that attempts to generalize either the importance of standards in one state or the techniques used to implement them in other states have usually failed. Comparing standards in one state with those of another, or comparing standards to behavioral objectives or outcome-based education, is looking at the standards out of context.

Increased Parental Involvement and Control

Parents will continue to demand an increased role in determining the direction the local schools are taking, and this is good because increasing evidence exists that parents can significantly increase their children's cognitive attainment. For example, parents can provide useful insights into students' literacy behaviors in the home setting. Current trends indicate that parent–teacher conferences are becoming more centered around portfolios and focused on communicating student developmental progress, growth in independent reading, the development of attitudes and interests, and the ability to use reading and writing for a variety of purposes.

Teachers tend to draw the line when parents make suggestions about daily classroom operations such as teaching methodology and classroom management methods. Teachers generally feel that most parents lack the expertise required to make decisions of this nature. Keeping parents from interfering while honoring the fact that the schools belong to the parents and other members of the community is a fine balance that twenty-first-century administrators and teachers will need to maintain as the trend toward increased desire for parental control continues. Administrators and teachers must continue to improve communications with parents. A review of research and literature shows that teachers use specific strategies to involve parents. As we mention throughout this book, technology is playing an ever-increasing role. However, there is no substitution for regularly scheduled events that bring teachers face-to-face with parents. As Claus (1999, p. 14) has pointed out:

> The literature suggests that the more teachers and parents know each other on a personal basis, and the more educators understand and appreciate the perspectives of parents, the greater the likelihood the two groups will be able to collaborate and, in times of disagreement, achieve constructive compromise.

Another way that parents are becoming involved in some parts of the country is through the forming of parent-teacher-administrator networks, joining to form "families." These families may involve several schools. The Los Angeles public school district has more than two dozen such school families. These networks can generate a sense of efficiency, which is required for maximum improvement.

Interstate New Teacher Assessment and Support Consortium (INTASC)

Many turn-of-the-century education programs sought to improve teaching by increasing performance standards. During the 1980s and early 1990s this approach focused primarily on student performance. The 1990s brought an increased emphasis on teacher preparation. One of the earliest of these programs was the Interstate New Teacher Assessment and Support Consortium (INTASC). Whereas most 1980s education reform had focused on strengthening teacher preparation in the content areas (particularly science and mathematics), INTASC was aimed at improving teachers' ability to integrate their content knowledge with pedagogical knowledge.

INTASC developed the following set of core standards designed to be used as a framework in teacher preparatory programs (CCSSO, 2005):

1. The teacher understands the central concepts, tools of inquiry, and structures of the discipline(s) he or she teaches and can create learning experiences that make these aspects of subject matter meaningful for students.
2. The teacher understands how children learn and develop and can provide learning opportunities that support their intellectual, social, and personal development.
3. The teacher understands how students differ in their approaches to learning and creates instructional opportunities that are adapted to diverse learners.
4. The teacher understands and uses a variety of instructional strategies to encourage students' development of critical thinking, problem solving, and performance skills.
5. The teacher uses an understanding of individual and group motivation and behavior to create a learning environment that encourages positive social interaction, active engagement in learning, and self-motivation.
6. The teacher uses knowledge of effective verbal, nonverbal, and media communication techniques to foster active inquiry, collaboration, and supportive interaction in the classroom.
7. The teacher plans instruction based upon knowledge of subject matter, students, the community, and curriculum goals.
8. The teacher understands and uses formal and informal assessment strategies to evaluate and ensure the continuous intellectual, social, and physical development of the learner.
9. The teacher is a reflective practitioner who continually evaluates the effects of his/her choices and actions on others (students, parents, and other professionals in the learning community) and who actively seeks out opportunities to grow professionally.
10. The teacher fosters relationships with school colleagues, parents, and agencies in the larger community to support students' learning and well-being.

In the late 1990s, INTASC began developing a similar set of standards for each of several content areas. In several states INTASC personnel have joined efforts with the respective state departments of education to enhance teachers' understanding of the INTASC standards and to improve teachers' ability to design portfolios to support this goal. In 2009, INTASC received funding to update the standards, with expectations of a final draft in 2010, and feedback is requested. For further information on the INTASC standards, including their compliance with NCLB requirements, visit their Web site (http://www.ccsso.org).

Privatizing Public Schools

The country's fascination with the *privatization* of its schools grew out of its dissatisfaction with the public schools. Among the many arguments for turning the public schools over to private organizations, the two most common are the beliefs that (1) anyone can do better with the schools than the public sector has been doing, and (2) private firms can do the job at less cost.

Those who prefer to retain the public schools argue that both of these proposed benefits are really not benefits because they are based on false premises. First, the argument that anyone could do better than the public schools have done is based on the assumption that the single purpose of schools is to raise test scores. We must remember that the role of our schools is much greater than raising test scores; our schools are charged with building a better and better society. Although business should participate in school reform, its narrow perspective should prevent it from leading the reform initiative. The public has never favored school privatization. The 40th Phi Delta Kappa/Gallup Poll of the Public's Attitudes toward The Public Schools (Bushaw & Gallup, 2008) reported that the public wants education leaders, not business leaders, to develop policies for the public schools.

The World of Work

In the new millennium, Americans are vitally concerned with ensuring that students acquire those skills and understandings essential to performing successfully on the job. In 1991, the Secretary of Labor's Commission on Achieving Necessary Skills (SCANS) produced the document *What Work Requires of Schools*, focusing on standards that address higher-order thinking, interpersonal skills, personal traits, and communication skills.

The American Society for Training and Development (ASTD) polled its 50,000 members to identify those skills most desired by employers. The result was a list of 16 skill areas including traditional academic skills and also nontraditional skills and traits such as high self-esteem, negotiation skills, and interpersonal skills. The results of this work were published in the pamphlet *Workplace Basics: The Essential Skills Employers Want* (Carnevale, Gainer, & Meltzer, 1990).

Although preparing graduates with the skills needed to get a job is important, critics are quick to point to the shortsightedness of this goal—those skills needed to get a job may become obsolescent before the new employee has settled comfortably into the new position. To combat this problem of viewing the purpose of schools as being only job preparation, the Carl Perkins Vocational and Technical Education Act of 1998, which funds vocational education, was amended to require that all funded programs integrate academic and vocational education through coherent sequences of courses so that students achieve both academic and occupational competencies. In 2005, this act was renamed the Carl D. Perkins Career and Technical Education Improvement Act of 2005. The new law requires states to disaggregate data and report the performance levels of secondary and post-secondary groups of students by the special populations as described in ESEA (Elementary and Secondary Education Act of 1965) specifications.

The Southern Regional Education Board's *High Schools That Work* program goes far beyond preparing their graduates to get jobs. These schools start by requiring each student to take a rigorous science, math, and technology-based curriculum (Bottoms, 2007). Their 1,200 schools are located in 32 states. Weekend and after-school instruction is offered to students who need additional time to meet academic goals. Students work with interdisciplinary teaching teams to plan their curricula. The goal is to prepare students for college while preparing them for work by increasing the academic rigor of their curricula. For example, the Academic Academy Foundation (AAF) has over 600 academies spread over 41 states (Hoachlander, 2007).

Such integrated approaches have the power to motivate many students to become involved with the academic side of their education, students who otherwise might remain turned off to all academics. These include students who suffer from cultural dissonance. As Grubb (1996, p. 544) explained:

> Changing teaching so that intrinsic motivation is improved by producing meaningful contexts for students themselves has rarely been proposed. However, a recent analysis of teaching and learning for disadvantaged children has concluded that more active, student-centered approaches are the most promising ways of teaching such students. And these methods are consistent with contextualized and integrated teaching.

This current approach of integrating academics and work skills, coupled with authentic assessment and broad theme approaches, offers a promising route to the diverse student populations of the twenty-first century.

Global Education

Vivien Stewart, vice president for education at the Asia Society (2007, p. 10), states that today's U.S. high school graduates will sell to the world, buy from the world, and work for international companies. Many employees from other countries collaborate with people from all over the world in joint ventures, compete with people on the other side of the world for jobs and markets, and tackle global problems such as AIDS, Asian flu, pollution, and disaster recovery.

Many states are becoming proactive in promoting international skills and knowledge. Ohio, Indiana, and Wisconsin have collaborated to create global communities and promote global education. North Carolina and Vermont have developed commissions. Delaware, Massachusetts, and Washington have developed statewide summits, and Delaware and Idaho are revising their standards to reflect global concerns. New Mexico and Virginia are similarly revising their graduation requirements. Kentucky is adding critical foreign languages in its virtual high schools. Ohio and Texas are adding an international dimension to their STEM (science, technology, engineering, and mathematics) schools. More and more U.S. schools are offering Chinese language courses. Based on a list provided by the

Asia Society, about 264 schools in the United States now offer Chinese classes (*People's Daily Online,* 2009). According to the Modern Language Association (2007), language enrollments rose 13% between 1998 and 2007, with Arabic up 127%, Chinese up 51%, and Korean up 37%. The number of institutions of higher learning offering Arabic has nearly doubled since the last survey (from 264 in 2002 to 466 Arabic programs offered in 2006).

Physical distances are no longer barriers to learning and sharing information about different cultures, languages, and traditions. Internet technologies have bridged the geographic distance that separates global communities, raising the importance of developing the skills needed for communicating and collaborating with people from different countries. Students, therefore, need opportunities to take advantage of the communications and collaboration tools available in today's wired classrooms to engage in projects and dialogue with their international peers. Just as students can deepen their knowledge when teamed with their peers in the classroom, students can both broaden their perspective and enrich their understanding of the world through relationships with their international counterparts. Making this connection will be vital to navigating the global marketplace (The Partnership for 21st Century Skills, 2009a).

Vouchers and School Choice

Since the landing of the Pilgrims, Americans have always had a voice in public education. The idea that no single type of schooling is best for all locales led the writers of the Constitution, through purposeful omission, to grant the power to each state to establish and maintain its own school programs. The voucher movement reflects Americans' desire to choose their children's schools (public or private) and use public-school allocations to pay the tuition. *Vouchers* are government-issued notes that parents can use to pay all or part of the tuition at a private or church-related school. The majority of the public (60%) does not believe that parents should be allowed to choose a private school for their child to attend at the public's expense. Two-thirds (67%) oppose paying all the tuition for attending private schools, yet half (52%) support paying part of the tuition (Rose & Gallup, 2007). The 2008 polling still found the majority of Americans opposing the use of taxes to support private schools, but the minority who favored it rose to 46% (Bushaw & Gallup, 2008). If this minority becomes a majority, the nature of funding public education in this country will substantially change (McCarthy, 2008).

Traditionally, some parents have chosen to send their children to private schools at their own expense. Proponents of voucher plans argue that those parents who choose to send their children to private schools should be able to take the tax money that is currently allotted to the local public schools to educate their children and use that money to pay the school of their choice to do the job. Voucher plans are not a new idea; Canada has been a leader in their use during recent decades. In 1999 Florida became the first state to issue a statewide voucher plan that allows public funding of private schools.

Since 1990, parents in Milwaukee, Wisconsin, have had the option of using vouchers to send their children to private schools. During the 1994–1995 school year, vouchers averaging $3,200 for each student were used in 12 Milwaukee private schools (Witte & Thorn, 1994). The academic achievement of these students has not differed significantly from that of their counterparts who remained in the public schools, but the parents are much more pleased with the private schools.

Overall, in America vouchers have barely survived legislation battles. Although they have recently gained political and legal support, vouchers remain highly controversial. Critics of the voucher plan worry that it will exacerbate the inequality of educational opportunities, hurting most those children who attend the poorest schools. This concern is based on the fact that a disproportionate number of children in the poorest schools come from broken homes, or homes where parents cannot afford to take off from work to attend school meetings, or homes with parents who lack the ability to choose wisely among the options available. Put succinctly, these critics worry that vouchers will improve opportunities for the fortunate but will grossly worsen opportunities for the less fortunate. Even those students who can afford the transportation might suffer. Schlechty (2008) has noted, "Commuting to school in another district can often present students with insurmountable obstacles in terms of time, and money" (p. 55).

Proponents of the voucher system say that this system will force all schools to compete for students and that the competition will bring improvement to all schools. They say that teachers will have to cooperate to save their jobs and that teachers will not be able to afford to ever give up on a student. Furthermore, advocates for voucher programs point out that since the school is chosen by the parents, this gives the parents leverage to entice their children to perform well. Conversely, the school can eject students who fail to perform properly. Viewed positively, giving students some choice in the schools they attend should increase their satisfaction with their school and entice them to work hard to continue as a member of the school.

The early twenty-first century is characterized by hot debates over whether public taxes should be spent this way. In fact, the public is almost evenly split on this issue. Vouchers that would pay all the tuition were supported by 44% of the public in 2008, up 2% from the previous year (Rose & Gallup, 2008). At least for the near future, the use of vouchers will continue to occur here and there throughout the country, and debates over their value will also continue.

Cooperative Learning

The literature is replete with definitions of cooperative learning, and these definitions vary from general to specific. Lindblad (1994, p. 292) offered a general definition when he said, "In its purest form, *cooperative learning* is merely a few people getting together to study something and produce a single product." At the opposite end of the continuum, Johnson and Johnson (1989–1990) listed five specific basic elements of all cooperative learning programs: positive interdependence, face-to-face interaction, individual accountability, collaborative skills, and group processing.

Cooperative learning offers several advantages. Because the success of each member is contingent upon the other members succeeding, this technique has strong motivation potential and, consequently, promotes higher achievement. Cooperative learning also increases students' self-esteem.

When implementing cooperative learning, teachers need to play a guiding role rather than a dominating, leadership role. Lindblad (1994, p. 293) explains:

> Too often the traditional teacher feels the need to be part of everything going on in the class. Let students handle their own team progress. When the teacher stays removed from minor discord, the team members are forced to deal with those problems themselves.

The following guidelines can be used to implement cooperative learning:

1. Give students the freedom they need to run their groups.
2. Plan a short group assignment and introduce it early in the lesson.
3. Assign three or four students to each group.
4. Put domineering students together so that they will be forced to listen part of the time.
5. Put reserved students together so that they will be forced to assume leadership roles part of the time.
6. Explain that it is to everyone's advantage to help other group members.
7. Consider teaming with another teacher when implementing cooperative learning.
8. Help students learn how to ask productive questions.
9. Encourage students to ask questions.
10. Listen carefully to student-generated questions.

The Web provides a wealth of information and resources on cooperative learning, among them:

- http://edtech.kennesaw.edu/intech/cooperative learning.htm
- http://www.co-operation.org/pages/cl.html
- http://www.newhorizons.org/strategies/cooperative/front_cooperative.htm

Multiple Intelligences

Most of our understanding about intelligence comes from work done at the end of the nineteenth century and the beginning of the twentieth century. Many of the intelligence tests we use today were developed at that time. Although IQ scores are unstable until late adolescence and have largely been discredited for determining a single, generalized ability quotient (Murdoch, 2007), many schools still use these tests to sort students and determine expectations (Olson, 2008).

More recently, though, an increasing number of educational psychologists have been accepting and promoting the idea of *multiple intelligences* (Armstrong et al., 2009). Howard Gardner (1993) believes that humans possess the following seven distinct and separate kinds of intelligence:

- logical-mathematical
- linguistic
- musical
- spatial

- bodily-kinesthetic
- interpersonal
- intrapersonal

Summarizing the effects of Gardner's work, Jensen (2008) says that "While subjected to two decades of criticism, Gardner's work has made and continues to make a profound and positive difference in education worldwide" (p. 414).

Other theories of multiple intelligences have also been proposed. For example, Robert Sternberg (2007/2008) proposed a triarchic theory of intelligence, which includes *componential intelligence* (the ability to learn by separating relevant and irrelevant information), *contextual intelligence* (the ability to adapt to new experiences and solve problems in new situations), and *experiential intelligence* (the ability to deal with novel situations and the ability to turn new situations into routine procedures).

Teachers who accept the multiple intelligences concept do not restrict their classroom activities to the goal of acquiring information. Such teachers have the ability to see and appreciate potentials in their students that were not recognized by most teachers only a few years ago. Perhaps most important, multiple intelligences theory is causing teachers to appreciate and promote a wide range of abilities among their students.

The old narrow concept of giftedness has taken on additional dimensions, too. As new theories continually emerge, new types of human potential are being discovered that should provoke teachers to continuously search for "hidden" potential among their students, never giving up on a student who a few years ago might have been typecast as a slow student. An awareness of multiple intelligences theory should motivate teachers to expand their planning to include a variety of ways to help students use their creativity to discover and understand important content introduced in the classroom.

Evaluating Textbooks and Ancillary Materials

Other sections of this text have warned against the overuse of textbooks—a proclivity of many teachers to let the textbook virtually determine the curriculum. While this has been a prevailing problem over the years, such practice will be more flagrant and visible in the future since we now have content standards that teachers, through their representatives in their learned societies, have agreed to accept. Although overreliance on the textbook for determining curriculum direction is a major problem, there are other concerns about textbooks that also demand attention. Among these is the need to help teachers select textbooks and ancillary materials that promote the acceptance of ethnic diversity (people from all geographic regions, both outside and within the country); gender equity; physically, mentally, and emotionally challenged students; gifted students; and senior citizens.

Textbook Selection

One of the most controversial issues in education today is textbook selection. Typically, teachers play a variety of roles in selecting textbooks for their local district and state. Dr. Connie Mather, a nationally recognized expert on textbook selection, provides the following information and advice:

The most important thing to know in evaluating instructional materials is having a clear picture of what you want. This means you evaluate only selected content that fulfills one or more of the following criteria:

- essential to your curriculum
- coverage of your students' weakest areas
- something you personally dislike teaching, but you must
- something controversial
- something small enough so that a thorough examination can be made without you becoming confused

Have the committee define and describe the ideal. What is quality instruction or content in the desired new materials? How are the current materials being used? Remember, the committee is selecting materials for those who are not on the committee; those not serving may not teach the same way. A change in materials will not change how those materials are used—especially with those who have no voice in the selection.

Once the topic, concept, or skill is selected, based upon the above listed criteria, compare three publishers' materials at the same time and select the best match to what you have described as ideal. If you look at only one publisher, what are you comparing it to? Your old publisher? Then the new materials look pretty good. If you compare with two publishers, one is either good or bad. Three publishers gives you a nice comfortable triad. With four, you become confused.

You can remove publisher bias and make your study more scientific if you assign each publisher a color and duplicate that publisher's lesson in its designated color. Next, cut and tape the comparative lesson on a three-column form. You can immediately see differences (see tables 11.1 and 11.2).

When you label each publisher by its color, you can show these cut-and-tape evaluations to anyone: to other teachers who are not on the committee or even to students. Save your comparison charts, and if your district is ever challenged, you have clear evidence you selected the best materials to match your major curriculum goals.

There are many different evaluation strategies to use, but all are based on this same principle of choosing a topic, comparing three publishers, selecting the best, and photocopying the evidence. If your materials are hands-on programs, photocopy the teacher's additions. Whether it is audio, video, or software, you again try to compare apples to apples. I often ask three committee members to videotape the news for a specific evening on different stations. We then select the same story and compare the coverage. It's amazing the differences that can be seen quickly when comparing the same items.

The best evaluation strategy is what I call the "horizontal trace." However, this method is extremely time consuming, so I usually have the committee do the cut-and-tape small topic evaluations first. To do the horizontal trace, select the topic, concept, or skill exactly as you did before; however, instead of beginning with the instruction you begin with the measurement. How does your district test this item? How is it measured on state testing? The procedure is as follows:

- Take the test yourself.
- List everything the students will need to know or be able to do in order to succeed with the test.

- Go to the indices at the end of the first publisher's program and read (or photocopy) every page reference listed.
- Determine whether the instruction and content match what you're measuring.

Again, always compare three publishers, selecting the best match. (When you try to do more you'll forget what was in each publisher's version.) Photocopy evidence to support which publisher's material was best aligned with the test material. Share your results with others. Again, you'll have documentation in case you are challenged several years later.

Why do these evaluations work? What most people do not know is that authors do not necessarily write instructional materials. Most major publishers create their programs using "development houses" whose freelance authors write to each publisher's specifications. Ironically, development houses do not work with exclusivity contracts, which means they can be working for competing publishers at the same time. Since there are so many writers involved (which means a greater chance of error), and the materials all have to sound like they're written by one person in one voice, many instructional materials are boring. New programs must be created quickly in order to meet printer deadlines, for there are only about five major printers used by most companies. The pressure builds from adoption states, who preselect the instructional materials that can be purchased by teachers in that state. Deadlines are critical, for if a publisher misses getting material to the printer, the books are not submitted in time for state adoption, which automatically disqualifies them. Typically a publisher's program is written in one year, edited the next year, and then rushed to the printer. This leaves little or no time for field testing with students. Production is high-pressured and sales-driven, with some authors barely having time to read the text they are credited with writing. There are exceptions to all this, which is why comparing three publishers with your ideal will identify the best product.

Increased and Expanded Use of Technology

In the twenty-first century, both the number of people using technology and the number of ways of using it are increasing at an unprecedented rate (Armstrong et al., 2009). Paramount among these uses will be the expanded use of hypertext on the Internet. *Hypertext* is nonsequential written text that branches and allows choices on an interactive screen. As popularly conceived, this is a series of text chunks connected by links, which offers readers choices of different pathways.

Tomlinson and Doubet (2005, p. 15) remind us that "It's difficult to make curriculum relevant to lives that we don't understand." Youngsters thrive on instant gratification, and the best tool ever for giving instant gratification is the Internet. Through WebQuests, online simulations, podcasting, blogs, and other information technology, teachers can capitalize on students' desire to move faster. By observing students' habits, such as using e-mail and instant messaging, and by keeping abreast of new technologies, teachers can use these new technologies to involve students in ways that will motivate, challenge, and enlighten.

Electronic games are powerful motivators because they challenge students to perform better and better. Jenkins (2005) says that games create a social context that connects learners to others who share their interests. Discussions about

Table 11.1 A Comparison of Three Publishers' Coverage of Discrimination against Japanese Americans

Social Studies • Japanese Americans • Grade 8

	Pink, p. 615
Title	***The Relocation of Japanese Americans***
Introduction	At the start of the war, about 120,000 Japanese Americans lived on the West Coast of the United States. At least two-thirds of them were American-born citizens, known as Nisei. After the surprise attack by Japan on Pearl Harbor, many people believed rumors that Japanese Americans were involved in acts to aid the enemy. Although false, the rumors led to widespread mistreatment of West Coast Japanese Americans.
Roosevelt	On February 20, 1942, President Roosevelt gave in to public pressure and issued an order allowing the army to move West Cost Japanese Americans to "relocation camps." Forced to sell their homes, farms, and businesses quickly, many families suffered heavy losses.
Living Conditions	The relocation camps proved to be little better than prison camps, mostly in isolated desert areas. They were surrounded by barbed wire and patrolled by armed troops. Families were crowded into small wooden barracks covered with tar paper. (See Reading 24A.)
Supreme Court Ruling	None
Japanese Americans in the Armed Services	Despite this mistreatment, Japanese Americans remained loyal to the United States. Over 33,000 of them volunteered to serve in the armed forces. Japanese Americans made up the 442nd Regimental Combat Team, the most decorated unit in American military history.

Gray, p. 634	*Blue, p. 839*
Tragedy for Japanese Americans	***None***
The worst discrimination, however, was felt by Japanese Americans. Most Japanese Americans lived on the West Coast. Many were successful farmers and business people. For years, they had faced racial prejudice in part because of their success. After the attack on Pearl Harbor, many white Americans distrusted Japanese Americans. They warned that Japanese Americans on the West Coast could act as spies and help Japan invade the United States.	The demand for weapons and supplies finally ended the Great Depression. American industry had slowly been climbing out of the depression, helped by European war needs. Now great expanded production was needed. Hundreds of thousands of new workers were needed to produce the tools of war. Men and women flocked from farms, towns, and great cities to jobs in shipyards, steel plants, former automobile factories, and aircraft plants. About 6 million women were employed during the wear. Farmers also experienced boom times. The demand for food to feed American and Allied troops was enormous. Farm income more than doubled during the war. World War II had great popular support. Almost no one questioned the decision to fight the Axis powers.
The president agreed to an order to move Japanese Americans away from the coast to "relocation" camps farther inland. Over 100,000 Japanese Americans on the West Coast were ordered to sell their homes, land, and belongings.	This enthusiasm led to a serious blot on the Roosevelt record of civil liberties: treatment of Japanese Americans. Unfounded suspicion forced about 112,000 living on the West Coast to move to internment camps in a barren section of the country. There was absolutely no evidence that the Japanese Americans were less loyal than other Americans.
In relocation camps, Japanese Americans had to live behind barbed wire. Housing was poor.	None
The people did not understand why they, as American citizens, were singled out. Americans of German and Italian backgrounds were not sent to camps. In 1944, the Supreme Court ruled that the camps were a necessary wartime measure.	None
Only when an Allied victory seemed certain were Japanese Americans allowed to return to their homes. At first, Japanese Americans were barred from serving in the military. Later, this policy was changed. More than 10,000 Japanese Americans volunteered for service. Many were cited for their bravery. One unit of Japanese Americans used the slogan "Go for broke!" It became a popular rallying cry across the nation.	None

Table 11.2 A Comparison of Three Publishers' Coverage of the Boston Massacre

Social Studies • Boston Massacre • Grade 5

	White '09
Introduction	*The Boston Massacre* In 1767, Parliament ordered a tax on British glass, paint, paper, silk, and tea. British tax collectors, with soldiers to guard them, arrived in the colonies. Again the colonists protested. This time the protests led to violence.
Chronology of Event	The first incident took place in Boston. For years, Boston colonists had made fun of the red-coated British soldiers by calling them lobsterbacks. In 1770, however, this sport turned ugly. A crowd of colonists gathered around a lobsterback who was guarding the tax office. Colonists began shouting and throwing snowballs, some packed around ice or rocks. Other soldiers rushed to help the guard. In the confusion, soldiers fired into the crowd, killing five people including a black sailor named Crispus Attucks.

games by students is called *metagaming*, and this is a good way to encourage student collaboration. Jenkins also says that games lower the threat of failure and motivate students to do additional research and learning.

Many new ways that technology is changing the educational experience have already been discussed. For an interesting scenario of some future uses of technology, review the second half of chapter 2 on technical foundations of curriculum.

Summary of Trends across the Disciplines

Due to space limitations, this discussion of trends across the disciplines has been cursory and far from exhaustive. Most curriculum workers find the ever-changing nature of their profession exciting. Some choose one or two trends and follow these in the literature throughout their professional lives. Now let's examine several trends that are occurring within the disciplines.

Yellow '09	Green '09
The Boston Massacre In 1768, during the argument over the Townshend duties, Parliament got worried. They feared that the colonial protests were out of control. They sent soldiers to Boston. Some colonists welcomed the soldiers. They believed the soldiers might help keep order. Other colonists were angry. They charged that the soldiers were a danger to the rights of colonists.	**B. Tempers Flare in Boston** *British Troops* After the French and Indian War, the British government had sent thousands of troops to the colonies. They said that the soldiers were needed to defend the colonists against Indian attack. However, instead of going to the frontier where the Indians were, most of the soldiers remained in the cities near the coast. The colonists were angered by the sight of soldiers on their streets day and night. They jeered at the soldiers, made fun of them, and made their lives miserable. In several cities, fights broke out between colonists and soldiers.
Anger over the soldiers finally exploded in violence. On March 5, 1770, about 100 Bostonians moved toward some soldiers guarding the customs house. One of the Bostonians' leaders was a black man named Crispus Attucks. The crowd yelled, then threw rocks and snowballs. Fearing for their safety, the soldiers opened fire. They killed Attucks and four other colonists.	On the evening of March 5, 1770, a crowd of men and boys in Boston gathered around a lone British soldier on guard duty. They shouted insults and threw snowballs at him. Some of the snowballs had rocks inside them. The frightened soldier called for help. Then more British soldiers arrived. The crowd grew larger. And the shouts, dares, and insults grew louder and angrier. *Boston Massacre* Suddenly someone—no one knows who—called out "Fire!" The soldiers turned their guns on the crowd and shot. When the smoke cleared, five colonists lay dead, their blood staining the snow-covered street. One of them was Crispus Attucks, a runaway slave who worked as a sailor. Attucks was the first African American to die for the cause of American liberty, but not the last.

Trends within the Disciplines

The landmark education reform report, *A Nation at Risk* (National Commission on Excellence in Education, 1983), exposed the enduring practice of letting textbooks shape (and in many instances determine) elementary and secondary curricula, pointing to the absolute unreliability and failure of textbooks to contain the essential content in their respective fields (for further elaboration, see chapter 1).

Various segments of society, including educational societies, are calling for national standards. Although there is national agreement across content areas that elementary and secondary schools need help in upgrading the content in their curricula, and that some sort of national minimum standards should be set, the learned societies representing the disciplines do not agree on what those standards should be designed to do. A major area of disagreement is over whether the standards should be designed to prepare high school graduates to pursue further study in their chosen disciplines or whether the standards should be designed to bring all students to a minimum level required to function in our society. Armstrong and colleagues (2009) noted that most states expect their teachers to meet the goals set by professional societies of the disciplines. As early as 2004, most of these societies had set their own standards for teacher education programs. Individual disciplines are discussed below.

Mathematics

The National Council of Teachers of Mathematics (NCTM) set a precedent for other content organizations when it published a document setting forth what students should know at the various levels (K–4, 5–8, and 9–12). The 1989 publication, titled *Curriculum and Evaluation Standards for School Mathematics*, also tells how students might best demonstrate this knowledge in the classroom. In May 1995, NCTM published another document, titled *Assessment Standards for School Mathematics*. This document is organized around six major standards: important mathematics, enhanced learning, equity, openness, valid inferences, and coherence. It provides guidelines to help teachers use assessment to make instructional decisions, monitor student progress, evaluate student achievement, and evaluate programs. To access NCTM standards online, visit their Web site (http://standards.nctm.org/).

In general, mathematics programs are demanding increasingly higher levels of thinking. This change is reflected in a discussion of the Interactive Mathematics Program, a National Science Foundation funded program. According to Alper, Fendel, Fraser, and Resek (1996, p. 19):

> A major premise of the Interactive Mathematics Program (IMP) is that most students are capable of thinking about Mathematics and Understanding. This is a change from the philosophy of many traditional programs in which students do mostly rote work. . . . One of the features of the program . . . is the expansion of the curriculum to include new topics. For example, students learn about normal distribution and standard deviation, regression and curve fitting, and matrix algebra for both equation solving and geometric transformations—areas of mathematics that most high school students never see.

Twenty-first-century mathematics teachers will continue to use a variety of programs such as the IMP but, instead of focusing their attention on trying new programs, many teachers will continuously strive to experiment with new approaches and continue to learn more about teaching. Schifter (1996, p. 499) explains:

> For many teachers, this approach implies a change in their relationship to their own profession. Instead of concentrating on technique and strategy—keeping up with the latest trends—the new pedagogy means developing an attitude of inquiry toward classroom processes.

As mentioned in chapter 5, the sequencing of topics gives meaning to the curriculum. Unfortunately, U.S. math curricula lack coherence because of state-to-state variance, and because of the tendency of our mathematics curricula to cover the same concepts at different grade levels. Consistent with the No Child Left

FYI Helping All Math Students Move Forward

William L. Phillips • Eastern Kentucky University

Math learning communities were created at a P–12 laboratory school to diminish math anxiety while concomitantly moving top math students forward. At the beginning of each semester, students were given a pretest to determine current math ability and then assigned to learning communities with one strong math student, two average math students, and one weak math student in each group. Teacher presentations were calculated to teach at the level of the most gifted math students in the class. Then the teacher allowed the learning communities to discuss the presentations and solve the math problems. These learning communities helped students see how gifted math students processed and questioned new information. The teacher responded to questions posed by the learning communities while individual student questions were discussed and answered by the math learning community. Dual testing was used to make sure that both the group and the individual learned. Twenty-five percent of students' grades came from the scores on group tests and fifty percent of their grades came from individual testing.

Behind legislation, some mathematics teachers are learning to use only those methods that enhance results on exams and to cover fewer topics, spending much more time on each major concept. Mathematics teachers are purposefully increasing their pedagogical knowledge base. Historically, minority students have experienced a less rigorous mathematics curriculum. The NCLB legislation will ensure that all students take more rigorous mathematics classes.

Although we know that unlike the students in high math-achievement countries, our students cannot explain in their own terms the mathematics they are studying, our students are still using tests that do not let them explain their perceptions. When asked what curriculum changes are needed in math and science, Heidi Hayes Jacobs (see Perkins-Gough, 2004) said, "The overwhelming majority of assessments in math classes are still quizzes and tests. The rarest form of assessment in math is the formal examination of students' ability to retell in their own speech what they are doing" (p. 15).

Science

Like the mathematics curriculum, the science curriculum also suffers from redundancy. Problem solving continues to be a favored approach to teach science. It meets the NCLB requirement of being a scientifically based method. When we make time for discussion, we get a more thorough understanding of each student's interpretation of concepts or facts.

As noted in chapter 5, to be effective, problems must be authentic, students must have some ownership, and students must be given time to discuss. The problems do not have to be student initiated, and the teachers do not have to be experts on the proposed solutions. One teacher proved these assertions by having his students identify the most dangerous intersections they passed on the way to school. The students attained ownership by brainstorming a list of possible solutions to this problem.

Efforts to develop content standards in the sciences have been both vigorous and diverse. Leading this drive as major sources are the National Committee on Science Education Standards and Assessment (NCSESA), the American Association for the Advancement of Science (AAAS), and the National Science Teachers Association (NSTA).

NCSESA produced the document titled *National Science Education Standards*; AAAS's Project 2061 produced *Benchmarks for Science Literacy*, providing more than 60 literacy goals in science, math, and social studies; and NSTA published *The Content Core: A Guide for Curriculum Designers* (1993) with an addendum entitled *Scope, Sequence, and Coordination of National Science Education Standards* (1995). The standards may be accessed online (www.nap.edu/catalog/4962.html).

Trends in science include a continuing emphasis on covering less content while using a multidisciplinary hands-on approach with the goal of developing deeper understanding. Inquiry or problem solving are used in a constructivist context to enable students to tie newly discovered information to previously learned knowledge and to content across the curriculum.

Students need opportunities to share their projects. Science fairs continue to provide a good forum for enticing students to reflect on their projects and explain them to others. Now students can also post their findings online on Web sites and blogs (Hubbell & Kuhn, 2007).

Research-tested science programs in the form of kits continue to be popular, but only when teachers have received the necessary staff development required for the understanding and implementation of such programs. The twenty-first century should see plenty of staff development for science teachers. Koba (1996, p. 17), who used an NSF-funded, constructivist, community-based project titled "Solving Problems and Revitalizing Curriculum" (SPARCS), reports:

> Clearly . . . student achievement has risen, with fewer failures among African American students who were formally tracked in fundamentals classes. In addition, our own attitudinal surveys indicate that students now enjoy science more, feel more comfortable in the science classes, and perceive science as being more important than they ever did before. Most important, we now see learning as a way to make a difference—in our own lives, in our community, and in our world.

As the twenty-first century proceeds, expect to see more interdisciplinary, integrated, community-based science programs in both elementary and secondary schools. Although the terms *interdisciplinary curriculum* and *integrated curriculum* are sometimes used interchangeably, they are different. An interdisciplinary curriculum has the focus on one discipline, and other discipline(s) support or facilitate content in the first domain. An integrated curriculum is one with explicit assimilation of concepts from more than one discipline with equal attention to two or more disciplines.

Both the National Council of Teachers of Mathematics and the National Science Education standards emphasize constructivist teaching and learning techniques.

Language Arts

"Literacy is thinking; thinking is literacy. We think only through the medium of words" (Roberts & Billings, 2008, p. 32). In 1992, the Office of Research and Improvement funded a three-year project entitled the Standards Project for the English Language Arts (SPELA). The National Council of Teachers of English (NCTE), the International Reading Association (IRA), and the Center for the Study of Reading (CSR) proposed to conduct SPELA as a collaborative program, but because they failed to make substantial progress, the support was withdrawn. IRA and NCTE planned to continue the project even without federal support.

Although not purporting to write standards, the National Assessment of Educational Progress (NAEP) has produced several documents describing the nature of and format for writing language arts standards. For example, NAEP's *Description of Writing Achievement Levels—Setting Process and Proposal Achievement Level Definitions* (1993) gives examples of basic, proficient, and advanced performance in writing. In the area of reading, NAEP's *Reading Framework for the National Assessment of Educational Progress: 1992–2000* provides a detailed description of what students should know and be able to do at various levels and details the types of materials students should be able to read.

In 2002, NAEP administered a writing assessment to approximately 276,000 students in grades 4, 8, and 12 throughout the nation. For details and results, visit the National Center for Education Statistics Web site (http://nces.ed.gov/nationsreportcard/writing).

NCLB legislation includes reading and literacy programs entitled Early Reading First and Reading First, aimed at having all students read at grade level by the end of third grade. Students must be tested in grades 3 through 8. Data show that integrated programs are far more successful than pull-out programs. For complete program information, visit the U.S. Department of Education Web site at http://www.ed.gov/ programs/earlyreading/index.html (for Early Reading First) and http://www.ed.gov/programs/readingfirst/index.html (for the Reading First program).

Foreign Languages

The American Council on the Teaching of Foreign Language (ACTFL) and several foreign language associations produced National Standards for Foreign Language Education (April, 1995). The document gives standards under five goal areas for students: communicate in languages other than English; gain knowledge and understanding of other cultures; connect with other disciplines and acquire information; develop insight into one's own language and culture; and participate in multilingual communities. To access the standards online, visit the ACTFL Web site (http://www.actfl.org).

It appears that the public's understanding of students' needs exceeds the willingness of legislators to provide them. A full 85% of the public thinks that all children should learn a second language (Rose & Gallup, 2007). Unfortunately, only about half of our students study a foreign language (Stewart, 2007a). However, this situation has recently been improving and, for obvious reasons, will continue to do so. The global awareness mandated in the twenty-first century has resulted in more and more schools offering foreign language courses in Arabic and Chinese, for example.

English Language Arts

The English language arts include speaking, listening, reading, writing, and viewing. In recent years, educators have recognized that students draw meaning from the integration of these arts, although disadvantaged learners have difficulty with vocabulary and reading. Concerned with the narrowness of traditional standardized tests, especially objectively scored tests, Palmer and Pugalee (1999) emphasized the need for new assessment measures in the English language arts curriculum. Some future trends predicted by Palmer and Pugalee include:

1. continued use of standardized tests;
2. improved efficiency in the use of standardized tests;
3. greater scrutiny of unfair test use;
4. continued exploration of better ways to measure multiple ways students learn;
5. increased use of bibliotherapy (use of reading and writing for therapeutic value);
6. increased use of story writing, reading, and telling to improve critical, creative, and reflective thinking; and
7. increased parental involvement in portfolio assessment.

To access the standards for English language arts, visit the National Council of Teachers of English (NCTE) Web site (http://www.ncte.org/about/over/standards/110846.htm).

The NCLB Act of 2001 has ensured a continuing emphasis on a standards-based approach to reading, the same as with other subjects. While this emphasis on standards militates against the need to personalize lessons, a growing number of high school teachers in the content areas are using metacognition strategies to discover their own reading barriers and are leading their students to do likewise. Some teachers invite students to bring to class unfamiliar books for the teacher and others to read for the first time, and to collaboratively decipher meaning. Their reading is driven by their own questions.

Fine Arts

In spite of the current emphasis NCLB places on mathematics, the fine arts are still appreciated. Eighty percent of the public is worried that the arts and other subjects will be short-changed (Rose & Gallup, 2007). Substantial and successful efforts have been made to provide content standards in the fine arts. The U.S. Department of Education funded a grant to the National Endowment for the Arts and the National Endowment for the Humanities to identify standards for the arts. In 1994, the Consortium of National Arts Education Associations published *What Every Young American Should Know and Be Able to Do in the Arts*. This document gives standards for dance, music, theatre, and the visual arts organized into K–4, 5–8, and 9–12 grade clusters. To view the complete standards online, visit http://artsedge.kennedy-center.org/ teach/standards.cfm.

As the trend toward multidisciplinary programs continues, art is the perfect discipline to blend with all other disciplines. Unfortunately, funds to support the arts continue to dwindle, forcing art teachers to use some of their creative talents to garner support from the local community. Involving the arts with other disciplines produces positive changes in student attitudes. Infusing art into the curriculum provides students with therapy and motivation. It also gives students important tools for learning from, and communicating with, their world. Most important, it nurtures a sense of confidence that they can succeed in school and in life.

The arts can be used to stimulate creative thinking (Jensen, 2008). Furthermore, artists stretch themselves and their audiences through deliberate ambiguities in their work (Boix-Mansilla & Gardner, 2008). Unfortunately, the importance of the arts is not realized by many, especially twenty-first-century education reformers, and therefore people who believe in the importance of teaching the arts must continue to fight to maintain a place in the curricula for the arts in schools throughout the country. Twenty-first-century educators are using the arts to help at-risk children improve their social skills and academic performance (Camilleri, 2007). Programs such as Prevention and Education through the Arts (PEAK) and ArtSmarts have proved to be effective in this regard.

Social Studies

The National Council for the Social Studies (NCSS) has taken responsibility for setting broad social studies curriculum standards and has designated the setting of content standards to the individual disciplines within the social studies. In its 1994 publication, *Expectations of Excellence: Curriculum Standards for Social Studies*, NCSS lists 10 thematic strands, including culture, time, continuity and change, and individual development and identity. For these 10 strands, 241 performance expectations are described. As of this writing, the latest (fall, 2008) NCSS draft revision of the standards and thematic strands is available online, including an executive summary explaining the reasons for the proposed update (http://www.socialstudies.org/system/files/StandardsDraft10_08.pdf).

The use of performance assessment in social studies will continue. Because many of the social studies activities involve discourse (for example, participation in mock trial teams), future social studies teachers will need to be skilled in developing rubrics (specific guidelines that clearly spell out performances required to earn specific grades) to evaluate or score discourse. Students should be involved in developing rubrics. W. C. Parker (1996) offered the performance criteria shown in table 11.3 for civic discourse activities and the corresponding rubric shown in table 11.4 for scoring such discourse. (Both tables appear on the following page.)

History

The National Center for History in the Schools Web site features links to history standards for K–4 and 5–12 (http://nchs.ucla.edu/standards/toc.html). Some needed changes in the history curriculum include a shift in emphasis on state history to national and world. Few students who are in school today will spend all of their lives in the state where they were born. As is also true of other disciplines, history needs better curriculum alignment, and curricula that don't repeat the same concepts at different grade levels but instead build on the concepts learned in prior years. Also informative is *Building a History Curriculum: Guidelines for Teaching History in Schools* prepared by the Bradley Commission on History in Schools (Second Edition, 2005) at http://www.nche/net.docs/NCHE_BAHC.pdf.

Table 11.3 Performance Criteria for Civic Discourse

Substantive	Procedural
• States and identifies issues • Uses foundational knowledge • Stipulates claims or definitions • Elaborates statements with explanations, reasons, or evidence • Recognizes values or value conflict • Argues by analogy	*Positive* • Acknowledges the statements of others • Challenges the accuracy, logic, relevance, or clarity of statements • Summarizes points of agreement and disagreement *Negative* • Makes irrelevant, distracting statements • Interrupts • Monopolizes the conversation • Engages in personal attack

Table 11.4 Scoring Rubric for Assessing Civic Discourse

Substantive

Exemplary (3)	Adequate (2)	Minimal (1)	Unacceptable (0)
Weighs multiple perspectives on a policy issue and considers the public good; or uses relevant knowledge to analyze an issue; or employs a higher-order discussion strategy, such as argument by analogy, stipulation, or resolution of a value conflict.	Demonstrates knowledge of important ideas related to the issue, or explicitly states an issue for the group to consider, or presents more than one viewpoint, or supports a position with reasons or evidence.	Makes statements about the issue that express only personal attitudes, or mentions a potentially important idea but does not pursue it in a way that advances the group's understanding.	Remains silent, or contributes no thoughts of his or her own, or makes only irrelevant comments.

Procedural

Exemplary (3)	Adequate (2)	Minimal (1)	Unacceptable (0)
Engages in more than one sustained interchange, or summarizes and assesses the progress of the discussion. Makes no comments that inhibit others' contributions, and intervenes only if others do this.	Engages in an extended interchange with at least one other person, or paraphrases important statements as a transition or summary, or asks another person for an explanation or clarification germane to the discussion. Does not inhibit others' contributions.	Invites contributions implicitly or explicitly, or responds constructively to ideas expressed by at least one other person. Tends not to make negative statements.	Makes no comments that facilitate dialogue, or makes statements that are primarily negative in character.

Geography

Teachers who enjoy teaching geography are more fortunate than other social studies teachers in that the Geography Education Standards Project has delineated 18 standards articulated for grades K–4, 5–8, and 9–12. You can view the standards online (http://www.nationalgeographic.com/resources/ngo/education/standardslist.html). The standards are organized into six areas: the world in spatial terms, places and regions, physical systems, human systems, the environment and society, and the uses of geography. These standards are published in *Geography for Life: National Geography Standards* (National Council for Geographic Education [NCGE], 1994). At the time of this writing the draft of a forthcoming second edition is available for downloading, and reader comments are solicited (http://www.ncge.org/files/public/draft_standards_review2.pdf). The NCGE is a nonprofit organization that works to enhance the status and quality of geography teaching and learning, and their Web site offers much useful information for educators. The Partnership for the 21st Century Skills has developed a map to illustrate the intersection between twenty-first-century skills and geography (http://www.21stcenturyskills.org/documents/21stcskillsmap_geog.pdf), offering educators, administrators, and policy makers concrete examples of how these skills can be integrated into core subjects.

Another source for standards in geography is NAEP's Item Specifications (1992) for its 1993 *Geography Assessment Framework for the 1994 National Assessment of Educational Progress* (http://nccs.ed.gov/pubs96/web/96810.asp).

Evidence that our students are ready for this challenge is seen in the increased interest in learning languages beyond the commonly taught Spanish. For example, 2,400 high schools expressed interest in offering the new advanced placement course in Chinese (Stewart, 2007a).

Civics

In 1994, the Center for Civic Education (CCE) published *National Standards for Civics and Government* (http://www.civiced.org/stds.html). This document gives some 70 standards for K–4, 5–8, and 9–12 students. Each content standard lists key concepts essential to meeting the standard. These standards are organized into the following areas: civic life, politics and government, the foundations of the U.S. political system, the values and principles of U.S. constitutional democracy, the relationship of U.S. polities to world affairs, and the role of the citizen.

The national social studies standards should be used in all schools, including private schools. We need a set of standards (or state-level sets) that will lead to a frame of mind that can include a variety of foundational notions.

Elliott Self (2003/2004) is concerned that current social studies programs based on state standards and textbooks do not adequately address the core civic topics necessary for students to understand what it means to live in a democratic society. He recommends programs such as Understanding by Design, which develop *enduring understandings*. The program uses six strategies to help students to:

- demonstrate their understanding,
- explain what they have learned,

- interpret a given document,
- apply their knowledge to a real situation,
- approach a problem from different viewpoints,
- empathize with others, and
- reflect on how their learning helps them understand more about their strengths, abilities, and civic responsibilities.

As mentioned in Chapter 7, civics should be expanded to include concern for helping, and ability to helping improve human conditions throughout the world (Stewart, 2007a).

Health and Physical Education

Since 1995, the major trend has been to make these curricula not just standards-based but also skills-based (Pateman, 2003/2004). The greatest benefit to educators has been the hands-on professional development opportunities to align standards assessment and instructional strategies (CCSS, 2003). In December of 2000, the federal government recognized the need to promote innovative physical education programs by making available some $400 million in incentive grants over five years through the Physical Education for Progress (PEP) Act (Jensen & Overman, 2003).

In 2007, the Joint Health Education Standards Committee published *National Health Education Standards: Achieving Excellence,* which identifies eight standards. Each has "performance indicators" for students at grades Pre-K–2, 3–5, 6–8, and 9–12. To access the standards online, visit the Web site (http://www.aahperd.org/aahe/pdf_files/standards.pdf).

In 2004, the National Association for Sports and Physical Education (NASPE) published the second edition of *Moving into the Future: National Standards for Physical Education* (available online at http://www.aahperd.org/naspe/template.cfm?template=publications-nationalstandards.html). This document identifies six standards with benchmarks at grades K, 2, 4, 6, 8, 10, and 12.

To access the American Alliance for Health, Physical Education, Recreation and Dance's content standards in physical education, visit http://www.aahperd.org/naspe/pdf_files/input_standards.pdf.

Ironically, at a time when NCLB has caused many schools to reduce the amount of physical activity in order to increase the amount of learning, brain research studies are showing that physical activity enhances cognition (Jensen, 2008). By increasing the amount of the flow of blood to the brain, exercise automatically increases student alertness.

But perhaps the concern for learning should take second place of our concern for children's health. Because of current lifestyles, mainly the strong tendency of today's youth to be overeaters and underactive, for the first time in our nation's history our children's life expectancies are less than those of their parents (Belluck, 2005).

Too many states have been relaxing their physical activity requirements. On the positive side, however, some states are beginning to strengthen their exercise and nutritional policies and practices. The Center for Science in the Public Interest recently graded states in how they write and implement policies that govern nutritional standards. The leading state was Kentucky, followed by Alabama, Arkansas, California, and New Mexico (Daniels et al., 2007). Because obesity is largely a result of family behavior, some argue that it is a family responsibility and, therefore, should be dealt with by the family. But, as Ringer and Crittenden (2007) have noted, both meeting the needs of the child and dealing with the parent can be difficult. Hopefully, our future policies will support teachers who, better than anyone else, understand that our schools exist to nurture growth in all areas.

Conclusion

Following is a summary of some of the advances made and concerns raised about the topics discussed in this chapter.

Advances

- In the twenty-first century, great strides are being made in the areas of home schooling, school safety, self-directed learning, and improved educational opportunities for gifted and special-needs students.
- A rebirth of emphasis on constructivism is causing more teachers to use interdisciplinary curricula.
- Learners in inclusive classrooms are performing better than ever on academic tests.
- Twenty-first-century teachers are using several effective methods, such as letting reading be driven by the students' own questions and creating small communities in their classrooms.

Concerns

- Traditionally, teachers have been reluctant to use interdisciplinary curricula; yet its successful use requires teacher support.
- More than one student in ten needs special help to achieve, and all students require high expectations.
- Emphasis on standards militates against the need to personalize lessons.

As the second decade of the twenty-first century unfolds, education is being radically reformed, and curriculum planners must be aware of current trends and major changes.

Authentic assessment is playing an important role in shaping curricula; it is designed to measure students' ability to apply what they have learned to real-life problems. Some of the new assessments include performance evaluation, self-assessment, and continuous assessment, all known as alternative assessments.

Because the reform report writers of the 1980s succeeded in convincing society that the education system in this country was inferior, it is not surprising that the issues of tenure and certification processes were viewed as systems that protect inept teachers and promote an inferior education system. This conflict between education critics and teachers is one to be watched as the new century proceeds.

Concern for ethnic diversity and gender equity continue to grow. Concerns about fairness to all citizens are broadening to include attempts to eliminate geographic stereotyping and to promote the fair treatment of senior citizens.

Several new programs have been developed in response to the criticisms of schools. Included among these are magnet schools with unique curricula, charter schools with permission to ignore restrictions that limit other schools, and vouchers that let students and parents choose their schools.

Concern for children with disabilities continues as these students are being placed in classrooms with students who do not have disabilities, a process called inclusion. The inclusion process differs from mainstreaming in that included students are given special help through individually designed education programs.

Some programs that show signs of continuing in the future include cooperative learning and concern for multiple intelligences.

The various disciplines are being shaped by national standards and benchmarks. Although the teachers developing these standards disagree on whether the purpose of school is to prepare all students for citizenship or to prepare students to become experts in the disciplines, there is widespread agreement that national standards are needed.

ADDITIONAL LEARNING OPPORTUNITIES

1. How does teaching interdisciplinary curricula contribute to implementing constructivism?
2. Of the several curriculum programs introduced during the 1980s and 1990s to respond to educational criticisms, which do you believe improve the system most?
3. What do you believe will be the result of attempts to abolish teacher tenure, and on what do you base your belief?
4. Do you believe it wise to take funds away from some schools in order to support magnet schools?
5. On what basis would you defend teacher tenure?
6. What is the social injustice that you would most like to see corrected, and how can the schools contribute to this adjustment?
7. What are the major liabilities of having national standards, and how can these be overcome?

SUGGESTED ACTIVITIES

1. Choose the current curriculum trend that you believe will have the greatest impact on twenty-first-century schools, research this trend, and prepare a written report on it.
2. Curriculum innovations are seldom pure and detached from one another. Select two contemporary trends in education and explain how they interact with each other.

3. Prepare a statement that both challenges and defends the concept of national educational standards.
4. Develop a strategy that teachers can use to affirm ethnic diversity in the classroom and in teachers' broader professional arena.
5. For each of the national standards in your discipline, select those benchmarks that you believe adequately represent and ensure attainment of the standards.
6. Reexamine the trends that this chapter has identified in each discipline and identify those trends that reflect constructivist philosophy.

GLOSSARY

This book has emphasized the perspective of the constructivists, which holds that no knowledge is permanent. As an experienced educator, you may already have a basic level of understanding of all of these terms. However, as your understanding grows, your vocabulary must be revised accordingly. Therefore, you may wish to compare and contrast your definitions with those offered here, paying particular attention to the ways in which your definitions of many of these terms are changing.

• • •

A Nation at Risk—A 1983 report (written by the Secretary of Education's National Commission on Excellence in Education Committee) that blamed the U.S. schools for letting the nation fall behind Russia in science and technology.

abstraction—Something that is not concrete; a theoretical construct.

action research—Classroom-based or school-based inquiry that teachers undertake to understand and improve their own practice.

advance organizers—Oral or written statements at the beginning of a lesson intended to orient learners to the content and/or procedures used, in order to facilitate learning and comprehension of new material.

affective domain—The part of human learning that involves changes in interests, attitudes, and values.

alternative assessment—Any of many types of assessment that replace traditional testing.

alternative curricula—Curricula that offer students choices from a menu of courses.

analysis-level objective—Requires students to work with concepts and principles.

application-level objective—Objective requiring students to use principles or generalizations to solve a concrete problem.

articulation—The flow (absence of disruptions) of a curriculum either vertically or horizontally.

assistive technology—any item, piece of equipment, or system, whether acquired commercially, modified, or customized, that is commonly used to increase, maintain, or improve functional capabilities of individuals with disabilities.

at-risk students—Students whose probability of dropping out of school is above average.

authentic tests—Assessment that requires students to apply new knowledge to solve life-like problems.

axiology—The philosophical structure concerned with pursuing the study of values and ethics.

balanced curriculum—Equal emphasis on disciplines; for example the arts and sciences, or vocational courses and college preparatory courses.

benchmark assessments—*See* interim assessments

blog—From "weblog," a publicly accessible journal available on the Web, created by using software allowing people with little or no technical background to update and maintain it.

Bloom's Taxonomy of Educational Objectives: *Handbook 1*, Cognitive Domain—A system developed by Benjamin Bloom and others for the purpose of classifying learning objectives.

Boston English Classical School—The first public high school in America, established in 1821.

broad-fields curriculum—A curriculum designed to replace the subject-centered curriculum and lead to understanding the broad content generalizations that spread among two or more subjects.

bulletin board—An Internet-accessed public forum created with software that supports multiple simultaneous users, where participants can post and comment on messages from other participants.

Cardinal Principles of Secondary Education—The National Education Association's aims for elementary and secondary schools.

Carnegie unit—120 clock hours of instruction.

case study—Method of using actual or contrived classroom experiences to connect theory and practice.

catechisms—Religious rhymes used extensively in Colonial times to teach morality.

charter schools—Schools given special permission to experiment with unique curricula.

CIPP model—A curriculum evaluation model that focuses on the content, input, process, and product.

coercive power—Power based on the ability to punish or give rewards.

cognitive dissonance—Differences in expectations at school and expectations at home that produce learning barriers.

cognitive domain—The part of human learning that involves changes in intellectual skills, such as assimilation of information.

cognitive objectives—Instructional objectives that stress knowledge and intellectual abilities and skills.

collaborative research—Professors and teachers working together as equal action research partners.

commonsense approach—The unscientific practice of drawing conclusions based only on personal experience.

comprehension-level objective—Requires students to translate, interpret, or predict.

comprehensive schools—Large secondary schools with diversified curricula.

concept maps—Drawings that show connections among related concepts (ideas).

concepts—Those major understandings within each discipline characterized by recurring patterns such as a common physical characteristic or common utility.

concrete operations—Piaget's third level of development (ages 8 to 11) at which the subject can perform first-order operations and think deductively.

connectionism—A learning theory which says that the most effective approach to learning and therefore to curriculum development is to connect newly acquired information to prior understandings.

constructivism—A philosophy of curriculum as connected concepts, based on psychologists' view that new information must be related to previously acquired understanding (knowledge) before it can become meaningful.

content—Information that has been selected for inclusion in the curriculum.

cooperative learning—Students working in groups to learn. The success of each member depends on the success of all members.

core curriculum—A curriculum design that has a common core of content and/or activities required of all students and other content and activities that are electives.

criterion-referenced evaluation—Evaluation that measures success by the attainment of established levels of performance. Individual success is based wholly on performance of the individual without regard to the performance of others. A *criterion-referenced test* measures a student's performance with reference to specified criteria or to that individual's previous level of performance.

cultural discontinuity—Problems that minority students face caused by conflicting expectations of family and school.

culture—The capacity for constantly expanding the range and accuracy of one's perception of meanings. An attempt to prepare human beings to continuously add to the meaning of their experiences.

curriculum—The total experiences planned for a school or students.

curriculum alignment—Matching learning activities with desired outcomes, or matching what is taught to what is tested.

curriculum arena—Location and level at which curriculum decisions are made.

curriculum coherence—The fitting together or meshing of curriculum components.

curriculum compacting—Strengthening parts of the curriculum for gifted students.

curriculum components—Any of the following: aims, goals, objectives, philosophy statement, student activities, teacher activities, content, and tests.

curriculum continuity—The quality of a curriculum that links parts together in a sequence for easier learning. Vertical articulation.

curriculum guide—A written statement of objectives, content, and activities to be used with a particular subject at specified grade levels; usually produced by state departments of education or local education agencies.

curriculum mapping—A procedure for collecting data about the operational curriculum in a school and in a district.

curriculum scope—The breadth of a curriculum.

curriculum sequence—The order in which content and activities in a curriculum are arranged.

Dalton Plan—An early twentieth-century school that had a highly individualized curriculum.

dame schools—Private homes where the colonial mother taught her children and her neighbors' children. Also called kitchen schools.

deductive logic—Reasoning that starts with the general and moves to the specific.

deep learning—A variety of strategies that cause students to gain additional insights into the topics being studied.

dilectic logic—Reasoning that begins with a thesis, moves to an antithesis, and then moves to synthesis.

direct instruction—An instructional approach to academic subjects that emphasizes the use of carefully sequenced steps that include demonstration, modeling, guided practice, and independent application.

dissatisfier—A factor that is a prerequisite to the operation of motivators but which itself does not motivate.

distance learning—Learning that takes place when the instructor and student are separated by space and/or time, bridging the gap through the use of technology (e.g., audiotapes, videoconferencing, satellite broadcasts, and online technology). *See also* eLearning.

dual language programs—Immersion programs that actually teach content in two languages so that the students will be fully prepared to speak both languages.

eLearning—Education via the Internet, network, or stand-alone computer, covering a wide set of applications and processes such as Web-based learning, computer-based learning, virtual classrooms, and digital collaboration—delivered via the Internet, intranet/extranet, audio- or videotape, satellite, and CD-ROM.

education—The process through which individuals learn to cope with life.

Education for All Handicapped Children Act—A 1977 legislative act requiring all states to provide special services for handicapped students at public expense and under supervision and direction.

education reform—An organized attempt to substantially improve the schools in a district, state, or nation.

education technology—Any combination of technologies (computer or other hardware, software and content applications, and media) used to provide all students the opportunity to meet educational goals.

educational aims—Lifetime aspirations that provide long-term directions for students.

educational consortium—A group of schools that join together, usually led by a university or other organization. By uniting their resources, these schools can afford programs that, by themselves, none of the schools could afford.

educational taxonomy—A hierarchical system for classifying educational objectives.

effective schools—Those schools whose students are high academic achievers.

effective teaching—Teaching that results in high learner achievement.

Eight-Year Study—A study from 1933 to 1941 conducted by Harvard University to compare the success of child-centered education with the success of traditional education.

electronic walks (e-walks)—Walks throughout the schools using a handheld electronic device to monitor rates of progress in school goals.

Elementary and Secondary Education Act of 1965—Forerunner to later rewrites, including the Title I programs and the No Child Left Behind Act. This act provided comprehensive support and regulations for American education.

Émile—Book written by Jean Jacques Rousseau on child rearing the natural way.

ends–means planning—Beginning curriculum planning by determining the desired outcomes. Also called the Tylerian curriculum model.

engaged time—Time actually spent in the classroom learning a topic.

English language learners (ELLs)—Students with little or no knowledge of the English language.

epistemology—That structure which pursues the study of truth.

essentialism—That structure which focuses on the knowledge that is needed for a successful adult life.

evaluation—Making measurements plus providing value judgments.

evaluation-level objective—The highest-level cognitive objective. Requires students to define criteria and then assess how well they were met.

existentialism—That structure that focuses on the present, promoting the belief that life is only what you make of it and you must live for the moment.

experiential education—A philosophy and methodology in which educators purposefully engage with learners in direct experience and focused reflection in order to increase knowledge, develop skills, and clarify values.

expert power—Power that derives from the possession of specialized skills or knowledge.

formal operations—Piaget's fourth level of development (ages 11 to 15 and older), during which adolescents perform second-order operations and use flexible thinking.

formative evaluation assessment—Evaluation that occurs before or during instruction and whose sole purpose is to promote learning by improving study skills, instructional strategies, or the curriculum.

forums—Online discussion groups (also called newsgroups, web boards, or message boards) where people exchange ideas about common interests.

Franklin Academy—A pragmatic school that by the end of the Revolutionary War replaced the Boston Latin Grammar School as the most important secondary school in America.

Gary Plan—Early twentieth-century experimental school that operated as a miniature community.

gender equity—Treating females and males fairly, having similar expectations for both.

generalizability—The ability of a concept, theory, principle, or event to be applied to a variety of circumstances

global awareness—Being cognizant of the needs of people throughout the world and of the effects of our behavior on the planet and its inhabitants.

goal displacement—Inadvertently letting the attainment of the goal replace the purpose for having the goal.

goals—Desired learning outcomes stated for a group of students and requiring from several weeks to several years to attain.

grading—The act of using a combination of types of student performance to indicate a student's overall level of success.

grassroots movement—A movement advocating change that is introduced within and conducted at schools, rather than from outside sources.

heterogeneous grouping—Grouping high-ability students with low-ability students.

hidden curriculum—The messages given by schools and teachers via the school climate and the teachers' behavior.

home schooling—When a parent assumes responsibility for teaching his or her children at home.

homogeneous ability grouping—Grouping students with similar abilities.

hornbook—A board with Biblical rhymes (catechisms) and other simple curriculum content, covered by a thin, transparent material, used in the dame schools.

human development—The idea that schools should improve society by improving individual learners.

hypertext—Any computer-generated "text" (including words, phrases, photos, and icons) that contains links to other documents (mouse clicking on hypertext causes the related documents to be retrieved and displayed).

idealism—A belief that reality lies in ideas and that there are universal truths and values.

inclusion—Placing challenged students in classrooms with their nonchallenged peers and giving them special instructional support.

inclusion (or full inclusion)—The practice of placing students with special needs in regular classrooms throughout the day, providing assistance and a welcoming climate.

individualized instruction—Instruction designed to meet the needs of all students.

inductive logic—Reasoning that moves from the specific to the general.

information literacy—The skills necessary to locate, access, and use information in today's society.

information-processing model—A mental model based on the computer, used to explain the mechanisms that allow individuals to develop, think, and learn.

information technology—A general term used to describe technologies that help produce, manipulate, store, communicate, or disseminate information.

in-service teachers—Teachers who have graduated and are teaching full time.

integrated curriculum—A curriculum that features explicit assimilation of concepts from more than one discipline with equal attention to two (or more) disciplines.

interclass ability grouping—Matching the performance of one class against another class of similar ability.

interdisciplinary curriculum—A curriculum that focuses on one discipline, with other discipline(s) supporting or facilitating content in the first domain.

interim assessments—Tests followed by immediate feedback to facilitate learning.

internationalization. *See* global awareness.

intraclass ability grouping—Grouping students of similar ability within a class.

intrinsic motivator—Incentive that comes from within or from one's own values.

Kalamazoo Case—A law passed in 1874 giving state legislatures the right to levy taxes to support schools.

kitchen school—*See* dame school.

knowledge—Meaningful information that the learner has related to prior understanding.

knowledge base—The research-derived knowledge and other knowledge that supports the practice of a profession.

knowledge-level objectives—Lowest level of cognitive objectives, requiring only memorization.

Latin Grammar School—Forerunner of modern high schools that prepared young men for entrance to Harvard College.

learning—More or less permanent change in behavior as a result of experiences.

learning cycle theory—A learning approach that involves exploration, concept introduction, and application.

learning experiences—Student activities that are made meaningful by tying these activities to prior experiences.

learning for mastery (LFM)—A particular type of teacher-paced, group-based mastery learning program.

learning styles—Conditions that favor learning for an individual student.

learning unit—A curriculum plan that usually covers 1 or 2 weeks of elementary study or 6 to 18 weeks of middle school or high school program.

legitimate power—Organizationally sanctioned ability to influence others.

lesson plan—A teaching outline of the important points of a lesson arranged in the order in which they are to be presented; it may include objectives, points to be made, questions to ask, references to materials, assignments, and evaluation methods or tools.

life certification. *See* tenure

long-range planning—Curriculum planning that covers several days, weeks, or years.

looping—The repetition of program instructions until a conditional exit situation is encountered.

magnet school—School with special curricula not available in other local schools. Attended part of each school week by students from neighboring schools.

mainstreaming—The practice of placing students with special needs in regular classrooms throughout the day without giving them assistance or a welcoming climate.

Maslow's hierarchy of needs—A model of human motivation assuming that people are primarily motivated by a desire to satisfy specific needs that are arranged in a specific hierarchy.

mastery learning—Technique of instruction whereby pupils are given multiple opportunities to learn using criterion-based objectives, flexible time, remediation, and instruction that matches the learners' styles.

measurement—The nonqualitative part of evaluation.

measurement-driven instruction (MDI)—Teaching to the test.

message board—A script on a Web site with a submission form that allows visitors to post messages on a Web site for others to read. These messages are usually sorted within discussion categories or topics, chosen by the host or possibly the visitor. A message board is also called a "web board" or a "forum."

meta-analysis—An organized process for analyzing many studies on a common topic.

metacognition—Knowledge of how one's mind works; thinking about ways to improve one's own ability to think and learn. The study of one's own learning processes.

metaphysical explanation—A proposition that cannot be tested.

mission statement—A statement of an institution's purpose.

model—A written or drawn description used to improve the understanding of its subject.

motivation—Arousal, selection, direction, and continuation of behavior.

multiculturalism—Commitment to helping students learn to appreciate and work with members of other cultures.

multidisciplinary education—Education directed at themes that cover two or more disciplines.

multiple intelligences (theory of)—The idea that individuals have more than one type of intelligence.

multipurpose activity—An activity that serves to attain two or more objectives.

national standards—Minimal educational standards set at the national level for all schools.

nature of knowledge—A study of how information is related to form knowledge.

naysayers—Teachers or others who oppose changes of all types, declaring any proposed changes undesirable and/or impossible.

needs hierarchy model—*See* Maslow's hierarchy of needs.

newsgroups—Online discussion groups, forums, or bulletin boards usually devoted to a specific topic. Found primarily on USENET, newsgroups post collections of related user messages to a news server, which then distributes them to other participating servers.

No Child Left Behind Act of 2001—A comprehensive piece of federal legislation that requires documentation that adequate progress is being made by learners from ethnic minorities, from homes in which English is not the first language, from economically impoverished backgrounds, and by learners with disabilities.

norm-referenced evaluation—A student's performance is evaluated by comparing it to the performance of others.

normal learning curve—A symmetrical, bell-shaped curve that shows the distributions of learners' abilities.

Northwest Ordinance of 1787—A law requiring that one section (one-sixteenth) of every township be set aside to be used to support public schools.

objective—*See* performance objective.

official curriculum—A school's planned curriculum.

Old Deluder Satan Act—A Massachusetts Colony law passed in 1647 which required every town of 50 or more families to hire a teacher and every town of 100 or more households to build a school.

outcomes-based education—Curriculum design that begins by determining or identifying desired learning outcomes.

perennialism—The philosophical structure that focuses on the knowledge that is retained through the years.

performance assessment—Assessment that requires students to apply information, as opposed to testing only for recall of information.

performance-based assessment—The practice of basing grades on measured performance.

performance objective—Objective that requires students to perform at specific levels under specified conditions; also called behavioral objective or instructional objective. *See also* analysis-level objective; application-level objective; evaluation-level objective; knowledge-level objective.

personalized instruction—Instruction designed to meet the needs of the whole child (as opposed to meeting only the academic needs).

pertinent concepts—Those concepts whose understanding is a prerequisite to understanding the discipline being studied.

philosophy—The love, study, and pursuit of wisdom.

podcasting—An online broadcast of audio content that can be converted to an MP3 file or other audio file format for playback in a digital music player.

portfolio—A diversified combination of samples of a student's quantitative and qualitative work.

power—*See* coercive power; expert power; legitimate power; punishment power; referent power; reward power.

pragmatism—The structure that emphasizes the practical.

praxis—Curriculum theory that brings together theory and practice.

preoperational period—Piaget's second level of development (ages 2 to 7), during which children develop symbolic modes of presentation.

privatization—The practice of a school district contracting with a private business or industry to educate its students.

professional development—Opportunities for professional education faculty to develop new knowledge and skills through in-service education, conference attendance, sabbatical leave, summer leave, intra- and inter-institutional visitations, fellowships, and work in P–12 schools, etc.

professionalism—Putting the client's welfare first.

progress reports—Ongoing assessment to promote learning.

Progressive Education Movement—The era spanning the early 1920s to the early 1940s, when the curriculum was student-centered and activities-centered.

psychomotor domain—The part of human learning that involves motor skills.

punishment power—The ability to punish others who fail to comply with your requests.

Quincy System—The nation's first school district to use a child-centered curriculum.

readiness—The stage of development required to perform mental and physical operations.

reading across the curriculum—Giving multidisciplinary reading assignments to enhance learning.

realism—The belief that people should pursue truth through use of the scientific method.

reconstructionism—That philosophical structure which is dedicated to using education to rid society of its ills.

referent power—The ability to influence others because they identify with you or want to be like you.

research-based teaching—*See* action research.

restructuring—Changing a school's entire program and procedure, as opposed to changing only one part of the curriculum.

reward power—The ability to reward others when they do what you want them to.

safe schools—Schools that have taken formal, proactive measures to reduce the probability of violence.

school culture—A school's somewhat permanent climate or ethos. The way things are done at a particular school.

school transformation—Completely reorganizing the changes needed to make an ineffective school effective.

science—An organized way to study the world or any part of it.

scientific method—A systematic approach to pursue truth through using the five senses.

scientism—Placing faith in science to do everything.

self-assessment—Student maintenance of an ongoing record of their own academic progress.

self-directed learning—Individualized, self-paced instruction that is initiated and implemented by the learner.

sensorimotor period—Piaget's first level of development (birth to age 2), during which infants develop the ability to use symbolic thought.

service learning—A type of learning program whereby students achieve academic expectations by providing service activities to their community.

set—An individual's readiness to act.

simulation (or simulation games)—Enactments that place students in lifelike roles; results in higher learning retention rates for students.

site-based decision making—The practice of using a council of teachers, administrators, and parents to run the school.

social contract—A written agreement signed by teacher and student to improve student behavior.

special students—Students who are either unusually challenged or who are unusually gifted.

spiral curriculum—A curriculum that introduces the same topic at different levels because students were not able to deal with some of the abstractions at a lower level (younger age).

standardized test—Based on norms derived from the average scores of thousands of students who have taken the test.

stanine scores—Reporting scores in categories of one-ninth of the normal curve.

statement of rationale—A statement of justification (created by the teacher) that uses students' values to convince them of the worth of a topic of study.

subject-centered curricula—Curricula consisting of specific courses usually delivered by using lectures and textbooks.

summative evaluation assessment—Evaluation that occurs following instruction and is used to determine grades and promotion.

Summerhill—A famous English school that practices almost complete permissiveness.

synthesis-level objectives—Cognitive objectives that require students to take parts of a whole and reassemble them to form an new whole.

Taba's inverted model—A curriculum model that begins with teachers who design learning units; considered opposite or inverted from traditional top-down models.

table of specifications—Chart to ensure coverage of varying levels of desired objectives, knowledge, and skills.

tabula rasa—Literally "blank slate." John Locke's idea that everyone is born with a blank mind and the only way to fill it is through direct experience.

taxonomy of educational objectives—A classification scheme that puts educational objectives into three major domains or groups: affective, cognitive, and psychomotor.

Taylorism—Applying efficiency engineering theory to education.

teacher empowerment—An attempt, associated with education reform, to increase teachers' involvement in decisions that affect the entire school.

teacher-proof curricula—Learning programs that do not require a teacher's help.

tenure—Also called life certification, a principle guaranteed by law in some states and as policy in some school districts, ensuring that employed teachers who reach certain minimum experience requirements can only be dismissed under specific, stipulated situations and providing them with due process in appealing a negative employment decision.

testing—Measuring student performance or measuring the degree to which students meet a curriculum's objectives.

Trump Plan—A curriculum design by Lloyd Trump which requires all students to use a combination of large group instruction, small group instruction, and independent study.

two-factor motivation theory—Herzberg's theory that there is a set of factors that when absent can block performance but when present do not motivate performance.

two-way bilingual immersion—Programs that take place in two languages, with non-English being used at least 50% of the time in both the classroom and homework assignments.

Tylerian curriculum model—A curriculum model that begins by identifying desired learning outcomes and designing the curriculum accordingly.

unit plan—A plan for learning a major section or topic within a course. Usually learned over a period of weeks and limited to one topical area.

USENET—A worldwide "bulletin-board system" or network of forums/newsgroups that can be accessed through the Internet or through many online services.

virtual—An adjective that refers to objects, activities, etc. that exist or are carried on in cyberspace—a colloquial way to refer to a computer process that is comparable to a real, physical function. (e.g., virtual schooling, virtual field trips).

vision statement—A written explanation of an institution's purpose.

vouchers—Government-issued notes that parents can use to pay all or part of the tuition for their children at a private or church-related school.

weblog—*See* blog.

WebQuest—An inquiry-oriented lesson format in which most or all the information that learners work with comes from the Web.

wiki—A Web page that can be directly edited by anyone with access to it, allowing multiple users to create, modify, and organize Web-page content in a a collaborative manner.

Winnetka Plan—An early twentieth-century curriculum planning model that involved teachers.

wisdom—The knowledge of things beautiful, first, divine, pure, and eternal.

Woods Hole Conference—A meeting of 35 scientists, educators, and business leaders in 1959 to redesign the curricula in American schools.

world of work—Purposefully designing curricula to prepare students to work.

writing across the curriculum—Giving multidisciplinary writing assignments to enhance learning in other disciplines.

REFERENCES

Abell, S. K. (2007, November 1). On reading in science [Perspectives Column]. *Science and Children,* 45(3), 56–57.

Abruscato, J. (1993, February). Early results and tentative implications from the Vermont portfolio project. *Phi Delta Kappan, 74*(6), 474–477.

Ackerman, R. A., & Mackenzie, S. V. (2006, May). Uncovering teacher leadership. *Educational Leadership 6*(8), 66–71.

ACT. (2006). *Benefits of a high school core curriculum.* Retrieved May 8, 2009, from http://www.act.org/research/policymakers/pdf/core_curriculum.pdf

Albanese, A. (2004). Google launches scholarly search service. *Publishers Weekly,* November 22.

Alberg, J., Cook, L., Fiore, T., Friend, M., Sano, S., et al. (1992). *Educational approaches and options for integrating students with disabilities: A decision tool.* Triangle Park, NC: Research Triangle Institute.

Allen, T. (2004). No school left unscathed. *Phi Delta Kappan, 85*(5), 396–397.

Alliance for Excellent Education. (n.d.). *Every child a graduate.* Retrieved February 17, 2005, from http://www.all4ed.org/college_prep/initiative.html

Alper, L., Fendel, D., Fraser, S., & Resek, D. (1996). Problem-based mathematics: Not just for the college-bound. *Educational Leadership, 53*(8), 18–21.

Alvarez, M. C. (1993). Imaginative uses of self-selected cases. *Reading Research and Instruction, 32*(2), 1–18.

Ambrosie, F., & Hanley, P. W. (1991, October). The role of the curriculum specialist in site-based management. *NASSP Bulletin, 75*(537), 73–81.

Amrein-Beardsley, A. (2007). Recruiting great teachers into hard-to-staff schools. *Phi Delta Kappan, 89*(1), 64–67.

Anchorage School District. (2002). *School business partnership report (2000–2002)* [Memorandum]. Anchorage, AK: Author.

Anderson, L. W. (2009). Upper elementary grades bear the brunt of accountability. *Phi Delta Kappan, 90*(6), 413–417.

Andrade, H. (2007/2008). Self-assessment through rubrics. *Educational Leadership, 65*(4), 60–63.

Antin, M. (1912). *The promised land.* Boston: Houghton Mifflin.

Apple, M. W. (1990). Is there a curriculum voice to reclaim? *Phi Delta Kappan, 71*(7), 526–530.

Applebee, A. N., Langer, J. A., & Mullis, I. V. S. (1987). *The nation's report card: Literature and U. S. history.* Princeton, NJ: Educational Testing Service.

Aratani, L. (2006, August 26). With a changing world comes an urgency to learn Chinese. *Washington Post,* A01.

Archbald, D., & Newmann, F. (1988). *Beyond standardized testing: Authentic academic achievement in the secondary school.* Reston, VA: NASSP Bulletin.

Arlin, M. (1984, Spring). Time, equality, and mastery of learning. *Review of Educational Research, 54*, 71–72.

Armstrong, D. G., Henson, K. T., & Savage, T. V. (2009). *Teaching today* (8th ed.). Upper Saddle River, NJ: Pearson.

Armstrong, L., Berry, M., & Lamshed, R. (2003). *Blogs as electronic journals.* Retrieved July 20, 2009, from http://playpen.moodle.com.au/moodle/mod/resource/view.php?id=219

Asher, N. (2007). Made in the (multicultural) USA: Unpacking tensions of race, culture, gender, and sexuality in America. *Educational Researcher, 36*(2), 65–73.

Asia Society. (2007). *Global education in U.S. schools: The world is thinking* [TV transcript]. Retrieved May 29, 2009, from http://fora.tv/fora/fora_transcript_pdf.php?cid=1037

Baines, L. (2007). Learning from the world: Achieving more by doing less. *Phi Delta Kappan, 89*(2), 98–100.

Baker, E. T., Wang, M. C., & Walberg, H. J. (1994/1995). The effects of inclusion on learning. *Educational Leadership, 52*(4), 33–35.

Banks, C. A. McGee, & Banks, J. A. (1995). Equity pedagogy: An essential component for multicultural education. *Theory into Practice, 34*(3), 152–158.

Banks, J. A. (2006). *Race, culture and education: The selected works of James A. Banks.* London & New York: Routledge.

Barber, B. R. (2004). Taking the public out of education. *The School Administrator, 61*(5), 10–13.

Barell, J. (2007). *Problem-based learning: An inquiry approach.* Thousand Oaks, CA: Corwin.

Barth, R. S. (1990). *Improving schools from within: Teachers and students can make a difference*. San Francisco, Oxford: Jossey-Bass.

Barton, P. E. (2007/2008). The right way to ensure growth. *Educational Leadership, 65*(4), 70–73.

Basom, R. E., & Crandall, D. P. (1991). Implementing a redesign strategy: Lessons from educational change. *Educational Horizons, 69*(2), 73–77.

Bauer, S. (2007, January 25). More public schools dividing boys and girls. *Houston Chronicle.*

Beauchamp, G. A. (1981). *Curriculum theory* (4th ed.). Itasca, IL: Peacock.

Behrmann, M. (1998, May 1). Assistive technology for young children in special education: It makes a difference. Retrieved June 18, 2009, from the Edutopia Web site: http://www.edutopia.org/assistive-technology-young-children-special-education

Bell, T. H. (1993). Reflections one decade after "A Nation at Risk." *Phi Delta Kappan, 74*(8), 592–600.

Bellamy, T., & Goodlad, J. (2008, April). Continuity and change in pursuit of a democratic public mission for our schools. *Phi Delta Kappan, 89*(8), 565–571.

Belluck, P. (2005, March 17). Children's life expectancy being cut short by obesity. *New York Times*. Retrieved June 23, 2009, from http://www.nytimes.com/2005/03/17/health/17obese.html

Bennett, C. K. (1993). Teacher-researchers: All dressed up and no place to go. *Educational Leadership, 51*(2), 69–70.

Berliner, D. C. (1984). The half-full glass: A review of research on teaching. In. P. A. Hosford (Ed.), *Using what we know about teaching*. Alexandria, VA: Association for Supervision and Curriculum Development.

Berliner, D. C., & Nichols, S. (2007). High-stakes testing is putting the nation at risk. *Education Week, 26*(27), 36–38.

Berman, J. J. (2003). *Cross-cultural differences in perspectives of the self.* Lincoln: University of Nebraska Press.

Berman, S. H. (2003). Practicing democracy in high school. *Educational Leadership, 61*(1), 35–38.

Bernauer, J. A. (1999). Emerging standards: Empowerment with purpose. *Kappa Delta Pi Record, 35*(2), 68–70, 74.

Bestor, A. E. (1953). *Educational wastelands*. Urbana: University of Illinois.

Betts, J., & Tang, Y. E. (2008, December). Charter schools and student achievement: A review of the evidence. In R. Lake (Ed.), *Hopes, fears, & reality: A balanced look at American charter schools in 2008* (chap. 1). Retrieved May 14, 2009, from the Center on Reinventing Public Education Web site: http://www.crpe.org/cs/crpe/view/csr_pubs/254

Bialo, E. R., & Sivin-Kachala, J. (1996). The effectiveness of technology in schools: A summary of recent research. Quoted in Stockard (2001), *Methods and resources for elementary and middle-school social studies*, Long Grove, IL: Waveland Press.

Billig, S. H., & Waterman, A. S. (Eds.). (2003). *Studying service-learning: Innovations in education research methodology*. Mahwah, NJ: Lawrence Erlbaum.

Bintz, W. P., & Dillard, J. (2007). Teachers as reflective practitioners: Examining teacher stories of curricular change in a 4th grade classroom. *Reading Horizons, 47*(3), 203–227.

Black, S. (2003, December). Engaging the unengaged. *American School Board Journal, 190*(12), 58–60.

Blendinger, J. (2010). Project-centered parental involvement. In K. T. Henson, *Supervision: A collaborative approach to instructional improvement* (p. 320). Long Grove, IL: Waveland Press.

Block, J. H., Efthim, H. E., & Burns, R. B. (1989). *Building effective mastery learning schools*. New York: Longman.

Block, J. H., & Henson, K. T. (1986, Spring). Mastery learning and middle school instruction. *American Middle School Education, 9*(2), 21–29.

Bloom, B. S. (1956). Taxonomy of educational objectives. *The classification of educational goals, Handbook I. Cognitive domain*. New York: McKay.

Bloom, B. S., Hastings, J. T., & Madaus, G. F. (1971). *Handbook of formative and summative evaluation of student learning*. New York: McGraw-Hill.

Bloom, B. S., Hastings, J. T., & Madaus, G. F. (1981). *Evaluation to improve learning*. New York: McGraw-Hill.

Blum, R. W. (2005). A case for school connectedness. *Educational Leadership 62*(7), 16–21.

Boix-Mansilla, V., & Gardner, H. (2008). Disciplining the mind. *Educational Leadership, 65*(5), 14–19.

Boles, K. C., & Troen, V. (2007). How to improve professional practice. *Principal, 87*(2), 50–53.

Bonar, B. D. (1992, Fall). The role of laboratory schools in American education. *National Association of Laboratory Schools Journal, 17*(1), 42–53.

Borko, H., & Elliott, R. (1999). Hands-on pedagogy versus hands-off accountability. *Phi Delta Kappan, 80*(5), 394–400.

Boss, S. (2008, July 21). Global Learning: Connecting the World with ePals. *Edutopia Magazine*. Retrieved March 9, 2009, from http://www.edutopia.org/epals-online-community-pen-pals

Boston Digital Bridge Foundation. (2006). *Case study: O'Donnell School SY '05–'06. Technology Goes Home @ School builds parental involvement*. Retrieved May 13, 2009, from http:www.cityofboston.gov/bra/digitalbridge/pdf/TGHCaseStudy6.pdf

Bottoms, G. (2007). Treat all students like the "best" students. *Educational Leadership, 64*(7), 34–35.

Bracey, G. W. (1991). Why can't they be like we were? *Phi Delta Kappan, 73*(2), 104–117.

Bracey, G. W. (1993). Tips for researchers. *Phi Delta Kappan, 75*(1), 84–86.

Bracey, G. W. (2003). The condition of public education. *Phi Delta Kappan, 85*(2), 148–164.

Bracey, G. W. (2007). The first time everything changed. *Phi Delta Kappan, 89*(2), 119–136.

Brady, M. (2008). Cover the material—or teach students to think? *Educational Leadership, 65*(5), 64–67.

Brewster, C., & Fager, J. (2000). *Increasing student engagement and motivation: From time-on-task to homework*. Portland, OR: Northwest Regional Educational Laboratory. Retrieved June 19, 2009, from http://www.nwrel.org/request/oct00/textonly.html

Brogdon, R. E. (1993). Darlene's story: When standards can hurt. *Educational Leadership, 50*(5), 76–77.

Brookhart, S. M. (2007/2008) Feedback that fits. *Educational Leadership, 65*(4), 54–59.

Brown, K. (2004). Technology: Building interaction. *TechTrends, 48*(5), 34–36.

Bruner, J. S. (1960). *The process of education*. Cambridge, MA: Harvard University Press.

Buck, F. (2007). Saving time and paper with basic technology. *Principal, 96*(3), 18–21.

Bunting, C. (2007). Principals as classroom leaders. *Principal, 86*(3), 39–41.

Burke, W. J. (1967). *Not for glory*. New York: Cowles Education Corporation.

Burns, R. B. (1979). Mastery learning: Does it work? *Educational Leadership, 37*, 110–113.

Bushaw, W. J., & Gallup, A. M. (2008). Americans speak out—Are educators and policy makers listening? The 40th Annual Poll of the Public's Attitudes toward the Public Schools. *Phi Delta Kappan, 90*(1), 9–20.

Camilleri, J. (2007). *Healing the inner city child: Creative arts therapies with at-risk youth*. London: Jessica Kingsley.

Campano, G. (2007). Honoring student stories. *Educational Leadership, 65*(4), 48–54.

Campbell, J. K. (1967). *Colonel Francis Parker: The children's crusader.* New York: Columbia University Teachers' College Press.

Cardelle-Elawar, M. (1993). The teacher as researcher in the classroom. *Action in Teacher Education, 15*(1), 49–57.

Carnevale, A. P., Gainer, L. J., & Meltzer, A. S. (1990). *Workplace basics: The essential skills employers want.* San Francisco: Jossey-Bass.

Carraher, D. (2003, April 9). *Weblogs in Education.* Retrieved June 15, 2005, from http://blogs.law.harvard.edu/carraher/stories/storyReader$6

Carroll, J. B. (1963). A model of school learning. *Teachers College Record, 64*, 723–733.

Carson, T. (1990). What kind of knowing is critical action research? *Theory into Practice, 29*(3), 167–173.

Caswell, H. L., & Campbell, D. S. (1935). *Curriculum development*. New York: American Book Company.

Cearley, A., & Bennett, A. (2008, November 25). Parental involvement goes high-tech. *USC News*. Retrieved April 29, 2009, from the University of Southern California Web site: http://www.usc.edu/ uscnews/stories/16000.html

Center for Applied Linguistics. (2009). *Directory of two-way bilingual immersion programs in the U.S.* Retrieved April 30, 2009, from http://www.cal.org/twi/directory/table.htm

Center on Education Policy. (2006, March). *From the capital to the classroom: Year 4 of the No Child Left Behind Act*. Retrieved June 18, 2009, from http://www.cccfiles.org/shared/publications/downloads/CEP-Capital%20to%20the%20Classroom%20Report-4.pdf

Center on Education Policy and the American Youth Policy Forum. (2000). *Do You Know the Good News about American Education?* Retrieved February 25, 2005, from http://www.ctredpol.org

Chappuis, J. (2009). The seven strategies of assessment for Learning. Portland, OR: ETS Assessment Training Institute.

Chappuis, S., & Chappuis, J. (2007/2008). The best value in formative assessment. *Educational Leadership,65*(4), 20–25.

Chattin-McNichols, J., & Loeffler, M. H. (1989). Teachers as researchers: The first cycle of the teachers' research network. *Young Children, 44*(5), 20–27.

Children's Defense Fund. (2008). Statistics taken from the *What Is NAREN?* Web site. Retrieved May 12, 2009, from http://www.atriskeducation.net/index.html

Christensen, C., Aaron, S., & Clark, K. W. (2005). Can schools improve? *Phi Delta Kappan, 86*(7), 545–551.

Christie, K. (2008). Dat's story: Things have got to change. *Phi Delta Kappan, 89*(9), 469–471.

Clark, R. W. (2004). Beyond the classroom. *Kappa Delta Pi Record, 41*(1), 26–29.

Claus, J. (1999). You can't avoid the politics: Lessons for teacher education from a case study of teacher-initiated tracking reform. *Journal of Teacher Education, 50*(l), 5–16.

Clement, M., & Vandenberghe, R. (2000, January). Teacher's professional development: A solitary or collegial (ad)venture? *Teaching and Teacher Education, 16*(1), 81–101.

Clinchy, E. (1998). The educationally challenged American school district. *Phi Delta Kappan, 80*(4), 272–277.

Cloud, J., & Morse, J. (2001). Home Sweet School. *Time.com*—seceding from school. Retrieved February 11, 2005, from http://www.time.com/covers/1101010827/cover.html

Conant, J. B. (1951). *Science and common sense.* New Haven, CT: Yale University Press.

Conant, J. B. (1959). *The American high school.* New York: McGraw-Hill.

Conroy, P. (1972). *The water is wide.* New York: The Old New York Book Shop. (Reprint, 1991).

Consortium of National Arts Education Associations. (1994). *National standards for arts education: What every young American should know and be able to do in the arts.* Reston, VA: Music Educators National Conference.

Cooper, H. (2006, March 7). Duke study: Homework helps students succeed in school, as long as there isn't too much. *Dukenews.* Retrieved April 23, 2009, from http://www.dukenews.duke.edu/2006/03/homework.html

Cooper, H., Robinson, J. C., & Patall, E. A. (2006). Does homework improve academic achievement? A synthesis of research, 1987–2003. *Review of Educational Research, 76,* 1–62.

Cooper, K. (1989, May 23). Education secretary calls for restructuring of public schools. *Center Daily Times*, p. 1.

Costa, A. C. (2008). The thought-filled curriculum. *Educational Leadership, 65*(5), 20–24.

Council of Chief State School Officers (CCSSO). (2005). *Next steps: Moving towards performance-based licensing into teaching.* Retrieved May 27, 2009, from http://www.ccsso.org/publications/details.cfm?PublicationID=86

Council of Chief State School Officers (CCSSO). (2008, April 28–May 1). *Report and recommendations for educational policy leaders.* The Pearson Foundation/CCSSO International Conference on Science and Mathematics Education, Singapore. Retrieved May 29, 2009, from http://www.pearsonfoundation.org/PDF/PF-CCSSO_Report.pdf

Counts, G. S. (1932). *Dare the schools build a new social order?* New York: John Day.

Cuban, L. (1992). Managing dilemmas while building professional communities. *Educational Researcher, 21*(1), 4–11.

Cuban, L. (1993). The lure of curricular reform and its pitiful history. *Phi Delta Kappan, 75*(2), 182–185.

Cunningham, R. D., Jr. (1991, September). Modeling mastery teaching through supervision. *NASSP Bulletin, 75*(536), 83–87.

Curtis, D. (2008). Disabled bodies, able minds: Giving voice, movement, and independence to the physically challenged. *Edutopia Magazine.* Retrieved May 14, 2009, from http://www.edutopia.org/print/1241

Curts, J. (2004). A constructivist approach to teaching how polls work. In K. T. Henson (Ed.), *Constructivist teaching strategies for diverse middle-level classrooms.* Boston: Allyn & Bacon.

Dallman-Jones, A. S. (2002, Spring). A case for separate at-risk education standards. *Journal of School Improvement, 3*(1), 32–34.

Daniels, D. Y., Queen, J. A., & Schumacher, D. (2007). Obesity and poverty: A growing challenge. *Principal, 86*(3), 42–47.

Daniels, H., & Zemelman, S. (2003/2004). Out with textbooks: In with learning. *Educational Leadership, 61*(4), 36–40.

Danielson, C. (2007). *Enhancing professional practice: A framework for teaching* (2nd ed.). Alexandria, VA: ASCD.

Darder, A., Baltodano, M., & Torres, R. (Eds.). (2003). *The critical pedagogy reader.* London & New York: Routledge.

Darder, A., Baltodano, M. P., & Torres, R. (Eds.). (2008). *The critical pedagogy reader* (2nd ed.). New York: Routledge.

Daresh, J. C. (2007). *Supervision as proactive leadership* (4th ed.). Long Grove, IL: Waveland Press.

Darling-Hammond, L. (1996). The quiet revolution: Rethinking teacher development. *Educational Leadership, 53*(6), 4–10.

Darling-Hammond, L. (2003). Keeping good teachers: Why it matters, what leaders can do. *Educational Leadership, 60*(8), 13.

Darling-Hammond, L., & Baratz-Snowden, J. (2007). A good teacher in every classroom: Preparing the highly qualified teachers our children deserve. *Educational Horizons, 85*(2), 111–132.

David, J. I. (2008). What research says about grade retention. *Educational Leadership, 65*(6), 83–84.

Davies, L. (2002). *Education and conflict: Complexity and chaos.* London: RoutledgeFalmer.

Davis, G. A. (1993). Creative teaching of moral thinking: Fostering awareness and commitment. *Middle School Journal, 24*(4), 32–33.

Davis, R. (2010). Know your faculty. In K. T. Henson, *Supervision: A collaborative approach to instructional improvement* (p. 8). Long Grove, IL: Waveland Press.

DeLuca, K. (2005). *Blogging Provides Classrooms Another Route to Web.* Red and Black Publishing Co. Retrieved June 15, 2005, from http://www.redandblack.com/

DeRoma, V. M., & Nida, S. (2004). A focus on hands-on, learner-centered technology and The Citadel. *TechTrends, 48*(5), 37–41.

DeVoe, J. F., Peter, K., Kaufman, P., Ruddy, S. A., Miller, A. K., Planty, M., Snyder, T. D., Duhart, D. T., & Rand, M. R. (2002). *Indicators of school crime and safety.* Washington, DC: U. S. Departments of Education and Justice.

Dewey, J. (1916). *Democracy in education.* New York: Macmillan.

Dewey, J. (1939). *Experience and education.* New York: Macmillan.

DeWitt, D. (2010). Breaking logjams. In K. T. Henson, *Supervision: A collaborative approach to instructional improvement* (p. 128). Long Grove, IL: Waveland Press.

Dick, R. (1999). *What is action research?* Retrieved May 12, 2009, from http://www.scu.edu.au/schools.gcm/ar/whatisar.html

DiMartino, J., & Castaneda, A. (2007). Assessing applied skills. *Educational Leadership, 64*(7), 38–42.

Dlott, A. M. (2007). A (Pod)cast of thousands. *Educational Leadership, 64*(7), 80–82.

Doll, R. C. (1996). *Curriculum improvement: Decision making and process* (9th ed.). Boston: Allyn & Bacon.

Doorey, N., & Harter, B. (Dec. 2002/Jan. 2003). From court order to community commitment. *Educational Leadership, 60*(4), 22–25.

Downey, C. J., Steffy, B. E., & Poston, W. K., Jr. (2009). *50 ways to close the achievement gap.* Thousand Oaks, CA: Corwin.

Dunn, R., & Dunn, K. (1999). *The complete guide to the learning styles in-service system.* Boston: Allyn & Bacon.

Dunn, R., Dunn, K., & Perrin, J. (1994). *Teaching young children through their individual learning styles.* Boston: Allyn & Bacon.

Dunn, R., Griggs, S. A., Olson, J., Gorman, B., & Beasley, M. (1995). A meta-analytic validation of the Dunn and Dunn learning styles model. *Journal of Educational Research, 88*(6), 353–362.

Dunn, R., & Klavas, A. (1992). *Homework disc.* Jamaica, NY: St. John's University's Center for the Study of Learning and Teaching Styles.

Echlin, H. (2007, September). *Digital discussion: Take your class to the Internet—How to set up a blog in your classroom.* Retrieved July 17, 2009, from the Edutopia Web site: http://www.edutopia.org/digital-discussion-take-your-class-to-internet?page=2

Education Commission of the States. (1983). *Action for excellence: A comprehensive plan to improve our nation's schools.* Task Force on Education for Economic Growth. Denver, CO: Authors.

Education Portal. (2007). *High school students taking the core curriculum are not college ready.* Retrieved May 22, 2009, from portal.com/articles/High_School_Students_Taking_the_Core_Curriculum_are_Not_College_Ready.html

Educational Technology. (2009). *Limitations.* Retrieved May 28, 2009, from the Educational Technology Web site: http://edtech.twinisles.com/limitations.html

Edutopia staff. (2008). *Why should schools embrace integrated studies?: It fosters a way of learning that mimics real life.* Retrieved March 9, 2009, from the Edutopia Web site: http://www.edutopia.org/integrated-studies-introduction

Egan, K., & Judson, G. (2008). Of whales and wonder. *Educational Leadership, 65*(6), 21–25.

Einstein, A. (1951). Autobiographical notes (P. A. Schilpp, Trans.). In E. A. Schilpp (Ed.), *Albert Einstein: Philosopher-scientist* (p. 7). The Library of Living Philosophers (Vol. VII). New York: Tudor.

Eisner, E. W. (1985). *The educational imagination* (2nd ed.). New York: Macmillan.

Eisner, E. W. (2001). What does it mean to say a school is doing well? *Phi Delta Kappan, 82*(5), 367–372.

Eisner, E. W. (2004). What do kids know and misunderstand about science? *Educational Leadership, 61*(5), 34–37.

Elam, S. M. (1996). Phi Delta Kappa's young leaders of 1980 tackle today's issues. *Phi Delta Kappan, 77*(9), 610–614.

Epstein, A. S. (2008). An early start on thinking. *Educational Leadership, 65*(5), 38–43.

Fahner-Vihtelic, A. (2006). *Engaging students for success.* Retrieved May 13, 2009, from http://beryl.educ.psu.edu/pds_download/2006InquiryProjects/fahnerVihtelicA.pdf

Ferrero, D. J. (2005). Does "research based" mean "value neutral"? *Phi Delta Kappan, 86*(6), 425–432.

Fisher, D., Grant, M., Frey, N., & Johnson, C (2007/2008). Taking formative assessment schoolwide. *Educational Leadership, 65*(4), 64–69.

Foshay, A. W. (1969). Changing interpretations of the elementary curriculum. In H. G. Shane (Ed.), *The American elementary school.* Thirteenth yearbook of the John Dewey Society.

Franco, S. (2007). Reauthorization of NCLB: Time to reconsider the scientifically based research requirement. *Third Education Group Review Essays, 3*(6). Retrieved April 29, 2009, from http://www.thirdeducationgroup.org/Review/Essays/v3n6.pdf

Franklin, J. (2005, February). Blogging and benefiting: Teachers go hi-tech to share tips and strategies. *Education Update, 47*(2). Retrieved July 20, 2009, from the Association for Supervision and Curriculum Development Web site: http://www.ascd.org/publications/newsletters/education_update/feb05/vol47/num02/Blogging_and_Benefiting.aspx

Frymier, J. (1979, February). Keynote speech at Southwest Educational Research Association, Houston, TX.

Fugate, C. (2007) Vonnegut warned us. *Phi Delta Kappan, 89*(1), 71–72.

Fullan, M. G. (1999). Education reform on the move. In B. Day (Ed.), *Teaching and learning in the new millennium*. Indianapolis: Kappa Delta Pi.

Gaither, M. (2008, December 24). *Breaking news! New NCES homeschool data!* Retrieved May 21, 2009, from http://gaither:worldpress.com/2008/12/24breaking-news-new-nces-homeschool-data

Gallup, Inc. (2009). *Children and violence*. Retrieved April 24, 2009, from the Gallup, Inc. Web site: http://www.gallup.com/poll/1588/Children-Violence

Gardner, H. (1993). *Multiple intelligences: The theory in practice*. New York: Basic Books.

Gay, G. (1990). Achieving educational equality through curriculum desegregation. *Phi Delta Kappan, 72*(1), 61–62.

Gay, G. (2004). The importance of multicultural education. *Educational Leadership, 61*(4), 30–35.

Gay, G. (2006). Connections between classroom management and culturally responsive teaching. In C. Evertson & C. Weinstein (Eds.), *Handbook of classroom management: Research, practice, and contemporary issues*. Mahwah, NJ: Erlbaum.

Geisert, G., & Dunn, R. (1991, March–April). Effective use of computers: Assignments based on individual learning style. *The Clearing House, 64*(4), 219–223.

Genesee, F., Lindholm-Leary, K. J., Saunders, W., & Christian, D. (2006). *Educating English language learners: A synthesis of empirical evidence*. New York: Cambridge University Press.

Gentile, J. R., & Lalley, J. P. (2003). *Standards and mastery learning: Aligning teaching and assessment so all children can learn*. Thousand Oaks, CA: Corwin.

Geography Education Standards Project. (1994). *Geography for life: National geography standards*. Washington, DC: National Geographic Research and Exploration.

George Lucas Educational Foundation. (2008). Readers survey, 2008. Retrieved May 27, 2009, from the *Edutopia* Web site: http://www.edutopia.org/readers-survey-2008

Gibbons, M. (2004). Pardon me, didn't I just hear a paradigm shift? *Phi Delta Kappan, 85*(6), 461–467.

Gibbons, M. (2008). *Empowering students to act: Motivating students and teaching them to motivate themselves*. Retrieved April 24, 2009, from http://www.selfdirectedlearning.com/article2.html

Gibbs, G. (2010). Using authentic data. In K. T. Henson, *Supervision: A collaborative approach to instructional improvement* (p. 374). Long Grove, IL: Waveland Press.

Gibran, K. (1923). *The prophet*. New York: Alfred A. Knopf.

Gilbert, S. L., & Smith, L. C. (2003). A bumpy road to action research. *Kappa Delta Pi Record, 39*(2), 80–83.

Glanzer, P. L. (2008). Harry Potter's provocative moral world: Is there a place for good and evil in moral education? *Phi Delta Kappan, 89*(7), 525–528.

Glatthorn, A. (2004). *Developing a quality curriculum*. Long Grove, IL: Waveland Press.

Glod, M., & Chandler, A. (2008, August 27). Scores stable as more minorities take SAT. *The Washington Post*, B01. Retrieved April 28, 2009, from http://www.washingtonpost.com/wp-dyn/content/article/2008/26/AR2008082601468_pf.html

Goldys, P., Kruft, C., & Subrizi, P. (2007). Action research: Do it yourself! *Principal, 86*(4), 60–63.

Gollnick, D. M., & Chinn, P. C. (2002). *Multicultural education in a pluralistic society* (6th ed.). Upper Saddle River, NJ: Merrill.

Gonzales, P. (2008). *Highlights from TIMSS 2007: Mathematics and science achievements of U.S. fourth- and eighth-grade students in an international context*. NCES 2009-001.

U.S. Department of Education. Retrieved May 29, 2009, from http://www.eric.ed.gov/ERICDocs/data/ericdocs2sql/content_storage_01/0000019b/80/41/e7/24

Good, T. L., & Brophy, J. E. (2008). *Looking in classrooms* (10th ed.). Boston: Allyn & Bacon.

Goodlad, J. I. (1984). *A place called school*. New York: McGraw-Hill.

Goodlad, J. I. (1997). *In praise of education*. New York: Teachers College Press.

Goodlad, J. I. (2003/2004). Teaching what we hold sacred. *Educational Leadership, 61*(4), 18–21.

Goodman, J. (1992). Towards a discourse of imagery: Critical curriculum theorizing. *Educational Forum, 56*(3), 269–289.

Gootman, E. (2008, December 20). In cramped spaces, small school benefits. *The New York Times*. Retrieved July 17, 2009, from http://www.nytimes.com/2008/12/21/education/21shared.html

Gorski, P. C. (2009). *Stages of multicultural school transformation*. Retrieved May 13, 2009, from EdChange, Multicultural Pavilion Web site: http://www.edchange.org/multicultural/resources/school_transformation.html

Gough, P. B. (1993). A view from the outside. *Phi Delta Kappan, 74*(9), 669.

Grubb, W. N. (1996). The new vocationalism: What it is, what it could be. *Phi Delta Kappan, 77*(8), 535–546.

Guskey, T. R. (2003). How classroom assessments improve learning. *Educational Leadership, 60*(50), 6–11.

Guskey, T. R., & Gates, S. L. (1986). Synthesis of research on the effects of mastery learning in elementary and secondary classrooms. *Educational Leadership, 45*(8), 73–80.

Haberman, M. (1992, November). The role of the classroom teacher as a curriculum leader. *NASSP Bulletin, 76*(547), 11–19.

Haberman, M. (1999). The anti-learning curriculum of urban schools. Part 2: The solution. *Kappa Delta Pi Record, 35*(2), 71–74.

Haberman, M., & Bracey, G. W. (1997). The anti-learning curriculum of urban schools. Part l: The problem. *Kappa Delta Pi Record, 33*(3), 88–89.

Habley, W. R., & McClanahan, R. (2004). *What works in student retention—Four-year private colleges*. Retrieved September 8, 2008, from The American College Testing Program (ACT) Web site: http://act.org/path/postsec/droptables/pdf/FourYearPrivate.pdf

Halverson, D. (2010). Curriculum Evaluation Walkthroughs. In K. T. Henson, *Supervision: A collaborative approach to instructional improvement* (p. 194). Long Grove, IL: Waveland Press.

Hanson, S., & Moir, E. (2008). Beyond mentoring: Influencing the professional practice and careers of experienced teachers. *Phi Delta Kappan, 89*(6), 453–459.

Harris, S. (2010). Finding common ground. In K. T. Henson, *Supervision: A collaborative approach to instructional improvement* (p. 58). Long Grove, IL: Waveland Press.

Harvey, O. J., Hunt, D. E., & Schroder, H. M. (1963). *Conceptual systems and personality organization*. New York: Wiley.

Henson, K. T. (1996). Teachers as researchers. In J. Sikula, T. J. Buttery, & E. Guyton (Eds.), *Handbook of research on teacher education* (2nd ed.). Arlington, VA: Association of Teacher Educators.

Henson, K. T. (Ed.) (2004). *Constructivist teaching strategies for diverse middle-level classrooms*. Boston: Allyn & Bacon.

Henson, K. T. (2006). *Curriculum planning: Integrating multiculturalism, constructivism and education reform* (3rd Ed.). Long Grove, IL: Waveland Press.

Henson, K. T. (2010). *Supervision: A collaborative approach to instructional improvement*. Long Grove, IL: Waveland Press.

Henson, K. T., & Eller, B. F. (1999). *Educational psychology for effective teaching*. Belmont, CA: Wadsworth.

Herzberg, F., Mausner, B., & Snyderman, B. (1959). *The motivation to work*. New York: John Wiley.

Hewett, S. M. (2004). Electronic portfolios: Improving instructional practices. *TechTends, 48*(5), 24–28.

Hoachlander, G. (2007).New rigor for career education. *Educational Leadership, 64*(7), 34–35.

Hoffman, D., & Levak, B. A. (2003). Personalizing schools. *Educational Leadership, 61*(1), 30–34.

Holmes, T. C. (2006). Low test score plus high retention rates equal more dropouts. *Kappa Delta Pi Record, 42*(2), 56–58.

Holzman, M. (1992, February). Do we really need "leadership"? *Educational Leadership, 49*(5), 36–40.

Hoover, J. J. (1990, March). Curriculum adaptation: A five step process for classroom implementation. *Academic Therapy, 25*(4), 407–416.

Hopkins, G. (2004). Is community service a waste of time? *Education World.* Retrieved May 29, 2009, from http://www.educationworld.com/a_curr/curr/88.html

Howlett, J. (2008). Industrial arts: Call it what you want, the need still exists. *Phi Delta Kappan, 89*(7), 522–524.

Hubbell, E. R., & Kuhn, M. (2007). Using technology to promote science inquiry. *Principal, 87*(2), 24–27.

Huggest, A. J., & Stinnett, T. M. (1958). *Professional problems of teachers*. New York: Macmillan.

Institute for Children and Poverty. (2008). *National data on family homelessness*. Retrieved May 22, 2009, from http://www.icpny.org/index,asp?CID=7

Interstate New Teacher Assessment and Support Consortium (INTASC). (1992). *Model standards for beginning teacher licensing, assessment and development: A resource for state dialogue.* Retrieved June 18, 2009, from http://www.cccso.org/content/pdfs/corestrd.pdf

Interstate New Teacher Assessment and Support Consortium (INTASC). 2005. *Model standards for beginning teacher licensing, assessment and development: A resource for state dialogue*. Retrieved July 20, 2009, from http://www.ccsso.org/content/pdfs/corestrd.pdf

Jackson Nakazawa, D. (2004). *Does anybody else look like me?: A parent's guide to raising multiracial children*. Cambridge, MA: Da Capo Press.

Jenkins, H. (2005). Getting into the game. *Educational Leadership,* 62(7), 48–51.

Jensen, C. R., & Overman, S. J. (2003). *Administration and Management of Physical Education and Athletic Programs*. Long Grove, IL: Waveland Press.

Jensen, E. P. (2008). A fresh look at brain-based education. *Phi Delta Kappan, 89*(6), 408–417.

Johnson, D. W., & Johnson, R. (1989–1990). Social skills for successful group work. *Educational Leadership, 47*(4), 29–33.

Julik, J. A. (1981, April). *The effect of ability grouping on secondary school students*. Paper presented at the American Educational Research Association, Los Angeles.

Kant, I. (1974). *On the old saw: That may be right in theory but it won't work in practice* (E. B. Ashton, Trans.). Philadelphia: University of Pennsylvania Press. (Original work published 1793)

Keefe, J. W., & Amenta, R. B. (2005). Whatever happened to the Model Schools Project? *Phi Delta Kappan, 86*(7), 536–544.

Kerlinger, F. (1973). *Foundations of behavioral research* (2nd ed.). New York: Holt, Rinehart, & Winston.

King, A. (1990, November–December). Reciprocal questioning: A strategy for teaching students how to learn from lectures. *The Clearing House, 64*(2), 131–135.

King, A., & Rosenshine, B. (1993). Effects of guided cooperative questioning on children's knowledge construction. *Journal of Experimental Education, 61*(2), 127–148.

Kinnaman, D. (2007, October 31). Small schools, big benefits. Retrieved July 17, 2009, from *District Administration Magazine* Web site: http://www.districtadministration.com/pulse/commentpost.aspx?news=no&postid=48619

Kladifko, R. (2010). Get personal. In K. T. Henson, *Supervision: A collaborative approach to instructional improvement* (p. 269). Long Grove, IL: Waveland Press.

Knapp, M. S., & Shields, P. M. (1990, June). Reconceiving academic instruction for the children of poverty. *Phi Delta Kappan, 71*(10), 753–758.

Koba, S. B. (1996). Narrowing the achievement gap in science. *Educational Leadership, 53*(8), 14–17.

Kohn, A. L. (2007). Rethinking homework. *Principal, 86*(3), 35–38.

Kowal, J. (1991). Science, technology, and human values: A curricular approach. *Theory Into Practice, 30*(4), 267–272.

Kowalski, T. J. (2002). *Contemporary school administration: An introduction*. Boston: Allyn & Bacon.

Kowalski, T. J., & Reitzug, U. C. (1993). *Contemporary school administration: An introduction*. New York: Longman.

Krathwohl, D. R., Bloom, B. S., & Masia, B. B. (1964). *Taxonomy of educational objectives: The classification of educational goals. Handbook II: The affective domain.* New York: McKay.

Kretovics, J., Farber, K. S., & Armaline, W. D. (2004). It ain't brain surgery: Restructuring schools to improve the education of children placed at risk. *Educational Horizons, 82*(3), 213–225.

Krugman, P. (2008, February 18). *Poverty is poison*. Retrieved June 18, 2009, from http://www.nytimes.com/2008/02/18/opinion/18krugman.html

Laboard, K. L. (2003, September 22). From teacher-centered to learner-centered curriculum: Improving learning in diverse classrooms. *Education, 124*(1).

Lacireno-Paquet, N., & Holyoke, T. T. (2007). Moving forward or sliding backward: The evolution of charter school policies in Michigan and the District of Columbia. *Educational Policy, 21*(1), 185–214.

Lacireno-Paquet, N., Holyoke, T. T., & Moser, M. (2002). Creaming versus cropping: charter school enrollment practices in response to market incentives. *Educational Evaluation and Policy Analysis, 24*(2), 145–158.

Latham, A. S. (1998). Gender differences on assessments. *Educational Leadership, 55*(4), 88–89.

LeDoux, J. (1996). *The emotional brain: The mysterious underpinnings of emotional life.* New York: Simon & Schuster.

Lehman, R., & Conceição, S. (2001, December). Involving the deaf community in distance learning using blended technologies and learning objects. *Teaching With Technology Today, 8*(3).

Levin, D., & Arafeh, S. (2002). The digital disconnect: The widening gap between Internet-savvy students and their schools. Pew Internet Project. Retrieved July 17, 2009, from http://www.pewinternet.org/~/media//Files/Reports/2002/PIP_Schools_Internet_Report.pdf.pdf

Levin, H. M. (2007, June). On the relationship between poverty and curriculum. *North Carolina Law Review,* 85(5). Retrieved June 18, 2009, from http://studentorgs.law.unc.edu/nclrev/issues/vol85/issue5/levin.aspx

Levine, M. (2007). The essential cognitive backpack. *Educational Leadership, 64*(7), 15–22.

Lindblad, A. H., Jr. (1994). You can avoid the traps of cooperative learning. *The Clearing House, 67*(5), 291–293.

Linder, D. (2002). *The Scopes trial: An introduction*. Retrieved March 22, 2005, from http://www.law.umkc.edu/faculty/projects/ftrials/scopes/scopes.htm

Lindholm-Leary, K. J. (2005). The rich promise of two-way immersion. *Educational Leadership, 62*(4), 56–59.

Lleras, C. (2009, February). Ability grouping in elementary school hampers minority students' literacy. *American Journal of Education*. Retrieved April 23, 2009, from http://www.eurekalert.org/pub_releases/2009-04/uoia-agi042109.php

Lobkowicz, N. (1967). *Theory into practice*. Notre Dame, IN: University of Notre Dame Press.

Long Island School-to-Work and Parental Choice. (2003). Retrieved June 24, 2005, from http://www.aypf.org/tripreports/1995/tr101995.htm

Lounsbury, J. H. (1991). A fresh start for the middle school curriculum. *Middle School Journal, 23*(2), 3–7.

Lowery, L. (1908). *The relation of superintendents and principal to the training and professional improvement of their teachers*. Seventh Yearbook for the National Society for the Study of Education, Part I. Chicago: University of Chicago Press.

Lunenburg, F. C., & Ornstein, A. C. (2004). *Educational administration: Concepts and practice* (5th ed). Belmont, CA: Wadsworth/Thomson.

Macdonald, J. B., & Leeper, R. R. (1965). *Theories of instruction*. Washington, DC: Association for Supervision and Curriculum Development.

Maddox, H., & Hoole, E. (1975). Performance decrement in the lecture. *Educational Review, 28*, 17–30.

Mangione, L. (2008). Is homework working? *Phi Delta Kappan, 89*(8), 614–615.

March, T. (2003, Dec./2004, Jan.) The learning power of webquests. *Educational Leadership,* 61(4), 42–47. Retricved June 18, 2009, from http://tommarch.com/writings/wq_power.php

Marsh, C. J., & Willis, G. (2003). *Curriculum: Alternative approaches, ongoing issues* (3rd ed.). Upper Saddle River, NJ: Merrill/Pearson/Prentice-Hall.

Marshak, D. (2004). No child left behind: A foolish race to the past. *Phi Delta Kappan, 85*(3), 229–231.

Marshall, C. (1991 March–April). Teachers' learning styles: How they affect student learning. *The Clearing House, 64*(4), 225–227.

Martinez, M. E. (2006). What is metacognition? *Phi Delta Kappan, 87*(9), 696–699.

Maslow, A. H. (1943). A theory of human motivation. *Psychological Review, 50*(4), 370–396.

Mathews, J. (2008, November 28), Should teachers ignore poverty's impact? *The Washington Post*. Retrieved March 19, 2009, from http://www.washingtonpost.com/wp-dyn/content/article/2008/11/28/AR2008112801130_pf.html

Mayo, K. E., & Whitley, C. (2004). Professional learning communities: A constructive approach to professional development. In K. T. Henson (Ed.), *Constructivist teaching strategies for diverse middle-level classrooms*. Boston: Allyn & Bacon.

McCarthy, M. (2008). Increased support for vouchers. *Phi Delta Kappan, 90*(1), 16.

McCarthy, M., & Kuh, G. D. (2006). Are students ready for college? What student engagement data say. *Phi Delta Kappan, 87*(9), 664–669.

McConachie, S. M., Hall, M., Resnick, L., Ravi, A., Bill, V., Bintz, J, & Taylor, P. (2006). Task, text and talk: Literacy for all subjects. *Educational Leadership, 64*(2), 8–14.

McCutcheon, C., & Jung, B. (1990). Alternative perspectives on action research. *Theory into Practice, 29*(3), 144–151.

McElroy, L. (1990). Becoming real: An ethic at the heart of action research. *Theory into Practice, 29*(3), 209–213.

McKernan, J. (1988). Teacher as researcher: Paradigm or praxis. *Contemporary Education, 59*(3), 154–158.

McNeil, J. D. (2003). *Curriculum: The teacher's initiative* (3rd ed.). Upper Saddlc River, NJ: Merrill/Prentice-Hall.

McTighe, J., & Thomas, R. S. (2003). Backward design for forward action. *Educational Leadership, 60*(5), 52–55.

Mediratta, K., Fruchter, N., & Lewis, A. C. (2002). *Organizing for school reform: How communities are finding their voice and reclaiming their public schools*. New York: Institute for Education and Social Policy, New York University.

Meek, A. (1998). America's teachers: Much to celebrate. *Educational Leadership, 55*(5), 12–16.

Meier, D. (2004). Smallness, autonomy, and choice: Scaling up. *Educational Horizons, 82*(4), 290–299.

Mercurius, N. (2003). *Redefining the role of computers in education: The vendors' curricula.* Retrieved June 14, 2005, from http://www.techlearning.com/story/showArticle.jhtml?articleID=12803457.

Merkley, D., Schmidt, D., Dirksen, C., & Fulher, C. (2006). Enhancing parent–teacher communication using technology: A reading improvement clinic example. *Contemporary Issues in Technology and Teacher Education, 6*(1). Retrieved January 15, 2009, from http://www.citejournal.org/vol6/iss1/languagearts/article1.cfm

Merrow, J. (2008). Message to charter schools. *Phi Delta Kappan, 90*(1), 18.

Metcalf, K. K., Theobald, N. D., & Gonzalez, G. (2003). State university roles in the charter school movement. *Phi Delta Kappan,* 84(7), 542–545.

Meyer, C. F., & Rhodes, E. K. (2006). Multiculturalism: Beyond food, festival, folklore, and fashion. *Kappa Delta Pi Record, 42*(2), 82–87.

Miller, J. A., & Dunn, R. (1997, November/December). The use of learning styles in sonography. *Journal of Diagnostic Medical Sonography, 13*(6), 304–308.

Mills, C. K. (2007). Building curriculum with digital materials. *Principal, 86*(3), 26–28.

Milner, N. (2007). Race, culture, and researcher position—Working through dangers seen, unseen, and unforeseen. *Educational Researcher, 36*(7), 388–400.

Modern Language Association (MLA). (2007, November). *Enrollments in languages other than English in United States institutions of higher education, fall, 2006.* Retrieved June 23, 2009, from http://www.mla.org/pdf/release11207_ma_feb_update.pdf

Moody, J., & Kindel, T. (2004). Technology in The Citadel School of Business Administration: Success, failures, and future steps. *TechTrends, 48*(5), 42–47.

Murdoch, S. (2007). *IQ: A smart history of a failed idea.* Hoboken, NJ: John Wiley.

Myrick, P., & Jones, R. (1991, September). How instructional leaders view staff development. *NASSP Bulletin, 75*(536), 1–6.

Nagel, G. K. (1998). Looking for multicultural education: What could be done and why it isn't. *Education, 119*(2), 253–262.

Nasir, N. (2008). Everyday pedagogy: Lessons from basketball, track, and dominos. *Phi Delta Kappan, 89*(7), 529–533.

National Assessment of Education Progress Science Consensus Project. (1993). *Science assessment and exercise specifications for the 1994 national assessment of educational progress.* Washington, DC: National Assessment Governing Board.

National Association for Gifted Children. (2005). *Parallel curriculum model (PCM): Support materials and distance learning opportunity.* Retrieved June 3, 2005, from http:// www.nagc.org/pcmlearning/pcmindex.htm

National Center for Children in Poverty. (2008, October). *Basic facts about low-income children: Fact sheet.* Retrieved May 27, 2009, from http://www.nccp.org/publications/pub_849.html

National Center for Education Statistics (NCES). (2002). *The condition of education.* Washington, DC: Author.

National Center for Education Statistics (NCES). (2006, November). *Internet access in U.S. public schools and classrooms: 1994–2005.* Retrieved July 20, 2009, from http://nces.ed.gov/pubs2007/2007020.pdf

National Center for Education Statistics (NCES). (2007, December). *Indicators of school crime and safety 2007* (NCES 2008-021). U.S. Department of Education, Institute of Education Sciences. Retrieved April 23, 2009, from http://nces.ed.gov/programs/crimeindicators/crimeindicators2007/index.asp

National Center for Education Statistics (NCES). (2009a). *The condition of education: Student effort and educational progress*. Retrieved June 19, 2009, from http://nces.ed.gov/programs/coe/2009/section3/indicator18.asp

National Center for Education Statistics (NCES). (2009b). *The nation's report card: Long-term trends 2008*. Retrieved May 29, 2009, from http://nces.ed.gov/pubsearch/pubsinfo.asp?pubid=2009479

National Coalition for the Homeless. (2000). *Homeless youth: NCH fact sheet #13*. Retrieved May 22, 2009, from http://www.nationalhomeless.org/factsheets/youth.html

National Commission on Excellence in Education. (1983). *A nation at risk: The imperative for educational reform*. Washington, DC: U.S. Government Printing Office.

National Council of Teachers of Mathematics. (1989). *Curriculum and evaluation standards for school mathematics*. Reston, VA: Author.

National Forum on Information Literacy. (2009). *Announcing the campaign for national recognition of National Information Literacy Week*. Retrieved May 28, 2009, from http://www.infolit.org/news/campaign.html

National Service-Learning Clearinghouse. (2008). *A–Z list of service-learning fact sheets*. Retrieved May 13, 2009, from http://www.servicelearning.org/instant_info/fact_sheets/a-z_list/index.php

Neihart, M. (2007). The socio-affective impact on acceleration and ability grouping: Recommendations for best practices. *The Gifted Child Quarterly, 51*(4), 330–341.

Neil, A. S. (1960). *Summerhill*. New York: Hart.

Neill, M. (2003). The dangers of testing. *Educational Leadership, 60*(5), 43–45.

Nicaise, M., & Barnes, D. (1996). The union of technology, constructivism, and teacher education. *Journal of Teacher Education, 47*(3), 205–212.

Nichols, S. L., & Berliner, D. C. (2007). *Collateral damage: How high-stakes testing corrupts America's schools*. Cambridge, MA: Harvard Education Press.

Noddings, N. (2008). All our students thinking. *Educational Leadership, 65*(5), 8–13.

Obama, B. (2009, February 24). Speech before Joint Session of Congress. Retrieved March 16, 2009, from http://blogs.suntimes.com/sweet/2009/02/obamas_speech_before_joint_ses.html

O'Donnell, T., & Danserau, D. F. (1993). Learning from lectures: Effects of cooperative review. *Journal of Experimental Education, 61*(2), 116–125.

O'Neal, M., Earley, B., & Snider, M. (1991). Addressing the needs of at-risk students: A local school program that works. In R. C. Morris (Ed.), *Youth at risk* (pp. 122–125). Lancaster, PA.: Technomic Publishing Co.

Oldenski, T. (2010). Assessing assessment. In K. T. Henson, *Supervision: A collaborative approach to instructional improvement* (p. 299). Long Grove, IL: Waveland Press.

Oliva, P. F. (1992). *Developing the curriculum* (3rd ed.). Glenview, IL: Scott Foresman.

Oliva, P. F. (2009). *Developing the curriculum* (7th ed.). Upper Saddle River, NJ: Pearson.

Oliva, P. F., & Pawlas, G. E. (2007). *Supervision for today's schools* (8th ed.). Danvers, MA: John Wiley & Sons.

Olson, K. (2008). The wounded student. *Educational Leadership, 65*(6), 45–49.

Orlich, D. C. (2000). Education reform and limits to student achievement. *Phi Delta Kappan, 81*(6), 468–472.

Ornstein, A. C., Behar, L. S., & Pajak, E. F. (2003). *Contemporary issues in curriculum* (3rd ed.). Boston: Allyn & Bacon.

Ornstein, A. C., & Hunkins, F. P. (2004). *Curriculum: Foundations, principles, and issues.* Boston: Allyn & Bacon.

Oyserman, D. (2008). Possible selves: Identity-based motivation and school success. In H. W. Marsh, R. G. Craven, & D. M. McInerney (Eds.), *Self-processes, learning and enabling human potential: Dynamic approaches* (pp. 112–125). Charlotte, NC: Information Age Publishing.

Oyserman, D., Bybee, D., & Terry, K. (2006). Possible selves and academic outcomes: When and how possible selves impel action. *Journal of Personality and Social Psychology, 91*, 188–204.

Ozmon, H. A., & Craver, S. M. (1999). *Philosophical foundations of education* (6th ed.). Columbus, OH: Merrill.

Ozmon, H. A., & Craver, S. M. (2008). *Philosophical foundations of education* (8th ed.). Upper Saddle River, NJ: Pearson/Merrill/Prentice-Hall.

Palmer, L. B., & Gau, R. (2005). Charter school authorizing: Policy implications from a national study. *Phi Delta Kappan, 86*(5), 352–357.

Palmer, W. S., & Pugalee, D. K. (1999). Assessment and the English language arts: Present and future perspectives. In B. Day (Ed.), *Teaching and learning in the new millennium.* Indianapolis, IN: Kappa Delta Pi.

Pare, V. (2004, Summer). Exploring the conflicts involved with ability grouping. *The National Research Center on the Gifted and Talented Newsletter.* Retrieved April 23, 2009, from the University of Connecticut Web site: http://www.gifted.ucon.edu/nrcgt/newsletter/summer04/sumer042.html

Parkay, F. W., Hass, G., & Anctil, E. J. (2010). *Curriculum leadership: Readings for developing quality educational programs* (9th ed.). Boston: Pearson/Allyn & Bacon.

Parker, W. C. (1996). Trends in social studies. *Educational Leadership 52*(8), 84–85.

Partnership for 21st Century Skills. (2009a). *Route 21: 2009 cyber summit on 21st century skills.* Retrieved May 14, 2009, from http://www.21stcenturyskills.org/route21/index.php?option=com_content&view=article&id=18&Itemid=164

Partnership for 21st Century Skills. (2009b). *21st century learning environments white paper.* Retrieved March 9, 2009, from http://www.21stcenturyskills.org/documents/le_white_paper-1.pdf

Parton, B. S. (2004). Distance education brings deaf students, instructors, and interpreters closer together: A review of prevailing practices, projects, and perceptions. *International Journal of Instructional Technology and Distance Learning.* Retrieved July 20, 2009, from http:// www.itdl.org/Journal/Jan_05/article07.htm

Pateman, B. (2003/2004). Healthier students: Better learners. *Educational Leadership, 61*(4), 70–74.

People's Daily Online. (2009, March 8.) More U.S. schools, universities, offer Chinese classes. Retrieved May 14, 2009, from http://English.people.com/cn.90001/900776/90883/6608876.html

Pepi, D., & Scheurman, G. (1996). The emperor's new computer: A critical look at our appetite for computer technology. *Journal of Teacher Education, 47*(3), 229–236.

Perkins, D., & Blythe, T. (1994). Putting understanding up-front. *Educational Leadership, 51*(5), 4–7.

Perkins-Gough, D. (2004). Creating a timely curriculum: A conversation with Heidi Hayes Jacobs. *Educational Leadership, 61*(4), 12–17.

Peske, H., & Haycock, K. (2006). *Teaching inequality: How poor and minority students are shortchanged on teacher quality.* Washington, DC: The Education Trust. Retrieved July 17, 2009, from http://www2.edtrust.org/NR/rdonlyres/010DBD9F-CED8-4D2B-9E0D-91B446746FED3/0/TQReportJune2006.pdf

Phillips, W. L. (2010). E-walks. In K. T. Henson, *Supervision: A collaborative approach to instructional improvement* (p. 204). Long Grove, IL: Waveland Press.

Piaget, J. (1952). *The origins of intelligence in children.* New York: International University Press.

Platoni, K. (2008, October 29). Internet explorers: Virtual field trips are more than just money savers. *Edutopia Magazine*. Retrieved May 28, 2009, from http://edutopia.org/virtual-field-trips

Popham, W. J. (2005). Squandered instructional zeal. *Educational Leadership, 62*(7), 92.

Popham, W. J. (2007/2008). What's "valid"? *Educational Leadership, 65*(5), 78–79.

Popham, W. J., & Baker, E. L. (1970). *Systematic instruction.* Englewood Cliffs, NJ: Prentice-Hall.

Poplin, M. S. (1992, February). The leader's new role: Looking to the growth of teachers. *Educational Leadership, 49*(5), 10–11.

Potter, L., Carruthers, M., & Green, K. (2002). Special education challenges for the principal: Be prepared. *Middle Ground, 5*(5), 43–44.

Powell, B. A. (2008, February). Black/white/other: Helping multiracial kids find their way. *Edutopia Magazine.* Retrieved May 4, 2009, from http://www.edutopia.org/black-white-other

Prensky, M. (2008). Turning on the lights. *Educational Leadership, 65*(6), 40–45.

Protheroe, N. (2007). Alternatives to retention in grade. *Principal, 96*(3), 30–33.

Publictechnology.net. (2005). *Teachers see IT, Internet and imagination replace the three Rs.* Retrieved July 20, 2009, from http://www.publictechnology.net/modules.php?op=modload&name=News&file=article&sid=2326

Purcell, J. H., Burns, D. E., & Leppien, J. H. (2002). The parallel curriculum model (PCM): The whole story. *Teaching for high potential: Developing students' gifts and talents, IV(1).* National Association for Gifted Children. Retrieved May 27, 2009, from http://staff.nebo.edu/~carol.day/Microsoft%20Word%20-%20parallel%20currciulum%20model.pdf

Purvis, J. R., & Boren, L. C. (1991, September). Planning, implementing a staff development program. *NASSP Bulletin, 75*(536), 16–24.

Pytel, B. (2007, September) *College entrance scores down: ACT scores are up—SAT scores are down.* Retrieved May 22, 2009, from Suite101.com Web site: http:;//educationalissues.suite101.com/article/cfm/college_entrance_scores_down

Qualifications and Curriculum Authority. (n.d.). *Parent power.* Accessed January 29, 2009, from http://www.innovation-unit.co.uk/images/stories/qca-06-2723-parent-power.pdf

Rebell, M. A. (2008). Equal opportunity and the courts. *Phi Delta Kappan, 89*(6), 432–439.

Rebora, A. (2009, March 16). Reinventing professional development in tough times. *Teacher Professional Development Sourcebook, 2*(2), 24–27.

Reed, C. (2010). Applying models and metaphors to the real world. In K. T. Henson, *Supervision: A collaborative approach to instructional improvement* (p. 337). Long Grove, IL: Waveland Press.

Reeves, D. B. (2008). Effective grading. *Educational Leadership, 65*(5), 85–87.

Reich, R. B. (1991). *The work of nations: Preparing ourselves for the 21st century capitalism.* New York: Knopf.

Reinstein, D. (1998). Crossing the economic divide. *Educational Leadership, 55*(4), 28–29.

Richards, J. (2007). How effective principals encourage their teachers. *Principal, 86*(3), 48–50.

Richardson, D., & Mancabelli, R. (2007). The read/write web: New tools for a new generation of technology. *Principal, 86*(3), 12–17.

Richardson, W. (2008, November). Giving students ownership of learning: Footprints in the digital age. *Educational Leadership 66*(3), 16–19.

Ringer, F., & Crittenden, P. (March, 2007). Eating disorders and attachment: The effects of hidden family processes on eating disorders. *European Eating Disorders Review, 15*(2), 119–130.

Ritchhart, R., & Perkins, D. (2008). Making thinking visible. *Educational Leadership, 65*(5), 57–61.

Robelen, E. W. (2007, October 10). Hands-on learning. *Education Week 27*(7). Retrieved May 29, 2009, from http://www.edweek.org/ew/articles/2007/10/10/07chicago.h27.html

Roberts, J. (2008). Talent development: A must for a promising future. *Phi Delta Kappan, 89*(7), 501–506.

Roberts, T., & Billings, L. (2008). Thinking is literacy, literacy is thinking. *Educational Leadership, 65*(5), 32–36.

Robinson, V. (2010). Using magic to build vision. In K. T. Henson, *Supervision: A collaborative approach to instructional improvement* (p. 223). Long Grove, IL: Waveland Press.

Rooney, J. (2007). Who owns teacher growth? *Educational Leadership, 64*(7), 87–88.

Rose, L. C., & Gallup, A. M. (2004). The 36th annual Phi Delta Kappa/Gallup poll of the public's attitudes toward the public schools. *Phi Delta Kappan, 86*(1), 41–48.

Rose, L. C., & Gallup, A. M. (2007). The 39th annual Phi Delta Kappa/Gallup poll of the public's attitudes toward the public schools. *Phi Delta Kappan, 89*(1), 33–48.

Rosenzweig, R., (1998). Afterthoughts: Everyone a historian. In R. Rosenzweig & D. Thelen, *The presence of the past: Popular uses of history in American life.* New York: Columbia University Press. Retrieved June 18, 2009, from http://www.chnm.gmu.edu/survey/index.html

Roth, K. J., & Garnier, H. (2007). How five countries teach science. *Educational Leadership, 64*(4): 16–23.

Rothstein, R. (2004). A wider lens on the black-which achievement gap. *Phi Delta Kappan, 96*(2), 104–110.

Rousseau, J. J. (1979). *Émile.* (Alan Bloom, Trans.). New York: Basic Books.

Rubenstein, G. (2006, March 1). World party: Cultivating a student's global consciousness. *Edutopia Magazine.* Retrieved May 12, 2009, from http://www.edutopia.org/world-party

Sagor, R. (2008). Cultivating optimism in the classroom. *Educational Leadership, 65*(6), 26–31.

Sanger, J. (1990). Awakening a scream of consciousness: The critical group in action research. *Theory into Practice, 29*(3), 174–178.

Saylor, J. G., & Alexander, W. M. (1966). *Curriculum planning for modern schools.* New York: Holt, Rinehart, & Winston.

Scherer, M. (1998). The discipline of hope: An interview with Herbert Kohl. *Educational Leadership, 56*(1), 8–13.

Schifter, D. (1996). A constructivist perspective on teaching and learning mathematics. *Phi Delta Kappan, 77*(7), 492–499.

Schlechty, P. C. (1990). *Schools for the 21st century: Leadership imperatives for educational reform.* San Francisco: Jossey-Bass.

Schlechty, P. C. (2008). No community left behind. *Phi Delta Kappan, 89*(8), 552–559.

Schmoker, M. (2007). Reading, writing, and thinking for all. *Educational Leadership, 64*(7), 63–66.

Schwahn, C., & Spady, W. (1998). Why change doesn't happen and how to make sure it does. *Educational Leadership, 55*(7), 45–47.

Scott, P. (1993). Unpublished manuscript. Tallahassee, FL.

Searby, L. (2010). Using spreadsheets to personalize. In K. T. Henson, *Supervision: A collaborative approach to instructional improvement* (p. 26). Long Grove, IL: Waveland Press.

Selekman, H. R. (1999). A teacher's class. In K. T. Henson and B. F. Eller (Eds.), *Educational psychology for effective teaching*. Belmont, CA: Wadsworth.

Self, E. (2003/2004). Social studies revived. *Educational Leadership, 61*(4), 54–59.

Seligmann, J. (1989, Winter–Spring). Variations on a theme. *Newsweek, 22*(2), 38–46.

Sergiovanni, T. J., & Starratt, R. J. (2002). *Supervision: A redefinition* (7th ed.). New York: McGraw-Hill.

Shaffer, C. R., & Anundsen, K. (1993). *Creating community anywhere.* New York: Jeremy P. Tarcher/Putman Sons.

Shane, H. (1977). *Curriculum change toward the 21st century.* Washington, DC: National Education Association.

Sharp, A. M. (2002). *Philosophy for children: Transformation in the classroom*. Retrieved July 20, 2009, from http://www.studyoverseas.com/america/usaed/philos.htm

Shen, J. (1998). Do teachers feel empowered? *Educational Leadership, 55*(7), 35–36.

Siegel, M. A., & Davis, D. M. (1986). *Understanding computer-based education.* New York: Random House.

Simpson, E. J. (1972). The classification of educational objectives in the psychomotor domain. *The psychomotor domain,* Vol. 3. Washington, DC: Gryphon House.

Sincero, P. (2006). *What is inquiry-based learning?* Retrieved May 8, 2009, from http://www.inquirylearn.com/Inquirydef.htm

Singham, M. (2003). The achievement gap: Myths and reality. *Phi Delta Kappan, 84*(8), 586–591.

Slavin, R. E. (1989, April). On mastery learning and mastery teaching. *Review of Educational Research, 50*, 77–79.

Slavin, R. E. (2006). *Educational psychology: Theory and practice* (8th ed.). Boston: Allyn & Bacon.

Sleeter, C. (2002, Winter). Multicultural education: Technology as a tool in multicultural teaching. *Multicultural Education.* Retrieved March 17, 2009, from http://findarticles.com/p/articles/mi_qu3935/is_200201/ai_n9059183

Sloan Consortium. (2009). *K–12 online learning: A 2008 follow-up of the survey of U.S. school district administrators.* Retrieved May 27, 2009, from http://www.sloan-c.org/publications/survey/k–12online2008

Smart, M. P. (2008a, October 8). In one ear: iTunes U puts iPods to good use. Retrieved April 29, 2009, from the *Edutopia Magazine* Web site: http://www.edutopia.org/itunes-u-professional-development

Smart, M. P. (2008b, November 12). Listening to themselves: Podcasting takes lessons beyond the classroom. *Edutopia Magazine.* Retrieved April 29, 2009, from http:///www.edutopia.org/podcasting-student-broadcasts

Smart, M. P. (2008c, December 10). The word and the world: Technology aids English-language learners. *Edutopia Magazine*. Retrieved May 29, 2009, from http://www.edutopia.org/technology-software-english-language-learners

Smith, B. O., Stanley, W. O., & Shores, J. H. (1957). *Fundamentals of curriculum development: Renewal*. New York: Harcourt, Brace, Jovanovich.

Smith, F. (2009, February). Why arts education is crucial, and who's doing it best. Retrieved June 22, 2009, from the *Edutopia* Web site: http://www.edutopia.org/arts-music-curriculum-child-development

Spencer, H. (1861). *Education: Intellectual, moral and physical*. New York: D. Appleton.

Spiclhagen, F. R. (2007). *Debating single-sex education: Separate and equal?* Lanham, MD: Rowman & Littlefield Education.

Spielvogel, J. J. (2006). *Western civilization: Volume II* (6th ed.). Belmont, CA: Thompson/Wadsworth.

Starr, L. (2005, October 7). Parents and teachers working together. Retrieved March 17, 2009, from the *Education World* Web site: http://www.education-world.com/a_curr/profdev124.shtml

Steers, R. M., Ungson, G. R., & Mowday, R. T. (1985). *Managing effective organizations.* Boston: Kent.

Stefanich, G. P. (1990, November). Cycles of cognition. *Middle School Journal, 22*(2), 47–52.

Sternberg, R. J. (2007/2008). Assessing what matters. *Educational Leadership,65*(4), 20–27.

Stewart, V. (2007a). Becoming citizens of the world. *Educational Leadership, 64*(7), 8–15.

Stewart, V. (2007b). The essential cognitive backpack. *Educational Leadership, 64*(7), 16–22.

Stiggins, R. (2008). *An introduction to student-involved assessment for learning* (5th ed.). Upper Saddle River, NJ: Pearson/Merrill.

Stinchfield, T. A., Hill, N. R., & Kleist, D. M. (2007). The reflection of triadic supervision: Defining an emerging modality. *Counselor Education and Supervision, 46*(3), 172–183.

Stockard, J. W., Jr. (2001). Using technology in social studies. In *Methods and resources for elementary and middle-school social studies* (pp. 205–233). Long Grove, IL: Waveland Press.

Strom, P. S., & Strom, R. (2004). Entitlement: The coming debate on higher education. *The Educational Forum, 68*(4), 325–335.

Suarez-Orozco, M. M., & Sattin, C. (2007). Wanted: Global citizens. *Educational Leadership, 64*(7), 58–62.

Susko, J. (2010). Using exit cards to teach concepts. In K. T. Henson, *Supervision: A collaborative approach to instructional improvement* (p. 391). Long Grove, IL: Waveland Press.

Swartz, R. J. (2008). Engaging learning. *Educational Leadership, 65*(5), 26–31.

Taba, H. (1962). *Curriculum development: Theory and practice.* New York: Harcourt Brace Jovanovich.

Talleyrand, R. M., & Kitsantas, A. (2003). Multicultural pedagogy and web-based technologies. *Academic Exchange Quarterly, 7*(1), 23–28.

Tanner, D., & Tanner, L. N. (1994). *Curriculum development: Theory into practice* (3rd ed.). New York: Macmillan.

Teacher Magazine. (2009, Spring). *Teacher professional development sourcebook.* Retrieved May 27, 2009, from http://teachermagazine.org/tsb/toc/2009/03/16/index.html

TeachingTips.com. (2008). *50 useful blogging tools for teachers*. Retrieved March 9, 2009, from http://www.teachingtips.com/b.oh/2008/07/21/50-useful-blogging-tools-for-teachers

Thomas, M. D., & Bainbridge, W. L. (June, 2002). No Child Left Behind: Facts and fallacies. *Phi Delta Kappan, 85*(10), 781–782.

Thompson, G. (2008). Beneath the apathy. *Educational Leadership, 65*(6), 50–54.

Thompson, S., & Gregg, L. (1997, May). Reculturing middle schools for meaningful change. *Middle School Journal, 28*(5), 27–31.

TIMSS Video Mathematics Research Group. (2003). Understanding and improving mathematics teaching: Highlights from the TIMSS 1999 Video Study. *Phi Delta Kappan, 84*(10), 768–775.

Tomlinson, C. A. (2007/2008). Learning to love assessment. *Educational Leadership, 65*(4), 8–13.

Tomlinson, C. A., & Doubet, K. (2005). Reach them to teach them. *Educational Leadership, 62* (7), 9–15.

Tomlinson, C. A., Kaplan, S. N., Renzulli, J. S., Purcell, J. H., Leppien, J. H., & Burns, D. E. (2002). *The parallel curriculum: A design to develop high potential and challenge high-ability learners.* National Association for Gifted Children. Thousand Oaks, CA: Sage Publications.

Townsend, N. C. (1999). A teacher's class. In K. T. Henson & B. F. Eller (Eds.), *Educational psychology for effective teaching* (p. 346). Belmont, CA: Wadsworth.

Tripp, D. H. (1990). Socially critical action research. *Theory into Practice, 29*(3), 158–166.

Tuttle, H. G. (2007, May 1). Avoid teacher technology integration, work with students directly. Education with Harry G. Tuttle [Blog entry]. Retrieved July 17, 2009, from http://eduwithtechn.wordpress.com/2007/05/01/avoid-teacher-technology-integration-work-with-students-directly/

Tyson, H., & Woodward, A. (1989). Why students aren't learning very much from textbooks. *Educational Leadership*, 14–17.

U.S. Census Bureau. (2008). *Poverty: 2006 highlights.* Retrieved June 18, 2009, from http://www.census.gov/hhes/www/poverty/poverty06/pov06hi.html

U.S. Department of Education. (2004, August 26). *The importance of arts education.* Retrieved March 17, 2009, from http://www.ed.gov/print/teachers/how/tools/initiative/updates/040826.html

U.S. Department of Education. (2004). *National Education Technology Plan: Toward a new golden age in American education—How the Internet, the law and today's students are revolutionizing expectations*. Retrieved July 20, 2009, from http://www.ed.gov/about/offices/list/os/technology/plan/2004/site/theplan/edlite-intro.html

U.S. Department of Education. (2008, December). Distance education at degree-granting postsecondary institutions: 2006–07. First look. Retrieved July 20, 2009, from http://nces.ed.gov/pubs2009/2009044.pdf

Value of CTE. (2008). *Techniques, 82*(3), 50–53. Retrieved April 29, 2009, from http://www.highbeam.com/doc/1G1-177101182.html

Van Scoter, J., Ellis, D., & Railsback, J. (2001). *Technology in early childhood education: Finding the balance*. Northwest Regional Educational Library. Retrieved June 24, 2005, from http://www.nwrel.org/request/june01/

Villa, R. A., & Thousand, J. S. (Eds.). (2005). *Creating an inclusive school*. Alexandria, VA: Association for Supervision & Curriculum Development.

Walker, R. J. (2008). Twelve characteristics of effective teachers. *Educational Horizons, 87*(1), 61–68.

Wang, M. C., Haertel, G. D., & Walberg, H. J. (1998). Models of reform: A comparative guide. *Educational Leadership, 55*(7), 66–71.

Ward, M. W. (1969). Learning to generalize. *Science Education, 53,* 423–424.

Waters-Adams, S. (2006). *Action research in education*. Retrieved May 12, 2009, from http://www.edu.plymouth.ac.uk/resined/actionresearch/arhome.htm

Watson, C., Beliveau, J., & Nelsen, M. (2004). Assessment and learning: Meeting everyone's expectations. In K. T. Henson (Ed.), *Constructivist teaching strategies for diverse middle-level classrooms* (3rd ed., p. 345). Boston: Allyn & Bacon.

Weishaar, M. K., Borsa, J. C., & Weishaar, P. M. (2007). *Inclusive educational administration: A case-study approach* (2nd ed.). Long Grove, IL: Waveland Press.

Weiss, I. R., & Pasley, J. D. (2004). What is high quality instruction? *Educational Leadership, 61*(5), 24–28.

Weller, L. D., Jr., Hartley, S. H., & Brown, C. L. (1994). Principles and TMQ: Developing vision. *The Clearing House, 67*(5), 298–301.

Westchester Institute for Human Services Research. (2002, July). Ability grouping. *The Balanced View, 6*(2). Retrieved April 23, 2009, from http://www.sharingsuccess.org/code/bv/abilitygrouping.pdf

What Does a Network Do? (n.d.). Retrieved February 23, 2003, from http://www.historyoftheinternet.com/chap3.html

Wherry, J. H. (2007). Getting parent support for standardized test success. *Principal, 87*(2), 12.

Whitehead, A. N. (1911). *An introduction to mathematics* (p. 157). New York: Holt, Rinehart, & Winston.

Wiggins, G. (1989, April). Teaching to the authentic test. *Educational Leadership, 46*(7), 41–47.

William, D. (2007). Content then process: Teacher learning communities in the service of formative assessment. In D. B. Reeves (Ed.), *Ahead of the curve: The power of assessment to transform teaching and learning.* Bloomington, IN: Solution Tree.

Wiliam, D. (2007/2008). Changing classroom practice. *Educational Leadership, 65*(4), 36–41.

Willis, S. (2002, March). Creating a knowledge base for teaching: A conversation with James Stigler. *Educational Leadership, 59*(6), 6–11.

Wilson, B., & Corbett, D. H. (2000). *"I didn't know I could do that": Parents learning to be leaders through the Commonwealth Institute for Parent Leadership.* Lexington, KY: Commonwealth Institute for Parent Leadership. Retrieved May 27, 2009, from http://www.cipl.org/pubs.html

Wirth, A. C. (1993, January). Educational work: The choice we face. *Phi Delta Kappan, 74*(5), 361–366.

Wise, D. (2010). On target. In K. T. Henson, *Supervision: A collaborative approach to instructional improvement* (p. 150). Long Grove, IL: Waveland Press.

Witte, J. F., & Thorn, C. A. (1994, December). *Fourth year report: Milwaukee Parental Choice Program.* Madison: University of Wisconsin, Department of Political Science and the Robert La Follette Institute of Public Affairs.

Wolfe, P., & Brandt, R. (1998). What do we know from brain research? *Educational Leadership, 56*(3), 8–13.

Wolk, R. (2004). Think the unthinkable. *Educational Horizons, 82*(4), 268–283.

Wood, P. (2002). *No Child Left Behind Act of 2001.* Westerville, OH: National Middle School Association.

Woolfolk Hoy, A., & Hoy, W. K. (2009). *Instructional leadership* (3rd ed.). Boston: Allyn & Bacon.

Worksheet Library.com. (2007). *Inquiry-based learning.* Teaching tip articles. Retrieved May 13, 2009, from http://www.worksheetlibrary.com/teachingtips.inquiry.html

Wright, R. (1985). Motivating teacher involvement in professional growth activities. *The Canadian Administrator, 5*, 1–6.

Young, J. H. (1985). The curriculum decision-making preferences of school personnel. *The Alberta Journal of Educational Research, 25*, 20–29.

Zais, R. S. (1976). *Curriculum: Principles and foundations.* New York: Harper & Row.

Zwiers, J. (2005). The third language of academic English. *Educational Leadership, 62*(4), 60–63.

NAME INDEX

SUBJECT INDEX

diff. between
concept
theory
model

model
systematic development to curr.
design + org.